Guide to Movies on Videocassette

Joe Blades and
the Editors of Consumer Reports Books

Consumers Union
Mount Vernon, New York

With grateful acknowledgment to
the editors of Consumer Reports Books

Maureen Tracy
Sarah Uman
Chris Kuppig

Copyright © 1986 by Joe Blades and Consumers Union of United States, Inc.
Mount Vernon, New York 10553

Library of Congress Cataloging-in-Publication Data

Blades, Joe.
Guide to movies on videocassette.
Includes index.
1. Video recordings—Catalogs. 2. Moving-pictures—Catalogs.
3. Video recordings—Reviews. 4. Moving-pictures—Reviews.
I. Consumer Reports Books.
II. Title.
PN1992.95.B5   1986   016.79143   86-70833
ISBN 0-89043-060-8

Design by Joy Taylor

First Printing, December 1986

Manufactured in the United States of America

Guide to Movies on Videocassette is a Consumer Reports Book published by Consumers Union, the nonprofit organization that publishes *Consumer Reports,* the monthly magazine of test reports, product Ratings, and buying guidance. Established in 1936, Consumers Union is chartered under the Not-For-Profit Corporation Law of the State of New York.

The purposes of Consumers Union, as stated in its charter, are to provide consumers with information and counsel on consumer goods and services, to give information on all matters relating to the expenditure of the family income, and to initiate and to cooperate with individual and group efforts seeking to create and maintain decent living standards.

Consumers Union derives its income solely from the sale of *Consumer Reports* and other publications. In addition, expenses of occasional public service efforts may be met, in part, by nonrestrictive, noncommercial contributions, grants, and fees. Consumers Union accepts no advertising or product samples and is not beholden in any way to any commercial interest. Its Ratings and reports are solely for the use of the readers of its publications. Neither the Ratings nor the reports nor any Consumers Union publications, including this book, may be used in advertising or for any commercial purpose. Consumers Union will take all steps open to it to prevent such uses of its material, its name, or the name of *Consumer Reports.*

To my favorite people

Dalton
Edna
Mary Frances

Contents

Introduction

In April 1947, *Consumer Reports* published its first Movie Poll stating: "The moving picture industry is one of America's biggest, and the price of movie admissions takes a good-sized bite out of the average family's dollar. To help *Reports* readers get Best Buys for their movie money, CU presents movie Ratings made up with the aid of some two thousand movie-going CU subscribers." Those who participated in the initial Movie Poll were supplied with a form postcard, and as soon as they saw a movie they mailed in the card indicating whether they considered the picture Excellent, Good, Fair, or Poor. Some of the movies that were considered good to excellent at that time were *Notorious* starring Cary Grant and Ingrid Bergman, *Best Years of Our Lives* with Frederic March and Myrna Loy, and *Two Years Before the Mast* featuring Alan Ladd and William Bendix.

Today's *Consumer Reports* Movie Poll is developed in a similar manner. Now, however, approximately three thousand readers are regular participants, augmented by almost four hundred members of the Media Educators Association—a nonprofit organization comprising teachers and media professionals who view movies prior to theatrical release. These days the editors select the movies to be reviewed, and those readers who want to participate in the poll are invited to write to the magazine for computerized ballots. Once the reader has viewed six to seven recent films that appear in the poll, they return the ballots and the total number of opinion-votes received for each movie is calculated.

Since that April 1947 issue, respondents have contributed Ratings on more than fifteen thousand movies. It is from that extensive list that we have selected the movies appearing in this guide, choosing only those motion pictures that were rated Very Good to Excellent and that are now available on videocassette.

The national average price for a single movie ticket today is almost four dollars, which translates into an expensive few hours of entertainment for a medium size family—an economic reality not that very different from 1947. But now, with the introduction of the videocassette recorder, or VCR, millions of Americans have dramatically changed their filmviewing habits. Instead of forming lines at movie theaters, people are renting and buying movies to view in the privacy and convenience of their homes. Thirty percent of American households already have a VCR, and the Electronics Industry Association predicts that by 1993, two-thirds of American households will be equipped with at least one VCR. A survey among *Consumer Reports* subscribers published in September 1985, indicated that "The viewing of rented films accounts for about one-third of the playback time." So, while movie attendance is down and broadcast television films draw smaller audiences, the amount of sales and rentals of motion pictures on cassettes for home viewing continues to grow at a rapid rate.

According to the National Video Clearinghouse, there are well over fifty-thousand cassette titles available from some nine hundred fifty distributors.

This superabundant selection of movies from which to choose can make a visit to the video store both confusing and annoying. Although many video stores list recently acquired releases, those listings most often consist only of movie titles. Unless the prospective viewer has previous knowledge of a particular film, he or she is taking a chance in buying or renting the videocassette. Rental fees for movies may vary between urban, suburban, and rural areas of the country, however, those videos priced to sell can range from twenty to eighty dollars; an expense one does not want to leave to chance.

The subject classifications contained in *Guide to Movies On Videocassette* are Biographies, Comedies, Dramas, Family Viewing/Children's, Foreign Language, Horror and Science Fiction, Musicals, Suspense and Mystery, War, and Westerns. Listed alphabetically with a synopsis for every film, the entries range from the huge box-office successes to the major award winners, as well as some minor classics both old and new, plus an appendix of pre-1946 movies chosen by the editors of Consumer Reports Books. Each of the entries contains the title, the year the film was released, the videocassette distributor, the director of the film, a listing of the cast, whether the movie is in black and white or color, a mention of awards it may have won, and a plot summary along with other noteworthy information.

How the Movies Were Selected

Over the decades, opinion-votes in the Movie Poll have been charted in various ways. *Consumer Reports* editors tallied responses in the earlier years by providing these rating breakdowns:

Excellent   Good   Fair   Poor

More recently, the distinction has evolved into

with the left-side symbols (◐ and ◑) representing Excellent and Very Good. These two classifications form the basis for the entries in the following pages. Films deemed by CU Movie Poll participants Good, Fair, or Poor have been excluded.

Here, then, are the criteria for inclusion in the book:

1. Was the film released in 1946 or thereafter? (Although the column began in 1947, a small number of 1946 movies were reader-rated.)

2. Did it receive either an Excellent or Very Good rating (or score in the top two classes of the current five-point scale) in Consumer Reports' Movie Poll?

3. Is the film available on videocassette?

4. Is it a fictional (i.e., nondocumentary) film? (Documentaries, including concert movies, are not abundantly featured in CU polls—and when they have appeared, they rarely ranked at the top. Consequently, we have eliminated the entire category.)

If all four answers are "yes," then the film is listed and discussed in the following pages.

About the Price of Videocassettes

Because prices and discount practices vary widely, they have not been suggested here. Some industry analysts predict that with the increase in VCR sales, the sale of movies on videocassettes may constitute as much as twenty-five percent of industry revenues this year. A lower sale price for new movies on videocassette could very well result.

Availability of Movies on Videocassette

From time to time, manufacturers may temporarily withdraw certain movies from the market. But, like out-of-print books, videocassettes very often are made available again, sometimes from a different distributor, or several new distributors. (Films that are in public domain are frequently offered by more than one distributor.) Although titles may be unavailable at one given time, many video store owners are of the opinion that movies in demand will probably be rereleased.

Membership in a Video Club

From the inception of video stores some five years ago, the club concept of videocassette rental has been promoted in various ways. As the rental market continues to boom, other retailers have joined in. Now, in many places it's possible to rent videocassettes in drugstores and variety stores—even convenience stores and supermarkets have entered the market.

The video club is still appealing from the videocassette merchandiser's point of view. While the particulars of membership vary widely, most often there is a provision for an annual membership fee or prepayment against which rentals are made. In some cases, members are provided with premiums (such as a number of free initial rentals, film guides, or catalogs rights to reserve videocassettes, or periodic special rates— "festivals" of a particular star or director's films or a discount or two-for-one night— even reduced prices on blank videocassettes and other video equipment). From the dealer's point of view, the club means certain income in the form of prepayments or membership fees, customers who are "obligated" to rent or buy videocassettes by virtue of their membership, and a built-in ongoing promotion for video hardware and other items offered to members at discounts.

What are the advantages to membership for the consumer? In the past, club membership generally meant reduced rates over single cassette rentals. By prepaying, members qualified for prices as low as $1.00 per rental, a significant savings over the $3.50 to $5.00 generally charged for single rentals. Of course, the interest that may have otherwise been earned on the prepayment or membership fee goes into the dealer's pocket, but given the level of the club member's investment in video entertainment at any given time—generally $100 tops—the additional cost in foregone interest income doesn't tip the balance against club membership.

A second advantage is convenience. Most video clubs depend on a computer database to keep track of their members and cassette rentals. If you are a member, your account can be quickly called up on a computer terminal and the cassette of your choice checked out to you. If you're not a member, a major credit-card voucher is usually requested and paperwork may be required.

Preferential treatment is another membership plus. Usually members can reserve new releases, which, while likely to be stocked in multiple copies, may otherwise be difficult to obtain for some time because they're in high demand.

The other discounts sometimes offered as a benefit of membership—blank cassettes, video hardware, purchase of recorded cassettes, etc.—may or may not be worthwhile given the volatile nature of discounting in the whole video market. It may pay to shop around before you buy a favorite film for your permanent cassette library.

As more and more non-video stores branch into rentals as an additional service, the costs of individual rentals have become more competitive with club prices. Depending on your tastes and the frequency with which you view films, you may be able to do better with single rentals from these outlets than with a club membership. However, in most cases, the stores dealing in cassettes as their stock and trade are likely to have much wider and more current selections than the non-specialty stores.

Keep in mind, too, that club membership terms and benefits may differ widely in your area. The total number of cassettes available in any club is also a consideration, as well as the club's hours and proximity to your home. It's best to do some research before committing.

What's the downside? With either club or single rentals, you're generally bound by contract to return the cassette by the end of the following business day or be faced with a late charge (many clubs stay open seven days a week, so there's no two-day weekend rental in these cases). Renting videocassettes obligates you to the terms stated in the agreement you sign—whether for a single rental or a club membership. Read it carefully. You are generally obligated to return the cassette on time and in good condition, or you may be charged (out of your prepayment or credit-card deposit) up to the full retail price of the cassette. If you get a cassette home and it does not play in your VCR, call the video store immediately, if possible, and notify the dealer of the problem. You should not be charged for the rental if the cassette is defective and you return it any time within the rental period. The store may be able to supply you with a good copy if you call right away.

A Word on Library Videocassette Collections

Increasing numbers of municipal libraries have begun to amass videocassette collections. While their holdings are generally not as large or as up to date as the commercial video stores, many worthwhile and classic films may be available from your local library free as a privilege of your library membership. In some cases, VCRs may also be checked out overnight for viewing cassettes; and some libraries have even invested in on-premise video viewing rooms for the enjoyment of library patrons.

Know the Law

It is a violation of U.S. law to duplicate any recorded videocassette that carries a copyright notice, whether rented or purchased for personal use. To do so may result in civil and criminal penalties.

Frequently Cited
Cassette Manufacturers

Abbreviations

CBS	CBS/Fox
Charter	Charter Entertainment
Continental	Continental Video
Disney	Walt Disney Home Video
Electric	Electric Video
Embassy	Embassy Home Entertainment
Key	Key Video
Learning	Learning Corp. of America
MCA	MCA Home Video
Media	Media Home Entertainment
MGM	MGM/UA Home Video
MPI	MPI Home Video
New	New World Video
Nostalgia	Nostalgia Merchant
Paramount	Paramount Home Video
RCA	RCA/Columbia Pictures Home Video
Republic	Republic Home Video
RKO	RKO Home Video
Thorn	Thorn EMI/HBO Video
Time	Time Life Video
United	United Home Video
Vestron	Vestron Video
VidAm	VidAmerica
Vid Dim	Video Dimensions
Warner	Warner Home Video

Other Distributors

Active Home Video
Admit One Video
BFA Educational Media
Blackhawk Films
Budget Video
Cable Films
Children's Video Library
Cinema Concepts
Classic Video Cinema Collectors Club
Corinth Films
Discount Video Tapes
Festival Films
Glenn Video Vistas
Goodtimes Home Video Corp.
Hal Roach Studios
Hollywood Home Theatre
Image Magnetic Associates
Kartes Productions
King of Video
Lightning Video
Magnetic Video
Monterey Home Video
Movie Buff Video

Pacific Arts Video
Paragon Video Productions
Playhouse Video
Prism
Regal Video
Sheik Video
Texture Films
Touchstone Home Video
Unicorn Video
U.S.A. Home Video
VC II Inc.
Video Award Motion Pictures, Inc.
Video Connection
Video Gems
The Video Station
Video Tape Network
Video Treasures
Video Yesteryear
Western Film and Video, Inc.
Wizard Video, Inc.
World Video Pictures
Worldvision Home Video

Key to Award Symbols

British Academy Award ★

Cannes Film Festival ❋

César ▲

Genie ♣

National Society of Film Critics ✪

New York Film Critics ❋

Oscar ◆

Biographies

The **A**ctress   1953   (MGM)   *Black-and-White*
Director: George Cukor
Starring: Spencer Tracy, Jean Simmons, Teresa Wright, Anthony Perkins, Ian Wolfe, Mary Wickes

Ruth Gordon's autobiographical play, *Years Ago,* was brought to the screen by MGM as a vehicle for Spencer Tracy. The film version, dubbed *The Actress,* also served as a showcase for Jean Simmons, whose popularity, until 1951, was largely restricted to Great Britain. A warm-hearted period (circa 1912) comedy, *The Actress* evinces teenage Gordon's home life in Quincy, Massachusetts—and her emergent theatrical aspirations just before she set off for New York to establish herself in what became an enduring and fruitful career. Simmons has the title role, and her costars are Teresa Wright (who played her mother again in 1970 in *The Happy Ending*) and Tracy, as the cantankerous father who equates actors with sin and therefore opposes young Ruth's newfound career. Miss Gordon did her own screenplay adaptation. Anthony Perkins's film debut.

Agatha   1979   (Warner)   *Color*
Director: Michael Apted
Starring: Dustin Hoffman, Vanessa Redgrave, Timothy Dalton, Helen Morse, Celia Gregory, Paul Brooke

For Agatha Christie the year 1926 was a tragic one: the death of her mother, the shakeup of her marriage, and a virtual nervous breakdown. The final blow arrived in December when her husband revealed he was seeking a divorce so he could legally unite with his long-time paramour. Shortly after, Agatha became the focus of a ten-day missing persons case. Her real-life disappearance sparked this cinematic speculation—with Vanessa Redgrave in the title role, Timothy Dalton as her caddish spouse, and Dustin Hoffman as a mystery man. There are lavish costumes combined with period detail on which to feast the eyes. *Agatha* may not be an accurate reflection of pre–Dame Agatha or her domestic difficulties, but it is entertaining.

Al Capone   1959   (Key)   *Black-and-White*
Director: Richard Wilson
Starring: Rod Steiger, Fay Spain, James Gregory, Murvyn Vye, Nehemiah Persoff, Martin Balsam

Prohibition-era Chicago was the stage for the rise of scarfaced hoodlum king Capone. This biography, penned by Malvin Wald and Henry Greenberg, has the texture of a documentary. The low budget, actually, is a plus—with Richard Wilson's blunt, primitive directorial style perfectly conveying the period, as well as the essence of his primitive subject. Steiger, who had been appearing in features since 1951 (with *On the Waterfront* one of his rare A-film appearances), had his first substantial starring role herein—and he seized the opportunity.

Amadeus   1984   (Thorn)   ◆   *Color*
Director: Miloš Forman
Starring: F. Murray Abraham, Tom Hulce, Elizabeth Berridge, Simon Callow, Roy Dotrice, Christine Ebersole, Jeffrey Jones, Charles Kay

The big-screen version of one of the most acclaimed productions in Broadway history—Peter Shaffer's biography of Wolfgang Amadeus Mozart. The title notwithstanding, *Amadeus* focuses on rival composer Antonio Salieri's envious hatred for the musical genius. Director Miloš Forman traces the last decade of the prodigy's life—his marriage to Constanze Weber, court intrigues, and Mozart's mysterious death in poverty and disrepute two months before his thirty-sixth birthday. It's quite a mélange: grand music, melodrama, and (by virtue of Patrizia von Brandenstein's production design and Miroslav Ondriček's location photography in Czechoslovakia) visual spectacle. Nominated in eleven Oscar categories, *Amadeus* was victorious in eight: film, direction, actor (Abraham as Salieri), screenplay adaptation (Shaffer), art direction (von Brandenstein), costume design (Theodor Pistek), and for both sound and makeup.

Anne of the Thousand Days   1969   (MCA)   *Color*
Director: Charles Jarrott
Starring: Richard Burton, Geneviève Bujold, Irene Papas, Anthony Quayle, John Colicos, Peter Jeffrey, Michael Johnson, William Squire

One thousand days. The duration of the tempestuous courtship and marriage of Henry VIII and Anne Boleyn. *Anne of the Thousand Days* dramatizes that period (roughly 1533 to 1536)—against a backdrop of political ferment arising from Henry's dispute with the churches of Rome and England concerning his *outré* marital customs. Richard Burton, as Henry—the prototypal *Dieu et mon droit* monarch—bellows "I am the King of England. When I pray, God answers. Let no man dare question that." (". . . or woman!" someone quickly appends.) But Anne Boleyn did defy the king her husband—and paid with her life. Inspired by Maxwell Anderson's 1948 verse drama, this screen adaptation adheres to the fashion expected of cerebral pageants *(Becket, A Man for All Seasons)*. William Squire, as Thomas More, does his best to place Paul Scofield in shadow. Upon completion of *Anne*, director Charles Jarrott went immediately into another historical project: *Mary, Queen of Scots*.

Becket   1964   (United; MPI)   ◆   *Color*
Director: Peter Glenville
Starring: Richard Burton, Peter O'Toole, Sir John Gielgud, Sir Donald Wolfit, Martita Hunt, Pamela Brown, Sian Phillips, Paolo Stoppa, Gino Cervi, David Weston, Felix Aylmer, Niall MacGinnis

From the internationally acclaimed stage work by Jean Anouilh, *Becket* revels in the power and beauty of language. (The screen adaptation brought Edward Anhalt an

Oscar.) The film, varying little from the playscript, depicts the love-hate relationship between King Henry II (Peter O'Toole) and the Archbishop of Canterbury, Thomas à Becket (Richard Burton)—the libertine turned man of God. Becket's adherence to "the honor of God" places him directly in defiance of his king (and former friend). Their philosophical collisions produce the central tensions of the film. Producer Hal Wallis had Canterbury Cathedral reconstructed to approximate its twelfth-century look and a replica of a French village from the Middle Ages built and placed in working order. Geoffrey Unsworth is responsible for the cinematography. Peter Glenville, director of the Broadway version starring Anthony Quinn (Henry) and Laurence Olivier (Becket), here repeats that role. Footnote: in *The Lion in Winter* (1968), O'Toole again plays Henry II, some twenty years after the events in *Becket.*

Birdman of Alcatraz   1962   (RCA)   *Black-and-White*
Director: John Frankenheimer
Starring: Burt Lancaster, Karl Malden, Thelma Ritter, Betty Field, Neville Brand, Edmond O'Brien, Hugh Marlowe, Telly Savalas, Crahan Denton, James Westerfield, Chris Robinson, Whit Bissell

This deliberately slow-paced account of two-time murderer Robert Stroud commands one's attention. Guy Trosper's fact-based screenplay, from a book by Thomas E. Gaddis, dramatizes Stroud's life as an Alcatraz inmate who, in solitary confinement, became an ornithologist. In time he was known, even far beyond the prison walls, as the "Birdman of Alcatraz." Burt Lancaster assumed the title role right in the middle of his most productive period. Two years earlier he had received the Oscar for *Elmer Gantry,* then gone on to *The Young Savages* (the first of his many films with John Frankenheimer), and followed that with *Judgment at Nuremberg.* Thelma Ritter plays Stroud's mother. Charles Crichton began the film, but Frankenheimer took over when "creative differences" arose.

The Boston Strangler   1968   (CBS)   *Color*
Director: Richard Fleischer
Starring: Tony Curtis, Henry Fonda, George Kennedy, Mike Kellin, Murray Hamilton, Hurd Hatfield, Jeff Corey, Sally Kellerman, William Marshall

Gerold Frank's nonfiction best-seller gets Hollywood screen treatment. *The Boston Strangler* traces in near-documentary style the manhunt, capture, and ultimate confession of Albert De Salvo, the psychotic plumber who murdered thirteen women. Tony Curtis, sporting a false nose, portrays De Salvo and there is assistance from Henry Fonda as the principal criminal investigator. The dogged detective work is well delineated. Director Richard Fleischer has contributed other film versions of famous murder cases: *Compulsion, 10 Rillington Place,* and *The Girl in the Red Velvet Swing.* Postscript: De Salvo, after being sentenced to life imprisonment, was stabbed to death by other inmates in 1973.

Bound for Glory   1976   (MGM)   ◆   *Color*
Director: Hal Ashby
Starring: David Carradine, Ronny Cox, Melinda Dillon, Gail Strickland, Randy Quaid, John Lehne, Ji-Tu Cumbuka, Lee McLaughlin

Hal Ashby's film evokes *The Grapes of Wrath* and *Bonnie and Clyde*—in both terrain and time frame. The hero is composer–folk singer Woody Guthrie. During his young manhood in the Depression, Guthrie to a large extent became the voice of the down-trodden masses—urban laborers, migrant farm workers, union organizers, Dust Bowl victims. Adapted by Robert Getchell from the Guthrie autobiography, *Bound for Glory* features a powerful interpretation of Woody by David Carradine. The star sings many Guthrie standards, including his trademark "This Land Is Your Land." Melinda Dillon plays two roles: Guthrie's first wife, Mary, and his singing partner, Memphis Sue. The movie is distinguished by Haskell Wexler's pioneering use of Steadycam, the hand-held camera that glides evenly to give a more fluid look. Wexler won his second Academy Award for *Bound for Glory*. (His first: *Who's Afraid of Virginia Woolf?*) An additional Oscar went to Leonard Rosenman for music adaptation.

Brother Sun, Sister Moon   1973   (Paramount)   *Color*
Director: Franco Zeffirelli
Starring: Graham Faulkner, Judi Bowker, Alec Guinness, Leigh Lawson, Kenneth Cranham, Lee Montague, Valentina Cortesa, Adolfo Celi

Italy at the dawn of the thirteenth century is the setting for this biography of the young Francis of Assisi. Franco Zeffirelli's follow-up to *Romeo and Juliet* is in the same lush, romantic mode—with visual lyricism and adolescent leads. Joining Suso Cecchi d'Amico, Zeffirelli's usual script collaborator, are Lina Wertmuller and Kenneth Ross; they dramatize Francis's conversion to asceticism, his espousal of poverty, and his love for nature. Graham Faulkner stars as Francis, and Alec Guinness plays Pope Innocent III. Musical score by Donovan.

Coal Miner's Daughter   1980   (MCA)   ◆   *Color*
Director: Michael Apted
Starring: Sissy Spacek, Tommy Lee Jones, Beverly D'Angelo, Levon Helm, Phyllis Boyens, William Sanderson, Robert Elkins, Bob Hannah, Jennifer Beasley, Jessica Beasley

This musical biography dramatizes the early life of country singer Loretta Lynn. As the coal miner's daughter travels from the backwoods of Kentucky to the stage of the Grand Ole Opry, she is observed as wife, mother, and (gradually) country-western star. Based on Loretta Lynn's autobiography, the screenplay is by Tom Rickman. Sissy Spacek, in her Oscar-winning performance, convincingly presents the title figure as both hill girl and mature woman—while bravely doing her own singing in preference to lip-synching Miss Lynn's records. Also admirable in an equally difficult role is Tommy Lee Jones, as her husband-manager. Through their interplay, Spacek and Jones bolster what might have been a standard rags-to-riches scenario. In memorable support are Levon Helm as Loretta's father and Beverly D'Angelo as Patsy Cline. Veteran Grand Ole Opry star Ernest Tubb appears as himself.

Conrack   1974   (Playhouse Video)   *Color*
Director: Martin Ritt
Starring: Jon Voight, Paul Winfield, Madge Sinclair, Tina Andrews, Antonio Fargas, Ruth Attaway, James O'Reare, Hume Cronyn

Conrack is the true story of Pat Conroy, based on his memoirs, *The Water Is Wide*. In the late sixties, Conroy, a white teacher, went to an island off the coast of South Carolina and there, in a weather-damaged two-room schoolhouse, attempted to educate underprivileged black children. His efforts—ultimately semisuccessful—were met with suspicion and negativity by locals, both black and white. In the movie, Jon Voight plays Conroy. The film's title? The children have difficulty pronouncing their new teacher's surname, so they wind up dubbing him "Conrack." In mood and texture the picture can be regarded as a companion to Martin Ritt's earlier work, *Sounder. Conrack* was developed for the screen by Irving Ravetch and Harriet Frank, Jr., who—also for Ritt—adapted *Hud; Hombre; Norma Rae; The Long, Hot Summer;* and *The Sound and the Fury.*

Cross Creek   1983   (Thorn)   *Color*
Director: Martin Ritt
Starring: Mary Steenburgen, Peter Coyote, Rip Torn, Alfre Woodard, Dana Hill, Joanna Miles, Ike Eisenmann, Cary Guffey, Norton Baskin, Malcolm McDowell

This film biography begins in 1928 with Marjorie Kinnan Rawlings's desertion of her comfortable middle-class existence in New York for the wilderness of the Florida Everglades. Here, secluded in a house on Cross Creek, Rawlings wrote *The Yearling* and other works of fiction and nonfiction. Director Martin Ritt documents the influences on the author: the wildlife, the swamp families, the crushing poverty, the creek itself. The script by Dalene Young, from Rawlings's memoirs, traces the subject's evolution on two levels—as a woman and as a writer. Mary Steenburgen represents the central figure with a will of iron, championing individual rights yet sensitive to the codes of the backwoods community. Among her costars are Rip Torn and Alfre Woodard, both Oscar nominees for their portrayals of two Cross Creek residents. Malcolm McDowell, Steenburgen's real-life husband, plays editor Maxwell Perkins; Peter Coyote enacts Rawlings's suitor (and eventual husband) Norton Baskin; and Norton Baskin himself, now a widower, does a bit as a front-porch philosopher. John A. Alonzo's cinematography features the region's bayous, dappled skies, lush greenery, and seemingly impenetrable stands of flora.

The **D**esert Fox   *Listed under War.*

The Diary of Anne Frank   1959   (CBS)   ◆   *Black-and-White*
Director: George Stevens
Starring: Millie Perkins, Joseph Schildkraut, Shelley Winters, Ed Wynn, Richard Beymer, Gusti Huber, Lou Jacobi, Diane Baker, Douglas Spencer, Dody Heath

Anne Frank was a teenage Jewish girl who fled Hitler's Germany with her parents and elder sister. For two years the Frank family hid from the Nazis in a warehouse attic in Amsterdam. During this time Anne kept a diary, which was published in 1947—three years after she was caught and eventually killed by the Nazis. Anne's writing inspired the Frances Goodrich-Albert Hackett stage play, from which this film was adapted. A solemn story, focusing wholly on the hiding place, the film was directed by George Stevens. Millie Perkins, in her screen debut, plays Anne, and Joseph Schildkraut plays her father Otto, who alone survived the concentration camps. Shelley Winters won her first supporting actress Oscar for her depiction of Mrs. Van Daan, another hideaway. Other Academy Award recipients were William C. Mellor for his cinematography and the art direction/set decoration technicians.

The **E**lephant Man   1980   (Paramount)   ★   *Black-and-White*
Director: David Lynch
Starring: Anthony Hopkins, John Hurt, Anne Bancroft, John Gielgud, Wendy Hiller, Freddie Jones, Hannah Gordon

John Merrick, who was born in England late in the nineteenth century, was a horribly deformed man—a victim of neurofibromatosis. Beneath the deformity resided a gentle, intelligent soul, though at first no one suspected as much. (Merrick was cruelly exhibited in carnival sideshows.) His salvation came by way of a compassionate surgeon, Dr. Frederick Treves, who supervised Merrick's education and introduced him to fashionable society. This true story forms the basis for a disturbing movie—an adaptation separate from the Broadway drama, though adopting several incidents from Bernard Pomerance's playscript. Before *The Elephant Man*, David Lynch had directed *Eraserhead* (he has since directed *Dune* and *Blue Velvet*). His screenplay, with Christopher De Vore and Eric Bergren, dramatizes Merrick's pitiable tale. The squalor and poverty of Victorian London are captured by cameraman Freddie Francis, who also shot *Room at the Top, Sons and Lovers,* and *The Innocents. The Elephant Man* was honored with several British Academy Awards, including best film and best actor (John Hurt as Merrick).

Frances   1982   (Thorn)   *Color*
Director: Graeme Clifford
Starring: Jessica Lange, Kim Stanley, Sam Shepard, Jeffrey De Munn, Jordan Charney, Bart Burns, Lane Smith, Jonathan Banks, Sarah Cunningham

Frances Farmer, who came from the New York stage in the era of The Group Theatre, was a Hollywood leading lady from 1936 to 1942. But most in the Hollywood community considered her too candid, independent, and unconventional to fit into the rigid studio system. She was never at home in Hollywood—or in her actual home, dominated by her mother. This biography of the ill-fated actress, written by Eric Bergren, Christopher De Vore, and Nicholas Kazan, traces her rocky career, the mother-daughter collisions, and her ultimate self-destruction. *Frances* is a harrowing portrait of a woman's disintegration, and scenes depicting Farmer's sojourn in an asylum are not for the squeamish. Supporting Lange are Kim Stanley as the mother, Jeffrey De Munn as dramatist Clifford Odets, and Sam Shepard, playing an amalgam of personalities associated with the subject. Susan Blakely starred in a 1983 television film of *Will There Really Be a Morning?*, based on Farmer's autobiography. It aired concurrently with the national release of *Frances*.

Funny Girl   *Listed under Musicals.*

Gandhi   1982   (RCA)   ◆ ✳ ★   *Color*
Director: Richard Attenborough
Starring: Ben Kingsley, Candice Bergen, Edward Fox, John Gielgud, Trevor Howard, John Mills, Martin Sheen, Rohini Hattangandy, Ian Charleson, Athol Fugard, Roshan Seth, Saeed Jaffrey, John Ratzenberger

Eight Academy Awards, including best picture and best actor, went to this sweeping biography of Mahatma Gandhi, India's revered spiritual leader. Richard Attenborough's production, piloted by the John Briley screenplay, spans more than fifty years, dramatizing Gandhi's lifelong struggle for his country's independence through nonviolence. The cinematography is by Billy Williams and Ronnie Taylor. Beyond its Oscar accolades, *Gandhi* was also cited by the New York Film Critics Circle, the British Academy of Film and Television Arts, and (in the foreign film category) the Hollywood press corps with the Golden Globe.

Give 'Em Hell, Harry!   1975   (Worldvision Home Video)   *Color*
Director: Steve Binder
Starring: James Whitmore

Give 'Em Hell, Harry!, written by Samuel Gallu, is a one-man show that James Whitmore toured in for several years, alternating with his popular *Will Rogers' U.S.A.* This rendition—videotaped, transferred to 35mm film, and now back on tape—captures a live performance, with Harry Truman as the hell-raising title figure. Whitmore immerses himself in the personality and physiognomy of our thirty-third president. The audience is invited into the White House oval office as Truman reminisces, in mostly comic terms, about his private and political life. Peter H. Hunt directed the stage edition; Steve Binder receives credit for recording this film version. Whitmore's tour de force inspired an Academy Award nomination for best actor, but the 1975 winner was Jack Nicholson for *One Flew Over the Cuckoo's Nest.*

The Glenn Miller Story   1954   (MCA)   ◆   *Color*
Director: Anthony Mann
Starring: James Stewart, June Allyson, Charles Drake, George Tobias, Harry Morgan, Frances Langford, Louis Armstrong, Gene Krupa, Ben Pollack, Barton MacLane, Sig Rumann, Irving Bacon, James Bell, Kathleen Lockhart, Katharine Warren, Dayton Lummis, Marion Ross, The Modernaires

A biography of the celebrated trombone-playing bandleader of the swing era. The script by Valentine Davies and Oscar Brodney presents James Stewart as Glenn Miller and June Allyson as his wife, Helen. Supporting them, under Anthony Mann's direction, are a number of musical greats playing themselves: Frances Langford, Louis Armstrong, and Gene Krupa. (Joe Yuki is the offscreen dubber when Stewart slides the trombone.) Musical director Joseph Gershenson and arranger Henry Mancini uncannily reproduce the Miller sound—and the music track erupts in a forties hit parade: "In the Mood," "String of Pearls," "Little Brown Jug," "Moonlight Serenade," "Pennsylvania 6-5000," and "Chattanooga Choo Choo." An Oscar went to Leslie Carey for his sound recording. *The Glenn Miller Story* remains one of James Stewart's most appealing films—and one of seven he and director Mann collaborated on from 1950 to 1955; five of them are Western classics: *Winchester '73, Bend of the River, The Naked Spur, The Far Country,* and *The Man from Laramie.*

The Great Caruso   1951   (MGM)   ◆   *Color*
Director: Richard Thorpe
Starring: Mario Lanza, Ann Blyth, Dorothy Kirsten, Jarmila Novotna, Richard Hageman, Carl Benton Reid, Eduard Franz, Ludwig Donath, Alan Napier, Paul Javor, Carl Milletaire, Shepard Menken, Nestor Paiva, Peter Edward Price, Mario Siletti, Angela Clarke, Ian Wolfe, Yvette Dugay

Italian tenor Enrico Caruso is spotlighted in this semifictional biography. Caruso, whose power and range made him a legendary star of grand opera, is here portrayed by Mario

Lanza. In the film (as scripted by Sonya Levien, MGM's story editor, and William Ludwig) music prevails—including the Verdi and Puccini arias for which Caruso is chiefly remembered. One new (for 1951) song gets an airing: Paul Francis Webster's "The Loveliest Night of the Year," based on the melody of the Viennese waltz "Over the Waves." Veteran director Richard Thorpe later guided Elvis Presley in his thespic forays. The MGM sound recording department received an Academy Award on behalf of *The Great Caruso.*

Gypsy   *Listed under Musicals.*

The **I**nn of the Sixth Happiness   1958   (CBS)   *Color*
Director: Mark Robson
Starring: Ingrid Bergman, Curt Jurgens, Robert Donat, Michael David, Athene Seyler, Ronald Squire, Moultrie Kelsall, Richard Wattis, Peter Chong, Tsai Chin, Edith Sharpe, Joan Young, Noel Hood, Burt Kwouk

Ingrid Bergman triumphs as an English housemaid who becomes a missionary in pre–World War II China. Working in an isolated mission, she falls in love with a Chinese army officer. As the Japanese troops advance, she leads a band of orphaned children on a journey. This biography of Gladys Aylward derives from the novel *The Small Woman* by Alan Burgess. Isobel Lennart contributed the screenplay and Mark Robson the direction. Supporting Miss Bergman are Curt Jurgens as her Chinese lover, Linnan, and—in his last movie—Robert Donat, cast against type as the mandarin. Rugged North Wales doubles for 1930s China.

Jim Thorpe, All-American   1951   *Black-and-White*
    (Image Magnetic Associates)
Director: Michael Curtiz
Starring: Burt Lancaster, Charles Bickford, Steve Cochran, Phyllis Thaxter, Dick Wesson, Jack Bighead, Suni Warcloud, Al Mejia, Hubie Kerns, Nestor Paiva

According to an Associated Press poll of sportswriters and broadcasters, Jim Thorpe (1888–1953) was the greatest U.S. athlete of the first half of the century. Thorpe, a Sac and Fox Indian, rose from humble Oklahoma beginnings to international fame as an All-American college halfback—and by winning the pentathlon and decathlon in the 1912 Stockholm Olympics. Thorpe excelled at them all—track and field, baseball, and football. This film account, directed by Michael Curtiz from a Douglas Morrow-Everett Freeman-Frank Davis script, casts athletic Burt Lancaster as the sports titan. Phyllis Thaxter costars as his wife. Adapted from the biography written by Thorpe and Russell J. Birdwell, *Jim Thorpe, All-American* honors the subject without over-glorifying him.

Joan of Arc   1948   (VidAmerica)   ◆   *Color*
Director: Victor Fleming
Starring: Ingrid Bergman, José Ferrer, George Coulouris, Richard Derr, Ray Teal, Roman Bohnen, Robert Barrat, Jimmy Lydon, Rand Brooks, Selena Royle, Francis L. Sullivan, Irene Rich, Nestor Paiva, Gene Lockhart, Richard Ney, Leif Erickson, John Emery, Ward Bond, John Ireland, J. Carrol Naish, Dennis Hoey, Hurd Hatfield, Cecil Kellaway, Morris Ankrum, Philip Borneuf, Alan Napier, George Zucco

Adapted by Andrew Solt and Maxwell Anderson from the latter's playscript, *Joan of Lorraine*, this Walter Wanger production tells the life story of France's national heroine. The Academy Award–winning visuals of this film (Joe Valentine's cinematography and the costume designs by Dorothy Jeakins and Karinska) don't overshadow the majesty of the drama. Ingrid Bergman plays the Maid of Orléans, whose visions from God propel her to lead France against British oppression; her Oscar-nominated performance was bested by Jane Wyman's in *Johnny Belinda*. Supporting her are Hurd Hatfield as Father Pasquerel, Francis L. Sullivan as Pierre Cauchon, and, in his motion picture debut, José Ferrer, playing the Dauphin. Directed by Victor Fleming—the final film of a career that stretched back to 1920 and included *Bombshell*, *Treasure Island*, *Reckless*, *Captains Courageous*, *The Wizard of Oz*, most of *Gone with the Wind*, *Dr. Jekyll and Mr. Hyde* (the Spencer Tracy version), *Tortilla Flat*, and *A Guy Named Joe*.

Lady Sings the Blues   1972   (Paramount)   *Color*
Director: Sidney J. Furie
Starring: *Diana Ross, Billy Dee Williams, Richard Pryor, James Callahan, Paul Hampton, Sid Melton*

Diana Ross made her acting debut in this hard-hitting depiction of legendary blues singer Billie Holiday, and received an Oscar nomination. Ross plays Lady Day from adolescence to her death of heroin addiction in 1959. Avoiding most of the clichés of star bio-melodramas, the screenplay (by Terence McCloy, Chris Clark, and Suzanne de Passe) faithfully adheres to Holiday's 1956 autobiography, *Lady Sings the Blues*, written with William Duffy. The film, then, is an account of the highs and lows of a too-brief life. Michel Legrand composed the original music, but the story incorporates some of the standards from Holiday's repertoire (interpreted by Ross): "Strange Fruit," "Willow Weep for Me," and "Ain't Nobody's Business If I Do." In a rare noncomic role, Richard Pryor plays the star's accompanist, Piano Man.

Lawrence of Arabia   1962   (RCA)   ◆   *Color*
Director: David Lean
Starring: *Peter O'Toole, Alec Guinness, Anthony Quinn, Jack Hawkins, Claude Rains, Anthony Quayle, Arthur Kennedy, José Ferrer, Omar Sharif, Michel Ray, John Dimech, I. S. Johar, Donald Wolfit, Norman Rossington, Howard Marion Crawford*

The saga of T. E. Lawrence (1888–1935), the legendary British adventurer, is told in flashbacks from the occasion of Lawrence's accidental death. The film—scripted by Robert Bolt and directed by David Lean—concentrates on the hero's aid to the Arabs in their revolt against the Turks in World War I. Peter O'Toole, in his first leading role, is dashing as Lawrence, and he is seconded by Omar Sharif in the part that made him a star: Lawrence's friend, Sherif Ali ibn el Kharish. Seven Academy Awards: best picture; director (only five years after Lean's win for *The Bridge on the River Kwai*); cinematography (Frederick A. Young); editing (Anne Coates); music score (Maurice Jarre); sound; and art direction/set decoration.

Lenny   1974   (Key)   *Black-and-White*
Director: Bob Fosse
Starring: *Dustin Hoffman, Valerie Perrine, Jan Miner, Stanley Beck, Gary Morton*

Comedian Lenny Bruce (1925–66) is the subject of this stinging biography, director Bob Fosse's first nonmusical. Under analysis are the comedian's success, his brushes with the law (mostly on counts of public obscenity), and his ultimate self-destruction with narcotics. The no-holds-barred presentation juxtaposes events from the comic's life with his nightclub act; the explicit language at the forefront of Bruce's routines is here replicated, in part, by Julian Barry's screenplay—remodeled from his Broadway stage success. A showcase for the performances of Valerie Perrine as Honey, Lenny's stripper-wife; Jan Miner as Sally Marr, his mother; and Dustin Hoffman, remarkable— in rise and fall—as the title figure.

A **M**an for All Seasons   1966   (RCA)   ◆   *Color*

Director: Fred Zinnemann
Starring: Paul Scofield, Wendy Hiller, Susannah York, Leo McKern, Robert Shaw, Orson Welles, John Hurt, Nigel Davenport, Corin Redgrave, Cyril Luckham

Six Academy Awards went to this drama about the life and martyrdom of Sir Thomas More (1478–1535). *A Man for All Seasons* was named best picture, and additional Oscars went to Paul Scofield for his leading performance, Fred Zinnemann for direction, Robert Bolt for the adaptation of his stage play, Ted Moore for cinematography, and Elizabeth Haffenden and Joan Bridge for their costume designs. The film's central conflict arises when the protagonist, a man of conscience and a devout Catholic, refuses to sanction Henry VIII's Act of Supremacy, which would make Henry the head of the Church of England—and allow him to wed again. Among the virtues of the production are Georges Delerue's score and the supporting cast: Robert Shaw as young, virile Henry; Wendy Hiller and Susannah York as More's wife and daughter; Leo McKern as Thomas Cromwell; John Hurt as Richard Rich; Corin Redgrave as William Roper; and, in an unbilled appearance, Vanessa Redgrave as Anne Boleyn.

Melvin and Howard   1980   (MCA)   ◆ ✳ ❍   *Color*

Director: Jonathan Demme
Starring: Paul Le Mat, Jason Robards, Mary Steenburgen, Jack Kehoe, Pamela Reed, Dabney Coleman, Michael J. Pollard, Gloria Grahame, Elizabeth Cheshire, Martine Beswick

This biography begins as Melvin Dummar (Paul Le Mat), a hand-to-mouth-existence factory worker, gives a lift to a bum hitchhiking in the Nevada desert. The hitchhiker turns out to be Howard Hughes, who eventually bequeaths his chauffeur-rescuer a substantial portion of his multimillion-dollar estate. Only no one believes the will Melvin has is authentic. A comic slice of Americana, *Melvin and Howard* is directed by Jonathan Demme—remembered for *Citizens' Band* (also known as *Handle with Care*) and *Stop Making Sense*—from a screenplay by Bo Goldman. Among its many awards: best picture (National Society of Film Critics); best director (New York Film Critics Circle); and Oscars to scenarist Goldman and to supporting actress Mary Steenburgen, who plays the hero's first wife. The real Melvin Dummar has a walk-on as a counterman in a bus depot cafeteria.

The Miracle Worker   1962   (MGM)   ◆   *Black-and-White*

Director: Arthur Penn
Starring: Anne Bancroft, Patty Duke, Victor Jory, Inga Swenson, Andrew Prine, Kathleen Comegys, Beah Richards, Jack Hollander, Judith Lowry

The Miracle Worker took a circuitous path to the motion picture screen. Adapted by William Gibson from Helen Keller's *The Story of My Life*, it was first an unproduced ballet in 1953, next—in 1957—a "Playhouse 90" teledrama (starring Teresa Wright as Annie Sullivan and Patty McCormack as Helen), then in 1959 a Broadway play. For the film, Anne Bancroft and Patty Duke re-create their stage performances as Annie and Helen. Gibson's biographical fragment focuses on the early childhood and education of the blind, deaf girl who is rescued from oblivion by miracle-working tutor Annie Sullivan. Bancroft and Duke won Oscars for their work. In yet another manifestation—a 1979 TV movie—"The Miracle Worker" starred the grown-up Patty Duke as Annie, with Melissa Gilbert assuming the role of Helen.

My Brilliant Career   1979   (Vestron)   *Color*
Director: Gillian Armstrong
Starring: Judy Davis, Sam Neill, Wendy Hughes, Robert Grubb, Max Cullen, Pat Kennedy, Aileen Britton, Peter Whitford, Carole Skinner, Alan Hopgood, Julia Blake

One of the most successful Australian films to reach American shores in the last decade, *My Brilliant Career* commends the pluck of headstrong farm girl Sybylla Melvyn (Judy Davis) in her aspirations to be a writer. Refusing to obey her family's wishes that she marry a local landowner, Sybylla applies pen to paper—and finally carves herself a literary career. Eleanor Witcombe's scenario derives from a 1910 autobiographical novel by "Miles Franklin," the male nom de plume for the real-life Sybylla. The picture marks Gillian Armstrong's feature-length directing debut. (She has since completed *Starstruck* and *Mrs. Soffel*.) The turn-of-the-century Australian bush is captured by Don McAlpine's cinematography.

Nicholas and Alexandra   1971   (RCA)   *Color*
Director: Franklin Schaffner
Starring: Michael Jayston, Janet Suzman, Tom Baker, Harry Andrews, Laurence Olivier, Michael Redgrave, Alexander Knox, Jack Hawkins, Curt Jurgens, John Wood, Michael Bryant, Irene Worth, Alan Webb

Franklin Schaffner's lavish historical pageant, following James Goldman's screenplay of the Robert K. Massie biography, covers the last fourteen years of the Romanov reign. The story opens with the birth of the czar and czarina's only son, then focuses on the royal couple and their children—while events outside the palace build inexorably to the Revolution. Many crises pass under the filmmakers' scrutiny: the czarevitch's hemophilia; the influence of the mesmeric monk, Rasputin; the rise of Lenin, Trotsky, and Stalin. The finale comes in 1918, with the execution of the royal family. The performers include Michael Jayston and Janet Suzman in the title roles, with Tom Baker (of TV's "Dr. Who") as Rasputin. The cinematographer is Frederick A. Young; the production designer, John Box.

Night and Day   1946   (Key)   *Color*
Director: Michael Curtiz
Starring: Cary Grant, Alexis Smith, Monty Woolley, Ginny Simms, Jane Wyman, Eve Arden, Carlos Ramirez, Donald Woods, Mary Martin, Victor Francen, Alan Hale, Dorothy Malone, Tom D'Andrea, Selena Royle, Henry Stephenson, Paul Cavanagh, Sig Rumann

Cole Porter is the subject of this fictionalized biography. The film, directed by Michael Curtiz from a script by Charles Hoffman, Leo Townsend, and William Bowers, provides a golden opportunity to recall some of Porter's best compositions: "In the Still of the Night," "Let's Do It," "You Do Something to Me," "Miss Otis Regrets," "I've Got You Under My Skin," "I Get a Kick Out of You," "Easy to Love," "Begin the Beguine," "My Heart Belongs to Daddy" (interpreted by Mary Martin), and, of course, "Night and Day." Cary Grant plays the composer—and even sings "You're the Top." Alexis Smith plays his wife, Linda. LeRoy Prinz staged the dance numbers.

Out of Africa   *Listed under Dramas.*

Papillon   1973   (CBS)   *Color*
Director: Franklin J. Schaffner
Starring: Steve McQueen, Dustin Hoffman, Victor Jory, Don Gordon, Anthony Zerbe, George Coulouris, Robert Deman, William Smithers, Woodrow Parfrey

Henri Charrière (also known as Papillon—Butterfly) is a French safecracker sentenced to life exile on Devil's Island for killing a pimp. This autobiographical film (adapted from Charrière's memoirs by Dalton Trumbo and Lorenzo Semple, Jr.) dramatizes the prisoner's various attempts to escape the island penal colony—and his ultimate victory. A gruesome but fascinating depiction, *Papillon* features Steve McQueen as Charrière and Dustin Hoffman as another convict, a counterfeiter named Louis Degas. The cinematographer is Fred Koenekamp. (To date Papillon is the only prisoner ever to escape from Devil's Island.)

Patton   1970   (CBS)   ◆   *Color*
Director: Franklin J. Schaffner
Starring: George C. Scott, Karl Malden, Stephen Young, Michael Strong, Frank Latimore, James Edwards, Lawrence Dobkin, Michael Bates, Tim Considine

Perfect warrior . . . a sixteenth-century man . . . a magnificent anachronism . . . a romantic warrior out of place in contemporary times . . . Old Blood and Guts. That's how General George S. Patton, Jr., was revered and reviled by his colleagues, his adversaries, and his troops. George C. Scott, portraying Patton in Franklin Schaffner's film, displays the multiple facets that account for those diverse personal evaluations. Here is the military historian and tactician; here also is a marvelously ambiguous personality, one capable of embracing both religiosity and exquisite profanity. Coauthors Francis Ford Coppola and Edmund H. North, working with factual materials by General Omar Bradley and Ladislas Farago, trace Patton's career in the North African, Sicilian, and European campaigns. Academy Awards: best picture, actor (an honor Scott refused), director, original screenplay, editing (Hugh S. Fowler), sound (Douglas Williams, Don Bassman), and art direction/set decoration (Urie McCleary, Gil Parrondo, Antonio Mateos, Pierre-Louis Thevenet).

Raging Bull   1980   (CBS)   ◆   *Black-and-White*
Director: Martin Scorsese
Starring: Robert De Niro, Cathy Moriarty, Joe Pesci, Frank Vincent, Nicholas Colasanto, Theresa Saldana

Raging Bull is a movie biography of middleweight boxing champ Jake La Motta. Adapted by Paul Schrader and Mardik Martin from La Motta's ghosted autobiography, the film is tough, violent, profane, and bloody. In the course of the reenactment, Jake (Robert De Niro) meets and marries sexy Vickie (Cathy Moriarty), throws a fight for the Mafia, wins then loses the middleweight title, opens a Florida night club (where he performs as a standup comic), and finally retires—all the while battling with his manager-brother Joey (Joe Pesci). De Niro's performance and Thelma Schoonmaker's editing were rewarded with Oscars. The grit and grime that permeate director Martin Scorsese's films from *Who's That Knocking at My Door?* to *The Color of Money* are on display here, too.

Reds   1981   (Paramount)   ◆   *Color*
Director: Warren Beatty
Starring: Warren Beatty, Diane Keaton, Jack Nicholson, Edward Herrmann, Maureen Stapleton, Jerzy Kosinski, Paul Sorvino, Nicolas Coster, Gene Hackman

In this film biography, journalist John Reed (Warren Beatty) and feminist Louise Bryant (Diane Keaton) are lovers, political comrades, and, ultimately, witnesses to the 1917 Bolshevik Revolution. *Reds,* as scripted by Trevor Griffiths and Warren Beatty, then directed by the latter, is a testament to the protagonists' romance and idealism—followed by disillusionment. A daring, ambitious work in the tradition of *Lawrence of Arabia* and *Doctor Zhivago,* the picture attempts to join Reed and Bryant's private lives to the sweep of history; it lasts for over three hours, but the period details and the performances should keep one riveted. Jack Nicholson is cast as Eugene O'Neill and Maureen Stapleton as anarchist Emma Goldman. Stapleton won an Oscar, as did Beatty for his direction, and Vittorio Storaro for the cinematography.

The Right Stuff   1983   (Warner)   ◆   *Color*
Director: Philip Kaufman
Starring: Sam Shepard, Scott Glenn, Ed Harris, Dennis Quaid, Fred Ward, Barbara Hershey, Kim Stanley, Veronica Cartwright, Pamela Reed, Scott Paulin, Charles Frank, Lance Henriksen, Donald Moffat, Levon Helm, Mary Jo Deschanel, Scott Wilson, Kathy Baker, Royal Dano, David Clennon, Jeff Goldblum, Harry Shearer, John P. Ryan, John Dehner

History is explored in this three-and-a-half-hour exposition of the early days of the U.S. space program. Based on Tom Wolfe's best-seller, *The Right Stuff* salutes "the last true American heroes": test pilot Chuck Yeager (Sam Shepard) and Project Mercury astronauts Gordon Cooper (Dennis Quaid), John Glenn (Ed Harris), Alan Shepard (Scott Glenn), Scott Carpenter (Charles Frank), Gus Grissom (Fred Ward), Wally Schirra (Lance Henriksen), and Deke Slayton (Scott Paulin). Among the highlights in the adaptation by screenwriter-director Philip Kaufman are Yeager's flight through the sound barrier; the astronauts' rigorous training; a view of their personal lives; their introduction to the press corps; the initial suborbital flights; Glenn's three orbits of the earth and his brush with death on descent; and—climactically—Yeager's ability to prove again that he has the right stuff in a near-fatal attempt to set a new speed record in the NF-104 airplane. Four Academy Awards: original score (Bill Conti), editing, sound, and sound effects editing.

Running Brave   1983   (Disney)   *Color*
Director: D. S. Everett
Starring: Robby Benson, Pat Hingle, Claudia Cron, Jeff McCracken, August Schellenberg,
Denis Lacroix, Graham Greene, Kendall Smith

A sports biography about Billy Mills, a Sioux Indian, who is a gifted cross-country runner. When he wins a scholarship to a Kansas university, he leaves his South Dakota reservation. After gaining recognition at the college level, he achieves record-books glory—winning a gold medal in the 10,000 meter run at the 1964 Tokyo Olympics. In the film, written by Henry Bean and Shirl Hendryx, performers include Robby Benson as the title character, Pat Hingle as Billy's university coach, and Jeff McCracken as his schoolmate, Dennis. D. S. Everett, the director, is a pseudonym for Canadian filmmaker Donald Shebib *(Goin' Down the Road, Heartaches)* who, after viewing the release print, asked that his name be removed from the credits.

Sacco and Vanzetti   1971   (United Home Video)   *Color*
Director: Giuliano Montaldo
Starring: Gian Maria Volontè, Riccardo Cucciolla, Milo O'Shea, Cyril Cusack, Rossana
Fratello, Geoffrey Kean

In the politically volatile 1920s, the Sacco-Vanzetti murder trial was a cause célèbre. Italian immigrants (and confessed anarchists) Nicola Sacco and Bartolomeo Vanzetti were arrested for the slaying of a paymaster and his guard in South Braintree, Massachusetts. The resulting trial unearthed contradictory evidence, but the men were found guilty and, after many delays, were executed. An indictment of political hysteria and miscarriage of justice, this Italian film, under the stewardship of director Giuliano Montaldo, presents the history of the Sacco-Vanzetti case. Montaldo, revered in this country for the TV miniseries "Marco Polo" and known in his native Italy for many other films, here directs an international cast from a screenplay he cowrote with Favrizio Onofri. Thanks primarily to Montaldo's guidance and the performances of Gian Maria Volontè and Riccardo Cucciolla in the title roles, *Sacco and Vanzetti* stays on course as a solid, affecting biography. Joan Baez performs the theme song.

Serpico   1973   (Paramount)   *Color*
Director: Sidney Lumet
Starring: Al Pacino, John Randolph, Jack Kehoe, Tony Roberts, Biff McGuire, Cornelia
Sharpe, Barbara Eda-Young, Lewis J. Stadlen

Inspired by the Peter Maas biography, this police exposé drama centers around New York City undercover cop Frank Serpico (Al Pacino). Departmental corruption is the theme. Serpico joins the force as an idealistic rookie but is soon overwhelmed by the rampant deceit among his fellow officers; he discovers that brutality, bribe-taking, and graft are all part of the day's work. Serpico's eyewitness account of these injustices helps lead to the formation of the Knapp Commission. These real-life events are dramatized, without adornment, in the Waldo Salt-Norman Wexler screenplay and captured by Arthur J. Ornitz's camera. *Serpico* is directed by Sidney Lumet, who returned to this genre in *Prince of the City*.

Silkwood   1983   (Embassy)   *Color*
Director: Mike Nichols
Starring: Meryl Streep, Kurt Russell, Cher, Craig T. Nelson, Diana Scarwid, Fred Ward, Ron Silver, Charles Hallahan, Sudie Bond, Henderson Forsythe, E. Katherine Kerr, Bruce McGill

Karen Silkwood is the subject of this screen biography. In the early seventies, Silkwood worked at an Oklahoma plutonium plant. On November 13, 1974, she was killed in a car accident just as she was about to expose unsafe practices in the nuclear industry. In the film, written by Nora Ephron and Alice Arlen, emphasis is placed on Karen's workaday existence and her unconventional personal life. Depicting the title figure, in a critically lauded performance, is Meryl Streep; Cher and Kurt Russell costar as her housemates. Under Mike Nichols's direction, *Silkwood* is both a historical re-creation and a suspenseful drama—even though the conclusion is foreknown.

Sister Kenny   1946   (Blackhawk Films)   *Black-and-White*
Director: Dudley Nichols
Starring: Rosalind Russell, Alexander Knox, Dean Jagger, Philip Merivale, Beulah Bondi, Charles Dingle, John Litel, Doreen McCann, Fay Helm, Charles Kemper, Dorothy Peterson

And They Shall Walk is the autobiography of Australian nurse Elizabeth Kenny, whose research of infantile paralysis ultimately led to the treatment for polio. In the screen adaptation, fashioned by Dudley Nichols, Alexander Knox, and Mary McCarthy, and directed by Nichols, the title role is assumed by Rosalind Russell. After a string of career-woman comedies, Russell made a major departure herein. Her interpretation of the courageous nurse and her crusades makes *Sister Kenny* a stirring biographical drama. Notable in the supporting cast is Philip Merivale, playing the obdurate Dr. Brack, who refuses to acknowledge Elizabeth Kenny's therapy. This film is one of three that veteran scenarist Nichols directed in the forties; also to his credit are *Government Girl* (1943) and, again with Russell as leading lady, *Mourning Becomes Electra* (1947).

The Spirit of St. Louis   1957   (Warner)   *Color*
Director: Billy Wilder
Starring: James Stewart, Murray Hamilton, Patricia Smith, Bartlett Robinson, Robert Cornthwaite, Sheila Bond, Marc Connelly, Arthur Space, Harlan Warde, Dabbs Greer, Paul Birch, David Orrick, Robert Burton, Aaron Spelling, Virginia Christine

This reconstruction of Charles A. Lindbergh's historic transatlantic solo flight is based on the aviator's 1953 Pulitzer Prize memoir. (Wendell Mayes, Charles Lederer, and Billy Wilder reworked the book into a screenplay, and Wilder directed.) James Stewart stars as Lindbergh, the "Lone Eagle." The hero's 1927 New York-to-Paris trip—3,600 miles flown nonstop in 33½ hours—is the film's centerpiece; flashbacks amplify the pre-1927 story. Of particular interest is the development of *The Spirit of St. Louis,* Lindbergh's specially constructed plane, by B. F. Mahoney (Bartlett Robinson). A grand adventure, with photography by Robert Burks, J. Peverell Marley, and (in the air) Thomas Tutwiler.

Till the Clouds Roll By   *Listed under Musicals.*

The Trial of the Catonsville Nine   1972   (RCA)   *Color*
Director: Gordon Davidson
Starring: Ed Flanders, Richard Jordan, Douglass Watson, Peter Strauss, Nancy Malone, William Schallert

This film transcript of the documentary play by Daniel Berrigan records the trial of the Catonsville Nine—seven men and two women who burned 378 draft records at Catonsville, Maryland, in 1968. The antiwar activists—including the author, a priest, and his brother Father Philip Berrigan—were subsequently jailed. It was from his prison cell that Daniel Berrigan wrote the playscript. (He and Saul Levitt collaborated on the screen version.) A fascinating series of testimonies give *The Trial of the Catonsville Nine* its foundation. Directed by Gordon Davidson and photographed by Haskell Wexler.

Viva Zapata!   1952   (Key)   ◆   *Black-and-White*
Director: Elia Kazan
Starring: Marlon Brando, Jean Peters, Anthony Quinn, Joseph Wiseman, Arnold Moss, Alan Reed, Margo, Lou Gilbert, Harold Gordon, Mildred Dunnock, Frank Silvera

Written by John Steinbeck and directed by Elia Kazan, this biography traces the rise of Mexican revolutionary Emiliano Zapata (as portrayed by Marlon Brando). Born in the late 1870s, Zapata was an Indian tenant farmer who, in 1908, began leading revolts in an effort to reclaim government-expropriated lands. In time, he became a hero to the peasants of southern Mexico—and before his assassination in 1919 he was revered throughout the nation. The Steinbeck-Kazan collaboration gives a sweeping, declamatory presentation of the hero's life and times. Costar Anthony Quinn won an Oscar for his interpretation of Zapata's older brother; four years later, Quinn took his second statuette, also in the supporting actor category, for *Lust for Life.*

Walking Tall   1973   (Lightning Video)   *Color*
Director: Phil Karlson
Starring: Joe Don Baker, Elizabeth Hartman, Rosemary Murphy, Gene Evans, Noah Beery, Felton Perry, Brenda Benet, Lurene Tuttle, Ed Call

Joe Don Baker stars as Buford Pusser in this documentary-drama of fact-based villainy set in McNairy County, Tennessee. Pusser was a baseball bat–wielding sheriff who cleaned up corruption in his hometown—for a while. A glorification of vigilantism, the film, directed by Phil Karlson from Mort Briskin's script, presents Pusser in his crusade against syndicate-backed gambling and prostitution operations. Aiding the hero in his strong-arm pursuit of justice are his wife (Elizabeth Hartman) and a black deputy (Felton Perry). By answering violence with violence, the lawman becomes a local hero: judge, jury, and executioner. This feature was ultimately such a hit it inspired two sequels—*Part 2, Walking Tall* (1975) and *Final Chapter—Walking Tall* (1977)—then a made-for-TV movie, *A Real American Hero* (1978), followed by a weekly series (1981).

The Wrong Man   *Listed under Suspense and Mystery.*

Comedies

Adam's Rib   1949   (MGM)   *Black-and-White*
Director: George Cukor
Starring: Spencer Tracy, Katharine Hepburn, Judy Holliday, Tom Ewell, David Wayne, Jean Hagen, Hope Emerson

Another George Cukor-Spencer Tracy-Ruth Gordon collaboration, *Adam's Rib* is a comedy classic. Tracy and Hepburn are married attorneys who find themselves on opposite sides of a domestic dispute case. Judy Holliday has shot her philandering husband (Tom Ewell)—and it's Tracy for the prosecution, Hepburn for the defense. Holliday's daffy blonde defendant role was a precursor to her Billie Dawn of *Born Yesterday*. Basis for the short-lived 1973 television series of the same title. Ken Howard and Blythe Danner starred as the lawyer spouses.

All About Eve   1950   (CBS)   ◆   *Black-and-White*
Director: Joseph L. Mankiewicz
Starring: Bette Davis, Anne Baxter, George Sanders, Celeste Holm, Gary Merrill, Hugh Marlowe, Thelma Ritter, Marilyn Monroe, Gregory Ratoff, Barbara Bates

After a series of mediocre roles in less than memorable pictures, Bette Davis reached new heights as Margo Channing. (Claudette Colbert, the studio's initial choice, had injured her back, so the role went to Miss Davis.) Her portrayal of a fortyish stage star facing difficult career decisions stands as one of her most powerful. Director-writer Mankiewicz created memorable moments for his entire cast, noteworthily Anne Baxter as the duplicitous ladder-climbing ingenue, Eve Harrington. The screenplay brims with epithets, trade chatter, venomous retorts, and even a double entendre or two or three. Watch for Marilyn Monroe, in an early appearance, as a starlet whom George Sanders introduces as "a graduate of the school of Copacabana." Six Oscars: best picture, director, screenplay, supporting actor (Sanders), costume design, sound recording.

All of Me   1984   (Thorn)   *Color*
Director: Carl Reiner
Starring: Steve Martin, Lily Tomlin, Madolyn Smith, Richard Libertini, Dana Elcar, Jason Bernard, Selma Diamond, Eric Christmas, Victoria Tennant

The amazing story of how recently deceased dowager Edwina Cutwater (Tomlin) inhabits half the body of lawyer Roger Cobb (Martin). Edwina's master plan at the point

17

of death was the teleportation of her soul into another earthly vessel. Through a colossal mix-up, however, she gets inside Roger—literally. His initial reaction: "I must be picking up 'General Hospital' in my fillings." And she wants to possess *all* of his (or somebody's) body, not merely half. The means by which these entanglements are straightened out spark what is to many fans one of the funniest comedies in decades. Phil Alden Robinson wrote the screenplay from his unpublished novel. Veteran actor-turned-director Reiner's supreme achievement to date.

American Graffiti   1973   (MCA)   *Color*
Director: George Lucas
Starring: Richard Dreyfuss, Ronny Howard, Paul LeMat, Charlie Martin Smith, Cindy Williams, Candy Clark, Mackenzie Phillips, Wolfman Jack, Harrison Ford, Manuel Padilla, Jr.

The "Where were you in '62?" movie was a sleeper hit in '73. Surely not even director Lucas or his cowriters Gloria Katz and Willard Huyck could have anticipated the enormous success awaiting *American Graffiti*. But apparently audiences were only too ready to rediscover the early sixties—and vicariously relive their high school years. The story unfolds one hot summer night, sunset to sun-up, in a small California town. A celebration of the icons of the age (ponytails, ducktails, flashy cars, the drive-in hangout, and the best of rock 'n' roll), *American Graffiti* has both the lingo and the look of those years. *American Graffiti* yields surprises even on second or third or fourth viewings—and allows an early look at an ensemble of actors that went on to further acclaim and, for certain individuals, stardom. In bits: Kathleen Quinlan, Debralee Scott, and Suzanne Sommers (as the blonde in the T-Bird).

And Now for Something Completely Different   *Color*
    Great Britain 1971; U.S. 1972   (RCA)
Director: Ian MacNaughton
Starring: Graham Chapman, John Cleese, Eric Idle, Terry Gilliam, Terry Jones, Michael Palin, Carol Cleveland, Connie Booth

This comic sampler introduced American moviegoers to the English satirical performers known collectively as Monty Python. Individually, they are five ex-Oxbridge writer-comics, abetted by American cartoonist Terry Gilliam. The troupe delighted BBC televiewers beginning in the late sixties; when their series, "Monty Python's Flying Circus," was brought to the United States by PBS, a cult developed. *And Now for Something Completely Different* assembles many of the old TV revue sketches and restages them for the motion picture camera. All the trademark skits are here: "Blackmail," "Hell's Grannies," "I'm a Lumberjack," "Dead Parrot," "Say No More—Nudge, Nudge," "The Joke That Kills," and "The Upper-Class Twit of the Year Competition." Dialogue sample (of Terry Jones as a boardinghouse landlady greeting her guests): "I won't shake hands. I was just putting lard on the cat's boil."

Annie Hall   1977   (CBS)   ◆   *Color*
Director: Woody Allen
Starring: Woody Allen, Diane Keaton, Tony Roberts, Colleen Dewhurst, Shelley Duvall, Carol Kane, Janet Margolin, Paul Simon, Christopher Walken

Woody Allen's breakout film. Alvy Singer, Allen's depressive, neurasthenic hero, falls in love with struggling singer-actress Annie Hall (Diane Keaton). Their bittersweet affair blossoms (then fades) to the accompaniment of forays around Manhattan, insights on New York versus Los Angeles, quotations from *The Sorrow and the Pity* (Alvy's favorite film), and revelations about the difficulty of maintaining relationships. Allen's working title was *Anhedonia*—the chronic inability to experience pleasure. Anhedonia finally takes its toll on Alvy and Annie, but their story continues to give lots of pleasure to others. Oscars: best picture, best director, best actress, and best screenplay (Marshall Brickman was the coauthor). The cinematography is by Gordon Willis, with whom Allen has worked frequently.

Any Which Way You Can   1980   (Warner)   *Color*
Director: Buddy Van Horn
Starring: Clint Eastwood, Sondra Locke, Geoffrey Lewis, Harry Guardino, William Smith, Michael Cavanaugh, Ruth Gordon

A continuation of *Every Which Way But Loose*—which means more pratfalls, more down-home humor, more bare-knuckles brawling. Most of the *Loose* cast reassemble as Clint battles shady gamblers and a tough motorcycle gang. It's been suggested by more than one critic that Clyde the orangutan has most of the good lines. For fisticuffs fanatics, the climactic battle between Clint and main bad guy William Smith ranks as one of the best staged fights on film.

The Apartment   1960   (RCA)   ◆   *Black-and-White*
Director: Billy Wilder
Starring: Jack Lemmon, Shirley MacLaine, Fred MacMurray, Ray Walston, David Lewis, Jack Kruschen, Joan Shawlee, Edie Adams, Hope Holiday

Jack Lemmon stars as an insurance company junior executive on the rise who will do anything for his superiors. He's only too pleased to make his bachelor apartment available for romantic trysts. After falling for Shirley MacLaine, he's caught between conscience and career opportunism when boss Fred MacMurray courts Shirley. *The Apartment*, by Billy Wilder and his longtime script partner I. A. L. Diamond, is a sardonic depiction of Madison Avenue morality. Edie Adams made her screen debut, as an executive secretary. Awards: five Oscars (directing, writing, editing, art direction/ set decoration—*and* the top honor). The musical theme from *The Apartment* ("Lonely Room") by Adolph Deutsch stayed on the record charts for years, and the sheet music is still a big seller. The film itself provided the inspiration for the Broadway musical hit *Promises, Promises*.

The Apprenticeship of Duddy Kravitz   1974   (Paramount)   *Color*
Director: Ted Kotcheff
Starring: Richard Dreyfuss, Jack Warden, Randy Quaid, Micheline Lânctot, Joseph Wiseman, Denholm Elliott, Joe Silver

This comedy-drama presents Richard Dreyfuss as a teenage wheeler-dealer in Montreal in the 1940s. Duddy Kravitz wants to climb out of the Jewish ghetto and he isn't exactly subtle in scaling the walls. He finally realizes success—but pays the price. Dreyfuss followed his showy central role in *American Graffiti* with this performance; hustling, wheedling Duddy may be the actor's most substantial film work. Screenplay by Mordecai Richler from his popular Canadian novel. Ted Kotcheff, in whose career *The Apprenticeship of Duddy Kravitz* remains a high point, went on to direct (among others) *Fun with Dick and Jane, Someone Is Killing the Great Chefs of Europe, North Dallas Forty, First Blood,* and *Uncommon Valor.*

The April Fools   1969   (Key)   *Color*
Director: Stuart Rosenberg
Starring: Jack Lemmon, Catherine Deneuve, Peter Lawford, Jack Weston, Harvey Korman, Sally Kellerman, Charles Boyer, Myrna Loy

Jack Lemmon is a stockbroker trapped in a loveless marriage with community- , family- , kultur- , sociopsychology-oriented Sally Kellerman. ("Oriented" is her favorite word.) Catherine Deneuve is the bored jet-set wife of Wall Street tycoon Peter Lawford. The ads tell the story: "He has a wife. She has a husband. With so much in common, they just had to fall in love." Hal Dresner's script is laced with an amalgam of styles (farce, satire, situation comedy). Lawford, as the villain of the piece, and Harvey Korman, as a lecherous, drunken commuter, are perhaps most memorable.

Around the World in 80 Days   1956   (Warner)   ◆   *Color*
Director: Michael Anderson
Starring: David Niven, Cantinflas, Robert Newton, Shirley MacLaine, Charles Boyer, Joe E. Brown, Martine Carol, John Carradine, Charles Coburn, Ronald Colman, Noël Coward, Marlene Dietrich, Ava Gardner, Sir John Gielgud, Sir Cedric Hardwicke

And Glynis Johns, Buster Keaton, Beatrice Lillie, Peter Lorre, Jack Oakie, George Raft, Gilbert Roland, Cesar Romero, Frank Sinatra, Red Skelton. And *more*—as guest stars by the score parade by for cameo service in this Michael Todd extravaganza from Jules Verne's source novel. Phileas Fogg, an imperturbable English gentleman, bets the members of his London club that he can circle the globe in eighty days. And, as recorded by the Todd-AO screen process, he does—thereby absorbing the splendors of the French Riviera, India, Hong Kong, Pakistan, Siam, Japan, San Francisco, and on and on, before returning to London in the allotted time. The prologue contains the 1902 Georges Méliès version of Verne's *A Trip to the Moon. Around the World in 80 Days* was the Oscar winner as best picture of the year; the Victor Young score was also cited. Others honored by the Academy: the screenwriters, the editing crew, and Lionel Lindon for his cinematography.

Arthur   1981   (Warner)   ◆   *Color*
Director: Steve Gordon
Starring: Dudley Moore, Liza Minnelli, Sir John Gielgud, Geraldine Fitzgerald, Jill Eikenberry, Stephen Elliott, Ted Ross, Barney Martin

An exercise in reviving thirties comedy—but underscored with contemporary tones. Arthur is a madcap millionaire who is given an ultimatum: marry according to the family's wishes and keep the fortune or defy them and lose it. Dudley Moore, as the frivolous and frequently inebriated title character, won new fans—while John Gielgud, as Arthur's sarcastic manservant, charmed movie patrons. Liza Minnelli plays the working-class waitress who steals Arthur's heart. The Oscar-nominated original screenplay by Steve Gordon (whose directing debut this was) hinted at equally sprightly movie milestones to come; unfortunately, Gordon died only a few years after *Arthur*'s premiere. On Academy Awards night Gielgud won, in absentia, a best supporting actor prize. Another *Arthur* victory came in the original song category: Burt Bacharach-Carole Bayer Sager-Christopher Cross-Peter Allen "Arthur's Theme (Best That You Can Do)."

Auntie Mame   *Listed under Musicals.*

Baby Doll   *Listed under Dramas.*

The Bachelor and the Bobby-Soxer   1947   ◆   *Black-and-White*
    (Blackhawk Films; Nostalgia)
Director: Irving Reis
Starring: Cary Grant, Myrna Loy, Shirley Temple, Rudy Vallee, Ray Collins, Harry Davenport, Johnny Sands, Don Beddoe, Lillian Randolph, Veda Ann Borg

Cary Grant is the bachelor. Shirley Temple is the bobby-soxer infatuated with him. And Myrna Loy is Shirley's level-headed sister—a judge who orders Cary to date the teen and to end her infatuation. Comedy that maintains its light touch almost throughout. Director Irving Reis, before turning to *The Bachelor and the Bobby-Soxer,* was chiefly known in the industry for his craftsmanlike approach to the Falcon suspense series, starring George Sanders. And afterward he concentrated on dramas like *Enchantment* and *All My Sons.* Oddly, in the final directing stint before his death—the Rex Harrison-Lilli Palmer vehicle, *The Fourposter*—he returned to comedy. Sidney Sheldon's original screenplay, his first Hollywood credit, brought him an Academy Award. Over twenty-five years later, Sheldon's best-selling novels—*Bloodline, Rage of Angels, The Other Side of Midnight*—made him a household name.

Back to the Future   1985   (MCA)   ◆   *Color*
Director: Robert Zemeckis
Starring: Michael J. Fox, Christopher Lloyd, Lea Thompson, Crispin Glover, Thomas F. Wilson, Claudia Wells, Marc McClure, Wendie Jo Sperber, George DiCenzo, Frances Lee McCain, James Tolkan

Midwest teen Marty McFly (Michael J. Fox) is hurtled back in time from 1985 to 1955. From this vantage he observes his high school–age parents and attempts to amend future events before they actually happen. His accomplice: crackpot inventor Christopher Lloyd. *Back to the Future* was the biggest movie money maker of 1985. As of this writing, it has brought in over $94 million at U.S. and Canadian box offices. This Steven Spielberg science-fiction comedy was written by Bob Gale and Robert Zemeckis—and directed by the latter. (Gale and Zemeckis have been a filmmaking team since Spielberg financed them on *I Wanna Hold Your Hand.*) One clever scene: the young hero's request for a Tab or a Pepsi Free at the fifties drug store soda fountain. Vintage music that runs the gamut from "Mr. Sandman" to "Johnny B. Goode" to "The Ballad of Davy Crockett." Original songs: "Back in Time" and the Oscar-nominated "The Power of Love" are performed by Huey Lewis and the News. Academy Award: sound effects editing.

The Bad News Bears   1976   (Paramount)   *Color*
Director: Michael Ritchie
Starring: Walter Matthau, Tatum O'Neal, Vic Morrow, Joyce Van Patten, Jackie Earle Haley, Alfred Lutter, Brandon Cruz, Ben Piazza

Morris Buttermaker, once a minor-league ballplayer, has been paying rent by cleaning swimming pools. He is hired to coach a bumbling Little League baseball team and lift it out of its slump. Because the oddball kids are such lousy players, as well as major misfits, Buttermaker brings in tomboy Tatum O'Neal as star pitcher. Learning this, the foul-mouthed Bears's repartee and ethnic jokes reach new lows. Bill Lancaster's story and dialogue are partly shocking, but almost entirely credible. Michael Ritchie is the director whose pre-*Bears* credits include *Downhill Racer, The Candidate,* and *Smile.* Matthau as the seedy coach is a natural. To accompany the John A. Alonzo visuals, Jerry Fielding's score works some variations on Bizet's *Carmen* to good effect. Critical and public support of *The Bad News Bears* prompted two sequels.

The Bad News Bears in Breaking Training   1977   (Paramount)   *Color*
Director: Michael Pressman
Starring: William Devane, Jackie Earle Haley, Clifton James, Jimmy Baio, Chris Barnes

In this installment, the Bears go to the Houston Astrodome—and William Devane, as tough kid Jackie Earle Haley's estranged father, becomes the new coach. Devane and Haley are a perfect match; their mutual antagonism and ultimate reconciliation are touching. This second picture also made a healthy profit. The series went downhill the third time, though; after the lackluster *The Bad News Bears Go to Japan* (1978, John Berry), the team retired except for a one-season (1979–80) comeback in the TV series, starring Jack Warden as Morris Buttermaker.

Bananas   1971   (CBS)   *Color*
Director: Woody Allen
Starring: Woody Allen, Louise Lasser, Carlos Montalban, Natividad Abascal, Jacobo Morales, Miguel Suarez, David Ortiz, René Enriquez, Charlotte Rae, Conrad Bain

Woody Allen's second feature, after *Take the Money and Run,* as writer-director-star. *Bananas* introduces Allen as products-tester Fielding Mellish, who—all for love—gets involved in guerrilla warfare to combat a dictatorship in the small South American state of San Marcos. Allen and his coscenarist Mickey Rose have devised spoofs of TV ads and programs. Sportscaster Howard Cosell reports play-by-play on the marital consummation of Fielding and his beloved (Louise Lasser). The "Wide World of Sports" indeed! Marvin Hamlisch's comic theme song, "Quiero la Noche," is interpreted by the Yomo Toro Trio—and punctuated by machine gun fire; his serious theme (with Howard Liebling), " 'Cause I Believe in Loving," is sung by Jake Holmes. Sylvester Stallone plays a no-nonsense street hood and Allen Garfield is the man on the cross colliding with Fielding over a parking space. Most Woody Allen devotees point to *Bananas* as his first masterpiece.

Barefoot in the Park   1967   (Paramount)   *Color*
Director: Gene Saks
Starring: Robert Redford, Jane Fonda, Charles Boyer, Mildred Natwick, Herbert Edelman, Mabel Albertson, Fritz Feld, James Stone

The screen transfer of Neil Simon's long-running Broadway hit (1,532 performances). The joke building here is sophisticated—and the humor is derived from an authentic situation: loving (then spatting) newlyweds moving into a five-story walkup in an East Side brownstone. Redford and Fonda make a handsome romantic comedy team. Mildred Natwick, however, as Fonda's protective mother, benefits from all of Simon's best lines. (Redford, Natwick, and phone repairman Herb Edelman were in the original cast when the play opened in New York in 1963.) The music is by Neal Hefti, who next scored *The Odd Couple*. This was actor Gene Saks's debut as a film director. Other Neil Simon movies guided by Saks: *The Odd Couple*, *The Last of the Red Hot Lovers*, and *Brighton Beach Memoirs*.

The Battle of the Sexes 1960 (Electric) *Black-and-White*
Director: Charles Crichton
Starring: Peter Sellers, Robert Morley, Constance Cummings, Jameson Clark, Ernest Thesiger, Moultrie Kelsall, Alex Mackenzie, Roddy McMillan, Donald Pleasence

The inspiration for this Charles Crichton satire is "The Catbird Seat," James Thurber's 1942 short story, originally published in *The New Yorker*. The film rates as a comedy of ideas, successfully capturing that bizarre Thurber combination of gentleness and acerbity. Scotsman Peter Sellers, the old retainer of a venerable Edinburgh kilts company, is appalled when a female efficiency expert wages an office-improvement campaign. Before long Sellers is pondering murder. Sellers is marvelous in yet another oddball role, and there are fine turns by Robert Morley as the gouty boss and Constance Cummings as the interloper with the bright ideas. Crichton is a former editor who turned to directing in the mid-forties. Other comedies made by Crichton during the heyday of the Ealing Studios include *The Lavender Hill Mob* and *The Titfield Thunderbolt*.

Beat the Devil 1954 (RCA) *Black-and-White*
Director: John Huston
Starring: Humphrey Bogart, Jennifer Jones, Gina Lollobrigida, Robert Morley, Peter Lorre, Edward Underdown, Ivor Barnard, Bernard Lee, Marco Tulli

This parody must be seen to be believed. John Huston, who directed and cowrote the script with Truman Capote, once remarked, "The formula of *Beat the Devil* is that everyone is slightly absurd." The reports that Capote doled out the dialogue piecemeal—day-by-day, in fact—may be apocryphal, but that would help to explain the improvisatory quality of the finished product. In Hitchcockian terms, the MacGuffin is a uranium deposit about which too many greedy parties learn. The search is on— from the Italian Riviera to British East Africa. Among the participants: husband and wife Bogart and Lollobrigida, swindlers Lorre and Morley, puzzled C.I.D. inspector Bernard Lee, perky Jennifer Jones and her British spouse Edward Underdown. *Beat the Devil* met with poor box office reception in its day; since 1954, though, a cult audience has developed. Audiences drawn to John Huston's *Prizzi's Honor* will probably greet his earlier spoof warmly too.

Bedazzled 1967 (CBS) *Color*
Director: Stanley Donen
Starring: Peter Cook, Dudley Moore, Eleanor Bron, Raquel Welch, Michael Bates, Howard Goorney

This imaginative updating of the Faust legend centers on bashful fry-cook Dudley Moore's desire to woo waitress Eleanor Bron, who is blind to his infatuation. Dapper Peter Cook enters the scene to grant the remainder of the fantasy, as inept Dudley keeps making a bungle of his wishes. Along the way, he meets Raquel Welch as one of the Seven Deadly Sins—Lillian Lust, "the babe with the bust." *Bedazzled* is both funny and, at times, irreverent; at one juncture, thanks to some devilish intervention, the stars become nuns in the Order of the Leaping Berelians. (The magic words are "Julie Andrews.") Peter Cook wrote the screenplay, "from an idea" he and Dudley Moore shared. Moore, for his behind-camera labor, created the musical score.

Bedtime for Bonzo   1951   (MCA)   *Black-and-White*
Director: Frederick de Cordova
Starring: Ronald Reagan, Diana Lynn, Walter Slezak, Jesse White, Lucille Barkley, Herbert Vigran, Brad Johnson, Ann Tyrrell

Bedtime for Bonzo is a situation comedy primarily remarkable nowadays because its handsome leading man, at this writing, resides in the White House. College professor Peter Boyd (Ronald Reagan) is engaged in an experiment in heredity. In order to validate his theory that early environment greatly influences how one develops, the professor adopts a chimpanzee and treats him like a child. The following year, Cary Grant traversed much of the same terrain in Howard Hawks's *Monkey Business*. There was a 1952 sequel—*Bonzo Goes to College*—With Fred de Cordova repeating as director, but with an all new cast.

Being There   1979   (CBS)   ◆   *Color*
Director: Hal Ashby
Starring: Peter Sellers, Shirley MacLaine, Jack Warden, Melvyn Douglas, Richard Dysart, Richard Basehart, James Noble, David Clennon

Chance, an illiterate gardener living in Washington, D.C., finds himself homeless when his benefactor dies. By accident he winds up in the mansion of a dying political luminary, who mistakes Chance's feebleminded taciturnity for acumen. The truth, in Hal Ashby's satire derived from the Jerzy Kosinski novel, provides black humor: the poor gardener is simply spouting TV jargon he has ingested over the years; talking straight-faced before the rich and the mighty in the nation's capital, he is taken for a modern-day Messiah. *Being There* was another tour de force for Peter Sellers. Melvyn Douglas received his second Oscar designation as best supporting actor (his first came with *Hud*) as the dying political adviser who provides a foster home for Chance. Kosinski himself wrote the screenplay. *Being There* was filmed chiefly at the late George Vanderbilt's Biltmore House castle near Ashville, North Carolina.

Bell, Book, and Candle   1958   (RCA)   *Color*
Director: Richard Quine
Starring: James Stewart, Kim Novak, Jack Lemmon, Ernie Kovacs, Hermione Gingold, Elsa Lanchester, Janice Rule, Philippe Clay, Howard McNear

In this screen version of John Van Druten's Broadway comedy, James Stewart is a Manhattan publisher who falls under the spell of a beguiling witch (Kim Novak), whose only desire is to be normal. When she, in turn, falls in love with Stewart—and learns how to cry—she gratefully forsakes all her magical powers. Jack Lemmon plays her brother, a warlock. Other members of the coven are Elsa Lanchester and Hermione Gingold, while Ernie Kovacs is a wacky author. Ailurophiles will reserve best acting citations for Pyewacket—Miss Novak's feline familiar. James Wong Howe is responsible for the color cinematography. A former actor and dancer who evolved into a director, Richard Quine had other successes with several Jack Lemmon comedies, *My Sister Eileen* (1955) and *Operation Mad Ball* (1957); several Kim Novak melodramas; and—with Lemmon and Novak together again—*The Notorious Landlady* (1962).

The Belles of St. Trinian's   1954   (Thorn)   *Black-and-White*
Director: Frank Launder
Starring: Alastair Sim, George Cole, Joyce Grenfell, Hermione Baddeley, Betty Ann Davies, Renee Houston, Beryl Reid, Irene Handl, Mary Merrall

English comedy fans should respond with laughter to *The Belles of St. Trinian's*. The aforementioned institution is a country girls' school fallen on hard times. In order to stave off bankruptcy, the headmistress turns for financial expertise to her brother—a bookie. Alastair Sim enacts both roles! His headmistress is particularly amusing. Director Frank Launder and his partner-scenarist, Sidney Gilliat, found dual inspiration for this film: first, Ronald Searle's popular cartoons about the hellions in knee socks enrolled in St. Trinian's; second, the hugely successful stage farce, *The Happiest Days of Your Life*, about adolescent girls erroneously billeted at a boys' school—which Launder and Gilliat brought to the screen in 1950. Three Launder-Gilliat sequels resulted: *Blue Murder at St. Trinian's* (1957), *The Pure Hell of St. Trinian's* (1960), and *The Great St. Trinian's Train Robbery* (1966).

Beverly Hills Cop   1984   (Paramount)   *Color*
Director: Martin Brest
Starring: Eddie Murphy, Judge Reinhold, John Ashton, Lisa Eilbacher, Ronny Cox, Bronson Pinchot, Steven Berkoff, James Russo, Steven Elliot, Paul Reiser

A Detroit street cop goes undercover in Beverly Hills, seeking to avenge the murder of a friend. This comedy-drama punctuated with gore and violence cleaned up at the box office: to date, *Beverly Hills Cop* has accumulated $108 million in film rentals (the U.S. and Canada tally alone). His third leading part—after *48 Hrs.* and *Trading Places*—also confirmed Eddie Murphy as one of the superstars of the eighties. In the dominant role, Murphy capitalizes on the brash, fast-talking, no-respect persona he nurtured in comedy clubs and on "Saturday Night Live." Among the supporting players, Judge Reinhold and Bronson Pinchot manage to seize a moment or two. The Oscar-nominated screenplay by Daniel J. Petrie, Jr., was directed by Martin Brest, whose earlier *Going in Style* features George Burns, Art Carney, and Lee Strasberg. Harold Faltermeyer's score won a Grammy for best movie soundtrack.

The Big Chill   1983   (RCA)   *Color*
Director: Lawrence Kasdan
Starring: Tom Berenger, Glenn Close, Jeff Goldblum, William Hurt, Kevin Kline, Mary Kay Place, Meg Tilly, JoBeth Williams, Don Galloway, James Gillis

Like the John Sayles 1980 independent production, *Return of the Secaucus Seven*, *The Big Chill* is a constructive, positive film about the late sixties dropout generation continuing the process of self-discovery in the eighties. And, even taking into account its opening sequence at a funeral, it is essentially lighthearted. Director Lawrence Kasdan's screenplay with Barbara Benedek makes sure of that. The scenario: seven bosom buddies—University of Michigan alumni—are reunited after one of their friends has committed suicide. After the funeral the mourners assemble for the weekend in the South Carolina antebellum mansion now owned by two members of the group. Revelations and reminiscences (mostly comic) accompany the booze, food, and football games. Lawrence Kasdan's screenwriting successes *(The Empire Strikes Back, Raiders of the Lost Ark, Continental Divide, Return of the Jedi)* made him a bankable entity in the new Hollywood. His auspicious directorial debut was *Body Heat*. *The Big Chill* came next.

The Bingo Long Traveling All-Stars and Motor Kings   1976   *Color*
(MCA)
Director: John Badham
Starring: Billy Dee Williams, James Earl Jones, Richard Pryor, Ted Ross, DeWayne Jessie,
Stan Shaw

The title characters are itinerant baseball players. Disillusioned by the lack of serious
competition, they defect from the old Negro National League and begin barnstorming,
challenging white teams on the circuit. At first, there is considerable prejudice against
the All-Stars and Motor Kings, but their athletic prowess—and showmanship—can't
be denied. Their reputation grows. This comedy-drama boasts a strong sense of time
and place (the rural South just before World War II). Richard Pryor is an All-Star who
is forever changing his appearance, his nationality, and his *nom de beisbol*. Badham
acquired several television credits—*The Gun, The Law, Reflections of Murder*—before
turning to this, his first directing job on a theatrical movie; his next assignment was
Saturday Night Fever. Screenplay by Hal Barwood and Matthew Robbins.

The Black Marble   1980   (Embassy)   *Color*
Director: Harold Becker
Starring: Robert Foxworth, Paula Prentiss, Harry Dean Stanton, Barbara Babcock, John
Hancock, Raleigh Bond, Judy Landers, James Woods

A combination love story/cop story, *The Black Marble* is a romantic comedy with a
police procedural subtext. Yet another screen adaptation of Joseph Wambaugh *(The*
New Centurions, The Choirboys, The Onion Field), the film represents a departure: less
violence, more complex characters—with an undercurrent of black humor. Paula Prentiss is a policewoman newly teamed with alcoholic Robert Foxworth, whose Russian
ancestry has bred a soul both joyous and sorrowful; his behavior is, at best, erratic—
often at inappropriate times for his fellow law enforcers. Harry Dean Stanton plays a
nutty dognapper. Before directing *The Black Marble*, Harold Becker brought Wambaugh's harrowing (though more conventional) *The Onion Field* to the screen. Neither
was a commercial hit.

Blazing Saddles   1974   (Warner)   *Color*
Director: Mel Brooks
Starring: Cleavon Little, Gene Wilder, Harvey Korman, Madeline Kahn, David Huddle-
ston, Alex Karras, Slim Pickens, Burton Gilliam, John Hillerman, Liam Dunn, Carol
Arthur, Dom De Luise, Mel Brooks

Cleavon Little plays a chain-gang fugitive who is recruited as sheriff in a small frontier
town where sheriffs traditionally haven't lasted long. (Some didn't even make it to
sundown.) Mel Brooks's burlesque of movie Westerns incorporates humor that ranges
from inspired to sophomoric to downright raunchy. Pratfalls, double- and triple-takes,
ethnic (and *reverse* ethnic) jokes, and deliberate anachronisms are abundant. (Richard
Pryor was among the team of scenarists assisting Brooks with this screenplay.) Gene
Wilder plays a fast-draw artist, and Madeline Kahn costars as a barroom *chanteuse*—a
sexy, outlandish lampoon of Marlene Dietrich. Coming after the low box office returns
of cult favorites *The Producers* (1968) and *The Twelve Chairs* (1970), *Blazing Saddles*
gave Brooks his first smash hit. The mock-Western theme song is performed by Frankie
Laine.

Blue Collar 1978 (MCA) *Color*
Director: Paul Schrader
Starring: Richard Pryor, Harvey Keitel, Yaphet Kotto, Cliff De Young, Ed Begley, Jr.,
Harry Bellaver, George Memmoli

This comedy-drama traces the misadventures of three Detroit auto workers struggling to stretch the weekly paycheck. Richard Pryor, Harvey Keitel, and Yaphet Kotto are the overworked, underpaid trio who discover it's not just management who's exploiting them, it's their union as well, so they concoct a plot to rob the union. Paul Schrader's earlier screenplays—*The Yakuza, Taxi Driver, Rolling Thunder*—are all populated with proletarian heroes; a movie like *Blue Collar* seems more than providential as his directing debut. Schrader's script, with his brother Leonard (who also helped shape *Old Boyfriends* and *Mishima*), takes a downbeat look at management, unionism, and the excruciating rigors of the workday. The material is fortified by Pryor's role; the most complex of the leading characters, he evolves into a turncoat—making him a far cry from Pryor's customarily audience-pleasing roles. Jack Nitzsche's abrasive music is a perfect underscoring of the assembly line activities of *Blue Collar*.

The Blues Brothers 1980 (MCA) *Color*
Director: John Landis
Starring: John Belushi, Dan Aykroyd, Cab Calloway, John Candy, Ray Charles, James
Brown, Carrie Fisher, Aretha Franklin, Kathleen Freeman, Henry Gibson, Charles Na-
pier

Jake and Elwood Blues, those singing siblings, are on a mission from God: save the bankrupt neighborhood orphanage (and their childhood parish). To accomplish this, they reunite their old band and stage a fund-raiser. Before the climactic concert comes to pass, the brothers—not the most accomplished motor vehicle operators—have demolished half of Chicago. Dan Aykroyd and John Landis devised this comedy; the latter directed. Cameos from Steve Lawrence, Frank Oz, Steven Spielberg, Twiggy, and others spark the proceedings. A parade of the finest soul singers alive appears in the musical sequences. Aretha Franklin, waitressing in a diner, does a show-stopping rendition of "Think."

Blume in Love 1973 (Warner) *Color*
Director: Paul Mazursky
Starring: George Segal, Susan Anspach, Kris Kristofferson, Shelley Winters, Marsha
Mason, Paul Mazursky

Blume (George Segal) is in love. In fact, he loves being in love. He's a Los Angeles divorce lawyer whose sexual wanderlust kills his own marriage. After he and his wife (Susan Anspach) part and enter other relationships, Blume realizes his loss. *Blume in Love* then depicts the hero's attempts to regain his wife. Writer-director Paul Mazursky is a keen-eyed satirist whose targets are L.A., modern marriage, and the nature of commitment (from *Bob & Carol & Ted & Alice* to *Down and Out in Beverly Hills*). *Blume in Love* was Marsha Mason's debut in films; she appears as a likable character who has an affair with the divorced Blume. As Anspach's love interest, Kris Kristofferson plays the most sympathetic of Mazursky's characters. A hippie drifter whose sunny disposition never fades, he is so genial and disarming that even Blume—in the throes of anguish—eventually likes him.

Born Yesterday   1950   (RCA)   ◆   *Black-and-White*
Director: George Cukor
Starring: Judy Holliday, Broderick Crawford, William Holden, Howard St. John, Frank Otto, Larry Oliver, Barbara Brown, Grandon Rhodes, Claire Carleton

Harry Brook (Broderick Crawford), an unscrupulous scrap iron tycoon on a working vacation in Washington, D.C., brings along his mistress, Billie Dawn (Judy Holliday), an ex–chorus girl. Brook hires a young journalist (William Holden) to educate Billie so she can maneuver in proper society. The scheme backfires when the girl absorbs more about democracy and personal independence than Harry intends. Garson Kanin's stage hit is now considered a screen comedy classic, too. Above all, it is a permanent record of Holliday repeating her Broadway incarnation of Billie Dawn—the dizzy (but deep-down intelligent) blonde, a prototype she parlayed into a sixteen-year career. She won an Oscar over stiff competition from Gloria Swanson *(Sunset Boulevard)* and Bette Davis and Anne Baxter *(All About Eve)*.

Brazil   1985   (MCA)   *Color*
Director: Terry Gilliam
Starring: Jonathan Pryce, Robert De Niro, Katherine Helmond, Ian Holm, Bob Hoskins, Michael Palin, Ian Richardson, Peter Vaughan, Jim Broadben, Kathryn Pogson, Kim Greist

Brazil presents a bizarre near-future Anglo world as envisioned by Terry Gilliam and his coscenarists Tom Stoppard and Charles McKeown. Their satirical screenplay defines an Orwellian universe—and the tragic consequences that occur when a young Ministry of Information records clerk named Sam Lowry (Jonathan Pryce) rebels against an oppressive bureaucratic system. Also involved in the proceedings are Jack Lint (Michael Palin), Sam's surgeon friend; Jill Layton (Kim Greist), the protagonist's dream girl—a truck driver in real life; a malevolent repairman (Bob Hoskins); Harry Tuttle (Robert De Niro), a fugitive commando; and Ida (Katherine Helmond), the hapless hero's socialite mother. This black comedy vision of totalitarianism was chosen best movie of 1985 by the Los Angeles Film Critics Association, which also cited the three screenwriters and the director. Gilliam, animator for Monty Python's Flying Circus and director of *Time Bandits,* has called his film "Walter Mitty Meets Franz Kafka." He and director of photography Roger Pratt are responsible for the picture's visual style. The main musical theme is "Brazil," the popular Ary Barroso-Bob Russell samba from 1939.

Breakfast at Tiffany's   1961   (Paramount)   ◆   *Color*
Director: Blake Edwards
Starring: Audrey Hepburn, George Peppard, Patricia Neal, Buddy Ebsen, Martin Balsam, John McGiver, Alan Reed, Dorothy Whitney, Beverly Hills, Mickey Rooney

The "Moon River" movie. Henry Mancini and Johnny Mercer's hit parade perennial was introduced in *Breakfast at Tiffany's*—and claimed an Oscar. (Mancini picked up another statuette for his musical scoring.) Audrey Hepburn's incarnation of amoral pixie Holly Golightly remains one of her best loved screen performances. Holly's misadventures in Manhattan society are witnessed by a struggling young writer (George Peppard) who is captivated by her madcap ways. The screenplay by George Axelrod is derived from a considerably quieter (and darker) short story by Truman Capote. Under Blake Edwards's direction, the comic escapades and slick happy ending ultimately betray the Capote source. Patricia Neal costars as Peppard's rich patroness; Martin Balsam plays the noisy Hollywood agent; and Buddy Ebsen plays Ozark farmer Doc Golightly.

Breaking Away   *Listed under Family Viewing/Children's.*

Broadway Danny Rose   1984   (Vestron)   *Black-and-White*
Director: Woody Allen
Starring: Woody Allen, Mia Farrow, Nick Apollo Forte, Milton Berle, Sandy Baron, Jackie Gayle, Morty Gunty, Will Jordan, Corbett Monica, Jack Rollins, Howard Storm, Craig Vandenburgh

Danny Rose is a small-time talent agent with a heart of gold. He has a knack for discovering one-of-a-kind specialty acts. Among his clients are a one-armed juggler, a one-legged tap dancer, a stuttering ventriloquist, a blind xylophone player, skating penguins, a woman who makes music by rubbing the rims of water glasses, and a hypnotist who isn't too adept at bringing subjects out of a trance. Danny's latest find: Lou Canova, an overweight lounge singer making his comeback. (Lou's one hit single, "Agita," was about indigestion.) *Broadway Danny Rose,* starring its writer-director Woody Allen, features Nick Apollo Forte in his screen debut (as Lou) and Mia Farrow as his beloved—a gangster's widow. Woody's salute to show biz heralded his one-shot return to madcap comedy after a string of comparatively serious efforts *(Interiors, Manhattan, Stardust Memories, A Midsummer Night's Sex Comedy,* and *Zelig).*

Bus Stop   1956   (CBS)   *Color*
Director: Joshua Logan
Starring: Marilyn Monroe, Don Murray, Arthur O'Connell, Betty Field, Eileen Heckart, Robert Bray, Hope Lange, Hans Conried, Casey Adams, Henry Slate

Marilyn Monroe's incarnation of Cherie, the mediocre saloon singer whose ambition is to be a "chantoosie," is probably the high point of her career. (You've never experienced "That Old Black Magic" till you hear Cherie warble it.) Parenthetically—or perhaps not—*Bus Stop* was Monroe's first film after studying at Lee Strasberg's Actor's Studio. Bo (Don Murray), a young rodeo cowboy, wants to hogtie Cherie's affections. With marriage and family on his mind, he abducts her from Phoenix and they set off on a bus for his ranch. Halfway there, the bus gets snowbound—so they and other travelers take refuge in a roadside diner. Grace's diner was the single setting for William Inge's playscript; screenwriter George Axelrod's opening up of the stage play stands as a how-to model. Veteran theater producer-director Joshua Logan had just filmed Inge's *Picnic; Bus Stop* gave him two Hollywood hits in a row. Play and film were the basis for a controversial 1961–62 TV series; Inge was script consultant on the show, which starred Marilyn Maxwell and Joan Freeman in the waitress roles assumed in the movie by Betty Field and Hope Lange.

Butterflies Are Free   1972   (RCA)   ◆   *Color*
Director: Milton Katselas
Starring: Goldie Hawn, Edward Albert, Eileen Heckart, Mike Warren, Paul Michael Glaser

Another transcribed Broadway comedy provides yet another screen showcase for Goldie Hawn. Her Oscar-winning *Cactus Flower* was followed with *There's a Girl in*

My Soup—both stage-derived. In Leonard Gershe's *Butterflies Are Free,* Goldie plays a fledgling actress whose handsome next-door neighbor is a blind songwriter. After years of self-sufficiency, the young man is still hovered over by his protective mother (Eileen Heckart). It's one of the mother's periodic visits that sets the comic plot in motion. This was Edward Albert's big screen debut; he and director Milton Katselas worked together again the following year in *Forty Carats.* Heckart, reviving her Broadway role, was named best supporting actress by the Academy.

Cactus Flower   1969   (RCA)   ◆   *Color*
Director: Gene Saks
Starring: Ingrid Bergman, Walter Matthau, Goldie Hawn, Jack Weston, Rick Lenz, Vito Scotti, Irene Hervey

Two women figure in dentist Walter Matthau's daily routine: his seemingly staid—and taken-for-granted—receptionist (Ingrid Bergman) and his wild and ceaselessly energetic mistress (Goldie Hawn). After a series of crazy encounters with both women, the receptionist begins to seem preferable to the mistress. Accordingly, Matthau turns his romantic attentions to Bergman. She, in turn, blossoms like the cactus flower on her office desk. This sweet-natured comedy, screenscripted by I. A. L. Diamond, was derived from Abe Burrows's Broadway hit (and an earlier French farce by Pierre Barillet and Jean-Pierre Gredy). "Laugh-In" alumna Goldie Hawn, as Matthau's pixilated girlfriend, collected most of the critical acclaim in 1969; indeed, she won a supporting actress Oscar for this, her second screen role (having debuted in the 1968 Disney musical, *The One and Only Genuine Original Family Band*).

Caddyshack   1980   (Warner)   *Color*
Director: Harold Ramis
Starring: Chevy Chase, Rodney Dangerfield, Ted Knight, Michael O'Keefe, Bill Murray, Cindy Morgan, Sarah Holcomb, Scott Colomby, Brian Doyle-Murray, Douglas Kenney

Bushwood Country Club, a bastion of snobbery, provides the setting for this irreverent comedy. Sight gags and verbal sparring hold dominion when a golf pro (Chevy Chase) tangles with a loudmouth (Rodney Dangerfield) and an obnoxious club president (Ted Knight). Meanwhile, one of Bushwood's caddies (Michael O'Keefe) tries to seduce the club president's daughter. And out on the greens, Bill Murray as a subversive groundskeeper grows more demented by the hour—he declares open warfare on an elusive gopher. For his directorial debut, Harold Ramis chose a film targeted to teen and young-adult audiences, and—with the assistance of cowriters Brian Doyle-Murray and Douglas Kenney—he scored a bull's-eye. (Made for less than two million, *Caddyshack* brought in over ten times that amount in North America alone.) The film, through its writers, director, and leading players, has roots in *National Lampoon,* Second City improvisationals, and "Saturday Night Live."

California Suite   1978   (RCA)   ◆   *Color*
Director: Herbert Ross
Starring: Alan Alda, Michael Caine, Bill Cosby, Jane Fonda, Walter Matthau, Elaine May, Richard Pryor, Maggie Smith, Gloria Gifford, Sheila Frazier, Herb Edelman, Denise Galik

A Neil Simon omnibus: four playlets, all taking place at the Beverly Hills Hotel. On stage, the episodes—two farces, two "serious" comedies—were separate; for the film adaptation, Simon and Herbert Ross, his director, interweave them. Jane Fonda plays the "Visitor from New York," in L.A. to discuss with ex-husband Alan Alda which of them will retain custody of their daughter. Walter Matthau, the "Visitor from Philadelphia," and his wife (Elaine May) will soon discover a dead-drunk hooker in the room. Maggie Smith, as an English actress nominated for an Oscar, and husband Michael Caine are the "Visitors from London." In the "Visitors from Chicago," Bill Cosby and Richard Pryor play buddies who are competitive tennis players. In *California Suite*, her character loses the Academy Award competition; but Maggie Smith truly won an Oscar (her second) for her delineation of the tipsy actress. Other Neil Simon-Herbert Ross collaborations: *The Sunshine Boys, The Goodbye Girl, I Ought to Be in Pictures*, and *Max Dugan Returns*. Only the last was written expressly for the screen.

The Captain's Paradise   1953   (Thorn)   *Black-and-White*
Director: Anthony Kimmins
Starring: Alec Guinness, Yvonne de Carlo, Celia Johnson, Charles Goldner, Miles Malleson, Bill Fraser, Nicholas Phipps, Ferdy Mayne, George Benson

Bigamy is played for farce in *The Captain's Paradise* and Alec Guinness creates an unforgettable character. Guinness, as master of *The Golden Fleece*, pilots his ferry steamer about the Mediterranean. In one port, he is husband to sultry Yvonne de Carlo; in another port, he is wed to homebody Celia Johnson. ("Two women!" the captain sighs. "Each with half of the things a man wants!") The script from Alec Coppel and Nicholas Phipps keeps piling coincidence upon coincidence. Comedy director Anthony Kimmins maintains the pace.

Casey's Shadow   1978   (RCA)   *Color*
Director: Martin Ritt
Starring: Walter Matthau, Alexis Smith, Robert Webber, Murray Hamilton, Andrew A. Rubin, Stephan Burns, Michael Hershewe

In this family comedy-drama, Walter Matthau plays an impoverished racehorse trainer whose wife has deserted him. Living with his three sons in a timeworn farmhouse, Matthau barely makes ends meet. His fortunes change when his youngest son—named Casey—grows fond of a colt. When the animal returns the little boy's affection—indeed follows him everywhere—he is dubbed Casey's Shadow. And under that moniker he becomes an estimable quarter horse. Carol Sobieski's script is derived from a John McPhee story called "Ruidoso." A formula racing picture with contemporary style (franker dialogue, for instance) and genuine emotions, *Casey's Shadow* was itself overshadowed in 1978 by another Walter Matthau movie that premiered the same week: *House Calls*.

Cat Ballou   1965   (RCA)   ◆   *Color*
Director: Elliot Silverstein
Starring: Jane Fonda, Lee Marvin, Michael Callan, Dwayne Hickman, Nat King Cole, Stubby Kaye, Tom Nardini, John Marley, Reginald Denny, Jay C. Flippen, Arthur Hunnicutt, Bruce Cabot, Burt Mustin, Paul Gilbert

The year is 1890—and, as the song tells it, they're hanging Cat Ballou in Wolf City, Wyoming. Flashbacks reveal why: Cat Ballou is a schoolmarm who has turned to outlawry to avenge her father's death. This lampoon of Western movie traditions presents Jane Fonda as the title character, while Oscar-winner Lee Marvin both aids and opposes her in two roles. In one, Marvin plays Kid Shelleen, Cat's ally and surely the most booze-befogged gunslinger in the Old West; he also plays Shelleen's lookalike brother, Tim Strawn, a deadly scoundrel with an artificial silver nose (the real one having been bitten off in a fight). The Walter Newman-Frank R. Pierson screenplay, based on the novel by Roy Chanslor, reaches its peak when Shelleen and Strawn meet for a gun duel. Nat King Cole and Stubby Kaye are bar-room balladeers whose lyrics comment on the action. Those funny songs were penned by Mack David and Jerry Livingston. Frank DeVol's music provides a lighthearted touch throughout.

Caveman   1981   (CBS)   *Color*
Director: Carl Gottlieb
Starring: Ringo Starr, Barbara Bach, Randy Quaid, Shelley Long, Jack Gilford, Avery Schreiber, John Matuszak

Debuting director Carl Gottlieb is no stranger to comic pandemonium. Although he first gained attention for his *Jaws* and *Jaws II* scripts, he also collaborated with Steve Martin on *The Jerk*. He has also been a script doctor on other comedies, as well as a humor writer for television. Actually, *Caveman* seems to have drawn its inspiration from TV—and the popular "Alley Oop" comic strip. Gottlieb and Rudy De Luca, his coscenarist, have devised a fifteen-word language for the cave dwellers; the actors, some of them unexpectedly skilled farceurs, put all fifteen words to good use. Ringo Starr plays the prehistoric protagonist; in the course of the film, which covers only a few days, Ringo learns how to stand erect and he discovers fire, cooking, the wheel, and music (drums are his specialty). "Cheers" star Shelley Long plays the shy heroine who considers curvaceous Barbara Bach a threat to her passions for Ringo. Former Oakland Raider John Matuszak makes a funny giant. David Allen and his special effects associates are responsible for the dinosaurs, including one that becomes domesticated.

Champagne for Caesar   1950   (United)   *Black-and-White*
Director: Richard Whorf
Starring: Ronald Colman, Celeste Holm, Vincent Price, Barbara Britton, Art Linkletter, Gabriel Heatter, George Fisher, Byron Foulger, John Eldredge, Lyle Talbot

Ronald Colman plays a genius in this satire of the television industry. He decides to appear on a quiz show sponsored by the soap company against which he holds a grudge. To everyone's amazement but his own, he becomes an invincible contestant—risking double or nothing. His wealth increases, as well as his national celebrity. Vincent Price, as the president of the sponsor company, sends Celeste Holm to distract the contestant. Colman's urbanity was put to use in this Hans Jacoby-Fred Brady script. The veteran actor retired from films after this role, though—and made only two brief cameo appearances thereafter: *Around the World in 80 Days* (1956) and *The Story of Mankind* (1957). Richard Whorf, an actor and director throughout the forties, inspired other funny performances too; in a clever bit of casting, Art Linkletter is the game show emcee. *Champagne for Caesar* was considered by many as the best feature Whorf worked on as director. Until his death in 1966, he was actively involved in series television, helming scores of "Rawhide" and "The Beverly Hillbillies" episodes.

Chapter Two   1979   (RCA)   *Color*
Director: Robert Moore
Starring: James Caan, Marsha Mason, Joseph Bologna, Valerie Harper, Alan Fudge, Judy Farrell, Debra Mooney

Widower George (James Caan) and divorcée Jennie (Marsha Mason) meet, fall in love, and get married. Chapter two of their lives looks rosy—except George can't forget his first wife. After anguish, altercations, and separation, George learns—with Jennie's help—to "stare happiness in the face . . . and embrace it." This transcription of Neil Simon's semiautobiographical play presents Caan as Simon and the then Mrs. Simon, with fictional liberties, playing herself. *Chapter Two* bears similarities to another post-divorce comedy released the same year: Alan Pakula's *Starting Over*. Other Simon scripts realized for the screen by Robert Moore: *Murder by Death* and *The Cheap Detective*.

The Committee   1969   (Pacific Arts Video)   *Color*
Director: Del Jack
Starring: Peter Bonerz, Barbara Bosson, Garry Goodrow, Carl Gottlieb, Jessica Myerson, Christopher Ross, Melvin Stewart, Don Sturdy

The Committee was a San Francisco–based comedy troupe/improvisational theater inspired by Chicago's seminal Second City. Developed by Alan Myerson in 1963 and continuing for a decade, The Committee became a fertile training ground for such actors as Peter Bonerz, Melvin Stewart, and Howard Hesseman (then going under the stage name of Don Sturdy). The group released three records, appeared frequently on TV, organized a Broadway edition of their material, and became the subject of two theatrical films. *Funnyman*, from 1971, is a backstage comedy starring Peter Bonerz as a stand-up comic. The earlier *The Committee* (also known as *A Session with the Committee*) is essentially an anthology composed of "The Best of. . . ." The skits, developed through improvisation, are satiric looks at politics, depersonalization, the dating and mating games, and sixties radicalization. Two of the funniest sketches involve a passionate couple on a stalled elevator and a blind date who turns out to be really blind. This production, directed by Del Jack, had an interesting metamorphosis: it was initially video-taped at a performance (and featured audience reactions), then transferred to 35mm film stock for theatrical release. Now it's back on tape for home viewing. The image clarity is not great—a graininess resulted in the video-to-film blowup.

Continental Divide   1981   (MCA)   *Color*
Director: Michael Apted
Starring: John Belushi, Blair Brown, Allen Goorwitz, Carlin Glynn, Tony Ganios, Val Avery, Liam Russell, Everett Smith

He is a city slicker, a nationally syndicated columnist from Chicago. She is an outdoorswoman, a naturalist whose current studies involve bald eagles in the Rockies. In this city mouse–versus–country mouse comedy, patterned upon the Tracy-Hepburn classics, the couple meet, hate one another, then (during confinement in a mountain cabin) fall in love. Can their romance survive the dichotomous environmental demands of their chosen fields? (He gets asphyxiated on pure air; she can't abide asphalt.) Lawrence Kasdan wrote this screenplay between stints with the *Star Wars* saga (and while he was working on his own *Body Heat*). The script, funny and touching in turns, represented a departure both for him and for John Belushi, here in a low-key role far from his *Animal House*/"Saturday Night Live" persona. Allen Goorwitz is Allen Garfield by his real name; he's since gone back to Garfield.

The Court Jester   1956   (Paramount)   *Color*
Directors: Norman Panama and Melvin Frank
Starring: Danny Kaye, Glynis Johns, Basil Rathbone, Angela Lansbury, Cecil Parker, Mildred Natwick, Robert Middleton, John Carradine, Edward Ashley, Michael Pate, Alan Napier

Before embarking on solo careers, Norman Panama and Melvin Frank had a productive partnership as writers, producers, and directors of comedy films. A partial credit list includes favorites such as *Road to Utopia, Mr. Blandings Builds His Dream House, White Christmas, That Certain Feeling, L'il Abner,* and *The Facts of Life.* The crowning achievement of their collaboration could very well be *The Court Jester,* a spoof of Merrie Olde England fondly regarded even by those not ordinarily susceptible to Danny Kaye's humor. The protagonist is a would-be Robin Hood—except he's too meek. In order to dethrone a tyrannical king (Cecil Parker) and install the rightful heir, Kaye enters the castle disguised as a court jester. Assisting him is Glynis Johns; opposing him are Angela Lansbury, Basil Rathbone, and as a formidable jousting rival, Robert Middleton. Romance, complex misunderstandings, plots and counterplots ensue. Panama and Frank wrote the tongue-tripping dialogue, which includes the memorable litany: "The pellet with the poison's in the vessel with the pestle; the chalice from the palace holds the brew that is true." Songs by Sylvia Fine and Sammy Cahn.

The Devil and Max Devlin   1981   (Disney)   *Color*
Director: Steven Hilliard Stern
Starring: Elliott Gould, Bill Cosby, Susan Anspach, Adam Rich, Julie Budd, David Knell, Charles Shamata, Ronnie Schell

This comedy-fantasy is a contemporary variation on Faustian themes. Max Devlin (Elliott Gould), an unprincipled apartment house manager, is killed when he collides with a crosstown bus. He wakes up in hell, where the devil (Bill Cosby) proposes a bargain: Max can regain his life if, within two months, he persuades three young people to sell their souls. Max agrees to take the devil on. As Mary Rodgers's screenplay evolves, Max also has to resort to a good deal of trickery to ensure a happy ending for the devil's three pawns. Steven Hilliard Stern, known to some for his television movies ("Draw!," "Mazes and Monsters," and "Hostage Flight") directed.

Diary of a Mad Housewife   1970   (MCA)   *Color*
Director: Frank Perry
Starring: Richard Benjamin, Frank Langella, Carrie Snodgress, Lorraine Cullen, Frannie Michel, Lee Addoms, Peter Boyle, Katherine Meskill, The Alice Cooper Band

Eleanor Perry's screenplay, from Sue Kaufman's comic novel, is a dual observation on modern urban marriage and the success ethic of postwar baby boomers. Richard Benjamin is cast as an over-achieving attorney whose callousness toward his wife (Carrie Snodgress) exhaustively redefines male chauvinism. In retaliation, the wife finds herself drawn into an affair with a novelist (Frank Langella). The fling is short-lived because the novelist, a narcissist filled with braggadocio, is not much of an improvement on her husband. So the mad housewife, still in quest of the feminine mystique, turns to a consciousness-raising group. *Diary of a Mad Housewife* is a product of the seventies. This was the last collaboration between Eleanor and Frank Perry; she wrote and he directed, among other works, *David and Lisa* and *Last Summer*. Shot on location in New York by Gerald Hirschfeld.

A Different Story 1978 (Embassy) *Color*
Director: Paul Aaron
Starring: Perry King, Meg Foster, Valerie Curtin, Peter Donat, Richard Bull, Barbara Collentine

A Different Story describes the romance between a gay male hustler and a lesbian real estate agent. Perry King and Meg Foster are cast as an unlikely pair thrown together as roommates, *à la The Goodbye Girl*. They marry in order to prevent King's deportation, then begin a platonic relationship, and eventually become lovers—and parents. This comedy-drama was written by Henry Olek. David Frank created the musical score.

Diner 1982 (MGM) *Color*
Director: Barry Levinson
Starring: Steve Guttenberg, Daniel Stern, Mickey Rourke, Kevin Bacon, Timothy Daly, Ellen Barkin, Paul Reiser, Kathryn Dowling, Michael Tucker, Jessica James, John Aquino, Colette Blonigan, Kelle Kipp, Richard Pierson

This comedy-drama is filled with nostalgia for the fifties. Barry Levinson's epigrammatic script takes place in 1959 Baltimore and focuses on a clique of post–high school boys, some now in college, and their bull sessions in a local diner. The boys' conversations are as contemporary as they are hilarious and bittersweet. Comprising the core group of french-fry-chomping buddies are Steve Guttenberg, Mickey Rourke, Kevin Bacon, Timothy Daly, and Daniel Stern (the married one, a rock 'n' roll addict whose passion is not shared by his wife)—and, on the fringes, Paul Reiser.

Doctor at Sea 1955 (VidAm; Learning) *Color*
Director: Ralph Thomas
Starring: Dirk Bogarde, Brigitte Bardot, Brenda de Banzie, James Robertson Justice, Maurice Denham, Michael Medwin, Hubert Gregg, Raymond Huntley, Geoffrey Keen, George Coulouris, Jill Adams, James Kenney

The origin for this British farce lies in Richard Gordon's novel, *Doctor in the House*, and the series, literary and cinematic, that grew therefrom. The 1954 movie of *Doctor in the House* led to a spate of *Doctor . . .* sequels (*At Large, In Love, In Distress, In Clover, and In Trouble*). These pictures chart the madcap medical misadventures of Simon Sparrow (Dirk Bogarde) and other doctors from St. Swithin's Hospital. *Doctor at Sea,* second in the series, finds Simon Sparrow eluding a forced marriage by signing on a cargo steamer as medical officer. The freighter also carries passengers—among them a curvaceous French girl (Brigitte Bardot). *Doctor at Sea* is a well-crafted comedy of errors. Prolific Nicholas Phipps wrote the script with Jack Davies. Bruce Montgomery, revered by many mystery readers under the name Edmund Crispin, composed the score. Ralph Thomas directed this and all the *Doctor* movies.

Dr. Strangelove, Or: How I Learned to   *Black-and-White*
     Stop Worrying and Love the Bomb   1964   (RCA)
Director: Stanley Kubrick
Starring: Peter Sellers, George C. Scott, Sterling Hayden, Keenan Wynn, Slim Pickens,
Peter Bull, Tracy Reed, James Earl Jones, Jack Creley, Frank Berry, Shane Rimmer

Stanley Kubrick's irreverent black comedy is in the tradition of Swiftian satire-bur-
lesque. Based (remotely) on Peter George's novel *Red Alert,* the target here is atomic
holocaust. On that pretext, scenarists Kubrick, George, and Terry Southern aim pot-
shots at the entire politico-military complex. Their story begins when General Jack D.
Ripper (Sterling Hayden), a deranged Air Force officer, launches a nuclear attack on
the Soviet Union. Scurrying about to mend the situation are General Buck Turgidson
(George C. Scott), Colonel Bat Guano (Keenan Wynn), and an assortment of defense
strategists, presidential advisers, and representatives of the U.S.S.R. Peter Sellers takes
three roles: U.S. President Merkin Muffley; Lionel Mandrake, an RAF group captain;
and Dr. Strangelove, a crippled German-American scientist and megalomaniac who
rolls his wheelchair around the Pentagon war room—while trying to control his in-
stinctual "heil, Hitler" salute. (Sellers's robotic interpretation of the black-gloved title
character is reportedly inspired by Dr. Rotwang in Fritz Lang's *Metropolis.*) Introduced
belatedly is Air Force Major T. J. "King" Kong (Slim Pickens), a good ole boy from
Texas who, after a fashion, rides to the rescue.

Educating Rita   1983   (RCA)   *Color*
Director: Lewis Gilbert
Starring: Michael Caine, Julie Walters, Michael Williams, Maureen Lipman, Jeananne
Crowley, Malcolm Douglas

Susan, a married hairdresser in her late twenties, decides to make some salient changes
in her life. One of the first changes, as she acquires the formal education that has
eluded her, is to rechristen herself Rita—in honor of Rita Mae Brown, her favorite
author. At the local university she meets Dr. Frank Bryant, a burnt-out English professor. Rita, a product of the English working classes, has a funny vulgarity that amuses
the professor—and her naïve enthusiasm for the world of knowledge sparks him.
Bryant, who had given up on formal education, becomes Rita's mentor and she blossoms
into a new woman. *Educating Rita* is based on the long-running West End comedy by
Willy Russell, who also wrote the screenplay. This 1980s variation on *Pygmalion* was
a surprise hit that resulted in Oscar nominations for Michael Caine (Professor Bryant),
Julie Walters (her screen debut as Rita), and screenwriter Russell. Shot in and around
Dublin and on the campus of Trinity University.

The Electric Horseman   *Listed under Dramas.*

The End   1978   (CBS)   *Color*
Director: Burt Reynolds
Starring: Burt Reynolds, Dom De Luise, Sally Field, Kristy McNichol, Robby Benson,
David Steinberg, Norman Fell, Carl Reiner, Myrna Loy, Pat O'Brien, Joanne Woodward

Although Burt Reynolds directed *The End,* he also plays the lead, a middle-aged
Californian who learns that he is dying of cancer. Before death claims him, he decides
to make last minute corrections in his life; among the people with whom he attempts

(unsuccessfully) to settle the score: parents, daughter, divorced wife, mistress. Finally he opts for suicide. But he can't successfully accomplish that either. Written by Jerry Belson, *The End* is a comedy. Dom De Luise, as the protagonist's schizophrenic roommate in a sanitarium, steals the show.

Entertaining Mr. Sloane   1970   (Thorn)   *Color*
Director: Douglas Hickox
Starring: Beryl Reid, Harry Andrews, Peter McEnery, Alan Webb

Joe Orton's plays—*Loot, What the Butler Saw,* and *Entertaining Mr. Sloane*—certainly placed him ahead of (or out-of-synch with) his time. The screen version of *Entertaining Mr. Sloane* unites a small ensemble of British stage and film veterans. Beryl Reid plays Kath, a middle-aged woman who shares her London dwelling with her older brother, Ed (Harry Andrews). Kath and Ed decide to take in a boarder. A kinky triangle develops when handsome young Mr. Sloane invades the house and becomes a lust object for both sister and brother. Peter McEnery plays the young hustler who realizes that his bread is buttered on both sides. This black comedy was screenwritten by Clive Exton and directed by Douglas Hickox, whose most recent credit is the 1986 telefilm "Sins." (Orton's *Loot* was brought to the screen in 1972 by Silvio Narizzano, with a cast that includes Lee Remick, Richard Attenborough, and Milo O'Shea.)

Every Which Way But Loose   1978   (Warner)   *Color*
Director: James Fargo
Starring: Clint Eastwood, Sondra Locke, Geoffrey Lewis, Beverly D'Angelo, Walter Barnes, George Chandler, Roy Jensen, James McEachin, Bill McKinney, William O'Connell, Dan Vadis, Geoffrey Walcott, Ruth Gordon

This star vehicle was carefully programmed for Clint Eastwood and his legion of fans. The strategy worked: the movie grossed $120 million worldwide. Eastwood enacts an L.A. trucker who shares his tumbledown home with his senile mother (Ruth Gordon) and Clyde, a kissing orangutan. A freewheeling comedy, *Every Which Way But Loose* actually allows its leading man to be loose, in a parody of his sober-faced macho roles. With brawls and car smashes galore, it plays like an episode of "The Dukes of Hazard." The screenplay by Jeremy Joe Kronsberg has been directed by James Fargo. This Clint-and-Clyde farce was followed in 1980 by *Any Which Way You Can,* which rigorously conformed to the blueprint of the original.

The F̲armer's Daughter   1947   (CBS)   ◆   *Black-and-White*
Director: H. C. Potter
Starring: Loretta Young, Joseph Cotten, Ethel Barrymore, Charles Bickford, Rose Hobart, Rhys Williams, Harry Davenport, Tom Powers, William Harrigan, Lex Barker, Harry Shannon, Keith Andes, Thurston Hall, Art Baker, Don Beddoe, Anna Q. Nilsson

Katrin Holstrum is a farm girl of Swedish descent who lands a job in Washington, working as a maid for her home-state congressman. Ultimately, Katy, never shy with her opinions, winds up competing with the man she loves for a congressional seat. *The Farmer's Daughter* is another feather in the cap of comedy director H. C. Potter *(Hellzapoppin, Mr. Blandings Builds His Dream House, Three For the Show).* The script is by Allen Rivkin and Laura Kerr. Leader of the frivolity is Loretta Young, as the title character; Katy is the role for which she won her best actress Oscar. Joseph Cotten is cast as Congressman Morley and Ethel Barrymore plays his mother. Among the young actors playing Katy's brothers are James Aurness, who later dropped the *u*, and a pre-Tarzan Lex Barker. *The Farmer's Daughter* was the basis for a three-season (1963–66) television sitcom starring Inger Stevens as Katy and William Windom as the congressman.

Father Goose   1964   (Republic)   ◆   *Color*
Director: Ralph Nelson
Starring: Cary Grant, Leslie Caron, Trevor Howard, Jack Good, Verina Greenlaw, Pip Sparke, Jennifer Berrington, Stephanie Berrington, Laurelle Felsette, Nicole Felsette, Sharyl Locke, Simon Scott, John Napier, Richard Lupino, Ken Swofford

In this World War II–set comedy, Cary Grant plays a South Seas drifter named Walter Eckland. Walter is strong-armed by the Australian Navy into becoming a plane spotter. For his sky-watching, he must go to a remote island. To his chagrin, his new home is also occupied by a French schoolteacher and several refugee students. When danger strikes, Walter is cast as a reluctant Father Goose, but he slowly warms to his adolescent charges. A family comedy, *Father Goose* is the creation of Peter Stone and Frank Tarloff, who were awarded the 1964 Oscar for best original screenplay. Ralph Nelson, esteemed for *Requiem for a Heavyweight, Lilies of the Field, Soldier in the Rain,* and *Charly,* is the director. The Oscar-nominated theme song, "Pass Me By," has music by Cy Coleman and lyrics by Carolyn Leigh.

First Monday in October   1981   (Paramount)   *Color*
Director: Ronald Neame
Starring: Walter Matthau, Jill Clayburgh, Barnard Hughes, Jan Sterling, James Stephens, Joshua Bryant

First Monday in October, the Jerome Lawrence-Robert E. Lee Broadway comedy starring Henry Fonda and Jane Alexander, hypothesized the appointment of the first woman to the U.S. Supreme Court. By the time the film version, also penned by Lawrence and Lee, was released, Sandra Day O'Connor had turned fiction into fact. With Walter Matthau and Jill Clayburgh assuming the Fonda-Alexander roles, the movie is a frothy battle-of-the-sexes lark. Matthau represents the voice of liberalism; Clayburgh is an arch-conservative. Their clash of wills (and budding romance) will remind some viewers of movies featuring Spencer Tracy and Katharine Hepburn. The supporting cast includes Barnard Hughes, Jan Sterling, and James Stephens (law student James T. Hart on TV's "The Paper Chase").

The Flim-Flam Man   1967   (Playhouse Video)   *Color*
Director: Irvin Kershner
Starring: George C. Scott, Michael Sarrazin, Sue Lyon, Harry Morgan, Jack Albertson, Alice Ghostley, Slim Pickens, Albert Salmi

As the adage goes, there's a sucker born every minute—and aiming to prove P. T. Barnum correct is the flim-flam man. Based on Guy Owen's novel, as scripted by William Rose, this rural comedy-drama runs the gamut from pathos to knockabout farce. George C. Scott, as the hoodwinker of the title, is joined by Michael Sarrazin, playing a conscience-stricken apprentice who, it turns out, is an army deserter. He's also too honest to survive the flim-flam game. The tale is deftly enacted, while the lion's share of laughs is generated by Scott, Sarrazin, and, as one of their victims, Harry

Morgan. Veteran second-unit director Yakima Canutt staged some of the action scenes (e.g., the car chases), but Irvin Kershner is the official director. Other Kershner credits include *The Hoodlum Priest, Eyes of Laura Mars,* the TV docudrama "Raid on Entebbe," *The Empire Strikes Back,* and *Never Say Never Again,* Sean Connery's return (and farewell) to Bond.

Forty Carats   1973   (RCA)   *Color*
Director: Milton Katselas
Starring: Liv Ullmann, Edward Albert, Gene Kelly, Binnie Barnes, Billy Green Bush, Nancy Walker, Deborah Raffin, Don Porter, Natalie Schafer, Rosemary Murphy

Forty Carats originated in the French stage farce by Pierre Barillet and Jean-Pierre Gredy, the coauthors of *Cactus Flower.* After a tenure on Broadway under its present title (starring Julie Harris), the Leonard Gershe comedy was transcribed for film by Milton Katselas, the director who shot Gershe's earlier playscript, *Butterflies Are Free.* *Forty Carats* is a May-December romance. This time the elder party is the woman—fortyish Liv Ullmann. Her lover, Edward Albert, is in his mid-twenties. The humor resides in how they explain the situation to her family, including ex-husband Gene Kelly.

Foul Play   1978   (Paramount)   *Color*
Director: Colin Higgins
Starring: Goldie Hawn, Chevy Chase, Burgess Meredith, Dudley Moore, Rachel Roberts, Eugene Roche, Marilyn Sokol, Billy Barty, Bruce Solomon

Gloria Mundy (Goldie Hawn) is a San Francisco librarian whose peaceful life is interrupted by a succession of dead bodies. But the corpses always disappear before the police arrive. This comedy-mystery, written and directed by Colin Higgins *(Nine to Five),* features Chevy Chase as the only police detective in San Francisco to believe Gloria's wild tales. Ultimately, the two heroes fall in love and uncover a conspiracy: the pope is to be assassinated at a performance of *The Mikado. Foul Play* is a union of murder and romance in the light Hitchcock vein *(To Catch a Thief, North by Northwest, Family Plot*—and with direct references to the 1956 *The Man Who Knew Too Much).* The city by the bay provides an atmospheric backdrop to the mayhem. The Academy Award–nominated theme song, "Ready to Take a Chance Again," with music by Charles Fox and lyrics by Norman Gimbel, is interpreted by Barry Manilow.

The Four Musketeers   1975   (U.S.A. Home Video)   *Color*
Director: Richard Lester
Starring: Oliver Reed, Raquel Welch, Richard Chamberlain, Michael York, Frank Finlay, Christopher Lee, Geraldine Chaplin, Jean-Pierre Cassel, Roy Kinnear, Sybil Danning, Gitty Djamal, Simon Ward, Faye Dunaway, Charlton Heston

Subtitled *The Revenge of Milady,* this irreverent comedy is a continuation of Richard Lester's *The Three Musketeers.* Indeed, *Four* was filmed in 1973 at the same time as *Three*—when the two were originally conceived as one long movie. The action picks up where the earlier film left off, with the title heroes—D'Artagnan, Athos, Porthos, and Aramis—at their swashbuckling best, getting revenge against Rochefort and Lady De Winter. The personnel behind Lester remain the same. For the record: screenplay by George MacDonald Fraser, cinematography by David Watkin, production design by Brian Eatwell; this time, however, the music is credited to Lalo Schifrin. (Michel Legrand scored the first feature.)

The Four Seasons   1981   (MCA)   *Color*
Director: Alan Alda
Starring: Alan Alda, Carol Burnett, Len Cariou, Sandy Dennis, Rita Moreno, Jack Weston, Bess Armstrong, Elizabeth Alda, Beatrice Alda, Robert Hitt, Kristi McCarthy, David Stackpole

Kate and Jack, Claudia and Danny, Annie and Nick. For seven years these three New York married couples have banded together for group vacations. Near the beginning of *The Four Seasons,* one of the six original partners, Annie, is replaced—when she and Nick divorce. But the group holidays continue as another participant is introduced: Ginny, Nick's girlfriend (later, wife). Ginny's presence brings about a period of adjustment—and a reconsideration of relationships—for all the others. Alan Alda's schematic script presents these seven characters over a year's time, framed by four eventful episodes (the outings), spring through winter, and underscored by Vivaldi's *The Four Seasons.* The seasons are conveyed by cinematographer Victor J. Kemper. Under Alda's direction, this is a warm and wise comedy about marriage and friendship. In the outstanding ensemble: Alda himself as Jack, the perennial toastmaker; Carol Burnett as his trip-organizing wife, Kate; Len Cariou and Sandy Dennis as Nick and Annie; Bess Armstrong as Ginny; Rita Moreno as Claudia; and Jack Weston as Danny. For the short-lived 1984 teleseries, only Weston reprised his role.

Fun with Dick and Jane   1977   (RCA)   *Color*
Director: Ted Kotcheff
Starring: George Segal, Jane Fonda, Ed McMahon, Dick Gautier, Allan Miller, John Dehner, Hank Garcia, Mary Jackson, Thalmus Rasulala, Sean Frye, Sarah Cunningham

Dick and Jane Harper (George Segal and Jane Fonda) are an affluent young couple living in Los Angeles. Dick is an aerospace engineer. Jane is a housewife. And their spaniel is named Spot. All is fine in the Harpers' suburban, upwardly mobile, credit-card-payment existence until Dick is fired. To maintain the style to which they have become accustomed, Dick and Jane turn to armed robbery—though, Robin Hood–inspired, they steal only from the rich, like the telephone company. This satire, written by David Giler, Jerry Belson, and Mordecai Richler, is based on an earlier script by Gerald Gaiser. Directed by Ted Kotcheff, the picture manages to be madcap while uttering some home truths about contemporary stress.

Genevieve   Great Britain 1953; U.S. 1954   *Color*
     (Embassy; Learning Corp. of America)
Director: Henry Cornelius
Starring: Dinah Sheridan, John Gregson, Kay Kendall, Kenneth More, Geoffrey Keen, Joyce Grenfell, Michael Medwin, Harold Siddens, Arthur Wontner, Reginald Beckwith

Genevieve is a 1904 Darracq roadster, and the film bearing her name is a comedy. This contemporary (i.e., 1953) romp concerns two vintage car owners (John Gregson and Kenneth More) whose friendly rivalry reaches its peak each year with the London-Brighton rally. William Rose's script pits Gregson and his wife (Dinah Sheridan), riding in Genevieve, against More and his girlfriend (Kay Kendall) for the cross-country race.

The characters' dilemmas en route may provoke frustration in them, but it inspires laughter from the audience. Muir Mathieson is credited as musical director, but the harmonica score was composed and played by Larry Adler. Directed by Henry *(Passport to Pimlico, I Am a Camera)* Cornelius.

Gentlemen Prefer Blondes   *Listed under Musicals.*

Ghostbusters   1984   (RCA)   *Color*
Director: Ivan Reitman
Starring: Bill Murray, Dan Aykroyd, Sigourney Weaver, Harold Ramis, Rick Moranis, Annie Potts, William Atherton, Ernie Hudson, David Margulies, Steven Tash, Jennifer Runyon, Michael Ensign, Alice Drummond

Who ya gonna call? Bill Murray, Dan Aykroyd, and Harold Ramis star as buddies who have formed an agency to eradicate evil spirits from Manhattan. They're sort of parapsychological hitmen. The ghost-hunting trio face their most rigorous challenge when a malevolent spirit invades a penthouse on Central Park West. Director Ivan Reitman, whose earlier features range from *Foxy Lady* and *Cannibal Girls* to *Meatballs* and *Stripes*, struck gold this time around. *Ghostbusters* was a box-office phenomenon; as of this writing, Columbia Pictures has collected almost $129 million in theater rentals. Aykroyd and Ramis penned the scenario, but generously handed the plum role to Murray, the "Big Spooker." Many viewers believe the best performance is by Rick Moranis as Sigourney Weaver's nerdy neighbor. The title song is written and performed by Ray Parker, Jr.

Going in Style   1979   (Warner)   *Color*
Director: Martin Brest
Starring: George Burns, Art Carney, Lee Strasberg, Charles Hallahan, Pamela Payton-Wright

Three pensioners living together in Queens decide to brighten their lackluster retirement by robbing a Manhattan bank. Before any of them can voice serious objection, they purchase Halloween masks and phony pistols—and, lo and behold, execute their plan. What's engineered as a lark turns into a bonanza. The old guys make a getaway and later learn that their haul exceeds their wildest dreams. This tenderhearted comedy-drama, written and directed by (then) twenty-eight-year-old Martin Brest, features George Burns, Art Carney, and Lee Strasberg as the late-blooming stickup artists who convey old age in its aches and anguish, its wisdom and triumph.

Good Sam   1948   (Republic)   *Black-and-White*
Director: Leo McCarey
Starring: Gary Cooper, Ann Sheridan, Ray Collins, Edmund Lowe, Joan Lorring, Ruth Roman, Clinton Sundberg

In this low-key situation comedy, a mild-mannered businessman gives vent to his generosity and becomes an overzealous good Samaritan. But Sam (played by Gary Cooper) is too magnanimous for his own good. He thrusts his small Midwest community into havoc and himself into bankruptcy. Ken Englund wrote the script. Directed by Leo McCarey, best known for *The Awful Truth, Going My Way,* and *The Bells of St. Mary's.*

The Goodbye Girl   1977   (MGM)   ◆   *Color*
Director: Herbert Ross
Starring: Richard Dreyfuss, Marsha Mason, Quinn Cummings, Paul Benedict, Barbara Rhoades, Theresa Merritt, Michael Shawn, Patricia Pearcy

An aspiring New York actor and a divorced chorus girl find themselves as unlikely apartment mates in this Neil Simon comedy, written directly for the screen. Richard Dreyfuss plays Elliott Garfield, the wisecracking thespian with a chip on his shoulder. Marsha Mason as Paula McFadden, the insecure divorcée, is always the loser when affairs of the heart turn sour; the perennial goodbye girl, just once *she* wants to be the one to break a heart. Simon's battle-of-the-sexes badinage provides the ammunition for Mason and Dreyfuss as they discover, after all, that they're really in love. *The Goodbye Girl* afforded Dreyfuss a best actor Oscar. In cameos: Powers Booth as one of the *Richard III* cast members and Nicol Williamson as a director who gives the Dreyfuss character a chance at film stardom.

The Graduate   1967   (Embassy)   ◆   *Color*
Director: Mike Nichols
Starring: Anne Bancroft, Dustin Hoffman, Katharine Ross, William Daniels, Murray Hamilton, Elizabeth Wilson, Brian Avery, Walter Brooke, Norman Fell, Elizabeth Fraser, Alice Ghostley, Buck Henry, Marion Lorne

Mike Nichols's second film as director confirmed the promise of *Who's Afraid of Virginia Woolf?* and established Dustin Hoffman as one of the leading actors of his generation. As Benjamin Braddock, Hoffman struck a note with audiences everywhere. Anne Bancroft plays the seductive Mrs. Robinson, and Katharine Ross, the Robinsons' daughter and Ben's beloved. This tale of corrupted innocence is based on Charles Webb's novel. Aided by a saucy and sexually frank screenplay by Calder Willingham and Buck Henry, Nichols orchestrates *The Graduate* into a landmark comedy. For his efforts he won the 1967 best director Oscar—although *In the Heat of the Night* was proclaimed best picture. The integral Paul Simon song score, performed by Simon and Garfunkel, includes "Mrs. Robinson," "Scarborough Fair," and "The Sounds of Silence."

The Great Race   1965   (Warner)   ◆   *Color*
Director: Blake Edwards
Starring: Tony Curtis, Jack Lemmon, Natalie Wood, Peter Falk, Keenan Wynn, Arthur O'Connell, Vivian Vance, Dorothy Provine, Larry Storch, Ross Martin, George Macready, Marvin Kaplan, Denver Pyle

This farce is intended as a paean to silent comedy. The Arthur Ross and Blake Edwards story, directed by the latter, dramatizes a 1908 New York-to-Paris car race. The leading competitors are Leslie Gallant III (Tony Curtis), hero of heroes, and dastardly Professor Fate (Jack Lemmon). The elaborate production spotlights duels, bar-room brawls, pie fighting, and desperate chicanery on the open road. Two Henry Mancini songs, with lyrics by Johnny Mercer, are notable: "The Sweetheart Tree" and Dorothy Provine's interpretation of the saloon sing-along, "He Shouldn't-a, Hadn't-a, Oughtn't-a Swang on Me." Vivian Vance, little seen in motion pictures either before or after her Ethel Mertz years, plays Hester Goodbody. Academy Award: sound effects (Tregoweth Brown).

Guess Who's Coming to Dinner   *Listed under Dramas.*

The **H**eartbreak Kid   1972   (Media)   *Color*
Director: Elaine May
Starring: Charles Grodin, Cybill Shepherd, Jeannie Berlin, Eddie Albert, Audra Lindley,
William Prince, Art Metrano

The anxieties of the newly married are given comic treatment in this Neil Simon satire, an expansion of Bruce Jay Friedman's short story "A Change of Plan." Charles Grodin and Jeannie Berlin are a New York couple honeymooning in Miami. When she gets sunburned and is confined to the hotel room, he finds himself attracted to another young vacationer (Cybill Shepherd), then pursues her—all the way to her family's home in Minneapolis. The second directorial credit of comedienne Elaine May (*A New Leaf* came first), *The Heartbreak Kid* is a harsh, unloving portrait of all the characters; but there is engaging acting by Eddie Albert, Audra Lindley, Grodin in the title role, and Berlin—May's daughter—as the abandoned bride.

Heaven Can Wait   1978   (Paramount)   *Color*
Directors: Warren Beatty, Buck Henry
Starring: Warren Beatty, Julie Christie, James Mason, Charles Grodin, Dyan Cannon,
Jack Warden, Vincent Gardenia, Joseph Maher, Dolph Sweet, Buck Henry

After a car accident, L.A. Rams quarterback Joe Pendleton (Warren Beatty) is prematurely whisked off to heaven. When the error is discovered by roll-keeper Mr. Jordan (James Mason), Joe is sent back to earth with a new identity: a billionaire—who falls in love with an English ecologist (Julie Christie). *Heaven Can Wait*, as scripted by Elaine May (with additions by Beatty), is a romantic comedy coupled with reincarnation fantasy—a remake of *Here Comes Mr. Jordan* (1941), which starred Robert Montgomery as Joe Pendleton (a pugilist) and Claude Rains as his celestial protector.

High Anxiety   1977   (CBS)   *Color*
Director: Mel Brooks
Starring: Mel Brooks, Madeline Kahn, Cloris Leachman, Harvey Korman, Dick Van Patten, Ron Carey, Howard Morris, Murphy Dunne, Jack Riley, Charlie Callas

Nobel Prize–winning Harvard psychiatrist Dr. Richard Thorndyke suffers from acrophobia. Unluckily, he has just been hired as the new director of the Psycho-Neurotic Institute for the Very, Very Nervous, a California sanitorium—situated atop an oceanside cliff. In a trice, Dr. Thorndyke has high anxiety. And that's before he learns that the institute is the breeding ground for a murder plot. *High Anxiety* is a spoofy amalgam of *Psycho, Vertigo, The Birds, Spellbound,* and *North by Northwest.* Regular Mel Brooks devotees will not be disappointed, while film connoisseurs may appreciate the allusions to Hitchcock's plotting and camera stylistics. Brooks's writing team on *Silent Movie*— Rudy De Luca, Ron Clark, and Barry Levinson—helped him with this one, too; also attending the reunion was composer John Morris, who has written a parody of Bernard Herrmann scores. In the acting company: Madeline Kahn, Cloris Leachman, Harvey Korman, and the director himself as Dr. Thorndyke.

Hobson's Choice   1954   (Thorn)   *Black-and-White*
Director: David Lean
Starring: Charles Laughton, Brenda de Banzie, John Mills, Richard Wattis, Helen Haye, Daphne Anderson, Prunella Scales

In this most famous screen incarnation of the venerable Harold Brighouse comedy, Charles Laughton plays a turn-of-century Lancashire bootmaker—a despot whose marriageable daughters provide him with cheap labor. His eldest daughter (Brenda de Banzie) finally rebels. The Norman Spencer-Wynard Browne screenplay provides scene-stealing opportunities for Laughton as the drunken shop owner and more subdued moments for de Banzie as his canny offspring. Cinematography by Jack Hildyard and art direction by Wilfrid Shingleton. Among other adaptations: a 1931 British version and a 1983 American TV movie, reset in New Orleans, and starring Richard Thomas, Sharon Gless, and Jack Warden.

Homebodies   1975   (Embassy)   *Color*
Director: Larry Yust
Starring: Peter Brocco, Ruth McDevitt, Ian Wolfe, Frances Fuller, Paula Trueman, William Hansen, Linda Marsh, Douglas Fowley

The protagonists of this black comedy are six elderly Cincinnatians. When they learn that their brownstone is to be razed in the wake of so-called urban renewal, they activate their tenants' league. After several conventional attempts to save their apartments fail, they resort to an unconventional plan. To quote the ad slogan: "A murder a day keeps the landlord away!" The script, by Howard Kaminsky, Bennett Sims, and Larry Yust (and directed by Yust), follows in the tradition of Hitchcock's *The Trouble with Harry*. Grisly humor and suspense combine as the mild-mannered elders protect their home. Filmed on location in Cincinnati.

Hopscotch   1980   (Embassy)   *Color*
Director: Ronald Neame
Starring: Walter Matthau, Glenda Jackson, Ned Beatty, Sam Waterston, Herbert Lom, David Matthau, George Baker, Ivor Roberts, Lucy Saroyan, Severn Darden, George Pravda, Mike Gwilym

This comedy-adventure reunites the *House Calls* team of Walter Matthau and Glenda Jackson. Adapted from Brian Garfield's 1975 book, winner of the Mystery Writers of America's Edgar Award as best novel, *Hopscotch* tells the story of maverick CIA agent Miles Kendig (Matthau). When he is unjustly demoted by an unsympathetic new boss, Kendig opts for revenge. An out-in-the-cold veteran superspy, he starts writing a manuscript that discloses trade secrets. His evolving memoirs could be a source of embarrassment to the CIA, the FBI, and the KGB—all of whom are in hot pursuit. The major capitals of Europe provide the backdrop for Kendig's game of hopscotch. Getting laughs in this parody of espionage fiction are Matthau, Glenda Jackson (as a friendly widow living in Vienna), Ned Beatty (a flustered CIA director), and Sam Waterston (a former company colleague who is amused by Kendig's capers). Garfield himself wrote the first-draft screenplay, which was then revised by Bryan Forbes.

The Hospital   1971   (CBS)   ◆   *Color*
Director: Arthur Hiller
Starring: George C. Scott, Diana Rigg, Barnard Hughes, Nancy Marchand, Richard Dysart, Stephen Elliott, Roberts Blossom, Robert Walden

This comedy about a New York hospital won Paddy Chayefsky a best screenplay Oscar. The locale is Metropolitan Hospital, where calamity piles upon calamity. In addition to the chaos created by misadministration and medical incompetency, there is now a homicidal maniac loose in the corridors who is killing doctors and nurses. George C. Scott, as the potentially suicidal chief of staff, has a lot of problems—private and professional—to solve. Diana Rigg is a femme fatale who both helps and hinders his progress. Viewers should be warned that there is much grimness amidst the laughter. Directed by Arthur Hiller, who also brought Chayefsky's *The Americanization of Emily* to the screen.

The Hot Rock   1972   (CBS)   *Color*
Director: Peter Yates
Starring: Robert Redford, George Segal, Ron Leibman, Paul Sand, Zero Mostel, Moses Gunn, William Redfield, Topo Swope, Charlotte Rae, Graham Jarvis, Harry Bellaver, Seth Allen, Robert Levine, Christopher Guest

Bungling criminal John Dortmunder is the mastermind hero of several caper comedies by mystery novelist Donald E. Westlake. Herein Dortmunder and his inept gang purloin a priceless diamond from the Brooklyn Museum. The band of bumblers get the jewel easily enough, then in a series of farcical and suspenseful developments lose and keep trying to reclaim it. There are vivid characterizations by Robert Redford (Dortmunder), George Segal, Paul Sand, and Ron Leibman as the robbers. Scenarist William Goldman and director Peter Yates are more renowned for their stark dramas, but *The Hot Rock* maintains an amusingly frenetic touch throughout.

House Calls   1978   (MCA)   *Color*
Director: Howard Zieff
Starring: Walter Matthau, Glenda Jackson, Art Carney, Richard Benjamin, Candice Azzara, Dick O'Neill, Thayer David

Medical satire and romantic comedy fuse in this entertainment. Walter Matthau, playing a widowed doctor, begins courting one of his patients, divorcée Glenda Jackson. Because they are both so independent, it's a rocky romance. Meanwhile, back at the office, Matthau must contend with a senile head of surgery (Art Carney). Screenplay credits go to Max Shulman, Julius J. Epstein, Alan Mandel, and Charles Shyer. Under the direction of Howard Zieff (*Slither, Hearts of the West, Private Benjamin, Unfaithfully Yours*), the three leads are engaging—and there's a noteworthy supporting performance by Richard Benjamin. Basis for the 1979–82 TV sitcom, also called "House Calls," starring Wayne Rogers and Lynn Redgrave (and later Sharon Gless).

How to Marry a Millionaire   1953   (CBS)   *Color*
Director: Jean Negulesco
Starring: Betty Grable, Marilyn Monroe, Lauren Bacall, David Wayne, Rory Calhoun, Cameron Mitchell, Alex D'Arcy, Fred Clark, William Powell, George Dunn, Harry Carter, Robert Adler, Tudor Owen, Maurice Marsac, Jan Arvan, Dayton Lummis, Charlotte Austin, Merry Anders

Loco, Pola, and Schatze are three glamourous gold diggers who set themselves up in a Park Avenue apartment in hopes of snaring eligible bachelors—or, at least, sugar daddies. This stylish movie, with a screenplay by Nunnally Johnson, provides opportunities for Betty Grable, Lauren Bacall, and Marilyn Monroe to demonstrate their

prowess as comediennes. William Powell plays one of several millionaires they en-
counter. A highlight in the career of Twentieth Century-Fox house director Jean
Negulesco. *How to Marry a Millionaire* later became a syndicated TV series, starring
Lori Nelson, Merry Anders, and Barbara Eden in the Monroe part.

The Hunter   1980   (Paramount)   *Color*
Director: Buzz Kulik
Starring: Steve McQueen, Eli Wallach, Kathryn Harrold, LeVar Burton, Ben Johnson,
Tracey Walter, Richard Venture, Tom Rosales, Theodore Wilson, Ray Bickel, Bobby Bass,
Kevin Hagen, Luis Avalos

Chases—by car, foot, and atop a moving train—highlight this action comedy about a
modern-day bounty hunter, Ralph "Papa" Thorson. Based on a biography of Thorson
written by Christopher Keane, the movie presents its protagonist (Steve McQueen)
on the run and at home with his pregnant girlfriend (Kathryn Harrold). In one suspenseful exchange, Thorson's private and professional lives entwine: his girl is held
hostage by a raving madman. For most of its running time, though, *The Hunter* is
played for laughs. This is McQueen's last film. Papa Thorson himself appears as a
bartender. Shot in and around Chicago from a screenplay by Ted Leighton and Peter
Hyams.

I'm All Right, Jack   Great Britain 1959; U.S. 1960   *Black-and-White*
     (Thorn)
Director: John Boulting
Starring: Ian Carmichael, Peter Sellers, Terry-Thomas, Richard Attenborough, Dennis
Price, Margaret Rutherford, Irene Handl, Liz Fraser, John Le Mesurier, Marne Maitland,
Sam Kydd

Social criticism is a hallmark of British comedies of the fifties and sixties. In this
production from twin brothers John and Roy Boulting (*Private's Progress, Brothers in
Law, Lucky Jim, Heavens Above*) the targets are trade unions and big business manage-
ment. Working at cross-purposes are shop steward Peter Sellers, personnel manager
Terry-Thomas, and young-man-on-the-rise (and nephew to the boss) Ian Carmichael.
When the latter upsets a crooked business scheme, he brings about a national strike.
The script is by Frank Harvey and John Boulting (from Alan Hackney's novel, *Private
Life*).

The In-Laws   1979   (Warner)   *Color*
Director: Arthur Hiller
Starring: Peter Falk, Alan Arkin, Richard Libertini, Nancy Dussault, Penny Peyser, Ar-
lene Golonka, Michael Lembeck, Paul Lawrence Smith, Ed Begley, Jr., Sammy Smith, Car-
mine Caridi, James Hong, Barbara Dana, Rozsika Halmos, Alvaro Carcano, David
Paymer

Everybody has prenuptial jitters in this farce—especially the fathers. Sheldon Kornpett
(Alan Arkin) is a conservative Manhattan dentist. What Vince Ricardo (Peter Falk)
does for a living isn't immediately apparent; his wife knows only that he does "some
kind of international consulting work; he travels a lot." Vince travels a lot because he
is mysteriously involved with the CIA, the Mafia, and hitmen-counterfeiters. On the
eve of their children's wedding, Vince and an unwilling Sheldon participate in the

aftermath of a U.S. Mint truck robbery—and they embark on a New York-to-Latin America escapade. Scenarist Andrew Bergman and director Arthur Hiller provide high hilarity most of the way. The musical score is by John Morris. Semisequel: *Big Trouble*, again starring Arkin and Falk, this time for John Cassavetes.

Indiscreet   1958   (Republic)   *Color*
Director: Stanley Donen
Starring: Cary Grant, Ingrid Bergman, Cecil Parker, Phyllis Calvert, David Kossoff,
Megs Jenkins, Oliver Johnston, Middleton Woods

Broadway's *Kind Sir*, starring Charles Boyer and Mary Martin, becomes *Indiscreet* in this drawing room comedy set in London's Mayfair. In the Boyer-Martin roles are Cary Grant and Ingrid Bergman. He's Philip Adams, an American diplomat; she's Ann Kalman, an actress. The premise, as adapted by Norman Krasna from his own playscript, has wedding-shy Philip protecting himself from romantic involvements by a blanket falsehood—that he's already married. The ruse proves unfortunate (and leads to hilarious complications) when he really falls in love with Ann. Grant and Bergman, who also starred in Hitchcock's *Notorious*, are models of sophistication here. Theme song by Sammy Cahn and James Van Heusen.

Inside Moves   1980   (CBS)   *Color*
Director: Richard Donner
Starring: John Savage, David Morse, Diana Scarwid, Amy Wright, Tom Burton, Bill
Henderson, Bert Remsen, Harold Russell

Max's bar is the meeting place for a disparate group of urban misfits. The latest member of the unofficial club is a young suicide survivor (John Savage), who is redeemed by the others—all of whom are in some way physically or mentally afflicted. (Another participant in the roundtable is Harold Russell, the handicapped soldier in *The Best Years of Our Lives*.) The tragicomic script is another collaboration of husband-and-wife team Valerie Curtin and Barry Levinson (*. . . And Justice for All, Best Friends*). The dialogue alternates between self-deprecation and life-affirmation. The score is by John Barry and Laszlo Kovacs handles the cinematography.

Irma La Douce   1963   (CBS)   *Color*
Director: Billy Wilder
Starring: Jack Lemmon, Shirley MacLaine, Lou Jacobi, Bruce Yarnell, Herschel Bernardi,
Hope Holiday, Joan Shawlee, Grace Lee Whitney, Paul Dubov, Howard McNear, Cliff
Osmond, Diki Lerner, Herb Jones

Another entertainment from the writing team of I. A. L. Diamond and Billy Wilder, this raucous adult comedy adds another honor to their collaborations: *Love in the Afternoon, Some Like It Hot, The Apartment*, and *One, Two, Three*—to list only the pre–*Irma La Douce* credits. In this tale of Parisian prostitute Irma and her gendarme lover Nestor, Shirley MacLaine and Jack Lemmon reactivate their chemistry from *The Apartment*. To maintain his hold on Irma, Nestor becomes her *mec* (pimp), and therefrom spring the complications of the tale. Based on the stage musical, this *Irma La Douce* is presented without the songs—though the original themes, as scored by André Previn, are heard as part of the background. Look for Bill Bixby as a tattooed sailor and James Caan in a walk-on.

It Should Happen to You   1953   (RCA)   *Black-and-White*
Director: George Cukor
Starring: Judy Holliday, Peter Lawford, Jack Lemmon, Michael O'Shea, Vaughn Taylor

Jack Lemmon's film debut came in one of Judy Holliday's best comedies. In the movie, scripted by Garson Kanin and Ruth Gordon, Holliday plays Gladys Glover, an unemployed New York model who becomes her own publicity agent—by having her name painted on a billboard, which overlooks Columbus Circle. Instant celebrity arises, and so does a romance with photographer Lemmon. George Cukor also directed several other Kanin-Gordon screenplays, including *Adam's Rib, A Double Life*, and *Pat and Mike*.

It's a Mad, Mad, Mad, Mad World   1963   (CBS)   *Color*
Director: Stanley Kramer
Starring: Spencer Tracy, Milton Berle, Sid Caesar, Buddy Hackett, Ethel Merman, Mickey Rooney, Dick Shawn, Phil Silvers, Terry-Thomas, Jonathan Winters, Edie Adams, Dorothy Provine, Eddie "Rochester" Anderson, Jim Backus, Ben Blue, Alan Carney, Barrie Chase, William Demarest, Peter Falk, Paul Ford, Leo Gorcey, Edward Everett Horton, Buster Keaton, Don Knotts, Carl Reiner, The Three Stooges

Literally scores of other comic actors and comedians appear in this movie. This return to madcap chase pictures of the silent era, with a screenplay by William and Tania Rose, focuses on various money-hungry characters who search for a cache of stolen bank loot. Spencer Tracy plays the captain of detectives who follows them cross country. Stanley Kramer's production concentrates on pratfalls, demolition, and high-speed chases. Among other guest stars in cameos: Jack Benny, Joe E. Brown, Jimmy Durante, Jerry Lewis—a nonstop roll call of comedy greats.

Joe   1970   (Vestron)   *Color*
Director: John G. Avildsen
Starring: Peter Boyle, Dennis Patrick, K Callan, Audrey Caire, Susan Sarandon, Patrick McDermott

Joe is a right-wing, blue-collar bigot. A foul-mouthed construction worker by day and a domestic tyrant at night, Joe is especially intolerant of hippies. One day at his favorite bar, Joe encounters an affluent advertising executive who is shaken by the fact that he has just murdered his daughter's drug-addicted boyfriend. When Joe, who advocates home-made law and order, learns this, he elevates the businessman to hero status. Norman Wexler's screenplay, a savage satire, is directed by John G. Avildsen, best known for *Rocky* and *The Karate Kid*. *Joe*, however, is brutal, at times bloody, certainly profane in its realistic depiction of the title character, and frequently funny. Unforgettable performances by Peter Boyle as Joe, Dennis Patrick as the killer-businessman, and K Callan and Audrey Caire as their wives.

Kelly's Heroes   1970   (MGM)   *Color*
Director: Brian G. Hutton
Starring: Clint Eastwood, Telly Savalas, Don Rickles, Donald Sutherland, Carroll O'Connor, Gavin MacLeod, Stuart Margolin, Harry Dean Stanton, Dick Davalos

This slam-bang action-comedy rematches the star (Clint Eastwood) and director (Brian G. Hutton) of *Where Eagles Dare* for a lighthearted modification of *The Dirty Dozen*. Under Eastwood's command, a band of GI's advance behind German lines in World War II. Their mission: steal a $20 million gold shipment from the enemy. Suspense and laughter take their turns in Troy Kennedy Martin's script, with Eastwood as platoon leader Kelly and Telly Savalas and Don Rickles among his heroes. Viewers may be puzzled by the presence of long-haired hippie enlisted man Donald Sutherland in the 1940s setting—a concession to 1970 audiences which now simply defies logic. Second-unit director: Andrew Marton.

Kind Hearts and Coronets   1949   (Thorn)   *Black-and-White*
Director: Robert Hamer
Starring: Dennis Price, Valerie Hobson, Joan Greenwood, Alec Guinness, Audrey Fildes, Miles Malleson, Clive Morton, Cecil Ramage, John Penrose, Hugh Griffith, Arthur Lowe

Director Robert Hamer's masterpiece, this satirical black comedy is based on the 1907 novel *Noblesse Oblige* by Roy Horniman. The film's adaptation is by Hamer and coscenarist John Dighton. Dennis Price stars as a distant relative of the titled d'Ascoyne family. He aspires to the Dukedom of Chalfont, but eight others (all played by Alec Guinness) precede him in the line of succession. So our hero decides to eliminate them. Guinness has a field day with his eight roles, each with an obligatory death scene; women's suffrage spokesman Lady Agatha d'Ascoyne is perhaps his most priceless characterization.

A King in New York   Great Britain 1957; U.S. 1973   *Black-and-White*
     (CBS)
Director: Charles Chaplin
Starring: Charles Chaplin, Dawn Addams, Oliver Johnston, Maxine Audley, Harry Green, Jerry Desmond, Sidney James, Michael Chaplin

King Shadhov (Charles Chaplin), a penniless European ruler fleeing a civil revolution, comes to America during the McCarthy witchhunt era. He carries with him a plan for the peaceful use of atomic energy. However, no one—least of all the Atomic Energy Commission—is interested. In order to survive, the king becomes a TV commercial pitchman, endorsing a brand of whiskey. He fluffs a take when, after imbibing, he coughs; the whiskey company airs this version anyway and the king becomes a celebrity. He also is subpoenaed to appear before the House Un-American Activities Committee. *A King in New York* (shot in London) was released abroad in 1957, when Chaplin—for his political views—was unpopular in America; it had its belated theatrical release here in 1973. Written, directed, and with music by Chaplin, the film costars Dawn Addams as the advertising woman who guides Shadhov's TV career and ten-year-old Michael Chaplin as a discontented progressive school student—whose parents are political radicals.

King of Hearts   France 1966; U.S. 1967   (CBS)   *Color*
Director: Philippe de Broca
Starring: Alan Bates, Geneviève Bujold, Jean-Claude Brialy, Françoise Christophe, Julien Guiomar, Pierre Brasseur, Micheline Presle, Michel Serrault, Adolfo Celi, Marc Dudicourt, Daniel Boulanger

The small French town of Marville at the end of World War I. Private Charles Plimpick (Alan Bates), a Scottish soldier, is sent to Marville to dismantle a bomb that the Germans have left behind. When he arrives, the private discovers the village abandoned by the enemy—and overtaken by local asylum inmates. The loonies are soon convinced that Charles is the prodigal King of Hearts. This comic fantasia, written by Daniel Boulanger and directed by Philippe de Broca, works as whimsy and as an antiwar statement. The score is by Georges Delerue.

The Lavender Hill Mob   ◆   *Black-and-White*
Great Britain 1951; U.S. 1952   (Thorn; Learning)
Director: Charles Crichton
Starring: Alec Guinness, Stanley Holloway, Sidney James, Alfie Bass, Marjorie Fielding, Edie Martin, John Gregson, Gibb McLaughlin

Another Ealing Studios gem. This comedy by T. E. B. Clarke, who received an Oscar for his screenplay, stars Alec Guinness as a timorous bank clerk in charge of a shipment of gold bullion delivered to the Bank of England. With three partners in crime (Stanley Holloway, Sidney James, Alfie Bass), the clerk robs the bullion and has it shipped to France—as Eiffel Tower souvenir paperweights. Veteran comedy director Charles Crichton (*The Titfield Thunderbolt, Law and Disorder, The Battle of the Sexes*) brings his expert pacing to the project. Watch for Audrey Hepburn in a small role.

Life with Father   1947   (Media; Hal Roach Studios;   *Color*
Video Yesteryear; Budget Video; Video Connection; Sheik Video; Discount Video Tapes; Cinema Concepts; King of Video)
Director: Michael Curtiz
Starring: William Powell, Irene Dunne, Elizabeth Taylor, Edmund Gwenn, ZaSu Pitts, Jimmy Lydon, Emma Dunn, Moroni Olsen, Elisabeth Risdon, Derek Scott, Johnny Calkins, Martin Milner, Queenie Leonard, Nancy Evans, Clara Blandick

A screen adaptation of the Howard Lindsay-Russel Crouse Broadway comedy (it ran from 1939 to 1947), *Life with Father* portrays a New York family in the 1880s. The anecdotal script, adapted by Donald Ogden Stewart, centers on irascible, eccentric Clarence Day (William Powell), his wife Vinnie (Irene Dunne), and their four sons, one of them, John, played by a very young Martin Milner. Directed by Michael Curtiz, this family comedy devotes much of its plot to the tyrannical father's refusal to be baptized. (Motion picture censorship in 1947 prevented Powell from uttering the play's famous curtain line: "I'm going to be baptized, damn it!") A television series ran in half-hour installments from 1953 to 1955 and featured Leon Ames and Lurene Tuttle as the Day parents.

A Little Romance   1979   (Warner)   ◆   *Color*
Director: George Roy Hill
Starring: Laurence Olivier, Diane Lane, Thelonious Bernard, Arthur Hill, Sally Kellerman, David Dukes, Broderick Crawford

Two adolescents, a French boy and a young American girl living in Paris, fall in love and run away together in this comedy taken from a novel by Patrick Cauvin. In the screenplay by Alan Burns (Mary Tyler Moore's TV producer-writer who also directed her in *Just Between Friends*), Laurence Olivier is a garrulous boulevardier (and pickpocket) who befriends the two runaways. Their dream is to pledge their eternal love beneath the Bridge of Sighs in Venice—at sunset, just as the bells toll. The European locales are captured in Pierre William Glenn's color cinematography. Georges Delerue won an Academy Award for his score.

Local Hero   1983   (Warner)   *Color*
Director: Bill Forsyth
Starring: Burt Lancaster, Peter Riegert, Fulton MacKay, Denis Lawson, Norman Chancer, Peter Capaldi, Rikki Fulton, Alex Norton, Jenny Seagrove, Jennifer Black, Christopher Rozycki, Christopher Asante, John Jackson, Dan Ammerman, Tam Dean Burn

Aspiring junior executive Mac MacIntyre (Peter Riegert) is dispatched to Scotland by his petrochemical company boss, Felix Happer (Burt Lancaster). Mac's assignment: to persuade the citizens of a sleepy fishing village to sell their land to Knox Oil so that a refinery can be constructed there. The young man expects to meet powerful resistance from the laid-back locals. But in this deadpan comedy, written and directed by Bill Forsyth (the creator of *Gregory's Girl*), Mac's preconceptions are punctured right and left. Contributing to the befuddlement are Gordon Urquhart (Denis Lawson), an innkeeper who doubles as an accountant; a black African minister named Macpherson (Christopher Asante); an ingénue with webbed feet—she is appropriately named Marina (Jenny Seagrove); and many others. Music by Mark Knopfler. Devotees of *Gregory's Girl* will spot the hero of that film (Gordon John Sinclair) in the small role of Ricky.

Lolita   1962   (MGM)   *Black-and-White*
Director: Stanley Kubrick
Starring: James Mason, Shelley Winters, Peter Sellers, Sue Lyon, Marianne Stone, Diana Decker, Jerry Stovin, Lois Maxwell

When *Lolita* was released, late-night TV promos touted it as the movie "you'll never see on television." Stanley Kubrick's cinematic treatment has a screenplay by Vladimir Nabokov, reshuffling events from his controversial novel. The plot remains essentially the same: Lolita (Sue Lyon in heart-shaped sunglasses) is a nymphet who prefers older men. Her most recent conquest is visiting college professor Humbert Humbert (James Mason); in order to be close to Lolita, Humbert marries her mother, Charlotte (Shelley Winters). Lolita, embodying both innocence and carnality, accepts Humbert's devotion almost passively. Much of this dark slapstick is hinged on their cross-country romantic interlude—with mysterious writer Quilty (Peter Sellers) in pursuit.

Lonely Hearts   *Listed under Dramas.*

Love and Death   1975   (CBS)   *Color*
Director: Woody Allen
Starring: Woody Allen, Diane Keaton, Harold Gould, Alfred Lutter, Olga Georges-Picot, Zvee Scooler, Georges Adel, Despo, Frank Adu

In *Love and Death* Woody Allen, who also directed from his original script, plays a condemned man. In 1812 Russia, the prisoner, a draft evader in the Napoleonic Wars, reflects on his misspent life. His flashbacks—personalized with uniquely Allenesque humor—focus on the pretentious, great-works-of-literature-quoting cousin (Diane Keaton) whom he's loved from afar. En route to its hilarious finale, *Love and Death* satirizes Russian novels, pokes fun at Bonaparte, and sends up Ingmar Bergman films. Music by Prokofiev.

Love at First Bite   1979   (Warner)   *Color*
Director: Stan Dragoti
Starring: George Hamilton, Susan Saint James, Richard Benjamin, Dick Shawn, Arte Johnson, Sherman Hemsley, Isabel Sanford

This horror film spoof ponders what would happen if Count Dracula fled Communist-controlled Transylvania and emigrated to present-day New York City. The main merrymakers are George Hamilton, as the protagonist—a suave, seductive Dracula whose Old World, gentlemanly charm makes him an anachronism; Susan Saint James, a fashion model in love with the count; Richard Benjamin, a psychiatrist who, in trying to expose the vampire, gets his monster-repelling lore confused; and Arte Johnson, the count's devoted manservant, Renfield—still fond of the occasional housefly or spider snack. Robert Kaufman's script (which *does* get the vampire lore straight) is directed by Stan Dragoti.

Love in the Afternoon   1957   (CBS)   *Black-and-White*
Director: Billy Wilder
Starring: Audrey Hepburn, Gary Cooper, Maurice Chevalier, John McGiver, Van Doude, Lise Bourdin

This sophisticated comedy set in Paris is the first of many films director Billy Wilder cowrote with I. A. L. Diamond. (Their collaboration continued in *Some Like it Hot; The Apartment; One Two Three; Irma La Douce; Kiss Me, Stupid; The Fortune Cookie; The Private Life of Sherlock Holmes; Avanti!*; and *Buddy, Buddy*.) Their script for *Love in the Afternoon* harkens back to the romantic comedies of Ernst Lubitsch. A French cello student (Audrey Hepburn) and her father, a private eye (Maurice Chevalier), match wits and exchange drolleries with an American playboy (Gary Cooper). The plot revolves around the cellist's warning the American Casanova that an enraged husband is planning to shoot him.

Mad Wednesday   1947   (Prism; Video   *Black-and-White*
Yesteryear; Budget Video; Discount Video Tapes; Glenn Video Vistas; Sheik Video; Cable Films; King of Video; Video Connection; Western Film & Video Inc.; Classic Video Cinema Collector's Club; Hal Roach Studios; Kartes Productions)
Director: Preston Sturges
Starring: Harold Lloyd, Jimmy Conlin, Raymond Walburn, Edgar Kennedy, Arline Judge, Franklin Pangborn, Lionel Stander, Margaret Hamilton, Frances Ramsden

This madcap farce was comedian Harold Lloyd's final motion picture. In it the funnyman reprises the hero of his classic silent, *The Freshman*—the last reel of which is used as the preface to *Mad Wednesday*. Harold Diddlebock (Lloyd), once a college football star, is now a middle-aged bookkeeper—and a bumbler. Written, produced, and directed by veteran comedy filmmaker Preston Sturges, *Mad Wednesday* also stars Frances Ramsden as Miss Otis, Jimmy Conlin as Wormy, Raymond Walburn as E. J. Waggleberry, Edgar Kennedy as the bartender, Franklin Pangborn as Formfit Franklyn, Lionel Stander as Max, and Margaret Hamilton as Harold's sister; a lion named Jackie plays the ferocious beast that figures in the rollicking climax. Alternate title: *The Sin of Harold Diddlebock*—which constitutes the studio-edited version not authorized by Sturges.

Make Mine Mink   1960   (Sheik; VidAmerica)   *Black-and-White*
Director: Robert Asher
Starring: Terry-Thomas, Athene Seyler, Hattie Jacques, Billie Whitelaw, Elspeth Dux-
bury, Irene Handl, Jack Hedley, Raymond Huntley

A band of larcenous rooming house tenants are the unlikely heroes of this British
comedy. Michael Pertwee's script has dowager Athene Seyler and ex–military officer
Terry-Thomas as leaders of a team of Robin Hood–like fur thieves; the proceeds they
derive from stealing from the rich go to the poor. A perplexed detective, played by
Raymond Huntley, investigates—and, in one scene, Terry-Thomas must make a fast
getaway by stripping to his shorts and pretending he's a racewalking entrant. Inventive
absurdity sparks this production, with Robert Asher directing the comedians.

The Man in the White Suit   1951   (Thorn)   *Black-and-White*
Director: Alexander Mackendrick
Starring: Alec Guinness, Joan Greenwood, Cecil Parker, Michael Gough, Ernest Thesiger,
Howard Marion Crawford, Henry Mollison, Russell Waters, Joan Harben, Vida Hope,
Miles Malleson, George Benson, Edie Martin

Alec Guinness gives a winning deadpan performance in this farce about a chemist who
creates a miraculous fabric that will never rip, soil, or wear out. His invention creates
furor not only in the local textile plant, but throughout the garment industry. Both
union and management seek to destroy the scientist's formula. The script by Roger
MacDougall, John Dighton, and Alexander Mackendrick is a high watermark of Ealing
Studios comedy. Mackendrick, an American who forged his career in England, directed.
Comedienne Joan Greenwood manages to steal a few scenes from Guinness and his
indestructible white suit.

Manhattan   1979   (MGM)   ✳ *Black-and-White*
Director: Woody Allen
Starring: Woody Allen, Diane Keaton, Michael Murphy, Mariel Hemingway, Meryl
Streep, Anne Byrne, Karen Ludwig, Michael O'Donoghue, Victor Truro, Tisa Farrow,
Bella Abzug, Gary Weis, Charles Levin, Mark Linn-Baker, Damion Sheller, Kenny
Vance, Wallace Shawn, Ray Serra

This Manhattan Baedeker, crafted by Woody Allen and coscenarist Marshall Brickman,
introduces Isaac Davis, a TV comedy show gagsmith currently writing a serious novel.
In his breaks from writing, Isaac explores the Big Apple and has encounters with
friends (Michael Murphy, Anne Byrne), lovers (Diane Keaton, Mariel Hemingway),
and an ex-wife (Meryl Streep). A cerebral comedy marked by the director's confessional,
psychoanalytical pronouncements, and Gordon Willis's high-contrast black-and-white
cinematography—underscored by the strains of George Gershwin. *Manhattan* was
singled out by the New York Film Critics Circle for Allen's direction.

M*A*S*H   1970   (CBS)   ✳ ◐ *Color*
Director: Robert Altman
Starring: Donald Sutherland, Elliott Gould, Tom Skerritt, Sally Kellerman, Robert Du-
vall, JoAnn Pflug, René Auberjonois, Roger Bowen, Gary Burghoff, Fred Williamson,
John Schuck, Bud Cort, G. Wood

MASH is an acronym for the 4077th Mobile Army Surgical Hospital. Near the front
lines of the Korean conflict, a coterie of dedicated medics perform their self-termed

"meatball surgery" on battle casualties. The film *M*A*S*H* follows (to quote the camp's ever-present public address system) "the zany antics of our combat surgeons—snatching laughs and loves between amputations and penicillin. . . ." *M*A*S*H*, then, is a comedy, but filtered through the persona of director Robert Altman, a savage and deeply iconoclastic comedy. It quite neatly redefines antiestablishment. Hawkeye Pierce (Donald Sutherland), Trapper John McIntyre (Elliott Gould), and Duke Forrest (Tom Skerritt) are the three captain-surgeon-draftees who, with their shenanigans, drive the brass batty. By developing a wacky camaraderie, the trio withstand the atrocities of war; their after-hours pranks consist of helicoptering to Japan for a golf tourney, planning a suicide party for the unit's dejected Don Juan dentist, and devising a public broadcast of the noisy lovemaking of a chaplain and a chief nurse. The doctors' madness, however, is more than equaled by their proficiency in the operating room. Ring Lardner's Oscar-acknowledged script is inspired by the novel by Richard Hooker, the pseudonym for a real-life Korean War surgeon. The movie was the recipient of the Palme d'Or at Cannes and the best picture prize of the National Society of Film Critics. "M*A*S*H" the teleseries ran from 1972 to 1983.

Mr. Blandings Builds His Dream House   1947   *Black-and-White*
     (Media; Nostalgia)
Director: H. C. Potter
Starring: Cary Grant, Myrna Loy, Melvyn Douglas, Reginald Denny, Sharyn Moffett, Connie Marshall, Louise Beavers, Ian Wolfe, Harry Shannon, Tito Vuolo, Nestor Paiva, Jason Robards, Lurene Tuttle, Lex Barker

Jim Blandings (Cary Grant) and his wife Muriel (Myrna Loy) are a New York City couple who long for a dream home in the Connecticut countryside. Their fantasy turns to reality but they discover rural life isn't all it's cracked up to be. The Blandings's departure from the city very effectively spells an end to domestic bliss. The Norman Panama-Melvin Frank screenplay is derived from Eric Hodgkins' novel. The film's satiric theme represents a time-honored tradition that stretches—at the very least— from *George Washington Slept Here* (1942) to *The Money Pit* (1986).

Mr. Peabody and the Mermaid   1948   (Republic)   *Black-and-White*
Director: Irving Pichel
Starring: William Powell, Ann Blyth, Irene Hervey, Andrea King, Clinton Sundberg

William Powell and Ann Blyth portray the title characters in this fantasy comedy. The plot might be regarded as an early sketch for Ron Howard's *Splash* (or a minor variation on the 1947 British film *Miranda*). Mr. Peabody, a Boston businessman on a fishing trip in the Caribbean, encounters an amorous mermaid. So he takes her home to his bathtub. Screenwritten by Nunnally Johnson, from a novel by Guy and Constance Jones, *Mr. Peabody and the Mermaid* is directed by Irving Pichel (*The Most Dangerous Game, She, The Moon Is Down, Happy Land, The Miracle of the Bells, Destination Moon*). Russell Metty is the cinematographer.

Mister Roberts   1955   (Warner)   ◆   *Color*
Directors: John Ford and Mervyn LeRoy
Starring: Henry Fonda, James Cagney, William Powell, Jack Lemmon, Betsy Palmer, Ward Bond, Phil Carey, Martin Milner, Gregory Walcott, James Flavin, Jack Pennick, Duke Kahanamoko, Nick Adams, Ken Curtis, Harry Carey, Jr., Frank Aletter

The U.S.S. *Reluctant*, known by her crew as the *Bucket*, is a navy cargo ship in the Pacific during World War II. The ship's captain (James Cagney) is a strict disciplinarian. Lieutenant (jg) Doug Roberts (Henry Fonda) wants desperately to be transferred to a fighting zone. Aided by Doc (William Powell in his last role) and Ensign Pulver (Jack Lemmon in his first Oscar-winning role)—he makes the skipper's life miserable in order to have his request granted. Frank Nugent and Joshua Logan adapted the Broadway comedy by Logan and Thomas Heggen (from Heggen's earlier novel). Codirected by two seasoned pros, John Ford and Mervyn LeRoy, *Mister Roberts* is a noteworthy service comedy. Sequel: *Ensign Pulver* (1964), with Robert Walker as the title character.

Monsieur Verdoux   1947   (CBS; Playhouse Video)   *Black-and-White*
Director: Charles Chaplin
Starring: Charles Chaplin, Martha Raye, Isobel Elsom, Marilyn Nash, Irving Bacon, William Frawley, Mady Correll, Allison Roddan, Margaret Hoffman, Almira Sessions, Audrey Betz

This sardonic comedy is based on the ladykilling career of Landru, the French Bluebeard—who went to the guillotine in 1922, convicted of murdering ten women. He had wooed (and possibly done away with) many others. Reinterpreted by Charles Chaplin—as star, writer, and director—Landru becomes Verdoux, a bank cashier who marries and murders a series of rich ladies. The protagonist's cold-bloodedness has a compassionate root: he is trying to support his real-life wife, a cripple. Fans of Chaplin's lovable tramp should be warned that the bigamist antihero of this film is a radical departure.

Monty Python and the Holy Grail   1975   (RCA)   *Color*
Directors: Terry Gilliam and Terry Jones
Starring: Graham Chapman, John Cleese, Terry Gilliam, Eric Idle, Terry Jones, Michael Palin, Connie Booth, Carol Cleveland, Neil Innes, John Young

Nine hundred thirty-two A.D. King Arthur of England (Graham Chapman) rides through the countryside looking for knights to join his Round Table. Unluckily, the poor monarch has no mount so he must pretend, by skip-hopping, that he is astride a sturdy steed. Meanwhile, his lamebrained servant Patsy (Terry Gilliam) follows apace clapping coconut shells to simulate the sound of hoofbeats. This consideration of Camelot springs from the fertile satirical minds of the Monty Python troupe; they wrote the screenplay and two of their members—Terry Gilliam (now renowned for *Brazil*) and Terry Jones—directed the action. *Monty Python and the Holy Grail* is the group's first movie with something resembling a narrative. (See *And Now for Something Completely Different*.) With visual gags, non sequiturs, and straight-faced reactions to absurd situations, the Arthur-Lancelot-Galahad legend is parodied for all it's worth. Awaiting the pursuers of the Holy Grail: bloody sword fights, a three-headed knight, the eerie Castle Anthrax, the Gorge of Eternal Peril, an airborne killer rabbit, and much more.

Monty Python's Life of Brian   1979   (Warner)   *Color*
Director: Terry Jones
Starring: Graham Chapman, John Cleese, Terry Gilliam, Eric Idle, Terry Jones, Michael Palin, Carol Cleveland

Written by and starring the Monty Python six, this irreverent parody-parable is set in biblical times. The devout should be forewarned. Brian (Graham Chapman), a would-be Messiah, has a childhood that parallels a famed Nazarene carpenter. When he reaches his thirtieth birthday, he turns Judea and the Roman Empire topsy-turvy by joining the Judean Revolutionary People's Front. Brian's teachings fragmentize the populace and his enemies have him crucified. The Python team, in thrusting satiric barbs at the New Testament, rely on parody, surrealism, and sometimes scurrilous dialogue to make their points.

Monty Python's The Meaning of Life   1983   (MCA)   *Color*
Director: Terry Jones
Starring: Graham Chapman, John Cleese, Terry Gilliam, Eric Idle, Terry Jones, Michael Palin, Carol Cleveland, Simon Jones

Again sharing starring and screenwriting duties, the Monty Python players present a series of songs and skits dramatizing the seven ages of man. This brazen spoof includes odes to procreation, catholic doctrine, modern medicine, gluttony, and the Grim Reaper. (The latter arrives, in a Bergman-cum-Buñuel parody, at a fashionable dinner party.) Perhaps the most widely discussed episode features director Terry Jones as the fattest man in the world.

The Moon Is Blue   1953   (CBS)   *Black-and-White*
Director: Otto Preminger
Starring: William Holden, David Niven, Maggie McNamara, Tom Tully, Dawn Addams, Fortunio Bonanova

This romantic comedy was a censorship cause célèbre in 1953. It was denied a Production Code seal of approval because it contained such risqué words as "virgin," "seduce," and "mistress." The tale, scripted by F. Hugh Herbert from his Broadway hit, introduces Maggie McNamara as Patty O'Neill—a proud virgin, who refuses to be seduced or become the mistress of Donald Gresham (William Holden) or David Slater (David Niven). The pursuit, nonetheless, continues. New York is the setting, with an extended sequence atop the Empire State Building.

Morgan!   1966   (Thorn)   *Black-and-White*
Director: Karel Reisz
Starring: Vanessa Redgrave, David Warner, Robert Stephens, Irene Handl, Arthur Mullard, Newton Blick, Nan Munro, Bernard Bresslaw

Morgan Delt (David Warner) is a young Londoner obsessed with Marxism, King Kong, and Leonie (Vanessa Redgrave), his ex-wife. Morgan is an artist of sorts, though he rarely gets around to painting anything. He's too busy indulging in fantasies and giving vent to his simian concerns (he keeps a life-size stuffed gorilla in his studio). Archetypal sixties anarchism, this black comedy gave the two leads their first significant film roles. Three years later director Karel Reisz and Redgrave would reteam for *Isadora* (also known as *The Loves of Isadora*). *Morgan!*, subtitled *A Suitable Case for Treatment* remains the high point of David Warner's screen career, though he had supporting parts in later pictures (*The Bofors Gun, The Fixer, The Sea Gull, The Ballad of Cable Hogue, The Omen, Cross of Iron*).

The Mouse That Roared   1959   (RCA)   *Color*
Director: Jack Arnold
Starring: Peter Sellers, Jean Seberg, David Kossoff, William Hartnell, Monty Landis, Leo McKern, Macdonald Parke, Harold Kasket, Timothy Bateson

Leonard Wibberley's novel about the tiny Duchy of Grand Fenwick was the basis for this popular screen farce. In the adaptation by Roger MacDougall and Stanley Mann, Peter Sellers assumes three roles: a field marshal, a prime minister, and Grand Fenwick's adorably befuddled dowager, Duchess Gloriana. Directed by Jack Arnold, the picture concerns a small, impoverished country's declaration of war on the United States—with the intention of losing and thereby collecting Marshall Aid. Bright entertainment that inspired a 1963 sequel, *The Mouse on the Moon*, directed by Richard Lester and starring Margaret Rutherford as Gloriana.

Movie, Movie   1978   (RCA)   *Color*
Director: Stanley Donen
Starring: George C. Scott, Trish van Devere, Barbara Harris, Red Buttons, Barry Bostwick, Ann Reinking, Art Carney, Harry Hamlin, Kathleen Beller, Rebecca York, Michael Kidd, Jocelyn Brando, Eli Wallach

This parody of 1930s double features brings two movies for the price of one. First on the bill is a black-and-white prizefight melodrama, *Dynamite Hands*, a lampoon of *Golden Boy* that centers on Joey Popchick (Harry Hamlin), a poor law student who turns to boxing to finance his kid sister's operation. The second attraction is *Baxter's Beauties of 1933*, an all-talking, singing, and dancing Busby Berkeley pastiche starring George C. Scott as Broadway musical impresario Spats Baxter. Most of the actors appearing in the opening feature regroup for the second. Written by Larry Gelbart and Sheldon Keller and directed by Stanley Donen. Michael Kidd choreographed *Baxter's Beauties* and appears as Papa Popchick in *Dynamite Hands*.

Murder by Death   1976   (RCA)   *Color*
Director: Robert Moore
Starring: Eileen Brennan, Truman Capote, James Coco, Peter Falk, Alec Guinness, Elsa Lanchester, David Niven, Peter Sellers, Maggie Smith, Nancy Walker, Estelle Winwood

This Neil Simon mystery-movie parodies such fictional sleuths as Sam Spade, Miss Marple, Charlie Chan, and Nick and Nora Charles. The script has the world's greatest detectives assembling at the mansion of eccentric millionaire Lionel Twain (Truman Capote) to unravel a mystery he has devised. Whoever solves the weekend's whodunit will win a million dollars. Lunacy reigns, but, under Robert Moore's direction, the movie is full of distinctive genre patter and remains true to its 1930s settings. (Stephen Grimes is the production designer.) The music by Dave Grusin contributes to the spoofery.

My Bodyguard   1980   (CBS)   *Color*
Director: Tony Bill
Starring: Martin Mull, Ruth Gordon, Chris Makepeace, Adam Baldwin, Matt Dillon, John Houseman, Craig Richard Nelson, Tim Kazurinsky

A slice-of-life exposition of teenage friendship and rivalry turns into a sweet-natured comedy. The creators of *My Bodyguard*—writer Alan Ormsby and actor Tony Bill in his directing debut—present a fifteen-year-old Chicago high school student named Clifford Peache (Chris Makepeace). Cliff is being harassed by a class bully (Matt Dillon). In retaliation, he hires a bodyguard (Adam Baldwin), a hulking classmate with his own impressive reputation as a campus tough. Martin Mull and Ruth Gordon provide laughs as the pestered protagonist's father and grandmother. The score is by Dave Grusin.

My Dinner with André   1981   (Pacific Arts Video)   *Color*
Director: Louis Malle
Starring: André Gregory, Wallace Shawn, Jean Lenauer, Roy Butler

Written by and starring André Gregory and Wallace Shawn (as themselves), this film is a dialogue staged in a posh Manhattan restaurant. Premised as a reunion of two colleagues who have not seen one another for years, *My Dinner with André* simply presents the conversation between André, an avant-garde theater director, and Wally, an actor-playwright. The two old friends drink and dine, catch up on the missing years, and engage in philosophical arguments. It's an occasion for wit and—surprisingly—drama.

My Favorite Brunette   1947   (Prism; Video   *Black-and-White*
     Yesteryear; Budget Video; Sheik Video; Cable Films; Video Connection; Discount
     Video Tapes; Western Film & Video Inc.; Cinema Concepts; Kartes Productions)
Director: Elliott Nugent
Starring: Bob Hope, Dorothy Lamour, Peter Lorre, Lon Chaney, Jr., John Hoyt, Charles Dingle, Reginald Denny, Frank Puglia, Ann Doran, Willard Robertson, Jack La Rue, Charles Arnt, Garry Owen

Many viewers claim this is the best of the *My Favorite . . .* series starring Bob Hope. The spy spoof presents the comedian as photographer Ronnie Jackson. To help beautiful brunette Carlotta Montay (Dorothy Lamour) out of dire straits betwixt coded maps and murderers, Ronnie turns detective. Hope's high spirits (and the dialogue by Edmund Beloin and Jack Rose) make *My Favorite Brunette* a breakneck farce. The director is seasoned comedy creator Elliott Nugent (Hope's *The Cat and the Canary*). Appearing in cameos are Alan Ladd and Bing Crosby.

My Favorite Year   1982   (MGM)   *Color*
Director: Richard Benjamin
Starring: Peter O'Toole, Jessica Harper, Mark Linn-Baker, Joseph Bologna, Bill Macy, Lainie Kazan, Anne De Salvo, Lou Jacobi, Adolph Green, George Wyner, Selma Diamond, Cameron Mitchell, Gloria Stuart

A farce about the days of live-broadcast television in the fifties, *My Favorite Year* is at root an affectionate tribute to the ground-breaking *Your Show of Shows*. Peter O'Toole stars as Alan Swann, an Errol Flynnesque silver screen swashbuckler who is hired as a featured guest on a prime time comedy-variety hour. Problems arise because Alan, accustomed to retake after retake in the movies, doesn't realize the show will be telecast live. It may not matter anyway; Alan, a dashing rogue off-screen as well as on-, spends most of his time inebriated. Richard Benjamin's directorial debut coincides with the major film debut of Mark Linn-Baker as the harried writer who acts as Swann's unofficial chaperone. The screenplay is by Norman Steinberg and Dennis Palumbo.

Nashville   *Listed under Musicals.*

National Lampoon's Animal House   1978   (MCA)   *Color*
Director: John Landis
Starring: John Belushi, Tim Matheson, John Vernon, Verna Bloom, Thomas Hulce, Cesare Danova, Peter Riegert, Stephen Furst, Karen Allen, James Widdoes, Sarah Holcomb, Bruce McGill, Martha Smith, Mary Louise Weller, James Daughton, Kevin Bacon, Donald Sutherland

Faber College in the early 1960s is the setting for this farce pitting Dean Wormer (John Vernon) against the fraternity brothers of Delta House—Otter (Tim Matheson), Boon (Peter Riegert), Bluto (John Belushi), Flounder (Stephen Furst), D-Day (Bruce McGill), Hoover (James Widdoes), et al. Comic chaos rules when the Delts—mostly slobbish pranksters—play one-upmanship with the snobbish residents of Omega House. Raucous and raunchy are adjectives that might be applied to the screenplay by Harold Ramis, Douglas Kenney, and Chris Miller. The production provides a showcase for several future stars: Peter Riegert, Tom Hulce, Karen Allen, and Kevin Bacon. The movie inspired the short-lived TV sitcom "Delta House"—with Vernon, Furst, McGill, and Widdoes reprising their big screen roles.

Network   1976   (MGM)   ◆   *Color*
Director: Sidney Lumet
Starring: Faye Dunaway, William Holden, Peter Finch, Robert Duvall, Ned Beatty, Beatrice Straight, Wesley Addy, William Prince, Marlene Warfield, Roy Poole

Howard Beale (Peter Finch), a Universal Broadcasting System news anchorman, becomes the "mad prophet of the airwaves" in Paddy Chayefsky's satirical overview of American television and the ratings game. Beale, fed up with capitalism, materialism, *and* TV, goes berserk one night on a newscast and announces "I'm mad as hell, and I'm not going to take this anymore." (That diatribe turns into a rallying cry and Howard is soon a national hero—with the best ratings of his career.) This black comedy, directed by Sidney Lumet, won Oscars for Chayefsky's screenplay, supporting actress Beatrice Straight, leading actress Faye Dunaway, and—a posthumous recognition—Peter Finch as the foul-mouthed protagonist.

Nine to Five   1980   (CBS)   *Color*
Director: Colin Higgins
Starring: Jane Fonda, Lily Tomlin, Dolly Parton, Dabney Coleman, Elizabeth Wilson, Henry Jones, Lawrence Pressman, Marian Mercer, Ren Woods, Norma Donaldson, Peggy Pope, Richard Stahl, Ray Vitte, Sterling Hayden

From nine to five, even as during the rest of the day, Franklin Hart (Dabney Coleman) is an all-round bigot and chauvinist. As a vice-president at Consolidated Companies, he makes life intolerable for his private secretary, Doralee Rhodes (Dolly Parton) and her officemates, Violet Newstead (Lily Tomlin) and Judy Bernly (Jane Fonda). When Doralee, Violet, and Judy kidnap Hart and make him their prisoner, they are able to bring office efficiency to an all-time high. The chemistry of the three stars and the office truths of writer-director Colin Higgins's script turned this farce into a top moneymaker; to date it has earned over $60 million. Dolly Parton's title song was Oscar-nominated. The scenario inspired an ABC-TV series that ran sporadically from March 1982 through October 1983 before being reactivated for syndication in 1986.

No Time for Sergeants   1958   (Warner)   *Black-and-White*
Director: Mervyn LeRoy
Starring: Andy Griffith, Myron McCormick, Nick Adams, Murray Hamilton, Howard Smith, Will Hutchins, Sydney Smith, James Milhollin, Don Knotts, Jean Willes, Bartlett Robinson, Henry McCann, Dub Taylor, William Fawcett, Raymond Bailey, Jameel Farah, Malcolm Atterbury, Sammy Jackson, Rad Fulton

Will Stockdale (Andy Griffith), an uneducated but resourceful Georgia hillbilly, is the pivotal character in this service comedy. Based on the Mac Hyman novel and the subsequent TV and Broadway plays scripted by Ira Levin, the film adaptation—by John Lee Mahin—documents young Will's career as an army recruit. Unaccustomed to the world beyond his remote farm community, the young soldier becomes the butt of many jokes and inspires calamity wherever he goes, particularly for his platoon leader, Sergeant King (Myron McCormick). Griffith reprises his role from the TV and stage play; Nick Adams plays Will's cohort in cataclysm, the sweet-natured Ben Whitledge; and Will Hutchins portrays Lieutenant Bridges. Don Knotts's film debut gives him one funny scene with Griffith, his future TV costar. Jameel Farah, the actor portraying Lieutenant Gardella, soon changed his name to Jamie Farr. Sammy Jackson, who plays one of the inductees, graduated to the star part when "No Time for Sergeants" became a weekly series in the 1964–65 TV season.

North Dallas Forty   1979   (Paramount)   *Color*
Director: Ted Kotcheff
Starring: Nick Nolte, Mac Davis, Charles Durning, Dayle Haddon, G. D. Spradlin, Bo Svenson, Steve Forrest, Dabney Coleman, John Matuszak

A seriocomic dissection of professional football, this loose adaptation of the Peter Gent best-seller is written by Gent himself, in collaboration with Frank Yablans and director Ted Kotcheff. Labor abuse in the National Football League rates as the serious half of the film; the comedy arises in how the bruised, battered gridiron stars cope with the grueling game. *North Dallas Forty* unfolds with vignettes involving drugs, alcohol, and sexual escapades—so it's hardly an uplifting portrait of the sport or its participants; but the production has vitality. The actors—both veterans (Nick Nolte, Charles Durning, Steve Forrest, Dabney Coleman) and tyros (Mac Davis, John Matuszak)—lend conviction to the machismo. The score is by John Scott.

Ocean's 11   1960   (Warner)   *Color*
Director: Lewis Milestone
Starring: Frank Sinatra, Dean Martin, Sammy Davis, Jr., Peter Lawford, Angie Dickinson, Richard Conte, Cesar Romero, Patrice Wymore, Joey Bishop, Akim Tamiroff, Henry Silva, Ilka Chase, Buddy Lester, Richard Benedict, Jean Willes, Norman Fell

Frank Sinatra and members of his self-styled Rat Pack star in this crime caper. Five Las Vegas casinos are the target as Danny Ocean (Sinatra) and his wartime pals execute a major heist. Other members of the eleven-man team include Sam Harmon (Dean Martin), Josh Howard (Sammy Davis, Jr.), and Jimmy Foster (Peter Lawford). Screenwriters Harry Brown and Charles Lederer follow the formula (the robbery itself is relatively effortless), but then add surprises to the aftermath. *Ocean's 11* is a comedy-drama, packaged by longtime director Lewis Milestone (*All Quiet on the Western Front, The Front Page, Of Mice and Men, A Walk in the Sun, Pork Chop Hill*). The songs are by Sammy Cahn and Jimmy Van Heusen, and guest stars include Red Skelton, Shirley MacLaine, Hoot Gibson, and George Raft.

The Odd Couple   1968   (Paramount)   *Color*
Director: Gene Saks
Starring: Jack Lemmon, Walter Matthau, John Fiedler, Herbert Edelman, David Sheiner, Larry Haines, Monica Evans, Carole Shelley, Iris Adrian

Walter Matthau, the quintessential Neil Simon actor, reprises his Broadway role and Jack Lemmon takes over for Art Carney. A classic of the American stage, *The Odd Couple* dramatizes the clash of reluctant apartment-mates Oscar Madison (Matthau) and Felix Unger (Lemmon)—the slob and the perfectionist. In this screen adaptation, by Simon himself, the stars savor the comic melancholy of the situation. In splendid support are Carole Shelley and Monica Evans as the "Coo-Coo" Pigeon sisters and—enacting the odd couple's poker-playing buddies—Herb Edelman, David Sheiner, Larry Haines, and John Fiedler. Composer Neal Hefti created the score. Jack Klugman and Tony Randall inherited the leading roles in the subsequent television series (1970–75); Demond Wilson (Oscar) and Ron Glass (Felix), however, were unsuccessful as "The New Odd Couple," a short-run series of the 1982-83 season.

Oh, God!   1977   (Warner)   *Color*
Director: Carl Reiner
Starring: George Burns, John Denver, Teri Garr, Paul Sorvino, George Furth, Ralph Bellamy, Barnard Hughes, William Daniels, Donald Pleasence, Barry Sullivan, Dinah Shore, Jeff Corey, David Ogden Stiers

In his screen acting debut, John Denver plays a supermarket manager who becomes a modern-day Moses on whom God (embodied by George Burns) confers a message of hope. The young man is enlisted to spread the word that God is alive and well and living, for the moment, in L.A. Writer Larry Gelbart (*Tootsie*) has a facility for gags and repartee, and his script—inspired by Avery Corman's novel—generally strikes a tactful balance between piety and sacrilege. Burns reprised his role for two sequels: *Oh God, Book II* (1980) and *Oh, God! You Devil* (1984).

The One and Only   1978   (Paramount)   *Color*
Director: Carl Reiner
Starring: Henry Winkler, Kim Darby, Gene Saks, William Daniels, Polly Holliday, Hervé Villechaize, Harold Gould, Richard Lane

The one and only Gorgeous George is the subject of this heavily fictionalized biography set in the fifties. As the film opens, George is an impetuous college actor with fantasies of a career on the professional stage. For years fame eludes him as he tackles one harebrained show biz–related job after another. Only when he climbs into a wrestling ring with his hair dyed blond and set in curls does he hit the big time. Henry Winkler stars as the persistent and sometimes obnoxious central character, and Kim Darby appears as his patient wife. Carl Reiner, fresh from *Oh, God!* and en route to *The Jerk*, directed from a script by Steve Gordon, who later wrote and directed *Arthur*.

Operation Petticoat   1959   (Republic)   *Color*
Director: Blake Edwards
Starring: Cary Grant, Tony Curtis, Joan O'Brien, Dina Merrill, Gene Evans, Richard Sargent, Virginia Gregg, Robert F. Simon, Robert Gist, Gavin MacLeod, George Dunn, Dick Crockett, Madlyn Rhue, Marion Ross, Frankie Darro, Arthur O'Connell

This sprightly comedy recounts a fictional episode from World War II. Admiral Matthew Sherman (Cary Grant) is the commander of the *Sea Tiger*, a badly damaged submarine. Patched up and repainted, the vessel becomes the U.S. Navy's first shocking pink sub. On assignment in the South Pacific, Sherman and the *Sea Tiger*'s aggressively macho crew are aghast when five army nurses are placed aboard. The Stanley Shapiro-

Maurice Richlin script makes the most of its well-timed laughs. In supporting roles are "The Love Boat's" Gavin MacLeod (as Ernest Hunkle), Marion Ross of "Happy Days" (as Lieutenant Ruth Colfax), and former child star Frankie Darro (as a seaman named Dooley). *Operation Petticoat* later became a two-year TV sitcom, costarring—in the first season—John Astin and Jamie Lee Curtis.

The Out-of-Towners   1970   (Paramount)   *Color*
Director: Arthur Hiller
Starring: Jack Lemmon, Sandy Dennis, Sandy Baron, Anthony Holland, Anne Meara,
Carlos Montalban, Billy Dee Williams

One sunny spring afternoon, luggage-laden George and Gwen Kellerman (Jack Lemmon and Sandy Dennis) leave their suburban Ohio home and motor to the local airport. Destination: New York City. On the agenda (or so they think): a job interview for George; shopping and sightseeing for Gwen. They are *The Out-of-Towners*. When the Kellermans' delayed flight fails to land at a fog-bound Kennedy International, which results in their being rerouted to Boston for an early-morning return train to Gotham, they are greeted by an officious desk clerk who informs them that their hotel reservations have been cancelled. Meantime, their luggage has been misplaced. Accommodationless, George and Gwen are cast adrift in Manhattan's less fashionable districts, where they encounter a succession of looters, muggers, and kidnappers. The couple encounter mishaps and misfortunes that could only happen in New York. This Neil Simon comedy was originally conceived as one of the skits in his Broadway play *Plaza Suite*—then abandoned in the early stages of production.

Outrageous!   1977   (RCA)   *Color*
Director: Richard Benner
Starring: Craig Russell, Hollis McLaren, Richert Easley, Allan Moyle, David Meilwraith,
Jerry Salzberg, Andrée Pelletier, Helen Shaver

Outrageous! is a low-budget Canadian comedy that was well received in North America and later had long runs in European capitals. Shot in twenty-three days in January 1977 for $165,000, the film tells of Robin Turner (Craig Russell), a homosexual hairdresser who dreams of stardom as a female impersonator. In time he achieves success in Toronto and New York clubs—with impressions of Bette Davis, Mae West, Judy Garland, and Barbra Streisand. A subplot involving Robin's female roommate—a schizophrenic named Liza (Hollis McLaren)—contributes to the movie's aura of unpredictability. Russell's character in some ways parallels his own story, and there are interesting portrayals by McLaren, Allan Moyle (Martin), David Meilwraith (Bob, a New York cabbie), and Richert Easley. Written and directed by Richard Benner and loosely based on a Margaret Gibson story entitled "Making It." Music: Paul Hoffert.

Paper Moon   1973   (Paramount)   ◆   *Black-and-White*
Director: Peter Bogdanovich
Starring: Ryan O'Neal, Tatum O'Neal, Madeline Kahn, John Hillerman, P. J. Johnson,
Burton Gilliam, Randy Quaid

Moses Pray (Ryan O'Neal) is a phony Bible salesman plying his confidence tricks on residents of the Dust Bowl during the Depression. Unwillingly, he is saddled with nine-year-old Addie (Tatum O'Neal), who is quite possibly his illegitimate daughter. Addie becomes a star pupil and in no time equals Moses as a fast-talking con artist.

Their adventures on the road form the core of this comedy-drama, adapted from Joe David Brown's novel (called *Addie Pray*) by screenwriter Alvin Sargent and director Peter Bogdanovich. Bogdanovich and his cinematographer, Laszlo Kovacs, employ conventions of thirties filmmaking for the visual effects. Tatum O'Neal, as best supporting actress, is the youngest star ever to win an Oscar in a regular category. Madeline Kahn plays Trixie Delight. A 1974-season TV series of "Paper Moon" starred Jodie Foster as Addie and Christopher Connelly—Ryan O'Neal's brother on the "Peyton Place" saga—as Moses.

The Perils of Pauline   1947   (Prism; Hal Roach   *Black-and-White* Studios; Video Yesteryear; Budget Video; Movie Buff Video; Discount Video Tapes; Sheik Video; Cable Films; Media Home Entertainment; Video Connection; Kartes Productions)
Director: George Marshall
Starring: Betty Hutton, John Lund, Billy De Wolfe, William Demarest, Constance Collier, Frank Faylen, William Farnum, Paul Panzer, Snub Pollard, Creighton Hale, Chester Conklin, James Finlayson, Hank Mann, Bert Roach

Pearl White, queen of silent movie serials, is the subject of this fabricated biography that takes the form of a musical comedy. Slapstick routines, rather than facts, are the prominent feature. Betty Hutton stars as the resilient actress who plays heroine after heroine in cliffhanger after cliffhanger. Under George Marshall's direction of the P. J. Wolfson screenplay, *The Perils of Pauline* presents a comic look at backlot filmmaking in 1920s Hollywood. The picture profits from the appearance of comedians from the heyday of the silents and a Frank Loesser score which includes the Academy Award–nominated "I Wish I Didn't Love You So."

Pillow Talk   1959   (MCA)   ◆   *Color*
Director: Michael Gordon
Starring: Rock Hudson, Doris Day, Tony Randall, Thelma Ritter, Nick Adams, Julia Meade, Allen Jenkins, Marcel Dalio, Lee Patrick, Mary McCarty, Hayden Rorke, Valerie Allen, Jacqueline Beer, Arlen Stuart, Perry Blackwell, Don Beddoe, William Schallert

This film inspired a cycle of romantic comedies starring Doris Day; the actress was teamed most often with Rock Hudson, but sometimes with James Garner, and once (*That Touch of Mink*) with Cary Grant. Here Doris Day is cast as interior decorator Jan Morrow and Hudson plays Brad Allen, a wolf in sheep's clothing—two busy New Yorkers who hate one another, then fall in love on their telephone party line. The screenplay won an Academy Award for Stanley Shapiro, Maurice Richlin, Russell Rouse, and Clarence Greene. Crime and comedy specialist Michael Gordon (*Boston Blackie Goes to Hollywood, The Web, An Act of Murder, Portrait in Black, Boys' Night Out*) is the director. The title song, performed by Day, was written by Buddy Pepper and Inez James.

The Pink Panther   1964   (CBS)   *Color*
Director: Blake Edwards
Starring: David Niven, Peter Sellers, Robert Wagner, Capucine, Claudia Cardinale, Brenda de Banzie, Fran Jeffries, Colin Gordon, John Le Mesurier, Michael Trubshawe

The original French *sûreté* inspector Jacques Clouseau (Peter Sellers), a bungler, arrives in Switzerland in quest of the Phantom, a notorious jewel thief. The Phantom's own target: the Pink Panther, a precious diamond. Round and round they go until the Phantom is unmasked—no thanks to Clouseau, whose wife Simone (Capucine) is one of the thief's accomplices. With location photography by Philip Lathrop, this cat-and-mouse farce reaches its climax at a winter Alpine resort. Maurice Richlin and Blake Edwards concocted the plot, and the latter directed. Henry Mancini composed the music and cowrote the theme, "It Had Better Be Tonight" ("Meglio Stasera") with Johnny Mercer and Franco Misliacci. Clouseau's capers continued in *A Shot in the Dark*, *Inspector Clouseau* (in which Alan Arkin assumed the title role), *The Return of the Pink Panther*, *The Pink Panther Strikes Again*, *Revenge of the Pink Panther*, and—released after Peter Sellers' death—*Trail of the Pink Panther* and *Curse of the Pink Panther*.

The Pink Panther Strikes Again   1976   (CBS)   *Color*
Director: Blake Edwards
Starring: Peter Sellers, Herbert Lom, Colin Blakely, Lesley-Anne Down, Leonard Rossiter, Burt Kwouk, André Maranne, Marne Maitland

After a nervous breakdown (induced by Clouseau), Chief Inspector Dreyfus (Herbert Lom) plots his revenge. Dreyfus, who still twitches maniacally at the mere mention of Clouseau's name, assembles a band of criminals to eradicate his nemesis. A segment of the plot, devised by Frank Waldman and director Blake Edwards, deals with the Destruction Device, a ray gun powerful enough to wipe out the United Nations building. (The weapon also makes people and objects vanish, then reappear.) The fifth in the *Pink Panther* series if one includes *Inspector Clouseau*, made in 1968 without Edwards or Peter Sellers.

Play It Again, Sam   1972   (Paramount)   *Color*
Director: Herbert Ross
Starring: Woody Allen, Diane Keaton, Tony Roberts, Jerry Lacy, Susan Anspach, Jennifer Salt, Joy Bang, Viva

"Play it again, Sam" is the most famous nonexistent line from *Casablanca*. Even as a misquote, it is an appropriate title for this combination parody of and salute to the movies of Humphrey Bogart. Adapted by Woody Allen from his Broadway comedy, *Play It Again, Sam* offers the playwright-star as Allan Felix, a nebbishy San Francisco film critic whose wife (Susan Anspach) has deserted him. The grounds: "insufficient laughter." Allan has a recurring hallucination: the appearance of Bogie (Jerry Lacy)—clad in slouch hat and trenchcoat, enveloped in cigarette smoke, and ready to dispense advice to the lovelorn hero. The film, directed by Herbert Ross, also analyzes the strained marriage of a two-career couple—Dick (Tony Roberts) and Linda (Diane Keaton). Linda's brief romantic dalliance with Allan, only to return to her husband, brings the picture full circle to its *Casablanca* connection.

Plaza Suite   1971   (Paramount)   *Color*
Director: Arthur Hiller
Starring: Walter Matthau, Maureen Stapleton, Barbara Harris, Lee Grant, Louise Sorel, José Ocasio, Dan Ferraro, Jenny Sullivan, Tom Carey

The movie version of Neil Simon's Broadway hit revolves around Suite 719 in Manhattan's Plaza Hotel. (Directed by Arthur Hiller, the production was shot in Hollywood, but a number of New York exteriors have been added.) The elegant suite becomes the scene for three vignettes—all starring Walter Matthau. In "Visitor from Mamaroneck," a chirpy wife (Maureen Stapleton) recalls her Plaza honeymoon of twenty-three (or was it twenty-four?) years before. The "Visitor from Hollywood" is a jargon-spouting producer (Matthau) plotting a rendezous with an old flame (Barbara Harris), now a suburban matron and an ardent movie fan. Lee Grant costars in the third episode, "Visitor from Forest Hills," in which a mother and father (Matthau again) try to coax their daughter, a bride-to-be, out of a locked bathroom—while wedding guests grow restless in the ballroom. (Maureen Stapleton played all three women on Broadway; Lee Grant played them in the West Coast stage edition.)

Pocketful of Miracles 1961 (Key) *Color*
Director: Frank Capra
Starring: Glenn Ford, Bette Davis, Hope Lange, Arthur O'Connell, Peter Falk, Thomas Mitchell, Edward Everett Horton, Sheldon Leonard, Barton MacLane, Jerome Cowan, Mickey Shaughnessy, David Brian, Peter Mann, Mike Mazurki, Fritz Feld, John Litel, Snub Pollard, Jack Elam, Ann-Margret

A revamping by Frank Capra of his classic 1933 comedy, *Lady for a Day*, this version stars Bette Davis as Apple Annie, the gin-soaked queen of Broadway peddlers. Glenn Ford, Hope Lange, Peter Falk, and others play customers who help the old woman pose as a high-society matron when her long-unseen daughter comes to town. (Ann-Margret, in her screen debut, portrays the daughter.) The Hal Kanter-Harry Tugend screenplay is derived from Damon Runyon's "Madame La Gimp." The enterprise is directed by Capra with his accustomed finesse. However, in its initial release, it failed to attract an audience. *Pocketful of Miracles* was the director's last film.

The Prince and the Showgirl 1957 (Warner) *Color*
Director: Laurence Olivier
Starring: Marilyn Monroe, Laurence Olivier, Sybil Thorndike, Jeremy Spenser, Richard Wattis, Esmond Knight, Rosamund Greenwood, Maxine Audley, Daphne Anderson

Laurence Olivier and Marilyn Monroe's one and only screen teaming makes *The Prince and the Showgirl* an event. The story, as derived from Terence Rattigan's playscript, *The Sleeping Prince*, unfolds during the 1911 coronation of George V. An American chorus girl (Monroe) arrives in London, where she is romanced by the Prince Regent of Carpathia (Olivier). Complicating matters are the dowager queen (Sybil Thorndike), a stiff-necked minister (Richard Wattis), and the prince's haughty son (Jeremy Spenser). Adapted by Rattigan himself, *The Prince and the Showgirl*—thanks to Jack Cardiff's cinematography and the production design of Roger Furse—is rich in visual values. It's the only non-Shakespearean film Olivier has directed.

The Prisoner of Second Avenue 1975 (Warner) *Color*
Director: Melvin Frank
Starring: Jack Lemmon, Anne Bancroft, Gene Saks, Elizabeth Wilson, Florence Stanley, Sylvester Stallone

Mel Edison (Jack Lemmon) is a New York ad agency executive who is suddenly fired. And, as a result, he has a breakdown. Urban craziness turns Mel into a prisoner of his Upper East Side apartment. He and his wife Edna (Anne Bancroft) endure gridlock, a heat wave, a power failure, noisy neighbors—and Mel's paranoia. *The Prisoner of Second Avenue* is a rerun of themes from *The Out-of-Towners* and other Neil Simon anti–New York comedies, though here the playwright seems grimmer than usual. His screenplay is directed by Melvin Frank, the comic mind behind *Buona Sera, Mrs. Campbell* and *A Touch of Class*.

Private Benjamin   1980   (Warner)   *Color*
Director: Howard Zieff
Starring: *Goldie Hawn, Eileen Brennan, Armand Assante, Robert Webber, Sam Wanamaker, Barbara Barrie, Mary Kay Place, Harry Dean Stanton, Hal Williams, P. J. Soles, Albert Brooks*

Judy Benjamin (Goldie Hawn) is widowed on her wedding night. Finding herself at a crossroads, she decides to trade in her designer clothes for army khaki. As Private Benjamin, she discovers that life is hell—but after a grueling basic training, overseen by Captain Doreen Lewis (Eileen Brennan) and Sergeant Ted Ross (Hal Williams), Judy discovers self-esteem she never had. This service comedy with a feminist twist was written by Nancy Meyers, Charles Shyer, and Harvey Miller. It was directed by Howard Zieff of *Slither, Hearts of the West*, and *House Calls* fame. *Private Benjamin* was revised as a TV series for Lorna Patterson, with Brennan and Williams costarring in their original roles.

The Producers   1968   (Embassy)   *Color*
Director: Mel Brooks
Starring: *Zero Mostel, Gene Wilder, Dick Shawn, Kenneth Mars, Estelle Winwood, Lee Meredith, Renee Taylor, Christopher Hewett, Andreas Voutsinas, Michael Davis*

Lunatic Broadway producer Max Bialystock (Zero Mostel) makes most of his money by finding rich old lady investors and "giving them their last thrill on the way to the cemetery." An inspired con atist, Max hatches a new scheme. With the help of accountant Leo Bloom (Gene Wilder), he conspires to find "the worst play we can," then sell 25,000 percent of it; when the show—a guaranteed fiasco—closes overnight, they won't have to pay the backers anything: a foolproof bookkeeping swindle. The property they decide to produce is a musical called *Springtime for Hitler*—dedicated to "the Hitler you knew, the Hitler you loved, the Hitler with a song in his heart." It's the most offensive production ever to blacken the Great White Way. Unfortunately, the show is very favorably reviewed and becomes a hit. *The Producers*, too, was a hit, winning debuting writer-director Mel Brooks an Oscar for his screenplay. Music by John Morris.

The Purple Rose of Cairo   1985   (Vestron)   ★ ▲   *Color*
Director: Woody Allen
Starring: *Mia Farrow, Jeff Daniels, Danny Aiello, Dianne Weist, Milo O'Shea, Van Johnson, Deborah Rush, Zoe Caldwell, Irving Metzman, John Wood, John Rothman, Stephanie Farrow, Michael Tucker, Alexander H. Cohen, Annie Joe Edwards, Camille Saviola, Peter McRobbie, Karen Akers, Juliana Donald, Edward Herrmann*

In this comic fantasy from writer-director Woody Allen, a New Jersey diner waitress escapes the dreariness of the Depression through frequent visits to the local movie house. For Cecilia (Mia Farrow), happiness comes only from those movies. The current attraction at the Jewel Theatre is *The Purple Rose of Cairo*, a comedy about the idle rich and a pith-helmeted explorer named Tom Baxter (Jeff Daniels). One day when Cecilia is watching the film for the umpteenth time, Tom steps off the screen and sweeps her out of the cinema. The adventurer's behavior creates chaos not only for the film's other characters, but for the Jewel patrons and the real-life actor—Gil Shepherd (Jeff Daniels also)—playing Tom. *The Purple Rose of Cairo* (Woody's movie—not the 1930s movie within Woody's movie) was named best picture and given the best screenplay award by the British Academy; French César voters cited it as the best foreign film of the year.

Putney Swope   1969   (RCA)   *Color*
Director: Robert Downey
Starring: Arnold Johnson, Pepi Hermine, Ruth Hermine, Allen Garfield, Antonio Fargas,
Mel Brooks, Alan Abel

Putney Swope (Arnold Johnson) is a young black man who becomes the president of the Truth and Soul Agency, a powerful Madison Avenue advertising firm. His first order of business is to dismiss all but a few token white employees. In their wake arrives a staff of black militants. Reversal comedy is the name of the game in this iconoclastic feature written and directed by Robert Downey. (Other switcharounds: the agency's new owners turn down white applicants; a rich black couple have a lazy blonde maid.) With frank language and innuendo, *Putney Swope* continues the abrasive shock tactics that Downey used in his underground classic, *Chafed Elbows*. This time most of the fun is reserved for TV commercial parodies.

The Quiet Man   1952   (Republic)   ◆   *Color*
Director: John Ford
Starring: John Wayne, Maureen O'Hara, Barry Fitzgerald, Ward Bond, Victor McLaglen,
Mildred Natwick, Arthur Shields, Eileen Crowe, May Craig, Charles FitzSimmons,
Francis Ford, James Lilburn, Sean McClory, Jack MacGowran, Mae Marsh, Joseph O'Dea

John Ford called *The Quiet Man* his "first love story." It's that, but also a nostalgic comedy, based on the Maurice Walsh short story "Green Rushes" as adapted by Frank S. Nugent. The tale begins with Sean Thornton (John Wayne), an Irish-American boxer who, in the States, killed an opponent in the ring. Sean returns to the Emerald Isle to buy back the farm where he lived as a boy. Meanwhile, strong-willed Mary Kate Danaher (Maureen O'Hara) is the colleen who catches his eye. To wed her, Sean must convince not only the lady in question but her boisterous clan, led by brother Red Will (Victor McLaglen). This archetypal Ford film brought Oscars to the director and to cinematographers Winton C. Hoch and Archie Stout.

The Reivers   1969   (Key)   *Color*
Director: Mark Rydell
Starring: Steve McQueen, Sharon Farrell, Ruth White, Michael Constantine, Clifton
James, Juano Hernandez, Lonny Chapman, Will Geer, Rupert Crosse, Mitch Vogel, Dub
Taylor, Allyn Ann McLerie, Diane Ladd, Ellen Geer

Steve McQueen stars as Boon Hogganbeck, the William Faulkner hero who "borrows" his employer's car—a Winton Flyer—for a four-day joy jaunt from Jefferson, Mississippi to Memphis. Boon has two traveling companions—eleven-year-old Lucius Priest (Mitch Vogel) and livery hand Ned McCaslin (Rupert Crosse), who is a stowaway during the first part of the expedition. *The Reivers* (Yoknapatawpha County talk for thieves) explains what happens to the trio on the journey; following the lead of the Pulitzer Prize novel, it centers, via flashback narration, on Lucius. The film, directed by Mark Rydell upon Irving Ravetch and Harriet Frank, Jr.'s, script, depicts the young-ster's (partly unwilling) initiation into chicanery, prevarication, and adult deceit. His comic adventures with Boon and Ned lead him into a brawl with a bigoted lawman; a night in Miss Reba's brothel, where he fights for the honor of Miss Corrie (Sharon Farrell), Reba's prize prostitute; a stopover in a grimy Dixie jail; and a horse race in which he is a jockey. Burgess Meredith, as Lucius grown to manhood, provides the off-screen narration.

The Return of the Pink Panther   1975   (CBS)   *Color*
Director: Blake Edwards
Starring: Peter Sellers, Christopher Plummer, Catherine Schell, Herbert Lom, Burt Kwouk, Peter Arne, Grégoire Aslan, André Maranne, Victor Spinetti, Graham Stark, Peter Jef-frey, David Lodge

Chapter four in the biography of Inspector Clouseau. The fabled Pink Panther dia-mond—the national treasure of the Eastern state of Lugash—is purloined once again. But the thieves are at the mercy of the renowned French detective, who—though a buffoon—always seems to come out on top. The scenario of Blake Edwards (who again directs) and Frank Waldman invents sight gags galore; Clouseau creates ruination with a high-power vacuum cleaner, then performs some Chaplinesque maneuvers on a waxed dance floor. The Henry Mancini score and the opening title animations by Richard Williams and Ken Harris are highlights.

Return of the Secaucus Seven   1980   (RCA)   *Color*
Director: John Sayles
Starring: Bruce MacDonald, Maggie Renzi, Adam Lefevre, Maggie Cousineau, Gordon Clapp, Jean Passanante, Karen Trott, Mark Arnott, David Straithaim, John Sayles

For his first directing effort, novelist–short story writer–scenarist John Sayles created this comedy about graduates of the counterculture, a consideration of love and friend-ship that stands as a spiritual precursor to *The Big Chill*. Sayles' film is a mirror of the times, filled with authentic detail. In a weekend reunion in Vermont, a group of sixties college pals contemplate how their ideals and relationships have changed. Hosting the get-together are schoolteachers Michael and Katie (Bruce MacDonald and Maggie Renzi). Ten years earlier, they—along with five of their chums—were arrested in Secaucus, New Jersey, en route to an anti-Vietnam demonstration in Washington. Ever since, they have jokingly referred to themselves as "the Secaucus Seven." The cast includes Gordon Clapp (Chip), Jean Passanante (Irene), Mark Arnott (Jeff), Karen Trott (Maura), David Straitham (Ron), Maggie Cousineau (Frances), and Adam Lefevre (J.T.). Sayles himself, the screenwriter and editor as well as director, also takes the role of Howie. Shot on a shoestring for approximately $60,000.

Roman Holiday   1953   (Paramount)   ◆   *Black-and-White*
Director: William Wyler
Starring: Gregory Peck, Audrey Hepburn, Eddie Albert, Hartley Power, Laura Solari, Harcourt Williams, Margaret Rawlings, Tullio Carminati

Audrey Hepburn's Academy Award performance (and her American movie debut). She stars as a young princess (from a mythical country) on an official visit to Rome.

Weary of diplomatic red tape, Princess Anne escapes her royal trappings for a while and wanders incognito about the Eternal City. Joining her for the adventure are two American newspapermen (Gregory Peck and Eddie Albert). Her wish comes true when she is allowed to have ordinary, everyday experiences with the people she meets. The screenplay by Ian McLellan Hunter and John Dighton, realized by William Wyler, makes a perfect package of whimsicality.

Romancing the Stone   1984   (CBS)   *Color*
Director: Robert Zemeckis
Starring: Michael Douglas, Kathleen Turner, Danny De Vito, Zack Norman, Alfonso Arau, Manuel Ojeda, Holland Taylor, Mary Ellen Trainor, Eve Smith, Joe Nesnow, José Chavez

Romance novelist Joan Wilder (Kathleen Turner) is the heroine of this comic adventure. So far Joan's adventures have been confined to the pages of her historical bodice-rippers, set in exotic locales. But a real-life mystery involving her kidnapped sister sends Joan from her New York apartment into the treacherous jungles of Colombia. Once in South America she luckily tumbles into Jack Colton (Michael Douglas), a handsome fortune hunter with a knack for rescuing damsels in distress. Nonstop action in the vein of *Raiders of the Lost Ark* guides *Romancing the Stone*. The director is Robert Zemeckis (*Used Cars, Back to the Future*). Diane Thomas wrote the screenplay; cinematographer Dean Cundey shot the action on location—in Mexico. Sequel: *The Jewel of the Nile* (1985), reassembling Turner, Douglas, and De Vito for exploits in North Africa.

The Ruling Class   1972   (Embassy)   *Color*
Director: Peter Medak
Starring: Peter O'Toole, Alastair Sim, Arthur Lowe, Harry Andrews, Coral Browne, Michael Bryant, Carolyn Seymour, Nigel Green, William Mervyn, James Villiers

This farce, originally a London stage success, presents a young heir (Peter O'Toole) who, upon the death of his father, assumes the title of the fourteenth earl of Gurney. Jack, the young successor, now has a fortune, an estate, and a seat in the House of Lords. Unfortunately for all concerned, Jack—who has been cloistered in an asylum—also has the conviction that he is Jesus Christ. His family is aghast. And their efforts to cure him go sadly awry. The earl sinks deeper into madness and takes on a new guise: Jack the Ripper. Blood, laughter, and vaudeville songs commingle in this amalgam adapted by Peter Barnes from his playscript. Alastair Sim is cast as a stupefied bishop, Harry Andrews as the thirteenth earl of Gurney, and Arthur Lowe as his faithful manservant, benevolently rewarded in the will. Peter Medak, the director, numbers among his other credits *A Day in the Death of Joe Egg; Zorro, the Gay Blade;* and *The Men's Club.*

The Russians Are Coming! The Russians Are Coming!   1966   (CBS)
                                                                         Color
Director: Norman Jewison
Starring: Carl Reiner, Eva Marie Saint, Alan Arkin, Brian Keith, Jonathan Winters, Theodore Bikel, Paul Ford, Tessie O'Shea, John Phillip Law, Andrea Dromm, Ben Blue, Guy Raymond, Cliff Norton, Dick Schaal, Philip Coolidge, Parker Fennelly, Doro Merande, Michael J. Pollard

Based on Nathaniel Benchley's comic novel *The Off-Islanders*, this all-star feature pokes fun at the cold war. A Soviet submarine runs aground off Nantucket. When a landing party goes ashore, the summer vacationers assume America has been invaded. The Russians, meanwhile, are just as perplexed as the locals. Slapstick and wit alternate in William Rose's screenplay; he and director Norman Jewison construct some hilarious scenes. The players include Alan Arkin, in his film debut, as a cynical Russian sailor; Brian Keith, the town sheriff; Jonathan Winters, his bumpkin deputy; Carl Reiner and Eva Marie Saint as worried parents; and John Phillip Law and Andrea Dromm as the lovers.

Same Time, Next Year   1978   (MCA)   *Color*
Director: Robert Mulligan
Starring: Ellen Burstyn, Alan Alda

A translation of Bernard Slade's two-character Broadway comedy, *Same Time, Next Year* presents Ellen Burstyn in her stage role and Alan Alda in the part originated by Charles Grodin. Under observation in this romantic tale is an extramarital dalliance that lasts twenty-six years—but with a twist: the adulterous couple meet only once a year. It all begins innocently in 1951, when George, an accountant, and Doris, a young housewife, both of whom are in their mid-twenties, have a chance encounter at a seaside inn on the Northern California coast. After their one-night stand, they decide on an annual get-together. Slade, as playwright—here doubling as screenwriter—shows George and Doris over five-year intervals growing older and reflecting changes in American styles and attitudes. Marvin Hamlisch's theme song, "The Last Time I Felt Like This" (lyrics by Alan and Marilyn Bergman), is performed by Johnny Mathis and Jane Olivor.

Seems Like Old Times   1980   (RCA)   *Color*
Director: Jay Sandrich
Starring: Goldie Hawn, Chevy Chase, Charles Grodin, Robert Guillaume, George Grizzard, Harold Gould, Yvonne Wilder, T. K. Carter

Neil Simon's farce, written directly for the screen, places a lady lawyer (Goldie Hawn) in an intrigue with her ex-husband (Chevy Chase), a fugitive innocently involved with a bank robbery, *and* her current spouse (Charles Grodin), recently appointed district attorney. When they all meet under the same roof, there's laughter. Directed by Jay Sandrich (of "Mary Tyler Moore" fame), *Seems Like Old Times* is a salute to madcap movies of the thirties. David M. Walsh is the cinematographer and Marvin Hamlisch composed the score.

The Senator Was Indiscreet   1947   (Republic)   *Black-and-White*
Director: George S. Kaufman
Starring: William Powell, Ella Raines, Peter Lind Hayes, Arleen Whelan, Ray Collins, Allen Jenkins, Charles D. Brown, Hans Conried, Whit Bissell, Norma Varden, Milton Parsons

Comic playwright George S. Kaufman is the director of this political farce; it's his only directorial effort, but it's comparable to his work with Moss Hart: *Once in a Lifetime, You Can't Take It With You, The Man Who Came to Dinner, George Washington Slept Here*. *The Senator Was Indiscreet* capitalizes on the same kind of lunacy. Senator Melvin

Ashton (William Powell) is blazing the presidential campaign trail. He hires a press agent, then takes on the party bosses in his drive to gain the nomination. Kaufman and coscenarist Charles MacArthur (author, with Ben Hecht, of *The Front Page*) let fly with a volley of satiric barbs, and they create frenzy with one plot point: a scandal-ridden diary that spells embarrassment to all whose names are included; everybody scurries to gain possession of the incriminating document. In its heyday, this film was banned by over 300 Midwest cinemas because of the screenplay's "reflection on the integrity of every duly elected representative of the American people" which "could be used as vicious propaganda by subversive elements in this nation as well as our enemies abroad."

The Seven Year Itch   1955   (CBS)   *Color*
Director: Billy Wilder
Starring: Marilyn Monroe, Tom Ewell, Evelyn Keyes, Sonny Tufts, Robert Strauss, Oscar Homolka, Marguerite Chapman, Victor Moore, Donald McBride, Carolyn Jones, Butch Bernard, Doro Merande, Dorothy Ford

When his wife goes on a lengthy summer vacation, happily married Richard Sherman (Tom Ewell) suddenly succumbs to the seven year itch. A sexy blonde model (Marilyn Monroe) has moved into the apartment upstairs, and Richard fantasizes having an affair with her. The ensuing romance is staged only in Richard's mind—though viewers get to play eavesdropping voyeurs. A series of revue skits on the theme of summer bachelorhood, *The Seven Year Itch* is based on George Axelrod's Broadway comedy and adapted by Axelrod with director Billy Wilder. Set in New York City but mostly shot in Hollywood.

A Shot in the Dark   1964   (CBS)   *Color*
Director: Blake Edwards
Starring: Peter Sellers, Elke Sommer, George Sanders, Herbert Lom, Tracy Reed, Graham Stark, André Maranne, Douglas Wilmer, Vanda Godsell, Ann Lynn, David Lodge, Moira Redmond, Martin Benson

Inspired by the French stage farce by Marcel Achard and its American translation by Harry Kurnitz, *A Shot in the Dark* became, in revision, the second Inspector Clouseau screen comedy. (*The Pink Panther*, its predecessor, was released earlier in 1964.) Herein Clouseau (again Peter Sellers) investigates a murder. Evidence points to luscious Maria Gambrelli (Elke Sommer), a housemaid, as the guilty party, but the inspector is convinced of her innocence. Pratfalls, comedy of physical pain, and a foray through a nudist colony accrue before the actual murderer is pinpointed. *A Shot in the Dark*, as screenwritten by William Peter Blatty and director Blake Edwards, presents several characters who figure in later *Pink Panther* films: Hercule Lajoy (Graham Stark), François (André Maranne), Kato (Burt Kwouk), and Chief Inspector Charles Dreyfus (Herbert Lom), the twitchy police commissioner bedeviled by Clouseau. The character of Charlie, credited to actor Turk Thrust, is really played by director Bryan Forbes.

Silent Movie   1976   (CBS)   *Color*
Director: Mel Books
Starring: Mel Brooks, Marty Feldman, Dom De Luise, Bernadette Peters, Sid Caesar, Harold Gould, Ron Carey, Anne Bancroft, James Caan, Marcel Marceau, Liza Minnelli, Paul Newman, Burt Reynolds, Harry Ritz, Henny Youngman

Mel Funn (Mel Brooks) is a has-been Hollywood director. He regaled as a comic genius in the days of the silents, but talkies and alcohol spelled the end to his career. Now hoping for a comeback, Funn is hired by a studio chief (Sid Caesar) to shoot another silent movie. So the director and his minions begin preproduction work while petitioning superstars (like Anne Bancroft, Liza Minnelli, Paul Newman, Burt Reynolds, and others) to sign on for the project. Meanwhile, a conglomerate, Engulf & Devour, plots to annex the nearly bankrupt studio by sabotaging Mel Funn's production. Sheer lunacy from Brooks and his cowriters: Ron Clark, Rudy De Luca, Barry Levinson. Sharing in the fun on screen are Bernadette Peters as a sexy movie goddess, Marty Feldman, Dom De Luise, and many guest stars playing themselves.

Silver Streak   1976   (CBS)   *Color*
Director: Arthur Hiller
Starring: Gene Wilder, Jill Clayburgh, Richard Pryor, Patrick McGoohan, Ned Beatty, Ray Walston, Scatman Crothers, Clifton James, Richard Kiel, Valerie Curtin, Lucille Benson, Stefan Gierasch

As a luxury train hurtles cross country from Los Angeles to Chicago, one of the passengers reveals himself as a homicidal mastermind. Along for the ride (and centrally embroiled in the intrigue) are a publisher of how-to books (Gene Wilder), a crafty businessman (Patrick McGoohan), a thief (Richard Pryor), and the secretary of an art historian (Jill Clayburgh). It's the art historian's murder that sets the plot in motion. A comedy with pronounced thriller motifs, *Silver Streak* owes its inspiration to Hitchcock's lighthearted mystery escapades. Director Arthur Hiller (*The Out-of-Towners, Love Story, Plaza Suite, The Hospital*) works from a screenplay by Colin Higgins. (Higgins mined the comic mystery vein himself when he directed his own script for *Foul Play*.) Some violence and sexual badinage mar the fun briefly, but *Silver Streak* is pleasurable for most of the trip.

Slap Shot   1977   (MCA)   *Color*
Director: George Roy Hill
Starring: Paul Newman, Strother Martin, Michael Ontkean, Jennifer Warren, Lindsay Crouse, Jerry Houser, Andrew Duncan, Jeff Carlson, Steve Carlson, David Hanson, Yvon Barrette, Allan Nicholls, Brad Sullivan, Stephen Mendillo, Yvon Ponton, Matthew Cowles, Kathryn Walker, M. Emmet Walsh, Swoosie Kurtz, Paul D'Amato, Melinda Dillon, Ned Dowd, Paul Dooley

This brutal and raffish comedy focuses on the Charlestown Chiefs, a bush league ice hockey team. The Chiefs have endured a string of losses, and there is every chance they will fold. To prevent that, Reggie Dunlop (Paul Newman), the team's coach–star player, convinces the others that they must play dirty; with a few wins, a rich buyer will be found. Even the Chiefs' most scrupulous player, college-educated Ned Braden (Michael Ontkean), joins in the bone-crushing tactics. The results? A fast, funny, foul-mouthed movie directed by George Roy Hill from Nancy Dowd's script. Other attractions: the editing of Dede Allen and Elmer Bernstein's music.

Sleeper   1973   (CBS)   *Color*
Director: Woody Allen
Starring: Woody Allen, Diane Keaton, John Beck, Don Keefer, Mary Gregory, John Mc-Liam

America in the twenty-second century as observed by Woody Allen. Woody plays a Greenwich Village health food store proprietor who, in 1973, becomes a cryogenic guinea pig. He is deep-frozen as part of a minor operation, then wakes up in 2173. The brave new world of the future is a totalitarian state, where torture involves watching Howard Cosell telecasts and sex occurs in a step-in machine called the Orgasmitron. The hero decides he must escape. Collaborating with Allen on the script is Marshall Brickman, who went on to direct his own films: *Simon, Lovesick,* and *The Manhattan Project.* Cinematography by David M. Walsh; costume designs by Joel Schumacher; music by the director and the Preservation Hall Jazz Band.

Smokey and the Bandit   1977   (MCA)   *Color*
Director: Hal Needham
Starring: Burt Reynolds, Jackie Gleason, Sally Field, Jerry Reed, Mike Henry, Paul Williams, Pat McCormick

This first of the *Smokey* trilogy is a mile-a-minute chase comedy. The Bandit (Burt Reynolds) is a legendary Georgia bootlegger who bets that he can haul an illegal shipment of beer from Atlanta to Texarkana (and return to Atlanta) in twenty-eight hours. En route he picks up a runaway bride-to-be (Sally Field) who is being pursued by her irate fiancé (Mike Henry) and the fiancé's officious father—Sheriff Buford T. Justice (Jackie Gleason). The stars provide the charm; high-speed chases provide the humor. The screenwriters are James Lee Barrett, Charles Shyer, and Alan Mandel. *Smokey and the Bandit* is the directorial debut of stuntman Hal Needham. The sequels, with many of the original players, arrived in 1980 and 1983.

Some Like It Hot   1959   (CBS)   ◆   *Black-and-White*
Director: Billy Wilder
Starring: Marilyn Monroe, Tony Curtis, Jack Lemmon, George Raft, Pat O'Brien, Joe E. Brown, Nehemiah Persoff, Joan Shawlee, Billy Gray, George E. Stone, Dave Barry, Mike Mazurki, Harry Wilson, Beverly Wills, Barbara Drew, Edward G. Robinson, Jr., Tom Kennedy

Saxophonist Joe (Tony Curtis) and bass player Jerry (Jack Lemmon) are jazz musicians on the lam after witnessing the 1929 St. Valentine's Day Massacre. To flee Chicago, they disguise themselves as women—Joe becomes Josephine, Jerry calls himself Daphne— and they join an all-girl band, Sweet Sue and Her Society Syncopaters, headed for Miami. They both fall for the ensemble's ukulele-playing lead singer, Sugar Kane (Marilyn Monroe). This comedy, directed by Billy Wilder from his script with I. A. L. Diamond, contains strong performances—including the one by Joe E. Brown as Osgood Fielding III, a millionaire playboy smitten by Daphne. Brown gets to speak the film's memorable curtain line. Songs: "Running Wild," "I'm Through with Love," and "I Wanna Be Loved by You." A best costume design Oscar went to Orry-Kelly.

Splash   1984   (Touchstone Home Video)   *Color*
Director: Ron Howard
Starring: Tom Hanks, Daryl Hannah, Eugene Levy, John Candy, Dody Goodman, Shecky Greene, Richard B. Shull, Bobby Di Cicco, Howard Morris, Tony Di Benedetto, Patrick Cronin, Charles Walker

In this fantasy-comedy, Manhattan produce merchant Allen Bauer (Tom Hanks) is a disillusioned bachelor. Then, capitalizing on a childhood experience twenty years earlier on Cape Cod, he tumbles for the girl of his dreams—a mermaid (Daryl Hannah), who is promptly dubbed Madison, after the avenue. Theirs is a very special romance, endangered by a worrywart marine biologist (Eugene Levy) and government goons. Evolving from a screenplay by Lowell Ganz, Babaloo Mandel, and Bruce Jay Friedman, *Splash* owes much of its success to Ron Howard, here is directing his third theatrical film (*Night Shift* was the notable predecessor). Howard's guidance of the actors turns what could have been merely a rambunctious farce into a romantic comedy. The theme song, "Love Came for Me," was written by Will Jennings and Lee Holdridge.

Starting Over   1979   (Paramount)   *Color*
Director: Alan J. Pakula
Starring: Burt Reynolds, Jill Clayburgh, Candice Bergen, Charles Durning, Frances
Sternhagen, Austin Pendleton, Mary Kay Place, MacIntire Dixon, Jay Sanders, Charles
Kimbrough, Richard Whiting, Alfie Wise, Wallace Shawn, Daniel Stern, Helen Stenborg,
Anne De Salvo, Kevin Bacon

This romantic comedy stars Burt Reynolds as Phil Potter, a writer and college teacher hoping that love will be lovelier the second time around. Recently divorced, he can't forget the virtues of his former wife (Candice Bergen), a singer-songwriter. As the hero learns, starting over can be brutal. The James L. Brooks adaptation of Dan Wakefield's novel, as directed by Alan Pakula, is a dissection of contemporary conflicts in love and career—but, in observing the protagonist's struggles, there are many laughs. *Starting Over* also features Jill Clayburgh as a likable schoolteacher who may be the divorced writer's hope for the future. Music by Marvin Hamlisch. Sven Nykvist, Ingmar Bergman's cinematographer, is the director of photography.

State of the Union   1948   (MCA)   *Black-and-White*
Director: Frank Capra
Starring: Spencer Tracy, Katharine Hepburn, Van Johnson, Angela Lansbury, Adolphe
Menjou, Lewis Stone, Howard Smith, Maidel Turner, Raymond Walburn, Pierre Watkin,
Margaret Hamilton, Irving Bacon, Carl Switzer, Charles Lane, Art Baker, Arthur
O'Connell, Tor Johnson, Dave Willock

Howard Lindsay and Russel Crouse's stage hit became a movie match for Spencer Tracy, Katharine Hepburn, and director Frank Capra. The political comedy, screen-written by Anthony Veiller and Myles Connolly, begins with millionairess Kay Thorndyke (Angela Lansbury), a power-mad publisher who wants to be a president-maker. She convinces entrepreneur Grant Matthews (Tracy) to plunge into the presidential race; Grant's estranged wife, Mary (Hepburn), joins him for the campaign. The couple's idealism places them at war with the conniving politicos surrounding them.

The Sting   1973   (MCA)   ◆   *Color*
Director: George Roy Hill
Starring: Paul Newman, Robert Redford, Robert Shaw, Charles Durning, Ray Walston,
Eileen Brennan, Harold Gould, Dana Elcar, Jack Kehoe, Dimitra Arliss, Charles Dier-
kop, John Heffernan, Robert Earl Jones, Avon Long, Sally Kirkland

It's Chicago, 1936, and Doyle Lonnegan (Robert Shaw) is a ruthless mob king. More often than not his touch is lethal. In retaliation for the murder of a friend, two small-time bunco artists—Henry Gondorff (Paul Newman) and Johnny Hooker (Robert Redford)—scheme to put "the sting" on Lonnegan. Their elaborate swindle, they hope, will bankrupt the mobster and put him behind bars. In this Academy Award–winning caper comedy, confidence tricksters are the good guys, racketeers the bad guys. Written by David S. Ward and directed by George Roy Hill, *The Sting* basks in its evocation of the thirties, aided enormously by the cinema conventions of the period (irises, wipes, and intertitles) and by the use of Scott Joplin's piano rags, revised by Marvin Hamlisch. Oscars: best picture, director, screenplay, editing, costume design, score adaptation, and art direction/set decoration. Sequel: *The Sting II* (1983), with Jackie Gleason, Mac Davis, and Oliver Reed in the Newman, Redford, and Shaw roles.

Stir Crazy   1980   (RCA)   *Color*
Director: Sidney Poitier
Starring: Gene Wilder, Richard Pryor, Georg Stanford Brown, JoBeth Williams, Craig T. Nelson, Barry Corbin, Erland von Lidth de Jeude, Lee Purcell

In this farce, tailored to the talents of its two stars, Gene Wilder and Richard Pryor depict down-and-out New Yorkers who decide to try their luck in a warmer climate. Heading for California, they find themselves in the wrong place at the wrong time— as unwitting accomplices in a bank robbery. Framed, they are convicted and locked away in the Big House (for 125 years!). Lunacy prevails as the two pals go stir crazy. At last they fabricate an escape plan. A popular success for Wilder and Pryor—reunited after *Silver Streak*—*Stir Crazy* was written by Bruce Jay Friedman, scored by Tom Scott, and directed by Sidney Poitier. In 1982 Poitier directed Wilder again in *Hanky Panky*. As a television series, "Stir Crazy" had a brief life in 1985.

Stripes   1981   (RCA)   *Color*
Director: Ivan Reitman
Starring: Bill Murray, Harold Ramis, Warren Oates, P. J. Soles, Sean Young, John Candy, John Larroquette, Joe Flaherty, Dave Thomas

A service comedy that is a raunchy version of Abbott and Costello or Dean Martin-Jerry Lewis vehicles, *Stripes* pits Sergeant Hulka (Warren Oates), a calloused drill instructor, against a platoon of reluctant recruits. Enacting the heroes/comedy team this time are Bill Murray and Harold Ramis, the ringleaders for all the boot camp hijinks. The impudent protagonists effortlessly create turmoil in Today's Army. Canadian Ivan Reitman (*Meatballs, Ghostbusters, Legal Eagles*) directs from a script by co-star Ramis, Len Blum, and Dan Goldberg. Look for three Second City alumni: John Candy, Joe Flaherty, and Dave Thomas.

The Sunshine Boys   1975   (MGM)   ◆   *Color*
Director: Herbert Ross
Starring: Walter Matthau, George Burns, Richard Benjamin, Lee Meredith, Carol Arthur, Howard Hesseman, Ron Rifkin

The Sunshine Boys was the first collaboration between director Herbert Ross and Neil Simon, who adapted his own Broadway stage hit. (Ross later helmed Simon's *The Goodbye Girl, California Suite, I Ought To Be in Pictures,* and *Max Dugan Returns.*) The premise: Al Lewis (George Burns) and Willie Clark (Walter Matthau) were a vaudeville comedy team. After forty-three years in show business, they ended the partnership. As *The Sunshine Boys* opens, both men are in their seventies, their careers are inactive, and they haven't spoken to one another in eleven years. Ben Silverman (Richard Benjamin), Willie's nephew, persuades the cranky, semisenile pair to reunite for a television special. One for the record books: Burns, who had not made a movie since 1939, won an Oscar for his screen comeback.

Support Your Local Sheriff   1969   (CBS)   *Color*
Director: Burt Kennedy
Starring: James Garner, Joan Hackett, Walter Brennan, Harry Morgan, Jack Elam, Bruce Dern, Henry Jones, Gene Evans, Dick Peabody

This Western parody stars James Garner in a role not unlike his TV persona, Bret Maverick. An easygoing adventurer (Garner) wanders into a frontier town plagued by gold rush fever and takes on the job of sheriff. In time he proves himself a conscientious lawman—one who uses brains rather than fists or firepower. His methods seem unorthodox to the townsfolk, but finally he gains their support. The film, written by William Bowers and directed by Burt Kennedy, slyly punctures most movie Western clichés while providing comic bits for the character actors supporting the star. Another spoof, the 1971 *Support Your Local Gunfighter*, reunited Garner with director Kennedy and some of the featured players in *Sheriff*; but it isn't really a sequel.

The Sure Thing   1985   (Embassy)   *Color*
Director: Rob Reiner
Starring: John Cusack, Daphne Zuniga, Anthony Edwards, Boyd Gaines, Lisa Jane Persky, Tim Robbins, Viveca Lindfors, Nicollette Sheridan, Marcia Christie, Robert Anthony Marcucci, Sarah Buxton, Lorrie Lightle, John Putsch, Frantz Turner, Garry Goodrow

Walter Gibson (John Cusack) and Alison Bradbury (Daphne Zuniga) are two freshmen at an East Coast Ivy League college. Their relationship is not exactly promising as Alison is largely unimpressed with Gib's snappy patter. Gib's friend Lance (Anthony Edwards) invites him to Los Angeles for Christmas break. Lance promises to find a dream date—a sure thing—for his pal. On the cross-country journey Gib and Alison are unwillingly thrust together, as share-a-ride backseat passengers. (She's going to spend the holidays with her fiancé Jason (Boyd Gaines), a U.C.L.A. law student.) It's a sparring match all the way. From actor-turned-director Rob Reiner (*This Is Spinal Tap*), the film is scripted by Steven L. Bloom and Jonathan Roberts, photographed by Robert Elswit, and contains a music score by Tom Scott.

Susan Slept Here   1954   (United)   *Color*
Director: Frank Tashlin
Starring: Dick Powell, Debbie Reynolds, Anne Francis, Glenda Farrell, Alvy Moore, Horace McMahon

A Hollywood screenwriter (Dick Powell) who is researching juvenile delinquency gets firsthand experience when he accepts temporary custody of a teenage vagrant (Debbie Reynolds). The young woman, high-spirited but vulnerable, coaches the writer in the behavior of wayward youth—and she scandalizes his friends and colleagues. As their escapades continue, the two fall in love. This lighthearted romantic comedy is based on a play by Alex Gottlieb and Steve Fisher; Gottlieb did the screen adaptation. *Susan*

Slept Here was Powell's last movie role. After 1954, he focused on his directing career and on his multifarious television projects.

Take the Money and Run   1969   (CBS)   *Color*

Director: Woody Allen
Starring: Woody Allen, Janet Margolin, Marcel Hillaire, Jacquelyn Hyde, Lonny Chapman, Mark Gordon, Charlotte Rae, Louise Lasser

This is Woody Allen's directorial debut. Sparked by a screenplay by Allen and Mickey Rose, *Take the Money and Run* is a biography of would-be public enemy Virgil Starkwell—done in the mock documentary style of a TV news special. Virgil is a small-time hood, determined but all thumbs; his abiding frustration is that he never makes the ten-most-wanted list. He's a bumbling schlemiel with, moreover, poor penmanship. (After handing a bank teller a stickup note, he argues over whether he is holding a *gun* or a *gub*.) Spontaneity and improvisation are bywords here. Because the film is so packed with sight gags, one-liners, non sequiturs, and throwaway dialogue, viewers may complain some of the jokes misfire; even so, comic momentum arises from the rapid-fire delivery, so the next laugh is always just around the corner. Jackson Beck is the narrator of the pseudodocumentary on Virgil's rise and fall, and Marvin Hamlisch composed the score.

The Taming of the Shrew   1967   (RCA)   *Color*

Director: Franco Zeffirelli
Starring: Elizabeth Taylor, Richard Burton, Cyril Cusack, Michael Horden, Alfred Lynch, Alan Webb, Victor Spinetti, Michael York, Natasha Pyne

Before embarking on *Romeo and Juliet*, Franco Zeffirelli tested the waters with this big-budget edition of *The Taming of the Shrew*—filmed when Elizabeth Taylor and Richard Burton, direct from *Who's Afraid of Virginia Woolf?*, were at the height of their popularity. The Bard's battling Renaissance lovers are here embodied by twentieth-century counterparts. Kate (Taylor) is the independent elder daughter of a wealthy Padua merchant; Petruchio (Burton) is the robust rogue from Verona who wagers that he can tame her. In the screenplay by Paul Dehn, Suso Cecchi D'Amico, and Zeffirelli— "with acknowledgments to William Shakespeare without whom they would have been at a loss for words"—the emphasis is upon ribald comedy. Another acting team, Mary Pickford and Douglas Fairbanks, appeared in a 1929 condensation of the play.

10   1979   (Warner)   *Color*

Director: Blake Edwards
Starring: Dudley Moore, Julie Andrews, Bo Derek, Robert Webber, Dee Wallace, Sam Jones, Brian Dennehy, Max Showalter, Don Calfa, Nedra Volz, James Noble

George (Dudley Moore) is a middle-aged composer who rates women on a scale from one to ten. His male menopausal crisis is exacerbated by the plethora of gorgeous, but seemingly untouchable, women living in Southern California—and the fact that his homosexual lyricist-partner (Robert Webber) has a stable relationship. Then George spots the perfect ten—Jenny (Bo Derek)—unfortunately, on her wedding day. But completely smitten with her, he follows the newlyweds to their honeymoon hotel in Mexico. In a turnaround that surprises even him, George has his one-night-stand fantasy with Jenny. This situation comedy is written and directed by Blake Edwards and co-stars Mrs. Edwards—Julie Andrews as Sam(antha), the mature woman in George's love life.

Ten from Your Show of Shows   1973   *Black-and-White*
  (Media; Sheik Video)
Director: Max Liebman
Starring: Sid Caesar, Imogene Coca, Carl Reiner, Howard Morris, Louis Nye, Jack Russell, Ray Drakley, Dorothy Patten, Sven Svensen, Eleanor Williams

"Your Show of Shows," the legendary Saturday night comedy-variety series, was telecast by NBC from 1950 to 1954. Performed live, the ninety-minute weekly program was produced by Max Liebman, who engaged all the writers—including Mel Brooks, Neil Simon, Woody Allen, Larry Gelbart, Lucille Kallen, and Mel Tolkin. This compilation film—starring Sid Caesar, Imogene Coca, Carl Reiner and Howard Morris—assembles ten sketches taken from the kinescopes of those broadcasts. The skits: a housewife finds herself "Breaking the News" to her mate about an auto accident; two lovers have a spat "At the Movies" and an innocent bystander gets caught in the crossfire; a high-society concert is interrupted by the noisy husband of the hostess; a lunch hour in the corporate conference room obstructs "Big Business"; a roving reporter (Reiner) interviews Viennese aeronautical authority Professor Ludwig von Spacebrain (Caesar); mechanical figures strike the hour in a Bavarian village's prize clock; a Teutonic general and his valet (speaking Anglo-Germanic gobbledygook) prepare for the day; and there are three parodies—"From Here to Obscurity"; a silent screen spoof called "The Sewing Machine Girl"; and "This Is Your Story," in which a highly reluctant honoree has his "intimate inside story" telecast live nationwide.

Terms of Endearment   1983   (Paramount)   ◆   *Color*
Director: James L. Brooks
Starring: Shirley MacLaine, Debra Winger, Jack Nicholson, Jeff Daniels, John Lithgow, Lisa Hart Carroll, Danny De Vito

Inspired by Larry McMurtry's novel, this comedy-drama centers on a turbulent mother-daughter relationship as it evolves over a thirty-year period. Shirley MacLaine and Debra Winger star as Aurora Greenway and her free-spirited offspring, Emma. *Terms of Endearment* was proclaimed best film by several year-end award donors, including the Motion Picture Academy. Additional Oscar glory accrued to MacLaine (her first win), Jack Nicholson (his second), and debuting director James L. Brooks. Indeed, Brooks—the mastermind behind TV's "Taxi" and "Mary Tyler Moore"—was twice blessed, taking direction *and* adapted screenplay honors. Unsung hero: Jeff Daniels as Emma's unfaithful husband.

That Touch of Mink   1962   (Republic)   *Color*
Director: Delbert Mann
Starring: Cary Grant, Doris Day, Gig Young, Audrey Meadows, Alan Hewitt, John Astin, Richard Sargent, Joey Faye, Laurie Mitchell, John Fiedler, Willard Sage, Jack Livesey

In the late fifties and early sixties, Doris Day's teamings with Rock Hudson and, as here, Cary Grant were labeled sex comedies. A more appropriate description might be the avoidance-of-sex comedies. Cary is cast as urbane playboy-tycoon Philip Shayne; Doris plays Cathy Timberlake, a prim shopgirl holding out for a wedding ring—even during her whirlwind trip with Philip to Bermuda. The stars are light comedians and the script by Stanley Shapiro and Nate Monaster serves them well. Supporting actors are Gig Young as an alcoholic advertising genius; Alan Hewitt as his bewildered psychiatrist; and Audrey Meadows as the heroine's best friend, an Automat waitress. Guest stars Roger Maris, Mickey Mantle, and Yogi Berra appear as themselves.

Those Lips, Those Eyes   1980   (MGM)   *Color*
Director: Michael Pressman
Starring: Frank Langella, Glynnis O'Connor, Thomas Hulce, Kevin McCarthy, Jerry Stiller, Herbert Berghof, Joseph Maher

A Cleveland summer stock troupe in the 1950s gets affectionate treatment in this coming-of-age comedy. Assembled for a season of operetta are a once-promising matinee idol (Frank Langella), the company's resident ingénue (Glynnis O'Connor), and a stagestruck pre-med student (Thomas Hulce) interning as a prop boy. Their interrelationship provides the humor—and the poignancy. David Shaber's script is a tribute to summer theatricals. *Those Lips, Those Eyes* represents an intermission in Pressman's heavy action/raucous comedy career; his other directing credits include *Dynamite Women* (also known as *The Great Texas Dynamite Chase*), *The Bad News Bears in Breaking Training, Boulevard Nights, Some Kind of Hero, Doctor Detroit*, and, for TV, "The Impostor" and "Final Jeopardy."

Those Magnificent Men in Their Flying Machines   1965   (CBS)   *Color*
Director: Ken Annakin
Starring: Stuart Whitman, Sarah Miles, James Fox, Alberto Sordi, Robert Morley, Gert Frobe, Jean-Pierre Cassel, Eric Sykes, Terry-Thomas, Irina Demick, Benny Hill, Yujiro Ishihara, Flora Robson, Karl Michael Vögler, Sam Wanamaker, Gordon Jackson, John Le Mesurier, Jeremy Lloyd, Zena Marshall, Millicent Martin, Eric Pohlmann, Marjorie Rhodes, Michael Trubshawe, Tony Hancock, Red Skelton

Subtitled *How I Flew from London to Paris in 25 Hours and 11 Minutes*, this episodic slapstick exhibit ranks in many viewers' minds with *The Great Race, It's a Mad . . . World, The Russians Are Coming*, and other king-sized comedies of the sixties. Transcribed from a screenplay by Jack Davies and Ken Annakin (he also directed), *Those Magnificent Men* documents a 1910 London-to-Paris air race. Among those piloting the crates of early aviation are Orvil Newton (Stuart Whitman), an American cowboy; Richard Mays (James Fox), a stiff-upper-lip British chap; Count Emilio Ponticelli (Alberto Sordi), a wiry Italian; and Pierre Dubois (Jean-Pierre Cassel), a Frenchman more serious about amour than aviation. Red Skelton appears in the prologue as a Neanderthal man who craves to fly like the birds do. Music by Ron Goodwin; cinematography by Christopher Challis; special effects by Richard Parker.

A Thousand Clowns   1965   (CBS)   *Black-and-White*
Director: Fred Coe
Starring: Jason Robards, Barbara Harris, Martin Balsam, Barry Gordon, Gene Saks, William Daniels

Herb Gardner's nonconformist comedy was a Broadway hit in 1962 and has been a staple of summer stock and amateur and regional theater ever since. In its film adaptation, by Gardner himself, both the small scale and the laughs are retained. So is the star—Jason Robards, reprising his role of Murray Burns, the frustrated writer of a TV kiddie show. After years of inventing dialogue for Chuckles the Chipmunk (Gene Saks), Murray gets fed up and resigns. He holes up in his Manhattan apartment, determined no longer to work like "a thousand clowns"—or let his live-in teenage nephew (Barry Gordon) get trapped in a similar rat race. Murray's idyll is short-lived though: his ultra-conventional brother (Martin Balsam) and two social workers (Barbara Harris and William Daniels) entreat him "to return to reality." "I'll only go as a tourist," he replies. Fred Coe directs.

The Three Musketeers   *Listed under Dramas.*

Tom Jones   1963   (CBS)   ◆   *Color*
Director: Tony Richardson
Starring: Albert Finney, Susannah York, Hugh Griffith, Edith Evans, Joyce Redman, Diane Cilento, Joan Greenwood, David Tomlinson, Peter Bull, George Devine, David Warner, Wilfrid Lawson, Freda Jackson, Rachel Kempson, Rosalind Knight, John Moffat

A parodistic adaptation of Henry Fielding's 1749 novel, *Tom Jones* captured four Academy Awards. As best picture of 1963, it also brought Oscars to scenarist John Osborne, director Tony Richardson, and composer John Addison. Fielding's hero is a foundling who grows into a roguish seducer. He participates in the escapades of robust country squires and feels equally at home in lecherous London society. Richardson's free-form interpretation whirls along with sword fights, fisticuffs, and sexual encounters. It's a marriage of ribaldry and satire—made so, in part, by the camera work by Walter Lassally (*A Taste of Honey, Zorba the Greek*). Albert Finney enacts the picaresque protagonist; and there are memorable performances by Susannah York (as Sophia Western), Hugh Griffith (Squire Western), Edith Evans (the elder Miss Western), George Devine (Squire Allworthy), Joyce Redman (Mrs. Waters), Diane Cilento (Molly), David Warner (Blifil), David Tomlinson (Lord Fellamar), and Joan Greenwood (Lady Bellaston).

Tootsie   1982   (RCA)   ◆   *Color*
Director: Sydney Pollack
Starring: Dustin Hoffman, Jessica Lange, Teri Garr, Dabney Coleman, Charles Durning, Bill Murray, George Gaynes, Geena Davis, Doris Belack, Ellen Foley, Peter Gatto, Lynne Thigpen, Ronald L. Schwary, Debra Mooney, Estelle Getty, Christine Ebersole, Sydney Pollack

One of the most successful comedies in cinema history, *Tootsie* has amassed more than $96 million in U.S. and Canadian rentals. Michael Dorsey (Dustin Hoffman) is a New York actor down on his luck and with a reputation for being temperamental. In fact, as his agent insists, he's unemployable. The only role up for grabs is that of a female hospital administrator on a daytime soap opera, so on a dare Michael adopts the name Dorothy Michaels, disguises himself accordingly, and auditions for—and captures—the part. Only his roommate (Bill Murray) and his agent (director Sydney Pollack in a rare acting stint) know Dorothy's true identity. Murray Schisgal and Larry Gelbart are credited with the screenplay, an evolution of Gelbart and Don McGuire's original treatment; Elaine May, among other writers, also contributed ideas. The featured players include Teri Garr as a struggling actress, Dabney Coleman as a sexist TV director, Charles Durning as Dorothy's suitor, George Gaynes as the Teleprompter-transfixed soap actor, and—in her Oscar-winning role—Jessica Lange. The theme song, "It Might Be You," was written by Dave Grusin, with lyrics by Alan and Marilyn Bergman, and is performed by Stephen Bishop.

Topkapi   *Listed under Suspense and Mystery.*

A Touch of Class   1973   (CBS)   ◆   *Color*
Director: Melvin Frank
Starring: George Segal, Glenda Jackson, Paul Sorvino, Hildegarde Neil, Cec Linder,
K Callan, Mary Barclay

This sex farce about the exasperations of an extramarital love match provided Glenda Jackson with her second Oscar. (*Women in Love* accounted for her earlier Academy recognition.) Melvin Frank and Jack Rose's screenplay, as directed by the former, invents a married American businessman named Steve Blackburn (George Segal) and Vicki Allessio (Miss Jackson), an English divorcée who works as a dress designer. They meet in London, then take off on a business holiday to Marbella—away from the prying eyes of family and friends. Owing to circumstances, Marbella is far from a pleasure trip; the couple's first night together, intended as an amatory paradise, may be, in fact, one of the funniest disasters ever recorded on film. The music score is by John Cameron and two songs—the title number and "All That Love Went to Waste"—are contributed by George Barrie (music) and Sammy Cahn (lyrics).

Trading Places   1983   (Paramount)   *Color*
Director: John Landis
Starring: Dan Aykroyd, Eddie Murphy, Ralph Bellamy, Don Ameche, Denholm Elliott,
Jamie Lee Curtis, Paul Gleason, Kristin Holby, Jim Belushi

Is success more a matter of heredity or common sense? That's the question posed by investment broker brothers Randolph (Ralph Bellamy) and Mortimer Duke (Don Ameche). Randolph speculates that a person's environment determines behavior; Mortimer disagrees, insisting that behavior is inherited. To test their theories, the Duke brothers concoct a switch with two human guinea pigs: rich Philadelphia executive Louis Winthrope III (Dan Aykroyd) and ghetto hustler Billy Ray Valentine (Eddie Murphy). The world of high finance is shaken to its foundations when the two innocents are forced to trade place. A slapstick comedy, *Trading Places* was directed by John Landis from a screenplay by Timothy Harris and Herschel Weingrod. (The original scenario was entitled *Black and White*—and envisioned as another Richard Pryor-Gene Wilder vehicle.)

The Trouble with Harry   *Listed under Suspense and Mystery.*

The Twelve Chairs   1970   (Media)   *Color*
Director: Mel Brooks
Starring: Ron Moody, Frank Langella, Dom De Luise, Mel Brooks, Bridget Brice, Robert
Bernal, Diana Coupland

The Twelve Chairs, the Elie Ilf-Eugene Petrov novel, has inspired numerous comedy films—*Keep Your Seats, Please* (1936), *It's in the Bag* (1945), and *12 + 1* (1970), to name only three. To many the 1970 Mel Brooks version is the most madcap interpretation. The setting is post-revolutionary Russia. Three men are in pursuit of, and vying against one another to find, jewels which have been stuffed into one of twelve identical chairs. The fortune-chasers are a handsome swordsman (Frank Langella), a servant (Dom De Luise), and a bureaucrat (Ron Moody) who once belonged to nobility and whose mother-in-law hid the jewels. Brooks not only directed; he wrote the screenplay and appears in a featured role. His regular composer, John Morris, wrote the score.

Two-Way Stretch   1960   (Thorn)   *Black-and-White*
Director: Robert Day
Starring: Peter Sellers, Wilfrid Hyde-White, Lionel Jeffries, Liz Fraser, Maurice Denham,
Bernard Cribbins, Beryl Reid, David Lodge, Irene Handl, George Woodbridge

An antic British comedy, *Two-Way Stretch* pokes fun at the penal system. Three Cockney prisoners in a progressive jail devise the means whereby they can escape, steal a
diamond from a visiting maharajah, then return to the safety of their cells. It's a two-
way stretch, but if all goes according to plan, they'll never be suspected. Robert Day
directed the script by John Warren and Len Heath. Peter Sellers heads the merry cast.

Uptown Saturday Night   1974   (Warner)   *Color*
Director: Sidney Poitier
Starring: Sidney Poitier, Bill Cosby, Harry Belafonte, Calvin Lockhart, Flip Wilson,
Richard Pryor, Rosalind Cash, Roscoe Lee Browne, Paula Kelly

This raucous comedy is Sidney Poitier's third stint as a director (*Buck and the Preacher*,
in 1972, and *A Warm December*, in 1973, were the previous two). The complications
begin when two working stiffs (Poitier and Bill Cosby) are held up in an after-hours
gambling club. It turns out that a winning lottery ticket has been stolen along with the
heroes' hard-earned wages. So the two friends go *Uptown Saturday Night* to retrieve
the ticket. Richard Wesley's script dramatizes that fateful decision. The all-star cast
includes comedians Flip Wilson and Richard Pryor, along with Harry Belafonte, who—
as a black godfather—does a memorable Marlon Brando impersonation. Poitier, as
actor-director, reteamed with Cosby for further pranks in the appropriately titled *Let's
Do It Again* (1975) and *A Piece of the Action* (1977).

Welcome to L.A.   1976   (CBS)   *Color*
Director: Alan Rudolph
Starring: Keith Carradine, Sally Kellerman, Geraldine Chaplin, Harvey Keitel, Lauren
Hutton, Sissy Spacek, John Considine, Viveca Lindfors, Richard Baskin, Denver Pyle

Alan Rudolph, the writer and director of *Welcome to L.A.*, is a Robert Altman protégé.
Los Angeles is penetrated here much in the way Altman characterized the title city in
Nashville. The picture, which Rudolph conceived with composer Richard Baskin, takes
an episodic view of L.A.'s dizzy denizens and free-floating visitors—particularly those
related to the music and movie business. A frank, mature comedy that, time and again,
avoids an obvious laugh for the sake of realistic observation, *Welcome to L.A.* centers
on recent arrival Carroll Barber (Keith Carradine). Barber is a lyricist who hopes to
interest pop star Eric Wood in his latest composition, "City of the One-Night Stands."
(In a reverse-the-roles situation, Eric is played by Baskin himself, who wrote all the
music and songs.) Subsequent Alan Rudolph films—most in the same vein as this
feature: *Remember My Name* (1978), *Roadie* (1980), *Endangered Species* (1982), *Choose
Me* (1984), *Songwriter* (1984), and *Trouble in Mind* (1985).

We're No Angels   1955   (Paramount)   *Color*
Director: Michael Curtiz
*Starring: Humphrey Bogart, Aldo Ray, Peter Ustinov, Joan Bennett, Basil Rathbone, Leo
G. Carroll, Gloria Talbott, John Baer, John Smith*

Derived from the Broadway success by Sam and Bella Spewack (out of an earlier French farce—*La Cuisine des Anges* by Albert Russon), *We're No Angels* presents three Devil's Island escapees (Humphrey Bogart, Aldo Ray, and Peter Ustinov) and their comic escapades. In the Ranald MacDougall screenscript, directed by Michael Curtiz, the three convicts pause for a while with an oppressed French shopkeeper (Leo G. Carroll) and his family. Using rather unorthodox methods, the jovial protagonists help the family make a success of their business. *We're No Angels* rates as an offbeat treat, featuring Bogie; his foils, Ray and Ustinov; Joan Bennett as the mother; Gloria Talbott as the daughter; and Basil Rathbone as a scheming uncle.

What's Up, Doc?   1972   (Warner)   *Color*
Director: Peter Bogdanovich
Starring: Barbra Streisand, Ryan O'Neal, Kenneth Mars, Austin Pendleton, Madeline Kahn, Sorrell Booke, Michael Murphy, Liam Dunn, Mabel Albertson, John Hillerman, Randy Quaid, M. Emmet Walsh

What's Up, Doc? is Peter Bogdanovich's tribute to Hollywood comedy—a flashback to the Howard Hawks universe of the thirties. Energized by rapid-fire dialogue from Buck Henry, David Newman, and Robert Benton, the story takes place in modern-day San Francisco. An absent-minded musicologist (Ryan O'Neal) is vying for a twenty-thousand-dollar grant. During his stay in the city he becomes involved with rival scholars, his stuffy fiancée (Madeline Kahn), a madcap adventuress (Barbra Streisand), and a mix-up over stolen jewels, top secret documents, and four identical suitcases. The technical team includes cinematographer Laszlo Kovacs, production designer Polly Platt, and editor Verna Fields.

Wise Blood   1979   (MCA)   *Color*
Director: John Huston
Starring: Brad Dourif, Ned Beatty, Harry Dean Stanton, Daniel Shor, Amy Wright, Mary Nell Santacroce, John Huston, William Hickey

John Huston's translation of Flannery O'Connor's 1952 novel resharpens the original's satirical barbs. Hazel Motes (Brad Dourif) is an army veteran who has turned to street-corner evangelism. He returns to his rural Georgia hometown to propagate his self-founded sect: "The Church Without Christ." Ms. O'Connor's prose has been faithfully adapted by scenarists Benedict and Michael Fitzgerald. Assisting Huston on the technical end are cinematographer Gerry Fisher, editor Roberto Silvi, and costumer and sets supervisor Sally Fitzgerald. Alex North wrote the score. The featured actors include Harry Dean Stanton as phony preacherman Asa Hawks; Amy Wright as Sabbath Lily, Hazel's wicked fifteen-year-old mistress; and Dan Shor as the dim-witted Enoch Emery. *Wise Blood* was released briefly to good reviews but poor box-office, then relegated to the midnight movie circuit.

The World According to Garp   1982   (Warner)   *Color*
Director: George Roy Hill
Starring: Robin Williams, Mary Beth Hurt, Glenn Close, John Lithgow, Hume Cronyn, Jessica Tandy, Swoosie Kurtz, James McCall, Peter Michael Goetz, George Ede, Mark Soper, Kate McGregor-Stewart, Warren Berlinger, Susan Browning, Brandon Maggart, Amanda Plummer, John Irving

This adaptation of John Irving's runaway best-seller eulogizes T. S. Garp and his life of wonder and absurdity. With dialogue by Steve Tesich and direction by George Roy Hill, the picture stars Robin Williams as the protagonist; Glenn Close as his unorthodox mother, Jenny Fields; Mary Beth Hurt as his wife; and John Lithgow as transsexual Roberta Muldoon, a former linebacker for the Philadelphia Eagles. They and others are involved in a series of funny and life-affirming vignettes. The director of photography is Miroslav Ondriček.

The World of Henry Orient   1964   (Key)   *Color*
Director: George Roy Hill
Starring: Peter Sellers, Paula Prentiss, Angela Lansbury, Tom Bosley, Phyllis Thaxter, Tippy Walker, Merrie Spaeth, Bibi Osterwald, Peter Duchin, John Fiedler, Al Lewis, Fred Stewart, Philippa Bevans

Henry Orient (Peter Sellers) is an egotistical concert pianist and a ladies' man. He has also aroused the ardor of Valerie Boyd (Tippy Walker) and Marian Gilbert (Merrie Spaeth), fourteen-year-old Manhattan schoolgirls. The two adolescents pursue Henry all over town, creating fantasies about him as they go. Henry soon learns that it's a bother to be idolized. Comedy is king in the screenscript by Nunnally and Nora Johnson, derived from Nora's novel. Debuting actresses Walker and Spaeth keep things mirthful—right up to the poignant climactic twist. Music by Elmer Bernstein, whose score united with the plot to inspire the subsequent Broadway musical *Henry, Sweet Henry*.

The Wrong Arm of the Law   Great Britain 1962;   *Black-and-White*
      U.S. 1963   (Monterey)
Director: Cliff Owen
Starring: Peter Sellers, Lionel Jeffries, Bernard Cribbins, Davy Kaye, Nanette Newman, John Le Mesurier, Dennis Price, Bill Kerr

Another of the cycle of caper comedies that arrived from England in the fifties and sixties—and many viewers believe one of the funniest. The premise here is that several audacious Australian gangsters, operating in London, dress up as bobbies and confiscate loot from the robbers they apprehend. A local gang, led by Peter Sellers, and the real police are eager to trap the interlopers. A fast-paced spoof, *The Wrong Arm of the Law* has Cliff Owen directing a John Warren-Len Heath screenplay. (Owen, a madcap comedy specialist, also directed the screen version of *No Sex Please, We're British*.) Ernest Steward is the cinematographer and Richard Rodney Bennett supplies the score.

The Wrong Box   1966   (RCA)   *Color*
Director: Bryan Forbes
Starring: John Mills, Ralph Richardson, Michael Caine, Peter Cook, Dudley Moore, Nanette Newman, Wilfrid Lawson, Peter Sellers, Tony Hancock, Thorley Walters, Cicely Courtneidge, Irene Handl, John Le Mesurier, Gerald Sim, Norman Bird, Tutte Lemkow

Loosely based on a story by Robert Louis Stevenson and Lloyd Osbourne, *The Wrong Box*—scripted by Larry Gelbart and Burt Shevelove—is an archetypal British farce. The plot centers on two elderly Victorian brothers (John Mills and Ralph Richardson) intent on outliving each other. They are the only survivors of a tontine—which will provide a fortune to the last one alive. To accelerate fate, the siblings resort to murder attempts. Therein lies the outlandishness of this black comic tale. The ingredients include a train wreck, misplaced corpses, an insouciant hero (Michael Caine), a beauteous heroine (Nanette Newman), a crackpot doctor (Peter Sellers), mercenary relatives (Peter Cook and Dudley Moore), and a runaway funeral cortege. The director is Bryan Forbes, the cinematographer Gerry Turpin.

Young at Heart   1954   (Republic)   *Color*
Director: Gordon Douglas
Starring: Doris Day, Frank Sinatra, Gig Young, Ethel Barrymore, Dorothy Malone, Robert Keith, Elizabeth Fraser, Alan Hale, Jr.

Doris Day and Frank Sinatra, then at the peak of their pop-chart popularity, appear in this color remake of *Four Daughters* (1938). The daughters are now three; as portrayed by Doris Day, Dorothy Malone, and Elizabeth Fraser, they are the offspring of a small-town music teacher (Robert Keith). Romance and love songs are on the agenda; among the latter are "You, My Love," "Just One of Those Things," and the title tune— which remains part of Sinatra's repertoire to this day. Adapted by Liam O'Brien from Fannie Hurst's novel *Sister Act*, then scripted by Julius J. Epstein and Lenore Coffee.

Young Frankenstein   1974   (CBS)   *Black-and-White*
Director: Mel Brooks
Starring: Gene Wilder, Peter Boyle, Marty Feldman, Cloris Leachman, Teri Garr, Kenneth Mars, Madeline Kahn, Richard Haydn, Liam Dunn

Parody runs rampant in this sendup of the Dr. Frankenstein myth and movies. As the picture begins, Frederick Frankenstein (Gene Wilder), a brain surgeon and grandson of the nefarious baron of yore, returns to Transylvania to make a monster (Peter Boyle). The young doctor is attended by Igor (Marty Feldman), a hunchback whose hump mysteriously shifts sides; Frau Blücher (Cloris Leachman), the castle housekeeper who frightens the horses; and his beautiful fiancée (Madeline Kahn), who becomes the bride of the monster. Kahn's Elsa Lanchesteresque makeup and performance work in homage to *The Bride of Frankenstein* (1935), as does Gene Hackman's cameo of the blind hermit. Horror film fans will tick off other specific references in the script—a collaboration between leading man Wilder and director Mel Brooks. The imitative photography (Gerald Hirschfeld) and art direction (Dale Hennessy) are further reminders of those long-ago fright films.

Zorro, the Gay Blade   1981   (CBS)   *Color*
Director: Peter Medak
Starring: George Hamilton, Lauren Hutton, Brenda Vaccaro, Ron Leibman, Donovan Scott, James Booth, Clive Revill

This comedy, scripted by Hal Dresner and directed by Peter Medak, is a lampoon of Zorro, the swashbuckling adventurer of TV and motion picture fame. Set in Spanish California of the 1820s, the film introduces Don Diego de la Vega (George Hamilton), a wealthy womanizer who—in secret—dons a mask and sword to fight oppression. As Zorro, he is beloved by the peasants, despised by the authorities. Only his trusty sidekick Paco (Donovan Scott) knows that Don Diego and Zorro are one. However, when the crusading hero is bedridden after an accident, he must rely on his long-lost twin brother, giggling Bunny Wigglesworh. Hamilton plays the dual roles, and he is surrounded by farceurs—Scott, Ron Leibman, Brenda Vaccaro—and, as the love interest, Lauren Hutton. John A. Alonzo is the director of photography.

Dramas

Absence of Malice   1981   (RCA)   *Color*
Director: Sydney Pollack
Starring: Paul Newman, Sally Field, Bob Balaban, Melinda Dillon, Luther Adler, Barry Primus, Josef Sommer, Wilford Brimley, John Harkins

Five short years after *All the President's Men* immortalized newspaper reporters, Sydney Pollack's *Absence of Malice* provided a distinctly alternative view. This bristling portrait of journalistic responsibility features a top-notch performance by Paul Newman, who plays a Miami businessman mistakenly accused by reporter Sally Field of involvement in the disappearance of a labor leader. When he tries to defend himself, he confronts the power and privilege of the press. *Absence of Malice* reached the top of the box office charts during its initial end-of-1981 release and continued to do well into the new year. Oscar attention focused on Newman, Melinda Dillon (as another victim of the misleading story), and screenwriter Kurt Luedtke—none of them recipients of an award. Exteriors filmed in Miami.

Accident   1967   (Thorn)   *Color*
Director: Joseph Losey
Starring: Dirk Bogarde, Stanley Baker, Jacqueline Sassard, Delphine Seyrig, Alexander Knox, Michael York, Vivien Merchant

Harold Pinter's reputation as a major force in British theater was well-established when he began collaborating with Joseph Losey on some of the most thought-provoking movies of the late sixties and early seventies. Released after *The Servant* (1965), and before *The Go-Between* (1971), *Accident* is thought by many to be the most arcane of films. The original screenplay captures many of the comic eccentricities of Pinter's stage work (with particular resemblances to *The Homecoming*). Dirk Bogarde stars as an Oxford don whose dalliance with a student creates tragedy in several households. What follows is a study of several very enigmatic, slightly depraved, and exceedingly civilized characters.

Advise and Consent   1962   (Hal Roach)   *Black-and-White*
Director: Otto Preminger
Starring: Henry Fonda, Charles Laughton, Don Murray, Walter Pidgeon, Gene Tierney, Peter Lawford, Franchot Tone, Burgess Meredith, Lew Ayres, Paul Ford, George Grizzard, Betty White

Advise and Consent bears the trademarks of the climax of Otto Preminger's career; from roughly 1959 through 1975 (with the release of *Rosebud*), the director capitalized on commercial properties, controversial themes, and all-star casts. Culled from Allen Drury's best-seller by Wendell Mayes, the film provides a behind-the-scenes view of the Washington political machine. Risqué characters abound: a frivolous Don Juan; a mysterious hostess; a ruthless, dying president; a vindictive Southern statesman; an idealistic senator with a past. This was Charles Laughton's last performance, while Gene Tierney, Preminger's Laura, made her comeback herein. Most scenes were shot in actual locales.

An Affair to Remember   1957   (CBS)   *Color*
Director: Leo McCarey
Starring: Cary Grant, Deborah Kerr, Richard Denning, Cathleen Nesbitt, Neva Patterson, Robert Q. Lewis, Charles Watts

A shipboard romance turns into heartbreak on land. Cary Grant and Deborah Kerr are the two lovers who break off their engagement, but decide to meet again six months later. Little do they realize how tragedy will intervene. A Technicolor remake by Leo McCarey of his 1939 *Love Affair*, starring Charles Boyer and Irene Dunne. Performances by the leads and outstanding production values elevate this film above the typical big studio tearjerker. McCarey shares the screenplay credit with writer-director Delmer Daves.

The African Queen   1951   (CBS)   ◆   *Color*
Director: John Huston
Starring: Humphrey Bogart, Katharine Hepburn, Robert Morley, Peter Bull, Theodore Bikel, Walter Gotell, Peter Swanick

A slovenly riverboat captain and a "skinny, psalm-singing old maid" engage in the age-old battle of the sexes in German East Africa when war breaks out in 1914. The odd-couple roles were tailor-made for Humphrey Bogart and Katharine Hepburn; indeed, Bogie collected his one and only Oscar for embodying drunken skipper Charlie Allnutt. A tongue-in-cheek adventure classic, *The African Queen* is both funny and thrilling. Directed by John Huston, who coadapted the C. S. Forester novel with James Agee. The sometimes treacherous but beautiful location photography was accomplished by Jack Cardiff, whose later brief career as a director encompasses *Sons and Lovers* and *Young Cassidy*.

Agnes of God   1985   (RCA)   *Color*
Director: Norman Jewison
Starring: Jane Fonda, Anne Bancroft, Meg Tilly, Anne Pitoniak, Winston Rekert, Gratien Gélinas, Guy Hoffman, Gabriel Arcand, Françoise Faucher, Jacques Tourangeau, Janine Fluet, Norma Dell'Agnese

Agnes (Meg Tilly), a novice in a remote French Canadian convent, is accused of strangling her just-born infant. Dr. Martha Livingston (Jane Fonda), a court-appointed psychiatrist, is dispatched to examine the young nun and rule on her sanity. The determinedly secular doctor clashes with the convent's Mother Superior (Anne Bancroft), who insists that Sister Agnes has no memory of the pregnancy, let alone the infanticide. This film transfer of John Pielmeier's Broadway hit, screenwritten by the playwright himself, escalates into a debate between science and religion; both realms figure in the resolution, wherein the mystery behind Agnes's conception and delivery is hypothesized. Sobering drama, the picture contains one scene of comedy: chain-smoking Dr. Livingston and the Mother Superior, a former cigarette fiend, speculate on what kind of tobacco various saints would have smoked—or chewed. Directed by Norman Jewison and shot by Sven Nykvist.

Alfie   1966   (Paramount)   *Color*
Director: Lewis Gilbert
Starring: Michael Caine, Shelley Winters, Julia Foster, Jane Asher, Shirley Anne Field, Millicent Martin, Vivien Merchant, Alfie Bass, Denholm Elliott

Bill Naughton's popular West End comedy achieved worldwide recognition in its 1966 screen incarnation. The film, also written by Naughton, improved upon the play, providing increased depth and compassion for the characters—even the title one, a conniving Cockney lover boy whose amoral dalliances all round London are a source of both comedy and tragedy. *Alfie* evolves in vignettes, in the style of *La Ronde.* After ten years of supporting roles, Caine—by doing *The Ipcress File* and *Alfie* back-to-back— was an overnight success. In *Alfie* his bad-boy charm enlists sympathy for what is essentially a thoroughly ribald and unscrupulous character. Cilla Black sings the hit-parade theme song, "What's It All About, Alfie?"

Alice Doesn't Live Here Anymore   1974   (Warner)   ◆   *Color*
Director: Martin Scorsese
Starring: Ellen Burstyn, Kris Kristofferson, Billy Green Bush, Alfred Lutter, Diane Ladd, Jodie Foster, Vic Tayback, Valerie Curtin, Harvey Keitel

Housewife Alice Hyatt is left penniless when her construction worker husband is killed. With visions of being a vocalist like Alice Faye, this Alice heads west to embark on a singing career. She and her twelve-year-old son wind up in Phoenix—where Alice becomes a singer-waitress. *Alice Doesn't Live Here Anymore* is atypical Martin Scorsese, who specializes in taut, hard-hitting dramas; even so, it was one of his biggest hits. Robert Getchell's original screenplay was bested in the Oscar race by Robert Towne's *Chinatown,* but Ellen Burstyn won best actress. The film inspired the long-running teleseries (1976–85), with Vic Tayback re-creating his role as the cantankerous owner of Mel's Diner and, for one season, Diane Ladd (who played Flo in the movie) as a new character called Belle.

Alice's Restaurant   1969   (CBS)   *Color*
Director: Arthur Penn
Starring: Arlo Guthrie, Pat Quinn, James Broderick, Michael McClanathan, Geoff Out-law, Tina Chen, Shelley Plimpton

Founded on Arlo Guthrie's true-life blues ballad, "The Alice's Restaurant Massacree," Arthur Penn's episodic film is a freewheeling and heartfelt evocation of the world of hippies in the 1960s—focusing on the scene in Stockbridge, Massachusetts. Both song and motion picture begin with Guthrie's prosecution for littering one fine Thanksgiving day; then they dramatize his subsequent rejection for military service. Secondary emphasis is placed on newlyweds Alice and Ray Brock (Pat Quinn and James Broderick), who at the time inhabited an abandoned Stockbridge church and opened a restaurant "about a half a mile from the railroad track." The young couple become spiritual parents for a brood of social dropouts—with tragic results. On the record when Arlo sang

"You can get anything you want at Alice's restaurant—exceptin' Alice," most people roared with laughter. Quite a different response is sought in the film.

All Mine to Give   1957   (United)   *Color*
Director: Allen Reisner
Starring: Glynis Johns, Cameron Mitchell, Patty McCormack, Rex Thompson, Hope Emerson, Ernest Truex, Alan Hale

Movies like *All Mine to Give* are frequently associated with the sobriquet *soap opera.* In this instance the term diminishes a plausible family saga. This comedy-drama (emphasis on the latter) places viewers on an emotional roller coaster as a pioneer family confronts hardships in the winter wilds of Wisconsin. Farmer Cameron Mitchell and his wife (Glynis Johns) die young, leaving behind a houseful of children ranging in age from newborn to early teens. To say that this feature is based on a teleplay entitled "The Day They Gave the Babies Away" provides only part of the plot. The film was overlooked when new because RKO, in the final year of its decline, just barely released it. Directed by Allen Reisner, whose next film was *St. Louis Blues.*

All That Jazz   *Listed under Musicals.*

All the King's Men   1949   (RCA)   ◆   *Black-and-White*
Director: Robert Rossen
Starring: Broderick Crawford, John Derek, Joanne Dru, John Ireland, Mercedes McCambridge, Shepperd Strudwick, Jane Seymour, Ralph Dumke

Robert Penn Warren's Pulitzer Prize novel drew inspiration from real-life model Huey Long. Adapted for the screen by Robert Rossen, *All the King's Men* tells the story of the rise and fall of Southern governor Willie Stark, a self-styled "redneck hick." For many, this is one of the most unforgettable depictions of political demagoguery ever captured on film. The corruption of power is an old story, but producer-screenwriter-director Rossen (*Body and Soul, The Hustler*) reanimated it here. Broderick Crawford is the perfect screen embodiment of Stark, and for his performance he won the 1949 Oscar; Mercedes McCambridge as his tart-tongued aide won in the supporting actress category. And the film captured the top prize. Rossen, however, lost to Joseph L. Mankiewicz, cited as best director and writer for *A Letter to Three Wives.*

All the President's Men   1976   (Warner)   ◆   *Color*
Director: Alan Pakula
Starring: Robert Redford, Dustin Hoffman, Jason Robards, Martin Balsam, Jack Warden, Hal Holbrook, Jane Alexander, Stephen Collins, Meredith Baxter, Ned Beatty, Robert Walden

Adapted from the Bob Woodward-Carl Bernstein book by William Goldman, *All the President's Men* is an intricate dramatization of the journalistic reporting in the wake of the Watergate burglary. Alan Pakula's film follows Woodward (Robert Redford) and Bernstein (Dustin Hoffman) as they unravel the mystery that climaxed with President Nixon's resignation. Camerawork by Gordon Willis and editing by Robert L. Wolfe underline Pakula's quasi-documentary style. As 1976 was the year of that phenomenon named *Rocky*, *All the President's Men* missed out on the best picture Oscar; but individuals carried away honors: Jason Robards, as the *Washington Post*'s Ben

Bradlee, for best supporting actor; Goldman for his screenplay; and George Jenkins and George Gaines for their art direction and set decoration.

All the Right Moves   1983   (CBS)   *Color*
Director: Michael Chapman
Starring: Tom Cruise, Craig T. Nelson, Lea Thompson, Charles Cioffi, Paul Carafotes, Christopher Penn, Gary Graham, Sandy Faison

A football scholarship is high school athlete Tom Cruise's only way out of his dying mill town. But his hopes are dashed when he quarrels with coach Craig T. Nelson and is dropped from the team. His efforts to be reinstated and his romance with pretty Lea Thompson provide the core of the plot. *All the Right Moves,* from Michael Kane's script, features naturalistic elements and a feisty hero to root for. Cruise—one of the on-the-rise young stars of the eighties—is appealing in his second starring role. (*Risky Business* was released three months earlier.) The film represents the directing debut of cinematographer Michael Chapman (*Taxi Driver, Raging Bull*). Location shooting took place in Johnstown, Pennsylvania—which closely resembles the gray steel mill town in *The Deer Hunter.*

American Hot Wax   1978   (RCA)   *Color*
Director: Floyd Mutrux
Starring: Tim McIntire, Fran Drescher, Jay Leno, John Lehne, Laraine Newman, Jeff Altman, Chuck Berry, Jerry Lee Lewis, Screamin' Jay Hawkins

New York WINS deejay Alan Freed was a major force in promoting and establishing rock 'n' roll in the mid-fifties, and *American Hot Wax* concentrates on those happy days. Director Floyd Mutrux (*Dusty and Sweets McGee; Aloha, Bobby and Rose;* and *The Hollywood Knights*) and his scriptwriter, John Kaye, paint portraits of the milieu and the period. The climax comes when Freed emcees a legendary concert at the Brooklyn Paramount, and Mutrux captures some of the original artists performing: Chuck Berry, duckwalking through "Reelin' and Rockin'," is a highlight. Tim McIntyre plays Freed, Laraine Newman stars as a fledgling composer, Fran Drescher as a discordant girl Friday, Jay Leno as her boyfriend, and little Moosie Drier as the president of the Buddy Holly Fan Club.

. . . And Justice for All   1979   (RCA)   *Color*
Director: Norman Jewison
Starring: Al Pacino, Jack Warden, John Forsythe, Lee Strasberg, Jeffrey Tambor, Christine Lahti, Sam Levene, Robert Christian, Thomas Waites, Craig T. Nelson

Al Pacino is a Baltimore lawyer dedicated to reforming the criminal justice system. He is assigned to defend a powerful and potentially corrupt judge (Forsythe) on a rape charge. As evidence mounts on both sides, Pacino wrestles with a moral dilemma. Jewison, a seasoned director whose most recent work was *Rollerball* and *F.I.S.T.,* rebounded with . . . *And Justice for All.* Actress Valerie Curtin and director Barry Levinson, a husband-and-wife writing team, created the original script (and also wrote Jewison's next film, *Best Friends*). Levinson himself went on to direct *Diner, The Natural,* and *Young Sherlock Holmes.*

The Apprenticeship of Duddy Kravitz   *Listed under Comedies.*

Arch of Triumph   1948   (Republic)   *Black-and-White*
Director: Lewis Milestone
Starring: Ingrid Bergman, Charles Boyer, Charles Laughton, Louis Calhern, Curt Bois,
J. Edward Bromberg

A sweeping, old-fashioned drama of passion. Set in Paris just before the Nazi occupation, *Arch of Triumph* brings together Charles Boyer as a refugee doctor and Ingrid Bergman as a young woman with a mysterious past. This rendition of the novel by Erich Maria Remarque was a second teaming for Remarque and Milestone, who had established his cinema reputation by bringing to the screen *All Quiet on the Western Front*, the author's classic antiwar tale. *Arch of Triumph* was remade as a telemovie in 1985 with Anthony Hopkins and Lesley-Anne Down as the romantic leads.

The Asphalt Jungle   1950   (MGM)   *Black-and-White*
Director: John Huston
Starring: Sterling Hayden, Louis Calhern, Jean Hagen, James Whitmore, Sam Jaffe, John McIntire, Marc Lawrence, Barry Kelley, Anthony Caruso, Teresa Celli, Brad Dexter

What many movie fans call a classic heist drama, *The Asphalt Jungle* illustrates *dis*honor among thieves. John Huston separately introduces his band of felons—mastermind Sam Jaffe, society lawyer Louis Calhern, petty criminal Sterling Hayden, getaway driver James Whitmore, bookie Marc Lawrence, and cop-on-the-take Barry Kelley—then draws them together as participants in the burglary of a jewelry store. The robbery goes off without a hitch. Then greed overcomes them all. Dialogue unites with MGM's ultra-gloss (director of photography: Harold Rosson) to turn *The Asphalt Jungle* into one of Huston's most skillful accomplishments. The director adapted W. R. Burnett's crime novel with Ben Maddow. Marilyn Monroe, who started doing bit work in 1948, here had her first A-budget role as Calhern's girlfriend. *The Asphalt Jungle* was officially remade three times: *The Badlanders* (1958, Delmer Daves), *Cairo* (1963, Wolf Rilla), and *Cool Breeze* (1972, Barry Pollack).

Atlantic City   France 1980; U.S. 1981   (Paramount)   *Color*
Director: Louis Malle
Starring: Burt Lancaster, Susan Sarandon, Kate Reid, Hollis McLaren, Robert Joy, Michel Piccoli, Robert Goulet

This character study of an aging, small-time numbers runner is a tale of faded dreams and renewed aspirations—shot on location in Atlantic City, where a rejuvenated Boardwalk might spell a bright future. John Guare's script delineates the city's on-the-margin lovers and losers. And in Louis Malle he found an inspired directorial eye. Burt Lancaster stars as the over-the-hill hood. Also sharing the limelight are Susan Sarandon, a clam bar employee studying to be a croupier; Robert Joy, her drug-dealing brother; and Kate Reid, Lancaster's sometime mistress. Officially a coproduction of France and Canada, the film was released in some foreign markets in 1980 as *Atlantic City, U.S.A.*

Baby Doll   1956   (Warner)   *Black-and-White*
Director: Elia Kazan
Starring: Karl Malden, Carroll Baker, Eli Wallach, Mildred Dunnock, Lonny Chapman, Eades Hogue, Noah Williamson, Rip Torn

Tennessee Williams's comedy-drama presents a child bride and her jealous middle-aged husband languishing in their ramshackle Mississippi mansion waiting for Baby

Doll's twentieth birthday—when they plan to consummate the marriage. Carroll Baker stars as Baby Doll and Karl Malden plays her husband. Williams's passions are given full vent in this extension of his short play, *27 Wagons Full of Cotton*—and his scenario is populated with white trash, subservient blacks, faded gentility, the citizens of Benoit, Mississippi (where filmed)—and one outsider: cotton-gin owner Eli Wallach, whose lust for the teenage bride equals the husband's. The carnal goings-on allow a dress rehearsal for the more sophisticated *The Long Hot Summer*, Martin Ritt's Faulkner adaptation. Photography by Boris Kaufman. *Baby Doll* was the first picture from a major Hollywood studio (Warner Bros.) to be condemned by the Legion of Decency. Today's viewers may wonder what all the fuss was about.

The Bad and the Beautful   1952   (MGM)   ◆   *Black-and-White*
Director: Vincente Minnelli
Starring: Lana Turner, Kirk Douglas, Walter Pidgeon, Dick Powell, Barry Sullivan, Gloria Grahame, Gilbert Roland, Leo G. Carroll, Vanessa Brown, Paul Stewart, Sammy White, Elaine Stewart, Jonathan Cott

The Bad and the Beautiful charts the ruthless road to success in Tinseltown. Kirk Douglas plays a brilliant movie producer who is also a heel. His life story is presented in three versions by some of the people who know him most intimately: director Barry Sullivan, scriptwriter Dick Powell, and glamorous star Lana Turner. Charles Schnee's melo-dramatic screenplay constitutes a Hollywood self-exposé and affords witty observations in the *All About Eve* vein. An interesting footnote: ten years later Kirk Douglas, Charles Schnee, and director Vincente Minnelli joined forces again for *Two Weeks in Another Town*—a film with similar themes and which utilized clips from *The Bad and the Beautiful*. Five Oscars: Grahame for best supporting actress, Schnee for the script, Robert Surtees for black-and-white cinematography, Helen Rose for costuming, and the art direction/set decoration ensemble. In small roles: silent screen heartthrob Francis X. Bushman and Beaver Cleaver's mom, Barbara Billingsley.

Badlands   1973   (Warner)   *Color*
Director: Terrence Malick
Starring: Martin Sheen, Sissy Spacek, Warren Oates, Ramon Bieri, Alan Vint, Gary Littlejohn, John Carter

In a small South Dakota town in the early sixties, garbage collector Kit Carruthers (Martin Sheen) and high school majorette Holly Sargis (Sissy Spacek) fall in love. Each recognizes in the other a lonely soul. When Kit loses his job and Holly's father forbids her to continue the relationship, Kit shoots the old man and sets fire to the Sargis house. Kit and Holly then run away together and commence a headline-grabbing killing spree. This debut film of writer-producer-director-editor Terrence Malick is a subdued thriller modeled on the true story of the Charles Starkweather-Caril Ann Fugate case. What makes it different is the narration supplied by Holly. For years she has immersed herself in movie fan magazines and confession stories, and in those terms she now describes her life with Kit. ("Each lived for the precious hours when he or she could be with the other, away from the cares of the world.") Music: Carl Orff and Erik Satie.

Bang the Drum Slowly   1973   (Paramount)   *Color*
Director: John Hancock
Starring: Michael Moriarty, Robert De Niro, Vincent Gardenia, Heather MacRae, Barbara Babcock, Phil Foster, Tom Signorelli, Tom Ligon, Marshall Efron, Selma Diamond

A sports movie that redefines the genre. *Bang the Drum Slowly* documents a season with a (fictional) New York baseball club. From Mark Harris's fifties novel of the same name, the screen version updates the action to post-Vietnam. Henry Wiggen (Michael Moriarty) is the tall, lanky, fair-haired pitcher who does some writing in the off-season; Bruce Pearson (Robert De Niro) is the genial, near-illiterate Southern boy who is the team's catcher and Henry's roommate on the road. As the film begins, we learn that Bruce is doomed with Hodgkin's disease. Henry is the only other person who knows of Bruce's diagnosis. As the dying boy wants to play out the season, they pledge to keep his fate secret as long as possible. Upon this premise (screenscripted by novelist Harris himself) is constructed a powerful and poignant film. De Niro is a revelation as the heart-of-gold catcher, with Moriarty unforgettable in the less showy role of his saintly teammate. (In a 1956 "U.S. Steel Hour" television adaptation, Albert Salmi and Paul Newman assumed the catcher-pitcher roles.)

Barabbas 1962 (RCA) *Color*
Director: Richard Fleischer
Starring: Anthony Quinn, Silvana Mangano, Vittorio Gassman, Arthur Kennedy, Jack Palance, Ernest Borgnine, Katy Jurado, Valentina Cortesa

This lavish biblical spectacle is based on Pär Fabian Lagerkvist's novel, and the teleplay ("Give Us Barabbas") evolved from it. Director Richard Fleischer and his dialogist, Christopher Fry, render a chronicle of the Jewish thief who was replaced on the cross by Christ. Events both before and after that dramatic moment are invented, with particular emphasis on Barabbas's days as a gladiator. Anthony Quinn makes an ideal Barabbas. Director Richard Fleischer, son of cartoonist Max Fleischer, gained his early reputation making speedy, low-budget action pictures. The economical, seventy-minute *The Narrow Margin* (1952) is the purest example from that period. In graduating to big-time, big-cost projects like *Compulsion, Fantastic Voyage,* and, especially, *Barabbas,* Fleischer abandoned every conceivable notion of economy.

The Barefoot Contessa 1954 (CBS) ◆ *Color*
Director: Joseph L. Mankiewicz
Starring: Humphrey Bogart, Ava Gardner, Edmond O'Brien, Marius Goring, Valentina Cortesa, Rossano Brazzi, Elizabeth Sellars, Warren Stevens, Franco Interlenghi

Revealed in a series of flashbacks, *The Barefoot Contessa* is the story of a sexy flamenco dancer in a Madrid cabaret who is discovered and then groomed for stardom by an American film director. In Hollywood the cabaret dancer becomes a celebrated actress, has a string of unhappy love affairs, and enters into an equally unhappy, indeed tragic, marriage with an Italian count. Ava Gardner is the fiery *señorita*, Bogart the crackerjack director who becomes her mentor, and Edmond O'Brien won an Oscar as the syco-phantic publicity agent. *The Barefoot Contessa* represents another success for the cin-ematographer Jack Cardiff.

Barry Lyndon 1975 (Warner) ◆ *Color*
Director: Stanley Kubrick
Starring: Ryan O'Neal, Marisa Berenson, Patrick Magee, Hardy Krüger, Steven Berkoff, Gay Hamilton, Frank Middlemass, Godfrey Quigley, Diana Koerner, Murray Melvin, Marie Kean, Leon Vitali, David Morley

Barry Lyndon was one of William Makepeace Thackery's lesser-known novels—until filmmaker Stanley Kubrick reclaimed it from the obscurity of graduate school literary criticism courses. In Kubrick's adaptation, Ryan O'Neal is the handsome Irish rogue who climbs up the social ladder by marrying a rich widow; Marisa Berenson is Lady Lyndon. Four Oscars went to *Barry Lyndon* for photography (John Alcott), scoring adaptation (Leonard Rosenman), art direction/set decoration (Ken Adam, Roy Walker, Vernon Dixon), and costume design (Ulla-Britt Soderlund, Oilean Cononero). John Alcott's cinematography is the production's strong point; the only illumination in many night scenes comes from candlelight.

Becket   *Listed under Biographies.*

Ben-Hur   1959   (MGM)   ◆   *Color*
Director: William Wyler
Starring: Charlton Heston, Jack Hawkins, Stephen Boyd, Haya Harareet, Hugh Griffith, Martha Scott, Sam Jaffe, Cathy O'Donnell, Finlay Currie, Frank Thring, Terence Longden, André Morell

Ben-Hur is the single most honored film in the Motion Picture Academy's history: its record-establishing eleven Oscars have yet to be matched. Elected best picture of 1959, with the top male performance, this is the most widely known screen adaptation of General Lew Wallace's "tale of the Christ." (There were two silent versions.) Charlton Heston is Judah Ben-Hur, of a noble family, and Stephen Boyd is Messala, his boyhood friend and adult rival. Their story becomes inextricably linked with the life and crucifixion of Jesus. MGM's prerelease publicity announced: "Fifteen million dollars, ten years in preparation, a year in production, 496 speaking roles, 100,000 extras, eight hectares of sets, enough negative used to stretch around the world." Karl Tunberg wrote the screenplay, based on Wallace's 1880 novel, with uncredited help from Christopher Fry, Gore Vidal, and others. Veteran filmmaker William Wyler shot the dialogue scenes; Andrew Marton and Yakima Canutt were the second-unit directors who staged the chariot race and the sea battles. Joining the picture and Heston with Oscars were Wyler; supporting actor Hugh Griffith as the wily Sheik Ildeerim; the editors; director of photography Robert Surtees; the MGM sound department; the art direction/set decoration squad; Miklos Rozsa for his musical score; the special effects crew; and costume designer Elizabeth Haffenden.

The Best Years of Our Lives   1946   (Embassy)   ◆   *Black-and-White*
Director: William Wyler
Starring: Myrna Loy, Fredric March, Dana Andrews, Teresa Wright, Virginia Mayo, Cathy O'Donnell, Hoagy Carmichael, Harold Russell, Gladys George, Roman Bohnen, Ray Collins, Steve Cochran

Producer Samuel Goldwyn's timely film about veterans returning from World War II was a critical and popular success and continues to be one of the most beloved films of the forties. Three soldiers return to the States on the same plane: an Air Force bombardier (Dana Andrews); a sergeant who had been a banking executive (Fredric March); and a sailor who lost his hands in a bomb explosion (Harold Russell). The story follows their readjustment, individually and collectively, to the homes they left behind. Noteworthily, Harold Russell, a former paratrooper, actually lost his hands in the war; until his appearance in *Inside Moves* in 1980, *The Best Years of Our Lives* was his only screen work—and it netted him a best supporting actor Oscar. He was also presented with an honorary statuette "for bringing hope and courage to his fellow veterans." Other Academy Award recognition: best picture, actor (March had previously won for *Dr. Jekyll and Mr. Hyde*), director (William Wyler), screenplay (Robert Sherwood), music scoring (Hugo Friedhofer), and editing (Daniel Mandell).

Betrayal   1983   (CBS)   *Color*
Director: David Jones
Starring: Ben Kingsley, Jeremy Irons, Patricia Hodge

Harold Pinter's screen treatment of *Betrayal,* his three-character, London and New York stage hit, is superior in some respects to the original. This elegant, epigrammatic mood piece about a love triangle seems specially designed for the intimate exploration of a motion picture camera. Ben Kingsley is the husband. Patricia Hodge is his wife. Jeremy Irons is their best friend. Expressed through Pinteresque conundrums, *Betrayal* is an analysis of the dissolution of the Irons-Hodge love affair. The gimmick is that the story is played in reverse; each scene witnessed occurs chronologically just *before* the earlier one—so that the film's ending is the beginning of the betrayal. As the movie proceeds, though, it's apparent there are more betrayals than just the central one.

Between the Lines   1977   (Vestron)   *Color*
Director: Joan Micklin Silver
Starring: John Heard, Lindsay Crouse, Jeff Goldblum, Jill Eikenberry, Stephen Collins, Lewis J. Stadlen, Michael J. Pollard, Marilu Henner, Gwen Welles, Bruno Kirby

Joan Micklin Silver's second feature-length movie—after the popular *Hester Street. Between the Lines* is an anecdotal account of life at a small alternative newspaper in Boston. The staff—radicals of the sixties who have become admired journalists, editors, and photographers—learn that they are facing takeover by a conglomerate. The offices are thrown into turmoil. Working from a script by Fred Barron and David M. Helpern, Jr., the director creates a very credible milieu; the weekly *Mainline* (modeled on the Boston *Phoenix* and *The Real Paper*) rings true. Most prominent in the large cast are John Heard, who plays a prize-winning reporter; Stephen Collins as a successful writer who has emerged from the counterculture; Lewis J. Stadlen, who plays a representative of the Establishment; and Jill Eikenberry as the receptionist-secretary who is the unsuspected (until the climax) heart and soul of the newspaper.

The Big Chill   *Listed under Comedies.*

The Bingo Long Traveling All-Stars and Motor Kings   *Listed under Comedies.*

Birdy   1984   (RCA)   *Color*
Director: Alan Parker
Starring: Matthew Modine, Nicolas Cage, John Hawkins, Sandy Baron, Karen Young, Bruno Kirby, Nancy Fish, George Buck, Dolores Sage

Matthew Modine is Birdy, a shy young bird-fancier obsessed with learning how to fly. Nicolas Cage is his best friend, an extroverted athlete obsessed with learning about girls. In the novel by William Wharton, their story unfolds within the context of World

War II. In Sandy Kroopf and Jack Behr's screen adaptation, directed by Alan Parker, *Birdy* opens in a post-Vietnam mental hospital where the emotionally scarred title character is recovering from the effects of battle—and his friend, also a soldier, is trying to bring him back to reality. This antiwar fable has numerous moments of emotional power, but in updating the action Parker and his production designers get the nostalgic scenery boggled: vintage cars, clothes, and set pieces seem to derive from the fifties; yet when the film leaves the boys' Philadelphia neighborhood (presumably only a year or two later), it plunks the two heroes in the midst of the Vietnam era.

Black Narcissus   1947   (VidAm; Learning Corp. of America)   ◆   *Color*
Directors: Michael Powell and Emeric Pressburger
Starring: Deborah Kerr, David Farrar, Kathleen Byron, Flora Robson, Jean Simmons, Sabu, Esmond Knight

This drama about an order of Anglican nuns owes its inspiration to Rumer Godden's delicate 1939 novel of the same name. The film is yet another from writing-directing partners Michael Powell and Emeric Pressburger, responsible for *The Life and Death of Colonel Blimp, I Know Where I'm Going,* and *The Red Shoes.* Subtle characterizations are a hallmark of their productions, and *Black Narcissus* is no exception. Deborah Kerr is the sister superior in a mission hospital in the Himalayas. Even in this remote quarter, secular temptation arises—in the guise of Englishman David Farrar, who actually lures one of the sisters (Kathleen Byron) away. Oscars went to Jack Cardiff for color cinematography and Alfred Junge for art direction.

Blackboard Jungle   1955   (MGM)   *Black-and-White*
Director: Richard Brooks
Starring: Glenn Ford, Anne Francis, Louis Calhern, Margaret Hayes, John Hoyt, Richard Kiley, Emile Meyer, Warner Anderson, Basil Ruysdael, Sidney Poitier, Vic Morrow, Rafael Campos

A rundown vocational training school in a city slum is the breeding ground for juvenile delinquency. Novice teacher Glenn Ford tries to stamp it out. Adapted by Richard Brooks from Evan Hunter's novel, *Blackboard Jungle* is—even as it was in 1955—a terrifying look at urban secondary education. Ford is an idealist who, nonetheless, harbors no illusions about the monetary rewards of his profession. But he does wish to help his classroom of undisciplined, aggressive students. One of them, Sidney Poitier, finally sees the light. (In 1967, the tables were turned on Poitier, who played teacher in *To Sir, with Love.*) Future film director Paul Mazursky appears as Emmanuel Stoker, one of the rowdies. The music of Bill Haley and the Comets prominently features "Rock Around the Clock."

Bless the Beasts and Children   1971   (RCA)   *Color*
Director: Stanley Kramer
Starring: Billy Mumy, Barry Robins, Miles Chapin, Ken Swofford, Jesse White, Vanessa Brown, Bob Kramer

Six adolescent boys, all social misfits, band together for the summer at a rich kids' ranch camp. When they discover that a captive buffalo herd is to be slaughtered, they wage a campaign to save the beasts from corrupt sportsmen and politicians. Mac Benoff's spare adaptation of the Glendon Swarthout novel brings a freshness to this project. Of the actors, rebel Billy Mumy and Miles Chapin are the standouts. Mix in the splendors of the open spaces and the Barry De Vorzon-Perry Botkin, Jr., music—and voila! *Bless the Beasts and Children.*

Bloodbrothers 1978 (Warner) *Color*
Director: Robert Mulligan
Starring: Paul Sorvino, Tony Lo Bianco, Richard Gere, Lelia Goldoni, Yvonne Wilder, Michael Hershewe, Kenneth McMillan, Floyd Levine, Marilu Henner, Kristine De Bell, Kim Milford, Robert Englund

Urban family strife and male bonding are the dominant themes in *Bloodbrothers*, Walter Newman's Oscar-nominated adaptation of the Richard Price novel. Construction worker Tony Lo Bianco wants his son (Richard Gere) to follow in his footsteps. Gere, however, not only shuns a hardhat and high-rise girders, he wants to break entirely from the family. Newman has faithfully transcribed Price's depiction of blue-collar machismo. Director Robert Mulligan's more successful films are *To Kill a Mockingbird, Summer of '42, The Other.* As Lo Bianco's perceptive, compassionate brother, Paul Sorvino is commendable. The camera work is by Robert Surtees, whose forty-year career also encompasses *Ben-Hur, The Bad and the Beautiful, The Graduate, The Last Picture Show,* and *The Turning Point*—to name but a few.

Blow-Up 1966 (MGM) ✷ *Color*
Director: Michelangelo Antonioni
Starring: Vanessa Redgrave, David Hemmings, Sarah Miles, Peter Bowles, Verushka, Jane Birkin, Jill Kennington

Under Michelangelo Antonioni's scrutiny in his first English-language film is a London fashion photographer (David Hemmings) at the height of sixties mod. Strolling in the park, the bored young hero inadvertently takes pictures of a murder. Only he doesn't realize what he's photographed until he returns to his studio to develop the negatives. *Blow-Up* is on one level a psychological suspense tale—with the darkroom substituted for a forensics or ballistics lab. It is also a variation on Pirandellian reality-versus-illusion games. Antonioni's screenplay with Tonino Guerra was given an English adaptation by playwright Edward Bond; somewhere along the way, *Blow-Up* took several giant steps away from its inspiration: a short story by Julio Cortázar. Hemmings is the emotionally alienated protagonist, and top-billed Vanessa Redgrave plays the mystery woman who tries to buy the incriminating negatives. The cinematography is by Carlo di Palma, who subsequently went on to his own directorial career. Music: Herbie Hancock. Included among the international honors bestowed upon *Blow-Up* was the best picture designation at the 1966 Cannes Film Festival.

Blue Collar *Listed under Comedies.*

The Blue Lagoon 1980 (RCA) *Color*
Director: Randal Kleiser
Starring: Brooke Shields, Christopher Atkins, Leo McKern, William Daniels

Following a shipwreck, a boy and a girl are marooned on a South Seas island. Several years pass and the youngsters grow to maturity—ultimately exploring their awakening sexual feelings. This idyllic fantasy was extremely popular with young ticket buyers—its target audience. The leads, Christopher Atkins and Brooke Shields, became teen idols. Location filming took place in the Fiji Islands. The sun-drenched photography of Nestor Almendros merited an Academy Award nomination. A remake of the 1949 British film starring Jean Simmons and Donald Houston as the shipwrecked lovers, *The Blue Lagoon* represented director Randal Kleiser's second success in a row with teenage moviegoers: *Grease,* his 1978 theatrical debut, is one of the all-time box office record holders. Kleiser's subsequent movies aimed at the same audience were *Summer Lovers* and *Grandview U.S.A.*

Body and Soul   1947   (Republic)   *Color*
Director: Robert Rossen
Starring: John Garfield, Lilli Palmer, Hazel Brooks, Anne Revere, William Conrad, Joseph Pevney, Canada Lee, Lloyd Goff, Art Smith, James Burke, Virginia Gregg

At the center of the narrative is Charlie Davis (John Garfield), a boxer trying to punch his way out of the slum. In his ascent to the championship, he is approached and briefly led astray by racketeers. Finally, Charlie opts for the straight and narrow—having been redeemed by his love for his family and his girl (Lilli Palmer). *Body and Soul* is the best-known feature written by blacklisted screenwriter Abraham Polonsky, and one of the most admired by sometime scenarist Robert Rossen, whose second film as director it was. Rossen's supervision of the dialogue and the milieu makes *Body and Soul* among the most authentic prizefight pictures ever made. (The crisp camera work is by James Wong Howe.) George Bowers directed a 1981 remake starring black actors in the leading roles. Leon Isaac Kennedy played the Garfield character.

Bonnie and Clyde   1967   (Warner)   ◆   *Color*
Director: Arthur Penn
Starring: Warren Beatty, Faye Dunaway, Michael J. Pollard, Gene Hackman, Estelle Parsons, Denver Pyle, Dub Taylor, Evans Evans, Gene Wilder, James Stiver

A cinema milestone. Initially, Clyde Barrow is seen as a feckless drifter, a child of the Depression; Bonnie Parker as a bored small-town girl who likes Clyde's looks and decides to run off with him. They unite with auto mechanic C. W. Moss and Clyde's brother and sister-in-law, Buck and Blanche Barrow. Then the Barrow-Parker gang embark on a bank-robbing spree through Texas and the Dust Bowl of the prairie states. (Burnett Guffey's Oscar-winning cinematography captures the dusty, desolate qualities indigenous to the thirties Midwest.) The bridging of these sequences is accomplished by editor Dede Allen. "They're young . . . they're in love . . . and they kill people," rhapsodized the original print ads for the picture. But this violent film, while supposedly helping to usher in an era of screen permissiveness, is hardly a glorification of violence. The writing team of Robert Benton and David Newman use period touches, often for ironic effect (as with the clip of the "We're in the Money" production number from *Gold Diggers of 1933*). Under Arthur Penn's direction, humor and terror sometimes coincide—notably in the joy-riding scene with the undertaker played by Gene Wilder. An Oscar-honored performance by supporting actress Estelle Parsons in her movie debut. Filmed in and around Dallas.

Born Free   *Listed under Family Viewing/Children's.*

The Boys in Company C   *Listed under War.*

The Boys in the Band 1970 (CBS) *Color*
Director: William Friedkin
Starring: Frederick Combs, Leonard Frey, Cliff Gorman, Reuben Greene, Robert La Tourneaux, Laurence Luckinbill, Kenneth Nelson, Keith Prentice, Peter White

"*The Boys in the Band* . . . is not a musical." So went this film's ad campaign back in 1970. Mart Crowley's stage play about a group of homosexual men sharing their thoughts and feelings at a Greenwich Village birthday party transfers to the screen. While a more conventional theater piece than *Who's Afraid of Virginia Woolf?*, *The Boys in the Band* features an identical brand of acidic humor that culminates in emotion-charged confrontations.

Breaker Morant 1979 (RCA) *Color*
Director: Bruce Beresford
Starring: Edward Woodward, Jack Thompson, John Waters, Bryan Brown, Charles Tingwell, Vincent Ball, Lewis Fitz-Gerald

Harry "Breaker" Morant was an Australian poet and soldier who gained status as a folk hero. During the Boer War (1899–1902) Morant was court-martialed, with several other soldiers, for civilian murders. Bruce Beresford's film—from his screenplay with Jonathan Hardy and David Stevens—is a brooding, rational exploration of those events (with clear parallels to Vietnam's My Lai massacre). The movie reconstructs the court-martial and reaches its climax with the sentencing and aftermath. Edward Woodward plays Morant, with Jack Thompson as the defense attorney. Woodward is now TV's "The Equalizer," while Bryan Brown has made inroads into American television and motion pictures, notably as the special effects–designing hero of *F/X*. Beresford himself went on to direct *Tender Mercies* and *King David*.

The Breakfast Club 1985 (MCA) *Color*
Director: John Hughes
Starring: Emilio Estevez, Paul Gleason, Anthony Michael Hall, Judd Nelson, Molly Ringwald, Ally Sheedy, John Kapelos, Perry Crawford, Mary Christian, Ron Dean, Tim Gamble, Fran Gargano, Mercedes Hall

Five stir-crazy high school students, heterogeneous but for their ages, are forced to spend a Saturday in study hall detention together. Their assignment: write a self-analytical 1,000-word essay. They grumble, harass their officious teacher-supervisor, cavort in the halls, then talk out their problems with the group before finally applying pen to paper. The stars—Emilio Estevez, Anthony Michael Hall, Judd Nelson, Molly Ringwald, and Ally Sheedy—are leaders of Hollywood's so-called Brat Pack. The editing (by Dede Allen) and John Hughes's directorial tinkering (he also wrote the script) often give *The Breakfast Club* the semblance of a music video. (Of the many background songs, the Simple Minds' "Don't You," composed by Keith Forsey and Steve Schiff, became a hit.)

Brief Encounter 1946 (Learning) ✳ *Black-and-White*
Director: David Lean
Starring: Celia Johnson, Trevor Howard, Cyril Raymond, Joyce Carey, Stanley Holloway, Everley Gregg, Margaret Barton, Valentine Dyall, Irene Handl

Brief Encounter is David Lean's fourth film and his fourth collaboration with Noël

Coward. They had previously worked together on *In Which We Serve* (with Coward as codirector), *This Happy Breed,* and *Blithe Spirit.* Expanded from the dramatist's one-act "Still Life," *Brief Encounter* unfolds primarily at a suburban train station. Trevor Howard plays the doctor who removes a cinder from Celia Johnson's eye. Instantly attracted to one another (and unhappily married to others), they decide to meet weekly in the railway buffet. Coward performed the screenwriting duties, with the assistance of Lean and Anthony Havelock-Allan. Robert Krasker handled the camerawork. Celia Johnson was selected as best actress by the New York Film Critics Circle. A 1975 made-for-TV "Brief Encounter" starred Sophia Loren and Richard Burton as the star-crossed lovers.

The Browning Version   1951   (Learning)   ✳   *Black-and-White*
Director: Anthony Asquith
Starring: Michael Redgrave, Jean Kent, Nigel Patrick, Wilfrid Hyde-White, Ronald Howard, Brian Smith, Bill Travers, Paul Medland, Ivan Simpson

This production epitomizes the craftsmanship that marked British cinema of the 1950s. Terence Rattigan's screenplay, from his playscript, is interpreted by Anthony Asquith. (The director had earlier filmed Rattigan's *The Winslow Boy.*) At a tutorial the unpopular classics master (Michael Redgrave) of a provincial boys' school is confronted by what his students really think of him. Deeply introverted, he has closed himself off as a teacher—and as a husband. Coincidentally, he discovers that his wife has been having an affair with the very popular science master. Rattigan's study of repression is notable for its sensitivity and sophisticated dialogue. The key performance by Redgrave is flawless. At the 1951 Cannes Film Festival, the jury selected Redgrave as best actor and honored Rattigan for his screenplay.

Brubaker   1980   (CBS)   *Color*
Director: Stuart Rosenberg
Starring: Robert Redford, Yaphet Kotto, Jane Alexander, Murray Hamilton, David Keith, Morgan Freeman, M. Emmet Clark, Richard Ward, Tim McIntire, Linda Haynes, Albert Salmi, John McMartin

W. D. Richter's fact-inspired screenplay represents a plea for prison reform. The new warden at Wakefield Prison Farm is disturbed to learn of atrocities that occurred under a previous administration. Inmates were regularly beaten and tortured—and there are quite literally some skeletons to be uncovered. The idealistic warden then puts his job on the line to eradicate brutality and corruption. Robert Redford is the title character, a fictional counterpart of Thomas Murton, former superintendent of the Arkansas State Penitentiary. In the supporting cast, David Keith and Richard Ward are prominent as, respectively, youthful and elderly pawns of the Wakefield system. Grimmer and less romanticized than Stuart Rosenberg's earlier prison picture—*Cool Hand Luke.*

Buster and Billie   1974   (RCA)   *Color*
Director: Daniel Petrie
Starring: Jan-Michael Vincent, Pamela Sue Martin, Clifton James, Robert Englund, Joan Goodfellow

Rural Georgia is the setting for this evocation of high school passion. Over the objections of his peers, popular Buster (Jan-Michael Vincent) starts to date Billie (Joan Goodfellow). Billie is a girl from the wrong side of the tracks, with the wrong kind of reputation. Theirs is a rocky affair—agitated by pressure and prejudice from all sides. Writer Ron Turbeville gives *Buster and Billie* a mixture of comedy, poignancy, and foreboding. Knowledgeable performances from the two leads, and by Pamela Sue Martin as one of the in-crowd students, raise the level of the production too. The director is Daniel Petrie, who includes among his credits *A Raisin in the Sun, Lifeguard, Resurrection,* and, for TV, "Eleanor and Franklin," "Sybil," and "The Dollmaker."

The Caine Mutiny   1954   (RCA)   *Color*
Director: Edward Dmytryk
Starring: Humphrey Bogart, José Ferrer, Van Johnson, Fred MacMurray, Robert Francis, May Wynn, Tom Tully, E. G. Marshall, Arthur Franz, Lee Marvin, Warner Anderson, Claude Akins, Katherine Warren, Jerry Paris, Steve Brodie, Whit Bissell, James Best

The naval officers of the minesweeper *Caine* suspect that Captain Queeg, their skipper, is losing his mind. During a typhoon, the *Caine*'s executive officer relieves the captain of his command—an action which results in a court-martial. Is Captain Queeg mentally unbalanced? That's the question explored in Stanley Roberts's scenario, filled with authentic dialogue. Humphrey Bogart's embodiment of Queeg gave the actor his last great role—and he plays the paranoiac captain superbly. Van Johnson plays the essentially decent court-martialed officer and Fred MacMurray enacts a lieutenant who is, at bottom, a snake. Edward Dmytryk directed the proceedings as an exercise in tension—broken only by a minor romantic subplot involving Robert Francis and May Wynn. *The Caine Mutiny*'s source is Herman Wouk's Pulitzer Prize novel of the same name—and the subsequent Broadway play (entitled *The Caine Mutiny Court Martial*).

The Candidate   1972   (Warner)   *Color*
Director: Michael Ritchie
Starring: Robert Redford, Peter Boyle, Don Porter, Allen Garfield, Karen Carlson, Quinn Redeker, Morgan Upton, Pat Harrington, Jr., Melvyn Douglas

This cynical look at the manipulation behind campaign politics, coproduced by Robert Redford, stands as one of the actor's few box office disappointments. Jeremy Larner, a former speechwriter for Eugene McCarthy, won an Oscar for his original screenplay. Redford stars as Bill McKay, a John F. Kennedy type from California who is a U.S. Senate aspirant. Initially regarded as a dark horse, he keeps gaining popularity. (Even his campaign director has underrated McKay's charisma.) Not so surprisingly, he beats the elderly incumbent. Redford's closing line is a classic: "What do we do now?" Don Porter plays the shrewd rival; Melvyn Douglas plays McKay's father, a retired governor; and Peter Boyle portrays the weaseling campaign manager.

Casey's Shadow   *Listed under Comedies.*

Cat on a Hot Tin Roof   1958   (MGM)   *Color*
Director: Richard Brooks
Starring: Elizabeth Taylor, Paul Newman, Burl Ives, Jack Carson, Judith Anderson, Madeleine Sherwood, Larry Gates, Vaughn Taylor, Vince Townsend, Jr.

A plantation home in the Mississippi Delta is the setting for Tennessee Williams's Pulitzer Prize play. Patriarch Big Daddy has returned from the hospital with the knowledge that he is dying of cancer; visiting him now at his vast estate are various relatives who squabble over the anticipated inheritance. The one person who cares little about wealth is Brick, Big Daddy's alcoholic, but best-loved son, whose marriage to Maggie the Cat is troubled beyond repair. The dramatist's analysis of "mendacity" is softened in the Richard Brooks-James Poe screenplay. Big Daddy's profanity and his boorish humor are missing from the movie version. Elizabeth Taylor stars as Maggie; Paul Newman plays Brick; Judith Anderson portrays Big Mama; and Jack Carson and Madeleine Sherwood play Gooper and Mae, parents of the "no-neck monsters." Burl Ives re-creates his Broadway role of Daddy. He received the supporting actor Oscar in 1958—not for *Cat on a Hot Tin Roof,* but for *The Big Country.*

The Champ   *Listed under Family Viewing/Children's.*

Champion   1949   (Republic)   *Black-and-White*
Director: Mark Robson
Starring: Kirk Douglas, Marilyn Maxwell, Arthur Kennedy, Paul Stewart, Ruth Roman, Lola Albright, Luis Van Rooten, Harry Shannon, John Day, Ralph Sanford

Kirk Douglas's star-making performance contributes an element of realism that makes *Champion* a classic. The story of defiant boxer Midge Kelly (Douglas) is recounted in flashbacks. Initially, he and his brother (Arthur Kennedy) are companion hoboes hitching rides to California. Work in postwar L.A. is not ample, so as a lark Midge accepts a challenge to climb into the ring. The roar of the crowd soon infects him—and he builds up an enviable record. Traveling the circuit, he constantly defies fight fixers, refusing to knuckle under to threats. But in his climb to the top, Midge also rebuffs his family and friends. Former editor Mark Robson had his first major directing success in *Champion.* Carl Foreman's screenscript, from a story of the same title by Ring Lardner, is darker than *Body and Soul* or almost any prizefight picture before—and many since. Frank Planer's low-key, black-and-white cinematography further lends authority to the production.

Chariots of Fire   1981   (Warner)   ◆ ★   *Color*
Director: Hugh Hudson
Starring: Ben Cross, Ian Charleson, Nicholas Farrell, Nigel Havers, Ian Holm, Sir John Gielgud, Lindsay Anderson, Nigel Davenport, Cheryl Campbell, Alice Krige, Dennis Christopher, Brad Davis, Patrick Magee, Peter Egan, Struan Rodger, David Yelland, Yves Beneyton, Daniel Gerroll, Jeremy Sinden

The focal point here is the 1924 Olympics competition in Paris, where two remarkably dissimilar runners vie for fame—though, ultimately, not in the same contests. Devout Scotsman Eric Liddell runs for God's glory and Harold Abrahams, a Jewish student at Protestant Cambridge, races against prejudice. Romanticism, patriotism, and religious fervor are the major themes. A wealth of talents collaborated on this rousing film— with what were (then) unknown stars and an untried director. Ultimately, critical acclaim and word-of-mouth made a virtual sleeper into a substantial hit. Winner of four Academy Awards (best picture; best screenplay—by Colin Welland; best original score— Vangelis; and best costume design—Milena Canonero), *Chariots of Fire* was also honored by the British Academy (picture; costume design; and supporting actor—Ian Holm). David Watkin is the cinematographer. The cast includes Ben Cross, who plays

Abrahams; Ian Charleson as Liddell; Ian Holm, playing Abraham's coach, Sam Mussabini; and, as other British Olympians, Nigel Havers, Nicholas Farrell, and Daniel Gerroll.

The China Syndrome   1979   (RCA)   · *Color*
Director: James Bridges
Starring: Jane Fonda, Jack Lemmon, Michael Douglas, Scott Brady, Peter Donat, James Hampton, Wilford Brimley, James Karen, Richard Herd, Daniel Valdez

This nuclear-age thriller can be viewed as an analysis of the paranoia spreading through America in the wake of Three Mile Island. Ironically, the film was long completed—and just beginning its first week of national release—when the Three Mile Island emergency occurred. In the fictional representation, Jack Lemmon plays the controller of a California nuclear power plant; after discovering an operational flaw and bringing it to the attention of his superiors, he must battle an administrative cover-up. Trying to help Lemmon publicize this affront to public safety are a TV news reporter and her cameraman (Jane Fonda and Michael Douglas). The screenplay is attributed to Mike Gray, T. S. Cook, and James Bridges. The latter directed.

The Cincinnati Kid   1965   (MGM)   *Color*
Director: Norman Jewison
Starring: Steve McQueen, Edward G. Robinson, Ann-Margret, Karl Malden, Tuesday Weld, Joan Blondell, Rip Torn, Jack Weston, Cab Calloway, Jeff Corey, Theo Marcuse, Milton Selzer, Karl Swenson

This variation on *The Hustler*'s parvenu–versus–old pro motif presents Steve McQueen as the Cincinnati Kid and Edward G. Robinson as his nemesis. The Kid is a cardsharp with dreams of glory as a poker champion. He assembles with other dedicated card players in New Orleans for a marathon stud poker match—with Lancey Howard, longtime professional gambler, as the man to beat. For decades Lancey has been invincible, but now the up-and-coming Kid senses victory. As in the Richard Jessup source novel, suspense is generated in the turn of a card. (Ring Lardner, Jr., and Terry Southern were the screenwriters.) Philip Lathrop shot the New Orleans backgrounds, Hal Ashby edited. Ray Charles sings the title tune.

Clash by Night   1952   (United)   *Black-and-White*
Director: Fritz Lang
Starring: Barbara Stanwyck, Paul Douglas, Robert Ryan, Marilyn Monroe, J. Carrol Naish, Keith Andes, Silvio Minciotti

Clifford Odets's 1942 playscript is given cinema transcription in this romantic melodrama directed by Fritz Lang. Paul Douglas plays a naïve coastal village fisherman who shyly romances, then marries Barbara Stanwyck, a hometown girl hardened by the big city. Local movie projectionist Robert Ryan has eyes for Stanwyck, too. This romantic triangle evolves in contrast to the rosier union of youngsters Marilyn Monroe and Keith Andes. Alfred Hayes wrote the script. Nicholas Musuraca's high-contrast black-and-white cinematography is a bonus.

Cleopatra   1963   (CBS)   ◆   *Color*
Director: Joseph L. Mankiewicz
Starring: Elizabeth Taylor, Richard Burton, Rex Harrison, Pamela Brown, George Cole,
Hume Cronyn, Cesare Danova, Kenneth Haigh, Andrew Keir, Martin Landau, Roddy
McDowall, Robert Stephens, Francesca Annis, Grégoire Aslan, Herbert Berghof, Michael
Gwynne, Michael Hordern, John Hoyt

Cleopatra's production history has been chronicled far and wide. What began as a $1.2 million project (when, in 1958, it was to star Joan Collins on the Fox backlot) became a $40 million fiasco—given inflationary adjustments, probably the most expensive movie in Hollywood history. The postproduction sentiments of director Joseph L. Mankiewicz, after countless disputes with studio heads: "They could cut it into banjo picks if they want." Elizabeth Taylor, of course, ultimately became the queen of the Nile. Richard Burton, in his first picture with his future wife, was Marc Antony. Completing the triumvirate: the Julius Caesar of Rex Harrison. Based on various classical sources, the screenplay was pieced together by Mankiewicz, Ranald Mac-Dougall, Sidney Buchman, and uncredited others—Marc Brandel, Nunnally Johnson, and Lawrence Durrell, to name a few. Critics assaulted the film. Audiences, however, rose to its support—though not in sufficient numbers. A few days after the premiere, approximately twenty minutes were cut. (A bonus in the video edition of *Cleopatra* is the restoration of these scenes.) The movie collected four Oscars: cinematography (Leon Shamroy), costume design, special effects, and art direction/set decoration. Beyond reveling in the pageantry, fans of television's "Upstairs, Downstairs" and "All in the Family" may want to keep an eye peeled for Jean Marsh as Octavia and Carroll O'Connor as Casca.

The Color Purple   1985   (Warner)   *Color*
Director: Steven Spielberg
Starring: Danny Glover, Adolph Caesar, Margaret Avery, Rae Dawn Chong, Whoopi
Goldberg, Oprah Winfrey, Leonard Jackson, Willard Pugh, Desreta Jackson

The ad copy promoting *The Color Purple* was all-inclusive: "It's about life. It's about love. It's about us." But most audiences agreed with the sentiments. Steven Spielberg's adaptation of Alice Walker's story was a Christmas crowd pleaser that attracted patrons well into 1986. Miss Walker's epistolary novel brought her (among other distinctions) the Pulitzer Prize and the American Book Award. The screenplay by Menno Meyjes, while assuming a reverential stance toward the original, also clearly reiterates its life-affirming themes. Of primary consideration are two sisters who emerge from a black family in rural Georgia during the early years of this century. Their separation and growth away from (then back to) their roots constitute the drama of *The Color Purple,* which marks the screen debut of stage actress Whoopi Goldberg. She incarnates Celie, the sister who is enslaved by marriage. Nominated for eleven Academy Awards, *The Color Purple* encountered formidable competition from *Out of Africa* and wound up without a single win. It did, however, collect the best picture prize from the National Board of Review.

Come Back to the 5 & Dime, Jimmy Dean, Jimmy Dean   1982   *Color*
    (Embassy)
Director: Robert Altman
Starring: Sandy Dennis, Cher, Karen Black, Sudie Bond, Kathy Bates, Marta Heflin

Nineteen-seventy-five. The twenty-year reunion of the James Dean Fan Club is underway at a dime store in McCarthy, Texas. The attendees, half a dozen women, were schoolmates in 1955 when the movie idol came to Texas to shoot *Giant*. Because the location site was near McCarthy, the adolescent girls were directly affected, some of them irrevocably. In Robert Altman's movie rendering of Ed Graczyk's Broadway play (also directed by Altman), the reunion triggers recollections and revelations. Of the latter, not the most astounding is one woman's disclosure that her son (heard but unseen) is the progeny of James Dean. Altman's actresses, re-creating their Broadway performances, are Sandy Dennis, Cher, Karen Black, Kathy Bates, Marta Heflin, and, as the owner of the five and dime, the late Sudie Bond.

Coming Home   1978   (CBS)   ◆   *Color*
Director: Hal Ashby
Starring: Jane Fonda, Jon Voight, Bruce Dern, Robert Carradine, Penelope Milford, Robert Ginty, Charles Cyphers, Tresa Hughes, Mary Jackson, Willie Tyler, David Clennon

An aftermath-of-Vietnam drama, *Coming Home* is one of the most potent antiwar declarations ever issued from Hollywood. The story, scripted by Waldo Salt and Robert C. Jones from an earlier screenplay by Nancy Dowd, begins in Los Angeles in 1968. A paraplegic soldier (Jon Voight) in a veterans' hospital is embittered by his experience in Southeast Asia—and by his present helplessness. He falls in love with a former high school classmate who is now a volunteer nurse (Jane Fonda)—while her husband, a gung-ho Marine captain (Bruce Dern), is overseas. As the affair progresses, the soldier becomes stronger, the woman more radicalized. Together they campaign against the war and for the rights of veterans. Then the hawkish captain comes home. In delineating how the war affected those on the home front, this picture took a courageous early stand on behalf of America's Vietnam vets. The Oscar roster: Voight for best actor; Fonda for best actress (*Klute*, in 1971, was her first win); and the three screenwriters.

The Conqueror   1956   (MCA)   *Color*
Director: Dick Powell
Starring: John Wayne, Susan Hayward, Pedro Armendariz, Agnes Moorehead, Thomas Gomez, John Hoyt, William Conrad, Ted De Corsia, Leslie Bradley, Lee Van Cleef, Peter Mamakos, Leo Gordon, Richard Loo, Sylvia Lewis, Jarma Lewis, Billy Curtis

A royal caravan escorting a Tartar princess across the Gobi Desert is attacked. Many of the travelers are massacred, but the princess is spared by the leader of the assault: the Mongol chieftain Temujin—better known by his honorary title, Genghis Khan (Perfect Warrior). To the horror of the young woman, Temujin decides to take her as his bride. The last film produced by Howard Hughes, *The Conqueror* dramatizes the barbarian leader's empire-building and his rocky courtship and marriage. John Wayne plays the title character; Susan Hayward enacts his (red-haired, fair-skinned) Tartar bride. Oscar Millard wrote the screenplay. In this enterprise action is all—and *The Conqueror* has action to spare.

Cool Hand Luke   1967   (Warner)   ◆   *Color*
Director: Stuart Rosenberg
Starring: Paul Newman, George Kennedy, J. D. Cannon, Lou Antonio, Robert Drivas, Strother Martin, Jo Van Fleet, Clifton James, Morgan Woodward, Luke Askew, Marc Cavell, Robert Donner, Warren Finnerty, Dennis Hopper, John McLiam, Wayne Rogers, Charles Tyner, Anthony Zerbe

Lucas Jackson, nicknamed Cool Hand Luke, is a prisoner on a Southern chain gang. Having no respect for authority, being a hard worker, a gifted poker player, and prison record-holder for consuming fifty hard-boiled eggs at a time, he is esteemed by the other convicts. After his repeated escape attempts and subsequent brutal beatings by guards, indomitable Luke becomes a symbol to his comrades. The scenario by Donn Pearce and Frank R. Pierson, from Pearce's novel, takes both a naturalistic and alle-gorical/messianic view of the central character. In Luke, Paul Newman found one of the most celebrated roles of his career. Jo Van Fleet plays Luke's ma; Dragline, the chain gang leader, brought George Kennedy his supporting actor Oscar; and Strother Martin, cast as the sadistic captain of the guards, delivers one of those immortal lines of dialogue: "What we got here is failure to communicate." In bit parts: Joe Don Baker as Fixer; Harry Dean Stanton as a tramp; Ralph Waite as Alibi; Richard Davalos, James Dean's *East of Eden* brother, as Blind Dick; and Donn Pearce—who created it all—as the sailor. The director of photography: Conrad Hall.

The Cotton Club   1984   (Embassy)   *Color*
Director: Francis Coppola
Starring: Richard Gere, Gregory Hines, Diane Lane, Lonette McKee, Bob Hoskins, James Remar, Nicolas Cage, Allen Garfield, Fred Gwynne, Gwen Verdon, Joe Dallesandro

The renowned Harlem night spot of the twenties and thirties was a magnet for some of America's greatest black musicians—and Prohibition's most notorious white rack-eteers. Francis Coppola's musical drama concentrates on two years (1928–30) in the Cotton Club's history, providing sidelong glances at both the illustrious dancers and singers (notably Cab Calloway) and the underworld kingpins (Dutch Schultz, Lucky Luciano)—and many fictional characters from both camps. *The Cotton Club*'s troubled development and production have been well documented. Initially, producer Robert Evans was scheduled to direct; then he brought Coppola on board as a script doctor; before long, Coppola was at the helm. (Among other contributors to the screenplay: Mario Puzo and Pulitzer Prize winner William Kennedy.) The finished product owes a large part of its success to Gregory Hines's tapping toes and the atmospheric pro-duction design of Richard Sylbert.

Country   1984   (Touchstone Home Video)   *Color*
Director: Richard Pearce
Starring: Jessica Lange, Sam Shepard, Wilford Brimley, Matt Clark, Therese Graham, Levi L. Knebel, Jim Haynie, Sandra Seacat, Alex Harvey, Stephanie-Stacie Poyner, Jim Ostercamp, Robert Somers, Frank Noel, Jr.

Jessica Lange produced and starred in this drama about an Iowa farm community battling banks, the elements, and governmental bureaucracy. To retain their land, farmers have been given thirty days to repay bank loans. Among those families facing the deadline is the one headed by Jewell Ivy (Lange) and farmer-husband Gil (Sam Shepard). *Country* shares some plotting similarities with *The River* and *Places in the Heart*, also released at the end of 1984. Written by William (*The Black Stallion*) Wittliff and directed by Richard (*Heartland*) Pearce, the film gathers its primary strength from its actors—noteworthily Wilford Brimley and, in his screen debut, Levi L. Knebel, as Lange and Shepard's teenage son. Further authenticity arises in David M. Walsh's winter landscape cinematography.

The Country Girl 1954 (Paramount) ◆ *Black-and-White*
Director: George Seaton
Starring: Bing Crosby, Grace Kelly, William Holden, Anthony Ross, Gene Reynolds, Jac-queline Fontaine, Eddie Ryder, Robert Kent, John W. Reynolds, Ida Moore, Frank Scanell, Ruth Rickaby

For her traditional values and conservative wardrobe, Georgie Ellis is referred to, semijokingly, by her husband as a "country girl." Georgie was Grace Kelly's ticket to Oscar glory—with the future princess partially disguising her cool beauty behind horn-rimmed glasses and shapeless, well-worn sweaters. *The Country Girl,* Clifford Odets's Broadway drama, analyzes the complex relationships shared by Georgie, constant and sensible; her husband Frank, a once-great actor now dependent on the bottle; and Bernie Dodd, the brash young director who casts Frank in a show headed for Broadway. In the film version, screenwriter-director George Seaton tailored the washed-up actor role for Bing Crosby. Thus, Frank is a crooner as well. (Crosby's three songs, by Ira Gershwin and Harold Arlen, comment obliquely on the action: "The Pitchman," "Live and Learn," and "The Search Is Through.") William Holden plays Bernie, the director who's a whiz at interpreting playscripts but misinterprets everything about Frank and Georgie. For an interesting comparison of approaches, see the Group W/Showtime pay cable production (available from Thorn EMI/HBO Video), wherein Faye Dunaway, Dick Van Dyke, and Ken Howard take on Georgie, Frank, and Bernie.

Crossfire 1947 (Nostalgia Merchant) *Black-and-White*
Director: Edward Dmytryk
Starring: Robert Young, Robert Mitchum, Robert Ryan, Gloria Grahame, Paul Kelly, Sam Levene, Jacqueline White, Steve Brodie, George Cooper, Richard Benedict, Richard Powers, William Phipps, Lex Barker, Robert Bray

This influential drama stands with *Gentleman's Agreement* as an early (post–World War II) example of Hollywood's condemnation of anti-Semitism. Adopting the framework of a thriller, *Crossfire* tells of the murder of a recently demobilized GI. His body is discovered in a New York hotel, and three other soldiers become suspects. In solving the case, police detective Robert Young learns that the young soldier was killed merely because he was Jewish. The murderer, an ex-sergeant played by Robert Ryan, tries to evade the police by implicating a buddy. John Paxton did the screen adaptation of Richard Brooks's *The Brick Foxhole,* and Edward Dmytryk directed. Generally regarded as Dmytryk's best film, *Crossfire* was not an Oscar winner, but it was nominated in numerous categories, including best picture—where it lost to *Gentleman's Agreement.*

Cyrano de Bergerac 1950 (Prism; Republic; ◆ *Black-and-White*
Electric Video; Video Yesteryear; Cable Films; Video Connection; Budget Video; Western Film and Video, Inc.; Select-a-Tape; Discount Video Tapes; Classic Video Cinema Collector's Club)
Director: Michael Gordon
Starring: José Ferrer, Mala Powers, William Prince, Morris Carnovsky, Ralph Clanton, Lloyd Corrigan, Virginia Farmer, Edgar Barrier, Elena Verdugo, Don Beddoe, Percy Hel-ton, Virginia Christine, Jerry Paris

Edmond Rostand's celebrated play provided the vehicle for José Ferrer's Oscar win as best actor. Ferrer, a renowned stage performer (Iago to Paul Robeson's Othello), had done only a few movies before *Cyrano de Bergerac.* His interpretation of Rostand's romantic hero established him in Hollywood and in the years immediately thereafter, he was cast as Toulouse-Lautrec in *Moulin Rouge*, the clergyman in *Miss Sadie Thompson*, and the defending attorney in *The Caine Mutiny*. *Cyrano*, from Carl Foreman's screenplay by way of Brian Hooker's translation, is a faithful screen adaptation. The costumes and picturesque settings work as accoutrements to the poetry. There are admirable secondary performances, but Ferrer's dashing, big-nosed poet-soldier is appropriately at the center of the spectacle.

The Damned   1969   (Warner)   *Color*
Director: Luchino Visconti
Starring: Dirk Bogarde, Ingrid Thulin, Helmut Griem, Helmut Berger, Charlotte Rampling, Florinda Bolkan, Renaud Verley, René Koldehoff, Albrecht Schönhals, Umberto Orsini

The Damned has been alternately revered and reviled. Thirties Germany furnishes the backdrop for this explicit (originally X-rated) Luchino Visconti drama. Under the filmmaker's observation is a Krupp-like dynasty of industrialists. Viewed in microcosm, the family members are individually or collectively linked with the political ideologies of the Third Reich—and its decadent, psychotic underpinnings. Ingrid Thulin is cast as a vampirish mother who both corrupts and is corrupted by her dope-addicted transvestite son (Helmut Berger). Dirk Bogarde plays Thulin's lover—and her partner in a munitions manufacturing empire. Visconti's story, co-written with Nicola Badalucco and Enrico Medioli, is recounted in a style embracing both grand opera (specifically Wagner) and Grand Guignol.

The Dark Mirror   1946   (Republic)   *Black-and-White*
Director: Robert Siodmak
Starring: Olivia de Havilland, Lew Ayres, Thomas Mitchell, Richard Long, Garry Owen, Charles Evans

"The mirror is everything in reverse," a doctor explains to distraught Olivia de Havilland. Mirrors haunt the heroine of this melodrama—with de Havilland playing mirror-image twin sisters. One of them is (relatively) normal; the other is a demented murderess. A psychiatrist (Lew Ayres) and a police detective (Thomas Mitchell) join forces to determine which is which. Part of the sleuthing involves inkblot and word-association tests. Nunnally Johnson's screenplay, from an original story by Vladimir Posner, abounds in twists and red herrings; under Robert Siodmak's guidance, the story gathers momentum as it races toward the final revelation. *The Dark Mirror* became a movie for television in 1984, starring Jane Seymour, Stephen Collins, and Vincent Gardenia.

Darling   1965   (Embassy)   ◆   *Black-and-White*
Director: John Schlesinger
Starring: Julie Christie, Dirk Bogarde, Laurence Harvey, Roland Curram, Alex Scott, Basil Henson, José Luis de Villalonga, Trevor Bowen, Pauline Yates, Peter Bayliss

The title character is a London model and would-be actress. As she tells her life story to a magazine reporter, the camera flashes back on her adventures: an early marriage, an affair with a TV writer-interviewer, an abortion, a movie appearance, other affairs, travels on the continent, followed by another unhappy marriage—to an Italian prince with seven children. The antiheroine, played by Julie Christie, is a symbol of sixties despair, a victim of mod rootlessness. In fabricating her biography, scenarist Frederic Raphael also weaves a slashing social satire. (Raphael later wrote the teleplay "The Glittering Prizes," which was textured by some behind-the-scenes *Darling* anecdotes.) Directed by John Schlesinger, who had just worked with Julie Christie on *Billy Liar*. Oscars went to Christie and Raphael.

The Day of the Jackal   1973   (MCA)   *Color*
Director: Fred Zinnemann
Starring: Edward Fox, Alan Badel, Cyril Cusack, Michel Lonsdale, Ronald Pickup, Eric Porter, Delphine Seyrig, Donald Sinden, Michel Auclair, Tony Britton, Olga Georges-Picot, Barrie Ingham, Derek Jacobi, Maurice Denham, Anton Rodgers, Timothy West

Manhunt melodrama. Jackal is the code name for an English hitman hired by the OAS to assassinate General De Gaulle. Kenneth Ross's screenplay, based on the Frederick Forsyth best-seller, is set in 1963—so the climax is no surprise: De Gaulle lives. Still, director Fred Zinnemann generates an inordinate amount of suspense as the Jackal makes his elaborate preparations for the hit. Meanwhile, French and British police join ranks to trap the assassin. Edward Fox plays the cool, efficient professional gunman, while the performances by other key actors—Alan Badel, Cyril Cusack, Tony Britton—are on a par with their finest work. Other contributions are made by composer Georges Delerue and cameraman Jean Tournier.

The Day of the Locust   1975   (Paramount)   *Color*
Director: John Schlesinger
Starring: Donald Sutherland, Karen Black, Burgess Meredith, William Atherton, Geraldine Page, Richard A. Dysart, Bo Hopkins, Lelia Goldoni, Natalie Schafer, Jackie Earle Haley, Billy Barty

Nathanael West's dark satire of 1930s Hollywood—a grim and ambivalent novel—was inspired by the author's experiences as a screenwriter. In the film version, scripted by Waldo Salt, William Atherton plays West's stand-in, Tod Hackett, the narrator/bystander around whom all the major events occur. Tod, a young painter aspiring to a position in a studio art department, witnesses the eccentricities, the naked ambition, and the ruthlessness that surround the film community. Costarring with Atherton are Donald Sutherland as Homer Simpson, the repressed accountant from Iowa; Karen Black as Faye Greener, a would-be actress; and Burgess Meredith as Faye's father, a former vaudevillian who now sells miracle elixir door to door. The movie's chief distinctions are the photography of Conrad Hall and the production design by Richard MacDonald; they dramatically and visually transport the tawdriness (and latent violence) West described.

Days of Heaven   1978   (Paramount)   ◆   *Color*
Director: Terrence Malick
Starring: Richard Gere, Brooke Adams, Sam Shepard, Linda Manz, Robert Wilke, Jackie Shultis, Stuart Margolin, Tim Scott, Gene Bell, Doug Kershaw, Richard Libertini

Written and directed by Terrence Malick after his *Badlands* debut, *Days of Heaven* tells the story of three migrant workers who, in 1916, leave Chicago for the wheatfields of the Texas Panhandle. The three nomads are Bill (Richard Gere), his girl Abby (Brooke Adams), and his kid sister Linda (Linda Manz). In Texas they strike up an uneasy friendship with their employer (Sam Shepard), who asks them to remain after the harvesting. A tragic love triangle is born among Bill, Abby, and the farm owner. Little Linda narrates all these events (and their fiery climax). Malick's dialogue is lean and laconic, so Linda's deadpan, matter-of-fact narration gives the movie a balladlike quality— further amplified in the graceful camerawork of Nestor Almendros. (*Days of Heaven* was his first American film; when he had to leave a few weeks before shooting was finished, Haskell Wexler completed the cinematography.) For his endeavors, Almendros was awarded an Oscar.

Days of Wine and Roses   1962   (Warner)   ◆   *Black-and-White*
Director: Blake Edwards
Starring: Jack Lemmon, Lee Remick, Charles Bickford, Jack Klugman, Alan Hewitt, Debbie Megowan, Katherine Squire, Maxine Stuart, Jack Albertson, Ken Lynch, Tom Palmer, Gail Bonney

As this drama set in San Francisco unfurls, a formerly happy-go-lucky public relations man (Jack Lemmon) becomes an alcoholic. In desperation and almost as a gesture of companionship, his wife (Lee Remick) turns to the bottle, too. The husband's ultimate awakening sets him on a gradual course of recovery, but his wife is unable to give up her addiction. J. P. Miller's *Days of Wine and Roses,* adapted from his "Playhouse 90" telescript, is a grim update on *The Lost Weekend* and other stories, onscreen and off, dramatizing alcohol abuse. Charles Bickford gives a sensitive reading of Remick's straitlaced father. The Henry Mancini-Johnny Mercer title song won an Oscar; it was the second consecutive win for the team, whose "Moon River" was the 1961 best song.

Death Hunt   1981   (CBS)   *Color*
Director: Peter Hunt
Starring: Charles Bronson, Lee Marvin, Andrew Stevens, Angie Dickinson, Ed Lauter, Carl Weathers, Henry Beckman

Charles Bronson plays yet another loner hero in this action adventure set in Canada in 1931. Based on the story of a real-life trapper who was framed for murder, the screenplay of Michael Grais and Mark Victor validates the protagonist's innocence, then traces his escape into the Yukon—with the Mounties and others in pursuit. Bronson plays the unjustly accused trapper; Lee Marvin is cast as the leader of the RCMP posse. When *Death Hunt* was released, the film's publicists trumpeted the trapper's adventure as the largest manhunt in Canadian history. Angie Dickinson, whose coif and costume seem not at all in period, does a cameo.

Decameron Nights   1953   (Hal Roach Studios;   *Black-and-White*
     Video Gems; Discount Video Tapes; Video Treasures)
Director: Hugo Fregonese
Starring: Joan Fontaine, Louis Jourdan, Binnie Barnes, Joan Collins, Godfrey Tearle, Eliot Makeham, Marjorie Rhodes, Noel Purcell

This costume drama is, at heart, a compilation of risqué tales by fourteenth-century Italian storyteller Giovanni Boccaccio. Louis Jourdan plays Boccaccio, ardently pursuing his latest love (Joan Fontaine). To woo her, he narrates a series of witty (and moderately licentious) tales. The screenplay by George Oppenheimer dramatizes these stories, thus yielding Jourdan and Fontaine several roles beyond their initial ones. Guy Green, soon thereafter known for his directorial achievements (*The Mark, A Patch of Blue*), is credited with the black-and-white cinematography. In one of her first motion picture appearances, Joan Collins enacts a glamourous woman with a wicked tongue.

The Deer Hunter   1978   (MCA)   ◆ ✳   *Color*
Director: Michael Cimino
Starring: Robert De Niro, John Cazale, John Savage, Meryl Streep, Christopher Walken, George Dzundza, Chuck Aspergren, Rutanya Alda, Shirley Stoler, Amy Wright

The Deer Hunter opens on the last day of work for three young steel mill workers who are lifelong buddies. The trio (Robert De Niro, John Savage, Christopher Walken) are leaving their small Pennsylvania town, having enlisted in the 101st Airborne Division. After a wedding, a deer hunt, and a heavy drinking farewell party, they are off to training. When next we see them, they are prisoners of the Vietcong—and it is up to the De Niro character to animate his friends' will to survive. Two of the three heroes make it back to Pennsylvania. The third, we learn, is still alive in Vietnam. Michael Cimino's film, scripted by Deric Washburn, has many difficult-to-watch war sequences, marked by graphic prison camp tortures. But beyond its depiction of Vietnam, the film is, first and foremost, an absorbing examination of machismo. It earned the top New York Film Critics' prize and was awarded five Oscars: best picture, director, supporting actor (Walken), editing (Peter Zinner), and sound.

The Defiant Ones   1958   (CBS)   ◆   *Black-and-White*
Director: Stanley Kramer
Starring: Tony Curtis, Sidney Poitier, Theodore Bikel, Charles McGraw, Lon Chaney, Jr., King Donovan, Claude Akins, Lawrence Dobkin, Whit Bissell, Carl Switzer, Kevin Coughlin, Cara Williams

Two chained-together convicts, one black, one white, make a desperate break for freedom in this Stanley Kramer production. A groundbreaking movie in its depiction of racial themes, *The Defiant Ones* dramatizes the prisoners' encounters with various people along their escape route. Tony Curtis and Sidney Poitier turn the leading characters into men who are constantly surprised at their shifting emotions; their mutual hatred finally mellows when they realize their commonality. The picture was honored in two Oscar categories: cinematography (Sam Leavitt) and the original screenplay by Nathan E. Douglas (blacklisted actor Nedrick Young) and Harold Jacob Smith. Angus, one of the trackers, was the last film role of Carl "Alfalfa" Switzer, star of the "Our Gang" comedies. A TV remake of *The Defiant Ones* was aired in 1986, with Robert Urich and Carl Weathers in the Curtis-Poitier roles.

Deliverance   1972   (Warner)   *Color*
Director: John Boorman
Starring: Jon Voight, Burt Reynolds, Ned Beatty, Ronny Cox, Bill McKinney, Herbert "Cowboy" Coward, James Dickey, Ed Ramey, Billy Redden, Seamon Glass

This disquieting look at the rites of manhood frames its theme in a nightmarish melodrama. Four friends, Atlanta businessmen, go on a weekend canoe trip. The quartet little realize how deadly nature—or mankind—can be. Before the weekend concludes, they confront raging rapids, bestial mountaineers, and murder. The beauty of nature is recorded in the long, smooth takes of cinematographer Vilmos Zsigmond. The horror is supplied in the scenario and dialogue of James Dickey, derived from his best-selling novel. The four hapless protagonists are embodied by Burt Reynolds, Ned Beatty,

Ronny Cox, and Jon Voight—with the latter emerging as the most heroic. Novelist-screenwriter Dickey plays the sheriff in the film's concluding section. One of the best moments (and one of the few tranquil ones): the "Dueling Banjos" duet between Ronny Cox and a retarded mountain boy.

The Devil at 4 O'Clock   1961   (RCA)   *Color*
Director: Mervyn LeRoy
Starring: Spencer Tracy, Frank Sinatra, Kerwin Mathews, Jean-Pierre Aumont, Grégoire Aslan, Alexander Scourby, Barbara Luna, Cathy Lewis, Bernie Hamilton, Martin Brandt, Lou Merrill, Marcel Dalio

Max Catto's adventure novel is given a fiery screen rendition in this downbeat melodrama, scripted by Liam O'Brien. Father Matthew Doonan (Spencer Tracy) is an alcoholic missionary engaged in saving souls on a volcanic South Seas island. Part of his flock is a colony of leper children. Arriving to test Father Doonan's faith and challenge his benevolent authority are three escaped convicts. The precarious situation worsens when the long-dormant volcano starts erupting and the island must be evacuated. Under Mervyn LeRoy's direction, the climactic lava flow, captured by Joseph Biroc's camera, affords a blazing finale.

A Different Story   *Listed under Comedies.*

Diner   *Listed under Comedies.*

Doctor Zhivago   1965   (MGM)   ◆   *Color*
Director: David Lean
Starring: Geraldine Chaplin, Julie Christie, Tom Courtenay, Alec Guinness, Siobhan McKenna, Ralph Richardson, Omar Sharif, Rod Steiger, Rita Tushingham

Script streamlining diminished the scope and complexity of Boris Pasternak's novel, but David Lean's production is a bona fide epic, rooted in the upheavals leading to the Russian Revolution, while thrusting into the foreground the intimate human drama surrounding the title character. Particularly notable are Omar Sharif, Julie Christie, Tom Courtenay, and Geraldine Chaplin—at this juncture giving indications of what later became successful screen careers for them all. Oscars went to Robert Bolt's screenplay, Maurice Jarre's score, Freddie Young's cinematography, Phyllis Dalton's costumes, and to the art direction/set decoration team.

Dog Day Afternoon   1975   (Warner)   ◆   *Color*
Director: Sidney Lumet
Starring: Al Pacino, John Cazale, Charles Durning, James Broderick, Chris Sarandon, Carol Kane, Sully Boyar, Penny Allen, Florence Stanley

It's a sweltering dog day afternoon in the summer of 1972 when two would-be robbers decide to stick up a Brooklyn bank. Sonny (Al Pacino), a Vietnam veteran, is a former bank clerk; so he's in touch with the routine. Sal (John Cazale), his buddy, is in touch with reality—least of all reality. When an accomplice deserts them and there is hardly any money in the vault *and* a battalion of New York's finest dots the street outside, both Sonny and Sal grow increasingly unhinged. What is intended as a five-minute heist turns into a twelve-hour media event. Sonny, as a liaison between the police and the bank employee hostages, becomes an instant celebrity. Frank Pierson's script, taken from the Patrick Mann novel, dramatizes an actual event. In filmic context, *Dog Day Afternoon* is a tragicomedy, with heavy emphasis on the comedy. Pierson took home an Oscar for his screenplay.

A Double Life   1947   (Republic)   ◆   *Black-and-White*
Director: *George Cukor*
Starring: *Ronald Colman, Signe Hasso, Edmond O'Brien, Shelley Winters, Ray Collins, Philip Loeb, Millard Mitchell, Joe Sawyer, Charles La Torre, Whit Bissell*

Ronald Colman, whose career spanned more than thirty years, appeared in movies as diverse as *Arrowsmith, A Tale of Two Cities, Lost Horizon,* and *Random Harvest.* But it was only at the twilight of his film career, in 1947, that he gained Oscar recognition. Colman was named best actor for his interpretation of a brilliant, though paranoiac, thespian who begins to confuse real life with his stage role—Othello. He imagines that his actress-wife (Signe Hasso), who is also his Desdemona, is having an affair with their agent (Edmond O'Brien). His unfounded suspicions lead not only to his own madness but to tragedy for others. This melodrama was written by Ruth Gordon and Garson Kanin and directed by their frequent collaborator, George Cukor. Miklos Rozsa joined Colman as an Academy Award recipient; he was cited for "best scoring of a dramatic or comedy picture."

Downhill Racer   1969   (Paramount)   *Color*
Director: *Michael Ritchie*
Starring: *Robert Redford, Gene Hackman, Camilla Sparv, Karl Michael Vogler, Jim McMullan, Christian Doermer, Dabney Coleman, Joe Jay Jalbert, Timothy Kirk, Kathleen Crowley*

This lively sports film deals with the price of fame, the sacrifice of being a champion athlete. Robert Redford portrays a semipro who comes to Europe as a last-minute replacement on the U.S. Olympic ski team. Vying for the top spot in the downhill competitions, he does not deny his acquisitive, aggressive behavior. Location photography (by Brian Probyn) was accomplished at the 1968 Winter Olympics in Grenoble, France, and other scenic continental slopes. The caroming skiers are a breathtaking sight, and the downhill racing rivals the great chases in *Bullitt, The French Connection,* and any number of Bond films. Director Michael Ritchie, working from a screenplay by James Salter, adds new dimensions to the standard sports feature. *Downhill Racer* contains both adventure and psychological insight into the codes of competition. Gene Hackman plays the team-spirited coach.

The Dresser   1983   (RCA)   *Color*
Director: *Peter Yates*
Starring: *Albert Finney, Tom Courtenay, Edward Fox, Zena Walker, Eileen Atkins, Michael Gough, Lockwood West, Cathryn Harrison, Ann Manion, Ann Way*

Ronald Harwood's screenplay, from his West End and Broadway original, assesses an unstable Shakespearean actor-manager touring the hinterlands in World War II Britain (and modeled loosely on Sir Donald Wolfit). Sir, as he is known, counts Othello and King Lear as part of his repertory. Now past his peak, Sir is coddled by Norman, his manservant. Their mutually supportive and abusive relationship is the centerpiece of *The Dresser.* Under Peter Yates's direction, Albert Finney plays Sir, and Tom Courtenay portrays Norman. These character studies provide an insightful look at wartime England and the squalid milieu of second-rate provincial theatricals. Alan Boyle accomplished the makeup designs.

The Duellists   1977   (Paramount)   *Color*
Director: Ridley Scott
Starring: Keith Carradine, Harvey Keitel, Edward Fox, Cristina Raines, Robert Stephens, Diana Quick, Tom Conti, John McEnery, Alan Webb, Jenny Runacre, Meg Wynn-Owen, Albert Finney

Placed during the Napoleonic wars, Joseph Conrad's short story, "The Duel," covers a long-running fued between two French cavalry officers. One soldier imagines that the other has insulted him and challenges the offender to a duel. Only a slight injury results—and so, as the years pass, through war and peace, other duels take place between the two *sabreurs*. *The Duellists,* as the screen edition is called, is the first feature-length work of former TV director Ridley Scott, subsequently lauded for *Alien, Blade Runner,* and *Legend.* Keith Carradine stars as Lieutenant D'Hubert, the rational aristocrat, and Harvey Keitel as Lieutenant (ultimately General) Feraud, the spiteful antagonist from a lower class. Filling smaller roles are many British notables—Albert Finney, Tom Conti, and Edward Fox, to name three. Gerald Vaughan-Hughes wrote the screenplay, and Frank Tidy was the director of photography.

Earthquake   1974   (MCA)   ◆   *Color*
Director: Mark Robson
Starring: Charlton Heston, Ava Gardner, George Kennedy, Geneviève Bujold, Lorne Greene, Richard Roundtree, Marjoe Gortner, Victoria Principal, Barry Sullivan, Lloyd Nolan, Monica Lewis, Lloyd Gough, John Randolph, Scott Hylands, Kip Niven, Pedro Armendariz, Jr., Gabriel Dell

Los Angeles is shaken by a series of earthquakes. The third tremor causes major destruction. This Jennings Lang-Mark Robson production emerged in the heyday of disaster epics (*The Poseidon Adventure, The Towering Inferno,* the *Airport* cycle, et al.), and its principal claim to fame was its initial release in a process termed Sensurround: rumbling noises on the sound track that made the cinema seats quiver too. But in *Earthquake* the (Academy Award–winning) visual effects are the stars; freeways buckle, buildings implode, dams burst, the ground opens to yawning chasms. Amid the noise and devastation are such performers as Charlton Heston, Ava Gardner, Lloyd Nolan, Lorne Green, George Kennedy and Geneviève Bujold. In a bit, Walter Matuschanskayasky plays a bar-room drunk; the actor is better known under his adopted surname: Matthau. George Fox and Mario (*The Godfather*) Puzo wrote the script.

East of Eden   1955   (Warner)   ◆   *Color*
Director: Elia Kazan
Starring: Julie Harris, James Dean, Raymond Massey, Burl Ives, Jo Van Fleet, Richard Davalos, Albert Dekker, Lois Smith, Harold Gordon, Richard Garrick, Timothy Carey, Nick Dennis, Lonny Chapman, Barbara Baxley

John Steinbeck's *East of Eden* is a modern interpretation of the biblical Cain and Abel story—placed in California during World War I. The movie version, directed by Elia Kazan, is from an adaptation by Paul Osborn that pares down the text (by almost half) and takes much of the dialogue directly from Steinbeck. James Dean plays Cal; Richard

Davalos plays Aron; Raymond Massey portrays their stern father, Adam. Both sons compete for the old man's favor; their rivalry drives an even deeper wedge into the heart of the family. *East of Eden* is James Dean's first starring role. Other supporting players are Julie Harris, playing Abra, his girl, and Jo Van Fleet, who won an Oscar for her portrayal of Kate, the shadow figure of a mother—now running a nearby brothel. *East of Eden* became a seven-hour miniseries in the 1980–81 television season; Jane Seymour, Timothy Bottoms, and Bruce Boxleitner starred.

Easy Rider   1969   (RCA)   ❉   *Color*
Director: Dennis Hopper
Starring: Peter Fonda, Dennis Hopper, Luana Anders, Luke Askew, Toni Basil, Karen Black, Warren Finnerty, Sabrina Scharf, Robert Walker, Phil Spector, Jack Nicholson

Wyatt and Billy are easy riders (dope dealers). After concluding an unusually profitable haul, they celebrate by biking "in search of America," caroming eastward from L.A. across the desert southwest to their ultimate destination: New Orleans at Mardi Gras. This odyssey of the open road is a counterculture classic. When it premiered, audiences disillusioned by Vietnam took it to heart, reveling in Dennis Hopper's direction (and Donn Cambern's editing) and the power of Laszlo Kovacs's landscape shots. Written by leading players Hopper and Fonda, with contributions from Terry Southern, *Easy Rider* can now be viewed as a central artifact of the sixties. Jack Nicholson, heretofore cast in horror films and sex-cycle-and-drugs programs, plays a sometime lawyer and full-time civil rights advocate. Hopper was designated best new director at the 1969 Cannes Film Festival. On the soundtrack: Carole King, Jimi Hendrix, Bob Dylan, The Byrds, The Band, Steppenwolf, and many others.

The Electric Horseman   1979   (MCA)   *Color*
Director: Sydney Pollack
Starring: Robert Redford, Jane Fonda, Valerie Perrine, Willie Nelson, John Saxon, Nicolas Coster, Allan Arbus, Wilford Brimley

Meet Sonny Steele, an ex–rodeo rider and a has-been star of cowboy movies. Nowadays, Sonny is employed as the spokesman for a breakfast cereal company; so he tours the country decked out in neo-dude ranch apparel studded with twinkling lights—a parody of his former persona. At a glitzy Las Vegas convention, his abhorrence of show business sham reaches its peak when he learns that his employers' corporate mascot, a multimillion-dollar racehorse, has been pumped with steroids. Sonny's actions to save the thoroughbred bring on a man- and horsehunt across several states. *The Electric Horseman* is a comedy-drama with a moral, developed in a way by writer Robert Garland and director Sydney Pollack so that the message doesn't overwhelm the entertainment. The director of photography is Owen Roizman. In their third screen pairing, after *The Chase* and *Barefoot in the Park*, Robert Redford and Jane Fonda costar as the title character and the sympathetic newswoman who aids him. Their performances are bolstered by John Saxon and Nicolas Coster as villains, Valerie Perrine playing Sonny's wife, and Willie Nelson in his movie acting debut.

Elmer Gantry   1960   (CBS)   ◆   *Color*
Director: Richard Brooks
Starring: Burt Lancaster, Jean Simmons, Arthur Kennedy, Shirley Jones, Dean Jagger, Patti Page, Edward Andrews, John McIntire, Joe Maross, Everett Glass, Michael Whalen, Hugh Marlowe, Philip Ober

Elmer Gantry is a flamboyant and ruthless evangelist spreading the Gospel in the 1920s. Gantry teams up with Sister Sharon Falconer, a sincere minister-healer, and travels with her on the revival circuit throughout the Midwest. Muckraking journalist Jim Lefferts and Lulu Baines, a former girlfriend betrayed by Gantry, try to unmask the opportunism of the traveling religion show. Writer-director Richard Brooks's production is based on the classic 1927 novel by Sinclair Lewis. The cinematographer was John Alton and the art director Edward Carrere. Strong characterizations are contributed by all the actors. Oscar night brought three statuettes *Elmer Gantry*'s way: Shirley Jones, as Lulu Baines, was named best supporting actress; Brooks won in the adapted screenplay category; and Burt Lancaster claimed the best actor prize for his portrayal of Gantry.

Elvira Madigan   1967   (Thorn)   *Color*
Director: Bo Widerberg
Starring: Pia Degermark, Thommy Berggren, Lennart Malmert, Nina Widerberg, Cleo Jensen

Sweden, 1889. Count Sixten Sparre (Thommy Berggren) is an army lieutenant who longs for a time when men "will be allowed to make more than one life for themselves." Elvira Madigan (Pia Degermark) is a coquettish teenager who works as a circus tightrope dancer. The two young people fall in love, even though Sixten is already a husband and father. As their affair develops, the lieutenant deserts his regiment (and his wife and children). He and Elvira run away to the Danish countryside, where they hope to live in a sylvan paradise. But all is not idyllic. The lovers run out of money and wander hungry in the woods. Ultimately, plagued by their past but still madly in love, they enter a suicide pact. The legend of Sixten and Elvira is based on fact. The film version is the best-known feature film of writer-editor-director Bo Widerberg, who also directed *Joe Hill. Elvira Madigan* is enhanced by Jorgen Persson's cinematography. Much of the tale is underscored by the romantic strains of Mozart's Piano Concerto no. 21.

Equus   1977   (MGM)   *Color*
Director: Sidney Lumet
Starring: Richard Burton, Peter Firth, Colin Blakely, Joan Plowright, Harry Andrews, Eileen Atkins, Jenny Agutter, Kate Reid

This study in abnormal psychology begins when a seventeen-year-old stablehand blinds six horses with a steel spike. A psychiatrist is assigned to analyze the tragedy and learns that the boy worships the horse-god, Equus. Upon investigating further, the doctor pieces together the events that led up to the shocking incident. *Equus* is a kind of intellectual detective story—separate interviews with the stableboy, his parents, his employers, his girlfriend—punctuated by monologues from the psychiatrist. Volcanic emotions erupt in Peter Shaffer's screenplay, adapted from his London-to-New York stage success. Richard Burton, who, as Dr. Martin Dysart, replaced Anthony Perkins on Broadway, repeats the role here. Peter Firth, costar of both West End and New York original casts, plays the troubled teenager, Alan Strang.

Escape from Alcatraz   1979   (Paramount)   *Color*
Director: Don Siegel
Starring: Clint Eastwood, Patrick McGoohan, Roberts Blossom, Jack Thibeau, Fred Ward, Paul Benjamin, Larry Hankin

Clint Eastwood, in an uncharacteristically reflective role, plays Frank Norris, an inmate at the infamous Rock in San Francisco Bay. He and two other prisoners devise an escape plan, then execute it. *Escape from Alcatraz,* directed by Don Siegel, is based on real events surrounding a sixties breakout, as recounted in J. Campbell Bruce's book. The screenplay adaptation is by Richard Tuggle, who later directed Eastwood in *Tightrope.* As the gruff warden, Patrick McGoohan proves a vigorous adversary for the escapees. The finale duplicates the true story: After his successful (?) escape, Frank Norris was never heard from again.

Excalibur   1981   (Warner)   *Color*
Director: John Boorman
Starring: Nigel Terry, Helen Mirren, Nicol Williamson, Nicholas Clay, Cherie Lunghi, Corin Redgrave, Paul Geoffrey

Writer-director John Boorman and his coscenarist, Rospo Pallenberg, relate the Camelot legend as a three-generation saga: first, Uther Pendragon, king of Britain; then, Arthur, his illegitimate son, who must prove his right to be king; and finally, Mordred, Arthur's illegitimate son. Some familiar ingredients augment the Boorman-Pallenberg rendition: the magic of Merlin, Arthur's mentor; the hero's receipt of Excalibur, his powerful sword, from the Lady of the Lake; the wooing of Guinevere; the pageantry of the Round Table. In addition, *Excalibur* is a sexually charged depiction of the sorcery of Morgan Le Fay and the love affairs between Arthur and Guinevere, then Guinevere and Lancelot. The guiding vision here (Boorman's) is romantic; Alex Thomson's camera work and Anthony Pratt's sets contribute mightily. The major players: Nigel Terry (Arthur), Cherie Lunghi (Guinevere), Nicholas Clay (Lancelot), Helen Mirren (Morgan Le Fay), and Nicol Williamson (Merlin).

Exodus   *Listed under War.*

A Face in the Crowd   1957   (Warner)   *Black-and-White*
Director: Elia Kazan
Starring: Andy Griffith, Patricia Neal, Anthony Franciosa, Walter Matthau, Lee Remick, Percy Waram, Rod Brasfield, Charles Irving, Howard Smith, Paul McGrath, Kay Medford, Alexander Kirkland

Lonesome Rhodes, a cracker-barrel philosopher from Piggott, Arkansas, is the focal point for *A Face in the Crowd.* The character was introduced in Budd Schulberg's short story, "Your Arkansas Traveler." (When the film was released, the story was expanded for novelization tie-in purposes.) Andy Griffith, in his debut, portrays Lonesome. Patricia Neal plays the reporter who discovers him and promotes him into a national TV star. Lonesome hobnobs with the wealthy and the powerful—and his down-home humor and country songs thrust him into the limelight. At the peak of his celebrity, he hosts a network variety show. Unfortunately, as Lonesome scrambles up the status ladder, he also becomes megalomaniacal, almost fascistic. Schulberg's comedy-drama was directed by Elia Kazan. Beyond Griffith and Neal, there are characterizations by Anthony Franciosa, Walter Matthau, and, as baton-twirling champion Betty Lou Fleckum, Lee Remick. *A Face in the Crowd* was Remick's first movie, too.

Fail Safe   1964   (RCA)   *Black-and-White*
Director: Sidney Lumet
*Starring: Henry Fonda, Walter Matthau, Fritz Weaver, Dan O'Herlihy, Sorrell Booke,
Larry Hagman, Frank Overton, Edward Binns, Russell Collins, Bob Gerringer, Dom De
Luise*

Although *Fail Safe* is a melodrama, to many it is similar to the Kubrick comedy, *Dr.
Strangelove,* in premise, conflict, and resolution. Henry Fonda is cast as the U.S. president striving to avert thermonuclear warfare. One of our planes has been accidentally
ordered to bomb Moscow. To avoid a nuclear showdown between America and the
Soviet Union, Fonda has to agree to a horrifying retaliation. The screenplay, derived
from the Eugene Burdick-Harvey Wheeler novel, is by Walter Bernstein. Lumet's
direction is intense, and his actors are chilling.

Fanny   1961   (Warner)   *Color*
Director: Joshua Logan
*Starring: Leslie Caron, Maurice Chevalier, Charles Boyer, Horst Buchholz, Salvatore
Baccaloni, Lionel Jeffries, Raymond Bussières, Victor Francen, Georgette Anys, Joel
Flateau*

The Broadway musical of *Fanny* was inspired by Marcel Pagnol's classic film trilogy—
Marius (1931), *Fanny* (1932), and *César* (1936)—about several volatile characters on
the Marseilles waterfront. In adapting the musical for the screen, Josh Logan (and his
scenarist Julius J. Epstein) dropped the songs and used the music as underscoring. The
plot remains the same: Marius (Horst Buchholz), whose father, César (Charles Boyer),
runs a dockside bar, abandons his fiancée, Fanny (Leslie Caron), in order to travel the
seven seas. After he leaves, Fanny marries elderly Panisse (Maurice Chevalier) and
gives birth—to the child of Marius. The cinematography is by Jack Cardiff. (*Fanny*
was filmed on location in Marseilles, and at the Château d'If and Notre Dame de la
Garde.)

The Farmer's Daughter   *Listed under Comedies.*

First Blood   1982   (Thorn)   *Color*
Director: Ted Kotcheff
*Starring: Sylvester Stallone, Richard Crenna, Brian Dennehy, Bill McKinney, Jack Star-
rett, Michael Talbot, David Caruso, David Crowley, Chris Mulkey, Alf Humphries*

John Rambo (Sylvester Stallone), a former Green Beret who has had difficulty adjusting
to post-Vietnam America, is backpacking through the Pacific Northwest. Unjustly
imprisoned by a small town sheriff who doesn't like his looks, the veteran breaks out
of jail and leads local, state, and federal law enforcement officers on an action-filled
chase. Rambo, decorated for his service in Vietnam, is described as a "killing machine."
When his guerrilla tactics hold his pursuers at bay, his former Beret commander
(Richard Crenna) is flown in as an ameliorator. At the conclusion of David Morrell's
novel, *First Blood,* the hero was killed. In the Michael Kozoll-William Sackheim screenplay, directed by Ted Kotcheff, he survives—in anticipation of one of the most successful sequels in all of moviedom: *Rambo: First Blood, Part II* (1985).

F.I.S.T. 1978 (CBS) *Color*
Director: Norman Jewison
Starring: Sylvester Stallone, Rod Steiger, Peter Boyle, Melinda Dillon, Kevin Conway, David Huffman, Tony Lo Bianco, Cassie Yates, Peter Donat, Henry Wilcoxon, Ken Kercheval

This Norman Jewison-Gene Corman production, directed by the former, opens in Cleveland in 1930. Johnny Kovak (Sylvester Stallone), depleted by long hours and low pay, decides to rebel against management exploitation. He becomes a spokesman for the working class of Cleveland, then gains national prominence. As his exposure grows, so does his affiliation with racketeers. Finally, he is the target of a senator (Rod Steiger) and his investigating committee. This fictionalization of the rise and fall of a labor union boss is modeled closely on Jimmy Hoffa's career. (Steiger's role is based on Estes Kefauver.) Stallone, who cowrote the screenplay with Joe Eszterhas, evokes the cocksure flamboyance of the rabble-rousing leader. The title is an acronym for *Federation of InterState Truckers*.

Fort Apache, the Bronx 1981 (Vestron; Time) *Color*
Director: Daniel Petrie
Starring: Paul Newman, Edward Asner, Ken Wahl, Danny Aiello, Rachel Ticotin, Pam Grier, Kathleen Beller, Tito Goya, Miguel Piñero

The underbelly of the South Bronx is captured with conviction in this controversial police melodrama. Paul Newman plays the good cop who discovers that drugs, graft, prostitution, sadistic colleagues, and bureaucratic stupidities are all part of the day's work. Others in the cast: Ken Wahl as a rookie; Ed Asner as a fair-minded but hardnosed chief; and Danny Aiello as a psychopath—who, unfortunately, is protected by his badge and a code of silence. An exercise in ultra-violence, *Fort Apache, the Bronx* is a stark film with the look and impassivity of a documentary. Heywood Gould's screenplay, directed by Daniel Petrie, was labeled unfair and prejudicial by the NYPD.

The Fountainhead 1949 (Key) *Black-and-White*
Director: King Vidor
Starring: Gary Cooper, Patricia Neal, Raymond Massey, Kent Smith, Robert Douglas, Henry Hull, Ray Collins, Moroni Olson, Jerome Cowan, Paul Harvey, Harry Woods, Paul Stanton

Ayn Rand's mammoth novel (and her philosophy of objectivism—i.e., rational self-interest) reaches the screen somewhat diminished but not damaged. Rand herself did the screenplay, which highlights an idealist architect, modeled on Frank Lloyd Wright, who refuses to kowtow to public housing bureaucrats. Although some of Rand's neo-Nietzschianism has been removed, *The Fountainhead* is a powerful and thought-provoking film. The cinematography of Robert Burks is rife with Expressionist symbolism, and Max Steiner's score lionizes the hero, played with conviction by Gary Cooper. Patricia Neal costars as his lady love. Directed by veteran King Vidor (*The Big Parade, The Crowd, Our Daily Bread, Stella Dallas, Northwest Passage, War and Peace*).

The French Lieutenant's Woman 1981 (CBS) *Color*
Director: Karel Reisz
Starring: Meryl Streep, Jeremy Irons, Leo McKern, Hilton McRae, Emily Morgan, Patience Collier, Peter Vaughan, Charlotte Mitchell, Lynsey Baxter, Liz Smith, Penelope Wilton, Gerard Falconetti, David Warner

Sarah Woodruff is a young woman living in seaside Lyme Regis in the 1860s. She has been ostracized by the townspeople after a scandalous love affair with a French lieutenant. An enigmatic woman who now shuns human contact, Sarah becomes a focal obsession for Charles Smithson, a gentleman scholar. Before long, Charles has decided to forsake his fiancée and follow Sarah. This is Harold Pinter's adaptation of the multi-layered John Fowles novel. Pinter, in alliance with director Karel Reisz, has chosen to abandon the novel's multiple-truth, alternate-ending premise; instead, the screenplay presents a modern-day framework whereby Meryl Streep and Jeremy Irons play two roles: Sarah and Charles—*and* the two contemporary cinema actors, Anna and Mike, who portray the Victorian lovers. As the nineteenth-century and twentieth-century scenes are interspliced, life imitates fiction. Freddie Francis's cinematography re-creates the vistas of nineteenth-century Dorset.

Friendly Persuasion   1956   (CBS)   *Color*
Director: William Wyler
Starring: Gary Cooper, Dorothy McGuire, Anthony Perkins, Marjorie Main, Richard Eyer, Robert Middleton, Walter Catlett, Phyllis Love, Mark Richman, Richard Hale, Joel Fluellen, Theodore Newton, John Smith

This adaptation of Jessamyn West's novel by scenarist Michael Wilson and director William Wyler introduces a Quaker farm family striving to maintain religious convictions during the Civil War. A family drama starring Gary Cooper and Dorothy McGuire (the parents) and Anthony Perkins and Richard Eyer (the elder and younger sons), *Friendly Persuasion* focuses on a crisis of faith that arises when the boy played by Perkins contemplates enlisting in the army. Dimitri Tiomkin wrote the score and, with lyricist Paul Francis Webster, the theme song, "Thee I Love." *Friendly Persuasion* was remade as a 1975 television movie, directed by Joseph Sargent, featuring Richard Kiley, Shirley Knight, and Michael O'Keefe in the Cooper-McGuire-Perkins roles. Samantha, the pet goose, is seen and heard in both incarnations.

From Here to Eternity   1953   (RCA)   ◆   *Black-and-White*
Director: Fred Zinnemann
Starring: Burt Lancaster, Montgomery Clift, Deborah Kerr, Donna Reed, Frank Sinatra, Philip Ober, Mickey Shaughnessy, Harry Bellaver, Ernest Borgnine, Jack Warden, John Dennis, Merle Travis, Tim Ryan, Arthur Keegan, Barbara Morrison, Jean Willes, Claude Akins, Robert Karnes

Schofield Barracks in Honolulu, 1941. A peacetime infantry unit forms the backdrop for this character study. Several tormented lives are penetrated: Sergeant Warden (Burt Lancaster) in love with his commanding officer's wife (Deborah Kerr); bugler Private Prewitt (Montgomery Clift), who has accidentally killed a man in a boxing match; Lorene (Donna Reed), a prostitute whose heart opens to Prewitt; and hotheaded Maggio (Frank Sinatra), who becomes the constant target of a sadistic bully's wrath. Their personal crises are dramatically interrupted with the Japanese bombing of Pearl Harbor. Daniel Taradash's script is a reshaping and streamlining of the massive James Jones novel. *From Here to Eternity* was honored with eight Academy Awards. Proclaimed best picture of the year, it also brought glory to supporting actors Reed and Sinatra; director Zinnemann; screenwriter Taradash; cinematographer Burnett Guffey; the sound recordists at Columbia Pictures; and editor William Lyon. A six-hour television mini-series (which inspired a short-lived weekly series) debuted in 1979; the leading parts were taken by William Devane (Warden), Natalie Wood (Karen Holmes, the Deborah

Kerr role), Steve Railsback (Prewitt), Kim Basinger (Lorene), and Joe Pantoliano (Maggio).

The Front   1976   (RCA)   *Color*
Director: Martin Ritt
Starring: Woody Allen, Zero Mostel, Herschel Bernardi, Michael Murphy, Andrea Marcovicci, Remak Ramsay, Marvin Lichterman, Lloyd Gough, David Margulies, Joshua Shelley, Norman Rose, Charles Kimbrough, Josef Sommer, Danny Aiello, Georgann Johnson, Scott McKay, David Clarke, Julie Garfield

In this drama and black comedy, Woody Allen plays a delicatessen cashier named Howard Prince. Howard makes money on the side as a small-time bookmaker. Several of his friends are TV writers who are being blacklisted during the McCarthy witchhunts, so as a favor (and for a commission) he becomes a front: Howard sells their scripts under his name. Though he is circumspect, he still winds up before a congressional investigating committee. Here's a rare appearance by Woody Allen for another director (Martin Ritt) and his only starring role to date in a film that he did not write. Walter Bernstein, the scenarist for *The Front*, was himself blacklisted, as were Ritt and his supporting players, Zero Mostel, Herschel Bernardi, and Lloyd Gough. Photographed with a feeling for the texture of the fifties by Michael Chapman.

Gallipoli   *Listed under War.*

Giant   1956   (Warner)   ◆   *Color*
Director: George Stevens
Starring: Elizabeth Taylor, Rock Hudson, James Dean, Carroll Baker, Jane Withers, Chill Wills, Mercedes McCambridge, Dennis Hopper, Sal Mineo, Rodney Taylor, Judith Evelyn, Earl Holliman, Robert Nichols, Paul Fix, Alexander Scourby, Fran Bennett, Charles Watts, Elsa Cardenas, Carolyn Craig, Monte Hale, Mary Ann Edwards, Sheb Wooley

The screen adaptation of Edna Ferber's sprawling novel faithfully chronicles thirty years in the lives of a Texas ranch family—the Benedicts. Written by Fred Guiol and Ivan Moffatt and directed by George Stevens, *Giant* is as sweeping as the Texas landscapes captured by William C. Mellor's camera. Central to the conflict is the waning of ranch-style Texas in the face of nouveau riche oil interests. Rock Hudson and Elizabeth Taylor, as Bick and Leslie Benedict, represent the former; James Dean, as Jett Rink, symbolizes the latter. Beyond the performances of the three leads, the movie offers both Hollywood legends (Chill Wills, Mercedes McCambridge, Jane Withers) and 1956-vintage bright newcomers (Carroll Baker, Sal Mineo, Dennis Hopper, Earl Holliman, Rod Taylor). *Giant* was nominated in numerous Oscar categories, but only Stevens's direction was ultimately cited. (Dean's fatal auto crash occurred only a few days after production wrapped; a few of his scenes then had to be dubbed by his friend Nick Adams.)

Girlfriends   1978   (Warner)   *Color*
Director: Claudia Weill
Starring: Melanie Mayron, Anita Skinner, Eli Wallach, Christopher Guest, Bob Balaban, Mike Kellin, Amy Wright, Viveca Lindfors

This independent film, shot on a low budget in New York, analyzes the friendship of two young women. Melanie Mayron stars as a budding photographer cast temporarily adrift when her roommate (Anita Skinner) leaves to get married. The special link the two have forged is tested. Mayron, at first, feels abandoned, but her newfound privacy allows her to explore new dimensions of herself and her career. Vicki Polon's script sharply delineates how friendships endure when one friend marries and the other doesn't. The resultant changes, minutely observed by Polon and her director, Claudia Weill, form the core of *Girlfriends*. Musical score by Michael Small.

The Godfather   1972   (Paramount)   ◆   *Color*
Director: Francis Ford Coppola
Starring: Marlon Brando, Al Pacino, James Caan, Richard Castellano, Robert Duvall, Sterling Hayden, John Marley, Richard Conte, Diane Keaton, Al Lettieri, Abe Vigoda, Talia Shire, Gianni Russo, Al Martino, Morgana King

This violent and shattering portrait of an American gangster dynasty is one of the all-time box office successes; slightly over $86 million in receipts to date. The opening chapter of the Corleone saga, *The Godfather* introduces aging syndicate chieftain Don Vito and his sons: Sonny, groomed as heir; Michael, the educated one; and Fredo, the weak-willed one. Under Coppola's guidance, memorable performances abound—Marlon Brando as Vito; James Caan as Sonny; John Cazale as Fredo; Richard Castellano as Clemenza; Robert Duvall as the loyal family *capo*, Tom Hagen; and Al Pacino, a standout in the ultimately central role of Michael. The composer is Nino Rota, production designer, Dean Tavoularis, and the cinematographer is Gordon Willis. Three Academy Awards: best picture, best actor (Brando, who refused the Oscar), and best adapted screenplay (Puzo and Coppola).

The Godfather, Part II   1974   (Paramount)   ◆   *Color*
Director: Francis Ford Coppola
Starring: Al Pacino, Robert Duvall, Diane Keaton, Robert De Niro, John Cazale, Talia Shire, Lee Strasberg, Michael V. Gazzo, Richard Bright, G. D. Spradlin, Morgana King, Troy Donahue, Fay Spain, Roger Corman, Phil Feldman, William Bowers

The Sicilian code that spawned the Corleone family legend is explored in this violent sequel/prequel to *The Godfather*. *Part II* is both a continuation of Michael's underworld reign and a flashback to the early years of his father. The launching point is a 1958 senatorial investigation of organized crime; as Michael waits to testify, he reflects on his past—and his late father's. Given this structure, the Coppola-Puzo script spans sixty-odd years, presenting young immigrant Vito (Robert De Niro), escaping from Sicily to New York's teeming Little Italy at the turn of the century. Named best picture by the Academy, *Part II* also claimed five other statuettes: director, screenplay adaptation, supporting actor (De Niro), dramatic score (Nino Rota and Carmine Coppola), and art direction (Richard Sylbert and his crew).

Going in Style   *Listed under Comedies.*

Goodbye, Columbus   1969   (Paramount)   *Color*
Director: Larry Peerce
Starring: Richard Benjamin, Jack Klugman, Ali MacGraw, Nan Martin, Michael Meyers, Lori Shelle, Jan Peerce

When Neil Klugman meets Brenda Patimkin, it's love at first sight. At least for Neil, a college dropout working in a public library. Brenda, a Radcliffe student on her summer vacation, is amused by Neil's overtures. Soon she drops her defenses and they begin a summer affair. When she returns to school, she invites Neil to meet her nouveau riche family. End of affair. The Philip Roth novella *Goodbye, Columbus* focused on Jewish life in 1956. In the Arnold Schulman screen adaptation, directed by Larry Peerce, Neil and Brenda's story unfolds in 1969. Richard Benjamin and Ali MacGraw, in their film debuts, are the protagonists. Jack Klugman, Nan Martin, and Michael Meyers are Brenda's parents and brother. In a bit part Jaclyn Smith plays a model.

Great Expectations   Great Britain   ◆   *Black-and-White*
    1946; U.S. 1947   (Learning)
Director: David Lean
Starring: John Mills, Valerie Hobson, Bernard Miles, Finlay Currie, Martita Hunt, Jean Simmons, Alec Guinness, Francis L. Sullivan, Anthony Wager, Ivor Barnard, Freda Jackson, Hay Petrie, O. B. Clarence, George Hayes, Torin Thatcher, Eileen Erskine

Dickens's masterpiece is given lavish treatment in this British production, cowritten by Ronald Neame and director David Lean. Pip (Anthony Wager) is the impoverished orphan who meets an escaped convict on the Romney Marshes—and the encounter changes his life. As Neame and Lean recount the classic (leaving chunks of original dialogue intact), Pip gains great wealth from a mysterious donor and grows into a gentleman (John Mills). *Great Expectations* will enchant devotees of the novel, while introducing those not yet Dickens-initiated to a world classic. A Christmas 1946 presentation in London, it was released here in 1947 and garnered Academy Awards for cinematography (Guy Green) and art direction/set decoration (John Bryan and Wilfred Shingleton). Also noteworthy—in diction, comportment, and period evocation—are Finlay Currie as Magwitch, the convict; Bernard Miles and Freda Jackson as Joe and Mrs. Gargery; Jean Simmons, and then Valerie Hobson, as Estella; Martita Hunt as Mrs. Havisham; and Francis L. Sullivan as Jaggers (which he had also played in a 1934 Hollywood adaptation).

The Great Santini   1980   (Warner)   *Color*
Director: Lewis John Carlino
Starring: Robert Duvall, Blythe Danner, Michael O'Keefe, Lisa Jane Persky, Stan Shaw, David Keith, Theresa Merritt, Julie Anne Haddock

Introducing Bull Meechum, a career officer in the Marine Corps who runs his home like a boot camp. The year is 1962, and Meechum, a fighter pilot, has no enemies to subdue, so he turns on his family. Chief recipient of Bull's rage is his teenage son, Ben. Writer-director Lewis John Carlino's screenplay is inspired by the autobiographical novel by Pat (*Conrack*) Conroy. In the central role, the self-styled "great Santini" is played by Robert Duvall. Supporting Duvall's not very likable hero are Blythe Danner (as Mrs. Meechum), Michael O'Keefe and Lisa Jane Persky (as the brother and sister, Ben and Mary Anne), Stan Shaw (as Ben's black friend), and David Keith (as a local redneck).

The Great Waldo Pepper   1975   (MCA)   *Color*
Director: George Roy Hill
Starring: Robert Redford, Bo Svenson, Bo Brundin, Susan Sarandon, Geoffrey Lewis, Margot Kidder, Edward Herrmann, Philip Bruns, Roderick Cook, Kelly Jean Peters, Scott Newman

This nostalgic adventure movie, from an original screenplay by William Goldman, begins in Nebraska in 1926. Waldo Pepper, a former World War I flier, is now a barnstorming pilot who takes passengers up in his biplane for five dollars a ride. Waldo makes his way to Hollywood, where he is employed as an aerial stuntman—and where he meets German ace Ernst Kessler, also doing stunt work. The two daredevils become genial rivals, flying the skies over Hollywood in a match they never had in the war. Producer-director George Roy Hill unites whimsy and romance in *The Great Waldo Pepper,* while utilizing the talents of his *Butch Cassidy and the Sundance Kid* and *The Sting* star, Robert Redford. Robert Surtees is the cinematographer on and above ground.

The Greatest Show on Earth   1952   (Paramount)   ◆   *Color*
Director: Cecil B. De Mille
Starring: Betty Hutton, Cornel Wilde, Charlton Heston, Dorothy Lamour, Gloria Gra-hame, James Stewart, Henry Wilcoxon, Emmett Kelly, Lyle Bettger, Lawrence Tierney, John Kellogg, John Ridgely, Frank Wilcox, Bob Carson, Lillian Albertson, Julia Faye

Cecil B. De Mille's 1952 Oscar-winning all-star extravaganza was also crowned for its screen story by Fredric M. Frank, Theodore St. John and Frank Cavett. *The Greatest Show on Earth* represents the flamboyance of the Ringling Brothers-Barnum & Bailey Circus. Filmed in Sarasota, Florida, the troupe's home base, and during performances in Philadelphia, *The Greatest Show on Earth* features animals, clowns, high-wire artists— and suspenseful set pieces, most memorably a train wreck sequence. At the center of drama in and outside the three circus rings are Holly (Betty Hutton), a star aerialist; Brad (Charlton Heston), the financially plagued manager; Buttons (James Stewart), a man with numerous reasons to hide behind clown makeup; Klaus (Lyle Bettger), the jealous elephant trainer; Angel (Gloria Grahame), who rides the elephants and is the source of his jealousy; and Sebastian (Cornel Wilde), a performer injured in a high-wire accident. In cameos as themselves: John Ringling North, Bing Crosby, Bob Hope, and master clown Emmett Kelly. William Boyd appears as Hopalong Cassidy. The circus acts include Lou Jacobs, Felix Adler, The Liberty Horses, The Flying Concellos, Paul Jung, and The Maxellos.

The Greatest Story Ever Told   1965   (CBS)   *Color*
Director: George Stevens
Starring: Max von Sydow, Michael Anderson, Jr., Carroll Baker, Ina Balin, Pat Boone, Victor Buono, Richard Conte, Joanna Dunham, José Ferrer, Van Heflin, Charlton Hes-ton, Martin Landau, Angela Lansbury, Janet Margolin, Roddy McDowall, Dorothy McGuire, Sal Mineo, Nehemiah Persoff, Donald Pleasence, Sidney Poitier, Claude Rains, Gary Raymond, Telly Savalas, Joseph Schildkraut, John Wayne, Shelley Winters, Ed Wynn

Fulton Oursler's 3-million-copy best-seller, along with other sources, ancient and mod-ern, form the basis for this depiction of the life of Jesus. The screenplay is credited to James Lee Barrett and George Stevens, "in creative association with Carl Sandburg." Max von Sydow, in his first American film, plays Jesus. A Hollywood who's who supports him—ranging from Dorothy McGuire and Robert Loggia's Mary and Joseph through David McCallum's Judas Iscariot down to John Wayne's Roman centurion. Filmed in the Utah desert, Pyramid Lake, Nevada, and Death Valley, California.

The Grey Fox   Canada 1982; U.S. 1983   (Media)   ✛   *Color*
Director: Philip Borsos
Starring: Richard Farnsworth, Jackie Burroughs, Wayne Robson, Ken Pogue, Gary Rei-
neke, Timothy Webber

The Grey Fox, a Canadian film, has a very familiar plot, but the artists involved make it seem brand new. The year is 1903. "Gentleman bandit" Bill Miner (Richard Farnsworth) has just been given his freedom after thirty-three years in prison. The world, of course, has changed in the intervening decades—along with potential sources of income. Stagecoaches, for instance, are out; locomotives are in. Inspired by watching Edwin Porter's *The Great Train Robbery,* Bill Miner decides to adapt to the times. He has mixed success as a train bandit, but very good fortune romancing a lady photographer whose fierce independence matches his own. In this nostalgic Western, stuntman-turned-actor Farnsworth delivers on the promise he made in small roles in *Comes a Horseman* and other features. The picture won seven Genie Awards, the Canadian equivalent of the Oscar: best film, best foreign actor (Farnsworth), screenplay (John Hunter), director (Philip Borsos), supporting actress (Jackie Burroughs), art direction (Bill Brodie), and music score (Michael Conway Baker and The Chieftains).

Greystoke: The Legend of Tarzan, Lord of the Apes   1984   *Color*
     (Warner)
Director: Hugh Hudson
Starring: Ralph Richardson, Ian Holm, James Fox, Christopher Lambert, Andie Mac-
Dowell, Paul Geoffrey, Cheryl Campbell, Hilton McRae, John Wells, Nigel Davenport,
Ravinder, Ian Charleson, Nicholas Farrell, Richard Griffiths, Eric Langlois, Roddy
Maude-Roxby, Daniel Potts, David Suchet

The saga of John Clayton (also known as Tarzan) is one of triumph over adversity. As the infant child of Lord Jack and Lady Alice Clayton, he is orphaned in the African jungle. Raised by apes, he grows to manhood as their leader. When the Belgian explorer Philippe D'Arnot happens upon Tarzan, he comes to realize that he is the grandson of Lord Greystoke. In Hugh Hudson's version of the oft-filmed Edgar Rice Burroughs saga, P. H. Vazak (a pseudonym for Robert Towne) and Michael Austin are the screenwriters, and the leading role is taken by French actor Christophe(r) Lambert. Other members of the cast include Ian Holm as D'Arnot, and Ralph Richardson in his final film role as the Sixth Earl of Greystoke. John Alcott's cinematography contributes to the visual sophistication.

Guess Who's Coming to Dinner   1967   (RCA)   ◆   *Color*
Director: Stanley Kramer
Starring: Spencer Tracy, Sidney Poitier, Katharine Hepburn, Katharine Houghton, Cecil
Kellaway, Roy E. Glenn, Sr., Beah Richards, Isabel Sanford, Virginia Christine, Alexan-
dra Hay, Barbara Randolph, D'Urville Martin

This comedy-drama, an attack on racial intolerance, was Spencer Tracy's last film (released posthumously), his fourth time under Stanley Kramer's direction, and his ninth pairing with Katharine Hepburn. Hepburn's niece, Katharine Houghton, in her film debut, plays Joey Drayton, the daughter of a liberal couple in San Francisco (Tracy and Hepburn). When the daughter brings home her black fiancé (Sidney Poitier), the parents find their tolerance ebbing. The story is screenscripted by William Rose. Tracy's charismatic homespun decency is one of the film's most noteworthy elements. Hepburn, as his understanding wife, was the Oscar recipient though. (*Guess Who's Coming to Dinner* was her second of three best actress wins.) Rose also won for his screenplay.

Hamlet   1948   (Learning)   ◆   *Black-and-White*
Director: Laurence Olivier
Starring: Laurence Olivier, Basil Sydney, Felix Aylmer, Jean Simmons, Eileen Herlie, Terence Morgan, Norman Wooland, Peter Cushing, Stanley Holloway, John Laurie, Esmond Knight, Anthony Quayle

There have been many screen interpretations of Shakespeare's melancholy Dane, but Olivier's version, as star and director, is among the finest. Some critics would call it the greatest cinema adaptation of the Bard. As the title character, Olivier reveals the depths of the prince's quandary—expressing the tension between thought and action. His supporting company, mostly players from the Old Vic, are well-versed in Shakespearean tradition. During the production of *Hamlet*, Olivier received his knighthood. Upon its completion, he was awarded an Oscar as best actor. The film was additionally cited by the Academy as best picture and for its costume design (Roger K. Furse) and art direction/set decoration (Furse and Carmen Dillon).

Hard Times   1975   (RCA)   *Color*
Director: Walter Hill
Starring: Charles Bronson, James Coburn, Jill Ireland, Strother Martin, Maggie Blye, Michael McGuire, Robert Tessier

Hobo Chaney (Charles Bronson) is the hero of this sometimes violent melodrama set in Depression-laden Louisiana. Chaney, a reluctant street fighter, teams up with Speed (James Coburn), a compulsive gambler. It's a union of brawn and brains. After Speed realizes how talented—and profitable—his new pal is as a bare-knuckle brawler, he becomes Chaney's manager and they seek fame and fortune in New Orleans. *Hard Times* was the directorial debut of Walter Hill, who went on to *The Warriors, The Long Riders, Southern Comfort,* and *48 Hrs.,* among other action pictures. The scenario is by Hill, Bryan Gindorff, and Bruce Henstell.

The Harder They Come   *Listed under Musicals.*

The Harder They Fall   1956   (RCA)   *Black-and-White*
Director: Mark Robson
Starring: Humphrey Bogart, Rod Steiger, Jan Sterling, Mike Lane, Max Baer, Jersey Joe Walcott, Edward Andrews, Harold J. Stone

The main attraction of this brutal boxing exposé is Humphrey Bogart in his last performance. In Philip Yordan's adaptation of the Budd Schulberg novel, Bogie plays a former sportswriter engaged as a fight promoter. In his new job he witnesses firsthand how pathetically prizefighters are treated by their managers. The careful performances (by Bogart, Jan Sterling as his wife, and Mike Lane as the literal fall guy) provide grit;

the backgrounds, photographed by Burnett Guffey, contribute atmosphere. Director Mark Robson was also responsible for the 1949 square-ring classic, *Champion*.

Hawaii 1966 (CBS) *Color*
Director: George Roy Hill
Starring: Julie Andrews, Max von Sydow, Richard Harris, Carroll O'Connor, Elizabeth Cole, Diane Sherry, Heather Menzies, Torin Thatcher, Gene Hackman, John Cullum, Lou Antonio, Jocelyne La Garde, Malcolm Atterbury, George Rose, Michael Constantine, John Harding, Bette Midler

A film for lavish historical drama lovers, *Hawaii* is an abbreviated version of James Michener's epic novel. As scripted by Dalton Trumbo and Daniel Taradash, the story tells of pious Abner Hale (Max von Sydow), a Yale divinity student who becomes a missionary to the undeveloped Hawaiian islands of the 1820s. Julie Andrews plays the minister's wife; Richard Harris is the rough-hewn sea captain in love with her. Among the haunting ingredients of this adaptation are the scenery and the second unit work of Richard Talmadge. Sequel: *The Hawaiians* (1970), covering the period from 1870 to 1900.

The Heart Is a Lonely Hunter 1968 (Warner) *Color*
Director: Robert Ellis Miller
Starring: Alan Arkin, Sondra Locke, Laurinda Barrett, Chuck McCann, Biff McGuire, Stacy Keach, Percy Rodriguez, Cicely Tyson

This update of Carson McCullers's 1940 novel is about life in a small Southern town. With director Robert Ellis Miller (*Sweet November, Reuben, Reuben,* and *The Girl from Petrovka*) at the helm, the film rendition of McCullers was relatively faithful—in part because most of the movie was shot in Selma, Alabama. When first released, *Lonely Hunter* met with only moderate commercial acceptance. Beyond providing a rare dramatic outing for Alan Arkin (as deaf-mute John Singer, who helps everyone around him), the film features Sondra Locke's debut and glimpses of early work by Stacy Keach and Cicely Tyson, just before they achieved star status. Both Arkin and Locke were Oscar-nominated, but, in their respective categories, they lost to Cliff Robertson's *Charly* and Ruth Gordon's menacing neighbor in *Rosemary's Baby*.

The Heiress 1949 (MCA) ◆ *Black-and-White*
Director: William Wyler
Starring: Olivia de Havilland, Montgomery Clift, Ralph Richardson, Miriam Hopkins, Vanessa Brown, Mona Freeman, Ray Collins, Betty Linley, Selena Royle, Paul Lees, Harry Antrim, Russ Conway

Olivia de Havilland was a two-time winner of a best actress Oscar—first for *To Each His Own* (1946), second for this complex character study. Adapted from Henry James's novel *Washington Square* (by playwrights Ruth and Augustus Goetz), *The Heiress* dramatizes the romance between Catherine Sloper (de Havilland), a wealthy spinster, and Morris Townsend (Montgomery Clift), a handsome young fortune hunter. In addition to the star's recognition, Academy Awards went to Aaron Copland for his music, Edith Head and Gile Steele for costume design, and the art direction/set decoration team (John Meehan, Harry Horner, Emile Kuri).

Henry V   Great Britain 1944; U.S. 1946   ◆   *Color*
   (Sheik Video; Learning)
Director: Laurence Olivier
Starring: Laurence Olivier, Robert Newton, Leslie Banks, Renée Asherson, Esmond Kight,
George Robey, Leo Genn, Ernest Thesiger, Ivy St. Helier, Ralph Truman, Harcourt Wil-
liams, Max Adrian, Valentine Dyall, Felix Aylmer, John Laurie, Robert Helpmann, Niall
MacGinnis

Laurence Olivier's debut as a film director came with this Shakespeare chronicle play.
Olivier converted the Bard's heroic poetry into a hymn of patriotism—robustly intoned
by the Plantagenet ruler who defeated the superior armies of France at Agincourt. The
motion picture, with an adaptation by the director and Alan Dent, is a spectacle of
both realism and stylization (beginning and ending in a structural representation of the
Globe Theatre). Olivier plays Henry, and he is supported by Leslie Banks (Chorus),
Renée Asherson (the French princess), George Robey (Falstaff), Esmond Knight (Fluellen), and Robert Newton (Ancient Pistol). The first Shakespearean movie in color and
probably the first to frame soliloquies as thought—voice-overs rather than visibly
spoken. Olivier received an honorary Oscar "for his outstanding achievement as actor,
producer, and director in bringing *Henry V* to the screen."

Hester Street   1975   (Vestron)   *Black-and-White*
Director: Joan Micklin Silver
Starring: Steven Keats, Carol Kane, Mel Howard, Dorrie Kavanaugh, Doris Roberts, Ste-
phen Strimpell

Set in turn-of-the-century New York, this drama reflects the cultural adjustment endured by Jewish immigrants as they embark on new lives on the Lower East Side. Gitl
(Carol Kane) is a young Orthodox woman who joins her husband (Steven Keats),
already established in America. Reluctant to abandon her Old World beliefs and practices, Gitl begins to run afoul of her hot-tempered mate and his newfound friends.
Written and directed by Joan Micklin Silver, after a short story by Abraham Cahan,
Hester Street is a depiction of the human comedy, with a timeless quality to its observation
of the sexes.

Hide in Plain Sight   1980   (MGM)   *Color*
Director: James Caan
Starring: James Caan, Jill Eikenberry, Robert Viharo, Joe Grifasi, Barbra Rae, Kenneth
McMillan, Josef Sommer, Dany Aiello

This chilling, headline-inspired drama stands as James Caan's first (and to date only)
directorial stint. Caan plays a divorced man in search of his lost children. When his
former wife marries a mob informant, the family is secreted away as part of a witness
protection/relocation program. Both the government and the underworld conspire to
keep the location a secret. Spencer Eastman's screenplay, adapted from a book by
Leslie Waller, focuses on the protagonist's search for his lost children. Caan plays the
leading role.

Home of the Brave   1949   (Republic)   *Black-and-White*
Director: Mark Robson
Starring: Douglas Dick, Steve Brodie, Jeff Corey, Lloyd Bridges, Frank Lovejoy, James Ed-
wards, Cliff Clark

A sobering consideration of racial prejudice in the military, *Home of the Brave*, directed by Mark Robson, is another of producer Stanley Kramer's low-budget dramas of social realism. (*Champion*, also directed by Robson, and *The Men*, from Fred Zinnemann, spring from the same period.) In the World War II Pacific campaign, a black infantryman named Moss (James Edwards in his movie debut) is the victim of abuse from the white men in his platoon. Playing the platoon major is Douglas Dick, remembered for his roles as the good guy in Hitchcock's *Rope* and as the young lieutenant in *The Red Badge of Courage*. The screenplay by Carl Foreman derives from an Arthur Laurents play in which the intolerance is directed toward a Jewish soldier.

Honeysuckle Rose   *Listed under Musicals.*

Hud   1963   (Paramount)   ◆   *Black-and-White*
Director: Martin Ritt
Starring: Paul Newman, Melvyn Douglas, Patricia Neal, Brandon de Wilde, Whit Bissell, John Ashley, George Petrie, Sheldon Allman, Carl Low, Don Kennedy, Crahan Denton, Val Avery, Curt Conway, Yvette Vickers

The newspaper ads of the period gave this drama a hard sell: "Hud is a real hunk of man. . . . He drives a Cadillac with one hand, has a girl in the other . . . and gets what he wants, whatever it costs someone else." Inspired by Larry McMurtry's contemporary Western, *Horseman, Pass By*, the picture features Paul Newman as Hud Bannon, who lives on an arid Texas ranch with his father, Homer (Melvyn Douglas), his young brother, Lon (Brandon de Wilde), and their housekeeper, Alma (Patricia Neal). All of them become involved to some extent in Hud's business chicanery and his sexual exploits. Martin Ritt's direction of the Irving Ravetch-Harriet Frank, Jr., screenplay brought Oscars to Neal and Douglas. Newman, in the best actor race, lost to Sidney (*Lilies of the Field*) Poitier. An additional award went to James Wong Howe's cinematography.

The Hustler   1961   (Key)   ◆   *Black-and-White*
Director: Robert Rossen
Starring: Paul Newman, Jackie Gleason, Piper Laurie, George C. Scott, Myron McCormick, Murray Hamilton, Michael Constantine, Stefan Gierasch, Gordon B. Clarke, Alexander Rose, Carolyn Coates, Carl York, Vincent Gardenia, Willie Mosconi, Art Smith

In this suspenseful drama about backroom pool sharks, based on the novel by Walter Tevis, Paul Newman has one of the key roles of his career: Fast Eddie Felson. A pool hustler par excellence, Eddie hoodwinks players left and right; but in champion Minnesota Fats he finally has a formidable opponent. The conflict in this film, as plotted by Sidney Carroll and Robert Rossen (and directed by the latter), springs from two sources: Eddie's brush with a menacing gambler and his contest with Minnesota Fats. Briskly played by Newman in the title part, Piper Laurie as his girl, George C. Scott as the gambler, and Jackie Gleason as cool, collected Minnesota Fats; all four were in the Oscar race, though Scott refused his nomination. Winning for *The Hustler* were Eugen Shuftan (black-and-white cinematography) and Harry Horner and Gene Callahan (art direction/set decoration). Sequel: *The Color of Money*, directed by Martin Scorsese, with Newman returning as Fast Eddie.

I Am a Camera   1955   (Monterey)   *Black-and-White*
Director: Henry Cornelius
Starring: Julie Harris, Laurence Harvey, Shelley Winters, Ron Randell, Anton Diffring,
Patrick McGoohan, Peter Prowse

The nonmusical precursor to *Cabaret* also draws its inspiration from Christopher Isherwood's stories of pre–World War II Berlin (and the subsequent John Van Druten play). In the Henry Cornelius motion picture, scripted by John Collier, Julie Harris repeats her Broadway role as Sally Bowles. The title derives from the opening lines of *A Berlin Diary*, spoken in the film by Laurence Harvey: "I am a camera with its shutter open, quite passive, recording, not thinking. . . . Some day, all this will have to be developed, carefully printed, fixed." Shot in England, the film is faithful to its source and in its day was denied a Production Code seal of approval. (In 1955, the heroine was deemed promiscuous and the movie immoral.)

I Never Promised You a Rose Garden   1977   (Warner)   *Color*
Director: Anthony Page
Starring: Bibi Andersson, Kathleen Quinlan, Sylvia Sidney, Susan Tyrrell, Signe Hasso,
Diane Varsi, Ben Piazza, Lorraine Gary, Reni Santoni

Hannah Green's semiautobiographical novel recounts a teenager's treatment for schizophrenia. Sixteen-year-old Deborah Blake (Kathleen Quinlan) is both schizoid *and* suicidal. Guiding her back toward normalcy is a dedicated psychiatrist (Bibi Andersson). Anthony Page's direction and Bruce Logan's cinematography are forceful, unrelenting in depicting the pathos of madness (including scenes of self-mutilation with live cigarettes and jagged pieces of tin). The screenplay is a collaboration between Gavin Lambert and Lewis John Carlino.

I Remember Mama   1948   (RKO; Blackhawk; Nostalgia)   *Black-and-White*
Director: George Stevens
Starring: Irene Dunne, Barbara Bel Geddes, Oscar Homolka, Philip Dorn, Sir Cedric
Hardwicke, Edgar Bergen, Rudy Vallee, Barbara O'Neil, Florence Bates, Peggy McIntyre,
June Hedin, Steve Brown, Ellen Corby, Hope Landin, Edith Evanson, Tommy Ivo, Frank-
lyn Farnum

A celebration of immigrant family life in turn-of-the-century San Francisco. The Norwegian-American Hansen clan consists of Papa (Philip Dorn), Mama (Irene Dunne), and three children: Nels (Steve Brown), Katrin (Barbara Bel Geddes), and Dagmar (June Hedin). Constructed as Katrin's reminiscence of her youth (". . . most of all, I remember Mama"), the film is a mixture of comedy and drama. The screenscript, taken from John Van Druten's play and Kathryn Forbes's novel, *Mama's Bank Account,* is by De Witt Bodeen. The film inspired the long-running (1949–56) teleseries titled "Mama."

I Want to Live!   1958   (MGM)   ◆   *Black-and-White*
Director: Robert Wise
Starring: Susan Hayward, Simon Oakland, Virginia Vincent, Theodore Bikel, Wesley
Lau, Philip Coolidge, Lou Krugman, James Philbrook, Bartlett Robinson, Gage Clark, Joe
De Santis, John Marley, Dabbs Greer, Raymond Bailey, Alice Backes, Gertrude Flynn,
Gavin MacLeod, Peter Breck

A plea for the abolition of capital punishment, this prison drama recounts the true story of Barbara Graham, a prostitute and petty criminal who was convicted of murder and sentenced to death in a California gas chamber—in the face of mounting evidence of her innocence. Based on the convicted woman's letters and reports filed by San Francisco journalist Ed Montgomery, *I Want to Live!* was written for the screen by Nelson Gidding and Don Mankiewicz and directed by Robert Wise. A harrowing portrait of Graham's life both inside and outside prison walls; Lionel Lindon's lighting and photography lend a semidocumentary feel. Susan Hayward, rewarded with an Academy Award, plays the leading role. Simon Oakland costars as Ed Montgomery, while Bart Robinson, radio's Perry Mason, plays the district attorney.

Ice Castles 1978 (RCA) *Color*
Director: Donald Wrye
Starring: Robby Benson, Lynn-Holly Johnson, Colleen Dewhurst, Tom Skerritt, Jennifer Warren, David Huffman

Two small-town Iowa teenagers—he an ice hockey player and she a figure skater—are the romantic figures in this drama. Both Nick (Robby Benson) and Alexis (Lynn-Holly Johnson) have dreams of professional sports glory, but Alexis, on the brink of an Olympic championship, is blinded in a skating accident. Her recovery is guided by Nick, her loving father (Tom Skerritt), and a demanding coach (Colleen Dewhurst). David Huffman costars in the role of the ne'er-do-well who abandons Alexis. The musical theme, "Through the Eyes of Love," brought an Oscar nomination to Marvin Hamlisch and Carol Bayer Sager. Director of photography: Bill Butler.

If . . . 1969 (Paramount) *Color*
Director: Lindsay Anderson
Starring: Malcolm McDowell, David Wood, Richard Warwick, Christine Noonan, Rupert Webster, Robert Swann, Hugh Thomas, Michael Cadman, Peter Sproule, Peter Jeffrey, Arthur Lowe, Mona Washbourne, Mary MacLeod, Geoffrey Chater, Ben Aris, Graham Crowden, Charles Sturridge, Sean Bury

Originally rated X for its brief nudity and the violent finale, *If . . .* closely examines life in an English public school. On view are the headmaster, the matron, the chaplain, housemasters, various professors, the scums (new boys), the whips (prefects), and the rebels—self-appointed crusaders—who become the heroes of the tale: Mick (Malcolm McDowell), Johnny (David Wood), Wallace (Richard Warwick), and Bobby Philips (Rupert Webster). The conflict arises when the whips literally whip the crusaders for not conforming. Then, on the school's annual Speech Day, the crusaders turn from rebellion to all-out revolution. This comedy-drama—combining elements of realism, romanticism, allegory, fantasy, and satire—emerges from a screenplay by David Sherwin (derived from an earlier scenario by Sherwin and John Howlett). Lindsay Anderson directs Malcolm McDowell in this, his screen debut. The musical theme is "Sanctus" from the *Missa Luba*.

Inherit the Wind 1960 (CBS) *Black-and-White*
Director: Stanley Kramer
Starring: Spencer Tracy, Fredric March, Gene Kelly, Florence Eldridge, Dick York, Donna Anderson, Harry Morgan, Elliott Reid, Philip Coolidge, Claude Akins, Paul Hartman, Jimmy Boyd, Noah Beery, Jr., Ray Teal, Norman Fell, Hope Summers

The famous Scopes "monkey trial" of 1925 inspired dramatists Jerome Lawrence and

Robert E. Lee to write *Inherit the Wind*. (Scopes, a high school teacher, was accused of violating Tennessee state law when his classes studied Darwin's theory of evolution.) In Kramer's film, adapted from the playscript by Nathan E. Douglas and Harold Jacob Smith, Dick York portrays the John Scopes figure; Spencer Tracy plays his defender, Henry Drummond (modeled on Clarence Darrow); and Fredric March enacts prosecuting attorney Matthew Harrison Brady (read William Jennings Bryan). Florence Eldridge, Mrs. Fredric March, plays Mrs. Matthew Harrison Brady. Freedom of speech and fundamentalist religion collide in this drama directed by Kramer.

Interiors   1978   (MGM)   *Color*
Director: Woody Allen
Starring: Kristin Griffith, Mary Beth Hurt, Richard Jordan, Diane Keaton, E. G. Marshall, Geraldine Page, Maureen Stapleton, Sam Waterston, Missy Hope, Kerry Duffy, Henderson Forsythe

Woody Allen's homage to Ingmar Bergman centers on a sterile, noncommunicative family. The family—consisting of father, mother, and three grown daughters—is torn asunder when the parents divorce. Arthur (E. G. Marshall), the patriarch, a successful lawyer, eventually remarries and his life flourishes. Not so for his former wife, Eve (Geraldine Page), an interior decorator whose situation amasses the children's sympathy. All the while, the three sisters (Diane Keaton, Kristin Griffith, and Mary Beth Hurt) have their own private and professional conflicts. *Interiors* is the first of Allen's writing-directing projects in which he didn't also star.

Islands in the Stream   1977   (Paramount)   *Color*
Director: Franklin J. Schaffner
Starring: George C. Scott, David Hemmings, Claire Bloom, Susan Tyrrell, Gilbert Roland, Richard Evans, Hart Bochner, Julius Harris, Michael-James Wixted, Brad Savage

Taken from Hemingway's posthumous novel, this adaptation by Denne Bart Petitclerc, directed by Franklin Schaffner, stars George C. Scott as Thomas Hudson. Hemingway's protagonist is an expatriate artist living on a Bahamian island in 1940. His three sons, from two marriages (both dissolved), come to spend the summer with him. There has been a long period of estrangement, and Hudson must work overtime to bind the father-son ties. The film blends human drama with the panorama of the Bahamas paradise. Noteworthy performances arise from Scott, David Hemmings as his drinking companion, Claire Bloom as Hudson's first wife, Gilbert Roland as a Cuban fishing boat skipper, and the actors playing the three sons—Hart Bochner, Michael-James Wixted, and Brad Savage.

It's a Wonderful Life   1946   (Prism; Nostalgia; Republic; Media; Select-a-Tape; Sheik Video; Cable Films; Video Connection; Video Yesteryear; Budget Video; Discount Video Tapes; Western Film & Video Inc.; Cinema Concepts; Kartes Productions; Classic Video Cinema Collector's Club; Hal Roach Studios)
                                                                 Black-and-White
Director: Frank Capra
Starring: James Stewart, Donna Reed, Lionel Barrymore, Thomas Mitchell, Henry Travers, Beulah Bondi, Frank Faylen, Ward Bond, Gloria Grahame, H. B. Warner, Todd Karns, Samuel S. Hinds, Mary Treen, Frank Albertson, Virginia Patton, Charles Williams, Sara Edwards, Bill Edmunds, Lillian Randolph, Argentina Brunetti, Bobby Anderson, Sheldon Leonard, Carl "Alfalfa" Switzer

Flashbacks help to explain the story of George Bailey, the most beloved citizen of Bedford Falls. As this film opens—on Christmas Eve—George's lifelong spirit of generosity has backfired. Following a series of business misfortunes, he is contemplating suicide. Rallying to his support are friends, neighbors, and a 200-year-old guardian angel named Clarence Goodbody who wants to earn his wings by saving George. This comedy-drama (based on Philip Van Doren Stern's short story, "The Greatest Gift," and screen written by Frances Goodrich, Albert Hackett, Jo Swerling, and Frank Capra) is a hallmark in the careers of Capra and leading player James Stewart. Costarring are Donna Reed as George's steadfast wife, Henry Travers as the pixieish Clarence, Thomas Mitchell as George's Uncle Billy, and Lionel Barrymore, playing Henry Potter, "the richest and meanest man in the county." The Hal Roach Studios edition is computer-colorized.

Ivanhoe   1952   (MGM)   *Color*
Director: Richard Thorpe
Starring: Robert Taylor, Elizabeth Taylor, Joan Fontaine, George Sanders, Emlyn Williams, Robert Douglas, Finlay Currie, Felix Aylmer, Francis De Wolff, Guy Rolfe, Norman Wooland, Basil Sydney, Harold Warrender, Sebastian Cabot

Sir Walter Scott's 1820 historical romance gets royal treatment in this MGM-Pandro S. Berman production. It's a faithful adaptation—by Noel Langley and Aeneas MacKenzie—of Scott's novel set in twelfth-century Britain. Director Richard Thorpe (*Night Must Fall, The Great Caruso, The Prisoner of Zenda, The Student Prince, Knights of the Round Table, Quentin Durward*) captures all the pomp, pageantry, and chivalry. Robert Taylor stars as the dashing title hero; he is supported by Elizabeth Taylor and Joan Fontaine as Rebecca and Rowena respectively, knighthood's most ravishing maidens in distress. Supplying the villainy is George Sanders as De Bois-Guilbert. Particularly impressive work comes from Emlyn Williams as Wamba, Guy Rolfe as Prince John, and Norman Wooland as King Richard. A 1982 made-for-television movie cast Anthony Andrews as Ivanhoe.

Jagged Edge   1985   (RCA)   *Color*
Director: Richard Marquand
Starring: Glenn Close, Jeff Bridges, Peter Coyote, Robert Loggia, John Dehner, Karen Austin, Guy Boyd, Marshall Colt, Louis Giambalvo, Ben Hammer, Lance Henriksen, Sanford Jensen, James Karen, Leigh Taylor-Young, William Allen Young, Maria Mayenzet, Dave Austin, Richard Partlow, Al Ruscio, Sarah Cunningham, Brandon Call, Diane Erickson, Walter Brooke

Did San Francisco newspaper editor Jack Forrester (Jeff Bridges) slay his socialite wife? That's the key question propelling this whodunit-cum-courtroom melodrama written by Joe Eszterhas. Thomas Krasny (Peter Coyote), an overambitious district attorney, thinks Forrester is guilty; defense lawyer Teddy Barnes (Glenn Close) feels the case is built on circumstantial evidence. So she and her hard-bitten legman, private eye Sam Ransom (Robert Loggia), set out to prove the newsman's innocence. Meanwhile, Teddy falls in love with her client, an indisputable charmer. Director Richard Marquand's other work includes *The Legacy, Eye of the Needle,* and *Return of the Jedi.*

The Jazz Singer   *Listed under Musicals.*

Jeremiah Johnson   *Listed under Westerns.*

Johnny Belinda   1948   (U.S.A. Home Video)   ◆   *Black-and-White*
Director: Jean Negulesco
Starring: Jane Wyman, Lew Ayres, Charles Bickford, Agnes Moorehead, Stephen McNally,
Jan Sterling, Rosalind Ivan, Dan Seymour, Mabel Paige, Ida Moore, Alan Napier, Monte
Blue, Douglas Kennedy

Jane Wyman joined the ranks of Oscar winners for her leading performance in this
touching drama about Belinda McDonald, a deaf mute. A sheltered farm girl, Belinda
is known in the nearby fishing community as "the Dummy"; she lives with her father,
whose attitude is "What she don't know don't hurt her none." When the girl is raped
and bears the illegitimate child—Johnny Belinda—a sympathetic doctor, new to town,
works to improve life for mother and infant. Among Miss Wyman's costars: Lew Ayres
as Dr. Robert Richardson; Charles Bickford as Belinda's father; Jane Sterling in her
first film as the good-hearted tramp, Stella; and Stephen McNally, playing the unsavory
Locky McCormick. Irmgard von Cube and Allen Vincent based their screen adaptation
on the Elmer Harris playscript. Music: Max Steiner.

Johnny Got His Gun   1971   (Media)   *Color*
Director: Dalton Trumbo
Starring: Timothy Bottoms, Jason Robards, Jr., Marsha Hunt, Diane Varsi, Kathy
Fields, David Soul, Tony Geary, Donald Sutherland

A World War I army hospital is the principal setting for this grim antiwar tract written
by Dalton Trumbo, who also makes his directorial debut. Trumbo's targets include
capitalists, organized religion, and the military complex. Army medics are keeping a
young soldier (Timothy Bottoms)—who lost his arms, legs, and speech—alive and
hidden from public scrutiny despite his wish to die. Lying in the hospital, he recalls
his past (parents, girlfriend, battle experience), then imagines a conversation with Jesus
Christ (Donald Sutherland), who offers no solace: "Perhaps it would be better for you
to go away now. You're a very unlucky young man and perhaps it rubs off." Trumbo's
premise is horrifying—and relentlessly pessimistic to the final frame.

Judgment at Nuremberg   1961   (CBS)   ◆   *Black-and-White*
Director: Stanley Kramer
Starring: Spencer Tracy, Burt Lancaster, Richard Widmark, Marlene Dietrich, Maximil-
ian Schell, Judy Garland, Montgomery Clift, William Shatner, Edward Binns, Kenneth
MacKenna, Werner Klemperer, Alan Baxter, Torben Meyer, Ray Teal, Martin Brandt,
Virginia Christine

Adapted by Abby Mann from his TV playscript, this is a fictionalized interpretation
of the 1948 German war crimes trials. With Judge Dan Haywood (Spencer Tracy) of
the United States presiding, the trials explore national and individual responsibilities
for the commission of Nazi atrocities. (Some actual concentration camp footage is
shown.) Maximilian Schell won the best actor Oscar for his portrayal of the German
defense lawyer (and Mann won for his screenplay). Directed by Stanley Kramer and
filmed in stark black and white by Ernest Laszlo, the film also contains impeccable
performances by Marlene Dietrich as a German widow who befriends Haywood; Richard Widmark as the prosecutor; and as witnesses Burt Lancaster, Montgomery Clift,
and Judy Garland.

Julia 1977 (CBS) ◆ *Color*
Director: Fred Zinnemann
Starring: Jane Fonda, Vanessa Redgrave, Jason Robards, Hal Holbrook, Rosemary Murphy, Maximilian Schell, Dora Doll, Elisabeth Mortenson, Meryl Streep, John Glover, Lisa Pelikan, Susan Jones, Maurice Denham, Cathleen Nesbitt

A portion of Lillian Hellman's memoir, *Pentimento*, forms the inspiration for this fact-based drama set in the thirties. Jane Fonda portrays Hellman as a fledgling author and playwright; Jason Robards plays detective writer Dashiell Hammett, with whom she had a long love affair; and Vanessa Redgrave is her noble childhood friend-turned-political activist. Julia is committed to the anti-Nazi struggle—and she enlists Lillian's support. Alvin Sargent's script for *Julia*, a balance between action and reflection, centers on Hellman smuggling $50,000 into Germany to be used by the anti-Nazi underground. Sargent won a screenplay adaptation Oscar; the supporting actor winners were Redgrave and Robards (his second consecutive win in the category). Meryl Streep's screen debut.

The **K**arate Kid *Listed under Family Viewing/Children's.*

Key Largo 1948 (CBS) ◆ *Black-and-White*
Director: John Huston
Starring: Humphrey Bogart, Edward G. Robinson, Lauren Bacall, Lionel Barrymore, Claire Trevor, Thomas Gomez, Harry Lewis, John Rodney, Marc Lawrence, Dan Seymour, Monte Blue, Jay Silverheels, Rodric Redwing

John Huston directed and cowrote (with Richard Brooks) this adaptation of the Maxwell Anderson playscript. The film avoids some of the darker inflections of the original to concentrate on mood and melodrama. Humphrey Bogart plays Frank McCloud, a war veteran putting his life back together in the Florida keys. There, at a hotel retreat, he encounters racketeer Johnny Rocco (Edward G. Robinson) and his gang, who are terrorizing vacationers during a tropical storm. The action, shot by Karl Freund, dwells on the hurricane hazards, getaway plans, Rocco's death threats, and double- and triple-dealing. Supporting actress Claire Trevor won an Oscar for her depiction of Rocco's boozy moll. Music: Max Steiner.

The Killing Fields 1984 (Warner) ◆ ★ *Color*
Director: Roland Joffé
Starring: Sam Waterston, Dr. Haing S. Ngor, John Malkovich, Julian Sands, Craig T. Nelson, Spalding Gray, Bill Paterson, Athol Fugard, Graham Kennedy, Katherine Krapum Chey

This true-life tale of friendship and survival begins in 1973, when former *New York Times* correspondent Sydney Schanberg was filing dispatches from Phnom Penh, Cambodia, during the takeover by the Communist Khmer Rouge forces. Assisting him in reporting was Dith Pran, his devoted guide and interpreter. When foreigners were evacuated, Schanberg and his allies tried unsuccessfully to take Pran to safety. (Back in Cambodia, Pran survived the Khmer Rouge's reeducation camps and ultimately escaped to America.) *The Killing Fields* is drawn from Schanberg's Pulitzer Prize–winning coverage and his memoirs. The film swept the British Academy Awards, winning seven statuettes, including best picture and best actor (Dr. Haing S. Ngor as Dith Pran). Here it took three Oscars: supporting actor (Ngor again), cinematography

(Chris Menges), and film editing (Jim Clark). The script, a harrowing adaptation by Bruce Robinson, was realized by debuting director Roland Joffé.

Kiss of the Spider Woman   1985   (Charter)   ◆ ★   *Color*
Director: Hector Babenco
Starring: William Hurt, Raul Julia, Sonia Braga, José Lewgoy, Milton Gonçalves, Miriam Pirés, Nuño Leal Maia, Fernando Torres, Patricio Bisso

This adaptation of the Manuel Puig novel is set somewhere in present-day Latin America. Puig's unorthodox story, screenwritten by Leonard Schrader and directed, in English, by Brazilian Hector (*Pixote*) Babenco, centers on two cellmates—both jailed for their potentially subversive extremism. Valentín (Raul Julia) is a Marxist-Leninist revolutionary; Molina (William Hurt) is a window dresser imprisoned for his homosexuality. To pass the time, Molina amuses Valentín by recounting the scenarios of 1940s romantic movies (which get visual reenactment, starring Sonia Braga as various screen heroines). Finally, the ideological lines that separate the two prisoners (and the demarcation between reality and fantasy) become blurred. A phenomenal commercial success for a small, independently made film, *Kiss of the Spider Woman* has taken in more than $16 million at the national box office. William Hurt was recognized by both the American and British motion picture academies as 1985's best actor, the same honor he was accorded at Cannes. The Los Angeles Film Critics Circle crowned both Hurt and Raul Julia.

Knights of the Round Table   1954   (MGM)   *Color*
Director: Richard Thorpe
Starring: Robert Taylor, Ava Gardner, Mel Ferrer, Anne Crawford, Stanley Baker, Felix Aylmer, Robert Urquhart, Niall MacGinnis, Maureen Swanson

For MGM's first production in CinemaScope, studio executives chose to revive Sir Thomas Malory's *Le Morte D'Arthur*, the fifteenth-century romance which became the bible for all later versions of the Arthurian saga. With a screenplay by Talbot Jennings, Jan Lustig, and Noel Langley, this rendition again dramatizes the royal intrigues and private affairs of King Arthur (Mel Ferrer), Guinevere (Ava Gardner), Lancelot (Robert Taylor), Morgan Le Fay (Anne Crawford), and Mordred (Stanley Baker). With Richard Thorpe as director, *Knights of the Round Table* flourishes with pageantry and battle spectacle—aided by Miklos Rozsa's musical score.

Knock on Any Door   1949   (RCA)   *Black-and-White*
Director: Nicholas Ray
Starring: Humphrey Bogart, John Derek, George Macready, Allene Roberts, Susan Perry

Abridged from Willard Motley's hardboiled novel, this frank drama introduces John Derek (his second film) as Nick Romano, a young punk from the Chicago slums. When Nick is accused of murdering a cop, a liberal attorney (Humphrey Bogart) is called in to defend him. Under cult director Nicholas Ray's guidance, both Derek and Bogie give illuminating performances. The did-he-or-didn't-he plot, scripted by Daniel Taradash and John Monks, Jr., is intriguing—though encumbered by a flashback technique that, according to numerous later interviews, displeased even the director himself. Sequel: *Let No Man Write My Epitaph* (1960).

Kramer vs. Kramer   1979   (RCA)   ◆ ✸   *Color*
Director: Robert Benton
Starring: Dustin Hoffman, Meryl Streep, Jane Alexander, Justin Henry, Howard Duff,
George Coe, JoBeth Williams, Bill Moor

This child-custody drama, adapted from Avery Corman's novel, was designated best picture by the New York Film Critics Circle and the Motion Picture Academy. Additionally, both groups singled out Dustin Hoffman (best actor) and Meryl Streep (best supporting actress). The stars play Ted and Joanna Kramer, affluent Manhattanites in the throes of a divorce and a custody battle over their six-year-old son Billy (Justin Henry). Robert Benton (*Bad Company, The Late Show, Still of the Night,* and *Places in the Heart*) won Oscars for direction and screenplay adaptation. Among the supporting players: Jane Alexander as Margaret, the Kramers's neighbor whose allegiance shifts from mother to father, and JoBeth Williams as a colleague (and short-term romantic interest) of Ted's. Nestor Almendros is the cinematographer.

The Last Detail   1973   (RCA)   *Color*
Director: Hal Ashby
Starring: Jack Nicholson, Otis Young, Randy Quaid, Clifton James, Carol Kane, Michael
Moriarty, Luana Anders, Kathleen Miller, Nancy Allen, Don McGovern, Gerry Salsberg,
Pat Hamilton, Gilda Radner

Two naval petty officers are detailed as "chasers" to transport a young sailor to the brig in this raucous, profane comedy-drama, scripted by Robert Towne from the novel by Darryl Ponicsan. Signalman first class "Bad Ass" Buddusky (Jack Nicholson) and Mulhall (Otis Young), a gunner's mate, are the two officers-turned-shore patrolmen; their prisoner is eighteen-year-old Larry Meadows (Randy Quaid), who has been sentenced to eight years' imprisonment and a dishonorable discharge for attempting to pilfer forty dollars from a polio-donation box. As the trio travel, by bus and train, from the Norfolk, Virginia, Naval Center to the Portsmouth, New Hampshire, Marine prison (with brief stops in Washington, New York, and Boston), the officers take pity on Meadows—in his last few days of freedom. Their efforts to "show the kid a good time" result in four days of boozing, brawling, and whoring.

Last Summer   1969   (Key)   *Color*
Director: Frank Perry
Starring: Barbara Hershey, Richard Thomas, Bruce Davison, Catherine Burns, Ernesto
Gonzales, Ralph Waite, Conrad Bain

A seagull provides the central metaphor in Eleanor and Frank Perry's film, *Last Summer,* adapted from Evan Hunter's novel. Ms. Perry's script dramatizes a summer on Fire Island as spent by four well-to-do teenagers—two boys, two girls. Of the latter, Rhoda, the sensitive odd-girl-out played by Cathy Burns, is the human embodiment of the seagull. There are virtues in this end-of-innocence youth picture. *Last Summer* rose above its genre stamp during a flurry of similar teen movies. First-time viewers, nonetheless, might be warned that this tale of sexual experimentation and self-confessional "truth games" does have a brutal finale. (For fans of "The Waltons," there are glimpses of the future stars of that series: Richard Thomas and Ralph Waite.)

Lawrence of Arabia   *Listed under Biographies.*

The Left Hand of God   1955   (Key)   *Color*
Director: Edward Dmytryk
Starring: Humphrey Bogart, Gene Tierney, Lee J. Cobb, Agnes Moorehead, E. G. Marshall, Jean Porter, Carl Benton Reid, Victor Sen Yung, Philip Ahn, Benson Fong, Richard Cutting, Leon Lontok, Don Forbes, Peter Chong, Robert Burton, Candace Lee, Kam Tong, Sammee Tong

This version of the William E. Barrett novel, scenarized by Alfred Hayes, takes place in a tiny Chinese village in 1947. Father Jim Carmody (Humphrey Bogart) has just arrived to supervise a Catholic mission. What the villagers don't know is that the priest is, in reality, a heroic American fighter pilot who has escaped from a warlord. His religious garments were adopted as a disguise. *The Left Hand of God* gives Bogart the central role in a suspenseful melodrama, flavored by Edward Dmytryk's direction and the music score of Victor Young. (A year earlier Dmytryk directed Bogie in *The Caine Mutiny*.)

Lili   1953   (MGM)   ◆   *Color*
Director: Charles Walters
Starring: Leslie Caron, Mel Ferrer, Jean-Pierre Aumont, Zsa Zsa Gabor, Kurt Kasznar, Amanda Blake, Alex Gerry, Ralph Dumke, Wilton Graff, George Baxter

Helen Deutsch and Bronislau Kaper's lilting theme song, "Hi-Lili, Hi-Lo," didn't win the Oscar in 1953 ("Secret Love" from *Calamity Jane* took the honors); but Kaper won in the scoring category. The song is the centerpiece for this whimsical romance, derived by screenwriter Deutsch from a story by Paul Gallico. Lili Daurier (Leslie Caron) is the teenage orphan girl of the title. She joins a carnival traveling about the French countryside and falls in love with embittered puppeteer Paul Berthalet (Mel Ferrer). Lili's story is directed by Charles Walters and highlighted by the dream sequence in which she dances with the larger-than-life puppets. This film furnished the basis for the popular Broadway musical *Carnival*.

Lilies of the Field   1963   (Key)   ◆   *Black-and-White*
Director: Ralph Nelson
Starring: Sidney Poitier, Lilia Skala, Lisa Mann, Isa Crino, Francesca Jarvis, Pamela Branch, Stanley Adams, Dan Frazer

"It's been a long journey to this moment." With those words, Sidney Poitier accepted the Oscar for his leading role in *Lilies of the Field*. He was the first black actor to win an Academy Award, Hattie McDaniel's 1939 win for *Gone with the Wind* having made her the first black actress. Poitier portrays ex-GI handyman Homer Smith. As the focal point of *Lilies of the Field*, Homer finds himself in southern Arizona, where he helps to build a chapel for five German nuns. William E. Barrett's novel provided the inspiration for the James Poe screenplay. Ralph Nelson's understated direction and his star's earthy, exuberant performance enhance the tale. Nelson himself appears in the role of Ashton, the contractor. Sequel: "Christmas Lilies of the Field," a 1979 television movie, also directed by Nelson—and starring Billy Dee Williams as Homer Smith.

Limelight   1952   (Playhouse Video)   ◆   *Black-and-White*
Director: Charles Chaplin
Starring: Charles Chaplin, Claire Bloom, Nigel Bruce, Buster Keaton, Sydney Chaplin,

Norman Lloyd, André Eglevsky, Melissa Hayden, Marjorie Bennett, Wheeler Dryden, Charles Chaplin, Jr., Geraldine Chaplin, Michael Chaplin, Josephine Chaplin, Snub Pollard

Limelight brings humor and pathos to the story of Calvero (Charlie Chaplin), an aging British music hall entertainer in the twilight of his career. Calvero regains his confidence while taking care of Terry (Claire Bloom), a talented young ballerina who has attempted suicide; then guides her on the path to stardom. Although set principally in pre–World War II London, the film was shot in America—the last Chaplin made in this country. (He directed from his own screenplay.) Unfortunately, *Limelight*'s initial release coincided with its creator's lowest ebb in popularity. In fact, the picture wasn't even commercially released in Los Angeles until 1972—at which time Chaplin won an Academy Award for his original score. A highlight: a slapstick skit featuring the star and that other genius of silent comedy, Buster Keaton—the one and only time they appeared together. Also taking part are Chaplin's children: Sydney plays Neville; Charles, Jr., is a clown in the ballet; and Geraldine, Michael, and Josephine appear as street urchins.

The Lion in Winter   1968   (Embassy)   ◆   *Color*
Director: Anthony Harvey
Starring: Peter O'Toole, Katharine Hepburn, Jane Merrow, John Castle, Anthony Hopkins, Nigel Terry, Timothy Dalton

The scenario by James Goldman, barely revised from his Broadway playscript, imagines the 1183 court of Henry II and his family at Christmastime. Eleanor of Aquitaine (Katharine Hepburn) is there, released from exile for the occasion, and so are the royal sons. Henry (Peter O'Toole) is deliberating over a successor. Who will it be—Richard the Lionhearted (Anthony Hopkins), Prince John (Nigel Terry), or Prince Geoffrey (John Castle)? A series of squabbles, revelations, and metaphorical backstabbings ensue. *The Lion in Winter* is another historical drama, à la *Becket,* but with humor added. Academy Awards went to Hepburn (her third win), and to Goldman's screenplay, John Barry's score, and the art direction/set decoration ensemble.

Little Big Man   *Listed under Westerns.*

The Loneliness of the Long Distance Runner   1962   *Black-and-White*
     (Sheik)
Director: Tony Richardson
Starring: Michael Redgrave, Tom Courtenay, Avis Bunnage, Peter Madden, Alec McCowen, James Bolam, Joe Robinson, Julia Foster

Colin (Tom Courtenay), a teenage slum boy, is convicted of thievery and sent to a Borstal reformatory. Colin's only apparent talent is long-distance running. When the insidious reform school governor (Michael Redgrave) learns this, he pushes Colin to race in an important track contest. The young outcast's innate rebelliousness and his contempt for authority and tradition create dissension in the ranks. Derived by Alan Sillitoe from his renowned short story, *The Loneliness of the Long Distance Runner* is directed by Tony Richardson with an emphasis on character and milieu. The film stands as another example of the British kitchen-sink drama/neorealist school which Richardson helped establish in works such as *Look Back in Anger, The Entertainer,* and *A Taste of Honey.*

Lonely Hearts   Australia 1982; U.S. 1983   (Embassy)   *Color*
Director: Paul Cox
Starring: Wendy Hughes, Norman Kaye, John Finlayson, Julia Blake, Jonathan Hardy

Australian writer-director Paul Cox began his film career as a documentarist and this romantic comedy, coscripted with John Clarke, represents a departure for him. A dating service unites a shy bank clerk (Wendy Hughes) and a middle-aged piano tuner (Norman Kaye) with a penchant for theatrics. The seemingly mismatched pair discover they have some common interests—and similar histories: they've both been losers in love. The screenplay, juxtaposing farce and poignant drama, is a generally satisfying replay of elements from *A Touch of Class, Cousin, Cousine,* the Renee Taylor-Joseph Bologna *Made for Each Other*—and even *Harold and Maude* (without the age differential).

Long Ago, Tomorrow   1971   (RCA)   *Color*
Director: Bryan Forbes
Starring: Nanette Newman, Malcolm McDowell, Georgia Brown, Bernard Lee, Gerald Sim, Michael Flanders, Barry Jackson, Geoffrey Whitehead, Margery Mason, Michael Lees

Two residents at a home for the physically handicapped fall in love in this British drama, written and directed by Bryan Forbes from an autobiographical novel by Peter Marshall. The two paraplegics are a former soccer player (Malcolm McDowell), a misfit at the institution because of his arrogance and lower-class background, and an upper-class woman (played by Nanette Newman, Mrs. Bryan Forbes). Their developing affair is recorded with sincerity and delicacy. While some critics regard *Long Ago, Tomorrow* as a wheelchair-bound counterpart of Erich Segal's *Love Story,* Forbes and his actors avoid the clichés of the lovers-from-two-different-worlds genre. Stanley Myers composed the melodic score.

Long Day's Journey into Night   1962   ✳   *Black-and-White*
    (Republic)
Director: Sidney Lumet
Starring: Katharine Hepburn, Ralph Richardson, Jason Robards, Jr., Dean Stockwell, Jeanne Barr

Most of the original script is retained in Sidney Lumet's adaptation of the Eugene O'Neill stage masterpiece. Hovering together in their rambling Connecticut home, circa 1912, are the members of the Tyrone clan: James (Ralph Richardson), a legendary stage actor; Mary (Katharine Hepburn), his wife; and their sons, Jamie (Jason Robards) and Edmund (Dean Stockwell as the young O'Neill). *Long Day's Journey into Night* is a corrosive depiction of egotism, alcoholism, family in-fighting, morphine addiction, and madness. The cinematography is by Boris Kaufman, the production design by Richard Sylbert. For the execution of their demanding roles, the four leads received a joint award at the 1962 Cannes Film Festival.

The Longest Yard   1974   (Paramount)   *Color*
Director: Robert Aldrich
Starring: Burt Reynolds, Eddie Albert, Ed Lauter, Michael Conrad, Jim Hampton, Ber-

nadette Peters, Charles Tyner, Mike Henry, Henry Caesar, Richard Kiel, Robert Tessier, Malcolm Atterbury

Paul Crewe (Burt Reynolds), a former football pro, is imprisoned for drunkenness, car theft, and resisting arrest. The warden (Eddie Albert) coerces him into quarterbacking for the prison's team of misfit players. Ultimately, the hulking convicts will be matched up against the warden's hand-picked cadre of semipros. In Tracy Keenan Wynn's comic screenplay—with references to both *The Loneliness of the Long Distance Runner* and *The Dirty Dozen*—nothing goes as the tyrannical warden plans; Paul Crewe's squad of criminals become better football players than anybody ever imagined. A brutal and action-filled entertainment, with *The Dirty Dozen*'s Robert Aldrich as the director.

Love Is a Many-Splendored Thing   1955   (CBS)   ◆   *Color*
Director: Henry King
Starring: William Holden, Jennifer Jones, Torin Thatcher, Isobel Elsom, Murray Matheson, Virginia Gregg, Richard Loo, Soo Yong, Philip Ahn, Jorja Cutright, Donna Martell, Candace Lee, Kam Tong

Inspired by *A Many-Splendored Thing*, Han Suyin's autobiographical novel, this romantic drama is laid in Hong Kong during the Korean War. John Patrick's screenplay highlights the love affair of Han Suyin (Jennifer Jones), a Eurasian doctor, and war correspondent Mark Elliott (William Holden). Their bittersweet relationship unfolds against a background of Chinese-Eurasian strife. The director is veteran Henry King (*In Old Chicago, Alexander's Ragtime Band, Jesse James, Stanley and Livingston, The Song of Bernadette, Wilson, Twelve O'Clock High, The Gunfighter, Carousel, The Sun Also Rises,* and *Tender Is the Night*). Recipient of three Academy Awards: best score (Alfred Newman); best costume design (Charles Le Maire); and best original song (Sammy Fain and Paul Francis Webster's popular title theme).

Love Story   1970   (Paramount)   *Color*
Director: Arthur Hiller
Starring: Ali MacGraw, Ryan O'Neal, Ray Milland, John Marley, Katherine Balfour, Russell Nype, Sydney Walker

"Love means never having to say you're sorry" is perhaps the best-remembered line from Erich Segal's screenplay (and simultaneous novelization) of *Love Story*. The story, rendered in flashback, begins with the female character's death at twenty-five and examines the romance and marriage of wealthy law student Oliver (Ryan O'Neal) and Radcliffe student Jenny (Ali MacGraw), the daughter of a poor Italian widower. An Oscar went to Francis Lai for his original score. In 1977, Ryan O'Neal reprised his *Love Story* character in *Oliver's Story*, wherein he finally comes to terms with Jenny's death; joining him for the sequel was Ray Milland (repeating his interpretation of Oliver Barrett III).

Macbeth   1948   (Republic)   *Black-and-White*
Director: Orson Welles
Starring: Orson Welles, Jeanette Nolan, Dan O'Herlihy, Edgar Barrier, Roddy McDowall, Robert Coote, Erskine Sanford, Alan Napier, John Dierkes

Shakespeare's tragedy of Macbeth, Thane of Glamis, Cawdor, and "king hereafter," was brought to the screen in 1948 by Orson Welles. The adaptation was filmed in a record twenty-one days because, according to the director, "no one would give me any money for a further day's shooting." Faced with the tight production schedule, art director Fred Ritter worked, quite literally, with papier-mâché sets. The Welles stamp is distinguishable in the bizarre lighting, camera angles (John L. Russell is the cinematographer), and radical interpretations of the Bard's dramatis personae—with most of the actors speaking in authentic Scottish accents. Welles gives voice to the tragic hero; Jeanette Nolan plays Lady Macbeth; Edgar Barrier embodies Banquo and his ghost; and Dan O'Herlihy, as Macduff, vanquishes Macbeth and crowns Malcolm. Roman Polanski rendered his movie version of the Scottish tragedy in 1971—under a considerably larger budget.

Madame Bovary   1949   (MGM)   *Black-and-White*
Director: Vincente Minnelli
Starring: Jennifer Jones, Van Heflin, Louis Jourdan, Christopher Kent, Gene Lockhart, Frank Allenby, Gladys Cooper, John Abbott, Harry Morgan, George Zucco, Ellen Corby, James Mason

Gustave Flaubert published his masterwork, *Madame Bovary,* in 1857. This Vincente Minnelli film, from a Robert Ardrey screenplay, places a framework around the novel. It opens and closes with the scandal surrounding the book's appearance and the trial resulting therefrom. Prosecuted on moral grounds—for not condemning Emma Bovary "for introducing adultery and ruin into her home"—Flaubert (portrayed by James Mason) takes the stand. His self-defense segues to the story proper, with Jennifer Jones as Emma—the incurable romantic who sacrifices her respectable, but dull, husband (Van Heflin) for a more glamourous life. To many film critics the formal ball sequence is one of the highlights of Minnelli's career.

A Man for All Seasons   *Listed under Biographies*

The Man from Snowy River   Australia 1982; U.S. 1983   (CBS)   *Color*
Director: George Miller
Starring: Kirk Douglas, Tom Burlinson, Sigrid Thornton, Jack Thompson, Lorraine Bayly, Tommy Dysart, Bruce Kerr, Terence Donovan

This adventure, set in nineteenth-century Australian bush country, tells of the legendary man from Snowy River. His exploits, as chronicled in an epic Australian poem by A. B. "Banjo" Paterson, form the basis of the George Miller film. (John Dixon and Fred Cul Cullen are the dialogists.) The young hero must prove his talents as a ranchman to an empire-building cattle baron. In the course of his horse-taming apprenticeship, the man from Snowy River falls in love with the cattleman's beautiful daughter. Tom Burlinson plays the dashing title character and Kirk Douglas adds spark in two radically different roles.

The Man Who Would Be King   1975   (CBS)   *Color*
Director: John Huston
Starring: Sean Connery, Michael Caine, Christopher Plummer, Saeed Jaffrey, Shakira Caine, Jack May

Victorian India; greed and ambition; mountainous treks; foolhardy risks; narrow escapes—these are the epical ingredients of *The Man Who Would Be King,* John Huston's cinematic rendering of the Rudyard Kipling short story. Daniel Dravot (Sean Connery) and Peachy Carnehan (Michael Caine), two conmen—and former soldiers in Her Majesty's Indian Army—decide to cross the mountains into Kafiristan and establish Dravot as a sacred king among a remote religious tribe. Their ruse works until they try to deprive the natives of their temple treasures. Saeed Jaffrey plays Billy Fish, the misguided heroes' interpreter, and Christopher Plummer begins and ends the tale by playing young editor Rudyard Kipling. Huston wrote the screenplay with Gladys Hill; cinematography by Oswald Morris. Shot in Morocco.

Marty   1955   (CBS)   ◆ ❋ ❋   *Black-and-White*
Director: Delbert Mann
Starring: Ernest Borgnine, Betsy Blair, Esther Minciotti, Augusta Ciolli, Joe Mantell, Karen Steele, Jerry Paris, Frank Sutton, Walter Kelley, Robin Morse, Charles Cane, Minerva Urecal

Marty Pilletti (Ernest Borgnine) is a shy, lovelorn butcher from the Bronx. Clara Snyder (Betsy Blair) is an equally shy schoolteacher. When they meet at a Saturday night dance club, they try to overcome their fears. *Marty,* a comedy-drama scripted by Paddy Chayefsky from his "Goodyear TV Playhouse" production, ushered in an era of television-inspired motion pictures. (*The Catered Affair, The Bachelor Party,* both by Chayefsky, and *Twelve Angry Men,* among many others, were to follow.) A low-key, neorealist portrait, this Harold Hecht–produced film featuring naturalistic dialogue and lower middle-class locales looked revolutionary in its heyday. The Palme d'Or winner at Cannes and the New York Film Critics Circle's top choice, *Marty* went on to capture four Academy Awards: best picture, actor, screenplay, and director.

Mask   1985   (MCA)   ◆   *Color*
Director: Peter Bogdanovich
Starring: Cher, Sam Elliott, Eric Stoltz, Estelle Getty, Richard Dysart, Laura Dern, Micole Mercurio, Harry Carey, Jr., Dennis Burkley, Lawrence Monoson, Ben Piazza, Alexandra Powers, Craig King, Kelly Minter, Andrew Robinson, Barry Tubb

Screenwritten by Anna Hamilton Phelan and directed by Peter Bogdanovich, this picture evolved from the true story of teenager Rocky Dennis. Rocky, as played by Eric Stoltz, suffers from a rare and incurable disease called lionitis, a condition wherein calcium deposits build within the cranium, disfiguring the victim's face and ultimately preventing blood supply to the brain. In other respects, though, Rocky is as normal as any high schooler. His single-parent mother, Rusty (Cher), highly unconventional herself, tries to ensure that Rocky will live as conventionally as possible. Estelle Getty, the irrepressible Sophia of TV's "The Golden Girls," here plays Cher's mother. An Academy Award for makeup design went to Michael Westmore and Zoltan Elek for creating Rocky's lion face.

Mass Appeal   1984   (MCA)   *Color*
Director: Glenn Jordan
Starring: Jack Lemmon, Željko Ivanek, Charles Durning, Louise Latham, James Ray, Talia Balsam, Jerry Hardin, Alice Hirson, Lois de Banzie, F. William Parker, Helene Heigh

When seminarian Mark Dolson is placed on a special assignment with Father Tim

Farley, the young man freely admits that before embarking on a religious life he "enrolled in a three-year orgy that laid waste to every fibre of [his] character." But now he invites celibacy. Father Farley (Jack Lemmon) is a shrewd but complacent priest of a wealthy suburban parish. Idealistic, impertinent Mark (Željko Ivanek) calls him "a song and dance theologian, a phony, and a drunkard." A comic consideration of ecumenical conflict, *Mass Appeal* examines this turbulent relationship—mandated by a worrisome monsignor (Charles Durning). Adapted by Bill C. Davis from his two-character playscript.

Mean Streets   1973   (Warner)   ✱ ○   *Color*
Director: Martin Scorsese
Starring: Robert De Niro, Harvey Keitel, David Proval, Amy Robinson, Richard Romanus, Cesare Danova, George Memmoli, David Carradine, Robert Carradine

Martin Scorsese's independent, low-budget ($550,000) film reunites some of the characters of his earlier *Who's That Knocking at My Door?* (1968). It's an impressionistic excursion through the mean streets of Manhattan's Little Italy. Scorsese, in his script with Mardik Martin, explores the community's deep-grained Catholicism and its Mafia undercurrents. Charlie (Harvey Keitel), being groomed as a mafioso, is involved in his *capo* uncle's loan operation. Regrettably, Charlie's career advancements—and his life—are placed in jeopardy by his bosom buddy, a dimwitted punk named Johnny Boy (Robert De Niro). Johnny Boy's poolroom brawling and loan-welshing lead to eruptions of violence between Little Italy's warring factions—with he and Charlie caught in the middle. (Scorsese himself plays a hired killer in the climax.) De Niro was named best supporting actor by both the New York Film Critics and the National Society of Film Critics.

Medium Cool   1969   (Paramount)   *Color*
Director: Haskell Wexler
Starring: Robert Forster, Verna Bloom, Peter Bonerz, Marianna Hill, Harold Blankenship, Sid McCoy

In writer-director-cinematographer Haskell Wexler's *cinéma-vérité* exploration of the cool medium (i.e., television), documentary footage of the turbulent 1968 Democratic convention in Chicago provides texture to the fiction. Wexler's central character is a TV news cameraman (Robert Forster) who grows more emotionally detached as events around him become increasingly tumultuous. The focus of his romantic life is a young Appalachian widow and mother (Verna Bloom). *Medium Cool* juxtaposes their relationship with the real-life stories the cameraman shoots for the evening news. Originally rated X for its scenes of brief nudity, the picture endures principally as a reflection of the gloomy political climate of late sixties America.

Melvin and Howard   *Listed under Biographies.*

The Men   1950   (Republic)   *Black-and-White*
Director: Fred Zinnemann
Starring: Marlon Brando, Teresa Wright, Everett Sloane, Jack Webb, Richard Erdman, Arthur Jurado, Virginia Farmer, Dorothy Tree, Howard St. John, Nita Hunter, Patricia Joiner

Marlon Brando, critically acclaimed for his stage roles, made his screen debut in this semidocumentary drama. As Ken, a paraplegic war veteran striving to adjust to civilian life, Brando attained even greater glory. (Directly after *The Men,* he did the film version of *A Streetcar Named Desire* and thereafter never returned to legitimate theater.) Supporting him are Teresa Wright as Ellen, the protagonist's fiancée; Howard St. John and Dorothy Tree as her parents; and Everett Sloane as Dr. Brock. Carl Foreman's screenplay might be taken as a forerunner to Hal Ashby's *Coming Home.* Production, under Fred Zinnemann's direction, took place at the Birmingham Veterans Administration Hospital.

Midnight Cowboy 1969 (MGM)   *Color*
Director: John Schlesinger
Starring: Dustin Hoffman, Jon Voight, Brenda Vaccaro, John McGiver, Ruth White, Sylvia Miles, Barnard Hughes, Jennifer Salt, Bob Balaban, Georgann Johnson, Gary Owens, Jonathan Kramer, Jan Tice, Viva, Ultra Violet, Anthony Holland, Paul Jabara, Taylor Mead, Paul Morrissey

This retelling of Steinbeck's *Of Mice and Men,* set in New York, is a compassionate portrait of two society castoffs: Enrico Salvatore "Ratso" Rizzo, a crippled, tubercular bum from the Bronx, and Joe Buck, a twenty-five-year-old naïf from Texas. Ratso survives as a grifter; Joe has arrived to parlay his good looks into a career as a midnight cowboy—catering to the sexual needs of the city's rich women. The two loners meet and form an unusual and touching symbiotic relationship. Dustin Hoffman, already known as *The Graduate,* increased his reputation through his interpretation of Ratso, while Jon Voight, enacting personable and gullible Joe Buck, leapt to stardom. Waldo Salt's Academy Award–winning scenario, based upon the James Leo Herlihy novel, captures the ambience of Manhattan, particularly the squalid drug-and-prostitution Times Square haunts. Two other Oscars went to the production: best director (John Schlesinger) and best picture—the first (and, to date, only) X-rated feature to merit the top citation.

The Miracle of the Bells 1948 (Republic) *Black-and-White*
Director: Irving Pichel
Starring: Fred MacMurray, Alida Valli, Frank Sinatra, Lee J. Cobb, Charles Meredith

The titular miracle occurs when a renowned movie queen dies and is buried in her home town, an impoverished coal-mining community. Nationwide publicity attends the event, as an array of Hollywood types intermingle with the locals. Religious overtones surround this drama. The screenplay is a fundamental departure for Ben Hecht, a master of hard-edged comedies and mysteries. Appealing in the large cast are young Frank Sinatra (as a priest) and Italian discovery Alida Valli in her second English-language film (following Hitchcock's *The Paradine Case*).

Moby Dick 1956 (CBS) *Color*
Director: John Huston
Starring: Gregory Peck, Richard Basehart, Leo Genn, Orson Welles, James Robertson Justice, Harry Andrews, Bernard Miles, Noel Purcell, Edric Connor, Mervyn Johns, Joseph Tomelty, Francis De Wolff, Royal Dano, Friedrich Ledebur

In 1926 John Barrymore played Herman Melville's tormented, revengeful Captain Ahab in an adaptation of *Moby Dick* entitled *The Sea Beast*—and did so again in a 1930 talkie version. But most critics will claim it took Gregory Peck (abetted by Technicolor, writer-director John Huston, coscenarist Ray Bradbury, cinematographer Oswald Morris, and location shooting in Ireland, Wales, Madeira, and the Canary Islands) to deliver the definitive Ahab to the screen. As the skipper of the whaling vessel *Pequod*— determined to harpoon the great white whale that bit off his leg—Peck heads an ensemble that includes Orson Welles (Father Mapple), Leo Genn (Starbuck), Harry Andrews (Stubb), Friedrich Ledebur (Queequeg), and Richard Basehart (Ishmael, the narrator).

Mogambo   1953   (MGM)   *Color*
Director: John Ford
Starring: Clark Gable, Ava Gardner, Grace Kelly, Donald Sinden, Philip Stainton, Eric Pohlmann, Laurence Naismith, Denis O'Dea

Victor Marswell (Clark Gable) is a great white hunter headquartered in Kenya. Arriving on safari are Eloise Kelly (Ava Gardner), an American showgirl, and a British archaeologist and his wife—Donald and Linda Nordley (Donald Sinden, Grace Kelly). A romantic triangle develops among Victor and the two women. The screenplay by John Lee Mahin is a revision of his work on *Red Dust* (1932), which also starred Clark Gable; therein the other sides of the triangle were enacted by Jean Harlow and Mary Astor. Ava Gardner has the tart-tongued Harlow part. Filmed on location in East Africa.

Mutiny on the Bounty   1962   (MGM)   *Color*
Director: Lewis Milestone
Starring: Marlon Brando, Trevor Howard, Richard Harris, Hugh Griffith, Richard Haydn, Tarita, Percy Herbert, Duncan Lamont, Gordon Jackson, Chips Rafferty, Noel Purcell, Ashley Cowan, Eddie Byrne, Frank Silvera

Inspired by an actual incident, this colorful epic reconstructs the eighteenth-century voyage of the *Bounty*, a British war vessel, and the crew's mutiny against Captain Bligh. The 1962 version of the tale utilizes a portion of the *Bounty* trilogy of Charles Nordhoff and James Norman Hall, as scenarized by Charles Lederer. Starring as Bligh is Trevor Howard; playing Fletcher Christian, leader of the mutiny, is Marlon Brando. There are three other screen adaptations of the saga: *In the Wake of the Bounty*, a 1933 Australian feature; the famous 1935 MGM production of *Mutiny on the Bounty*, with Charles Laughton and Clark Gable as Bligh and Christian; and the succinctly titled *Bounty* (1984), which cast Anthony Hopkins and Mel Gibson in the leads. This Lewis Milestone edition is highlighted by Trevor Howard's performance and Robert Surtees's cinematography.

My Brilliant Career   *Listed under Biographies.*

The **N**atural   1984   (RCA)   *Color*
Director: Barry Levinson
Starring: Robert Redford, Robert Duvall, Glenn Close, Kim Basinger, Wilford Brimley, Barbara Hershey, Robert Prosky, Richard Farnsworth, Joe Don Baker, John Finnegan, Alan Fudge, Paul Sullivan, Jr., Bernie McInerney

Roger Towne and Phil Dusenberry adapted Bernard Malamud's baseball novel for the screen. Robert Redford plays Roy Hobbs, a talented but aging ballplayer trying to make a comeback after a fifteen-year layoff. That he's a natural no one can deny—especially New York Knights trainer Pop Fisher (Wilford Brimley), or the team's unscrupulous owner, The Judge (Robert Prosky). To fulfill the promise of his early career, Roy must overcome obstacles of greed, graft, and drugs. Iris (Glenn Close), his childhood sweetheart, inspires him to beat the odds. This fantasy drama, photographed by Caleb Deschanel and directed by Barry Levinson, features Redford, Brimley, Close, Richard Farnsworth (as Red Blow), Robert Duvall (as reporter Max Mercy), and the unbilled Darren McGavin as a shifty-eyed villain. Shot in and around Buffalo, New York.

Network   *Listed under Comedies.*

The Night of the Iguana   1964   (MGM)   *Black-and-White*
Director: John Huston
Starring: Richard Burton, Ava Gardner, Deborah Kerr, Sue Lyon, James Ward, Grayson Hall, Cyril Delevanti, Mary Boylan, Gladys Hill, Billie Matticks, Eloise Hardt

Tennessee Williams's Broadway drama, as screenwritten by Anthony Veiller and John Huston (and directed by the latter), dissects an assembly of characters who find themselves in a rundown hotel in coastal Mexico. The Reverend T. Lawrence Shannon (Richard Burton) is a defrocked clergyman working as a bus-tour guide; Maxine Faulk (Ava Gardner) owns the hotel where Shannon stays; Hannah Jelkes (Deborah Kerr) is a lonely spinster whose aged poet-father is dying; and Charlotte Goodall (Sue Lyon) is passing through the area on a student tour. The ex-minister is all three women's object of desire. The confrontation of these passions leads to a three-way conflict, with some cynical observations from sideline participants. A painful exploration of human agony and loneliness.

A Night to Remember   1958   (Learning)   *Black-and-White*
Director: Roy Baker
Starring: Kenneth More, Honor Blackman, Michael Goodliffe, David McCallum, George Rose, Anthony Bushell, Ralph Michael, John Cairney, Kenneth Griffith, Frank Lawton, Michael Bryant, Jill Dixon, Alec McCowen, Laurence Naismith, Ronald Allen, Robert Ayres

The night in question is April 14, 1912. On that date the *Titanic*, the luxury liner on its maiden voyage from England to New York, struck an iceberg in the waters off Newfoundland—and sank. Most of the 2,200 passengers died. This film version of the sea disaster is inspired by Walter Lord's book, and it's a convincing reenactment. The large cast is directed by Roy (Ward) Baker, a specialist in supernatural—rather than documentary—horror (*Five Million Years to Earth, The Vampire Lovers, Asylum, And Now the Screaming Starts*). But the human story takes primary importance here, with ignorance and apathy followed by shock and outright panic giving way to acts of courage and cowardice. A grim drama, *A Night to Remember* owes much to Eric Ambler's screenplay and Geoffrey Unsworth's cinematography.

The Ninth Configuration   1980   (New World Video)   *Color*
Director: William Peter Blatty
Starring: Stacy Keach, Scott Wilson, Jason Miller, Ed Flanders, Neville Brand, Moses Gunn, George Di Cenzo, Robert Loggia, Tom Atkins, Alejandro Rey, Joe Spinell, Steve Sandor, Richard Lynch

An offbeat psychoanalytical drama, *The Ninth Configuration* was founded upon William Peter Blatty's novel *Twinkle, Twinkle, Killer Kane* (and released briefly under that title). The picture contains vestiges of *One Flew Over the Cuckoo's Nest.* Set in an old castle used in secret by the U.S. government as an asylum, the story concerns the relationship of an unconventional chief doctor (Stacy Keach) to his psychiatric ward patients, high-ranking military misfits. The question of who is more lunatic—the psychiatrist or his inmates—ends in a draw. Blatty, of *The Exorcist* fame, is the enterprise's writer, producer, and director. Filmed in Hungary.

Norma Rae   1979   (CBS)   ◆   *Color*
Director: Martin Ritt
Starring: Sally Field, Beau Bridges, Ron Leibman, Pat Hingle, Barbara Baxley, Gail Strickland

A textile mill in a small Southern town is the battleground when gutsy young widow Norma Rae Webster becomes a union organizer. Martin Ritt's rousing drama is based on an actual incident. Husband-and-wife team Irving Ravetch and Harriet Frank, Jr., Ritt's frequent collaborators, wrote the screenplay. *Norma Rae* is given added distinction in the semidocumentary visual style adopted by cinematographer John A. Alonzo. Sally Field's title role performance, coupled with her 1977 Emmy for "Sybil," finally validated her as an acting force in Hollywood. And her Academy peers voted her best actress. Another Oscar went to *Norma Rae*'s theme song, "It Goes Like It Goes" (by David Shire and Norman Gimbel).

O**cean's 11**   *Listed under Comedies.*

An Officer and a Gentleman   1982   (Paramount)   ◆   *Color*
Director: Taylor Hackford
Starring: Richard Gere, Debra Winger, David Keith, Robert Loggia, Lisa Blount, Lisa Eilbacher, Louis Gossett, Jr., Tony Plana, Harold Sylvester, David Caruso, Victor French, Grace Zabriskie

Richard Gere plays perennial loser Zack Mayo in this coming-to-maturity story that seconds as a romantic drama. Zack enrolls in Naval Officer Candidate School as a last-ditch attempt to make something of himself. He is taught to accept responsibility by a tough drill sergeant, Emil Foley (Louis Gossett, Jr., in an Oscar-winning performance). At the same time, he and poor factory worker Paula Pokrifki (Debra Winger) begin a torrid affair. Douglas Day Stewart's screenplay is a blend of two plot lines—given force by salty dialogue and frank sexual situations. The supporting cast includes one unsung hero: David Keith, in a sensitive depiction of Zack's troubled classmate, Sid Worley. A second Academy Award went to the film for its theme song, "Up Where We Belong," with lyrics by Will Jennings and music by Jack Nitzsche and Buffy Sainte-Marie.

On Golden Pond   1981   (CBS)   ◆   *Color*
Director: Mark Rydell
Starring: Katharine Hepburn, Henry Fonda, Jane Fonda, Doug McKeon, Dabney Coleman, William Lanteau

Norman and Ethel Thayer have been married for forty-eight years. For most of that time they have spent their summers in a lakeside cottage in Maine. Joining them on Golden Pond this summer is their daughter Chelsea's thirteen-year-old stepson, Billy. Norman, observing his eightieth birthday, is at first a reluctant host to the teenager, but as the weeks pass, a special friendship grows between them. Henry Fonda and Katharine Hepburn (in their only screen appearance together) are a casting coup as the Thayers; both won Oscars for their work. An additional award went to Ernest Thompson for his adaptation of his Broadway playscript. Supporting the stars are Jane Fonda as the old couple's alienated daughter, Dabney Coleman as her new husband, and Doug McKeon as Billy. This comedy-drama, directed by Mark Rydell (*The Reivers, The Cowboys, The Rose, The River*), showcases Henry Fonda's last big-screen release; the 1981 telefilm, "Summer Solstice," costarring Myrna Loy, was his final film.

On the Waterfront 1954 (RCA) ◆ *Black-and-White*
Director: Elia Kazan
Starring: Marlon Brando, Karl Malden, Eva Marie Saint, Lee J. Cobb, Rod Steiger, Pat Henning, Leif Erickson, James Westerfield, Tony Galento, Tami Mauriello, John Hamilton

The winner of eight Academy Awards, the melodrama with a screenplay by Budd Schulberg based on nonfiction accounts by Malcolm Johnson, succeeds as both a racketeering exposé and a character study. Marlon Brando stars as Terry Malloy, a longshoreman caught between two factions. When Terry realizes that waterfront boss Johnny Friendly (Lee J. Cobb) is a murderous gangster, he gives incriminating testimony before the Crime Commission. At first Terry is marked as a stool pigeon by his coworkers; but the mob's stranglehold on the dockworkers' union is finally broken. Elia Kazan's direction provides a neorealist, semidocumentary touch. In addition to its best picture citation, *On the Waterfront* brought Oscars to Brando, Kazan, and Schulberg—as well as supporting actress Eva Marie Saint (in her film debut), cinematogapher Boris Kaufman, art director Richard Day, and editor Gene Milford. Music by Leonard Bernstein. Featured in small roles: Martin Balsam, Fred Gwynne, and Nehemiah Persoff.

One Flew Over the Cuckoo's Nest 1975 (Thorn) ◆ *Color*
Director: Miloš Forman
Starring: Jack Nicholson, Louise Fletcher, William Redfield, Brad Dourif, Michael Berryman, Peter Brocco, Scatman Crothers, Danny De Vito, Nathan George, Sydney Lassick, Christopher Lloyd, Louisa Moritz, Marya Small, Will Sampson

One Flew Over the Cuckoo's Nest is the second film in history, after *It Happened One Night*, to win Academy Awards in all the major categories. Its five Oscars went to leads Jack Nicholson and Louise Fletcher, screenwriters Laurence Hauben and Bo Goldman, and director Miloš Forman—while the picture itself was dubbed the year's best. The movie's hero is free-spirited Randle Patrick McMurphy (Nicholson), a state mental hospital inmate. McMurphy's nemesis is Nurse Ratched (Fletcher), a by-the-book administrator who will not brook McMurphy's insolence—or his attempts to get the other patients to assert themselves. Ken Kesey's 1962 novel and the subsequent Broadway drama are the sources of this hard-hitting, psychological study. Other major roles are taken by Brad Dourif (as Billy Bibbit), Will Sampson (Chief Broom), and Sydney Lassick (Cheswick). The future costars of TV's *Taxi*—Danny De Vito and Christopher Lloyd—play two other asylum residents.

One on One   1977   (Warner)   *Color*
Director: Lamont Johnson
Starring: Robby Benson, Annette O'Toole, G. D. Spradlin, Gail Strickland, Melanie
Griffith, Lamont Johnson

Henry (Robby Benson), a talented teen basketball player from Colorado, faces the
corrupt world of college athletics. With a beautiful young tutor (Annette O'Toole) to
help him elevate his grade point average and a tyrannical, unscrupulous coach (G. D.
Spradlin) to harass him, the kid's freshman year is far from dull. This overcoming-the-
odds scenario was written by young Benson and his father, Jerry Segal. The supporting
cast—particularly the women in Henry's life (O'Toole as the brainy upperclassman
and Gail Strickland as a nymphomaniacal college secretary)—brighten the proceedings.

Only When I Laugh   1981   (RCA)   *Color*
Director: Glenn Jordan
Starring: Marsha Mason, Kristy McNichol, James Coco, Joan Hackett, David Dukes,
John Bennett Perry, Kevin Bacon, Guy Boyd, Peter Coffield, Mark Schubb

This is a heavily revised version of Neil Simon's stage drama *The Gingerbread Lady*.
The film pivots on the role-shattering relationship of a mother and her teenage daughter.
Marsha Mason plays an alcoholic actress struggling to stay away from the bottle;
Kristy McNichol is her estranged daughter. Together they rebuild the mother's life.
Filmed on location in New York by director Glenn Jordan (*Mass Appeal* and TV's
"Heartsounds," "Toughlove," and "Dress Gray"). Noteworthy supporting actors in-
lude James Coco and, in her last movie role, Joan Hackett. Simon himself wrote the
screenplay.

Ordinary People   1980   (Paramount)   ◆ *Color*
Director: Robert Redford
Starring: Donald Sutherland, Mary Tyler Moore, Timothy Hutton, Judd Hirsch,
M. Emmet Walsh, Elizabeth McGovern, Dinah Manoff, Fredric Lehne, James B. Sikking,
Basil Hoffman, Quinn Redeker, Mariclare Costello, Meg Mundy, Elizabeth Hubbard,
Adam Baldwin, Richard Whiting

Judith Guest's best-selling novel is transformed into an Academy Award–winning
motion picture in this directing debut for Robert Redford. The Calvin Jarrett family
tries to adjust after the accidental drowning death of eldest son, Buck. The survivors—
Calvin (Donald Sutherland), an affluent tax attorney; Beth (Mary Tyler Moore), his
efficient homemaker-wife; and Conrad (Timothy Hutton), the second son—all undergo
recriminations and Conrad, who blames himself for surviving, attempts suicide. The
boy is helped in his emotional recovery by psychiatrist T. C. Berger (Judd Hirsch).
Academy Awards: best picture, director, supporting actor (Hutton), and screenplay
adaptation (Alvin Sargent).

Out of Africa   1985   (MCA)   ◆ *Color*
Director: Sydney Pollack
Starring: Robert Redford, Meryl Streep, Klaus Maria Brandauer, Michael Kitchen, Malick
Bowens, Joseph Thiaka, Stephen Kinyanjui, Michael Gough, Suzanna Hamilton, Rachel
Kempson, Graham Crowden, Leslie Phillips, Shane Rimmer, Mike Bugara, Job Seda, Mo-
hammed Umar, Donal McCann

This majestically shot romantic tale dramatizes the young womanhood of Danish novelist Isak Dinesen (then known under her real name, Karen Blixen). The screenplay by Kurt Luedtke, with some rewriting by David Rayfiel, focuses on the heroine's life on a coffee plantation in pre–World War I Kenya. Taken from Miss Dinesen's writings and other books, including the Judith Thurman biography *Isak Dinesen: The Life of a Storyteller*, *Out of Africa* presents Meryl Streep as Karen, the patrician plantation owner; Klaus Maria Brandauer as her husband in name only, Baron Bror Blixen; and Robert Redford as the English big-game hunter, Denys Finch Hatton, with whom she falls in love. Seven Academy Awards: best picture, screenplay, direction (Sydney Pollack), score (John Barry), cinematography (David Watkin), art direction/set decoration (Stephen Grimes, Josie MacAvin), and sound (Chris Jenkins, Gary Alexander, Larry Stensvold, Peter Handford).

The Outsiders 1983 (Warner) *Color*
Director: Francis Coppola
Starring: C. Thomas Howell, Matt Dillon, Ralph Macchio, Patrick Swayze, Rob Lowe, Diane Lane, Emilio Estevez, Tom Cruise, Leif Garrett, Tom Waits

Tulsa, Oklahoma, in the late sixties is the scene for this teenage conflict drama. A Francis Coppola production, *The Outsiders* is based on the popular S. E. Hinton novel, and adapted by screenwriter Kathleen Knutson Rowell. The plot stems from a deep-seated rivalry between the "socs" (society kids) and the "greasers." After presenting an initial accidental killing (and the flight of two innocents—played by C. Thomas Howell and Ralph Macchio), the film settles into a gang-rumble story. Upon completion of this production, Coppola and S. E. Hinton coadapted another of her young adult novels, *Rumble Fish*; Matt Dillon again took a leading role.

The Paper **Chase** 1973 (CBS) ◆ *Color*
Director: James Bridges
Starring: Timothy Bottoms, Lindsay Wagner, John Houseman, Graham Beckel, Edward Herrmann, Craig Richard Nelson, James Naughton, Bob Lydiard

The competitive first year of Harvard Law School; that's round one of the paper chase. In this comedy-drama, assimilated from John Jay Osborn's novel by writer-director James Bridges, James T. Hart (Timothy Bridges), the earnest hero, encounters Professor Charles Kingsfield (John Houseman in his Oscar-winning supporting role). The professor is the world's leading authority on contract law—and his course is the make-or-break one for freshmen. Hart makes a pressurized situation even worse: the young woman he is dating is Kingsfield's daughter, a temperamental divorcée (Lindsay Wagner). As the haughty Kingsfield, Houseman patented his withering stare on the subsequent TV series for CBS and Showtime.

Paper Moon *Listed under Comedies.*

Papillon *Listed under Biographies.*

A Passage to India 1984 (RCA) ✻ ◆ ★ *Color*
Director: David Lean
Starring: Peggy Ashcroft, Judy Davis, James Fox, Alec Guinness, Nigel Havers, Victor Banerjee, Richard Wilson, Michael Culver, Antonia Pemberton, Art Malik, Ann Firbank, Saeed Jaffrey, Clive Swift, Sandra Hotz, Roshan Seth

This multiple-award recipient was named best picture by the New York Film Critics Circle and the National Board of Review—and both bodies cited leading lady Peggy Ashcroft and director David Lean; additionally it was honored with several Oscars—for Maurice Jarre's score and Dame Peggy's (supporting) performance; meanwhile, the star won the British Academy Award in the best actress category. *A Passage to India*, derived from the E. M. Forster novel and the playscript by Santha Rama Rau, represents editor-screenwriter-director Lean's return to filmmaking. (There was a fourteen-year gap between *Ryan's Daughter* and this epic.) Forster's mystical tale occurs in the Chandrapore district of India during the British colonial rule of the 1920s. A naïve young woman (Judy Davis), away from England for the first time, arrives on the scene with her future mother-in-law (Ashcroft). The newcomers are befriended by a kindly, though social-climbing, doctor (Victor Banerjee) who escorts them on an elaborate excursion to the forbidding Marabar Caves—where the drama comes to a crisis.

Paths of Glory   *Listed under War.*

Patterns   1956   (Goodtimes Home Video Corp.)   *Black-and-White*
Director: Fielder Cook
Starring: Van Heflin, Everett Sloane, Ed Begley, Beatrice Straight, Elizabeth Wilson, Joanna Roos, Ronnie Welsh, Jr.

A large New York organization becomes the setting for corporate intrigue, fortune-making, and reputation-building (and demolition). *Patterns* is an expansion by Rod Serling of his 1955 *Kraft Television Theatre* script; most of the original TV actors reprise their performances for the film. Junior executive Frank Staples (Van Heflin) joins the high-pressure company and is assigned to work with veteran Bill Briggs (Ed Begley). Little does Frank realize that Bill is being set up for a fall. Jim Ramsey (Everett Sloane), the corporation president, intends to groom Frank as Bill's replacement. The patterns of power as they surface in board meetings provide the drama. *Patterns* was Fielder Cook's feature film directing debut; after several other movies—notably *A Big Hand for the Little Lady* and *From the Mixed-Up Files of Mrs. Basil E. Frankweiler*—he turned again to television, where his greatest successes lie (*Too Far to Go, I Know Why the Caged Bird Sings, Will There Really Be a Morning?*).

The Pawnbroker   1965   (Republic)   *Black-and-White*
Director: Sidney Lumet
Starring: Rod Steiger, Geraldine Fitzgerald, Brock Peters, Jaime Sanchez, Thelma Oliver, Juano Hernandez, Marketa Kimbrell, Baruch Lumet, Linda Geiser, Nancy R. Pollock, Raymond St. Jacques, Warren Finnerty

This parable is distinguished by Rod Steiger's searing performance as Sol Nazerman, a Jewish pawnbroker in Spanish Harlem. A survivor of a Nazi concentration camp where his wife and children perished, Sol remains detached from his customers and acquaintances. But even callousness can't minimize the torment of his memories. (The prison camp episodes are rendered, sometimes almost subliminally, in flashbacks.) Confronted with the violence on New York streets, Sol's present world begins to crumble, too. Director Sidney Lumet's firm grip is apparent throughout in this adaptation of Edward Lewis Wallant's novel. (David Friedkin and Morton Fine cowrote the screenplay.) In the supporting cast, Juano Hernandez as an old man starved for companionship stands out.

Payday   1973   (Thorn)   *Color*
Director: Daryl Duke
Starring: Rip Torn, Ahna Capri, Elayne Heilveil, Michael C. Gwynne, Cliff Emmich

This drama traces a day and a half in the life of country music singer Maury Dann (Rip Torn). On tour in the South, Maury travels in a chauffeur-driven Cadillac; his entourage rides in another car. En route to a one-night stand in Birmingham, the troupe encounters groupies, disc jockeys, and Maury's full-blown egotism. (He's successful and borderline psychotic in equal measure.) Completed in 1971, then shelved until early 1973, *Payday* is directed by Daryl Duke, later renowned for the television adaptations of *The Thorn Birds* and *Tai-Pai*. The screenplay, authentic in milieu and dialogue, is by novelist Don Carpenter.

A Place in the Sun   1951   (Paramount)   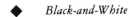   *Black-and-White*
Director: George Stevens
Starring: Montgomery Clift, Elizabeth Taylor, Shelley Winters, Anne Revere, Keefe Bras-selle, Fred Clark, Raymond Burr, Herbert Heyes, Shepperd Strudwick, Frieda Inescort, Kathryn Givney, Walter Sande, Ted De Corsia

An impoverished young man's longings for financial success and social acceptance underline this classic drama from director George Stevens. The source is Theodore Dreiser's *An American Tragedy*—filmed under its original title in 1931; but the setting here is modern (i.e., 1951). Montgomery Clift stars as George Eastman, a mill worker who romances (and impregnates) poor girl Alice Tripp (Shelley Winters), then sets his sight on society heiress Angela Vickers (Elizabeth Taylor). In order to woo Angela, he contemplates killing Alice. Ironically, when Alice drowns in a boating accident, George is charged with her murder. The Michael Wilson-Harry Brown screenplay tones down the social criticism of Dreiser's novel, but retains the overwhelming emotional impact. The film amassed six Academy Awards: direction, screenplay adaptation, cinematography (William C. Mellor), scoring (Franz Waxman), editing (William Hornbeck), and costume design (Edith Head).

Places in the Heart   1984   (CBS)   *Color*
Director: Robert Benton
Starring: Sally Field, Lindsay Crouse, Ed Harris, Amy Madigan, John Malkovich, Danny Glover, Lane Smith, Terry O'Quinn, Bert Remsen, Yankton Hatten, Gennie James, Ray Baker, Jay Patterson

Myth and nostalgia permeate this period drama from writer-director Robert Benton. Set in Benton's hometown of Waxahachie, Texas, in 1935, *Places in the Heart* focuses on a widow who has two small children—and a farm on which the bank is about to foreclose. After her husband is killed in an accident, Edna Spalding (Sally Field) must learn how to plant and harvest a cotton crop. Helping her are Moze (Danny Glover), a black hobo, and Mr. Will (John Malkovich), a blind man who becomes a boarder in the Spalding home. Other ingredients in Benton's recollection include a tornado, Ku Klux Klan coercion against Moze, and an extramarital affair that affects three essentially good-hearted people (Lindsay Crouse, Ed Harris, and Amy Madigan). What is basically a well-observed tale of the Depression is elevated to something considerably more in its final ninety seconds. The director of photography is Nestor Almendros, who worked with Benton on *Kramer vs. Kramer* and *Still of the Night*. Academy Awards went to Sally Field and to Benton for his original screenplay.

The Prime of Miss Jean Brodie   1969   (CBS)   ◆   *Color*
Director: Ronald Neame
Starring: Maggie Smith, Robert Stephens, Pamela Franklin, Celia Johnson, Gordon Jackson, Jane Carr

Miss Brodie (Maggie Smith), an unorthodox teacher at Marcia Blaine's School for Girls in 1932 Edinburgh, devotes her prime to her students—especially the select "Brodie set"—upon whom she exerts a benevolently despotic influence. ("I am putting old heads on your young shoulders, and all my pupils are the crème de la crème.") Director Ronald Neame herewith surpassed the reputation he established with *Tunes of Glory*, *The Chalk Garden*, and other films. Jay Presson Allen's screenplay, derived from her theatrical adaptation of Muriel Spark's novel, is a model of compression and restructuring. Maggie Smith's interpretation won her the best actress Academy Award.

Promises in the Dark   1979   (Warner)   *Color*
Director: Jerome Hellman
Starring: Marsha Mason, Ned Beatty, Susan Clark, Michael Brandon, Kathleen Beller, Paul Clemens, Donald Moffat

In this medical drama, Kathleen Beller portrays a teenager dying of cancer. Striving to ease her final hours is a compassionate doctor (Marsha Mason). As the girl's pain increases, the doctor undergoes a crisis of conscience. Ultimately, as directed by Jerome Hellman from a screenplay by Loring Mandel, *Promises in the Dark* makes a strong pro-euthanasia statement. A case history, the film contains sensitive performances by the two leading ladies and by Michael Brandon as Mason's love interest, Paul Clemens as the young patient's boyfriend, and Ned Beatty and Susan Clark as her parents.

The Proud Rebel   1958   (Embassy)   *Color*
Director: Michael Curtiz
Starring: Alan Ladd, Olivia de Havilland, Dean Jagger, David Ladd, Cecil Kellaway, Henry Hull, John Carradine, James Westerfield

A Civil War veteran (Alan Ladd), the titular Rebel, and his mute son (David Ladd) drift north. The father, while searching for expert medical help for the boy, accepts a job with a Yankee farm woman (Olivia de Havilland). *The Proud Rebel* is one of the senior Ladd's best post-*Shane* films; his son David, here in his screen debut, made a few more movies (notably *A Dog of Flanders*), then abandoned acting. A family Western, written by Joseph Patracca and Lillie Hayward, *The Proud Rebel* was directed by Michael Curtiz. Look for Harry Dean Stanton (then billed without the Harry) in a small role.

Providence   1977   (RCA)   ▲   *Color*
Director: Alain Resnais
Starring: Dirk Bogarde, John Gielgud, Ellen Burstyn, David Warner, Elaine Stritch

A dying novelist, whose pain eliminates all hope of sleep, lies awake imagining his final book. His dramatis personae include members of his family—who take on shocking larger-than-life characteristics. When the family assembles for the writer's seventy-eighth birthday, they are revealed as quite unlike the old man's imagination of them. John Gielgud plays the novelist; Dirk Bogarde his barrister son; Ellen Burstyn his daughter-in-law; David Warner his illegitimate son. David Mercer's complex screenplay commingles biography, French classic tragedy, Ingmar Bergmanesque introspection, and horror films. Ricardo Aronovich is responsible for the cinematography. At the year-end César (French Oscar) ceremonies, *Providence* was cited as best film and Alain Resnais proclaimed best director.

The **Q**uiet Man   *Listed under Comedies.*

Rachel and the Stranger   1948   (Nostalgia)   *Black-and-White*
Director: Norman Foster
Starring: Loretta Young, William Holden, Robert Mitchum, Tom Tully, Sara Haden, Gary Gray, Frank Ferguson

Actor-turned-director Norman Foster (he helmed B series like Mr. Moto and Charlie Chan) had his most notable brushes with class-A filmmaking in the 1942 *Journey into Fear* and with this Western comedy-drama. Based on a novel by Howard Fast and the screenplay by Martin Rackin, the picture concerns Rachel (Loretta Young), the taken-for-granted wife of a frontier backwoodsman (William Holden). A handsome wanderer (Robert Mitchum) passes through their remote settlement—and briefly complicates, then simplifies, the couple's life. When the stranger nearly woos Rachel away, her husband finally declares his love for her. Under Foster's direction, a slim premise becomes an appealing romance.

Rachel, Rachel   1968   (Warner)   ✻   *Color*
Director: Paul Newman
Starring: Joanne Woodward, James Olson, Kate Harrington, Estelle Parsons, Donald Moffat, Terry Kiser, Frank Corsaro, Bernard Barrow, Geraldine Fitzgerald, Nell Potts, Shawn Campbell, Violet Dunn, Izzy Singer

Rachel (Joanne Woodward) is a thirty-five-year-old spinster schoolteacher in a small New England community. She is plagued by boredom, sexual inhibition, and responsibility for her sickly mother (Kate Harrington); the two share an apartment over a funeral home where Rachel's late father worked as an embalmer. The summer in which the film takes place, Rachel tries to come out of her shell. A character study, the film is adapted by Stewart Stern from Margaret Laurence's novel, *A Jest of God.* James Olson plays a potential love match for Rachel, and Estelle Parsons plays one of her school colleagues. *Rachel, Rachel* was Paul Newman's first directorial outing, and he has subsequently directed his wife in TV adaptations of *The Shadow Box* and in *The Glass Menagerie.* In 1968 the New York Film Critics Circle cited both Woodward and Newman for *Rachel, Rachel.*

Raging Bull   *Listed under Biographies.*

Ragtime   1981   (Paramount)   *Color*
Director: Miloš Forman
Starring: James Cagney, Elizabeth McGovern, Howard E. Rollins, Jr., Mary Steenburgen, James Olson, Brad Dourif, Kenneth McMillan, Mandy Patinkin, Donald O'Connor, Pat O'Brien, Debbie Allen, Moses Gunn, Norman Mailer

This film treatment of the sweeping E. L. Doctorow novel interweaves historical events

with the lives of a (fictional) turn-of-the-century New York family. In the episodic interpretation by screenwriter Michael Weller and director Miloš Forman, such legends as
Harry Houdini, Evelyn Nesbit, Stanford White, and several real-life political figures
emerge in the passing parade. There is ultimate emphasis on black musician Coalhouse
Walker (Howard E. Rollins, Jr.) and his pursuit of justice and fight against prejudice—
and on the middle-class white family headed by James Olson and Mary Steenburgen.
In the small role of Police Commissioner Waldo, James Cagney made his comeback
(after an absence of twenty years) *and* his farewell movie appearance. (His last performance came in the 1984 telefilm, "Terrible Joe Moran.") Integral to *Ragtime*'s success
are Miroslav Ondriček's cinematography and the Randy Newman score.

A Raisin in the Sun   1961   (RCA)   *Black-and-White*
Director: Daniel Petrie
*Starring: Sidney Poitier, Claudia McNeil, Ruby Dee, Diana Sands, Ivan Dixon, John
Fiedler, Louis Gossett*

Lorraine Hansberry's prize-winning Broadway drama was adapted for the screen by
the playwright herself. Under examination is a black family from Chicago and their
efforts to abandon their overcrowded apartment for a home in an all-white neighborhood. The move is made possible by a $10,000 insurance benefit. But trouble—in the
form of fraud and racial prejudice—intervenes en route to the happy ending. Claudia
McNeil plays the family matriarch; Diana Sands is cast as her daughter, studying to be
a doctor; Sidney Poitier plays the elder son, longing to quit his chauffeur job; and
Ruby Dee portrays his wife.

Rambo: First Blood, Part II   1985   (Thorn)   *Color*
Director: George P. Cosmatos
Starring: Sylvester Stallone, Richard Crenna, Martin Kove, Charles Napier, Julia Nickson

More violent than its predecessor, *First Blood,* this revenge drama follows guerrilla
fighter John Rambo (Sylvester Stallone) as he destroys the Viet Cong and cleans up
at the box office. Nearly $100 million was registered in its initial release—and the
producers are still counting. The plot unfolds when Rambo is sent back to Vietnam
to search for Americans reported missing in action. The screenplay is by Stallone and
James Cameron, and directed by George P. Cosmatos. The two features inspired a
five-part TV cartoon miniseries, also called "Rambo," with the hero leading a strike
force against evildoers in a South American country.

Rebel Without a Cause   1955   (Warner)   *Color*
Director: Nicholas Ray
*Starring: James Dean, Natalie Wood, Sal Mineo, Jim Backus, Ann Doran, Corey Allen,
William Hopper, Rochelle Hudson, Dennis Hopper, Edward C. Platt, Virginia Brissac,
Ian Wolfe, Robert Foulk, Jack Simmons, Nick Adams*

Released a mere six months after *East of Eden,* this examination of youthful alienation
fueled the public's desire for more James Dean. His performance dominates the film,
directed by Nicholas Ray from his original story and a screenplay by Stewart Stern
and Irving Shulman. Dean plays Jim Stark, a misunderstood teenager yearning for
acceptance but driven to rebellion. His parents (Jim Backus, Ann Doran) aren't supportive, and the gangs at school only compound his misfit feelings. Knife fights, a
"chicken run" car race, and violent death provide the action in *Rebel Without a Cause;*

but there is sensitivity, too—in Dean's interpretation and in his relationship with two good-hearted high school chums (Natalie Wood and Sal Mineo). This depiction of tormented youth achieved cult status, owing partly to the star's fatal car crash in 1955.

The Red Badge of Courage   1951   (MGM)   *Black-and-White*
Director: John Huston
Starring: Audie Murphy, Bill Mauldin, Douglas Dick, Royal Dano, John Dierkes, Arthur Hunnicutt, Tim Durant, Andy Devine, Robert Easton, Glenn Strange, Whit Bissell

This adaptation of Stephen Crane's Civil War novel, from a screenplay by director John Huston and Albert Band, retells of Henry Fleming (Audie Murphy), the young soldier who questions his bravery, runs away during a battle, then returns, still uncertain, to the fray. When the youth receives a wound—his red badge of courage—he comes to terms with the possibility of death. A sobering depiction of war, this small-scale production was a struggle for Huston. (The Lillian Ross book, *Picture*, gives a full account of the rigors the director endured, including studio interference both during and after the shooting.) Cartoonist Bill Mauldin plays the loud soldier; Douglas Dick, the lieutenant; Royal Dano, the tattered man; and John Dierkes, the tall soldier. A 1974 television remake starred Richard Thomas.

The Red Shoes   1948   (Learning)   ◆   *Color*
Directors: Michael Powell, Emeric Pressburger
Starring: Anton Walbrook, Marius Goring, Moira Shearer, Robert Helpmann, Leonide Massine, Albert Basserman, Ludmilla Tcherina, Esmond Knight, Jean Short, Gordon Littman, Austin Trevor, Eric Berry, Irene Brown

This milestone British film, set in the world of classical dance, is not just for balletomanes. Devised by the writing-producing-directing team of Michael Powell and Emeric Pressburger (with additional dialogue by Keith Winter), it's the tale of middle-aged impresario Boris Lermontov (Anton Walbrook) and his obsession with young dancer Victoria Page (Moira Shearer in her film debut). Boris wants to develop Vicky as his prima ballerina and, because he demands complete dedication, he tries to sabotage her budding love affair with composer Julian Craster (Marius Goring). The director of photography is Jack Cardiff; the choreography is by Robert Helpmann, who also appears as Ivan Boleslawsky. Oscars went to Brian Easdale for his score and to Hein Heckroth and Arthur Lawson for art direction/set decoration.

Reds   *Listed under Biographies.*

The Right Stuff   *Listed under Biographies.*

The Robe   1953   (CBS)   *Color*
Director: Henry Koster
Starring: Richard Burton, Jean Simmons, Victor Mature, Michael Rennie, Jay Robinson, Dean Jagger, Torin Thatcher, Richard Boone, Betta St. John, Jeff Morrow, Ernest Thesiger, Dawn Addams, Leon Askin, Michael Ansara

The first film in CinemaScope, this religious epic, adapted by Philip Dunne from the Lloyd C. Douglas novel, stars Richard Burton as Marcellus Gallio, a Roman tribune in charge of Christ's crucifixion. The film chronicles the tribune's conversion to Christianity as he and others come in contact with the robe worn by Jesus. Helping Marcellus keep the robe from the clutches of Caligula (Jay Robinson) are Demetrius (Victor Mature), a slave; Diana (Jean Simmons), a young noblewoman; and Peter (Michael Rennie), the fisherman of Galilee. *The Robe* was enormously popular in its day and led to a sequel, *Demetrius and the Gladiators* (1954)—this time with Mature as the lead.

Robin and Marian   1976   (RCA)   *Color*
Director: Richard Lester
Starring: Audrey Hepburn, Sean Connery, Robert Shaw, Richard Harris, Nicol Williamson, Denholm Elliott, Ian Holm, Kenneth Haigh, Ronnie Barker, Bill Maynard, Esmond Knight, Peter Butterworth

A seemingly unlikely project for madcap comedy director Richard Lester, *Robin and Marian* is a romantic drama forged from the legends of the twelfth-century English outlaw. Central to James Goldman's screenplay is the love affair between aging Robin Hood—back from the Crusades—and Maid Marian, who has joined a convent. They have not seen one another in twenty years, and yet their romance is soon rekindled. Other familiar Sherwood Forest characters figure into the story too: Little John (Nicol Williamson), Will Scarlett (Denholm Elliott), and Friar Tuck (Ronnie Barker), and, though older, King John (Ian Holm) and the Sheriff of Nottingham (Robert Shaw).

Rocky   1976   (CBS)   ◆   *Color*
Director: John G. Avildsen
Starring: Sylvester Stallone, Talia Shire, Burt Young, Carl Weathers, Thayer David, Joe Spinell, Jimmy Gambina, George Memmoli, Bill Baldwin, Billy Sands, Burgess Meredith

The Oscar-winning best picture of 1976, *Rocky* brought additional statuettes to John Avildsen for his direction and to Richard Halsey and Scott Conrad for their editing. Three sequels and millions of dollars later, it's hard to remember that this film was a true sleeper that charmed both critics and ticket buyers. From star Sly Stallone's script, the picture relates a Cinderella story about an obscure club boxer from Philadelphia who vies for the heavyweight title. He's told it's a "million-to-one shot" and proceeds to narrow the odds. Sequels: *Rocky II* (1979), *Rocky III* (1982), and *Rocky IV* (1985).

Rocky II   1979   (CBS)   *Color*
Director: Sylvester Stallone
Starring: Sylvester Stallone, Talia Shire, Burgess Meredith, Burt Young, Carl Weathers

Rocky Balboa returns! And so do Adrian (Talia Shire), his wife; Paulie (Burt Young), his brother-in-law; and Mickey (Burgess Meredith), his trainer. Disillusioned by the commercialism that followed his bout with Apollo Creed (Carl Weathers), Rocky gears up for a rematch. Again Sylvester Stallone is both star and scenarist, though this time he also directs. Bill Conti again provides the stirring score. And again Irwin Winkler and Robert Chartoff are the producers. The new element: cinematographer Bill Butler.

Rocky III   1982   (CBS)   *Color*
Director: Sylvester Stallone
Starring: Sylvester Stallone, Talia Shire, Burgess Meredith, Burt Young, Carl Weathers, Tony Burton, Mr. T., Ian Fried, Al Silvani, Wally Taylor, Hulk Hogan

The Italian Stallion is trained by Apollo Creed (Carl Weathers), his former nemesis, for a championship bout with Clubber Lang (Mr. T.). Rocky, after years at the top, must learn to be hungry again. Directed by Stallone from his own screenscript and starring the cast of regulars. And the formula continues in *Rocky IV* (1985).

Romeo and Juliet   1954   (Learning)   *Color*
Director: Renato Castellani
Starring: Laurence Harvey, Susan Shentall, Flora Robson, Mervyn Johns, Bill Travers, Sebastian Cabot, Enzo Fiermonte, Norman Wooland, Aldo Zollo, Lydia Sherwood, Giulio Garbinetti, John Gielgud

Siena, Venice, and Verona provide the backdrops for this location-shot version of Shakespeare's drama. It's a visual spectacle as photographed by Robert Krasker. The pair of star-crossed lovers once more enact their story of woe—Romeo (Laurence Harvey), heir of the Montagues, and Juliet (Susan Shentall), daughter of the rival Capulets. They are supported by Sir John Gielgud, who speaks the prologue; Bill Travers as Benvolio; Flora Robson as the nurse; Mervyn Johns as Friar Laurence; and Sebastian Cabot as Capulet. Lenor Fini is the costume designer, and the musical score is by Roman Vlad. This 1954 Anglo-Italian rendition of *Romeo and Juliet* falls midway between the MGM mounting in 1936 and the Zeffirelli adaptation.

Romeo and Juliet   1968   (Paramount)   *Color*
Director: Franco Zeffirelli
Starring: Leonard Whiting, Olivia Hussey, Milo O'Shea, Robert Stephens, Natasha Parry, Michael York, Pat Heywood, Paul Hardwick, Bruce Robinson

Franco Zeffirelli's condensation of Shakespeare's play was hotly debated back in 1968. Scholars complained about the director's excisions, and opinion was divided on the leads. Teenage actors playing the title roles was a rarity—Leonard Whiting and Olivia Hussey were, respectively, seventeen and sixteen at the time. In fact, the film's youth appeal may have contributed to the box office success. Pat Heywood plays the nurse and John McEnery is Mercutio. The cinematographer is Pasquale de Santis and the score is by Nino Rota. (His theme, "What Is a Youth?," was so popular with young lovers that, for several years, it supplanted Mendelssohn's "Wedding March" as the preferred marriage ceremony melody.)

Room at the Top   1959   (Electric Video)   ◆   *Black-and-White*
Director: Jack Clayton
Starring: Laurence Harvey, Simone Signoret, Heather Sears, Donald Wolfit, Hermione Baddeley, Ambrosine Philpotts, Donald Houston, Raymond Huntley, John Westbrook, Allan Cuthbertson, Mary Peach

Joe Lampton (Laurence Harvey), an ex-Royal Air Force sergeant, is determined to make it to the top now that he's a civilian. He leaves the stifling slums of his native Yorkshire and moves to a nearby city where he becomes a clerk in the town hall. Joe is enthralled by class, money, and power. Venal and ambitious in equal measure, he conspires to woo and marry the daughter (Heather Sears) of the local tycoon (Donald Wolfit). Meanwhile, he abandons his mistress—and true love—Alice (Simone Signoret). This condensation and reconstruction of John Braine's *Angry Young Man* novel brought Oscars to screenwriter Neil Paterson and to Signoret as best actress. Also noteworthy in Jack Clayton's cast are Sears, Wolfit, Donald Houston, Hermione Baddeley, and Harvey, who for the occasion speaks with a Midlands accent. Joe Lampton's cynical opportunism resurfaced in two sequels: *Life at the Top* (1965) and *Man at the Top* (1973), the last also being the title of a British TV series that played the States on PBS stations.

The Rose   1979   (CBS)   *Color*
Director: Mark Rydell
Starring: Bette Midler, Alan Bates, Frederic Forrest, Barry Primus, Sandra McCabe, David Keith, Harry Dean Stanton, Will Hare, Rudy Bond, Don Calfa, James Keane, Doris Roberts, Sandy Ward, Michael Greer, Claude Sacha, Michael St. Laurent, Sylvester, John Dennis Johnston, Seamon Glass, Pat Corley, Hildy Brooks, Jack Starret, Chip Zien

Mary Rose Foster, known as The Rose (Bette Midler), is an alcoholic, drugged-out rock star who pleads with her manager (Alan Bates) for a year's vacation. When the hardnosed manager refuses, The Rose escapes anyway—for a bit. But she returns to fulfill concert dates in St. Louis and, climatically, Memphis, her home town. This dark portrait of a self-destructive Janis Joplinesque singer catapulted Bette Midler to screen stardom; her energy dominates the picture. (Frederic Forrest and David Keith are also commendable as a chauffeur and a soldier who befriend The Rose.) Bill Kerby and Bo Goldman devised the story, and their screenplay is peppered with acute observations and forthright language. The music is arranged and conducted by Paul Rothchild, and Bette sings, among other selections, "When a Man Loves a Woman," "Sold My Soul to Rock 'n' Roll," "Stay With Me, Baby," and the title song. Vilmos Zsigmond is the principal photographer, while other cinematographers share credit for the concert footage: Conrad Hall, Haskell Wexler, and Laszlo Kovacs.

Ryan's Daughter   1970   (MGM)   ◆   *Color*
Director: David Lean
Starring: Robert Mitchum, Trevor Howard, John Mills, Christopher Jones, Sarah Miles, Leo McKern, Barry Foster, Archie O'Sullivan, Marie Kean

The time is 1916, the place a coastal village in Ireland. Rosy Ryan (Sarah Miles) is the daughter of the local publican (Leo McKern). She marries a widowed schoolmaster (Robert Mitchum) twice her age, and—a romantic creature spoiled by her father—she is bored. Her boredom, however, wanes when a dashing British major (Christopher Jones) is assigned to the town's small garrison. Although Rosy's husband is unconcerned about the extramarital affair that develops, the townspeople turn against the girl. (They suspect Rosy and her father of passing IRA secrets to the British; finally, as punishment, they publicly strip her and cut off her hair.) The original screenplay by stage dramatist Robert Bolt (*A Man for All Seasons*) is directed by David Lean—his last film before *A Passage to India* (1984). *Ryan's Daughter* is distinguished by Freddie Young's cinematography, for which he won an Oscar—as did John Mills, featured in the role of Michael, the mute fool. Other performers, particularly Trevor Howard as the village priest, are notable too.

Samson and Delilah   1949   (Paramount)   ◆   *Color*
Director: Cecil B. De Mille
Starring: Hedy Lamarr, Victor Mature, George Sanders, Angela Lansbury, Henry Wilcoxon, Olive Deering, Fay Holden, Julia Faye, Rusty Tamblyn, William Farnum, Lane Chandler, Moroni Olsen, Mike Mazurki, George Reeves, Nils Asther, Karen Morley, Tom Tyler

Based on the Biblical chronicles of Samson and Delilah (Judges, chapters 13 to 16), this Cecil B. De Mille spectacular won Oscars for the costume designers, led by Dorothy Jeakins and Edith Head, and for the art directors and set decorators. Featuring De Mille's traditional opulence, high-charged drama, and special effects, the tale is an elaborate one. Victor Mature stars as the muscleman whose power is curtailed when Delilah, played by Hedy Lamarr, shears his locks. Also speaking the Jesse L. Lasky, Jr.-Frederic M. Frank dialogue are Angela Lansbury, as Delilah's sister, Semadar; Henry Wilcoxon as Ahtur; silent star William Farnum as Tubal; and George Sanders as the villainous Saran of Gaza. Music by Victor Young. George Barnes is the director of photography.

Saturday Night Fever   1977   (Paramount)   *Color*
Director: John Badham
Starring: John Travolta, Karen Lynn Gorney, Joseph Cali, Donna Pescow, Barry Miller, Paul Pape, Julie Bovasso, Bruce Ornstein, Martin Shakar, Val Bisoglio, Lisa Peluso, Sam J. Coppola, Nina Hansen, Monti Rock III, Denny Dillon, Fran Drescher

Tony Manero (John Travolta) dreams of escaping his working-class existence in Brooklyn's Bay Ridge. Nineteen years old, Tony works in a hardware store by day, then comes alive at night dancing in the 2001 Odyssey disco. By winning a Saturday night dance contest, he hopes to fulfill his fantasy—and make it big in Manhattan. Also offering major contributions are his costars, director John Badham, cinematographer Ralf D. Bode, editor David Rawlins, and the song score—performed (and for the most part created) by the Bee Gees. Norman Wexler's screeenplay was inspired by Nik Cohn's *New York* magazine article, "Tribal Rites of the New Saturday Night." Sequel: *Staying Alive,* in which Tony achieves Broadway stardom.

Sayonara   1957   (CBS)   *Color*
Director: Joshua Logan
Starring: Marlon Brando, Red Buttons, Ricardo Montalban, Miiko Taka, Miyoshi Umeki, Patricia Owens, James Garner, Martha Scott, Kent Smith, The Shochuku Kagekidan Girls Revue

Filmed on location in Kobe, Japan, this romantic drama is an adaptation of the James Michener novel. With a screenplay by veteran dramatist Paul Osborn and direction by Broadway dynamo Joshua Logan, *Sayonara* gives Marlon Brando one of his most sympathetic roles. Stationed in post–World War II Japan, Major Lloyd Gruver (Brando), an American pilot, falls in love with a geisha girl (Miiko Taka). The clash of cultures, added to the tensions of recent history, makes their affair difficult to sustain. A parallel love story involves Red Buttons and Miyoshi Umeki—in Oscar-winning supporting roles. Other Acadamy Award recipients: sound recordist George Groves, art director Ted Haworth, and set decorator Robert Priestly. Irving Berlin wrote the title song.

Scarecrow   1973   (Warner)   *Color*
Director: Jerry Schatzberg
Starring: Gene Hackman, Al Pacino, Dorothy Tristan, Ann Wedgeworth, Eileen Brennan, Richard Lynch

In this comedy-drama two drifters meet on a roadside and their lives become intertwined. Hitchhiking east from California is an ex-convict (Gene Hackman), destined for his sister's home in Denver, then for Philadelphia to open a car-wash establishment.

His companion, a demobilized sailor (Al Pacino), hopes to visit in Detroit with the little daughter he has never seen. Ultimately, the two loners decide to band together in the car-wash business. Directed by Jerry Schatzberg—whose credits include *The Panic in Needle Park*, *The Seduction of Joe Tynan*, and *Honeysuckle Rose*—this picture stands as a kind of peripatetic *Midnight Cowboy*. The screenplay is by Garry Michael White; Vilmos Zsigmond is the cinematographer.

The Seduction of Joe Tynan   1979   (MCA)   ✳   *Color*
Director: Jerry Schatzberg
Starring: Alan Alda, Barbara Harris, Meryl Streep, Melvyn Douglas, Rip Torn, Carrie Nye, Charles Kimbrough

Joe Tynan (Alan Alda), a young liberal senator earmarked for success, is torn between his personal life and his political aspirations. Tynan has long been faithful to his wife (Barbara Harris), but in Washington the road to political advancement includes an illicit liaison with a civil rights activist (Meryl Streep). The protagonist discovers that when his wedding vows are tarnished, so are his other principles. Alan Alda, as star and screenwriter, is essentially the *auteur* of this study of character and politics; Jerry Schatzberg is credited with the direction. The New York Film Critics Circle honored supporting actress Streep for her performance—and for another of her 1979 roles, the mother in *Kramer vs. Kramer*.

A Separate Peace   1972   (Paramount)   *Color*
Director: Larry Peerce
Starring: John Heyl, Parker Stevenson, Victor Bevine, William Roerick, Peter Brush, Scott Bradbury

John Knowles' *A Separate Peace*, required teen English class reading for the last twenty years (as a postscript to *The Catcher in the Rye*), tells of two New England boarding school students, circa 1942. Studious Gene and athletic Finny (Parker Stevenson and John Heyl) are Devon roommates who grow toward maturity in the closing years of World War II. A curious rivalry-friendship develops between them, leading to a tragic accident. Heyl and Stevenson make their screen debuts under Larry Peerce's direction.

Separate Tables   1958   (CBS)   ◆   *Black-and-White*
Director: Delbert Mann
Starring: Rita Hayworth, Burt Lancaster, Deborah Kerr, David Niven, Wendy Hiller, Gladys Cooper, Cathleen Nesbitt, Felix Aylmer, Rod Taylor, Audrey Dalton, May Hallatt, Priscilla Morgan, Hilda Plowright

The two one-act plays of Terence Rattigan's stage drama are interwoven in this film adaptation (by Rattigan with John Gay). An English seaside guest house is the setting for the conflict. Among the boarders taken in by the proprietress (Wendy Hiller) are Ann Shankland (Rita Hayworth) and John Malcolm (Burt Lancaster), a divorced couple who cannot live with or without one another; Sibyl Railton-Bell (Deborah Kerr), a shy spinster, and her mother (Gladys Cooper); newlyweds Charles and Jean (Rod Taylor and Audrey Dalton); and a mysterious man of military bearing who calls himself Major Pollock (David Niven). The actors etch unforgettable characters; Niven and Hiller, in their Oscar-winning roles, add particular dimension to the picture.

Serpico   *Listed under Biographies.*

The Servant   1963   (Thorn)   *Black-and-White*
Director: Joseph Losey
Starring: Dirk Bogarde, James Fox, Sarah Miles, Wendy Craig, Derek Tansley, Dorothy
Bromiley, Ann Firbank, Richard Vernon, Patrick Magee, Alun Owen, Catherine Lacey,
Harold Pinter

Perversity and moral degradation attend this study of the English class system. A well-
born but weak-willed London aristocrat (James Fox) is easily manipulated by his cal-
culating manservant (Dirk Bogarde). The valet preys on his master's weaknesses; what
begins as a power struggle soon leads to character destruction. In time, the two men
completely reverse roles. This moody, sexually suggestive film represents the first
collaboration of director Joseph Losey and playwright Harold Pinter, who later teamed
for *Accident* and *The Go-Between*. Pinter's script for *The Servant* is derived from the
novel by Robin Maugham. The acting by the leading men—and by Wendy Craig as
the gentleman's mistress and Sarah Miles as the valet's accomplice—is memorable.

The Seven-Per-Cent Solution   1976   (MCA)   *Color*
Director: Herbert Ross
Starring: Alan Arkin, Vanessa Redgrave, Robert Duvall, Nicol Williamson, Laurence Oliv-
ier, Joel Gray, Samantha Eggar, Charles Gray, Georgia Brown, Régine, Jeremy Kemp

Sigmund Freud attempts to cure Sherlock Holmes of his persecution complex and his
cocaine addiction in this comic pastiche. Nicholas Meyer wrote the screenplay, a translation of his own whimsical novel. Sir Arthur Conan Doyle's renowned consulting
detective and his doctor friend have appeared in many movie adventures, but *The
Seven-Per-Cent Solution* is one of the most memorable. The star-filled cast includes Nicol
Williamson as the illustrious Holmes; Robert Duvall as his foil (and the viewer's
representative on the screen), Dr. Watson; Alan Arkin as Freud; and Laurence Olivier
as the evil genius Moriarty (seen here in a slightly different light). London and Vienna,
circa 1890, are re-created by production designer Ken Adam.

Shoot the Moon   1982   (MGM)   *Color*
Director: Alan Parker
Starring: Albert Finney, Diane Keaton, Karen Allen, Peter Weller, Dana Hill, Leora
Dana, Viveka Davis, Tracey Gold, Tina Yothers

George and Faith Dunlap and their four daughters are the subjects of *Shoot the Moon*.
They live together in a farmhouse in Marin County, California—the setting for constant
bitter arguments as George (Albert Finney), a writer, and Faith (Diane Keaton) are in
the throes of a divorce. When the break finally arrives, the emotional wreckage is
severe—for parents, children, and even friends and lovers on the sidelines. The Dun-
laps' is not a civilized, sweetly spoken divorce; there is rage, psychological torment,
and physical abuse before George and Faith move on to new partners. Bo Goldman's
screenplay and Alan Parker's direction work at a slow pace, but the film's melodramatic
observations are never dull.

Short Eyes   1977   (Lightning Video)   *Color*
Director Robert M. Young
Starring: Bruce Davison, José Perez, Nathan George, Don Blakely, Shawn Elliot, Tito
Goya, Joe Carberry, Kenny Steward, Bob Maroff, Keith Davis, Miguel Piñero, Curtis
Mayfield, Freddie Fender

Based on the drama by Miguel Piñero, as presented by Joe Papp's Shakespeare Festival, *Short Eyes* (prison slang for child-molester) was shot in the Tombs—New York City's Men's House of Detention. Piñero's screenscript retains the raw, forceful dialogue of the original stage play. As the drama opens, a new prisoner, Clark Davis (Bruce Davison), is led into the cell block. It is revealed that Clark is a child-molester. To the other convicts—muggers, shoplifters, drug pushers, murderers—Clark's crime is the gravest of all. In turn, they ostracize, taunt, and torture him. The film is directed by Robert M. Young, who is known for his TV documentaries, including the NBC "White Paper" specials. Under his guidance: Davison; José Perez as Juan (Poet); Nathan George as Ice; Tito Goya as Cupcakes; Joe Carberry as Longshoe Murphy; Piñero himself as Go Go; composer Curtis Mayfield; and Freddie Fender as a singing inmate.

Silkwood   *Listed under Biographies.*

Slaughterhouse-Five   1972   (MCA)   *Color*
Director: George Roy Hill
Starring: Michael Sacks, Ron Leibman, Eugene Roche, Sharon Gans, Valerie Perrine, John Dehner, Holly Near, Sorrell Booke, Perry King, Roberts Blossom, Kevin Conway

Kurt Vonnegut's cult novel has been conscientiously adapted by screenwriter Stephen Geller and director George Roy Hill. A satirical fantasy, *Slaughterhouse-Five* centers around the life span of Billy Pilgrim, a suburban optometrist. Billy gets "unstuck in time" and finds himself time- and space-tripping from his present home back to his World War II experiences in Dresden and forward to an existence on the planet Tralfamadore. (In the war Billy is witness to the fire-bombing of Dresden, while on Tralfamadore he is mated with Hollywood starlet Montana Wildhack, who frequently goes topless.) The hero, a contemporary Everyman, is embodied by Michael Sacks; Valerie Perrine plays Montana; Ron Leibman is cast as Lazzaro, a maniacal GI and later a maniacal civilian; Eugene Roche represents Derby; Sharon Gans plays Billy's wife; and Holly Near and Perry King portray his children. Cinematography by Miroslav Ondriček; the editor is Dede Allen.

A Soldier's Story   1984   (RCA)   *Color*
Director: Norman Jewison
Starring: Howard E. Rollins, Jr., Adolph Caesar, Art Evans, David Alan Grier, David Harris, Denis Lipscomb, Larry Riley, Robert Townsend, Denzel Washington, William Allen Young, Wings Hauser, Scott Paulin, John Hancock, Trey Wilson, Patti LaBelle

Dramatist Charles Fuller adapted his own Pulitzer Prize stage hit, *A Soldier's Play*, for this film version. On a segregated Louisiana army base in 1944, within a unit of black GI's, Sergeant Vernon C. Waters (Adolph Caesar) is murdered with a .45-caliber automatic. Dispatched to investigate the incident is a military lawyer from Washington—Captain Richard Davenport (Howard E. Rollins, Jr.). Davenport is that World War II rarity: a black officer, and his color gets in his way as he tries to find Waters's murderer. Ultimately, though, justice triumphs. The gravel-voiced Adolph Caesar won both an Obie and a New York Drama Desk Award in 1982 for his performance in the stage edition, and he was nominated for a 1984 Oscar. Score is by Herbie Hancock.

Somewhere in Time　　1980　　(MCA)　　　　　　　　　　*Color*
Director: Jeannot Szwarc
Starring: Christopher Reeve, Jane Seymour, Christopher Plummer, Teresa Wright, George
Voskovec, Bill Ewin, Tim Kazurinsky

Romance and suspense dominate this story of lovers separated by time and space. While vacationing in Michigan, a young playwright (Christopher Reeve) stops by a luxury hotel on Mackinac Island. There he discovers a seventy-year-old portrait of an actress (Jane Seymour). Infatuated with the beautiful woman and determined to win her love, the playwright practices self-hypnosis and becomes a time-traveler. And the lovers are united in the past—though not without complications. A romantic fantasy, *Somewhere in Time* was screenwritten by Richard Matheson from his novel, *Bid Time Return*. Both book and movie salute the time-honored tradition of *Portrait of Jennie*, *Berkeley Square*, and *I'll Never Forget You*—with hints of *Laura*.

Sophie's Choice　　1982　　(CBS)　　　　　.　　　　*Color*
Director: Alan J. Pakula
Starring: Meryl Streep, Kevin Kline, Peter MacNicol, Rita Karin, Stephen D. Newman,
Greta Turken, Josh Mostel, Moishe Rosenfeld, Robin Bartlett, Eugene Lipinski, John
Rothman, Gunther Maria Halmer

Meryl Streep stars as Sophie Zawistowska, a Polish survivor of a Nazi concentration camp. When we meet Sophie, living in a Brooklyn boardinghouse in 1947, she is still haunted by murky secrets about the Holocaust. Writer-director Alan Pakula's abridgment of the William Styron novel dramatizes Sophie's intimacy with two other boarders: her mercurial lover, Nathan Landau (Kevin Kline), and their downstairs neighbor, Stingo (Peter MacNicol). Stingo, an aspiring young novelist, becomes Sophie's confidant—but soon learns that her confessional reminiscences are often riddled with lies. In time, though, he discovers the dark horror that, in Auschwitz, led to Sophie's choice. Streep won an Oscar for her interpretation; but there are equally noteworthy performances by Kline and MacNicol. The voice-over narration is read by Josef Sommer (playing Stingo as a middle-aged man). Cinematography by Nestor Almendros.

Spartacus　　1960　　(MCA)　　　　　　　　　　　*Color*
Director: Stanley Kubrick
Starring: Kirk Douglas, Laurence Olivier, Jean Simmons, Tony Curtis, Charles Laughton,
Peter Ustinov, John Gavin, Nina Foch, Herbert Lom, John Ireland, John Dall, Charles
McGraw, Joanna Barnes, Woody Strode, Harold J. Stone, Peter Brocco, Paul Lambert,
John Hoyt

Dalton Trumbo's script, sculpted from the novel by Howard Fast, lends prestige to this spectacular. Laid in first century B.C. Rome, the film extols Spartacus (Kirk Douglas), the gladiator who led an army of slaves in a revolt against the bastions of the city. An unusually humane motion picture from director Stanley Kubrick, *Spartacus* features performances by Douglas as the stalwart hero; Laurence Olivier as Roman general Marcus Crassus; Jean Simmons as the virtuous Varinia; Charles Laughton as the republican Gracchus; John Gavin as Julius Caesar; Tony Curtis as the slave Antonius; and—perhaps best—Peter Ustinov as Batiatus, a slave dealer. Ustinov won an Oscar, as did cinematographer Russell Metty, the costume designers, and the art direction/ set decoration corps. Since 1960, *Spartacus* has been the victim of frequently mutilated prints, but the footage is intact for the videocassette version.

Splendor in the Grass   1961   (Warner)   ◆   *Color*
Director: Elia Kazan
Starring; Natalie Wood, Warren Beatty, Pat Hingle, Audrey Christie, Barbara Loden, Zohra Lampert, Fred Stewart, Joanna Roos, Jan Norris, Gary Lockwood, Sandy Dennis, Crystal Field, Marla Adams, Lynn Loring, Martine Bartlett, Sean Garrison, William Inge, Phyllis Diller

Playwright William Inge and director Elia Kazan collaborated on this probing study of sexual repression among Midwest high school students. Set in a small Kansas town in the twenties, *Splendor in the Grass* focuses on the mutal attraction of two teenagers: Wilma Dean Loomis (Natalie Wood) and Bud Stamper (Warren Beatty in his film debut). Their relationship is ultimately a tragedy that is wrought by hypocrisy and parental obtuseness. In the large supporting cast, Gary Lockwood and Sandy Dennis play Wilma and Bud's school friends, Toots and Kay; Zohra Lampert is cast as Angelina, the poor girl destined for Bud: Pat Hingle portrays Bud's father; and (in a bit) Inge plays the minister. (He also collected an Oscar for his screenplay.) A 1981 television remake stared Melissa Gilbert and Cyril O'Reilly.

The Sterile Cuckoo   1969   (Paramount)   *Color*
Director: Alan J. Pakula
Starring: Liza Minnelli, Wendell Burton, Tim McIntire, Austin Green, Sandra Faison, Chris Bugbee, Jawn McKinely

A bittersweet college freshman romance, *The Sterile Cuckoo* emerges from the 1965 John Nichols novel, as adapted by Alvin Sargent. The film provided a star-making role for Liza Minnelli (her first Oscar-nominated performance) as well as the directing debut of producer Alan J. Pakula. Minnelli portrays Pookie Adams, whose mission in life is to expose and escape from weirdos, creeps, jocks, fanatic intellectuals, and anybody else not compatible with her nonconformist values. Pookie, enrolled in Hamilton College in upstate New York, falls in love with Jerry Payne (Wendell Burton), a first-year student at a neighboring boys' school. Afraid of being Jerry's discarded lover, Pookie victimizes the boy with a shower of affection and clings to him with all the steely determination her nineteen years can summon. Her passion finally drives a wedge into the relationship. Theme song: "Come Saturday Morning" by Fred Karlin (music) and Dory Previn (lyrics).

A Streetcar Named Desire   1951   (CBS; Warner)   ◆   *Black-and-White*
Director: Elia Kazan
Starring: Vivien Leigh, Marlon Brando, Kim Hunter, Karl Malden, Rudy Bond, Peg Hillias, Nick Dennis, Wright King, Edna Thomas

Vivien Leigh, who played Blanche DuBois on the London stage, here re-creates the role—the interloper in the marriage of her sister Stella (Kim Hunter) and brother-in-law Stanley Kowalski (Marlon Brando, reprising his Broadway performance). A re-pressed, aging Southern belle, Blanche wants "magic." But it is not to be found in the summer heat of New Orleans, or in the small tenement apartment belonging to Stanley and Stella. And in the course of Blanche's visit, brutish Stanley shatters all her remaining illusions. The Tennessee Williams playscript is adapted by director Elia Kazan, in association with Oscar Saul. The film's atmospheric, yet highly theatrical look is one of the key points in Harry Stradling's cinematography. Academy Awards went to Miss Hunter, Karl Malden (playing Mitch), Richard Day and George James for art direction and set decoration, and Leigh—whose first Oscar, twelve years earlier, came for another depiction of Southern womanhood. A 1984 tailored-for-television remake cast Ann-Margret as Blanche and Treat Williams as Stanley.

The Stunt Man   1980   (CBS)   *Color*
Director: Richard Rush
Starring: Peter O'Toole, Steve Railsback, Barbara Hershey, Chuck Bail, Allen Goorwitz, Adam Roarke, Alex Rocco, Sharon Farrell, Philip Bruns

Directed by Richard Rush from the Lawrence B. Marcus adaptation of Paul Brodeur's novel, this ambitious allegory asks the age-old question: What is illusion and what reality? A Vietnam veteran (Steve Railsback) who is a fugitive from justice joins a movie production when he accidentally causes the death of a seasoned stunt man. Eli Cross (Peter O'Toole), the picture's Svengali-like director, hires the runaway as the new stunt man. Cross is determined to make each shot perfect, even if it means another real-life death scene. This 1980 release was filmed in 1978, after a long preproduction struggle. Not a commercial success, *The Stunt Man* finally had its moment in the limelight when Rush, Marcus, and O'Toole were nominated for Oscars.

Suddenly, Last Summer   1959   (RCA)   *Black-and-White*
Director: Joseph L. Mankiewicz
Starring: Elizabeth Taylor, Katharine Hepburn, Montgomery Clift, Albert Dekker, Mercedes McCambridge, Gary Raymond, Mavis Villiers, Patricia Marmont, Joan Young

In this version of Tennessee Williams's one-act play, adapted by Williams himself with Gore Vidal, insanity and repression are again the themes. Suddenly, last summer Catherine Holly (Elizabeth Taylor) suffered a nervous breakdown while vacationing in Mexico with her homosexual cousin, Sebastian Venable. (It turns out that Catherine witnessed her cousin's murder.) Dr. Cukrowicz (Montgomery Clift), a young neurosurgeon, is engaged by Catherine's wealthy aunt (Katharine Hepburn) to perform a lobotomy on Catherine—to wipe out the details of Sebastian's death. As Cukrowicz interviews his patient, the specifics of the gruesome murder are revealed in flashbacks. A harrowing adult drama, *Suddenly, Last Summer* represents the third and final teaming of Taylor and Clift. (*A Place in the Sun* and *Raintree County* came before.) Among the picture's technical virtues are Jack Hildyard's cinematography and Oliver Messel's production designs.

Summer of '42   1971   (Warner)   *Color*
Director: Robert Mulligan
Starring: Jennifer O'Neill, Gary Grimes, Jerry Houser, Oliver Conant, Lou Frizell, Katherine Allentuck, Christopher Norris

This nostalgic coming-of-age drama takes place during World War II on an island off the New England coast. Herman Raucher's autobiographical screenplay, directed by Robert Mulligan, assembles three adolescent boys, island residents in the summer of 1942 and all yearning for sexual initiation. Hermie (Gary Grimes), Oscy (Jerry Houser), and Benjie (Oliver Conant) visit the local movie house to see *Now, Voyager*. The film fuels their romantic fantasies. Hermie, in particular, becomes infatuated with a young war bride (Jennifer O'Neill); to his astonishment, she returns his attention. A classic loss-of-innocence tale, *Summer of '42* is wistful; Michel Legrand's Oscar-winning score and the cinematography of Robert Surtees add to the mood.

Sunday, Bloody Sunday   1971   (Key)   *Color*
Director: John Schlesinger
Starring: Glenda Jackson, Peter Finch, Murray Head, Peggy Ashcroft, Tony Britton,
Maurice Denham, Vivian Pickles, Bessie Love, Frank Windsor, Thomas Baptiste, Harold
Goldblatt, Hannah Norbert, Richard Pearson, June Brown, Caroline Blakiston, Peter
Halliday, Richard Loncraine, Jon Finch

John (*Midnight Cowboy*) Schlesinger directed *Sunday, Bloody Sunday* from an original screenplay by writer and film critic Penelope Gilliatt. Set in contemporary London, the film traces a complex, at times painful, ménage à trois. Divorcée Alex Greville (Glenda Jackson) is an executive in a business-efficiency firm. Daniel Hirsh (Peter Finch) is a doctor. Though they have never met, they share a common lover: a handsome young furniture and sculpture designer named Bob Elkin (Murray Head). Adult topics are explored here, but without shock tactics. Billy Williams is the director of photography.

Sunset Boulevard   1950   (Paramount)   *Color*
Director: Billy Wilder
Starring; William Holden, Gloria Swanson, Erich von Stroheim, Nancy Olson, Fred
Clark, Jack Webb, Lloyd Gough, Cecil B. De Mille, Franklyn Farnum

Joe Gillis (William Holden) is an opportunistic (and penniless) writer. Pulling into a driveway on Sunset Boulevard, Joe comes upon the mansion of Norma Desmond (Gloria Swanson), a silent screen siren who retired when talkies arrived. Norma plans a comeback in her own adaptation of *Salome*—and she solicits Joe's help with polishing the script. Meanwhile, the once-glamorous star, lost among the mementoes of her past, remains secluded in her mansion, attended by Max (Erich von Stroheim), now her butler—but once her husband and director. Joe plays gigolo to Norma's great lady, and their relationship ends in tragedy. The screenplay is by Charles Brackett, D. M. Marshman, Jr., and director Billy Wilder. Many of the scenes were shot (by John F. Seitz) on the very Paramount backlot where Gloria Swanson starred in De Mille films from 1918 through the mid-twenties. De Mille is among those playing himself in *Sunset Boulevard*; other celebrities include Hedda Hopper, Buster Keaton, Anna Q. Nilsson, H. B. Warner, and songwriters Ray Evans and Jay Livingston. Louis B. Mayer's comment about Wilder's cynical portrait of Hollywood: "You have disgraced the industry that made you and fed you."

A **T**ale of Two Cities   1958   (Embassy;   *Black-and-White*
      Learning)
Director: Ralph Thomas
Starring: Dirk Bogarde, Dorothy Tutin, Cecil Parker, Stephen Murray, Christopher Lee,
Donald Pleasence, Ian Bannen, Athene Seyler, Rosalie Crutchley, Ernest Clark, Paul
Guers, Alfie Bass

"It was the best of times, it was the worst of times." So Dickens launched upon his 1859 tale of Paris and London, as they were during the French Revolution. The novel has had at least three other big screen adaptations—two silent versions (1917 and, as *The Only Way*, again in 1926) and the lavish 1935 MGM translation starring Ronald Colman as Sydney Carton; Chris Sarandon played the role in a 1980 TV movie. Taking the lead here is Dirk Bogarde; as Carton, the dissolute British lawyer who becomes a martyr in the Reign of Terror, he is an ideal romantic hero. This edition was written by T. E. B. Clarke and directed by Ralph Thomas, with cinematography by Ernest Steward.

Taps   1981   (CBS)   *Color*
Director; Harold Becker
Starring: George C. Scott, Timothy Hutton, Ronny Cox, Sean Penn, Tom Cruise, Brendan Ward, John P. Navin, Jr., Evan Handler

Young military academy cadets take war games seriously in this adaptation of Devery Freeman's novel, *Father Sky*. As screenwritten by Darryl Ponicsan and Robert Mark Kamen, the tale takes on overtones of a Vietnam allegory. When authorities threaten to close the academy, the students, in defense of the school and its traditions, initiate a strike. Media attention is gained, but misunderstandings, including violence and an accidental homicide, also result. The National Guard arrives—and the cadets prepare themselves for armed confrontation. George C. Scott plays the school's beloved headmaster; Timothy Hutton is cast as the cadet who leads the rebellion; Tom Cruise portrays a rabidly hawkish student; and Sean Penn plays the voice-of-reason classmate. *Taps* is not a lighthearted action picture; the tone is deadly earnest, and the finale is brutal.

Targets   1968   (Paramount)   *Color*
Director: Peter Bogdanovich
Starring: Boris Karloff, Tim O'Kelly, Nancy Hsueh, Peter Bogdanovich, James Brown, Sandy Baron, Arthur Peterson, Mary Jackson, Tanya Morgan, Monty Landis

Boris Karloff, in a slick bit of type-casting, plays a horror film star. The veteran actor (named Byron Orlok) is preparing to retire from pictures—partly because he feels there is too much violence in real life. It's a relevant observation: Orlok himself is destined to meet up with Bobby Thompson (Tim O'Kelly), a young gun-crazy sniper. The climax comes at a drive-in theater premiere of Orlok's latest bit of cinema ghoulery. The actor is there for a promotional appearance—but Bobby Thompson, continuing his killing spree, is a surprise guest. *Targets* is Peter Bogdanovich's debut; his screenplay and direction make it a suspenseful thriller with some pertinent asides about real-versus-fantasy violence. Bogdanovich costars as movie director Sammy Michaels. Director of photography: Laszlo Kovacs. *Targets*, Karloff's last American film, was also his last good feature; before his death in 1969, he shot four (virtually unreleased) horror quickies in Mexico.

A Taste of Honey   1962   (Electric Video)   *Black-and-White*
Director: Tony Richardson
Starring: Rita Tushingham, Dora Bryan, Murray Melvin, Robert Stephens, Paul Danquah, Moira Kaye

Shelagh Delaney's playscript is transferred with skill and integrity to the screen. (Ms. Delaney was only nineteen when she wrote *A Taste of Honey*.) Jo (Rita Tushingham) is a gangling teenager living with her brassy mother (Dora Bryan) in the slums of Salford in northern England. Temporarily abandoned by her parent, Jo has an affair with a black sailor (Paul Danquah) who impregnates, then deserts, her. She is befriended by Geoff (Murray Melvin), a lonely homosexual. He tends to Jo during her pregnancy and they set up house together. The film, scripted by Delaney with director Tony

Richardson, rates high as a comedy-drama of character and as a social document of British working-class life. Walter Lassally is the cinematographer and John Addison composed the score.

Taxi Driver   1976   (RCA)   ✳ ✳   *Color*
Director: Martin Scorsese
Starring: Robert De Niro, Jodie Foster, Albert Brooks, Harvey Keitel, Leonard Harris, Peter Boyle, Cybill Shepherd, Joe Spinell, Steven Prince, Richard Higgs, Diahnne Abbott, Martin Scorsese

Travis Bickle, the character Robert De Niro plays in *Taxi Driver,* is a collage of Charles Manson and Paul Kersey, the hero of the *Death Wish* series. Travis, a Vietnam veteran, is a cabbie who becomes an urban guerrilla to clean up New York City. Unbalanced and suffering from torturous headaches, he plans to assassinate a presidential candidate, then turns his attention to saving Iris (Jodie Foster), a twelve-year-old hooker, from her pimp—a long-haired muscle builder named Sport (Harvey Keitel). In an ironic turn of events, Travis becomes a media hero. Paul Schrader's screenplay, as realized by Martin Scorsese, depicts the squalid and brutal side of Manhattan. Accolades: the Palme d'Or at Cannes and the New York Film Critics' awards for best director and best actor. Longtime composer Bernard Herrmann, most frequently identified with Hitchcock films (*The Trouble with Harry, The Man Who Knew Too Much, The Wrong Man, Vertigo, North by Northwest, Psycho, Marnie*) completed the score for *Taxi Driver* the day he died.

Tell Them Willie Boy Is Here   1969   (MCA)   *Color*
Director: Abraham Polonsky
Starring: Robert Redford, Katharine Ross, Robert Blake, Susan Clark, Barry Sullivan, Charles McGraw, John Vernon, Charles Aidman

Abraham Polonsky is another Hollywood writer who, having run afoul of McCarthyism, coasted along with a very spotty career. Before the political interruption, he wrote the scripts for *Body and Soul* and *I Can Get It for You Wholesale* and both wrote and directed *Force of Evil. Tell Them Willie Boy Is Here,* in 1969, constitutes his first screen credit since 1950. (He may have worked pseudonymously in the interim.) The time is 1909; the place is California. Willie (Robert Blake), a young Paiute Indian, kills his future father-in-law in self-defense. An extensive manhunt is initiated, with a sheriff named Coop (Robert Redford), a hearty exponent of male bravado, as one of the trackers. Polonsky's script (from Harry Lawton's novel *Willie Boy*) is a reflection on racial intolerance in general, with specific reference to the white man's contemptuous treatment of Indians. The music is by Dave Grusin and the cinematography by Conrad Hall.

The Ten Commandments   1956   (Paramount)   ◆   Color
Director: Cecil B. De Mille
Starring: Charlton Heston, Yul Brynner, Anne Baxter, Edward G. Robinson, Yvonne De Carlo, Debra Paget, John Derek, Sir Cedric Hardwicke, Nina Foch, Martha Scott, Judith Anderson, Vincent Price, John Carradine, Eduard Franz, Olive Deering, Donald Curtis, Douglas Dumbrille, Lawrence Dobkin, H. B. Warner, Henry Wilcoxon, Julia Faye

This 1956 epic is a more elaborate remake of Cecil B. De Mille's 1923 silent version. Aside from the 1958 *The Buccaneer,* which he produced but didn't direct, it is De Mille's last movie. Culled from several sources, secular and ecclesiastical, the screenplay was written by Aeneas MacKenzie, Jesse L. Lasky, Jr., Jack Gariss, and Frederic M. Frank. The topic is the life of Moses. Fraser Heston plays the role of the baby in the bulrushes; Charlton, his more famous father, portrays Moses grown to manhood. The high points of the tale are the delivery of the tablets of commandments on Mount Sinai and the parting of the Red Sea—visual brio for which the picture claimed the special effects Oscar. Among the featured players are Yul Brynner (as King Ramses II); Anne Baxter (Nefertiri); John Derek (Joshua); Nina Foch (Bithiah), Judith Anderson (Memnet), Vincent Price (Baka), John Carradine (Aaron), Henry Wilcoxon (Pentaur), Julia Faye (Elisheba), Woody Strode (King of Ethiopia). Look for these tiny-role players: Clint Walker, Frankie Darro, Robert Vaughn, Michael Ansara, and Michael—then billed as Touch—Connors as the Amelekite herder.

Tender Mercies   1983   (Thorn)   ◆   *Color*
Director: Bruce Beresford
Starring; Robert Duvall, Tess Harper, Betty Buckley, Wilford Brimley, Ellen Barkin, Allan Hubbard

Screenwriter Horton Foote's protagonist, Mack Sledge, is a former country-western singer on the rebound from booze and hard times. After a drinking binge, he winds up in a small-town Texas roadside motel. He works as a handyman for (then ultimately marries) the motel owner, a young widow and mother. Eventually, he returns to his singing-songwriting roots. In fact, Robert Duvall, who plays Mack, wrote his own songs for *Tender Mercies*. (Other music is contributed by George Dreyfuss.) Duvall has said that the beauty of Horton Foote's writing is that "It's like Chekhov—simple but deep." Both the scenarist and Australian director Bruce Beresford, in his American film debut, capture the milieu with frankness and affection. *Tender Mercies* is a major movie with a minor budget ($4 million at a time when the average Hollywood production costs $15 million). Two Oscars: Duvall for best actor, Foote for best original screenplay. (Foote is also responsible for *Tomorrow, The Trip to Bountiful,* and the screen adaptation of *To Kill a Mockingbird*.)

Terms of Endearment   *Listed under Comedies.*

Tess   1980   (RCA)   *Color*
Director: Roman Polanski
Starring; Nastassia Kinski, Peter Firth, Leigh Lawson, John Collin, David Markham, John Bett, Tom Chadbon, Rosemary Martin, Sylvia Coleridge, Richard Pearson

Nastassia Kinski stars as Thomas Hardy's Tess of the d'Urbervilles, an innocent young farm girl sent to live with supposedly rich relatives. She tries to prove her noble lineage, but she is sidelined by her illegitimate child. Tess, in a sequence of rising and falling fortunes, becomes trapped between the morals of Victorian England and the irony of circumstance. In this Roman Polanski adaptation, Normandy stands in for Hardy's Wessex. Veteran cinematographer Geoffrey Unsworth (*A Night to Remember, Becket, 2001: A Space Odyssey, Cabaret, Superman*) died while shooting *Tess,* and principal photography was completed by Ghislain Cloquet. (Their collaboration brought forth an Oscar, and additional statuettes went to costume designer Anthony Powell and art directors Pierre Guffroy and Jack Stevens.) In France *Tess* captured the César for best film and best director. Gérard Brach and John Brownjohn worked on the screenplay with Polanski.

This Sporting Life   1963   (Sheik Video)   ❋   *Black-and-White*
Director: Lindsay Anderson
Starring: Richard Harris, Rachel Roberts, Alan Badel, William Hartnell, Colin Blakely,
Vanda Godsell, Arthur Lowe, Anne Cunningham, Jack Watson, Harry Markham, George
Sewell, Leonard Rossiter

This first feature film by critic-turned-documentarist Lindsay Anderson is another drama
from the British school of social realism. The working-class hero is Frank Machin
(Richard Harris), a young Yorkshire coal miner who becomes a professional rugby
player. The burly footballer's career advances, and he begins an affair with Mrs. Hammond (Rachel Roberts), the widow in whose house he lodges. David Storey's screenplay, faithfully constructed from his 1960 novel, concentrates on Frank's conflicts on
the playing field and his uneasy relationship with his mistress. *This Sporting Life* has
remarkable technical contributions by cinematographer Denys Coop, editor Peter Taylor, and sound editor Chris Greenham. Harris was honored as best actor at Cannes.

The Three Musketeers   1948   (MGM)   *Color*
Director: George Sidney
Starring: Lana Turner, Gene Kelly, June Allyson, Van Heflin, Angela Lansbury, Frank
Morgan, Vincent Price, Keenan Wynn, John Sutton, Gig Young, Robert Coote, Reginald
Owen, Ian Keith, Patricia Medina, Richard Stapley, Byron Foulger, Robert Warwick,
Marie Windsor, Tom Tyler, Kirk Alyn

"All for one, one for all." With that pledge, the three musketeers partake of one
swashbuckling adventure after another. In the reign of Louis XIII, the trio of Frenchmen—Athos (Van Heflin), Porthos (Gig Young), and Aramis (Robert Coote)—unite
with impoverished swordsman D'Artagnan (Gene Kelly) to fight for justice. This lavish
presentation of the Alexandre Dumas classic, scripted by Robert Ardrey and directed
by George Sidney, offers Lana Turner as Milady De Winter; June Allyson as Constance;
Frank Morgan as King Louis; Angela Lansbury as Queen Anne; and Vincent Price as
the nefarious Cardinal Richelieu. The spectacle is augmented by cinematographer
Robert Planck and art directors Cedric Gibbons and Malcolm Brown.

The Three Musketeers   1974   (U.S.A. Home Video)   *Color*
Director: Richard Lester
Starring: Oliver Reed, Raquel Welch, Richard Chamberlain, Michael York, Frank Finlay,
Christopher Lee, Geraldine Chaplin, Jean-Pierre Cassel, Roy Kinnear, Spike Milligan,
Simon Ward, Faye Dunaway, Charlton Heston

This version of the 1844 Dumas novel is directed by comedy specialist Richard Lester.
While adopting a tongue-in-cheek approach, this version is nonetheless faithful to the
spirit of the original. Bearing the subtitle *The Queen's Diamonds*, the story is a familar
one: the *four* heroes (Oliver Reed, Richard Chamberlain, Frank Finlay, and Michael
York) attempt to retrieve a diamond necklace belonging to Queen Anne of Austria
(Geraldine Chaplin) before its absence is noted. As before—in the (at least) half dozen
American film versions of *The Three Musketeers*—Lady De Winter and Cardinal Richelieu take the central roles of villainy. Here they are enacted by Faye Dunaway and
Charlton Heston. George MacDonald Fraser wrote the adaptation. It's a mosaic of
action, romance, and comedy. Sequel: *The Four Musketeers* (1975).

To Kill a Mockingbird   1962   (MCA)   ◆   *Black-and-White*
Director: Robert Mulligan
Starring: Gregory Peck, Mary Badham, Phillip Alford, John Megna, Frank Overton, Rosemary Murphy, Ruth White, Brock Peters, Estelle Evans, Paul Fix, Collin Wilcox, James Anderson, Alice Ghostley, Robert Duvall, William Windom, Crahan Denton, Richard Hale

An adult drama staged from a child's point of view, *To Kill a Mockingbird* is a multilevel experience. It is a mystery story about a rape trial and an attempted murder, but it's also a careful contemplation of childhood—with its nighttime terrors. The action occurs in 1932 in Maycomb, a small Alabama town rife with bigotries. Tom Robinson (Brock Peters) is a black sharecropper charged with the rape of a white woman, Mayella Ewell (Collin Wilcox). Defending Tom for what is ultimately revealed as a false accusation is local lawyer Atticus Finch (Gregory Peck), a widower with two children—Jem (Phillip Alford) and Scout (Mary Badham). The Robert Mulligan–directed picture is based on Harper Lee's Pulitzer Prize best-seller. As the Lincolnesque lawyer, Peck won a best actor Academy Award. The film was screenwritten by Horton Foote, who also created *Tomorrow, Tender Mercies,* and *The Trip to Bountiful.* Foote won an Oscar too—as did the art director/set decoration trio of Alexander Golitzen, Henry Bumstead, and Oliver Emert. Look for Robert Duvall in the role of Boo Radley.

Tomorrow   1972   (Monterey Home Video)   *Black-and-White*
Director: Joseph Anthony
Starring: Robert Duvall, Olga Bellin, Sudie Bond, Richard McConnell, Peter Masterson, William Hawley

Horton Foote has carved a reputation as a playwright and screenwriter who provides a voice for the common people. Both his original works—including *Tender Mercies, The Trip to Bountiful, 1918,* and *On Valentine's Day*—and his adaptations (*To Kill a Mockingbird*) celebrate the fortunes and tribulations of decent, God-fearing Southern families. In *Tomorrow,* a dramatization of a William Faulkner story, a sawmill caretaker (Robert Duvall) befriends an outcast pregnant woman (Olga Bellin). The two lonely misfits, in time, fall in love. Their story, touched with poignancy, culminates in violence and murder. Joseph Anthony, a former actor and dancer who turned to stage and film directing, also has *The Rainmaker, The Matchmaker,* and *Career* to his credit.

Trapeze   1956   (CBS)   *Color*
Director: Carol Reed
Starring; Burt Lancaster, Tony Curtis, Gina Lollobrigida, Katy Jurado, Thomas Gomez, Johnny Puleo, Minor Watson, Gerard Landry, Sidney James

Location photography at the renowned Paris Cirque d'Hiver highlights this circus drama. Inspired by the Max Catto novel *The Killing Frost,* the screenplay by Liam O'Brien and James R. Webb relates the tale of two aerialists—Mike Ribble (Burt Lancaster) and Tino Orsini (Tony Curtis)—and how their partnership is eclipsed with the arrival of a voluptuous new performer (Gina Lollobrigida). A romantic triangle, *Trapeze* is also a suspense drama: the stars work to perfect a death-defying mid-air triple somersault. Directed by Carol Reed, here reunited with cinematographer Robert Krasker, who worked with him on *Odd Man Out* and *The Third Man.*

The Trial   France-Italy-West Germay 1962; U.S. 1963   *Black-and-White*
   (Budget Video; Western Film & Video Inc.; Discount Video Tapes; Cable Films,
   Classic Video Collector's Club)
Director: Orson Welles
Starring: Anthony Perkins, Jeanne Moreau, Elsa Martinelli, Suzanne Flon, Madeleine
Robinson, Akim Tamiroff, Romy Schneider, William Kearns, Jess Hahn, Fernand Ledoux,
Michael Lonsdale, Orson Welles

Orson Welles's aura permeates this adaptation of the dense Franz Kafka novel. Welles,
as writer, director, and editor, weds his highly personal visual style to Kafka's 1915
nightmare tale. Joseph K (Anthony Perkins), a citizen of a nameless country, is arrested
on an unspecified charge. He is held for questioning, tried, and eventually convicted—
without ever knowing the nature of his crime. Welles, in dramatizing the protagonist's
anguish, constructs a surrealist maze of weird lighting and bizarre camera angles. After
Citizen Kane, The Trial is the only feature over which the filmmaker exercised complete
control, including the editing process. In the large featured cast, Romy Schneider plays
Leni; Elsa Martinelli is cast as Hilda; Jeanne Moreau portrays Miss Burstner; Akim
Tamiroff embodies Block; and Welles himself plays Hastler. Cinematographer: Edmond
Richard.

Tribute   1980   (Vestron)   *Color*
Director: Bob Clark
Starring: Jack Lemmon, Robby Benson, Lee Remick, Colleen Dewhurst, John Marley, Kim
Cattrall, Gale Garnett

When Scottie Templeton (Jack Lemmon), a much-loved Broadway press agent, learns
that he is dying of a rare blood disease, he attempts to make amends with his estranged
wife (Lee Remick) and their son (Robby Benson). The boy, in his twenty-odd years,
has barely seen his father; so he comes to New York to live with him for the summer.
Meanwhile, theatrical friends organize a testimonial evening to pay tribute to Scottie.
In the central role, Jack Lemmon resuscitates his Tony-winning stage performance.
The screenplay by Bernard Slade (*Same Time, Next Year*) adheres faithfully to his
Broadway script. Bob Clark, the film's director, may be better known for his subsequent
efforts: *Porky's, Porky's II: The Next Day,* and *A Christmas Story.*

The Trip to Bountiful   1985   (Embassy)   ◆   *Color*
Director: Peter Masterson
Starring: Geraldine Page, John Heard, Carlin Glynn, Richard Bradford, Rebecca De
Mornay, Kevin Cooney, Mary Kay Mars

Carrie Watts (Geradine Page), an old-age pensioner, occupies a portion of the Houston
apartment rented by her son (John Heard) and daughter-in-law (Carlin Glynn). The
vulnerable old woman, who grew up in the Gulf Coast town of Bountiful, is homesick.
Although Carrie has not seen Bountiful in decades, she decides to return by bus (and,
for the last few miles, by car) to the old home place. This film, adapted by Horton
Foote from his 1953 teleplay and covering a day and a half, dramatizes what happens
on that trip. Foote's dialogue, as in *Tomorrow, 1918,* and *To Kill a Mockingbird,* conveys
the texture of everyday lives. Former actor Peter Masterson (he co-stared in *Tomorrow*)
is the director. For her interpretation of lonely, hymn-singing Carrie, Geraldine Page
won the 1985 Oscar for best actress.

The Trojan Women   1971   (U.S.A. Home Video)   *Color*
Director: Michael Cacoyannis
Starring; Katharine Hepburn, Vanessa Redgrave, Geneviève Bujold, Irene Papas, Patrick Magee, Brian Blessed, Pauline Letts

This powerful denunciation of war, filmed at the peak of the Vietnam conflict, arises from the 416 B.C. drama by Greek tragedian Euripides. Shot in Spain, *The Trojan Women* recounts the aftermath of the fall of Troy. As the conquering Greeks lay siege to the city, four Trojan women bemoan their fate: Queen Hecuba (Katharine Hepburn); her daughter Cassandra (Geneviève Bujold), the seeress; Andromache (Vanessa Redgrave), Hecuba's daughter-in-law and the widow of the city's hero, Hector; and, finally and crucially, Helen (Irene Papas), the adulterous wife of King Menelaus of Sparta. Directed, from the translation by Edith Hamilton, by Michael Cacoyannis, who is best known for his direction of *Zorba the Greek.*

Tunes of Glory   1960   (Embassy; Learning)   *Color*
Director: Ronald Neame
Starring; Alec Guinness, John Mills, Susannah York, Kay Walsh, Dennis Price, John Fraser, Duncan Macrae, Gordon Jackson, Allan Cuthbertson

A power struggle between two career officers yields conflict in this military drama set in Scotland. The new commander (John Mills) of a Highland regiment is a strict disciplinarian, unlike his predecessor (Alec Guinness), a callous but careless older colonel. As the latter hands over the reins of command to the former, sparks fly. When other soldiers become involved and take sides, a court martial is the tragic consequence. A character study, *Tunes of Glory* has a screenplay by James Kennaway, based on his novel. Directed by Ronald Neame, whose later work includes *I Could Go on Singing, The Chalk Garden, Gambit, The Prime of Miss Jean Brodie, The Poseidon Adventure,* and *Hopscotch.*

The Turning Point   1977   (CBS)   *Color*
Director: Herbert Ross
Starring; Anne Bancroft, Shirley MacLaine, Tom Skerritt, Mikhail Baryshnikov, Leslie Browne, Martha Scott, Marshall Thompson, Anthony Zerbe, James Mitchell, Alexandra Danilova, Daniel Levans

Written and directed by Arthur Laurents and Herbert Ross respectively, *The Turning Point* is a valentine to the American Ballet Theatre (herein called American Ballet Company). The story focues on Emma (Anne Bancroft) and Deedee (Shirley MacLaine), rival ballerinas in their youth. Now, in middle age, only Emma has remained in the profession—to become the company's prima ballerina; Deedee, on the other hand, dropped out to settle in Oklahoma City and raise a family. After many years, the two women meet again. Envious of each other, they compare and contrast their lives. Meanwhile, the turning point has come for Deedee's daughter, Emilia (Leslie Browne), a promising teenage dancer who must decide if ballet will be her career. In the supporting cast: Tom Skerritt as Wayne, Deedee's husband; Martha Scott as Adelaide, the founder of the troupe; and, in his acting debut, Mikhail Baryshnikov, playing Yuri, Emilia's dancing partner. Photographed by Robert Surtees.

Twelve Angry Men   1957   (Key)   *Black-and-White*
Director: Sidney Lumet
Starring: Henry Fonda, Lee J. Cobb, Ed Begley, E. G. Marshall, Jack Warden, Jack Klugman, Edward Binns, Joseph Sweeney, Martin Balsam, George Voskovec, John Fiedler, Robert Webber, Rudy Bond, James A. Kelly, Bill Nelson, John Savoca

The angry men of the title are jurors deadlocked on a murder case in which there is a shadow of doubt. One holdout, Juror 8 (Henry Fonda), tries to convince the other men that the defendant (John Savoca) could not have killed his father. Sidney Lumet's feature film directing debut (he hailed from TV's golden age), *Twelve Angry Men* is an exercise in suspense. Except for a few seconds, the drama unfolds entirely within the jury deliberation room. The script is by Reginald Rose, an adaptation of his Emmy-winning "Studio One" teleplay of 1954—in which Robert Cummings starred as the dissenting juror. Boris Kaufman, who later worked with Lumet on *That Kind of Woman, The Fugitive Kind, Long Day's Journey into Night, The Pawnbroker, The Group,* and *Bye, Bye Braverman,* is the cinematographer.

Ulysses   1967   (Texture Films)   *Black-and-White*
Director: Joseph Strick
Starring: Milo O'Shea, Barbara Jefford, Maurice Roeves, T. P. McKenna, Martin Dempsey, Sheila O'Sullivan, Anna Manahan, Maureen Potter

James Joyce's *Ulysses* is the Homerian *Odyssey* in modern incarnation. A celebration of life, Joyce's massive novel takes place in Dublin in a twenty-four-hour period—June 16, 1904. The unity of time and locale provide the focus for this film condensation from director Joseph Strick. (Strick also prepared the screenplay with Fred Haines, and the adapters have retained some of the novel's explicit language.) Under scrutiny are salesman Leopold Bloom (Milo O'Shea), the drama's Everyman; his wife Molly (Barbara Jefford); and Stephen Dedalus (Maurice Roeves), hero of Joyce's *A Portrait of the Artist as a Young Man,* now a poet and teacher. *Ulysses,* the movie, makes a fine introduction to a classic of literary imagination.

Under Fire   1983   (Vestron)   *Color*
Director: Roger Spottiswoode
Starring: Nick Nolte, Gene Hackman, Joanna Cassidy, Ed Harris, Jean-Louis Trintignant, Richard Masur, René Enriquez, Hamilton Camp, Elpidia Carrillo

Set in 1979 Nicaragua, this political thriller dramatizes the fall of the Anastasio Somoza regime. Caught up in the turmoil of the dictator's last days is American photojournalist Russel Price (Nick Nolte), a daredevil when it comes to covering stories in the world's trouble spots. Sandanistan rebels promise him and another reporter (Joanna Cassidy) the first-ever photographs of a charismatic new leader named Raphael; but when the Americans arrive at a remote guerrilla camp, they learn that the man is dead. The rebels want a photo of Raphael anyway—so they can create the impression he is still living and leading the revolution. *Under Fire,* from an original script by Clayton Frohman as redrafted by Ron Shelton, is a variant on *The Year of Living Dangerously*—released earlier in the same year. Like that film, it relates a fictitious story with a background of real-life horror. Costarring with Nolte and Cassidy are Gene Hackman, Ed Harris, Richard Masur, and René Enriquez as Somoza. Directed by Roger Spottiswoode (*Terror Train, The Pursuit of D. B. Cooper,* and *The Best of Times*).

An Unmarried Woman   1978   (CBS)   *Color*
Director: Paul Mazursky
Starring: Jill Clayburgh, Alan Bates, Michael Murphy, Cliff Gorman, Lisa Lucas, Pat Quinn, Kelly Bishop, Linda Miller, Andrew Duncan, Penelope Russianoff, Daniel Seltzer

Written and directed by Paul Mazursky, this drama observes the dilemmas facing a recently divorced woman who has depended on a man all her life. Now, abandoned by her husband Martin (Michael Murphy), a Manhattan stockbroker, Erica Benton (Jill Clayburgh) struggles to maintain equilibrium. Her road to happiness involves psychiatry, a consciousness-raising group, her job in a SoHo Gallery, and—crucially—the love of her fourteen-year-old daughter, Patti (Lisa Lucas). When Erica meets artist Saul Kaplan (Alan Bates), he seems like Mr. Right. Martin, the ostensible villain, is portrayed by Michael Murphy, one of the components of the Robert Altman ensemble of the seventies; his breakdowns are harrowing to watch. Clayburgh, Mazursky's script, and the picture itself were nominated for Oscars.

The Verdict   1982   (CBS)   *Color*
Director: Sidney Lumet
Starring: Paul Newman, Charlotte Rampling, Jack Warden, James Mason, Milo O'Shea, Lindsay Crouse, Edward Binns, Julie Bovasso, Lewis J. Stadlen, Wesley Addy, Roxanne Hart, James Handy

Seedy Frank Galvin (Paul Newman) is an alcoholic Boston lawyer who, in his downward spiral, has lost pride, integrity, and solvency. He has even resorted to ambulance chasing to make a buck. With the help of his old friend, Judge Mickey Morrissey (Jack Warden), Frank regains his self-respect when he takes on a medical malpractice suit. Uncovering the incompetency behind a young hospital patient's death, he wages an impassioned courtroom fight for justice. Standing in his path is suave, opportunistic defense attorney Ed Concannon (James Mason). David Mamet's suspenseful screenplay is derived from the novel by Barry Reed. Director Sidney Lumet and his *Prince of the City* cinematographer Andrzej Bartkowiak teamed up again for this project.

The Vikings   1958   (MGM)   *Color*
Director: Richard Fleischer
Starring: Kirk Douglas, Tony Curtis, Ernest Borgnine, Janet Leigh, James Donald, Alexander Knox, Frank Thring, Maxine Audley, Eileen Way, Edric Connor, Dandy Nichols

This saga of tenth-century Scandinavia thrives on spectacle and violence. Twentieth-century Norway and Brittany provide the locales; hand-lopping and eye-gouging the violence. Einar (Kirk Douglas) and Eric (Tony Curtis) are rival half-brothers out to conquer new lands. Einar is the true barbarian son of Ragnar (Ernest Borgnine), while Eric has a softer side—especially when it comes to the fair Morgana (Janet Leigh). The siblings come together in a battle to the death over the kingdom of Northumbria. *The Vikings*, adapted from Edison Marshall's novel by Dale Wasserman, was screenwritten in final form by Calder Willingham. Narrated by Orson Welles.

Voyage of the Damned   1976   (CBS)   *Color*
Director; Stuart Rosenberg
Starring: Faye Dunaway, Oskar Werner, Max von Sydow, Malcolm McDowell, James Mason, Orson Welles, Katharine Ross, Ben Gazzara, Lee Grant, Sam Wanamaker, Julie Harris, Helmut Griem, Luther Adler, Wendy Hiller, Nehemiah Persoff, Maria Schell, Fernando Rey, Donald Houston, José Ferrer, Denholm Elliott, Janet Suzman, Lynne Fred-

erick, Laura Gemser, Victor Spinetti, Paul Koslo, Jonathan Pryce, Michael Constantine

An enormous cast unites for this fact-based drama excerpted from the book by Gordon Thomas and Max Morgan-Witts. In 1939 the Nazis allowed the *St. Louis* to sail from Hamburg, en route to Havana, with 937 Jewish passengers on board. But when the ship reached Cuba, authorities there refused to let the passengers disembark. The refugees were also barred from Florida. *Voyage of the Damned,* scripted by Steve Shagan and David Butler, dramatizes the plight of those homeless Jews as panic and tragedy invade the ship. Some of the standouts in the all-star ensemble are Max von Sydow, as the sympathetic captain of the *St. Louis,* Jonathan Pryce as a schoolteacher released from a concentration camp, Ben Gazzara as a representative for the Jewish Agency who is fighting bureaucracy to save the passengers' lives, and—as one of several romantic couples—Faye Dunaway and Oskar Werner

Wake of the Red Witch   1948   (Republic)   *Black-and-White*
Director: Edward Ludwig
Starring: John Wayne, Gail Russell, Gig Young, Adele Mara, Luther Adler, Eduard Franz, Grant Withers, Henry Daniell, Paul Fix, Dennis Hoey, Jeff Corey, Erskine Sanford, Duke Kahanamoku, Henry Brandon, Fernando Alvarado, John Wengraf, Myron Healey

This action-filled seafaring saga, localed in the East Indies, is founded on the novel by Garland Roark. In the Harry Brown-Kenneth Gamet adaptation, visualized in flashback by director Edward Ludwig, John Wayne stars as Captain Ralls, a veteran mariner who has been betrayed by his ship's owner. Both men are in quest of a sizable treasure but their bitter rivalry prevents either of them from laying claim to the fortune—lost in the South Seas and guarded by a giant octopus. Ralls establishes a plan to retrieve the treasure, but meanwhile bides his time with Angelique Desaix (Gail Russell), a beautiful island resident. The score for *Wake of the Red Witch* is by Nathan Scott, and the director of photography is Reggie Lanning.

War and Peace   1956   (Paramount)   *Color*
Director: King Vidor
Starring: Audrey Hepburn, Henry Fonda, Mel Ferrer, Vittorio Gassman, John Mills, Herbert Lom, Oscar Homolka, Anita Ekberg, Helmut Dantine, Barry Jones, Anna Maria Ferrero, Milly Vitale, Jeremy Brett, Lea Seidl, Wilfred Lawson, May Britt, Sean Barrett, Tullio Carminati

This large-scale adaptation of Tolstoy's epic comes to the screen through the efforts of six screenwriters: Bridget Boland, Robert Westerby, Mario Camerini, Ennio De Concini, Ivo Perilli, and King Vidor. Vidor, capping a forty-year career, also directs. (The battle scenes were staged by Mario Soldati.) A panorama of Russia during the Napoleonic Wars, the film culminates in the French emperor's invasion of Moscow in 1812. Primary focus in the interim is upon young Natasha (Audrey Hepburn) and the men in her life: Pierre (Henry Fonda), Anatole (Vittorio Gassman), and Prince Andrey (Hepburn's then-husband Mel Ferrer). Herbert Lom plays Napoleon. Shot in Italy and Yugoslavia by Jack Cardiff, with Aldo Tonti responsible for the battle sequences. Music by Nino Rota.

The Way We Were   1973   (RCA)   *Color*
Director: Sydney Pollack
Starring: Barbra Streisand, Robert Redford, Bradford Dillman, Murray Hamilton, Patrick O'Neal, Viveca Lindfors, Lois Chiles, Allyn Ann McLerie, Herb Edelman

Sydney Pollack, in realizing this popular love story, touches on three decades—beginning in 1937 and stretching, with an epilogue, into the mid-fifties. (Scenarist Arthur Laurents adapted his novel with uncredited assists from Alvin Sargent and David Rayfiel.) A romance about the attraction of opposites—in this case a female political radical who falls in love with the ostensible all-American boy—*The Way We Were* stars Barbra Streisand as Katie Morosky and Robert Redford as Hubbell Gardiner. They meet in college, where Hubbell is a jock with an unsuspected talent for writing and Katie is a poor Jewish girl fom New York who belongs to the Young Communists League. Their paths cross again in 1944, when Hubbell—still a budding novelist—is a navy officer on leave. They marry, move to Hollywood, and encounter the blacklist era. The photography by Harry Stradling, Jr., evokes the period(s) with a twist of nostalgia. Oscars went to Marvin Hamlisch's score and his title song (with lyrics by Alan and Marilyn Bergman).

When the Legends Die   1972   (Playhouse Video)   *Color*
Director: Stuart Millar
Starring: Richard Widmark, Frederic Forrest, Luana Anders, Vito Scotti, Herbert Nelson

This modern-day Western, suggested by Hal Borland's novel, focuses on Tom Black Bull (Frederic Forrest), a Ute Indian disenchanted with life on the reservation. An aging, hard-drinking cowboy (Richard Widmark) promises to make the young man a star on the rodeo circuit. The two misfits then cast their lot together. Even in the non-reservation world, though, Tom endeavors to preserve his heritage. This character study, scripted by Robert Dozier, marks the movie debut of Frederic Forrest and the first directorial outing for producer Stuart Millar. The score is by Glenn Paxton, the cinematography by Richard Kline.

The White Dawn   1974   (Paramount)   *Color*
Director: Philip Kaufman
Starring: Warren Oates, Timothy Bottoms, Lou Gossett, Simonie Kopapik, Joanasie Salomonie

An Arctic adventure, *The White Dawn* is based on a true story. As delineated in the James Houston-Tom Rickman screenplay, three American whalers (Timothy Bottoms, Warren Oates, and Lou Gossett), on an expedition in 1896, become lost when their boat fails them. Luckily, they are rescued by Eskimos (whose dialogue is rendered in subtitles). At first the whalers revel in their saviors' hospitality; then they begin to take unfair advantage of the situation—with tragic results. A moody, finally gloomy film, *The White Dawn* is elevated by the actors (particularly Bottoms as the gentle, sympathetic fisherman) and by Michael Chapman's location cinematography. Directed by Philip Kaufman, whose pre-1974 credits are *Goldstein, Fearless Frank,* and *The Great Northfield, Minnesota Raid*—and who later helmed *Invasion of the Body Snatchers, The Wanderers,* and *The Right Stuff.*

Who's Afraid of Virginia Woolf?   1966   (Warner)   ◆   *Black-and-White*
Director: Mike Nichols

Starring: Elizabeth Taylor, Richard Burton, Sandy Dennis, George Segal

A landmark film for its adult themes and frank language, *Who's Afraid of Virginia Woolf?* is a harrowing adaptation of the Edward Albee stage success. The four-character drama recounts a night-long drunken brawl between George (Richard Burton), a history professor, and Martha (Elizabeth Taylor), his combative but seductive wife. Witnesses to the fray are a young couple, Honey and Nick (Sandy Dennis and George Segal), newcomers to the small college community. The picture received five Academy Awards: best actress (Taylor's second statuette), best supporting actress (Dennis), cinematography (Haskell Wexler), costume design (Irene Sharaff), and art direction/set decoration (Richard Sylbert, George James Hopkins). Mike Nichols, in his debut as a director, was nominated—but didn't win until the next year, for *The Graduate.*

Whose Life Is It Anyway?   1981   (MGM)   *Color*
Director; John Badham
Starring: Richard Dreyfuss, John Cassavetes, Christine Lahti, Bob Balaban, Kenneth McMillan, Kaki Hunter, Janet Eilber, Thomas Carter

Brian Clark's right-to-die play, a London and New York success starring Tom Conti, was converted into a screen vehicle for Richard Dreyfuss. He plays Ken Harrison, a talented young sculptor who is paralyzed from the neck down after a car crash. Kept alive by drugs, injections, and machines, the quadriplegic decides to battle hospital authorities for his legal right to death with dignity. The screenplay, duplicating the original's complement of black comedy, is a collaboration between Clark and Reginald Rose. John Badham (*Saturday Night Fever, War Games*) is the director—and the cinematography is by Mario Tosi.

The Wild Duck   Australia 1983; U.S. 1985   (Vestron)   *Color*
Director: Henri Safran
Starring: Liv Ullmann, Jeremy Irons, Arthur Dignam, Lucinda Jones, John Meillon, Michael Pate, Colin Croft, Marion Edward, Peter De Salis, Jeff Truman, Clive Marshall

The Wild Duck, by Norwegian dramatist Henrik Ibsen, was first performed in 1884. This 1983 updated abbreviation by French-born Australian director Henri Safran is not the first film version of Ibsen's classic, but it is the one most widely distributed in America. Among the changes: the action is moved from Norway in the 1880s to Australia in 1913, and all the characters' names have been Anglicized. The plot is essentially unrevised: a man—here called Harold and played by Jeremy Irons—discovers that his beloved daughter (Lucinda Jones) is illegitimate and withdraws his affection. Safran's adaptation was accomplished by coscenarists Tette Lemkow, Dido Merwen, and Peter Smalley. The cinematographer is Peter James, the editor Don Saunders.

The Wild One   1954   (CBS)   *Black-and-White*
Director: Laslo Benedek
Starring: Marlon Brando, Mary Murphy, Robert Keith, Lee Marvin, Jay C. Flippen, Peggy Maley, Hugh Sanders, Ray Teal, John Brown, Will Wright, Robert Osterloh, Robert Bice, Jerry Paris, Alvy Moore

This influential melodrama about motorcycle hoodlums terrorizing a small California town was a shocker in its day. In fact, it was banned in England until 1968. The John

Paxton screenplay, suggested by Frank Rooney's story, "The Cyclists' Raid," revolves around Johnny (Marlon Brando), the gang's leader, and Chino (Lee Marvin), his rival. Kathie (Mary Murphy) is the virtuous local girl whose love *almost* redeems Johnny. Brando's enactment of antisocial behavior and his rebel image stamped a generation of young film actors. James Dean in *Rebel Without a Cause* was only a year away, *The Wild One* was directed by Laslo Benedek, whose other major film is the 1952 movie adaptation of *Death of a Salesman*.

Windom's Way   1957   (VidAmerica)   *Color*
Director: Ronald Neame
Starring: Peter Finch, Mary Ure, Natasha Parry, Robert Flemyng, Michael Hordern, Grégoire Aslan

Peter Finch, half English, half Australian, was a fixture in the cinema of both countries throughout the forties. After appearances in English and Anglo-American productions he was well-established as a leading man by 1957. In this melodrama taken from James Ramsay Ullman's popular novel, he plays an impassioned doctor working to squelch the communist takeover of a remote Malayan village. Directed by Ronald Neame from a screenplay by Jill Craigie (a renowned documentary filmmaker), *Windom's Way* is a truth-textured story of heroism. Neame's cinematographer is Christopher Challis.

Windwalker   Canada 1980; 1981   (CBS)   *Color*
Director: Kieth Merrill
Starring: Trevor Howard, Nick Ramus, James Remar, Serene Hedin, Silvana Gallardo, Billy Drago, Dusty Iron Wing McCrea, Rudy Diaz

This drama, set in late eighteenth-century Utah, gives a semidocumentary portrayal of the Crow and Cheyenne nations. Spanning several generations, *Windwalker* deals with the tribal life of the two nations—and their intense rivalry before white settlers arrived. A mystical element of the plot involves a deceased Cheyenne elder (Trevor Howard) who returns to life to protect his family from his vengeful son. Under Canadian director Kieth Merrill's guidance, the dialogue is spoken in Crow and Cheyenne, and there are English subtitles and narration. (Ray Goldrup's screenplay is adapted from the novel by Blaine Yorgason.)

The Winslow Boy   1949   (Thorn; Movie Buff Video)   *Black-and-White*
Director: Anthony Asquith
Starring: Robert Donat, Margaret Leighton, Cedric Hardwicke, Francis L. Sullivan, Frank Lawton, Basil Radford, Wilfrid Hyde-White, Ernest Thesiger, Jack Watling, Kathleen Harrison, Marie Lohr, Neil North

This courtroom drama, adapted from Terence Rattigan's fact-inspired playscript, is screenwritten by Rattigan with Anatole De Grunwald. The story begins with the expulsion of a Royal Naval College cadet (Neil North). The young man has been accused—unjustly, it develops—of theft. A top-level barrister (Robert Donat) comes to his defense. *The Winslow Boy* is directed by Anthony Asquith, who also brought to the screen Rattigan's *French Without Tears, While the Sun Shines, The Browning Version, The VIP's,* and *The Yellow Rolls-Royce*. As part-time writing-directing colleagues, Rattigan and Asquith were in the forefront of the English cinema's tradition of quality from 1939 through the peak years of the forties and into the sixties.

Wise Blood   *Listed under Comedies.*

Without a Trace   1983   (CBS)   *Color*
Director: Stanley R. Jaffe
Starring: Kate Nelligan, Judd Hirsch, David Dukes, Stockard Channing, Jacqueline
Brookes, Keith McDermott, Kathleen Widdoes, Daniel Bryan Corkill, Cheryl Giannini

Six-year-old Alex Selky (Daniel Bryan Corkill) lives only two blocks away from his
elementary school. One morning, while walking there, he disappears—without a trace.
Neither his estranged parents (Kate Nelligan and David Dukes) nor his schoolmates
have a clue as to his whereabouts. Then police detective Albert Menetti (Judd Hirsch)
enters the scene. This Brooklyn-set drama is based on the famous Etan Patz case that
occurred in Greenwich Village. That missing-child episode inspired Beth Gutcheon's
novel, *Still Missing*—which Gutcheon has here adapted for the screen. *Without a Trace*
is the directing debut for producer Stanley R. Jaffe. The director of photography is
John Bailey and the production designer, Paul Sylbert.

Women in Love   1970   (CBS)   ◆   *Color*
Director Ken Russell
Starring: Alan Bates, Oliver Reed, Glenda Jackson, Jennie Linden, Eleanor Bron, Alan
Webb, Vladek Sheybal, Catherine Willmer, Sarah Nicholls, Sharon Gurney, Christopher
Gable, Michael Gough, Nike Arrighi, James Laurenson, Michael Cox

Ken Russell brings to life the D. H. Lawrence classic about four individuals breaking
the bonds of sexual repression in the Midlands of the 1920s. Working from a script
by Larry Kramer, Russell celebrates the nonconformity of school inspector Rupert
Birkin (Alan Bates), his wealthy friend Gerald Crich (Oliver Reed), and the Brangwen
sisters—sculptress Gudrun (Glenda Jackson) and Ursula (Jennie Linden), the unimag-
inative schoolteacher and least daring of the quartet. The eroticism of the tale is given
visual underpinning in the period detail by Russell and his cinematographer, Billy
Williams. Georges Delerue supplied the music. For her portrayal of Gudrun, Jackson
won her first Academy Award.

The World According to Garp   *Listed under Comedies.*

The Yakuza   1975   (Warner)   *Color*
Director: Sydney Pollack
Starring: Robert Mitchum, Takakura Ken, Brian Keith, Richard Jordan, Herb Edelman,
Kishi Keiko

A swift and bloody action-adventure, written by Paul Schrader and Robert Towne, and
directed by Sydney Pollack. *The Yakuza* presents Robert Mitchum as Harry Kilmer,
an ex-GI and sometime private investigator. He returns to Japan in search of the
kidnapped daughter of his longtime friend (Brian Keith), a Los Angeles shipping
magnate. The *yakuza* (Japanese Mafia) are behind the abduction, so Harry enlists the
aid of a retired member of the organization (Takakura Ken, the star of over two hundred
films in Japan). This is the first American feature to explore the ancient—and extant—
code of the *yakuza*. Okazaki Kozo and Duke Callaghan collaborated on the cinematography.

The Year of Living Dangerously   Australia 1982; U.S. 1983   ◆   *Color*
(MGM)
Director: Peter Weir
Starring: Mel Gibson, Sigourney Weaver, Linda Hunt, Michael Murphy, Bill Kerr, Noel Ferrier, Bembol Roco

The political turmoil of Indonesia in 1965 provides the background for this suspense drama. An ambitious Australian journalist (Mel Gibson) is one of a small corps of foreign correspondents in Jakarta just before the ousting of Sukarno. To gather information the newsman relies on a British embassy attaché (Sigourney Weaver) and a mysterious photographer named Billy Kwan (played by actress Linda Hunt). Billy helps the Australian scoop his rivals, but the photographer's love for his poverty-stricken country also helps ignite the powderkeg that explodes into revolution. Director Peter Weir's script for *The Year of Living Dangerously* was developed with David Williamson and C. J. Koch, using the latter's novel as a guideline. Linda Hunt was an Oscar winner for her performance—to date the only actress to receive the award for enacting a male. Among the artists offscreen: cinematographer Russell Boyd, composer Maurice Jarre, and editor Bill Anderson. This picture was a precursor to *Under Fire* and *The Killing Fields,* two other hard-hitting political dramas with journalists as heroes.

Young at Heart   *Listed under Comedies.*

The Young Philadelphians   1959   (Warner)   *Black-and-White*
Director: Vincent Sherman
Starring: Paul Newman, Barbara Rush, Alexis Smith, Brian Keith, Diane Brewster, Billie Burke, John Williams, Robert Vaughn, Otto Kruger, Adam West, Paul Picerni, Robert Douglas, Frank Conroy

Tony Lawrence (Paul Newman) is a poor Philadelphia lawyer whose dash up the social ladder is interrupted by the Korean War. He and his affluent friend Chester (Robert Vaughn) return to Philly after the service, but Chester is framed on a murder charge. Tony defends him—forcing his way to the truth against lies, duplicity, and formidable blackmail threats. This picture is a precursor to glamorous post-sixties jet-set melodramas. The screenplay by James Gunn is derived from Richard Powell's best-selling novel *The Philadelphian.* Vincent Sherman directed. Vaughn's acclaimed performance as the murder defendant was Oscar-nominated but he lost to Hugh Griffith (*Ben-Hur*).

Zorba the Greek   1964   (CBS)   ◆   *Black-and-White*
Director: Michael Cacoyannis
Starring: Anthony Quinn, Alan Bates, Irene Papas, Lila Kedrova, George Foundas, Eleni Anousaki, Sotiris Moustakas, Takis Emmanuel, George Voyadjis

This adaptation by writer-director Michael Cacoyannis of the Nikos Kazantzakis novel presents Alexis Zorba (Anthony Quinn), an exuberant, life-embracing peasant on the island of Crete. Basil (Alan Bates), an English writer, is a recent arrival—and a bit standoffish at first. But Zorba extends his gregariousness to the scholarly young man and teaches him about life, lust, and the peculiarities of the Greek soul. Most prominent in the supporting cast are Irene Papas, as a widow with whom Basil falls in love, and Oscar-winning Lila Kedrova as Madame Hortense, an aging coquette. Other Academy Awards went to cinematographer Walter Lassally and art director Vassilis Fotopoulos.

The story was musicalized for the stage, debuting on Broadway in the 1968–69 season; Quinn and Kedrova re-created their screen roles in the 1980s revival.

Zulu   1964   (Charter)   *Color*
Director; Cy Endfield
Starring: Stanley Baker, Jack Hawkins, Ulla Jacobsson, James Booth, Michael Caine, Nigel Green, Ivor Emmanuel, Paul Danceman

A fact-based drama, *Zulu* depicts Britain's colonial expansion in nineteenth-century Africa. The John Prebble-Cy Endfield screenplay, directed by Endfield, builds to a bloody climax: the 1879 battle of Rorke's Drift, where a small garrison of English soldiers faced 4,000 Zulu warriors. The dramatic reconstruction concentrates on spectacle, African landscapes, studies of various individuals (Stanley Baker and Michael Caine as lieutenants, Jack Hawkins and Ulla Jacobsson as a fanatic missionary and his daughter)—and the insurmountable odds against the Britons. An epic with a foreknown unhappy ending, *Zulu* was photographed by Stephen Dade and has a score by John Barry. *Zulu Dawn*, a 1979 prequel (released in America in 1981), provided further historical background.

Family Viewing/
Children's

The **A**bsent-Minded Professor   1961   (Disney)   *Black-and-White*
Director: Robert Stevenson
Starring: Fred MacMurray, Nancy Olson, Keenan Wynn, Tommy Kirk, Ed Wynn, Leon Ames, Elliott Reid, Edward Andrews, Jack Mullaney

Special effects highlight this amiable family comedy from Walt Disney. Fred Mac-Murray, in the title role—a zany version of his patriarch on TV's "My Three Sons"—invents Flubber (flying rubber), and creates chaos in his suburban domicile. MacMurray, airborne in his trusty Model T Ford, is a sight that should tickle young audiences. Many Disney regulars appear in the supporting cast; most effective, perhaps, is Keenan Wynn as the villain out to steal the Flubber formula. Disney house director Robert Stevenson (*Old Yeller, Kidnapped, Mary Poppins*, et al) also was responsible for the equally popular sequel, *Son of Flubber* (1963). Originally released in black and white, *The Absent-Minded Professor*, in its 1986 videocassette version, is computer-colorized.

The Adventures of the Wilderness Family   1975   (Media)   *Color*
Director: Stewart Raffill
Starring: Robert Logan, Susan Damante Shaw, Hollye Holmes, Ham Larsen, George (Buck) Flower, William Cornford

Construction worker Robert Logan decides to leave behind the tension and noise of the city. So he and the family head out for a back-to-nature existence in the mountains of Utah. Though the scenery is breathtaking, danger lurks everywhere, yet after multiple soul-trying hardships, the wilderness family endures. This feature constitutes edge-of-the-seat entertainment for youngsters. It also spawned two direct sequels—*The Further Adventures of the Wilderness Family* (1978) and *Mountain Family Robinson* (1979), also starring Robert Logan. Stewart Raffilll also directed Logan in *Across the Great Divide*, in 1976, and, in 1978, *The Sea Gypsies* (aka *Shipwreck!*), two more family adventure tales.

The Apple Dumpling Gang   1975   (Disney)   *Color*
Director: Norman Tokar
Starring: Bill Bixby, Susan Clark, Don Knotts, Tim Conway, David Wayne, Slim Pickens, Harry Morgan, John McGiver, Don Knight, Clay O'Brien, Brad Savage, Stacy Manning, Dennis Fimple, Iris Adrian

In the Old West three orphans discover a large nugget in what everyone thinks is a played-out gold mine. Is it or isn't it? That's part of the fun in this Disney comedy caper about a gambler who inherits the three children. Bill Bixby and Susan Clark are the attractive adult leads. But even children and animals, both in abundant supply here, have difficulty stealing scenes from Don Knotts and Tim Conway. *The Apple Dumpling Gang* banked nearly $17 million (in the English-language market); but the sequel did only half that business, and any plans for continuing the series were quickly dissolved.

The Apple Dumpling Gang Rides Again   1979   (Disney)   *Color*
Director: Vincent McEveety
Starring: Tim Conway, Don Knotts, Tim Matheson, Kenneth Mars, Elyssa Davalos, Jack Elam, Robert Pine, Ruth Buzzi

Tim Conway and Don Knotts, the bumbling outlaws of *The Apple Dumpling Gang*, endeavor to go straight in this second slapstick adventure. They brush with spies, the U.S. Army, and train robbers. Puns and pratfalls ensue. A sturdy Disney cast of supporting players are foils for the stars' shenanigans. Though the Apple Dumpling gang disbanded at this juncture, Conway and Knotts joined forces again for non-Disney movies: *The Prize Fighter* (1979) and *The Private Eyes* (1980).

Bedknobs and Broomsticks   1971   (Disney)   *Color*
Director: Robert Stevenson
Starring: Angela Lansbury, David Tomlinson, Roddy McDowall, Sam Jaffe, John Ericson, Bruce Forsyth, Cindy O'Callaghan, Tessie O'Shea, Arthur E. Gould-Porter, Reginald Owen

During the London blitz, three children are evacuated to the quaint coastal village of Pepperings Eye. There they become the charges of Miss Eglantine Price—an apprentice witch. And they help Miss Price thwart a German invasion. Based on the book by Mary North, *Bedknobs and Broomsticks* is a live-action Disney musical, featuring animated sequences by Ward Kimball. The music and lyrics are from the Sherman brothers, of *Mary Poppins* fame. None of the songs has had a life after the movie, though one—"The Age of Not Believing"—has enduring charm. As Eglantine Price, Angela Lansbury actually seems to relish flying on her broomstick and antigravitational bed.

Benji   1974   (Vestron)   *Color*
Director: Joe Camp
Starring: Peter Breck, Christopher Connelly, Patsy Garrett, Tom Lester, Mark Slade, Herb Vigran, Deborah Walley, Frances Bavier, Edgar Buchanan, Terry Carter, Cynthia Smith, Allen Fiuzat, Ed De Latte

This family feature introduced moviegoers to that cuddly canine Benji (played by Higgins). He races to the rescue of two abducted children and in no time puts the bite on their kidnappers. Writer-director Joe Camp employed familiar TV faces in the leads: "Peyton Place's" Christopher Connelly, Edgar Buchanan from "Petticoat Junction," Terry Carter of "McCloud," Peter Breck of "The Big Valley" fame, and "The Andy Griffith Show's" Aunt Bee, Frances Bavier. (In the 1977 sequel, *For the Love of Benji*, only governess Patsy Garrett and the two children rejoined their hero). The result was big box office receipts: $17 million in U.S.-Canadian rentals. The story's focus is naturally on Benji; accordingly, much of the footage was shot at a height of eighteen inches from the ground—to dramatize the *real* star's point of view. "I Feel Love," the Euel and Betty Box theme song, was nominated for an Academy Award.

The Black Stallion   1979   (CBS)   *Color*
Director: Carroll Ballard
Starring: Kelly Reno, Teri Garr, Mickey Rooney, Clarence Muse, Hoyt Axton, Michael Higgins, Ed McNamara, Kristen Vigard, Fausto Tozzi, Leopoldo Trieste, Marne Maitland

From a shipwreck on a remote island and the rescue therefrom to a climactic championship race, *The Black Stallion* follows a young boy's adventures with a horse. The screenplay by Melissa Mathison, Jeanne Rosenberg, and William D. Witliff conveys the spirit of Walter Farley's boys' adventure tales. Little Kelly Reno stars as Alec Ramsay, Teri Garr plays mother Belle, and Mickey Rooney—in an Oscar-nominated performance—veteran horse trainer Henry Dailey. After directing several shorts and documentaries, Carroll Ballard came to his first feature film with Francis Coppola as executive producer—and a man of considerable talent behind the camera, Caleb Deschanel, whose work later included *The Natural* and *The Right Stuff*. Robert Dalva, the editor of this film, directed the 1983 sequel—*The Black Stallion Returns*.

The Boatniks   1970   (Disney)   *Color*
Director: Norman Tokar
Starring: Robert Morse, Stefanie Powers, Phil Silvers, Norman Fell, Mickey Shaughnessy, Wally Cox, Don Ameche, Joe E. Ross, Gil Lamb

Robert Morse is a Coast Guard ensign whose tour of duty at a Southern California marina is enlivened by a band of jewel thieves. While collecting clues and chasing suspects, the ensign finds time to court a pretty boat-rental lady (Stefanie Powers)—and together they ultimately nab the bad guys (Norman Fell, Mickey Shaughnessy, Phil Silvers). Arthur Julian wrote the screenplay. There is also the drollery of Morse, an accident-prone bungler who becomes a hero, and Phil Silvers, reviving his Bilko persona as the brains of the crime operation. Guiding the frivolity is Norman Tokar, who has spent much of his career with Disney, directing such films as *Big Red, The Ugly Dachshund, The Happiest Millionaire, Snowball Express,* and *The Apple Dumpling Gang.*

Born Free   1966   (RCA)   ◆   *Color*
Director: James Hill
Starring: Bill Travers, Virginia McKenna, Geoffrey Keen, Peter Lukoye, Omar Chambati, Bill Godden, Robert Cheetham

Joy Adamson's true life best-selling book recounted how she and her game warden husband raised Elsa, a lion cub, to maturity. The screen version, written by Gerald L. C. Copley and shot on location in Kenya, is a generally unsentimental translation. As George and Joy Adamson, husband-and-wife acting team Bill Travers and Virginia McKenna work effectively and intelligently together. The various animals representing Elsa as she grows are quite handsome too. James Hill, a former documentarist, is the director. Two Academy Awards went to *Born Free*: best original score (John Barry) and best song (Barry, with lyricist Don Black). In 1972, a sequel—*Living Free*—was released (with a new cast, except for Geoffrey Keen), documenting Elsa's life in the wild with her three cubs. Meanwhile, Travers and McKenna took the principal roles in two other animal films: *Ring of Bright Water* and *An Elephant Called Slowly*.

Breaking Away   1979   (CBS)   ◆   *Color*
Director: Peter Yates
Starring: Dennis Christopher, Dennis Quaid, Daniel Stern, Jackie Earle Haley, Barbara Barrie, Paul Dooley, Robyn Douglass, Amy Wright, John Ashton

Steve Tesich's comedy about a teenage bicycling enthusiast won him the 1979 original screenplay Oscar. Dave Stohler (Dennis Christopher) is from a working-class family in Bloomington, Indiana, where the university students classify the townies as cutters (emanating from the city's stone-cutting reputation). Dave's father, now a car salesman, was once a stone-cutter; thus the fraternity brothers' jibes hit home. So Dave dreams of making his mark by beating the university cycling team in a championship race. Before the big event, he and his lifelong buddies (Dennis Quaid, Daniel Stern, and Jackie Earle Haley) spend a summer grappling with present discontent and future prospects. *Breaking Away* constantly goes against one's expectations of the genre; even the adults—Paul Dooley and Barbara Barrie, as Dave's parents—come off sympathetically. As an ABC-TV series, "Breaking Away" existed but briefly in the 1980–81 season.

Bugsy Malone   1976   (Paramount)   *Color*
Director: Alan Parker
Starring: Scott Baio, Florrie Dugger, Jodie Foster, John Cassisi, Martin Lev, Albin Jenkins

This gangster film set in New York City in 1929 features several twists. First, it is a musical send-up of Prohibition mobster melodramas. Second, and most crucially, all the roles are played by children—most of them preteens. Open warfare exists between racketeers Fat Sam and Dandy Dan, but when the rival gangs clash, their Gatling Guns explode in whipped cream rather than bullets, their submachine guns splatter victims with marshmallows. Everything is scaled down; the vintage cars, for instance, are operated by pedal power. A true oddity from *The Terror of Tiny Town* school of filmmaking, *Bugsy Malone* is the screen debut of writer-director Alan Parker, who trained in British television. Composer-lyricist Paul Williams is also, through dubbing, the singing voice for many of the tykes.

Candleshoe   1977   (Disney)   *Color*
Director: Norman Tokar
Starring: David Niven, Helen Hayes, Jodie Foster, Leo McKern, Vivian Pickles, Veronica Gulligan, Ian Sharrock

Candleshoe is an estate in the English countryside. Helen Hayes, the last surviving family member, resides there, attended by a jack-of-many-trades manservant—David Niven. Rumors abound that a former occupant hid a fortune somewhere at Candleshoe, and two wily crooks (Leo McKern and Vivian Pickles) hatch a scheme to get an inside look: they force street-smart Jodie Foster to impersonate Miss Hayes's long-lost granddaughter. The comedy's plot ever so quickly thickens—thanks to David Swift and Rosemary Anne Sisson's screenplay, inspired by Michael Innes's mystery novel, *Christmas at Candleshoe*.

The Castaway Cowboy   1974   (Disney)   *Color*
Director: Vincent McEveety
Starring: James Garner, Vera Miles, Robert Culp, Eric Shea, Elizabeth Smith, Gregory Sierra

This period comedy finds Texas cowboy James Garner shanghaied on a Hawaiian island in the 1850s. Befriended by a poor widow (Vera Miles) with a young son, Garner decides to linger in paradise. Ultimately, he enters into partnership with the widow—converting her potato farm into a cattle ranch. Meanwhile, ne'er-do-well Robert Culp tries repeatedly to bilk the new partners out of their increasingly valuable property. Don Tait wrote the script. This was the second screen match-up for Garner and the Disney studios; *One Little Indian* (1973), in which the actor also played a cowboy smitten by Vera Miles, was the first.

The Cat from Outer Space   1978   (Disney)   *Color*
Director: Norman Tokar
Starring: Ken Berry, Sandy Duncan, McLean Stevenson, Harry Morgan, Roddy McDowall, Hans Conried, Ronnie Schell, Jesse White

An extraterrestrial feline named Jake lands on Earth and can't return to his own planet because his spaceship is out of commission. Seeking help with repairs, Jake enlists the sympathy and support of physicist Ken Berry. In due course, Jake is piloting his way home—but not before he has brushed with army brass and enemy spies. Ted Key wrote the witty script. Children and cat fanciers, above all, will be enchanted with the hero and his magic collar. Lalo Schifrin's bouncy score accompanies Jake's exploits.

The Champ   1979   (MGM)   *Color*
Director: Franco Zeffirelli
Starring: Jon Voight, Faye Dunaway, Ricky Schroder, Jack Warden, Arthur Hill, Strother Martin, Joan Blondell, Elisha Cook

A beyond-his-prime pugilist (Jon Voight), once a world-class champion, resides with his little son (Ricky Shroder) in reduced circumstances in Miami. A borderline alcoholic, he makes a living as a stableboy at the Hialeah race track. Life is not glamorous, but tolerable. His son's love and idolization buoy the champ. The glory days begin to haunt him, however, when his ex-wife (Faye Dunaway) spends a day at the races—and accidentally meets father and son. The boy's mother, now an affluent fashion designer, wants to provide a better life for her son—far from Florida. Walter Newman wrote this sentimental remake of the 1931 King Vidor classic (revised in 1953, as *The Clown*, for Red Skelton). Fred Koenekamp did the camera work.

Charlotte's Web   1973   (Paramount)   *Color*
Directors: Charles A. Nichols and Iwao Takamoto
Voices: Debbie Reynolds, Henry Gibson, Paul Lynde, Agnes Moorehead, Charles Nelson Reilly

Wilbur the pig is convinced that he is destined to be turned into breakfast bacon. For succor he turns to Charlotte, the resourceful barnyard spider. When Charlotte spins her magic web, she saves not only Wilbur but other farm animals as well. This animated musical is inspired by E. B. White's 1952 children's classic. The music and lyrics are by Richard and Robert Sherman, who contributed to many Disney features. The dialogue by Earl Hamner, Jr.—best known as the creator of TV's "The Waltons"—preserves White's wit and his compassionate depictions of the animal kingdom. *Charlotte's Web* comes from the studios of William Hanna and Joe Barbera, brainchildren behind such prominent cartoon creations as Tom and Jerry, Huckleberry Hound, Yogi Bear, the Flintstones, and the Jetsons.

A Christmas Carol   1951   (United)   *Black-and-White*
Director: Brian Desmond Hurst
Starring: Alastair Sim, Kathleen Harrison, Jack Warner, Michael Hordern, Mervyn
Johns, Hermione Baddeley, George Cole, Miles Malleson, Patrick Macnee

A Christmas Carol was, in the words of its creator, a "ghostly little book to raise the ghost of an idea." Among the plethora of movie and TV versions of Dickens's seasonal classic, this 1951 British production is generally regarded as most authentic—adhering more closely to the original's stark, spooky tone. The director, Brian Desmond Hurst, and his cinematographer, C. Pennington-Richards, enliven the period (mid-nineteenth-century London) and the author's style. Alastair Sim plays Ebenezer Scrooge, the neurotic miser who is reformed by four spectral visitors on Christmas Eve. Sim's interpretation is the yardstick by which all other Scrooges are measured.

Darby O'Gill and the Little People   1959   (Disney)   *Color*
Director: Robert Stevenson
Starring: Albert Sharpe, Janet Munro, Sean Connery, Jimmy O'Dea, Kieron Moore, Estelle
Winwood, Walter Fitzgerald, Denis O'Dea, J. G. Devlin, Jack MacGowran

A mischievous old caretaker named Darby O'Gill, widely known for his tall tales, falls down a well and tumbles into the land of the leprechauns. The King of Leprechauns allows Darby three wishes. Because the old man has spun so much blarney, no one believes his account of befriending the king—until a series of oddities occurs in the village. H. T. Kavanagh's Darby O'Gill stories are popular children's literature in Ireland, though unknown (or little known) here; but this Disney fantasy, filled with special effects and moments that are both whimsical and terrifying, affords a charming introduction to the protagonist. Screenwriter Lawrence Edward Watkin, collaborating with Oliver Wallace, has also created two songs for exploiting the lilting brogues at hand: "The Wishing Well" and "Pretty Irish Girl." The last-named is embodied by Janet Munro, playing Darby's daughter; her love interest is played by Sean Connery—three years before he soared to fame applying his secret agent skills against *Dr. No*. Character actor Albert Sharpe plays Darby, and Jimmy O'Dea portrays the king of the little people.

Doctor Doolittle   *Listed under Musicals.*

E.T., the Extraterrestrial   1982   (MCA in 1987)   ◆   *Color*
Director: Steven Spielberg
Starring: Dee Wallace, Henry Thomas, Peter Coyote, Robert MacNaughton, Drew Barry-more, K. C. Martel, Sean Frye, C. Thomas Howell

The phenomenon that literally redefined blockbuster, *E.T., The Extraterrestrial* is the undisputed high-grossing movie of all time ($228 million in rentals—not including foreign profits). The film is a warm family story about a ten-year-old boy's fascination with and loyalty to an extraterrestrial. When little E.T., the alien lifeform, is accidentally deserted by his interplanetary scouting party, he is befriended by Elliot, a suburban grade schooler. Adults intervene only to make the lovable extraterrestrial miserable. But, finally, Elliot and his friends help E.T. reunite with his colleagues from the spacecraft. This science fiction fantasy was written by Melissa Mathison, photographed by Allen Daviau, and performed by a lively ensemble of youngsters led by Henry Thomas as Elliot. Academy Awards: sound, sound editing, visual effects, and original score (John Williams).

The Earthling   1981   (Vestron)   *Color*
Director: Peter Collinson
Starring: William Holden, Ricky Schroder, Jack Thompson, Olivia Hamnett, Alwyn Kurts, Redmond Phillips, Willie Fennell, Roy Barrett

An Anglo-American-Australian coproduction, *The Earthling* is notable for its two stars, Ricky Schroder and William Holden, intersecting at the beginning and end of their respective careers. Basically a two-character rites of passage drama, woven from the familiar theme of age as instructor to youth, the tale is set in the Australian wilderness. Holden plays an embittered loner, terminally ill with cancer. When Schroder, who is cast as the quintessential city kid, is orphaned and gets lost in the wild, he abandons all hope; but a reluctant Holden teaches him survival tactics. Barely released in this country, *The Earthling* may now be discovered as an unforced back-to-nature adventure for all ages.

Escape to Witch Mountain   1975   (Disney)   *Color*
Director: John Hough
Starring: Eddie Albert, Ray Milland, Kim Richards, Ike Eisenmann, Donald Pleasence, Walter Barnes, Reta Shaw, Denver Pyle

Two orphans, a boy and a girl, discover that they possess paranormal powers. When an evil millionaire learns of the children's capabilities, he tries to harness their energies for his own devices. In this Disney adventure, the young hero and heroine, searching for their origins, are ultimately revealed as not of this earth. The screenplay by Robert Malcolm Young, from Alexander Key's novel, combines fantasy with hide-and-seek melodrama. Special effects are by Art Cruickshank. Ike Eisenmann and Kim Richards play the mysterious duo—and they engage in similar extrasensory feats in the 1978 sequel: *Return from Witch Mountain*.

For the Love of Benji   1977   (Vestron; Children's Video Library)   *Color*
Director: Joe Camp
Starring: Patsy Garrett, Cynthia Smith, Allen Fiuzat, Ed Nelson, Peter Bowles, Bridget Armstrong

The furry hero returns for the entertaining sequel to his 1974 debut. For this adventure, Benji and his owners are vacationing in Athens, where they cross paths with an international spy network. Benji, whose tattooed paw contains a secret formula, is the direct target. Fortunately, he is fleet of foot and keeps eluding his would-be captors. Fans of the first feature will not be disappointed in *For the Love of Benji,* also written and directed by Joe Camp. Young children should be advised that the first few scenes are English-subtitled condensations of the dialogue (mostly Greek). Afterwards, the English-speaking actors take over.

Freaky Friday   1976   (Disney)   *Color*
Director: Gary Nelson
Starring: Barbara Harris, Jodie Foster, John Astin, Patsy Kelly, Vicki Schreck, Dick Van Patten, Sorrell Booke, Alan Oppenheimer, Marie Windsor, Kaye Ballard, Ruth Buzzi

A teenager (Jodie Foster) yearns to trade places with her mother, a suburban housewife. The mother (Barbara Harris) has similar switching-places fantasies. Then one freaky Friday, both their dreams come true. For twenty-four hours mother and daughter magically switch personalities. Jodie becomes a fastidious homemaker, while Barbara attends classes, navigates by skateboard, and blows bubble gum till it bursts. This Disney farce, scripted by Mary Rodgers from her novel, is directed by Gary Nelson. (An action specialist, Nelson is best known for his TV movies—especially the two Mickey Spillane thrillers, "Murder Me, Murder You" and "More than Murder"—but he also directed *The Black Hole* for Disney.) John Astin, as Foster's father, and rival athletic coaches Ruth Buzzi and Kaye Ballard contribute to the comedy.

From the Mixed-Up Files of Mrs. Basil E. Frankweiler   1973   *Color*
     (BFA Educational Media)
Director: Fielder Cook
Starring: Ingrid Bergman, Madeline Kahn, Sally Prager, Johnny Doran, George Rose, Georgann Johnson, Richard Mulligan

This rarely seen, barely released fantasy features Ingrid Bergman in one of her last theatrical films. Aimed principally at children, the movie was perhaps a little too oddly rhythmed to appeal to a mass audience. (It was reissued as *The Hideaways.*) Just what is *From the Mixed-Up Files of Mrs. Basil E. Frankweiler?* The story concerns two twelve-year-old runaways (Sally Prager and Johnny Doran) who hide in the Metropolitan Museum of Art. They are befriended by a reclusive widow, Mrs. Basil E. Frankweiler (Miss Bergman), an art collector. Adapted from the well-reviewed novel by E. L. Konigsburg. Youngsters should be fascinated by the hide-and-seek escapades of the adolescent hero and heroine. Applauded for *Patterns* (1956), among other motion pictures, Fielder Cook, after *The Mixed-Up Files,* turned increasingly to television movies, where he directed such films as "A Love Affair: The Eleanor and Lou Gehrig Story" (1978), John Updike's "Too Far to Go" (1979), "I Know Why the Caged Bird Sings" (1979), "Gauguin the Savage" (1980), "Will There Really Be a Morning?" (1983), "Evergreen" (1985), and "Seize the Day" (1986).

Gentle Giant   1967   (Republic)   *Color*
Director: James Neilson
Starring: Dennis Weaver, Vera Miles, Clint Howard, Ralph Meeker, Huntz Hall

In the Florida Everglades a little boy and his family adopt an orphaned bear cub, name him Gentle Ben, then watch as he grows into a 700-pound giant. Fortunately, even fully grown, the pet retains his docility. He also becomes a lifesaver. Humorous and suspenseful, this family adventure is directed by James Neilson from a screenplay by

Edward J. Lakso and Andy White—in turn derived from Walt Morey's novel, *Gentle Ben*. Starring as young Mark Wedloe is Clint Howard, Ron Howard's little brother. Playing his parents are Dennis Weaver and Vera Miles. Weaver and Howard retained their father-son roles when the property was adapted for television; under the title "Gentle Ben," the series ran for two seasons, 1967–69.

The Great Muppet Caper   1981   (CBS)   *Color*
Director: Jim Henson
Starring: Charles Grodin, Diana Rigg, John Cleese, Trevor Howard, Robert Morley, Peter Ustinov, Jack Warden, and the Muppet performers (Jim Henson, Frank Oz, Dave Goelz, Jerry Nelson, Richard Hunt)

In this second feature in the Muppet movie cycle, Kermit the Frog and Fozzie Bear are reporters dispatched to London to solve the robbery of a fabulous jewel—the baseball diamond. But they don't make the voyage alone. Other regulars are here—Miss Piggy, Gonzo, and Rowlf—accompanied by some talented flesh-and-blood creatures, notably Diana Rigg and Charles Grodin. The caper, written by Tom Patchett, Jay Tarses, Jerry Juhl, and Jack Rose, is fun for all ages; the human guest stars blend deftly with the Muppets; and Joe Raposo's songs are melodic, particularly the Oscar-nominated "The First Time It Happens."

In Search of the Castaways   1962   (Disney)   *Color*
Director: Robert Stevenson
Starring: Maurice Chevalier, Hayley Mills, George Sanders, Wilfrid Hyde-White, Wilfrid Brambell, Michael Anderson, Jr., Keith Hamshire

This is the venerable Jules Verne story (*Captain Grant's Children*, adapted by Lowell S. Hawley) about an ill-assorted aggregate of diehards who—unscathed by wild animals, an earthquake, a flood, a tribe of hostile Indians, an avalanche, and a tidal wave—search for a castaway sea captain and his crew. Hayley Mills stars at the height of her popularity. Her romantic interest is Michael Anderson, Jr. Several songs by the Sherman brothers (Robert and Richard) are interpolated with the action and special effects, but they only hint at the popular scores the team would subsequently produce for *Mary Poppins* and *The Happiest Millionaire*.

The Incredible Journey   1963   (Disney)   *Color*
Director: Fletcher Markle
Starring: Emile Genest, John Drainie, Tommy Tweed, Sandra Scott, Syme Jago, Marion Finlayson, Muffey, Syn Cat, Rink

James Algar's adaptation of Sheila Burnford's popular adventure book is one of the features from the closing years of Walt Disney's reign. (He died in 1966.) Embarking on the title trek are three creatures who mistakenly believe they have been left behind when their owner leaves for a hunting trip. So the trio—Luath, a Labrador retriever (played by Rink); Bodger, a bull terrier (Muffey), and Tao, a Siamese cat (Syn Cat)—set off on a 250-mile journey across the Canadian wilderness to be reunited with their human family. Under Fletcher Markle's direction, this is an engaging novelty film. Rex Allen provides the voice-over narration.

The **K**arate Kid   1984   (RCA)   *Color*
Director: John G. Avildsen
Starring: Ralph Macchio, Noriyuki "Pat" Morita, Elisabeth Shue, Martin Kove, Randee Heller, William Zabka, Ron Thomas, Rob Garrison, Chad McQueen

Daniel, a fatherless teenager (Ralph Macchio), and his mother (Randee Heller) move from Newark, New Jersey, to Los Angeles. High school bullies, provoked by an over-enthusiastic karate instructor, make Daniel's life miserable until he is befriended by Mr. Miyagi (Pat Morita), the handyman at his apartment complex. Mr. Miyagi, a martial arts master, teaches the kid karate as a way of life—and as a way of warding off his classmates' taunts and physical abuse. Robert Mark Kamen's screenplay owes some of its inspiration to *Rocky*—a film directed by *The Karate Kid* director, John G. Avildsen. Another box-office smash for Avildsen.

The **L**ove Bug   1969   (Disney)   *Color*
Director: Robert Stevenson
Starring: Dean Jones, Michele Lee, David Tomlinson, Buddy Hackett, Joe Flynn, Benson Fong, Joe E. Ross, Iris Adrian

America's biggest box-office hit of 1969 (with over $20 million in rentals) concerned a self-motivated Volkswagen Beetle named Herbie. *The Love Bug*, written by Bill Walsh and Don da Gradi and directed by Robert Stevenson, details what happens when Herbie takes a liking to his new owner, a race car driver (Dean Jones), and propels him to fame. Pratfalls, stunts, and demolitions are major ingredients of this fast-moving Disney comedy. Three sequels resulted from this enormous success: *Herbie Rides Again* (1974), *Herbie Goes to Monte Carlo* (1977), and *Herbie Goes Bananas* (1980). Additionally, Dean Jones, the lead in two of the four entries in the series, found himself buckling up for a short-term (March to April 1982) TV sitcom adaptation called *Herbie, the Love Bug*.

Mary Poppins   1964   (Disney)   ◆   *Color*
Director: Robert Stevenson
Starring: Julie Andrews, Dick Van Dyke, David Tomlinson, Glynis Johns, Hermione Baddeley, Karen Dotrice, Matthew Garber, Elsa Lanchester, Ed Wynn, Arthur Treacher, Reginald Owen, Reta Shaw, Jane Darwell

Two precocious children, a flying nanny, a floating tea party, and a chorus of dancing chimney sweeps are a few of the components of Walt Disney's "supercalifragilisticex-pialidocious" musical fantasy. Julie Andrews, in her screen debut, portrays Mary Poppins, the "practically perfect" magical nursemaid of the books by P. L. Travers. Her two charges, from a straitlaced Edwardian London household, are Jane (Karen Dotrice) and Michael Banks (Matthew Garber). Their parents are a pompous banker (David Tomlinson) and an emergent suffragette (husky-voiced Glynis Johns). Joining in some of the adventures is Bert (Dick Van Dyke), Miss Poppins's jack-of-all-trades friend. The original songs by Richard M. and Robert B. Sherman include "Step in Time," "A Spoonful of Sugar," "Feed the Birds (Tuppence a Bag)," "Sister Suffragette," "Jolly Holiday," and the Academy Award–winning "Chim-Chim-Cheree." Julie Andrews emerged as a bright new movie star herein, captured the Oscar, and went on to even more acclaim the following year in *The Sound of Music*. Other Academy Awards went to Cotton Warburton for editing, the brothers Sherman for their score, and to the special visual effects team.

Melody   1971   (Embassy)   *Color*
Director: Waris Hussein
Starring: Jack Wild, Mark Lester, Tracy Hyde, Sheila Steafel, Kate Williams, Roy Kinnear

Mark Lester and Jack Wild, the adolescent stars of *Oliver!*, reteamed for this youth-geared English production. Written by future director Alan Parker, *Melody* features eleven-year-old Lester and twelve-year-old Tracy Hyde as a couple who want to run away and marry. When parents and school authorities present obstacles, Wild— playing Lester's more experienced school chum—tries to assist the young rebels. A co-producer of this comedy-drama is David Puttnam's appropriately named Goodtimes unit; preteens, in particular, may have good times with *Melody*. Songs by the Bee Gees.

Miracle on 34th Street   1947   (CBS)   ◆   *Black-and-White*
Director: George Seaton
Starring: Maureen O'Hara, John Payne, Edmund Gwenn, Gene Lockhart, Natalie Wood, Porter Hall, William Frawley, Jerome Cowan, Philip Tonge, James Seay, Harry Antrim, Thelma Ritter

A Christmas perennial, *Miracle on 34th Street* arises from Valentine Davies's story, as adapted and directed by George Seaton. In this fable of Kris Kringle, a Macy's employee (Edmund Gwenn) insists before skeptical little Susan Walker (Natalie Wood) that he really *is* Santa Claus. His assertions disturb parents and colleagues and he has to stand trial to prove his sanity. Academy Awards went to Davies, Seaton (as screenwriter), and Gwenn for their contributions. Filmed on location in New York City. A 1973 movie-for-television adaptation starred Sebastian Cabot as Kris Kringle.

The Muppet Movie   1979   (CBS)   *Color*
Director: James Frawley
Starring: Charles Durning, Austin Pendleton, Edgar Bergen, Milton Berle, Mel Brooks. James Coburn, Dom De Luise, Elliott Gould, Bob Hope, Madeline Kahn, Carol Kane, Cloris Leachman, Steve Martin, Richard Pryor, Telly Savalas, Orson Welles, Paul Williams, and the Muppet performers (Jim Henson, Frank Oz, Dave Goelz, Jerry Nelson, Richard Hunt)

Kermit, a singing frog, decides to abandon his Georgia swamp to pursue fame and fortune in Hollywood. The road to California is filled with weird characters, and there are enchanting moments en route. (The sight of Kermit on his bicycle should amuse children of all ages.) By the time the singing star has reached the movie capital, he's met up with Miss Piggy, Fozzie Bear, Gonzo, and others. The Muppets made their big screen debuts in this novelty film—written by Jerry Juhl and Jack Burns and featuring comedy, adventure, guest stars, and production numbers. One of the Paul Williams-Kenny Ascher songs, "The Rainbow Connection," was nominated for an Oscar. Later adventures include *The Great Muppet Caper* (1981) and *The Muppets Take Manhattan* (1984).

My Side of the Mountain   1969   (Paramount)   *Color*
Director: James B. Clark
Starring: Teddy Eccles, Tudi Wiggins, Paul Hebert, Cosette Lee, Ralph Endersby, George Allan, Frank Perry, Peggi Loder, Theodore Bikel

Sam (Teddy Eccles) is a thirteen-year-old Montreal boy who decides to leave the city to explore the Canadian wilderness. In this screen adaptation of the George Jean Nathan Award novel by Jean C. George, the young hero wants to be a naturalist. Accompanied by his pet raccoon, Gus, he begins his journey. He eats berries, catches fish, studies peregrine falcons, and gets trapped in a snowstorm. Denys Coop is responsible for the nature photography. Young Teddy Eccles is given strong support by Tudi Wiggins as the sympathetic librarian, Miss Turner, and by Theodore Bikel, playing Bando, a folksinging mountain man.

Never Cry Wolf   1983   (Disney)   *Color*
Director: Carroll Ballard
Starring: Charles Martin Smith, Brian Dennehy, Zachary Ittimangnaq, Samson Jorah, Hugh Webster, Martha Ittimangnaq, Tom Dahlgren, Walker Stuart

Farley Mowat's account of his life among Arctic wolves is the source of this Disney adventure. The screenplay by Curtis Hanson, Sam Hamm, and Richard Kletter changes the first-person narrator of Mowat's book into a fictional character named Tyler (Charles Martin Smith—Toad of *American Graffiti*). Tyler is a biologist on assignment for the Canadian government to study wolves and their suspected slaughter of caribou. He finds, ironically, that a symbiotic relationship exists between the animals—and that hunters are primarily responsible for the depletion of caribou herds. Practically a one-man show for Smith, *Never Cry Wolf* is highlighted by his performance—and by the scenery.

Night Crossing   1982   (Disney)   *Color*
Director: Delbert Mann
Starring: John Hurt, Jane Alexander, Beau Bridges, Ian Bannen, Glynnis O'Connor, Doug McKeon, Frank McKeon, Klaus Löwitsch, Geoffrey Liesik, Kay Walsh

This fact-based Disney production dramatizes the plight of two families as they escape from East Berlin to the west in a homemade hot-air balloon. Their preparation and perilous journey make for a bona fide adventure. (The real-life escape occurred in 1979.) *Night Crossing* is derived from a script by John McGreevey and was directed by Delbert Mann (*Marty, The Bachelor Party, The Dark at the Top of the Stairs, Lover Come Back*). Beau Bridges, Jane Alexander, Ian Bannen, and John Hurt head the international cast. Tony Imi's cinematography is noteworthy, particularly in the aerial sequences.

The North Avenue Irregulars   1979   (Disney)   *Color*
Director: Bruce Bilson
Starring: Edward Herrmann, Barbara Harris, Susan Clark, Karen Valentine, Michael Constantine, Cloris Leachman, Patsy Kelly, Douglas Fowley, Alan Hale, Jr., Virginia Capers

The Reverend Hill (Edward Herrmann), a Presbyterian minister, vows to wipe out organized crime in his community. Helping him are the FBI and a group of parish ladies. In the latter category are mothers who, for lack of babysitters, sometimes have to bring along the kids when collecting evidence against the syndicate. These unlikely crime-stoppers dub themselves the North Avenue Irregulars. This Disney comedy can be enjoyed by the entire family. Adapted by Don Tait from a novel by the Reverend Albert Fay Hill.

Old Yeller   1957   (Disney)   *Color*
Director: Robert Stevenson
Starring: Dorothy McGuire, Fess Parker, Tommy Kirk, Kevin Corcoran, Jeff York, Chuck Connors, Beverly Washburn, Spike

This heartwarming—and ultimately heartbreaking—Walt Disney drama centers around a pioneer farm family in 1850s Texas. Jim and Katie Coates (Fess Parker, Dorothy McGuire) have two sons: Travis (Tommy Kirk), a teenager, and Arliss (Kevin Corcoran), in grammar school. Travis adopts a yellow mongrel (Spike) that he hopes will be a top hunting dog. Old Yeller, as the new family member is called, fails in that regard; but time and again he is a veritable lifesaver. Robert Stevenson directs from a screenplay by William Tunberg and Fred Gipson, based on the popular novel by the latter. The animal fights are supervised by veteran second-unit man Yakima Canutt. Sequel: *Savage Sam* (1963).

Oliver Twist   Great Britain 1948; U.S. 1951   *Black-and-White*
        (Discount Video Tapes)
Director: David Lean
Starring: Alec Guinness, Robert Newton, John Howard Davies, Kay Walsh, Francis L. Sullivan, Anthony Newley, Henry Stephenson, Mary Clare, Gibb McLaughlin, Diana Dors, Ralph Truman

Dickens's Oliver Twist is a spindly foundling in a mid-nineteenth-century English workhouse who commits the unpardonable act of asking for more gruel. Sold to a hardhearted undertaker as a result, he flees to London and is befriended by a gang of young pickpockets. The child criminals are overseen by Fagin, an outcast Jew. This 1948 David Lean–directed version of the well-known tale was not shown in America until 1951 because Alec Guinness's interpretation of Fagin was considered anti-Semitic and the Production Code dispensers balked at the archfiend instructing his youthful band in thievery. That controversy aside, *Oliver Twist* can be viewed, now as then, as a careful pictorial representation of a beloved novel; the scenes of urban despair and poverty are unshakable. (Lean cowrote the screenplay with Stanley Haynes, while the cinematography is by Guy Green.)

The Parent Trap   1961   (Disney)   *Color*
Director: David Swift
Starring: Hayley Mills, Maureen O'Hara, Brian Keith, Charlie Ruggles, Una Merkel, Leo G. Carroll, Joanna Barnes, Cathleen Nesbitt, Ruth McDevitt, Crahan Denton, Linda Watkins, Nancy Kulp, Frank De Vol

In this Walt Disney comedy, Hayley Mills plays identical twins. Because of their parents' divorce, the two sisters—Susan and Sharon—have been separated since birth; each lives with one parent, unaware of the other's existence. When they accidentally meet at a summer camp, they scheme to rekindle the romance between their mother and father (Maureen O'Hara and Brian Keith). Inspired by Erich Kastner's novel *Das Doppelte Lottchen*, *The Parent Trap* is both scripted and directed by David Swift. There are three songs by Richard M. and Robert B. Sherman: "For Now, for Always," "Let's Get Together (Yeh, Yeh, Yeh)," and the title number, performed by Frankie Avalon and Annette Funicello. In the 1986 made-for-TV movie "The Parent Trap II," Hayley Mills reprises her roles as (the grown-up) Susan and Sharon.

Pete's Dragon   1977   (Disney)   *Color*
Director: *Don Chaffey*
Starring: *Helen Reddy, Jim Dale, Mickey Rooney, Red Buttons, Shelley Winters, Sean Marshall, Jane Kean, Jim Backus, Charles Tyner, Jeff Conaway, Joe Ross*

An amalgam of live action and fantasy, this Disney comedy, with music, takes place in 1900 Maine. Nine-year-old Pete (Sean Marshall) is an orphan with no friends his own age. The only adult who seems sympathetic to his needs is a pretty lighthouse keeper (Helen Reddy). In her absence, Pete relies on Elliott—a sometimes invisible flying dragon. Elliott is steadfast and protects the little boy from the village's criminal element. (Comedian Charlie Callas provides the dragon's voice.) The Malcolm Marmorstein screenplay is inspired by a treatment by Seton I. Miller and S. S. Field. Don Chaffey directs a cast that includes Jim Dale as an oily confidence man and Shelley Winters as the matriarch of a tribe of backwoods lowlife. The Al Kasha-Joel Hirschhorn song, "Candle on the Water," was nominated for an Oscar.

Pollyanna   1960   (Disney)   *Color*
Director: *David Swift*
Starring: *Hayley Mills, Jane Wyman, Richard Egan, Karl Malden, Nancy Olson, Adolphe Menjou, Donald Crisp, Agnes Moorehead, Kevin Corcoran, James Drury, Reta Shaw, Leora Dana*

Eleanor Porter's classic children's novel is the source for this Disney character comedy. It starts with twelve-year-old Pollyanna (Hayley Mills) arriving in a New England village to live with her aunt (Jane Wyman). In short order, Pollyanna, an optimistic orphan (she's termed "the glad girl"), has lifted the spirits of the community. She even wins over curmudgeons, misanthropes, and hypochondriacs. This is Hayley Mills's American film debut. *Pollyanna* is also the feature directing debut of David Swift, who wrote the screenplay. (To his later credit are *The Parent Trap* and *How to Succeed in Business Without Really Trying.*)

Race for Your Life, Charlie Brown   1977   (Paramount)   *Color*
Director: *Bill Melendez*
Voices: *Duncan Watson, Greg Felton, Stuart Brottman, Gail Davis, Liam Martin*

Once in a while the Peanuts gang, staples of newspaper comic strips and television specials, will venture onto the large screen. *A Boy Named Charlie Brown* (1969) set the feature film series in motion; *Snoopy, Come Home* (1972) arrived next. The third release, *Race for Your Life, Charlie Brown*, reunites the title character with the regulars—Lucy, Linus, Patty, Snoopy—for an antic adventure at summer camp. The climax finds the hero reluctantly participating in a raft race on a treacherous river. Creator Charles Schulz's humor is at the forefront of this animated comedy.

Robin Hood   1973   (Disney)   *Color*
Director: Wolfgang Reitherman
Voices: Brian Bedford, Peter Ustinov, Terry-Thomas, Phil Harris, Andy Devine, Monica Evans, Carole Shelley, Pat Buttram, George Lindsey, Roger Miller

Robin Hood, once played by Errol Flynn, really is a fox in this Disney animated feature. Under Wolfgang Reitherman's direction, the legend of Sherwood Forest is told from the animal kingdom's perspective. Balladeer Allan-a-Dale, for instance, is a rooster; real-life balladeer Roger Miller gives him a voice. Other characters are articulated by Brian Bedford (Robin), Monica Evans (Maid Marian), Andy Devine (Friar Tuck), Peter Ustinov (Prince John), Pat Buttram (Sheriff of Nottingham), and Phil Harris, who, as Little John, sings "The Phony King of England." "Love," another tune (with music by George Bruns and lyrics by Floyd Huddleston), was Oscar-nominated. The cast of famous voices makes this adaptation (from head writers Larry Clemmons and Ken Anderson) a treat. Viewers may, however, discover that the animation lacks the craftsmanship of the ancien régime at Disney; *Robin Hood* is computer-crafted.

The Secret of NIMH   1982   (MGM)   *Color*
Director: Don Bluth
Voices: Derek Jacobi, Elizabeth Hartman, Arthur Malet, Dom De Luise, Hermione Baddeley, Shannen Doherty, Wil Wheaton, Jodi Hicks, Ian Fried, John Carradine, Peter Strauss, Paul Shenar, Aldo Ray, Edie McClurg

This animated feature, produced by a group of former Disney artists, arises from the novel *Mrs. Frisby and the Rats of NIMH* by Robert C. O'Brien. (Director Don Bluth wrote the story adaptation with John Pomeroy, Gary Goldman, and Will Finn.) O'Brien's tale concerns a mouse named Mrs. Frisby (Elizabeth Hartman), a luckless, homeless widow who seeks aid from Nicodemus (Derek Jacobi), the King of the Rats. Nicodemus and his secret society of ultra-intelligent subjects help Mrs. Frisby and her son, ill with pneumonia. These characters reside in NIMH, an acronymic community beneath the National Institute of Mental Health. Also giving voice to the project are Hermione Baddeley as Auntie Shrew and John Carradine as the Great Owl.

The Shaggy Dog   1959   (Disney)   *Black-and-White*
Director: Charles Barton
Starring: Fred MacMurray, Jean Hagen, Tommy Kirk, Annette Funicello, Tim Considine, Kevin Corcoran, Cecil Kellaway, Alexander Scourby, Roberta Shore, James Westerfield, Jacques Aubuchon, Strother Martin

Wilby Daniels (Tommy Kirk) is a teenager fascinated by a scarab ring of the Borgias in the local museum. When he intones the Latin legend (*intra kapori transmuto*) inscribed on the ring, Wilby is transformed into an English sheepdog. His human and canine selves align to thwart a den of thieves. This Disney fantasy, scripted by Bill Walsh and Lillie Hayward, is inspired by Felix Salten's *The Hound of Florence*. Charles Barton, an expert at screen farce—and long associated with Abbott and Costello comedies—is the director. Sequel: *The Shaggy D.A.* (1976), in which the adult Wilby Daniels, now a lawyer and played by Dean Jones, speaks the magic syllables and turns hirsute all over again.

Snowball Express   1972   (Disney)   *Color*
Director: Norman Tokar
Starring: Dean Jones, Nancy Olson, Henry Morgan, Keenan Wynn, Mary Wickes, Johnny Whitaker, Michael McGreevey

A New York City accountant (Dean Jones) and his wife (Nancy Olson) are fed up with smog and rush-hour traffic. When they inherit a hotel in Colorado, they decide to trade the big city for the wilderness of the Rockies. Their fantasies of converting the guest house into a successful ski lodge are shattered when they arrive, with children and belongings in tow, and cast eyes on the dilapidated place. But it's too late to turn back. A Disney comedy, *Snowball Express* is based on Frankie and John O'Rear's novel, *Château Bon Vivant*—as adapted by Don Tait, Jim Parker, and Arnold Margolin. Another winner from ace Disney director Norman Tokar (*Big Red, Those Calloways, The Ugly Dachshund, The Happiest Millionaire, The Apple Dumpling Gang*).

Sounder   1972   (Embassy)   *Color*
Director: Martin Ritt
Starring: Cicely Tyson, Paul Winfield, Kevin Hooks, Carmen Matthews, Taj Mahal, James Best, Eric Hooks, Yvonne Jarrell, Janet MacLachlan

This Depression-set family drama is an adaptation by Lonnie Elder III of William H. Armstrong's celebrated novel. The Nathan Lee Morgan family are black sharecroppers in rural Louisiana. When Nathan Lee (Paul Winfield) is sentenced to a year of hard labor for stealing a ham, his wife Rebecca (Cicely Tyson) and preteen son David Lee (Kevin Hooks) must continue working the farm. In the course of the tale, David Lee is befriended by a dedicated schoolteacher (Janet MacLachlan) and a sympathetic white woman (Carmen Matthews)—both of whom seek to educate the boy to the world outside Louisiana. A deeply affecting movie about family ties, maturation, and roots. (Sounder, by the way, is David Lee's dog.) Sequel: *Part 2, Sounder* (1976), with a new cast under the direction of William A. Graham.

The Swiss Family Robinson   1960   (Disney)   *Color*
Director: Ken Annakin
Starring: John Mills, Dorothy McGuire, James MacArthur, Tommy Kirk, Kevin Corcoran, Cecil Parker, Janet Munro, Sessue Hayakawa

The famous children's novel by Johann Wyss makes a rousing romantic adventure by way of this Disney edition. (A low-budget version was released in 1940, and in 1975 a made-for-TV adaptation was aired.) In the early nineteenth century a Swiss family sailing to New Guinea is blown off course and shipwrecked. Cast upon a South Seas island, they convert it into a paradise. Working with a screenplay by Lowell S. Hawley and under Ken Annakin's direction, the cast is admirable. John Mills and Dorothy McGuire are cast as the parents; their sons are played by James MacArthur (as Fritz), Tommy Kirk (Ernst), and Kevin Corcoran (Francis); Sessue Hayakawa portrays a pirate leader.

The Sword in the Stone   1963   (Disney)   *Color*
Director: Wolfgang Reitherman
Voices: Sebastian Cabot, Alan Napier, Karl Swenson, Ricky Sorenson, Norman Alden

With veteran animators at the helm—Ollie Johnston, Milt Kahl, John Lounsbery, and Frank Thomas—there is technical precision in this Disney cartoon. The familiar tale revolves around an inscription on a majestic looking sword: "Whoso pulleth out this sword from this stone and anvil is rightwise King of England." A twelve-year-old boy named Wart does liberate the golden sword Excalibur. The rest is the legend of King Arthur. *The Sword in the Stone,* inspired by T. H. White's *The Once and Future King,* focuses on the young king's early years, his encounters with Merlin the Magician, and their various adventures. The screenplay is by Don Peet, the music by George Bruns.

That Darn Cat!   1965   (Disney)   *Color*
Director: Robert Stevenson
Starring: Hayley Mills, Dean Jones, Dorothy Provine, Roddy McDowall, Neville Brand, Elsa Lanchester, William Demarest, Frank Gorshin, Grayson Hall, Ed Wynn

An intrepid Siamese cat plays FBI agent in this slapstick romp from Disney. An evolvement from *Undercover Cat,* a novel by the Gordons, the husband-and-wife mystery writing team, the picture (cowritten by the authors and Bill Walsh) is a family adventure-comedy. Dean Jones is the human hero, who—in the course of a kidnapping investigation—becomes involved with two beautiful sisters (Hayley Mills and Dorothy Provine). They, with the undeniable aid of the feline protagonist (known principally as That Darn Cat), track and trap the kidnappers.

Time Bandits   1981   (Paramount)   *Color*
Director: Terry Gilliam
Starring: John Cleese, Sean Connery, Shelley Duvall, Katherine Helmond, Ian Holm, Michael Palin, Ralph Richardson, Peter Vaughan, David Warner, Kenny Baker, David Rappaport, Craig Warnock

In this recognition of the C. S. Lewis *Narnia* chronicles, a London schoolboy named Kevin (Craig Warnock) is whisked away by a band of thieving dwarfs, for an adventure through time. Kevin and the dwarfs keep falling through time holes in the universe. In the course of their adventures they meet up with Agamemnon (Sean Connery), Robin Hood (John Cleese), Napoleon Bonaparte (Ian Holm), the Supreme Being (Ralph Richardson), Satan (David Warner), and a continuing parade of unlucky lovers (all played by Michael Palin and Shelley Duvall). The Michael Palin-Terry Gilliam script, as directed by Gilliam, is more than a deft parody of children's adventure novels. It's an imaginative comic fantasy for all age groups.

Tom Sawyer   1973   (Playhouse Video)   *Color*
Director: Don Taylor
Starring: Johnnie Whitaker, Celeste Holm, Warren Oates, Jeff East, Jodie Foster

Of all the film adaptations of Mark Twain's classic piece of Americana, this 1973 version is one of the most faithful. As directed by Don Taylor, the screenplay of Richard and Robert Sherman (who also provide some songs) spins the oft-told tale of a boy's life in the Mississippi River town of Hannibal, Missouri, circa 1850. Tom Sawyer (Johnnie

Whitaker), an orphan, lives with his proper Aunt Polly (Celeste Holm), pals around with a scoundrel named Huckleberry Finn (Jeff East), becomes smitten with young Becky Thatcher (Jodie Foster), and—in a famous scene—fast-talks his way out of whitewashing a fence. Additionally, he and his fellow adventurers get involved with rascally Muff Potter (Warren Oates) and murder. Shot on location in Missouri by director of photography Frank Stanley.

Tom Thumb   1958   (MGM)   ◆   *Color*
Director: George Pal
Starring: Russ Tamblyn, June Thorburn, Peter Sellers, Terry-Thomas, Alan Young, Jessie Matthews, Bernard Miles, Ian Wallace

A special effects Oscar went to Tom Howard for his contributions to this Hollywood revamping of the Grimm brothers' fairy tale. Director George Pal uses live action, puppets, and animation to recount the legend of Tom Thumb (Russ Tamblyn), the five-inch-high forest boy adopted by a kindly old couple, then forced by thieves to rob the king's treasury. (Terry-Thomas and Peter Sellers are the Black Swamp villains who take advantage of the minuscule hero.) With a screenplay by Ladislas Fodor and cinematography by Georges Périnal, *Tom Thumb* is a lighthearted fantasy for children of all ages.

Treasure Island   1950   (Disney)   *Color*
Director: Byron Haskin
Starring: Bobby Driscoll, Robert Newton, Basil Sydney, Walter Fitzgerald, Denis O'Dea, Ralph Truman, Finlay Currie, Geoffrey Wilkinson

One of numerous adaptations—from silent days onward—of Robert Louis Stevenson's 1883 adventure novel, this version comes from Walt Disney. The time-honored tale, as screenwritten by Lawrence Edward Watkin, presents Bobby Driscoll as young Jim Hawkins, the cabin boy on the *Hispaniola*. The ship is infiltrated by a pirating band led by peg-legged Long John Silver (Robert Newton). And heroes and villains alike sail off to an island where buried treasure awaits. Directed by Byron Haskin, who in 1954 made a sequel in Australia—*Long John Silver*, with Newton reprising his title role interpretation.

20,000 Leagues Under the Sea   1954   (Disney)   ◆   *Color*
Director: Richard Fleischer
Starring: Kirk Douglas, James Mason, Paul Lukas, Peter Lorre, Robert J. Wilke, Carleton Young, Ted De Corsia, Percy Helton, Ted Cooper, Edward Marr, Fred Graham, J. M. Kerrigan

Jules Verne's 1870 nautical novel inspired this Disney adventure. The undersea kingdom of Captain Nemo is the principal setting. Nemo (James Mason), a mysterious recluse, challenges the British Navy from his futuristic submarine, the *Nautilus*. Taken aboard the sub are shipwreck victims Ned Land (Kirk Douglas), a robust harpooner; Professor Aronnax (Paul Lukas), a scientist; and Conseil (Peter Lorre), the professor's assistant. Directed by Richard Fleischer from a scenario by Earl Felton, the filming took place in New Providence, Bahamas; Long Bay, Jamaica—and in the Disney studio tank in Burbank. Academy Awards went to John Meehan and Emile Kuri's art direction and set decoration, and to the special effects team that created, among other wonders, an impressive looking giant squid.

Watership Down   1978   (Warner)   *Color*

Director: Martin Rosen
Voices: John Hurt, Richard Briers, Ralph Richardson, Denholm Elliott, Harry Andrews, Joss Ackland, Zero Mostel, Roy Kinnear, John Bennett, Simon Cadell

Animation and grand storytelling come together in this family adventure, derived from the best-selling Richard Adams novel. When their home is threatened by real-estate developers, a colony of rabbits begins a cross-country journey to find a new warren. In their odyssey, they encounter obstacles in man, nature, and other members of the animal kingdom. Directed by Martin Rosen from his screenplay, *Watership Down* affords offscreen opportunities for an array of well-known actors. Michael Hordern is the narrator; John Hurt is the voice of the rabbit leader; and Zero Mostel provides the voice of a friendly sea gull that accompanies the travelers. The animation was supervised by Tony Guy.

The **Y**earling   1946   (MGM)   ◆   *Color*

Director: Clarence Brown
Starring: Gregory Peck, Jane Wyman, Claude Jarman, Jr., Chill Wills, Clem Bevans, Margaret Wycherly, Henry Travers, Forrest Tucker, Donn Gift, Daniel White, Matt Willis, George Mann, Arthur Hohl, June Lockhart

This drama finds its source in Marjorie Kinnan Rawlings's novel about young Jody Baxter, a farmer's son, and his attachment to a pet fawn. Claude Jarman, Jr., in his film debut, plays Jody, and his father—a proud pioneer in the Florida Everglades—is played by Gregory Peck. Jody's yearling presents problems to the Baxter family, mother (Jane Wyman) included. Not the least of the difficulties is that it has a tendency to eat the crops. A tragic solution is proposed—based on Rawlings's real-life observations from her Cross Creek home. Paul Osborn wrote the screenplay, using much of the novelist's dialogue, and Clarence Brown directed. (Brown also directed Jarman in the 1949 Faulkner adaptation, *Intruder in the Dust.*) Academy Awards: cinematography (Charles Rosher, Leonard Smith, and Arthur Arling) and art direction/set decoration (Cedric Gibbons, Paul Goresse, and Edwin B. Willis).

Foreign Language

Aguirre, the Wrath of God   Germany 1972; U.S. 1976   *Color*
   (Continental)
Director: Werner Herzog
Starring: Klaus Kinski, Ruy Guerra, Helena Rojo, Cecilia Rivera, Peter Berling, Danny Ades

West Germany in the 1970s spawned three young filmmakers who went on to capture international reputations: Wim Wenders, Rainer Werner Fassbinder, and Werner Herzog. *Aguirre, the Wrath of God* represented Herzog's first big break in the American art house/foreign film circuit. Shot in Peru, it documents the attempts of Aguirre (Kinski), a half-crazed conquistador, to find the fabled seven cities of gold. The jungles of the Amazon prove his undoing. Herzog's production is beautiful to regard, though not in any conventional Hollywood way. And Kinski's Aguirre, a psychotic idealist and visionary, dramatizes the thin margin between compulsion and insanity.

Amarcord   1974   (Warner)   ◆   *Color*
Director: Federico Fellini
Starring: Magali Noël, Bruno Zanin, Luigi Rossi, Pupella Maggio, Armando Brancia, Giuseppe Lanigro, Josiane Tanzilla

Recalling some of Federico Fellini's early neorealist films, *Amarcord* (dialect for *I remember*) is a semi-autobiographical nostalgic look at an Italian seacoast town of the thirties. (Rimini, where Fellini grew up, was also the setting for *I Vitelloni*.) With longtime coscenarist Tonino Guerra, the filmmaker establishes a boy's perception of the village and its eccentric citizenry—while, for the most part, eschewing his trademark grotesqueries. Most memorable scene to many: the townspeople rowing out to see the luxury liner *Rex* as it passes in the foggy night. 1974 Oscar recipient for best foreign feature. Dubbed into English.

And God Created Woman   France 1956; U.S. 1957   *Color*
   (Vestron Video; Time-Life Video)
Director: Roger Vadim
Starring: Brigitte Bardot, Curt Jurgens, Jean-Louis Trintignant, Christian Marquand, Georges Poujouly, Jean Tissier

Brigitte Bardot's breakthrough film. A starlet and supporting player, usually as a brunette, beginning in 1952, she was hereafter a blonde sex kitten. As a young newlywed worshipped by her husband (Trintignant), chased by a tycoon (Jurgens), and physically ravished by husband's virile older brother (Marquand), Bardot displays not only undraped flesh but undisguised acting talent. Roger Vadim's first feature is essentially an old-fashioned melodrama with a modern (i.e., 1956) amoral twist. Vadim and his script collaborator Raoul Levy dramatize the new-versus-old moral code. But *And God Created Woman* endures expressly as an unapologetic showcase for Mlle. Bardot. St. Tropez in summery pastels is easy on the eyes too.

Autumn Sonata   1978   (Magnetic Video)   *Color*
Director: Ingmar Bergman
Starring: Ingrid Bergman, Liv Ullmann, Lena Nyman, Halvar Björk, Erland Josephson,
Gunnar Björnstrand

The Swedish master here reveals himself in an uncharacteristic naturalistic phase. Gone are the austerity, the unalterable pessimism, and the brooding metaphysical musings. In their place arrives a human comedy-drama depicted in straightforward narrative, recognizable characters, accessible motives, and episodes from "ordinary" life. *Autumn Sonata* outlines the uneasy reunion between a world-renowned concert pianist and her neglected daughter. Ingrid Bergman, in her first Swedish-language film role since 1938, is the mother; Liv Ullmann is the resentful daughter, married to a passionless clergyman. The supporting cast includes some of the director's career-long acting repertory; additionally, in *Autumn Sonata,* he is reteamed with Sven Nykvist, the sublime cinematographer who shot, among others, *The Virgin Spring, Winter Light, The Silence, Persona,* and *Cries and Whispers.* Filmed in Norway.

Beauty and the Beast   France 1946; U.S. 1947   *Black-and White*
(Vid Dim)
Director: Jean Cocteau
Starring: Jean Marais, Josette Day, Michel Auclair, Marcel André, Mila Parely, Nane
Germon, Raoul Marco

Cinematic wizardry from poet-painter-dramatist Jean Cocteau. *Beauty and the Beast,* his first full-length feature, is based on the children's fairy tale. The film is *not* for children only. Cocteau as prime mover, in league with associate director and technical adviser René Clément, refashions the fantasy of Beauty, who saves her father's life by sacrificing herself to Beast. Love, finally, saves all of them—and Beast is transformed into Prince Charming. The production moves from the storybook decor of the family farm where Beauty dwells to surreal sequences in Beast's domain; his haunted castle is a noteworthy achievement by the art direction and set decoration technicians, supervised by René Moulaert and Christian Bérard. Music is by Georges Auric; director of photography is Henri Alekan; Christian Bérard devised Beast's makeup. Jean Marais, Cocteau's protégé, is seen in three roles: Beast, Avenant, and the Prince.

Bed and Board   France 1970; U.S. 1971   (Key)   *Color*
Director: François Truffaut
Starring: Jean-Pierre Léaud, Claude Jade, Daniel Ceccaldi, Claire Duhamel, Mlle.
Hiroko, Barbara Laage, Jacques Jouanneau, Daniel Boulanger

The return of Antoine Doinel, Truffaut's semiautobiographical hero. Introduced as a mischievous schoolboy in *The 400 Blows,* Antoine, now a budding writer, has recently married and acquired a job with an American hydraulic company in Paris. *Bed and Board* traces the evolution of the marriage and Antoine's momentary after-hours dalliance with a fetching Japanese woman whom he meets at work. This episode is the fourth in the Doinel series (concluded with number five—*Love on the Run*—in 1979). It reveals Truffaut's style with personal, often comic situations in his alter ego's struggle toward maturity. One highlight: Antoine demonstrating his English by repeating absurd phrasebook sentences. Jean-Pierre Léaud, star of all five Doinel films, is again the embodiment of the protagonist—charming yet petulant, stoic yet romantic. Léaud, whom Truffaut deemed "the best French actor of his generation," has done other film work (*Last Tango in Paris, The Mother and the Whore,* several Godard projects, and Truffaut's non-Doinel *Two English Girls*).

The Bicycle Thief   1949   (Corinth Films)   ◆   *Black-and-White*
Director: Vittorio De Sica
Starring: Lamberto Maggiorani, Enzo Staiola, Lianella Carell, Elena Altieri, Gino Saltamerenda

The classic that catapulted Vittorio De Sica to the forefront of world cinema. A long-unemployed man (Lamberto Maggiorani) living in postwar Rome has just received work pasting up movie-publicity bills around the city. For the job he must use his bicycle, which, in the opening reel of the film, is stolen by a street gang. A futile chase ensues, and the local police offer no hope. So, accompanied by his seven-year-old son (Enzo Staiola), the laborer goes in search of his bike. A simple story—from De Sica's partner-scenarist, Cesare Zavattini, and imbued with almost Chaplinesque pathos. But De Sica frames these events more harshly than Chaplin would have. After *Shoeshine* in 1947, *The Bicycle Thief* was the second De Sica-Zavattini collaboration to find commercial acceptance in the States. Further, it validated the Italian neorealist school of filmmaking: shooting in the streets and buildings of Rome, rather than on constructed sets—and using unknown and nonprofessional actors. An American company proposed that Cary Grant star as the impoverished father; De Sica and Zavattini refused. *The Bicycle Thief* received a special Academy Award from the Board of Governors in 1949; the official foreign language Oscar category was not established until 1956.

Black Orpheus   1954   (CBS)   ◆ ✳   *Color*
Director: Marcel Camus
Starring: Bruno Mello, Marpessa Dawn, Adhemar Da Silva, Lourdes De Oliveira

Marcel Camus's French-Italian-Brazilian coproduction takes place in Rio de Janeiro at carnival time. The director, adapting a Brazilian stage play with Jacques Viot, offers the myth of Orpheus and Eurydice with a Bahia backdrop. In this incarnation, Orpheus is a streetcar conductor, Eurydice a naive country girl. Rio's exoticism is in full view as the two lovers cavort among the brightly costumed revelers—with Death in hot pursuit. Attempts to make this a quintessential art movie sometimes result in unintentionally funny dialogue. *Black Orpheus* is, at root, a potpourri of color and music that shouldn't be missed by fans of Latin American literature and rhythms. Among the accolades: Palme d'Or at Cannes, Academy Award for best foreign film.

Blue Country   France 1977; U.S. 1978   (RCA)   *Color*
Director: Jean-Charles Tacchella
Starring: Brigitte Fossey, Jacques Serrès, Ginette Garcin, Ginette Mathieu

Writer-director Jean-Charles Tacchella's *Cousin, Cousine* became one of the top-grossing imports ever to reach American shores. Throughout 1976 it broke box-office records, surmounting the narrow confines of art house fame—to play long runs everywhere. *Blue Country,* Tacchella's subsequent romantic comedy, unfortunately didn't duplicate that success. The rural, young singles counterpart to the earlier movie's urban, young marrieds scene, this film is the story of two lovers who want to retain their independence. Brigitte Fossey, a child star best remembered in America for the classic *Forbidden Games,* is radiant in what may be her most captivating adult role.

Carmen 1983 (Media) *Color*
Director: Carlos Saura
Starring: Antonio Gades, Laura del Sol, Paco de Lucia, Cristina Hoyos, Juan Antonio Jimenez, Sebastian Moreno

This contemporary update places the often filmed Prosper Mérimée classic in a theatrical setting. Spanish filmmaker Carlos Saura casts choreographer Antonio Gades *as* a choreographer named Antonio who is embroiled in auditions for a flamenco ballet version of *Carmen.* After tryouts, Antonio hires for the title role a young dancer (Laura del Sol), whose real name happens to be Carmen. Before long, a romance develops between Antonio and Carmen—with direct parallels to the theater piece they are rehearsing. A blend of drama and fiery dance, Saura's production transcends a narrow appeal to flamenco fans; it is accessible to all ages and tastes. Gades doubles as both choreographer and leading player. (He also cowrote the screenplay with the director.) Saura's film was part of an explosion of Carmen-related projects in late 1983 and early 1984; Francesco Rosi brought the Bizet opera to the screen with Placido Domingo and Julia Migenes-Johnson, and Jean-Luc Godard placed the heroine in a cops-robbers-kidnappers milieu for *Prénom: Carmen.*

Cat and Mouse France 1975; U.S. 1978 (RCA) *Color*
Director: Claude Lelouch
Starring: Michèle Morgan, Serge Reggiani, Philippe Léotard, Valérie Lagrange, Jean-Pierre Aumont

The scene is the topmost floor of a soon-to-be-completed Paris skyscraper, where a wealthy industrialist plunges to his death. Or does he? In a word, no. But that's how the businessman's wife, tired of his infidelities, imagines his demise. Within a few days, the same man is found shot to death at his lavish estate outside Paris—and his wife is considered the most likely suspect. Enter Inspector Lechat—for a game of cat and mouse with the wealthy widow. As the cat, Serge Reggiani stars as the spirited sleuth; Michèle Morgan, in a rare screen appearance, plays the ostensible mouse. Writer-director Claude Lelouch's whodunit affords a change of pace from the physically violent school of mystery movies. Lelouch is joined by two frequent collaborators: composer Francis Lai and director of photography Jean Collomb. English-dubbed.

Closely Watched Trains Czechoslovakia 1966; U.S. 1967   *Color*
  (RCA)
Director: Jiri Menzel
Starring: Vaclav Neckar, Jitka Bendova, Vladimir Valenta, Josef Somr, Libuse Havalkova, Vlastmil Brodsky, Jitka Zelenohorska

A tragicomedy laid in World War II Czechoslovakia. Deep in the background of the story line are the German Occupation and the sabotage of the Czech underground. At the forefront of the action is a teenage boy who takes on his first adult job at a rural railroad station. While apprenticing as a train dispatcher, the young hero also wants to lose his virginity. Opportunities, as they will, arise. Jiri Menzel, in his feature-length directing debut, combines uproarious moments with scenes of tenderness. (His screenplay with Bohumil Hrabal derives from the latter's rites-of-passage novel.) Vaclav Neckar plays the steadfast protagonist, abetted in one scene by director Menzel in the role of a sympathetic young doctor. *Closely Watched Trains* was cited by the Academy as the best foreign-language film of 1967—the second Czech feature in three years to be so honored. (See *The Shop on Main Street*.) To date it is the only Jiri Menzel film to be commercially released in the United States.

Cousin, Cousine   France 1975; U.S. 1976   (CBS)   *Color*
Director: Jean-Charles Tacchella
Starring: Marie-Christine Barrault, Victor Lanoux, Marie-France Pisier, Guy Marchand, Ginette Garcin, Sybil Maas, Jean Herbert, Pierre Plessis, Catherine Verlour, Hubert Gignoux

Writer-director Jean-Charles Tacchella has said of his second full-length comedy: "I only had one aim in making this film: to re-create life in the way it fascinates me most—as absurdity, funniness, and fragility." All those factors commingle when Marthe and Ludovic, two distant cousins, both with unfaithful spouses, meet at a family wedding. Dimly aware of one another at first, they begin a lengthy platonic relationship, followed by a fully blossoming love affair. Marie-Christine (niece of Jean-Louis) Barrault plays Marthe; Victor Lanoux plays Ludovic. Winner of the prestigious Louis Delluc Prize, *Cousin, Cousine* charmed audiences in its native France before becoming an international hit in 1976. It was that rare foreign language movie to be nominated in traditional Oscar categories—best actress (Barrault) and best original screenplay (Tacchella with Danièle Thompson)—in addition to its bid in the foreign film competition. Other contributing talents: Georges Lendi (cinematographer), Agnès Guillemot (editor), and Gérard Anfosso (for his music). Tacchella's follow-up: *Blue Country*.

The Cranes Are Flying   U.S.S.R. 1957;   ✳   *Black-and-White*
      U.S. 1959   (International Historic Films)
Director: Mikhail Kalatozov
Starring: Tatyana Samilova, Alexei Batalov, Vasily Merkuryve, A. Shovrin

A love story placed in the Soviet Union during World War II, *The Cranes Are Flying* marked a departure from the propagandistic motion pictures of the Stalinist era. A young woman and her fiancé are separated when he goes off to the front. She is raped by a brute, then reluctantly marries him. It's a loveless union; she keeps waiting for her lover's return. Eventually, she is evacuated to Siberia, where she becomes a nurse. After the war she is told that her beloved has been killed in action—but she refuses to believe the reports. Under the direction of veteran Soviet filmmaker Mikhail Kalatozov, Tatyana Samilova and Alexei Batalov star as the war-separated sweethearts. Kalatozov and *The Cranes Are Flying* received considerable acclaim in this country, during a period of active cultural exchange between America and the Soviet Union. With one exception, the director's later work is not widely known in the U.S. In 1971 Kalatozov's *The Red Tent*, about General Umberto Nobile's disastrous 1928 Arctic expedition, was released here. A Soviet-Italian coproduction, it starred Sean Connery,

Claudia Cardinale, Hardy Kruger, and (as Nobile) Peter Finch. *The Cranes Are Flying* was a prize winner at Cannes.

Cries and Whispers 1973 (Warner) ✲ ◆ *Color*
Director: Ingmar Bergman
Starring: Harriet Andersson, Ingrid Thulin, Liv Ullmann, Kari Sylwan, Erland Josephson, George Arlin, Henning Moritzen

This Ingmar Bergman period drama (circa 1900) relates the story of three sisters—the middle one, in her late thirties, dying of cancer in her country manor. She is attended by her married siblings and her faithful servant, Anna. Bergman dissects their interrelationships as "nothing but lies—a tissue of lies." But in the death of the one sister, the survivors begin a kind of rapprochement. There are outstanding performances from four actresses in the classic Bergman mode: Harriet Andersson as the dying woman, Ingrid Thulin and Liv Ullmann as her sisters, and Kari Sylwan as Anna. The film also represents a bold camera study by Sven Nykvist, emphasizing decors, props, and costumes of red, black, and white. (Scenes fade to red rather than black.) The New York Film Critics Circle named *Cries and Whispers* best film and Liv Ullmann best actress of 1973. Nominated for five Academy Awards, including picture, director, screenplay, and costume design, the film claimed only one—for Nykvist's cinematography. The videocassette represents the print of the film dubbed in English by most of the original stars.

Danton France/Poland 1982; U.S. 1983 (RCA) *Color*
Director: Andrzej Wajda
Starring: Gérard Depardieu, Wojciech Pszoniak, Patrice Chereau, Angela Winkler, Boguslaw Linda

Gérard Depardieu is perhaps the most internationally recognized young actor to have emerged from France in the last decade. A small sampling of the Depardieu films imported to America includes Bertolucci's *1900,* Truffaut's *The Last Metro,* Daniel Vigne's *The Return of Martin Guerre,* and two films by Bertrand Blier—*Going Places* and *Get Out Your Handkerchiefs*. In 1982 the actor collaborated with acclaimed Polish filmmaker Andrzej Wajda on this historical epic. *Danton* recounts the events leading to the French Revolution, then dramatizes the philosophical clash between two of its leading proponents—Georges Danton and Maximilien Robespierre. The latter forges a ruthless dictatorship, while Danton—still bolstered by revolutionary spirit—pledges to unseat him. In Wajda's hands, the Reign of Terror becomes a parallel to the contemporary Solidarity movement in Poland—and Danton is the equivalent of Lech Walesa.

Das Boot 1981 (RCA) *Color*
Director: Wolfgang Petersen
Starring: Jürgen Prochnow, Herbert Grönemeyer, Klaus Wennemann, Hubertus Bengsch, Martin Semmelrogge, Bernd Tauber, Erwin Leder, Martin May

Das Boot may be the most commercially successful German film to be released in America. The subject is a U-boat mission in World War II, where tedious day-to-day routines ultimately lead to heroism and self-sacrifice. Wolfgang Petersen, as writer and director, captures the claustrophobia inside the vessel and, more importantly, the visceral disillusionment with war that festers therein. (The screenplay is based on the autobiographical novel by Lothar-Günther Buchheim.) Petersen and his leading man, Jürgen Prochnow, have gone on to work in American movies and television. After *Das Boot*'s initial art house acclaim, a dubbed version (retitled *The Boat*) was created to play in most U.S. cinemas—and it is that edition, not the subtitled one, that is now available in videocassette.

Day for Night   1973   (Warner)   ◆ ✷ ◯   *Color*
Director: François Truffaut
Starring: Jacqueline Bisset, Valentina Cortese, Alexandra Stewart, Jean-Pierre Aumont, Jean-Pierre Léaud, François Truffaut, Jean Champion, Nathalie Baye, Dani, Bernard Menez, Nike Arrighi, Gaston Joly, Maurice Seveno, David Markham, Henry Graham

At the Victorine Studios in Nice, a famous French director is shooting a movie that reunites an alcoholic, middle-aged actress and her former silver screen seducer. Joining them are two young stars: a neurotic *jeune premier* and an American actress recovering from a nervous breakdown. This amiable comedy-drama documents the evolution of the film—a melodrama called *Meet Pamela*—while sneaking glimpses at the group and private lives of the participants. François Truffaut, who plays the director of *Meet Pamela,* is also the creator of *Day for Night,* coscripted by Jean-Louis Richard and Suzanne Schiffman. Henry Graham, who plays an insurance representative, is really author (and French Riviera resident) Graham Greene. The title derives from the cinematic custom of using filtered lenses in day shooting so that the resulting footage will look like night photography; the practice in France is termed *la nuit américaine.* Honors: Academy Award for best foreign film and—from both the New York Critics Circle and the National Society of Film Critics—best film, best director, and best supporting actress (Valentina Cortese).

Death in Venice   1971   (Warner)   ✷   *Color*
Director: Luchino Visconti
Starring: Dirk Bogarde, Silvana Mangano, Björn Andresen, Romolo Valli, Mark Burns, Nora Ricci, Marisa Berenson, Carole André, Leslie French, Franco Fabrizi, Luigi Battaglia

Venice, circa 1910, is the locale for this adaptation of the Thomas Mann novella, with a scenario by Luchino Visconti and Nicola Badalucco, who also collaborated on *The Damned.* The protagonist of *Death in Venice* is also one of the damned. Gustav von Aschenbach (Dirk Bogarde), a middle-aged German composer, is on holiday at a luxury hotel on the Lido when he falls under the spell of a beautiful young Polish boy, Tadzio (Björn Andresen). Unable to wrest himself from the boy's beauty, Aschenbach lingers in the city—even though he knows a cholera plague is imminent. To many, Visconti's slow pacing is a negative factor throughout; people believe the film is given visual distinction in the camera work of Pasquale de Santis. The soundtrack features the music of Gustav Mahler, whose death inspired Mann to write his novella. Winner of the Grand Prix at the 1971 Cannes Film Festival.

Diabolique   1955   (Hollywood Home Theatre)   *Black-and-White*
Director: Henri-Georges Clouzot
Starring: Simone Signoret, Véra Clouzot, Paul Meurisse, Charles Vanel, Jean Brochard, Thérèse Dorny, Michel Serrault, Jacques Varennes, Georges Chamarat, Henri Crémieux, Yves-Marc Maurin, Georges Poujouly, Noël Roquevort, Pierre Larquey

The Wages of Fear, Henri-Georges Clouzot's suspense classic, already a hit on the continent, opened to American acclaim (and financial rewards) early in 1955. A few months later, U.S. audiences were offered another Clouzot masterpiece of terror—*Diabolique.* Back-to-back, the director was responsible for two of the biggest foreign film successes in U.S. history. An exercise in Grand Guignol, *Diabolique* is an elaborate murder mystery set in a boys' school in the French provinces—under the directorship of an odious headmaster. Not even his wife and mistress, both on staff, can tolerate him. In fact, together they conspire to murder him and, during a holiday, set their plans in motion. Clouzot and his coscenarists Jérôme Géronimi, René Masson, and Frédéric Grendel adapted the famed Pierre Boileau-Thomas Narcejac novel, *Celle Qui N'Etait Plus.* The headmaster's wife is played by Clouzot's wife, Véra; Simone Signoret portrays her collaborator in crime; Paul Meurisse is their homicidal target; and Charles Vanel plays a tenacious detective. For first-time viewers, *Diabolique's* impact may be marginally diminished because it's one of the most imitated shockers of all time. One direct imitation is the TV-movie version, *Reflections of Murder,* directed by John Badham—and starring Tuesday Weld and Joan Hackett as the diabolical ladies.

The Discreet Charm of the Bourgeoisie   1972   (Media)   ◆   *Color*
Director: Luis Buñuel
Starring: Fernando Rey, Delphine Seyrig, Stéphane Audran, Jean-Pierre Cassel, Bulle Ogier, Paul Frankeur, Julien Berthau, Michel Piccoli, Claude Piéplu, Milena Vukotic

An Academy Award winner as best foreign feature, this 1972 Luis Buñuel masterpiece is yet another of the filmmaker's witty attacks on bourgeois institutions. The basic premise, concocted by the director and Jean-Claude Carrière, his frequent coscripter, is that an assortment of upper-crust friends are constantly trying to assemble for a meal. Several dinners are scheduled and each is interrupted—by everything from the army to terrorist threats. On one occasion the diners flee a restaurant when a corpse is found on the premises; on another they discover they aren't at a private dinner party, but onstage as a theater curtain lifts. As part of the surrealism, Buñuel proffers dreams within dreams. What is real and what is not? Only Buñuel knows. But the guessing can be fun.

Diva   France 1981; U.S. 1982   (MGM)   *Color*
Director: Jean-Jacques Beineix
Starring: Frédéric Andrei, Wilhelmenia Wiggins Fernandez, Richard Bohringer, Thuy An Luu, Jacques Fabbri, Chantal Deruaz, Anny Romand, Roland Bertin, Gérard Darmon, Dominique Pinon, Jean-Jacques Moreau

Jules (Frédéric Andrei) is an eighteen-year-old postal carrier working in Paris. He is also an opera buff with a particular passion for diva Cynthia Hawkins (American soprano Wilhelmenia Wiggins Fernandez), who has steadfastly refused throughout her career to make a recording. The film begins as Jules makes a bootleg audio tape of his idol's concert. By accident, he comes to possess another cassette: a murdered prostitute's confessions about a drug-and-prostitution ring. The teenage hero, with his two hot tapes, thus becomes the quarry of recording company agents who wish to market the pirated cassette *and* of ruthless killers who wish to retrieve the prostitute's incriminating evidence. This thriller, the feature debut of Jean-Jacques Beineix, becomes a merry manhunt all over Paris—shot by Philippe Rousselot. (The flashy interiors were created by production designer Hilton McConnico.) Contributing to the *outré* effects are a punk rock killer, a pretty Vietnamese shoplifter, an eccentric magnate into meditation, and a moped chase in the Paris métro. This fast-propelled game of wits derives from a novel, also called *Diva,* by Delacorta; Beineix wrote the screenplay with Jean Van Hamme. The original music is by Vladimir Cosma.

8½   1963   (Vestron)   ◆   *Black-and-White*
Director: Federico Fellini
Starring: Marcello Mastroianni, Claudia Cardinale, Anouk Aimée, Sandra Milo, Rosella Falk, Barbara Steele, Madeleine Lebeau, Jean Rougeul, Guido Alberti, Eugene Walter

"In my picture, everything happens," declares Guido Anselmi, filmmaker extraordinaire. But Guido has a creative block. So the movie is put on hold; the director, in the throes of a nervous breakdown, rests—and, in effect, psychoanalyzes himself. Episodes (dreams, recollections, pure fantasy) whir through his mind: his wife's maliciousness; school days in a religious college; a harem with an array of subservient wives; the beachside dance of a fat prostitute who tries to lure young boys. After days, perhaps weeks, of creative frustration, Guido finally realizes that his artistic future lies in creating more movies. Federico Fellini's *8½* is a mad compound of naturalism, surrealism, farce, and philosophy held together by Marcello Mastroianni, the focal point as Guido Anselmi. Fellini's own film output explains the title. Before 1963 he had shot three short and six full-length features. *8½,* then, is his 8½th movie. Academy Awards: best foreign language film and best costume design (Piero Gherardi). English-dubbed.

The Elusive Corporal   France 1962; U.S. 1963   *Black-and-White*
     (Video Yesteryear)
Director: Jean Renoir
Starring: Jean-Pierre Cassel, Claude Brasseur, Claude Rich, O. E. Hasse, Jean Carmet, Jacques Jouanneau, Conny Froboess, Guy Bedos

Master filmmaker Jean Renoir, whose 1936 classic, *Grand Illusion,* was the ultimate antiwar statement, looks again at the plight of Frenchmen held captive by the Germans—this time in World War II. And again his comic vision is tinged with both sarcasm and tenderness. The subjects are prisoners in a detention camp after the German blitzkreig conquest of France in 1940. Some of the POW's are indifferent to captivity; but one feisty little corporal (Jean-Pierre Cassel) tries repeatedly to escape. He is both penned-up and *pinned*-up (the original French title, *Le Caporal Epinglé,* is given amplification in the movie)—and he finally succeeds in breaking away. Renoir's coscenarist is Guy Lefranc. The score is by Hungarian composer Joseph Kosma, who provided the music for other works by the pioneer director—including *Grand Illusion.*

Fanny and Alexander   Sweden 1982; U.S. 1983   (Embassy)   ◆   *Color*
Director: Ingmar Bergman
Starring: Pernilla Allwin, Bertil Guve, Ewa Fröling, Erland Josephson, Jan Malmsjö, Gunn Wallgren, Borje Ahlstedt, Jarl Kulle, Allan Edwall, Mona Malm, Gunnar Björnstrand, Harriet Andersson

Fanny Ekdahl and her brother Alexander are children of a wealthy family who have made their fortune in commerce. The Ekdahls live in splendor in Uppsala. Ingmar Bergman's story about Fanny, Alexander, and their family unfolds as a series of interlinked episodes, beginning on Christmas Day 1907. A panoply of aunts, uncles, grandparents, cousins, and family friends parade through the household in holiday revelry. The film chronicles that momentous celebration, as well as the tragedy and comedy of the following year—expressed mostly through the point of view of ten-year-old Alexander. An amalgam of optimism and pessimism, reality and imagination, farce and high drama, *Fanny and Alexander* was hailed at the 1983 Academy Awards ceremony as best foreign film, and it also brought Oscars to Sven Nykvist (cinematography), Marik Vos (costume design), and Anna Asp and Susanne Lingheim (art direction/set decoration).

The Firemen's Ball   Czechoslovakia 1967; U.S. 1968   (RCA)   *Color*
Director: Miloš Forman
Starring: Jan Vostrcil, Josef Sebanek, Josef Valnoha, Josef Kolb, Vaclev Stockel, Josef Svet, Frantisek Debelka

A small Czechoslovakian community's annual firemen's ball is the setting for this character study. This year there's a threefold purpose to the event: to hold a raffle, to crown a beauty queen, and to present an honorary hatchet to the eighty-six-year-old retiring fire chief (Josef Svet). Everything goes awry: bit by bit, the raffle prizes are stolen; the girls of the town are reluctant participants in the beauty contest; and—before the aged (and fatally ill) chief can be eulogized—a fire breaks out nearby and an old man's home burns to the ground. After watching the latter spectacle, the citizens return to complete their revelries at the party. *The Firemen's Ball* is a dark comedy with close-to-life commentary on vanity, pettiness, and bureaucratic foul-ups. The screenplay is by Miloš Forman (who also directed), Ivan Passer, and Jaroslav Papoušek. The cinematography is by Miroslav Ondricek.

Forbidden Games   1952   (Vid Dim)   ◆   *Black-and-White*
Director: René Clément
Starring: Brigitte Fossey, Georges Poujouly, Amédée, Laurence Badie, Jacques Marin, Suzanne Courtal, Lucien Hubert

1940 France. During the Nazi Occupation, Paulette, a five-year-old orphan, is adopted by a peasant family and befriended by their eleven-year-old son, Michel. The two youngsters become playmates, while imitating the cruel adult life around them. When Michel's older brother is killed by a stampeding horse, the little ones begin to believe that dead people are buried to keep one another company—and to protect them from the rain. They start to collect dead animals (Paulette's pet dog, a mole, a beetle, a hen, a lizard) for their private cemetery. As an adjunct to their "forbidden games," they rifle the local cemetery for crosses to plant on the graves of their beloved creatures. When the villagers learn what the children have been doing, an outcry is raised. René Clément's screenplay, with Jean Aurenche and Pierre Bost, is a poignant end-of-childhood drama, noteworthy for its starkness and lack of sentimentality. Under Clément's direction, Brigitte Fossey and Georges Poujouly are the juvenile leads. Among the honors bestowed upon *Forbidden Games* were the top prize at the Venice Film Festival and the Academy Award as best foreign language film.

The 400 Blows   1959   (Key)   ✱   *Black-and-White*
Director: François Truffaut
Starring: Jean-Pierre Léaud, Claire Maurier, Albert Rémy, Guy Decomble, Georges Flamant, Patrick Auffay, Jeanne Moreau, Jean-Claude Brialy

This landmark film from the French New Wave is François Truffaut's first full-length feature, shot for less than $100,000. Further, it is the debut episode in the Antoine Doinel series. There are autobiographical overtones in Truffaut's account of a young Parisian boy who becomes an outcast at home and at school. Twelve-year-old Antoine is a lovable, if rascally, kid caught up with the anarchic impulses of adolescence. Essentially, the boy is a furtive loner who charms nearly everybody—but not his parents or schoolmaster. As punishment for his minor infractions, he is sent to a detention center near the seashore. To many viewers the final freeze-frame of Antoine on the beach after his mad dash for freedom is heartrending. Truffaut's cinematographer is Henri Decaë, his coscenarist Marcel Moussy. The nature of Truffaut's art, delicate and intricate, is apparent even at this early station in his career. He received the best director award at the 1959 Cannes Film Festival. Jean-Pierre Léaud portrays Antoine here and in all the subsequent Doinel stories: the "Antoine and Colette" sketch in *Love at Twenty* (1962), *Stolen Kisses* (1968), *Bed and Board* (1970), and *Love on the Run* (1979).

The **G**arden of the Finzi-Continis   1971   (RCA)   ◆   *Color*
Director: Vittorio De Sica
Starring: Dominique Sanda, Lino Capolicchio, Helmut Berger, Fabio Testi, Romolo Valli, Katina Morisani, Camillo Angelini-Rota, Katina Viglietti

The Garden of the Finzi-Continis is set in Ferrara, Italy, in 1938, when Mussolini's anti-Semitic edicts began to isolate the Jews from their communities. Among those snared in the Fascist web are the Finzi-Continis, an aristocratic family whose members live in a walled estate that, until their deportation, is a haven from the horrors outside. The film, photographed by Ennio Guarnieri, comes from an autobiographical novel by Giorgio Bassani; the adapters are Tullio Pinelli, Valerio Zurlini, Franco Brusati, Ugo Pirro, Vittorio Bonicelli, and Alain Katz. The primary behind-camera artist, however, is Vittorio De Sica. *The Garden of the Finzi-Continis* recalls the director's finest work— *The Bicycle Thief, Miracle in Milan, Two Women*. A haunting story, *The Garden of the Finzi-Continis* stars Dominique Sanda as Micòl, the eldest daughter; Helmut Berger, her sickly brother Alberto; Fabio Testi, Micòl's lover, Malnate; Lino Capolicchio, her would-be lover, Giorgio; and Romolo Valli, Giorgio's oppressed father. The score is by Manuel De Sica, Vittorio's son. Academy Award for best foreign language film.

General Della Rovere   Italy 1959; U.S. 1961   *Black-and-White*
(Budget Video)
Director: Roberto Rossellini
Starring: Vittorio De Sica, Hannes Messemer, Sandra Milo, Giovanna Ralli, Mary Greco, Linda Veras, Anne Vernon

This character examination represented a comeback for Roberto Rossellini, after five years away from the cinema; it was also a return to popularity, following low box-office receipts for *Voyage in Italy* and *Fear*, which starred Ingrid Bergman. *General Della Rovere* is a reflection of the neorealist classics that cemented the director's reputation in the forties. Set in World War II, Rossellini's scenario, cowritten with Sergio Amidei, Diego Fabbri, and Indro Montanelli, tells of a compulsive con artist who becomes an unlikely hero when he is forced—by the Germans—to impersonate a dead resistance leader, General Della Rovere. (The real general has been shot.) The trickster, played by Vittorio De Sica, becomes so captivated with his own role-playing that he adopts the dead man's integrity and code of honor. Also starring are Sandra Milo as Valeria, the con man's mistress, and Hannes Messemer as Colonel Müller.

Gervaise   France 1956; U.S. 1957   ✷   *Black-and-White*
     (Discount Video Tapes; Festival Films; Western Film & Video Inc.; Classic Video
     Cinema Collector's Club)
Director: René Clément
Starring: Maria Schell, François Périer, Suzy Delair, Armand Mestral, Jacques Harden,
Mathilde Casadesus, Ariane Lancell, Jacques Hilling, Jany Holt

Émile Zola's classic novel of naturalism, *L'Assommoir*, is the inspiration for this René Clément drama. The story, as adapted by screenwriters Jean Aurenche and Pierre Bost, recounts the misfortunes of a nineteenth-century Paris laundrymaid. The young woman (Maria Schell) struggles to support her family when her husband succumbs to alcoholism. Clément imparts a frightening anti-alcohol message while vividly evoking the lower depths of 1880s Paris; his director of photography is René Juillard, his art director Paul Bertrand. Austrian actress Schell, the sister of Maximilian, plays Zola's tragic heroine. The New York Film Critics Circle singled out *Gervaise* as best picture for 1957.

Get Out Your Handkerchiefs   1978   (Warner)   ◆ ○   *Color*
Director: Bertrand Blier
Starring: Gérard Depardieu, Patrick Dewaere, Carole Laure, Riton, Michel Serrault,
Eleonore Hurt, Sylvie Joly, Jean Rougerie

A reunion for the director, Bertrand Blier, and stars, Gérard Depardieu and Patrick Dewaere, of *Going Places*. *Get Out Your Handkerchiefs*, like the earlier work, is a comedy analyzing contemporary sexual attitudes. Herein, Raoul (Depardieu) tries everything imaginable to cheer up Solange, his bored, inscrutable, and sexually frustrated wife (Carole Laure). Then he decides to try the *un*imaginable—by finding her a potential lover. Stéphane (Dewaere) fits the bill for a while; but then Solange tires of him, too. Ultimately, she is capable of being aroused only by Christian (Riton), a thirteen-year-old schoolboy with a genius IQ. Blier's screenplay is affixed with elements of misogyny, misanthropy, amorality, and theater of the absurd. Michel Serrault plays a neighbor who first resents, then rejoices in, the bizarre ménage. *Get Out Your Handkerchiefs* was named best picture of the year by the National Society of Film Critics, then won an Oscar in the foreign language category. The video now available is of the dubbed print.

Going Places   France 1973; U.S. 1974   (RCA)   *Color*
Director: Bertrand Blier
Starring: Gérard Depardieu, Patrick Dewaere, Miou-Miou, Jeanne Moreau, Brigitte Fossey, Isabelle Huppert

Evil for evil's sake is an important ingredient of *Going Places*, directed by Bertrand Blier from his novel, *Les Valseuses*. Blier and his coscenarist Philippe Dumarçay tell of two loutish vagabonds—Jean-Claude (Gérard Depardieu) and Pierrot (Patrick Dewaere). They wander about France committing petty robberies, stealing cars for joy riding, and sharing (and abusing) women. Among their (partially willing) victims in the latter category: a kooky beautician (Miou-Miou) and a woman just released from prison (Jeanne Moreau). The antiestablishment theme of *Going Places* ensures that Jean-Claude and Pierrot are never placed in an altogether bad light. Blier records their escapades with whimsy, rather than moralistic judgment. The cinematography is by Bruno Nuytten. The violin score is composed and played by Stéphane Grappelli. Dubbed.

Happy New Year   1973   (Embassy)   *Color*
Director: *Claude Lelouch*
Starring: *Lino Ventura, Françoise Fabian, Charles Gérard, André Falcon*

Claude Lelouch's caper comedy revolves around the commission of a jewel heist. The target is the Cannes branch of Van Cleef & Arpels. Good guy thief Simon (Lino Ventura) devises the scheme. What he doesn't foresee is that he will fall in love with the beautiful lady (Françoise Fabian) who owns the antique shop next door. Further complicating matters is Simon's oafish accomplice (Charles Gérard, a cast regular in Lelouch films). Lelouch wrote the dialogue, and Jean Collomb is the cinematographer. The director incorporates footage from his earlier *A Man and a Woman*. Shot on location on the Côte d'Azur.

Hiroshima, Mon Amour   France 1959; U.S. 1960   ✳   *Black-and-White*
     (Budget Video; Vid Dim; Sheik Video; Hollywood Home Theatre; Discount
     Video Tapes; Western Film & Video Inc.; Video Award Motion Pictures, Inc.)
Director: *Alain Resnais*
Starring: *Emmanuelle Riva, Eiji Okada, Stella Dassas, Pierre Barbaud, Bernard Fresson*

In this New Wave classic, set in 1957 Hiroshima, a French actress appearing in a film about peace has a brief love affair with a Japanese architect. Their liaison is punctuated by both flashbacks and flash-forwards—as the actress recalls a tragic love of her youth in occupied Nevers; because of her romance with a German soldier, she was ostracized by the townspeople. The dialogue of Marguerite Duras is united to director Alain Resnais's experiments with narrative ellipsis. Newsreel footage of the A-bomb aftermath is interspersed with the present (1957) and war-based stories. *Hiroshima, Mon Amour,* conceived in continuous quick cuts—reflecting the thoughts flitting through the heroine's mind—revolutionized the medium. An art house success, the picture received numerous awards, including the New York Film Critics' designation as best foreign film.

Jules and Jim   1962   (Vid Dim; Sheik Video; Key)   *Black-and-White*
Director: *François Truffaut*
Starring: *Jeanne Moreau, Oskar Werner, Henri Serre, Vanna Urbino, Cyrus Bassiak, Sabine Haudepin, Marie Dubois, Jean-Louis Richard, Michel Varesano, Pierre Fabre, Danielle Bassiak, Bernard Largemains*

François Truffaut's third feature is this bittersweet comedy-drama, based on an autobiographical novel by Henri-Pierre Roché. Set (initially) in Paris before World War I, *Jules and Jim* traces the evolving friendship of the title characters—young dilettantes whose never-ending celebration of life, love, art, and literature leads to a meeting with Catherine (Jeanne Moreau), a mercurial, self-indulgent, but captivating Bohemian. For Jules the Austrian (Oskar Werner) and Jim the Frenchman (Henri Serre), Catherine becomes a focal point of joy—and her affections constantly shift between the two of them. The ménage à trois continues for twenty years. This lyrical (and, according to the Legion of Decency, immoral) work secured Truffaut's reputation in America. First-time viewers should be cautioned to keep alert from the first frame: *Jules and Jim* sets a speed record for packed exposition; Raoul Coutard's camera and Claudine Bouche's editing create a whirl of activity—while the voice-over narration by Michel Subor seems to be spoken double-time. Roché's only other novel, *Les Deux Anglaises et le Continent,* Truffaut also brought to the screen.

Kagemusha   1980   (CBS)   ❊   *Color*
Director: Akira Kurosawa
Starring: Tatsuya Nakadai, Tsutomu Yamazaki, Kenichi Hagiwara, Jinpachi Nezu,
Shuji Otaki

Akira Kurosawa's twenty-seventh feature takes place in sixteenth-century Japan. The story concerns feudal warfare, court machinations, and lines of succession. As a once-vigorous warlord lies dying from battle wounds, he orders his clan to keep his demise secret. In the interests of self-preservation, the subordinates force a thief (initially scheduled for execution) to impersonate the departed ruler—both at home and on the battlefield. (Among *Kagemusha*'s alternate titles in some countries are *The Double* and *Shadow Warrior.*) The film, with a screenplay by Kurosawa and Masato Ide, is one of the director's most imaginative works. A grand prize winner at Cannes, it is the most expensive production in the history of Japanese cinema. George Lucas and Francis Ford Coppola served as executive producers for the international release.

Knife in the Water   Poland 1960; U.S. 1963   *Black-and-White*
   (CBS; Video Yesteryear; Budget Video; Western Film & Video Inc.; Vid Dim;
   Sheik Video)
Director: Roman Polanski
Starring: Leon Niemczyk, Jolanta Umecka, Zygmunt Malanowicz

This, Roman Polanski's first feature-length film, is an unsettling three-character drama. On their way to a Sunday sailing outing, a married couple pick up a young hitchhiker and invite him to spend the day on their sailboat. The young man, close in age to the wife, accepts. On the boat various underlying tensions emerge: the hitchhiker's attraction to the wife; the husband's admiration for the virile youth; the wife's long-repressed boredom; and the two men's jockeying for domination—and favor in the woman's eyes. The screenplay by Polanski and his coscenarists, Jerzy Skolimowski and Jakob Goldberg, remains clinical, detached. Even with its few brief flurries of violence, *Knife in the Water* is far from the realm of melodrama. The movie has controlled performances by Leon Niemczyk (the husband), Jolanta Umecka (the wife), and Zygmunt Malanowicz (the hitchhiker) and excellent use of locale—the Polish lake country.

Kwaidan   1964   (Video Yesteryear)   *Color*
Director: Masaki Kobayashi
Starring: Rentaro Mikuni, Ganjiro Nakamura, Katsuo Nakamura, Michiko Aratama,
Keiko Kishi, Tatsuya Nakadai, Takashi Shimura

For the last fourteen years of his life, American expatriate Lafcadio Hearn (1850–1904) lived in Japan, where he eventually became a citizen. During that period, he wrote a dozen books, among them the exotic, macabre tales that form the basis of this portmanteau film. The four elegant stories represented—and moodily shot by Yoshio

Miyajima—contain colorful (and occasionally scary) depictions of ghosts, samurai, and mysterious monks. *Kwaidan* is that rare non-Kurosawa production from Japan to gain acceptance in this country. Its director, Masaki Kobayashi, is a prodigious filmmaker—though known in America only for this feature and for *Harikiri* (1962).

La Cage aux Folles France 1978; U.S. 1979 (CBS) *Color*
Director: Edouard Molinaro
Starring: Ugo Tognazzi, Michel Serrault, Michel Galabru, Claire Maurier, Remy Laurent, Benny Luke, Carmen Scarpitta, Luisa Maneri

La Cage aux Folles originated as a small-scale Paris stage farce, written by Jean Poiret. The story concerns two male lovers, Renato (played originally by Poiret, in the movie by Ugo Tognazzi) and Albin (Michel Serrault), who own a St. Tropez nightclub—La Cage aux Folles, a showcase for female impersonators. Albin, under his *nom de théâtre,* Zaza, is the star attraction. Poiret's plot—screenwritten by him, Francis Veber, Marcello Danon, and director Edouard Molinaro—evolves as a comedy of deception: Renato's son from a heterosexual liaison brings home his fiancée and her very conservative parents; the future father-in-law is, in fact, the secretary for the Union of Moral Order—so Renato and Albin must pretend to be equally conservative. Amassing over $40 million, *La Cage aux Folles* is almost certainly the most financially successful foreign film released in the United States. Two sequels, in 1980 and 1985, and a successful Broadway musical resulted. The video version is dubbed into English.

La Cage aux Folles II France 1980; U.S. 1981 (CBS) *Color*
Director: Edouard Molinaro
Starring: Ugo Tognazzi, Michel Serrault, Marcel Bozzuffi, Paola Borboni, Giovanna Bettorazzo, Glauco Onorato, Roberto Bisacco, Benny Luke, Michel Galabru

The antics continue in this sequel. For Part II, Renato (Ugo Tognazzi) and Albin (Michel Serrault) become involved in a caper comedy. Members of a spy ring invade St. Tropez and the two *La Cage aux Folles* heroes help the police capture the criminals. In this second script by Francis Veber, Jean Poiret, and Marcello Danon, emphasis is placed on Renato and Albin's involvement in the spy-police chase. (The videocassette represents the English-dubbed version.) Followed by *La Cage aux Folles 3: The Wedding* (1985), released in America in 1986.

La Dolce Vita Italy 1960; U.S. 1961 (Republic) ✻ *Black-and-White*
Director: Federico Fellini
Starring: Marcello Mastroianni, Anita Ekberg, Anouk Aimée, Alain Cuny, Yvonne Furneaux, Magali Noël, Nadia Gray, Lex Barker, Adriana Moneta, Carlo Di Maggio, Annibale Ninchi

Rome as a contemporary Sodom and Gomorrah is the setting for Federico Fellini's apocalyptic essay on *La Dolce Vita.* A principal participant in this sweet life is Marcello, a worldly-wise gossip columnist (played by Marcello Mastroianni). Fellini and his co-scenarists—Tullio Pinelli, Ennio Flaiano, Brunello Rondi—present Marcello in his forays around Rome and in association with the city's bewitching and sometimes decadent upper crust. Sharing a day (and night) in the journalist's life, viewers observe several episodes with him: the pursuit of a blonde bombshell (Anita Ekberg), inundated with paparazzi wherever she goes; a staged "miracle" in which two youngsters claim they have seen a vision of the Madonna; the failed suicide of Marcello's mistress; the visit of Marcello's father; several lovemaking adventures; and an orgy at a centuries-old castle—attended by the full panoply of indulgers in the soft life. A cynical portrait of a hedonistic society, *La Dolce Vita* won the Palme d'Or at the 1960 Cannes festival and went on to international acclaim.

La Ronde   1950   (Vid Dim)   *Black-and-White*
Director: Max Ophüls
Starring: Anton Walbrook, Simone Signoret, Serge Reggiani, Simone Simon, Daniel Gélin, Danièlle Darrieux, Fernand Gravey, Odette Joyeux, Jean-Louis Barrault, Isa Miranda, Gérard Philippe

Love is a merry-go-round in this adaptation of Arthur Schnitzler's playscript, *Reigen*. The often-filmed story achieves classic status here, with German filmmaker Max Ophüls (*Letter from an Unknown Woman, Caught, Madame de . . . ,* and *Lola Montès*) holding the directorial reins. *La Ronde* unfolds in fin de siècle Vienna, where a colorful array of personages engage in circular liaisons. A prostitute (Simone Signoret) meets a soldier (Serge Reggiani). The soldier has an affair with a chambermaid (Simone Simon). The chambermaid loves a student (Daniel Gélin). The student has an assignation with an older woman (Danièlle Darrieux). The woman goes home to her husband (Fernand Gravey). And so on. This stylized comedy-drama, screenwritten by Ophüls and Jacques Natanson, is held together by Anton Walbrook as the raconteur. The musical theme is by Oscar Straus.

La Strada   Italy 1954; U.S. 1956   (Embassy; Vid Dim)◆   *Black-and-White*
Director: Federico Fellini
Starring: Anthony Quinn, Giulietta Masina, Richard Basehart, Aldo Silvani, Marcella Rovere, Livia Venturini

This is one of Federico Fellini's most beloved works. Gelsomina (Giulietta Masina), a halfwit, is sold by her poor peasant mother to street performer Zampanò (Anthony Quinn); she will act as his aide-companion. But Zampanò is a brute; he mistreats Gelsomina as they wander along the road (*la strada*) from performance to performance—at last joining up with a circus where the gentlehearted Il Matto/The Fool (Richard Basehart) is a headliner as a high-wire artist. For a while, Il Matto is able to alleviate the misery of Gelsomina's life. *La Strada* represents another collaboration between the director and scenarists Ennio Flaiano and Tullio Pinelli. Quinn's magnetism is apparent in his role as the near-monosyllabic sideshow strongman and Masina is heartbreaking as the clown-faced waif. Winner of the 1956 Oscar for best foreign film—the first recipient in a category which had previously been honorary.

The Last Metro   France 1980; U.S. 1981   ▲   *Color*
Director: François Truffaut
Starring: Catherine Deneuve, Gérard Depardieu, Jean Poiret, Heinz Bennent, Andréa Ferréol, Paulette Dubost, Sabine Haudepin, Jean-Louis Richard, Maurice Risch, Richard Bohringer, Jean-Pierre Klein, Laszlo Szabo

This François Truffaut classic, cowritten with his collaborator, Suzanne Schiffman, revolves around a Paris theater during the Nazi Occupation. The troupe's renowned director-manager, a Jew, is believed to have fled; in fact, he has been secreted by his wife in the basement of the theater—where, through her, he continues his directorial activities. *The Last Metro* presents anecdotes of both comedy and suspense. It was nominated for twelve Césars (the French Oscar) and was the recipient of ten: best picture; actor (Gérard Depardieu as the company's leading man and a hero of the Resistance); actress (Catherine Deneuve as the wife of the absentee manager); supporting actor (Heinz Bennent as the director in hiding); supporting actress (Andréa Ferréol as the troupe's costume designer); screenplay; cinematography (Nestor Almendros); musical score (Georges Delerue); editing (Martine Barraque-Curie); art direction (Jean-Pierre Kohut-Svelko); and sound (Michel Laurent).

The Little Theatre of Jean Renoir   France 1969; U.S. 1974   *Color*
    (Texture Films)
Director: Jean Renoir
Starring: Jeanne Moreau, Nino Formicola, Roger Trapp, Roland Martin, Marguerite Cassan, Pierre Olaf, Jacques Dignan, Françoise Arnoul, Fernand Sardou, Jean Carmet

This compilation feature consists of three short films directed by Jean Renoir for French television. United under the umbrella title *Le Petit Théâtre de Jean Renoir,* the picture then had playdates in cinemas at home and abroad. The episodes are "The Last Christmas Dinner," inspired by Hans Christian Andersen's tale; "The Electric Floor Waxer," a comic opera about a bourgeois housewife's passion for her new appliance; and "Le Roi d'Yvêtot," centering around a love triangle, a cuckolded husband, and a game of *pétanque* as a test of honor. Providing continuity, Renoir appears as host and narrator— and there is a beguiling musical interlude spotlighting Jeanne Moreau as she sings "Quand l'Amour Se Meurt" by Oscar Crémieux. *The Little Theatre* represents the French master's farewell; he died in 1974.

Love And Anarchy   Italy 1973; U.S. 1974   (RCA)   *Color*
Director: Lina Wertmüller
Starring: Giancarlo Giannini, Mariangela Melato, Lina Polito, Eros Pagni, Pina Cel, Elena Fiore

This film, coupled with *The Seduction of Mimi,* helped to cement director Lina Wertmüller's reputation in America. Her screenplay, set in 1932 Italy, traces the misadventures of a bumbling country boy who goes to Rome convinced that he must assassinate Mussolini. His tribulations in the capital revolve around a bordello, where he meets and is enchanted by a prostitute who makes him rethink his assassination scheme. Wertmüller's directorial vision manifests itself in Baroque decors, unexpected comedy, her characters' raging passions, and an observance of society's moral decay. *Love and Anarchy* is not for every taste—but it is enhanced by the filmmaker's story-telling power and the performances of Giancarlo Giannini (a young Marcello Mastroianni) and Mariangela Melato as the hero and his inamorata.

Loves of a Blonde   Czechoslovakia 1965; U.S. 1966   *Black-and-White*
    (RCA)
Director: Miloš Forman
Starring: Hana Brejchova, Vladimir Pucholt, Vladimir Mensik, Josef Sebanek, Jan Vostrcil

This early comedy by Czech director Miloš Forman assembles the coscenarists he used on *Black Peter* and would again for *The Firemen's Ball:* Ivan Passer and Jaroslav Papoušek. Another low-key meditation on odd characters and their environment, the film tells of a teenage factory girl in a provincial, male-poor village. When a young musician visits, the heroine uses all her wiles to woo him. Her coworkers must take second best: a squadron of middle-aged army reservists who show up for a local dance. The movie is a mixture of anecdotes, situation comedy, and character exploration. Hana Brejchova plays the love-starved blonde.

Madame Rosa   France 1977; U.S. 1978   (Vestron)   ◆   *Color*
Director: Moshe Mizrahi
Starring: Simone Signoret, Samy Ben Youb, Claude Dauphin, Gabriel Jabbour, Michal Bat Adam, Bernard La Jarrige, Geneviève Fontanel, Costa-Gavras

Madame Rosa, an Auschwitz survivor, is an aging ex-prostitute whose Paris apartment is an unofficial nursery school for the offspring of day-shift streetwalkers. Her latest charge is a fourteen-year-old Arab boy. The boy's affection for Madame Rosa as she grows increasingly infirm forms the basis for writer-director Moshe Mizrahi's film— inspired by the award-winning Romain Gary novel (originally published under the pseudonym Émile Ajar). As the title character, Simone Signoret had her last major screen role. Costa-Gavras, of *Z* fame, who directed Signoret in *The Sleeping Car Murder* and *The Confession*, appears as Ramon. Academy Award for best foreign language film. The videocassette version is English-dubbed.

The Magician   1958   (Embassy)   *Black-and-White*
Director: Ingmar Bergman
Starring: Max von Sydow, Ingrid Thulin, Gunnar Björnstrand, Naima Wifstrand, Bibi Andersson, Ake Fridell, Lars Ekborg, Bengt Ekerot

Max von Sydow plays Dr. Vogler, a nineteenth-century mesmerist, in this dark tale of the supernatural written and directed by Ingmar Bergman. Vogler and his itinerant troupe arrive in a small Swedish town. The local police chief invites the travelers to give a performance at the home of a rich citizen. In the course of the evening, Vogler is exposed as a charlatan—and he plots a horrifying revenge. With Bergman as the guiding force, *The Magician* supplies parables of Christianity and art versus science. A difficult-to-decipher compendium of themes, but an absorbing film experience.

The Man Who Loved Women   1977   (RCA)   *Color*
Director: François Truffaut
Starring: Charles Denner, Brigitte Fossey, Nelly Borgeaud, Geneviève Fontanel, Nathalie Baye, Sabine Gläser, Valérie Bonnier, Nella Barbier, Jean Dasté, Roger Leenhardt, Leslie Caron

This comedy begins with the observation that "Women's legs, like the stems of a compass, circle around the globe, giving it balance and grace." The remark comes from Bertrand Morane (Charles Denner), an incurable romantic; neither a Casanova nor a macho monster, he is truly fond of all women. As perceived by François Truffaut (in his screenplay with Michel Fermaud and Suzanne Schiffman), Bertrand pursues women not only in his native Montpellier but all over France. Ultimately, he records his amorous feelings in an autobiography entitled *The Man Who Loved Women* and it becomes a best-seller. Brigitte Fossey, of *Forbidden Games* and *Blue Country*, plays Bertrand's editor and, in a rare screen appearance, Leslie Caron represents the hero's long-ago (and perhaps one true) love.

Masculine-Feminine   1966   (Discount Video Tapes)   *Black-and-White*
Director: Jean-Luc Godard
Starring: Jean-Pierre Léaud, Chantal Goya, Catherine-Isabelle Duport, Marlène Jobert, Michel Debord, Birger Malmsten, Eva Britt Strandberg, Elsa Leroy, Françoise Hardy, Brigitte Bardot, Antoine Bourseiller

Jean-Luc Godard referred to the protagonists of this film-essay as "the children of Marx and Coca-Cola." They are the students, revolutionaries, and left-wing intelligentsia on the brink of the May 1968 riots in Paris. But *Masculine-Feminine* is not heavy drama. Loosely based on two Guy De Maupassant short stories—"The Signal" and "Paul's Mistress"—the scenario, concocted and directed by Godard, tells of young journalist-interviewer Paul (Jean-Pierre Léaud), who is entranced by Madeleine (Chantal Goya), a pop singer. Unfortunately, Madeleine merely likes, but does not love, Paul. The main story, fashioned with Godardian constraint and detachment, pauses for monologues, essay excerpts, love lyrics, visual puns, and parody-interviews. An original concept in mixing genres, this discursive comedy-drama was Godard's eleventh motion picture (in seven years) and one of three released in 1966.

Mephisto   1981   (Thorn; The Video Station)   ◆   *Color*
Director: István Szabó
Starring: Klaus Maria Brandauer, Ildiko Bansagi, Krystyna Janda, Rolf Hoppe, Karin Boyd, Christine Harbot, Gyorgy Cserhalimi, Peter Andorai

A meditation on morality and the seamier aspects of life in the theater, *Mephisto* won the Academy Award as the best foreign language picture of 1981. Cowritten by Peter Donai and István Szabó, with the latter doubling as director, this Hungarian film presents Klaus Maria Brandauer (more widely recognized for his role in *Out of Africa*) as a provincial German actor who aspires to fame just as the Nazis are rising to power. His ambition leads him to sell his soul to Hitler in exchange for the directorship of the German State Theatre. Based on Klaus Mann's 1936 novel, which was inspired by the career of German actor Gustaf Gründgens.

Mon Oncle   1958   (Embassy; Budget Video;   ◆   *Color*
     Discount Video Tapes; Video Yesteryear)
Director: Jacques Tati
Starring: Jacques Tati, Jean-Pierre Zola, Adrienne Servantie, Lucien Frégis, Alain Bé-court, Betty Schneider, André Dino, Nicolas Bataille, Yvonne Arnaud

The return of Monsieur Hulot is also the occasion for Monsieur Tati's first film in color. With a screenplay by Jean L'Hôte, Jacques Lagrange, and director-star Tati, *Mon Oncle* is a sequel to *Monsieur Hulot's Holiday*. Here the gangling hero becomes his little nephew's object of devotion—while they contend with contemporary domestic gadgetry. (The boy's parents' chic new home is a monstrosity of over-mechanization.) Again Tati proves himself a master of comic timing. Like the earlier film, *Mon Oncle* harkens back to the era of silent slapstick. It received an Academy Award for best foreign picture.

Monsieur Hulot's Holiday   France 1953;   ✻   *Black-and-White*
     U.S. 1954   (Embassy; Video Yesteryear; Sheik Video; Vid Dim; Budget Video;
     Discount Video Tapes; Western Film & Video Inc.)
Director: Jacques Tati
Starring: Jacques Tati, Nathalie Pascaud, Michèle Rolla, Valentine Camax, Louis Per-rault, Lucien Frégis, André Dubois

In this French farce, a lanky, butterfingered bachelor surnamed Hulot is observed on his beach vacation in a resort town. Sight gags and inspired pantomime abound as Hulot, often unwittingly, creates havoc for other holiday revelers. Though sound effects are present, *Monsieur Hulot's Holiday* is in large part a silent movie. The script represents a collaboration between director Jacques Tati and Henri Marquet; Tati himself is the accident-prone protagonist. The picture won the Grand Prize at the Cannes Film Festival.

N**ever On Sunday**   1960   (MGM)   ◆   *Black-and-White*
Director: Jules Dassin
Starring: Melina Mercouri, Jules Dassin, Georges Foundas, Tito Vandis, Despo Diamantidou, Mitsos Liguisos

This adult fairy tale, written and directed by (and costarring) Jules Dassin, begins as an American scholar named Homer tours Greece. In the port city of Piraeus, Homer becomes infatuated with Illya (Melina Mercouri), a cheerful and golden-hearted prostitute. Delighted with Illya's body, the scholar also wants to improve her mind. The young woman embarks on a program of self-improvement (including the study of Greek literature); but all the culture-cramming backfires on Homer. *Never on Sunday* gave Mercouri her greatest recognition in America; she was nominated for an Academy Award, though lost to Elizabeth Taylor for her *Butterfield 8* performance. An Oscar did, however, go to Manos Hadjidakis for his title song. The film inspired the Broadway musical *Illya, Darling*, which also starred Mercouri.

O**ne Sings, the Other Doesn't**   1977   (RCA)   *Color*
Director: Agnès Varda
Starring: Valérie Mairesse, Thérèse Liotard, Robert Dadiès, Ali Raffi, Jean-Pierre Pellegrin, Mona Mairesse, Francis Lemaire, Gisèle Halimi, Dominique Ducros, Rosalie Varda, Joëlle Papineau, Micou Papineau, Doudou Greffier, François Wertheimer, Mathieu Demy

Writer-director Agnès Varda celebrates the women's movement by dramatizing the lives of two friends: Pauline (Valérie Mairesse), who sings, and Suzanne (Thérèse Liotard), who doesn't. Their story begins in 1962 Paris, when Pauline is a seventeen-year-old high school glee club star and Suzanne, five years older, is trapped in an oppressive relationship with a suicidal photographer. Pauline, a free spirit, takes on the *nom de théâtre* of Pomme and follows a singing career; Suzanne opts for motherhood. But throughout the sixties and seventies, their paths criss-cross as they rally for feminist causes. This seriocomic consideration of contemporary friendship is shot by cinematographer Charlie Van Damme. Music by François Wertheimer and the group Orchidée (Micou Papineau, Joëlle Papineau, and Doudou Greffier).

Open City   Italy 1945; U.S. 1946   (Discount Video   *Black-and-White*
Tapes, Video Yesteryear, Sheik Video, Budget Video, Western Film and Video Inc., Video Award Motion Pictures, Inc.)
Director: Roberto Rossellini
Starring: Aldo Fabrizi, Anna Magnani, Marcello Pagliero, Maria Michi, Vito Annicchiarico, Nanco Bruno, Francesco Grandjacquet, Harry Feist

Roberto Rossellini's neorealist document tells of the underground Resistance in Nazi-occupied Rome, the "open city." Planned in secret while the Germans still occupied the capital, the film was shot silent—film stock being exorbitantly expensive—and later dubbed. The story (given immediacy by Rossellini, Federico Fellini, and Sergio Amidei) introduces a Resistance leader named Manfredi (Marcello Pagliero) on the run from the Gestapo. In his attempt to deliver money to the underground, he is aided by a coworker (Francesco Grandjacquet), a pregnant widow (Anna Magnani), and a priest (Aldo Fabrizi). Rossellini's filmmaking style draws upon the methods of the newsreel and the documentary—partly out of necessity. *Open City* was the first postwar Italian feature to make its mark internationally. Then, as now, it is a testament to the fight against fascism.

Padre Padrone   1977   (RCA)   ✳   *Color*

Director: Vittorio and Paolo Taviani
Starring: Omero Antonutti, Saverio Marconi, Marcella Michelangeli, Fabrizio Forte, Marino Cenna, Stanko Molnar, Nanni Moretti

Written and directed by brothers Vittorio and Paolo Taviani, *Padre Padrone* is a contemplation of Gavino Ledda (Saverio Marconi), a Sardinian peasant boy who works as a shepherd for his abusive father (Omero Antonutti). Gavino's *padre* is, therefore, also his *padrone*. The old man distrusts literature and loathes civilization, and he tries to engender these prejudices in his son. Finally, the young man escapes from this oppression and grows up to be a scholar. *Padre Padrone,* based on Gavino Ledda's autobiography, is the first film to win both the Grand Prize and the Critics Prize at Cannes. Marked by persuasive, unemphatic acting and the Tavianis's languid, spare direction, the picture emerges first as a mood piece, then as a celebration of the triumph of the human spirit. Director of photography: Mario Masini.

Paisan   Italy 1946; U.S. 1948   (Video Award   *Black-and-White*
Motion Pictures, Inc.; Budget Video; Sheik Video; Cable Films; Video Yesteryear; Western Film and Video Inc.; Discount Video Tapes)
Director: Roberto Rossellini
Starring: Carmela Sazio, Gar Moore, Bill Tubbs, Maria Michi, Robert van Loon, Harriet White, Dale Edmonds, Carla Pisacane, Dots Johnson

War-torn Italy, 1943 to 1945, is the subject of this Roberto Rossellini multi-story drama. Filmed shortly after *Open City, Paisan*—cowritten by the director and Federico Fellini—presents six vignettes. The episodes depict the Occupation and subsequent liberation in Sicily, Naples, Rome, Florence, a Franciscan monastery, and the Po Valley. Professional and nonprofessional actors work side by side in these depictions, and there appears to be a lot of improvisation. Fellini, then a journalist in Rome, was an assistant director. The soundtrack is an equal mix of English and subtitled Italian.

Pardon Mon Affaire!   France 1976; U.S. 1977   (Embassy)   *Color*
Director: Yves Robert
Starring: Jean Rochefort, Claude Brasseur, Victor Lanoux, Guy Bedos, Danièle Delorme, Anny Duperey

This French comedy is created by Yves Robert, most renowned as the director of *War of the Buttons; Very Happy Alexander; Salut, L'Artiste;* and the two *Tall Blond Man* movies. This time Robert, abetted by his frequent coscenarist, Jean-Loup Dabadie, describes Etienne (Jean Rochefort), a happily married man who begins to frame extramarital thoughts when he meets a sexy model (Anny Duperey). As he fantasizes himself a Casanova, his tennis buddies (Claude Brasseur, Victor Lanoux, and Guy Bedos) provide commentary and engage in affairs of their own. Robert, Dabadie, and most of the cast reunited in 1977 for a sequel: *We Will All Meet in Paradise* (later retitled *Pardon Mon Affaire, Too*). Gene Wilder, in 1984, used the *Pardon Mon Affaire I* plot for his *The Woman in Red*.

Persona   Sweden 1966; U.S. 1967   (Video Award   *Black-and-White*
    Motion Pictures, Inc.; Video Yesteryear; Vid Dim; Sheik Video; Budget Video)
Director: Ingmar Bergman
Starring: Liv Ullmann, Bibi Andersson, Margaretha Krook, Gunnar Björnstrand

Elisabet Vogler (Liv Ullmann) is a famous actress who has been traumatized in some unspecified way. (Her physician diagnoses the phenomenon as Elisabet's recognition of her own falseness.) Sister Alma (Bibi Andersson), a nurse and admirer, is hired to take care of the actress. This Ingmar Bergman study examines the relationship of the two women as they spend a summer together in a secluded seaside cottage. A complex drama with cross-references to other Bergman puzzlers, *Persona* is his twenty-seventh film and his first with Liv Ullmann. Sven Nykvist is the cinematographer.

The Rape of Love   France 1978; U.S. 1979   (RCA)   *Color*
Director: Yannick Bellon
Starring: Nathalie Nell, Alain Fourès, Michèle Simonnet, Pierre Arditi, Daniel Auteuil, Bernard Granger

In this harrowing drama, based by writer-director Yannick Bellon on real-life case studies, a young nurse (Nathalie Nell) is raped by four drunks. Bellon is a prolific filmmaker whose work, stretching back to the late forties, is virtually unknown in the United States. *The Rape of Love*, however, was respectfully reviewed in several major American cities, then gained acceptance in art house and film society circles. It's a graphic depiction of an assault, then a depressing investigation of the aftermath. Bellon focuses on the emotional impact of the crime on the victim. A consciousness-raising vehicle as well as a drama, *The Rape of Love* surpasses similar American television portraits in its frankness and avoidance of easy resolutions.

Rashomon   Japan 1950; U.S. 1951   (Embassy)   ◆   *Black-and-White*
Director: Akira Kurosawa
Starring: Toshiro Mifune, Masayuki Mori, Machiko Kyo, Takashi Shimura, Minoru Chiaki, Kichijiro Uedo, Daisuke Kato, Fumiko Homma

An international blockbuster in its day (and the first American exhibition for Akira Kurosawa), *Rashomon* won an Oscar as best foreign film, then in 1964 was Americanized as a tale of the Old West in *The Outrage*. Kurosawa, elaborating on his recurrent theme of the gulf between illusion and reality, weaves a tale of medieval Kyoto inspired by the story "Inside a Bush" by Ryunosuke Akutagawa. A nobleman and his wife are traveling through a forest when they are detained by a bandit; while the husband watches, the young woman is raped by the bandit and the husband later is found dead. This violent episode is then recounted four times—by participants and eyewitnesses (including the dead nobleman, who testifies through a medium). Each interpretation of the crime is presented in flashback, and each flashback is radically different from the one before. Which witness holds the truth? Performed by Toshiro Mifune (bandit), Machiko Kyo (wife), Masayuki Mori (husband), and Fumiko Homma (medium). The Takashi Matsuyama score is a variation on Ravel's *Bolero.*

The Return of Martin Guerre   France 1982; U.S. 1983   (Embassy)   *Color*
Director: Daniel Vigne
Starring: Gérard Depardieu, Nathalie Baye, Maurice Barrier, Bernard-Pierre Donnadieu, Isabelle Sadoyan, Rose Thiery, Chantal Deruaz, André Chaumeau, Maurice Jacquemont, Roger Planchon

This French drama—which, as the narrator explains, is "not a tale of adventure, nor an imaginary fable; it is a true story"—begins in 1542. One August Sunday in that year, in the village of Artigat, young Bertrande de Rois is married to the equally young Martin Guerre, a bumbling peasant boy and something of a misfit in the little farming community. Shortly thereafter, Martin disappears. Nine years pass and Martin returns to Artigat as a self-assured, educated adult. He and Bertrande at last live together in harmony until someone challenges his claim that he is the real Martin Guerre. Is he or isn't he? That's the compelling conundrum behind the Daniel Vigne and Jean-Claude Carrière screenplay, directed by Vigne. Gérard Depardieu and Nathalie Baye play the grown-up Martin and Bertrande. Providing the authentic music and cinematography are, respectively, Michel Portal and André Neau. *The Return of Martin Guerre,* as packaged in cassette, has a soundtrack dubbed into English.

The Return of the Tall Blond Man with One Black Shoe   *Color*
   France 1974; U.S. 1975   (Prism; Cinema Concepts)
Director: Yves Robert
Starring: Pierre Richard, Mireille Darc, Michel Duchaussoy, Jean Rochefort, Jean Carmet, Paul Le Person

This sequel may please admirers of the 1972 *Tall Blond Man* comedy caper. The premise stays constant: a Clouseauesque klutz—also French like the inspector, but this time a classical musician—is mistakenly presumed to be a master spy. As this second adventure begins, the new intelligence chief (Jean Rochefort) calls for the elimination of the tall blond man (Pierre Richard), who blithely dodges bullets, daggers, and elaborate traps without realizing the dangers surrounding him. This time the action transpires in Rio as well as Paris. Another farcical espionage spoof from director Yves Robert and his cowriter Francis Veber—with most of the original cast reassembling. Note that *The Return* is offered in French with subtitles, while the first film—from a different cassette manufacturer—is dubbed into English.

Rififi   France 1954; U.S. 1955   (Video Award   *Black-and-White*
   Motion Pictures, Inc.; Movie Buff Video; Video Yesteryear; Budget Video; Dis-
   count Video Tapes; Cable Films; Western Film & Video Inc.; Hollywood Home
   Theatre)
Director: Jules Dassin
Starring: Jean Servais, Carl Möhner, Magali Noël, Robert Manuel, Marie Sabouret, Fernand Ledoux, Marcel Lupovici, Janine Darcey, Claude Sylvain, Perlo Vita, Robert Hossein

American filmmaker Jules Dassin directed this classic suspense drama from France.

Four hooligans from the vice-infested boîtes of Montmartre assemble to commit a jewel theft. The robbery of a *bijouterie* on the rue de Rivoli has been perfectly orchestrated down to the last detail. Or has it? Dassin stages the safe-cracking heist as a thirty-minute sequence during which not a word of dialogue is spoken. The dialogue, when it begins, is a collaboration of Dassin, René Wheeler, and August le Breton; the last-named wrote the source novel. *Rififi* (argot for *brawl* or *trouble*) presents Jean Servais as Tony, the ringleader; Carl Möhner (Jo); and Robert Manuel (Mario); the master safecracker César is played by the director under his acting pseudonym: Perlo Vita. This thriller is the antecedent of *Rififi in Tokyo, The Killing, Gambit, Topkapi* (also by Dassin), and *How to Steal a Million*.

The Roof   Italy 1957; U.S. 1959   (Budget Films;   *Black-and-White*
Festival Films)
Director: Vittorio De Sica
Starring: Gabriella Pallotta, Giorgio Listuzzi, Gastone Renzelli, Maria Di Rollo

In the interim between *The Gold of Naples* and *Two Women*, Vittorio De Sica made this less well-known feature. *The Roof* is a domestic drama about a penniless young couple in post–World War II Rome who have married against their parents' wishes. Without family support, they must fend for themselves in the overcrowded city. As the title suggests, their main worry is getting a roof over their heads. One evening, with the help of friends, the newlyweds begin building a serviceable one-room house. (Under Italian law, they will not be evicted as long as their dwelling has a roof and a functional front door.) The construction must be completed overnight—before the police arrive. De Sica and his traditional collaborator, author Cesare Zavattini, continue their neorealist observations here.

Sanjuro   1962   (Budget Video; Festival Films;   *Black-and-White*
Discount Video Tapes; Video Action)
Director: Akira Kurosawa
Starring: Toshiro Mifune, Tatsuya Nakadai, Takashi Shimura, Yuzo Kayama, Reiko Dan

This sequel to *Yojimbo* is vintage Kurosawa. Toshiro Mifune stars again as Sanjuro, the stoic samurai for hire. In the new adventure, also set in feudal Japan, the wandering warrior encounters a group of youngsters who want to be samurai. Sanjuro becomes their instructor and leads them in ridding their clan of its corrupt governors. The principal scoundrel (Tatsuya Nakadai) faces the hero in a climactic showdown. The finale, like the rest of the film, is violent, and serious and comic in almost equal proportion.

Scenes from a Marriage   1973   (RCA)   *Color*
Director: Ingmar Bergman
Starring: Liv Ullmann, Erland Josephson, Bibi Andersson, Jan Malmsjö, Anita Wall

Ingmar Bergman's reflection on the institution of marriage is a condensation of a six-part Swedish TV drama. Presented as six dialogues, the film centers upon Johan (Erland Josephson), a psychology professor, and his wife Marianne (Liv Ullmann), a divorce lawyer. Their conventional, middle-class union is seen initially in stark contrast to the sniping-match marriage of their friends, Peter and Katarina (Jan Malmsjö and Bibi

Andersson). In time, though—after years of quarrels, distrust, and misunderstanding—the presumably sturdy walls come tumbling down. Bergman's screenplay is rife with aphoristic observations on the nature of love, matrimony, adultery, divorce, and life after divorce. Dubbed into English.

The Seduction of Mimi   Italy 1972; U.S. 1974   (CBS)   *Color*
Director: Lina Wertmüller
Starring: Giancarlo Giannini, Mariangela Melato, Agostina Belli, Elena Fiore

The seduction here isn't purely sexual. It's political as well. The outrageous sense of humor, combined with clinical descriptions and depictions of sex, will not be embraced by all viewers. Giancarlo Giannini stars as Mimi, a laborer whose sympathy vacillates between the Mafia and the communists in his native Italy. Mariangela Melato, Giannini's co-star in *Love and Anarchy* and *Swept Away . . .* , plays his obstinate mistress. Wertmüller's screenplay, a potpourri, attacks machismo, politics, and the Sicilian concepts of honor. This version is dubbed into English. (*The Seduction of Mimi* inspired Richard Pryor's 1977 comedy, *Which Way Is Up?*)

Seven Beauties   1976   (RCA)   *Color*
Director: Lina Wertmüller
Starring: Giancarlo Giannini, Fernando Rey, Shirley Stoler, Elena Fiore, Enzo Vitale, Piero di Iorio

Pasqualino (Giancarlo Giannini) is a small-time hood in Naples at the outset of World War II. (Pasqualino, who has seven sisters, gets stuck with the nickname Seven Beauties.) In the course of this paradoxical comedy-drama, the protagonist becomes a mafioso, kills a rival, is sentenced to an insane asylum, joins and then deserts the Italian army, then is captured by German troops and placed in a concentration camp. Pasqualino, by hook and crook, survives it all. *Seven Beauties*, filled with gallows humor dialogue, is a testament to the life force and the will to endure—even when man's instincts for survival lead him to ludicrous and grotesque acts. With this picture Lina Wertmüller became the first woman ever nominated for an Oscar as best director. (She lost to *Rocky*'s John Avildsen; and her screenplay nomination was bested by Paddy Chayefsky for *Network*.) Wertmüller adherents call *Seven Beauties* her masterpiece. The cassette version comes from the English-dubbed print.

The Seven Samurai   1954   (Embassy; Budget Video;   *Black-and-White*
          International Historic Films; Sheik Video; Discount Video Tapes; Video Action)
Director: Akira Kurosawa
Starring: Takashi Shimura, Toshiro Mifune, Yoshio Inaba, Seiji Mayaguchi, Minoru Chicki, Daisuke Kato, Kuninori Kodo

The Seven Samurai, on video, is the full-length edition of three hours and twenty minutes. The Akira Kurosawa masterpiece was initially released in the United States in a truncated version (shorter by an hour) entitled *The Magnificent Seven*. A visually complex battle epic, the film is set in a sixteenth-century Japanese village—the target of an annual raid by bloodthirsty bandits. In defense, the townsfolk hire seven sturdy samurai. (Actually, there's an imposter in the group; the braggart hero played by Toshiro Mifune claims to be a samurai, but isn't.) Violence, spectacle, social criticism, historical treatise are all here, blended by Kurosawa and his writing collaborators, Shinobu

Hashimoto and Hideo Oguni. The story provided the outline for *The Magnificent Seven,* the 1961 John Sturges Western adaptation.

The Seventh Seal   1957   (Embassy)   *Black-and-White*
Director: Ingmar Bergman
Starring: Max von Sydow, Gunnar Björnstrand, Nils Poppe, Bengt Ekerot, Bibi Andersson, Gunnel Lindblom, Inga Gill, Maud Hansson

A medieval knight, his loyal squire, and the spectre of Death are the major players in this Ingmar Bergman allegory. *The Seventh Seal* is laid in fourteenth-century Sweden as the knight, Antonius Blok (Max von Sydow), returns from ten years in the Crusades. He and Jöns (Gunnar Björnstrand), his squire, journey homeward across a barren landscape. Disillusioned in battle, the knight is further disillusioned as he approaches his castle: Sweden has been ravaged by the plague. Death arrives to claim the two men, but Antonius challenges the black-cloaked figure to a life-or-death game of chess. One of Bergman's most ambitious productions, *The Seventh Seal* is permeated with visual highlights: the chess match on the seashore, the band of flagellants, the burning of a little girl condemned as a witch, and the climactic hilltop dance of death. Gunnar Fischer, who alternates with Sven Nykvist as Bergman's cinematographer, was behind the camera.

Shame   1968   (Sheik Video)   *Black-and-White*
Director: Ingmar Bergman
Starring: Liv Ullmann, Max von Sydow, Gunnar Björnstrand, Sigge Furst, Birgitta Valberg, Hans Alfredson

Global tensions in microcosm permeate this Ingmar Bergman fable about the loss of spirituality in modern society. A husband and wife (Max von Sydow and Liv Ullmann), both concert violinists, flee their native Sweden for a Baltic island because a civil war is raging on the mainland. The battle approaches the island retreat. Faced with ill health, physical horrors, and combat on their doorstep, the couple's insecure marriage erodes. *Shame* is a brooding and unheroic depiction of war. Sven Nykvist is the cinematographer.

The Shop on Main Street   1965   (RCA)   ◆   *Black-and-White*
Directors: Jan Kadar and Elmar Klos
Starring: Ida Kaminska, Josef Kroner, Hana Slivkova, František Svarik, Martin Gregor

The Shop on Main Street was part of a wave of Czech productions to reach American shores during the sixties. (*Closely Watched Trains, Loves of a Blonde,* and *The Firemen's Ball* were other comedy-dramas that achieved success here.) Based on a novel by Ladislav Grosman (who wrote the movie adaptation with the two directors), *Shop* takes place in 1942 in a small German-occupied Slovakian village. A young carpenter is named "Aryan controller" of a dry-goods store managed by an elderly Jewish widow. Because the old lady is practically deaf, she misinterprets the situation; the new manager, unable to explain, gradually adopts the widow's belief that he is her assistant. This is a comedy that contains at its core a nightmare vision of anti-Semitism. (British director Lindsay Anderson wrote the English subtitles.) Critically hailed, *The Shop on Main Street* also became the first Czech film to receive the best foreign film Oscar.

A Simple Story   France 1978; U.S. 1979   (RCA)   ▲   *Color*
Director: Claude Sautet
Starring: Romy Schneider, Bruno Cremer, Claude Brasseur, Arlette Bonnard, Roger Pigaut

Marie (Romy Schneider) is an industrial designer, a divorced mother on the brink of
forty. She learns that she is pregnant by her lover Serge (Claude Brasseur), a happy-
go-lucky but insecure companion. Almost simultaneously, she decides to have an abortion and to end her affair with Serge. And then her ex-husband Georges (Bruno
Cremer), a business magnate, reenters the picture. As depicted in director Claude
Sautet's screenplay with Jean-Loup Dabadie, Marie's relationships with her lover, husband, and friends provide a seemingly authentic slice of middle-class life. For her
enactment of Marie, the late Romy Schneider won the best actress César, the French
equivalent of the Oscar. Besides script collaborator Dabadie, two other frequent Claude
Sautet associates worked on the film: cinematographer Jean Boffety and composer
Philippe Sarde. In addition to *A Simple Story*, the director's major work includes *The
Things of Life* (1970), *César and Rosalie* (1972), *Vincent, François, Paul . . . and the Others*
(1974), and *Mado* (1976). English language soundtrack.

The Sleeping Car Murder   France 1965; U.S. 1966   *Black-and-White*
     (Movie Buff Video)
Director: Costa-Gavras
*Starring: Simone Signoret, Yves Montand, Jean-Louis Trintignant, Pierre Mondy, Michel
Piccoli, Claude Mann, Pascale Roberts, Charles Denner, Jacques Perrin, Nadine Alari,
Catherine Allégret*

Yves Montand's portrayal of Inspector Grazzi, a hardened but humane Paris cop, helps
lift this murder mystery to classic status. The story begins as the overnight Marseilles-
to-Paris express pulls into the Gare de Lyon—with the corpse of a young woman in
one of the sleeping compartments. In the days that follow the passengers who shared
the cabin with her are systematically murdered too. Inspector Grazzi races to save the
few remaining sleeping car occupants from almost certain death. This whodunit, based
on Sébastien Japrisot's acclaimed *roman policier Compartment Tueurs* (translated into
English as *The Sleeping Car Murders*), makes an auspicious debut film for Costa-Gavras.
The director here reveals the lightning pacing that became his trademark in *Z* and
other thrillers with political themes. (Costa-Gavras and Japrisot collaborated on the
adaptation.) The cinematographer is Jean Tournier, and the music score is by Michel
Magne.

Small Change   1976   (Warner)   *Color*
Director: François Truffaut
*Starring: Geory Desmouceaux, Philippe Goldman, Claudio Deluca, Franck Deluca, Rich-
ard Golfier, Laurent Devlaeminck, Bruno Staab, Sébastien Marc, Sylvie Grezel, Pascale
Bruchon, Corinne Boucart, Eva Truffaut, Laura Truffaut, Jean-François Stevenin*

François Truffaut's nineteenth movie is a reconsideration of *The 400 Blows*, offering a
breezier interpretation of the everyday passions and poignancies of youth. The action
begins in the French town of Thiers during the last month of the school year—then
reaches a climax in August in a summer camp. Participating in the events are a dozen
or so boys and girls, as well as their parents and teachers. In the resulting series of
sketches, Truffaut and his coscreenwriter Suzanne Schiffman dramatize various rites
of passage from early childhood to adolescence: bruises, misbehavior, peer pressure,
antisocial guises, infatuation, the first kiss.

A Special Day   1977   (RCA)   *Color*
Director: Ettore Scola
Starring: Sophia Loren, Marcello Mastroianni, John Vernon, Françoise Berd, Nicole Magny

The titular festivity occurs on May 8, 1938, when Hitler arrives in Rome to confer with Mussolini and celebrate the Rome-Berlin Axis. Most of the city's residents have fled their apartments to attend the day-long series of parades and rallies. Two neighbors, however, remain homebound. Though she idolizes Mussolini, an oppressed wife and mother (Sophia Loren) has too much housework to do; across the courtyard, a middle-aged radio announcer (Marcello Mastroianni) is preparing to commit suicide. A two-character movie, *A Special Day* dramatizes the meeting of the housewife and the announcer, who are drawn together by a fly-away mynah bird and pulled apart by their clashing opinions of Il Duce. Directed by Ettore Scola (*The Pizza Triangle, We All Loved Each Other So Much, Down and Dirty, Passione D'Amore, La Nuit de Varennes, Le Bal*) from his screenplay with Ruggiero Maccari and Maurizio Costanzo. English-dubbed soundtrack.

State of Siege   1973   (RCA)   *Color*
Director: Costa-Gavras
Starring: Yves Montand, Renato Salvatori, O. E. Hasse, Jacques Weber, Jean-Luc Bideau, Evangeline Peterson

Costa-Gavras, whose fifth feature this is, again tackles a controversial subject. (The writer-director, who began his film career with the whodunit *The Sleeping Car Murder*, emerged as an increasingly political moviemaker with *Shock Troops, Z*, and *The Confession*.) This fact-based drama probes the United States' clandestine involvement in and support of fascist activities in Uruguay. Kidnapping and assassination provided the climax to the real-life Dan Mitrione case. In *State of Siege* Mitrione is called Santore—and played by Yves Montand. Santore, an American representative of AID (Agency for International Development), is abducted by members of a left-wing underground organization seeking amnesty for all political prisoners. Authorities are told that Santore will be released when those demands are met. Unluckily for the kidnap victim, his captors come to realize that, contrary to appearances, he is in their country to train police in search-and-destroy missions against revolutionaries. Negotiations (and atrocities on both sides) continue, but the Uruguay government refuses to bargain for the American's life. Franco Solinas collaborated with Costa-Gavras on the screenplay, which is based in part on tapes made by the Tupamaros rebels who abducted Dan Mitrione. Music by Mikis Theodorakis, also of *Z* fame, and cinematography by Pierre-William Glenn. English-dubbed.

Stolen Kisses   France 1968; U.S. 1969   (RCA)   *Color*
Director: François Truffaut
Starring: Jean-Pierre Léaud, Claude Jade, Delphine Seyrig, Daniel Ceccaldi, Claire Duhamel, Michel Lonsdale, André Falcon, Harry Max, Catherine Lutz, Marie-France Pisier, Jean-François Adam, Serge Rousseau

Episode three in the unfolding memoirs of François Truffaut's surrogate—Antoine Doinel (again portrayed by Jean-Pierre Léaud). One of the most commercially successful works of Truffaut's middle period, *Stolen Kisses* picks up the adolescent hero of *The 400 Blows* ten years later, after his discharge from the army for being "temperamentally unfit for service." Back in Paris, Antoine becomes a hotel night clerk and a private investigator of astonishing ineptitude. The schoolboy rebel has turned into a genial but often maladroit young man. His foibles, professional and romantic, form the basis of this comedy. Assisting Truffaut on the screenplay are Claude de Givray and Bernard Revon; Denys Clerval is the cinematographer; and the music is by Antoine Duhamel. The next Antoine Doinel feature is *Bed and Board* (1970) and the series concludes with *Love on the Run* (1979).

The Story of Adèle H.   1975   (Warner)   ✳   *Color*
Director: François Truffaut
Starring: Isabelle Adjani, Bruce Robinson, Sylvia Marriott, Reubin Dorey, Joseph Blatchley, M. White, Carl Hathwell, Ivry Gitlis, Sir Cecil de Sausmarez, Sir Raymond Falla, Roger Martin

This sombre, disturbing film is perhaps the best of Truffaut's *oeuvre*. Detailing the all-consuming agonies of romantic passion and idealism, the story centers upon the second daughter of Victor Hugo. Adèle (Isabelle Adjani) is infatuated with Lieutenant Pinson (Bruce Robinson), a callow, caddish—but undeniably handsome—English officer. She follows him from the Channel Island of Guernsey, where the Hugo family lives in exile, to Nova Scotia and, ultimately, to Barbados. Her unrequited passion exacted a price: the loss of her sanity. Much of the screenplay by Truffaut, Jean Gruault, and Suzanne Schiffman is based on Adèle's journals. *The Story of Adèle H.* won the best screenplay award from the New York Film Critics Circle, the best foreign film designation from the National Board of Review, and the best actress award for Isabelle Adjani from both groups.

Sundays and Cybèle   France 1961; U.S. 1962   ◆   *Black-and-White*
(Budget Video; Discount Video Tapes)
Director: Serge Bourguignon
Starring: Hardy Krüger, Nicole Courcel, Patricia Gozzi, Daniel Ivernel

This Academy Award—winning French film derives from the Bernard Eschassériaux novel, *Les Dimanches de Ville D'Avray*—as adapted by the author, Antoine Tudal, and director Serge Bourguignon. Hardy Krüger stars as Pierre, a former pilot who is shell-shocked and amnesiac since crashing in flames in the Indo-China war. In Ville d'Avray, a Paris suburb, he encounters twelve-year-old Cybèle (Patricia Gozzi), a love-starved child who has been abandoned by her father. Pierre visits Cybèle at her convent school on Sundays. The little girl adopts the troubled young man as a father substitute. Their Sunday excursions are the source for magical idylls—but their relationship is misunderstood by certain petty-minded townspeople. The score is by Maurice Jarre and the photography by Henri Decaë. *Sundays and Cybèle* is the feature film debut for painter-turned-director Bourguignon.

Swept Away by an Unusual Destiny in the Blue Sea of August   *Color*
Italy 1974; U.S. 1975   (RCA)
Director: Lina Wertmüller
Starring: Giancarlo Giannini, Mariangela Melato

Love is a shouting match in Lina Wertmüller's sexually explicit *Swept Away by an Unusual Destiny in the Blue Sea of August,* shortened to *Swept Away. . . .* The passionate quarrelers are Raffaella (Mariangela Melato), an upper-class northern Italian *signora,* and Gennarino (Giancarlo Giannini), a lusty yacht steward from Naples who is employed by Raffaella and her husband for a Mediterranean cruise. When the two are shipwrecked and land on a deserted island, there is almost nonstop bickering. The leisure-class lady has little sympathy for Gennarino's communist leanings. He, in turn, can't abide her arrogance and shrewishness. At first Gennarino is clearly the underdog, but as castaways, the roles reverse. With his superior physical force, the lowly steward becomes the master. Wertmüller, as writer and director, and her leading players from *Love and Anarchy* and *The Seduction of Mimi* again pool their resources for a vitriolic comedy-drama. Ennio Guarnieri is the cinematographer. Dubbed into English.

The Tall Blond Man with One Black Shoe *Color*
France 1972; U.S. 1973   (RCA)
Director: Yves Robert
Starring: Pierre Richard, Mireille Darc, Bernard Blier, Jean Rochefort, Jean Carmet, Paul Le Person, Yves Robert, Colette Castel, Robert Castel, Robert Dalban

This madcap comedy from France was popular on both shores of the Atlantic. Directing from his screenplay with Francis Veber, Yves Robert introduces an absent-minded classical violinist (Pierre Richard) who becomes the unwitting decoy in an international spy-versus-spy contretemps. An upper-echelon intelligence agent (Bernard Blier) conspires to booby-trap an overly ambitious subordinate (Jean Rochefort). The tall blond violinist, shod for the day in one black and one brown shoe, is—without his knowledge—made to appear a secret agent. The complications build to a comic climax. Dubbed into English. The sequel, *Return of the Tall Blond Man with One Black Shoe*, is also available (in French with English subtitles). The 1985 American remake, starring Tom Hanks, is called *The Man with One Red Shoe*.

That Obscure Object of Desire   1977   (Embassy) *Color*
Director: Luis Buñuel
Starring: Fernando Rey, Carole Bouquet, Angela Molina, Julien Bertheau, André Weber, Milena Vukotic, Piéral

This is Luis Buñuel's final movie. The director's screenplay with Jean-Claude Carrière is a revision of the 1898 Pierre Louÿs novel, *La Femme et le Pantin (Woman and Puppet)*— previously filmed, with Marlene Dietrich, as *The Devil Is a Woman* and, retaining the novel's title, as a vehicle for Brigitte Bardot. In this Franco-Spanish coproduction, spoken in French, Fernando Rey (with the voice of Michel Piccoli) stars as Mathieu, a boulevardier with a taste for sadomasochism. Mathieu becomes obsessed with a young femme fatale named Conchita who is played in Jekyll and Hyde fashion by two actresses: Carole Bouquet and Angela Molina. Half Mathieu's age, Conchita represents daughter, prostitute, and lover—but not a lifelong mate. Ever elusive, she is *That Obscure Object of Desire*. Buñuel's insolent humor is slightly salacious and his motives aren't always clear, but this picture makes a fascinating finale to a successful film-making career.

The Tin Drum   1979   (Warner) *Color*
Director: Volker Schlöndorff
Starring: David Bennent, Mario Adorf, Angela Winkler, Daniel Olbrychski, Katharina Tahlbach, Heinz Bennent, Andréa Ferréol, Charles Aznavour

Oskar Matzerath (David Bennent) is a self-willed dwarf. Discontent with the society about him in pre–World War II Germany, Oskar, at the age of three, forces himself to stop growing. In this adaptation by director Volker Schlöndorff, Franz Seitz, and Jean-Claude Carrière of the 1959 Günter Grass novel, diminutive (twelve-year-old) David Bennent plays Oskar, the psychic drummer boy. The condensation of a challenging literary masterwork, *The Tin Drum* is a hard-hitting, often outrageous, parable on amorality and the rise of Nazism. Music by Maurice Jarre; director of photography is Igor Luther. *The Tin Drum* took the 1979 Academy Award as best foreign film.

Ugetsu Monogatari   1953   (Budget Video;   *Black-and-White*
    Sheik Video; Western Film & Video Inc.; Discount Video Tapes; Vid Dim; Video
    Action)
Director: Kenji Mizoguchi
Starring: Machiko Kyo, Masayuki Mori, Kinuyo Tanaka, Sakae Ozawa, Mitsuko Mito

Two sixteenth-century legends spur this Japanese ghost story. Genjuro (Masayuki Mori) is a village potter; his brother-in-law Tobei (Sakae Ozawa) is a farmer. Both young men go off to seek their fortune—Genjuro in the city and Tobei as a samurai. The former is seduced by a phantom lady (Machiko Kyo) and follows her to her mansion of apparitions; the latter finds his glory as a military warrior. *Ugetsu Monogatari* (translated as *Tales of the Pale and Silvery Moon After the Rain*) presents the parallel lives of the brothers-in-law, including their eventual return to their native village. A meditation on love and ambition, this Japanese feature is written by Yoshikata Yoda, Matsutaro Kawaguchi, and director Kenji Mizoguchi. Mizoguchi is probably the second best-known Oriental filmmaker (after Kurosawa) to Western audiences. A prolific *cinéaste*, he was active from the silent era till his death in 1956.

Umberto D   Italy 1952; U.S. 1955   (Budget Video; ✷   *Black-and-White*
    Discount Video Tapes)
Director: Vittorio De Sica
Starring: Carlo Battisti, Maria Pia Casilio, Lina Gennari

Another contribution to neorealism by Vittorio De Sica, *Umberto D* is a touching study of old age. Set in postwar Rome, the film (written by De Sica and his constant colleague, Cesare Zavattini) introduces seventy-year-old Umberto Domenico Ferrari (Carlo Battisti). Umberto is a former civil servant whose retirement pension is far too meager for his needs. He survives by living in a shabby furnished room and eating cheaply. Even so, his rent bill is overdue and his landlady (Lina Gennari) threatens eviction. He attempts to obtain money through begging, but his pride intervenes. In the end he is forced onto the street, abandoned by all but his faithful dog. *Umberto D* follows *Miracle in Milan* in the De Sica chronology. The director dedicated the picture to the memory of his father. *Umberto D* was cited by the New York Film Critics Circle as the best foreign language feature of the year.

The Umbrellas of Cherbourg   France 1964; U.S. 1965   *Color*
    (U.S.A. Home Video)
Director: Jacques Demy
Starring: Catherine Deneuve, Nino Castelnuovo, Anne Vernon, Marc Michel, Ellen Farner, Mireille Perrey

A contemporary romantic drama in the form of an operetta (every line of dialogue is sung), *The Umbrellas of Cherbourg* appeals to lovers of all ages. The film, written and directed by Jacques Demy and with music by Michel Legrand, follows the fate of Geneviève (Catherine Deneuve) and Guy (Nino Castelnuovo), two young citizens of Cherbourg. Geneviève works in an umbrella shop; Guy is a gas station attendant. They plan to marry when Guy returns from serving in Algeria. However, because Guy is sidelined with a war wound, the fiancés lose contact with one another. When Geneviève learns she is pregnant by Guy, she reluctantly marries Roland (Marc Michel), a middle-aged admirer who provides her and her child security and respect. But several more chapters of the tale remain. The lush camera work is by Jean Rabier. Two of the Demy-Legrand songs became popular in their English translations: "I Will Wait for You" and "Watch What Happens."

Viridiana   France 1961; U.S. 1962   ✳   *Black-and-White*
(Budget Video; Sheik Video; Discount Video Tapes)
Director: Luis Buñuel
Starring: Silvia Pinal, Francisco Rabal, Fernando Rey, Margarita Lozano, Teresa Rabal

This middle-period Buñuel drama was made when the director returned from Mexican exile to his native Spain. A winner of the Palme d'Or at the Cannes Film Festival, it was banned throughout Spain. (After the 1962 release of *The Exterminating Angel*, shot in Mexico, all Buñuel's remaining pictures were produced in France.) In *Viridiana* the title heroine is a novice nun (Silvia Pinal). Before she takes her final vows, she visits her uncle-by-marriage, Don Jaime (Fernando Rey). The uncle, a rich eccentric living on a remote estate, is taken by Viridiana's resemblance to his dead wife. Buñuel's trademark surrealism establishes itself at this point as *Viridiana* concentrates on lust, fetishism, attempted rape, and suicide. The director's fusion of religious and fable imagery works as a devastating assault on bourgeois values. The climactic "beggar's banquet," in which Don Jaime's servants assault the mansion, is one of the most discussed sequences in the filmmaker's repertoire.

The Wages of Fear   France 1953; U.S. 1955   ✳   *Black-and-White*
(Movie Buff Video; Budget Video; Video Yesteryear; Western Film & Video Inc.; Discount Video Tapes)
Director: Henri-Georges Clouzot
Starring: Yves Montand, Charles Vanel, Folco Lulli, Peter Van Eyck, Véra Clouzot, William Tubbs, Dario Moreno, Jo Dest

The Wages of Fear, Henri-Georges Clouzot's pre-*Diabolique* thriller, captured the Grand Prix at the 1953 Cannes Film Festival. It's the kind of movie for which the term hair-raising was invented. Skillfully adapted by Clouzot and Jérôme Géronimi from the novel by Georges Arnaud, the picture begins in a South American village named Las Piedras. O'Brien (William Tubbs), the manager of a U.S. oil installation in the jungle, learns that one of his wells—300 miles away—has caught fire. In hopes of extinguishing the fire by exploding it with nitroglycerin, O'Brien hires four down-and-out locals to truck the nitro to the disaster site. The convoy of trucks must follow a long and treacherous road to reach the destination. The four daredevils, who will collect $2,000 each if they succeed, are Bimba (Peter Van Eyck), a narcissistic German; Luigi (Folco Lulli), an Italian bricklayer; Mario (Yves Montand), a Corsican laborer; and Jo (Charles Vanel), a French thug who has quite literally killed to get the job. An exercise in sustained suspense, *The Wages of Fear* is photographed by Armand Thirard and contains a score by Georges Auric. Remade in 1977 by William Friedkin under the title *Sorcerer.*

Wifemistress   Italy 1977; U.S. 1979   (RCA)   *Color*
Director: Marco Vicario
Starring: Marcello Mastroianni, Laura Antonelli, Leonard Mann, Annie Belle, Gaston Moschin, William Berger

This erotic comedy from Italy centers around a young wife (Laura Antonelli) who has endured psychosomatic paralysis while her husband (Marcello Mastroianni) dallied with other women. The husband, an activist in the feminist/suffragette movement, is forced into hiding after a political murder. Only then does the wife emerge from her sexually repressed state and explore her husband's secret affairs. *Wifemistress* is written by Rodolfo Sonego and Marco Vicario—and directed by the latter. Vicario is also known in this country for the heist comedy-dramas *Seven Golden Men* and *Seven Golden Men Strike Again*—as well as the sex farces *Homo Eroticus (Man of the Year), The Swinging Confessors,* and *The Sensuous Sicilian.*

Wild Strawberries   1957   (CBS)   *Black-and-White*
Director: Ingmar Bergman
Starring: Victor Sjöström, Ingrid Thulin, Bibi Andersson, Gunnar Björnstrand, Folke Sundquist, Bjorn Bjelvestam, Naima Wifstrand, Jullan Kindahl

Isak Borg (Victor Sjöström), an elderly professor from Stockholm, recollects his life and loves in this Ingmar Bergman character study. Borg's interior journey is symbolically linked to his one-day motor trip to the university town of Lund, where he will receive an honorary degree. *Wild Strawberries* is a haunting mix of strange dreams and straightforward memories—all distilled through the protagonist's consciousness. Borg was one of the last roles played by veteran actor-filmmaker Sjöström (1879–1960), who under the name Seastrom directed some of the great classics of the American silent period: *He Who Gets Slapped, Name the Man, Confessions of a Queen, The Tower of Lies, The Scarlet Letter, The Divine Woman,* and *The Wind.* Bergman's cinematographer on *Wild Strawberries* is Gunnar Fischer.

Winter Light   1963   (Embassy)   *Black-and-White*
Director: Ingmar Bergman
Starring: Ingrid Thulin, Gunnar Björnstrand, Max von Sydow, Gunnel Lindblom, Allan Edwall

From the director of *Through a Glass Darkly* comes another drama examining the loss of faith. (These two films combine with Bergman's *The Silence* to form a trilogy on the theme.) Tomas Ericsson (Gunnar Björnstrand), a village clergyman, is at loose ends after the death of his wife. He feels affronted by what he calls "God's silence." On the Sunday under observation in *Winter Light,* Tomas celebrates Holy Communion with his parishioners, among them Märta (Ingrid Thulin), the schoolteacher he has taken as a mistress. To his great regret, he is not able to offer spiritual guidance to any of his flock, including a suicidal fisherman (Max von Sydow) and his wife (Gunnel Lindblom). *Winter Light* is a dour and chilly picture—graphically rendered in the cinematography of Sven Nykvist.

Woman in the Dunes 1964 (Festival Films; *Black-and-White*
Western Film & Video Inc.; Vid Dim)
Director: Hiroshi Teshigahara
Starring: Eiji Okada, Kyoko Kishida, Koji Mitsui, Hiroko Ito, Sen Yano

Suna No Onna, Kobo Abe's acclaimed allegorical novel, is the basis for this drama—
with a screenplay by Abe. A young entomologist (Eiji Okada) is persuaded by the
residents of a beach community to visit a widow (Kyoko Kishida) who lives in a shack
at the bottom of a deep sand pit. The woman's never-ending job is to shovel sand,
which the villagers haul up on pulleys and carry away. After spending a night with the
woman in the dunes, the entomologist is unable to leave. His curiosity has been
supplanted by sexual attraction, so he stays on as her lover and colaborer. A mysterious
and partly erotic film, *Woman in the Dunes* is distinguished by the leading players,
director Hiroshi Teshigahara, and cinematographer Hiroshi Segawa.

The World of Apu 1959 (Festival Films; *Black-and-White*
Budget Video; Video Yesteryear)
Director: Satyajit Ray
Starring: Soumitra Chatterjee, Sharmila Tagore, Alok Chakravarty, Swapan Mukherji

This is the climax of Satyajit Ray's Apu trilogy, begun with *Pather Panchali* and continued with *Aparajito* (*The Unvanquished*). The finale presents the title character in
adulthood. Apu (now played by Soumitra Chatterjee) is a university student in Cal-
cutta—and an aspiring writer. He marries his country cousin Aparna (Sharmila Tagore).
They live, for a time, in happiness until tragedy strikes. A poetic investigation of despair,
The World of Apu is, for many, the most rewarding chapter in the series. As with the
earlier installments, Ray himself wrote the screenplay, Subrata Mitra was the cinematographer, and Ravi Shankar created the score.

Yojimbo Japan 1961; U.S. 1962 (Budget Video; *Black-and-White*
International Historic Video Films; Sheik Video; Cable Films; Discount Video
Tapes; Video Yesteryear; Video Action)
Director: Akira Kurosawa
*Starring: Toshiro Mifune, Eijiro Tono, Seizaburo Kawazu, Isuzu Yamada, Hiroshi
Tachikawa, Ikio Sawamura*

Japan in 1860; a small town is ravaged by a long-going feud between two merchants.
The initial argument has centered on the rights to a gambling concession. Sanjuro
(Toshiro Mifune), a samurai, comes to town and sells his services to both factions of
the civil strife. Pledging to be a bodyguard for both groups, he helps them eliminate
one another. This tongue-in-cheek hero-for-hire drama, scripted and directed by Akira
Kurosawa, has been much imitated—and not only in Japan. Sergio Leone used *Yojimbo*
as the basis for his *A Fistful of Dollars*. Sanjuro's own comic adventures continued in
a Kurosawa sequel entitled, appropriately, *Sanjuro* (1962).

Z 1969 (RCA) ◆ ✳ ◯ *Color*
Director: Costa-Gavras
*Starring: Yves Montand, Irene Papas, Jean-Louis Trintignant, François Périer, Jacques
Perrin, Charles Denner, Pierre Dux, Georges Géret, Bernard Fresson, Marcel Bozzuffi,
Julien Guiomar, Magali Noël, Renato Salvatori, Jean Bouise*

Based upon Vassili Vassilikov's *roman à clef, Z* is a fictionalized account of the 1963 Lambrakis affair in Greece. Gregorios Lambrakis, a deputy and a University of Athens professor, was the target of a political assassination (disguised as an accident) when his pacifist notions rankled his enemies. Investigation traced the murder plot to right-wing elements supported by the army, police, and top-echelon officials. As a film, *Z* (the title derives from the Greek verb *zei*—meaning *he lives*) is a swift and compelling anatomy of fascism. Directed by Costa-Gavras and written by him and Jorge Semprun. Yves Montand plays the Lambrakis figure; Irene Papas, his widow; and Jacques Perrin and Jean-Louis Trintignant, a journalist and an examining magistrate who uncover the conspiracy. Selected as the top picture of 1969 by the New York Film Critics and the National Society, *Z* also won two Oscars: best foreign language film and best editing (Françoise Bonnot). Cinematographer: Raoul Coutard; music: Mikis Theodorakis. Dubbed into English.

Horror and Science
Fiction

Alien   1979   (CBS)   ◆   *Color*
Director: Ridley Scott
Starring: Tom Skerritt, Sigourney Weaver, Veronica Cartwright, Harry Dean Stanton,
John Hurt, Ian Holm, Yaphet Kotto

"In space no one can hear you scream." So went the print ad campaign for *Alien*. There was plenty of audible screaming in movie houses, though. Seven astronauts find an alien life force and, unaware that it is an indestructible killer, bring it aboard their spacecraft. This terror-in-space shocker, written by Dan O'Bannon, owes some of its intensity to crude slasher movies; for cast-iron stomachs, though, it afforded a warm-up for John Carpenter's *The Thing*. *Alien*'s visual effects team was honored by the Academy. Sequel: *Aliens* (1986).

Altered States   1980   (Warner)   *Color*
Director: Ken Russell
Starring: William Hurt, Blair Brown, Charles Haid, Bob Balaban, Thaao Penghlis,
Dori Brenner, Miguel Godreau, Drew Barrymore

Ken Russell, attempting to rebound from the poor box-office performance of his 1977 *Valentino*, seems to have tried to play it relatively safe in his next screen venture. He opted for a known property with conventional structure—to wit, Paddy Chayefsky's horror novel about a primal research scientist. The scientist (William Hurt) uses himself as a guinea pig in a sensory deprivation tank, where dreams turn to nightmares. Chayefsky wrote the screenplay himself, though he had his name removed from the credits just before the film's release. ("Sidney Aaron" gets the scenario credit.) A cautionary tale with some mesmerizing special effects.

An American Werewolf in London   1981   (MCA)   ◆   *Color*
Director: John Landis
Starring: David Naughton, Jenny Agutter, Griffin Dunne, John Woodvine, Brian Glover,
Lila Kaye, David Schofield

Two American college students, backpacking on the foggy, bleak English moors, are viciously attacked by a bloodthirsty beast whose bite spells disaster. One boy dies . . . or does he? John Landis, directing from his own screenplay, fashions a sendup of the werewolf genre while simultaneously creating another bona fide installment in it. The lycanthropy lore is honored, and there are genuine shocks—especially when hero David

Naughton undergoes a species shift and becomes the hirsute beast of folklore. But a definite undercurrent of spoofiness flows throughout; in one instance the soundtrack bursts into Creedence Clearwater Revival's "Bad Moon Rising" as the title character goes prowling. An Oscar for special effects went to Rick Baker, whose makeup designs for wolf transformations rank—with Rob Bottin's in *The Howling*—as the best ever executed for the movie camera.

The Andromeda Strain   1971   (MCA)   *Color*
Director: Robert Wise
Starring: Arthur Hill, David Wayne, James Olson, Kate Reid, Paula Kelly, George Mitchell, Ramon Bieri, Eric Christmas, Peter Hobbs

A satellite plunges to earth and, in a nearby desert town, all the inhabitants, save two, die. The two survivors—a wino and a baby with colic—are then transported to an underground research station, where a team of scientists observes them. The quarantine leads to the discovery of a biological menace: the Andromeda strain. The scientists must race to avert global catastrophe. Derived by Nelson Gidding from Michael Crichton's novel, *The Andromeda Strain* is a complex and suspenseful science fiction drama. Director Robert Wise *(The Day the Earth Stood Still)* returned to the science fiction genre after a string of big-star, big-budget extravaganzas, culminating in *The Sound of Music, The Sand Pebbles,* and *Star! The Andromeda Strain* is appropriately scaled down from those mega-productions, giving an almost documetary look at the workaday world of the microbiology research lab.

Asylum   1972   (Nostalgia)   *Color*
Director: Roy Ward Baker
Starring: Peter Cushing, Britt Ekland, Herbert Lom, Patrick Magee, Barry Morse, Barbara Parkins, Robert Powell, Charlotte Rampling, Sylvia Sims, Richard Todd, Geoffrey Bayldon

Omnibus terror flicks have been popular for more than thirty years in the British film industry. The seminal effort in the genre was, of course, *Dead of Night* in 1945. But only in the sixties did the production of these multi-part endeavors escalate—characteristically arising from two studios: Hammer or Amicus. Arguably the most lasting of the cycle was *Dr. Terror's House of Horrors* (1965, Freddie Francis). One of its direct descendants, with recurring formulas and a recurring stock company, is *Asylum*. This anthology film by *Psycho* creator Robert Bloch contains four episodes told from the point of view of four inmates: "Frozen Fear," "The Weird Tailor," "Lucy Comes to Stay," and "Mannikins of Horror." Around these is woven a fifth story as framework— a medical administrator's visit to the asylum. Directed by veteran suspense man Roy Ward Baker, who, in the seventies, gained visibility with high-class horror pictures *(The Vampire Lovers, The Scars of Dracula, Vault of Horror,* and *And Now the Screaming Starts).*

Back to the Future   *Listed under Comedies.*

The Bad Seed   1956   (Warner)   *Black-and-White*
Director: Mervyn LeRoy
Starring: Nancy Kelly, Patty McCormack, Henry Jones, Eileen Heckart, Evelyn Varden, William Hopper, Paul Fix, Jesse White, Gage Clark, Joan Croydon, Frank Cady

Angelic Rhoda Penmark, an eight-year-old in blonde pigtails, is really a cunning murderess. A chilling horror tale of evil in contemporary suburbia. This cinematic shocker, scripted by John Lee Mahin, was taken from the novel by William March and the Broadway dramatization written by Maxwell Anderson. Nancy Kelly repeats her Broadway performance as Rhoda's mother. Patty McCormack stars as the bad seed. For Production Code purposes, when the film was first released an epilogue was affixed—in effect assuring the audience that "all's well; we're just kidding, folks." Music by Alex North. The property was dusted off for TV movie treatment in 1985; Blair Brown, Carrie Wells, and David Carradine starred in, respectively, the Kelly, McCormack, and Henry Jones roles.

Battlestar Galactica   1978   (MCA)   *Color*
Director: Richard A. Colla
Starring: Lorne Greene, Richard Hatch, Dirk Benedict, Maren Jensen, Ray Milland, John Colicos, Patrick Macnee, Lew Ayres, Jane Seymour, Laurette Spang, Terry Carter

Battlestar *Galactica* is remembered primarily as an initially successful (then precipitously unsuccessful) series of the 1978–79 television season. The series pilot, however, was given a theatrical release in Canada and abroad, then shown in theaters stateside in 1979. The film occurs in the seventh millennium, A.D. *Galactica* is the only surviving battlestar after an attack by savage half-human, half-robots called Cylons, pledged to achieve "the final annihilation of the life force known as man." Combatting these villains are Commander Adama (Lorne Greene), his son Apollo (Richard Hatch), and ace pilot Starbuck (Dirk Benedict). These heroes lead other *Galactica* survivors on a journey to find refuge on an unexplored planet named Earth. Lasers, fighter squadrons, and last minute rescues abound. John Dykstra, one of the men behind *Star Wars*, devised the special effects.

Blade Runner   1982   (Embassy)   *Color*
Director: Ridley Scott
Starring: Harrison Ford, Rutger Hauer, Sean Young, Edward James Olmos, William Sanderson, Daryl Hannah, Joe Turkel, Joanna Cassidy, Brion James

A revision of Philip K. Dick's novel, *Do Androids Dream of Electric Sheep?*, this violent, futuristic thriller welds science fiction to the private detective canon. Former Los Angeles policeman Harrison Ford is a blade runner (that is, special enforcer); his current assignment: track down and destroy renegade replicants (androids) who have revolted "off-world" (in outer space) and returned to Earth as murderers. Among the most lethal of these beings is Rutger Hauer—a powerful killing machine. Ridley Scott's follow-up to *Alien* is a masterpiece of production design; L.A. in the next century glistens in neon and slimy rain. Ford's character is a departure from the tongue-in-cheek heroes of his Lucas and Spielberg films; Hauer plays a repellent replicant; and a pre-*Splash* Daryl Hannah appears as a martial arts monstrosity in punk regalia. Sharp-eyed viewers will catch William Sanderson ("Newhart's" Larry) and Edward James Olmos ("Miami Vice's" Castillo) here, before TV fame claimed them. Script adaptation: Hampton Fancher and David Peoples.

Carrie   1976   (CBS)   *Color*
Director: Brian De Palma
Starring: Sissy Spacek, Piper Laurie, William Katt, Amy Irving, Nancy Allen, Betty Buckley, John Travolta, P. J. Soles, Priscilla Pointer

Carrie White (Sissy Spacek) is a mousy teenager who is a social outsider at Bates High School. Mrs. White (Piper Laurie) is a religious fanatic who constantly berates her daughter about the wages of sin. Browbeaten at home and considered a laughingstock by the student body, Carrie has nowhere to turn. But then she discovers that she has telekinetic powers. She can, for instance, make butcher knives whiz around the kitchen. When she is invited to the prom—as a cruel joke—by the senior class hero, Carrie unleashes her powers. The lobby displays for Brian De Palma's film were direct: "If you've got a taste for terror . . . take Carrie to the prom." *Carrie,* with a screenplay by Lawrence D. Cohen from Stephen King's novel, is marked by De Palma's brand of humor (mixing horror and hijinks), his clinical depiction of characters, and his shock effects (executed by editor Paul Hirsch). As the title character, Sissy Spacek received her first Oscar nomination. Jack Fisk, one of De Palma's art directors here, later married Spacek—and directed her in *Raggedy Man* and *Violets Are Blue.*

Clash of the Titans   1981   (MGM)   *Color*
Director: Desmond Davis
Starring: Harry Hamlin, Judi Bowker, Burgess Meredith, Maggie Smith, Ursula Andress, Claire Bloom, Sian Phillips, Flora Robson, Laurence Olivier, Jack Gwyllim, Donald Houston, Freda Jackson

Greek mythology is the source for this heroic fantasy-adventure. Perseus, the mortal son of Zeus, endeavors to win Princess Andromeda. True love is thrown off course when evil sea goddess Thetis unleashes a horde of monsters. The gods on Mount Olympus watch as Perseus battles Medusa; a two-headed wolf-dog; Calibos, the horned Lord of the Marsh; and other assorted horrors—devised by special effects expert Ray Harryhausen. The technician behind *Mighty Joe Young* and *Jason and the Argonauts* (to cite two out of a score of achievements), Harryhausen is the master of stop-motion processing—as distinct from the current popular computerized effects. Laurence Olivier's Zeus is implacable and merciless. Burgess Meredith plays Ammon, the chronicler of the gods. Beverly Cross wrote the script.

A Clockwork Orange   1971   (Warner)   *Color*
Director: Stanley Kubrick
Starring: Malcolm McDowell, Patrick Magee, Adrienne Corri, Anthony Sharp, Warren Clarke, Aubrey Morris, James Marcus, Michael Tarn, Godfrey Quigley, Michael Bates, Philip Stone, Sheila Raynor

Stanley Kubrick's near-future satire, culled from the novel by Anthony Burgess, is an expression of society's attitudes toward violence. Kubrick, as adapter and director, introduces Alex, "our humble narrator"—a schoolboy who engages in acts of "ultra-violence." Accompanied by his "droogs" (buddies), Alex stomps an old man into insensibility and rapes his wife—crooning "Singin' in the Rain" all the while. Later, Alex breaks into another home and kills a woman. Imprisoned for his crimes, the young man is subjected to the Ludovico treatment, a criminal deterrent involving a forced witnessing of violent movies. *A Clockwork Orange* documents the change resulting from the treatment: upon his release, docile Alex becomes a victim of his former victims. But there is one more twist before the tale ends. As the pivotal character, Malcolm McDowell is a scary antihero, his vocabulary dotted with the mod language Burgess created specially for his novel—a curious amalgam of English and Russian. *A Clockwork Orange* is as compelling as it is complex. However, owing to the intense depictions of brutality (including sexual brutality), viewers are sharply divided as to its artistic merits.

Close Encounters of the Third Kind   1977   (RCA)   ◆   *Color*
Director: Steven Spielberg
Starring: Richard Dreyfuss, François Truffaut, Teri Garr, Melinda Dillon, Cary Guffey,
Bob Balaban, Roberts Blossom

A close encounter of the third kind represents direct alien contact. That's what happens in the final moments of this Steven Spielberg feature. Mixing fantasy and science fiction, Spielberg begins his story in Muncie, Indiana, where a lineman (Richard Dreyfuss) for an electrical power utility has a vision he doesn't fully comprehend. People in other parts of the country soon become obsessed with the same vision—which deals somehow with a cone-shaped object. The lineman's intuition and research lead him to the conical Devil's Tower in Wyoming, the presumed landing site for a UFO. The director of photography credit (and the Academy Award) went to Vilmos Zsigmond, although other cinematographers contributed: John Alonzo, William Fraker, Laszlo Kovacs, and Douglas Slocombe. Douglas Trumbull is the wizard behind the film's special effects. The video version of *Close Encounters of the Third Kind* is subtitled *The Special Edition*— Spielberg's 1980 rerelease print, which deletes footage from the middle section and adds to the finale, including some interior scenes of the spacecraft.

Cocoon   1985   (CBS)   ◆   *Color*
Director: Ron Howard
Starring: Don Ameche, Wilford Brimley, Hume Cronyn, Brian Dennehy, Jack Gilford,
Steve Guttenberg, Maureen Stapleton, Jessica Tandy, Gwen Verdon, Herta Ware, Tahnee
Welch, Barret Oliver

A Florida-set contemporary fairy tale that became one of 1985's top-grossing films. A group of St. Petersburg retirees (Don Ameche, Wilford Brimley, and Hume Cronyn) regularly take dips in a private swimming pool. As the story unfolds, something new has been added to the pool—in the form of large pods—and the men find that their favorite swimming hole is now a kind of fountain of youth. The secret of their rejuvenation is somehow connected to the arrival in St. Petersburg of several strange tourists. Ron Howard's film is a comedy in the mode of his earlier *Splash* but seasoned with elements of Spielberg's extraterrestrial movies. The Tom Benedek screenplay is derived from a novel by David Saperstein. Steve Guttenberg is the most visible young character. Don Ameche as the breakdancing septuagenarian won a supporting actor Oscar. (Another winner: the visual effects team.) Appearing in small parts are two second-generation Hollywoodites: Tyrone Power, Jr., as Pillsbury, and Tahnee Welch, Raquel's daughter, as Kitty.

Damien—Omen II   1978   (CBS)   *Color*
Director: Don Taylor
Starring: William Holden, Lee Grant, Robert Foxworth, Lew Ayres, Sylvia Sidney, Jona
than Scott-Taylor, Lucas Donat, Elizabeth Shepherd, Leo McKern

This is the middle segment of the trilogy that began with *The Omen*. Little Damien, the Antichrist, is now thirteen. His foster parents are William Holden and Lee Grant. Damien's connection with the grisly events of the first installment are clouded in mystery, and *Omen II* records his diabolic adventures at boarding school. Once again, Damien unleashes his evil powers—and gory shock effects splatter across the screen. The script by Stanley Mann and Michael Hodges, realized by Don Taylor, contains some unexpected heroes and villains. Damien, though, is unmistakably hellish, and he is played with a vengeance by Jonathan Scott-Taylor. The *Omen* cycle ground to a halt in 1981 with *The Final Conflict*, wherein Sam Neill played Damien in manhood.

The Day the Earth Caught Fire   1962   (Thorn)   *Black-and-White*
Director: Val Guest
Starring: Edward Judd, Janet Munro, Leo McKern, Michael Goodliffe, Arthur Christiansen, Bernard Braden, Reginald Beckwith, Austin Trevor, Renée Asherson, Edward Underdown

Two simultaneous atomic detonations—one U.S., the other Soviet—have a horrific aftermath: earth is thrown off its axis. Wrenched from its orbit, the planet is sent hurtling toward the sun. This fire-in-the-sky thriller takes place principally in London, where a team of Fleet Street journalists led by Edward Judd and science editor Leo McKern report the story. In telling their almost plausible yarn, Wolf Mankowitz and Val Guest rely upon wit and intelligence. Guest, who also directed, is revered by many science fiction fans for his other top-grade horror fables—notably the first two films in the Quatermass series, known in America as *The Creeping Unknown* and *Enemy from Space*. Not for hardcore action lovers, *The Day the Earth Caught Fire* is very much dialogue-based; the film works slowly and thoughtfully to its suspenseful conclusion.

The Day the Earth Stood Still   1951   (CBS)   *Black-and-White*
Director: Robert Wise
Starring: Michael Rennie, Patricia Neal, Hugh Marlowe, Sam Jaffe, Billy Gray, Frances Bavier, Frank Conroy, Lock Martin, Carleton Young, Fay Roope, Edith Evanson, Robert Osterloh, Tyler McVey, James Seay

A flying saucer lands on the Mall in Washington, D.C. From the craft steps an alien named Klaatu, who, endowed with human form, has come on a mission of peace—but with this added message: If the nations of earth don't stop their atomic testing, then, for the safety of the universe, earth will be demolished. Accompanying Klaatu is Gort, a robot who is programmed to destroy the planet if anything untoward happens to his master. Based loosely on the Harry Bates short story, "Farewell to the Master," *The Day the Earth Stood Still* is regarded by many fans as a science fiction classic. Robert Wise and his scenarist, Edmund H. North, not only tell a fascinating story; they present profound characters. Michael Rennie, as Klaatu, gives the action its cohesion; one can truly believe in the superior intelligence of this nonviolent visitor. Bernard Herrmann composed the score.

Dead of Night   Great Britain 1945; U.S. 1946   (Thorn)   *Black-and-White*
Directors: Alberto Cavalcanti, Charles Crichton, Basil Dearden, Robert Hamer
Starring: Mervyn Johns, Roland Culver, Mary Merrall, Googie Withers, Frederick Valk, Antony Baird, Sally Ann Howes, Robert Wyndham, Judy Kelly, Miles Malleson, Michael Allan, Barbara Leake, Ralph Michael, Esme Percy, Basil Radford, Naunton Wayne, Michael Redgrave, Hartley Power

This horror anthology from Michael Balcon's Ealing Studios introduces five stories—all linked by a framework narration. Several people gather in a drawing room to recount their most frightening nightmares. The recollections range from the macabre to the fantastic, while the final unifying tale is an outright ghost story. The screenplay by John Baines and Angus Macphail, with additional dialogue by T. E. B. Clarke, is a compendium of original material and adaptations of E. F. Benson and H. G. Wells. (The Wells derivation, a comic sketch about two rival golfers, was originally dropped from American release prints.) The most memorable episode stars Michael Redgrave as a ventriloquist dominated by his dummy. The score is by Georges Auric, and Michael Relph did the production designs.

The Dead Zone   1983   (Paramount)   *Color*
Director: David Cronenberg
Starring: Christopher Walken, Brooke Adams, Tom Skerritt, Herbert Lom, Anthony Zerbe, Colleen Dewhurst, Martin Sheen, Nicholas Campbell, Jackie Burroughs

Johnny Smith wakes up from a five-year coma to discover that he has the gift of second sight. To predict someone's future, he needs only make fleeting physical contact. But his gift becomes a curse when Johnny is expected to cure mankind's ills, so he runs away. But his past catches up with him when a psychotic politician (Martin Sheen) leads America to the brink of nuclear holocaust. A faithful adaptation of the Stephen King best-seller, Jeffrey Boam's script embraces several themes: telepathy, murder, children in jeopardy, political assassination. Walken, whose credits range from *Annie Hall* to *Brainstorm* to his Oscar-winning performance in *The Deer Hunter,* is cast as Johnny Smith. Tautly directed by Canadian horrormeister David Cronenberg, the picture is further strengthened by the work of Brooke Adams, Tom Skerritt, and Herbert Lom.

Destination Moon   1950   (Nostalgia)   *Color*
Director: Irving Pichel
Starring: John Archer, Warner Anderson, Tom Powers, Dick Wesson, Erin O'Brien Moore

"Whoever conquers the moon will control the Earth." That principle guides the U.S. astronauts in this ambitious account of man's first lunar voyage. Producer George Pal's *Destination Moon* pioneered Hollywood's science fiction boom of the fifties and, in turn, inspired a host of imitations. Derived from Robert A. Heinlein's juvenile novel, *Rocket Ship Galileo,* the story turns on the launching of the spacecraft, the rescue of a crewman adrift in space, the arrival on the moon, and explorations on the sandy, cratered lunar surface. The special effects contributions, which were awarded a 1950 Oscar, paved the way for more sophisticated motion pictures in the genre. Integral components of George Pal's technical team were veteran set designer Ernst Fegté and illustrator Chesley Bonestell, whose intricate drawings were used as backdrops for the rocket models.

Don't Look Now   1973   (Paramount)   *Color*
Director: Nicolas Roeg
Starring: Julie Christie, Donald Sutherland, Hilary Mason, Clelia Matania, Massimo Serato

Omens of death in Venice hover in this adaptation of Daphne du Maurier's macabre short story. A young English couple (Donald Sutherland and Julie Christie) are grieving over the accidental drowning of their little daughter. Two elderly sisters with psychic faculties claim they are in touch with the dead girl. The husband, an art restorer, is psychic too, though unsure of his powers; he knows only that he doesn't trust the two sinister sisters. Augmented by Anthony Richmond's languid camera and the baroque vision of director Nicolas Roeg, himself a former cinematographer, *Don't Look Now* was Roeg's third feature (after the cult films *Performance* and *Walkabout*—and before *The Man Who Fell to Earth*). Roeg uses a splintered intercutting of past, present, and future to propel his tale, scripted by Allan Scott and Chris Bryant. The technique stands out predominantly in one scene of particular sexual frankness, trimmed in U.S. release prints in order to avoid an X-rating. Unlike most shockers which preceded it, *Don't Look Now* provides no catharsis in its final frames.

Dracula   1979   (MCA)   *Color*
Director: John Badham
Starring: Frank Langella, Sir Laurence Olivier, Donald Pleasence, Kate Nelligan, Trevor Eve, Janine Duvitski, Jan Francis, Tony Haygarth

Bram Stoker's 1897 Gothic classic has been the source for innumerable horror pictures—from the silent *Nosferatu* to Werner Herzog's 1979 remake and beyond. Vampires are probably filmmakers' and filmgoers' most beloved monsters, and none is more durable than the centuries-old Transylvanian count. This 1979 Anglo-American retelling, scripted by W. D. Richter and directed by John Badham, draws additional inspiration from the popular stage play of Hamilton Deane and John Balderston. Dracula is played by Frank Langella, who also performed the role on Broadway. The count arrives in London and stalks fair damsels; he clouds the mind of poor Renfield; he is pursued by Jonathan Harker and Dr. Van Helsing. This is a romantic rendition of the legend, embellished by Peter Murton's cinematography and John Williams's music—marred only by an ending which rather nakedly paves the way for a sequel. The film was a commercial disappointment though, so all plans for *Dracula II* were dashed.

The Empire Strikes Back   1980   (CBS)   ◆   *Color*
Director: Irvin Kershner
Starring: Mark Hamill, Harrison Ford, Carrie Fisher, Billy Dee Williams, Anthony Daniels, David Prowse, Frank Oz, Alec Guinness, Jeremy Bulloch, John Hollis, Jack Purvis, Des Webb, Julian Glover

The intergalactic drama continues in this second film of the George Lucas *Star Wars* trilogy (subtitled *Episode V*). Luke Skywalker, Han Solo, and Princess Leia—after the destruction of the Empire's Death Star—have set up a base on the ice planet Hoth. However, the Empire's vengeful minions discover the heroes' whereabouts and launch an all-out attack. As the Empire strikes back, Luke is given advanced instruction in the ways of the Force; his mentor is Yoda, a mystic who has been training Jedi knights for centuries. Meanwhile, Darth Vader returns with more black-hearted deeds—and a startling secret that will affect Luke. *The Empire Strikes Back* represents writer Leigh Brackett's last completed work; the first draft of the screenplay was completed only days before her death, and Lawrence Kasdan was brought in for revisions. It's another space adventure, with so much action there is barely time for a romantic subplot involving Han and Leia. Mark Hamill, Harrison Ford, and Carrie Fisher reanimate Luke, Han, and Leia. Among the new actors, the most commanding is Billy Dee Williams, playing Lando Calrissian, lord of the cloud city of Bespin. James Earl Jones and Clive Revill supply the voices for, respectively, Darth Vader and the Emperor. *The Empire Strikes Back* won Oscars for sound and special effects.

E.T., The Extraterrestrial   *Listed under Family Viewing/Children's.*

The Exorcist   1973   (Warner)   ◆   *Color*
Director: William Friedkin
Starring: Ellen Burstyn, Max von Sydow, Jason Miller, Linda Blair, Lee J. Cobb, Kitty Winn, Jack MacGowran

William Peter Blatty's world-famous demonic possession shocker was a hardcover and paperback phenomenon. The novel's central character is twelve-year-old Regan MacNeil. She and her movie-star mother have just moved to Georgetown, where suddenly the little girl's body is invaded by a demon. Regan's desperate mother, an agnostic, turns to a Jesuit psychiatrist and an elderly ascetic priest (and exorcist)—whose archaeological diggings in Iraq somehow unearthed the evil. For William Friedkin's film, Blatty himself did the adaptation (and was awarded an Oscar). With Owen Roizman at the camera, there are careful delineations of the novel's sensational aspects: Regan's bouts with possession include levitation, head-rotation, foul language, and masturbation with a crucifix. For most viewers, *The Exorcist* is a nerve-jangling shocker, featuring Linda Blair (Regan), Ellen Burstyn (her mother), Jason Miller (Father Damien Karras), Lee J. Cobb (a police lieutenant), and Max von Sydow (as the title character). The production earned nearly $90 million at the box office, which encouraged a spate of imitators—most of them dubbed horrors from Europe (*Beyond the Door, Beyond the Door II, The Tempter, Exorcist's Daughter, House of Exorcism*, ad infinitum). A direct, though thoroughly miscalculated, sequel was released in 1977: *Exorcist II: The Heretic.*

Fantastic Voyage   1966   (CBS)   *Color*
Director: Richard Fleischer
Starring: Stephen Boyd, Raquel Welch, Edmond O'Brien, Donald Pleasence, Arthur O'Connell, William Redfield, Arthur Kennedy, Jean Del Val, Barry Coe, Ken Scott, Shelby Grant

One of the most popular science fiction films of the sixties, *Fantastic Voyage* charts a rescue mission not into space but into the human body. A high-level Czech scientist with military secrets is shot by enemy agents and suffers brain damage. To save his life, a team of doctors (and a submarine) are miniaturized to bacteria size and injected into the scientist's bloodstream. On their voyage to the brain, the doctors pass through arteries and confront corpuscles—and discover that there is a traitor in their midst. The screenplay is credited to Harry Kleiner, although Isaac Asimov had a hand in its development. In an early role, before fame in "Hotel" and "Marcus Welby, M.D.," James Brolin plays a lab technician.

The Final Countdown   *Listed under War.*

Flash Gordon   1980   (MCA)   *Color*
Director: Mike Hodges
Starring: Sam J. Jones, Melody Anderson, Ornella Muti, Max von Sydow, Topol, Timothy Dalton, Brian Blessed, Peter Wyngarde, Mariangela Melato, John Osborne, Richard O'Brien, John Hallam, Philip Stone, Suzanne Danielle

In this update of the comic strip and the thirties serials filmed by Universal, Flash Gordon is a quarterback for the New York Jets and Dale Arden is a travel agent. When evil Emperor Ming, of the planet Mongo, casts hot hail on the earth's surface, Flash and Dale join oddball scientist Dr. Hans Zarkov in his rocket mission to Mongo.

Will they be able to defeat Ming and save the Earth? Indubitably! The spoofy script is by Lorenzo Semple, Jr., with additions by Michael Allin. (The original Flash was the creation of Alex Raymond.) In the ensemble: Sam J. Jones (Flash), Melody Anderson (Dale), Ornella Muti (Princess Aura), Max von Sydow (Ming the Merciless), Topol (Dr. Zarkov), Timothy Dalton (Prince Barin), Brian Blessed (Prince Vultan), Mariangela Melato (Kala), and Peter Wyngarde (Klytus, the Emperor's robotlike henchman). Outstanding contributions are made by cinematographer Gil Taylor and Danilo Donati, the creator of the set and costume designs. The song score was composed and performed by Queen.

Halloween   1978   (Media)   *Color*

Director: *John Carpenter*
Starring: *Donald Pleasence, Jamie Lee Curtis, Nancy Loomis, P. J. Soles, Charles Cyphers, Kyle Richards, Brian Andrews, John Michael Graham, Nancy Stephens, Tony Moran*

For most fright film enthusiasts, *Halloween* is probably the definitive slasher movie. The plot is bookended by two Halloween nights in Haddonfield, Illinois—the first, in 1963, when six-year-old Michael Myers stabs his sister to death; the second, in 1978, when Michael escapes from a mental institution to start killing in his hometown again. As the children of Haddonfield conclude their trick-or-treating, Michael—wearing a fright mask—stalks several high school girls who are babysitting. John Carpenter's shocker, from his screenplay with Debra Hill, is terrifying. Jamie Lee Curtis stars as the smartest of Michael's would-be victims; Donald Pleasence is the psychiatrist. Sequel: *Halloween II*. How many other post-*Halloween*, calendar-derived horror movies can you name? Here's a start: *My Bloody Valentine; Friday the 13th* (I through *VI*); *April Fool's Day; Mother's Day; New Year's Evil; Don't Open Till Christmas; Silent Night, Deadly Night; The Day After Halloween.*

Jaws   1975   (MCA)   ◆   *Color*

Director: *Steven Spielberg*
Starring: *Roy Scheider, Robert Shaw, Richard Dreyfuss, Lorraine Gary, Murray Hamilton, Jeffrey Kramer, Susan Backlinie, Carl Gottlieb, Peter Benchley*

This triple-Oscar winner—for sound, John Williams's score, and Verna Field's editing—ranks, as of this writing, fifth on the list of all-time moneymakers (behind *E.T., The Extraterrestrial* and the *Star Wars* trilogy). Peter Benchley's blockbuster novel tells of the treacherous waters off the New England shore—where the citizens of Amity are plagued by shark attacks. In Steven Spielberg's movie realization, scripted by Benchley and Carl Gottlieb, three heroes go out after the man-eater: Brody (Roy Scheider), Amity's police chief, ichthyologist Roy Hooper (Richard Dreyfuss), and Quint (Robert Shaw), a battered sailor. The screenplay mixes character comedy with scares. Roy Scheider repeated his role for *Jaws 2* (1978), but an entirely new band of players tackled the contrivances of *Jaws 3-D* (1983).

Logan's Run   1976   (MGM)   *Color*

Director: *Michael Anderson*
Starring: *Michael York, Jenny Agutter, Richard Jordan, Roscoe Lee Browne, Farrah Fawcett-Majors, Peter Ustinov, Michael Anderson, Jr.*

The advertising slogan ran: "Welcome to the 23rd century. The perfect world of total pleasure." Perfect, that is, until you reach the age of thirty—then you're extinguished. That's the premise behind this futuristic fantasy, screenwritten by David Zelag Goodman from William F. Nolan and George Clayton Johnson's novel. Logan (Michael York) is a sandman (policeman) in the hedonistic crystal City of Domes. As his thirtieth birthday is rapidly approaching, Logan decides to flee the city for a purported utopia in the hinterlands—called Sanctuary. Gadgetry, dazzling sets, and state-of-the-art special effects provide the background for *Logan's Run*. Under the same title, it became a one-season television series, starring Gregory Harrison as Logan.

The Omen   1976   (CBS)   ◆   *Color*
Director: Richard Donner
Starring: Gregory Peck, Lee Remick, David Warner, Billie Whitelaw, Harvey Stephens, Leo McKern, Patrick Troughton, Martin Benson, Holly Palance, Anthony Nicholls

Robert Thorn (Gregory Peck) is appointed U.S. ambassador to Great Britain. He, his wife (Lee Remick), and their adopted son Damien (Harvey Stephens) move to an old mansion near London—where tragedy strikes again and again. This supernatural shocker by David Seltzer revolves around little Damien, who, one learns, is the Antichrist predicted in the Book of Revelation: the only begotten son of Satan. *The Omen* joins a parade of movies in recent years to have drawn inspiration from diabolism. Bloodthirsty Damien—smiling beatifically all the while—inspires a suicide by hanging, a graphic impalement, and an ingenious decapitation. (John Richardson is the creator behind these and other special effects.) Richard Donner, later responsible for *Superman*, *Ladyhawke*, and *The Goonies*, is the director. Jerry Goldsmith won an Oscar for his score. Sequels: *Damien—Omen II* (1978) and *The Final Conflict* (1981).

On the Beach   1959   (CBS)   *Black-and-White*
Director: Stanley Kramer
Starring: Gregory Peck, Ava Gardner, Fred Astaire, Anthony Perkins, Donna Anderson, John Tate, Lola Brooks, Lou Vernon, Guy Doleman, Ken Wayne, John Meillon

Radioactive fallout from a nuclear bomb has devastated most of the globe's population. Australia is one of the few spots yet untouched by the radioactive cloud. But even for those survivors death is inexorable. Awaiting the final hour are Dwight Towers (Gregory Peck), a submarine commander; Moira Davidson (Ava Gardner), his mistress; a young married couple (Anthony Perkins and Donna Anderson); and Julian Osborn (Fred Astaire), a race-car driver. Novelist Nevil Shute's antiwar message makes for a wrenching movie drama; the screenplay is by John Paxton and James Lee Barrett. Stanley Kramer directed. Most frightening sequence: the submarine crew's arrival in San Francisco to discover a depopulated ghost city.

Outland   1981   (Warner)   *Color*
Director: Peter Hyams
Starring: Sean Connery, Peter Boyle, Frances Sternhagen, James B. Sikking, Kika Markham, Clarke Peters, John Ratzenberger

A space-age sheriff (Sean Connery) is the hero of this futuristic chiller written and directed by Peter Hyams. The story unfolds in the twenty-first century on the third moon of Jupiter, where the lawman must confront professional hitmen hired by a corrupt mining company. Hyams may very well have conceived his film as *High Noon in Outer Space,* with Connery in the Gary Cooper part. In any case, *Outland* is an imaginative premise, given spark by the director's rapid pacing, his star's charisma, and the appearance of Frances Sternhagen as a grumpy but helpful doctor.

Planet of the Apes   1968   (Playhouse Video)   ◆   *Color*
Director: Franklin J. Schaffner
Starring: Charlton Heston, Roddy McDowall, Kim Hunter, Maurice Evans, James Whitmore, James Daly, Linda Harrison

In this science fiction movie, Charlton Heston stars as the leader of a team of astronauts who traverse a time warp and crash on a distant planet where apes are masters and humans are slaves. Loosely based on Pierre Boulle's novel of social satire, *Planet of the Apes* dramatizes the astronauts' rude induction into the simian society. In this civilization, orangutans are the ruling class and gorillas are members of the military. A kindhearted chimpanzee named Galen (played under heavy makeup by Roddy McDowall) befriends the newcomers. Rod Serling and Michael Wilson wrote the script; Franklin Schaffner directed. An Academy Award went to John Chambers for his makeup designs. There were four big-screen sequels (*Beneath . . . , Escape from . . . , Conquest of . . . ,* and *Battle for . . .*), then, for TV, a live-action series (1974), followed by a cartoon series (1975).

Poltergeist   1982   (MGM)   *Color*
Director: Tobe Hooper
Starring: JoBeth Williams, Craig T. Nelson, Beatrice Straight, Dominique Dunne, Oliver Robins, Heather O'Rourke, Zelda Rubinstein, James Karen

Richard Edlund's special effects highlight this haunted house melodrama. Though basically an exercise in terror, the film provides moments of humor and warmth. A California suburban community has been erected over a cemetery—and the orderly life of one family is shattered when supernatural forces from the world beyond invade their home. The malevolence is released, through the television set, by the family's youngest member (Heather O'Rourke), a five-year-old blonde cherub who announces "They're here!" She is then whisked away into another dimension by the angry spirits. Produced by Steven Spielberg from his script with Michael Grais and Mark Victor, *Poltergeist* is a chiller built on the theme of a child's nightmare. Directed by Tobe Hooper (*The Texas Chainsaw Massacre, Eaten Alive, Salem's Lot, The Funhouse,* and *Lifeforce*). Sequel: *Poltergeist II: The Other Side* (1986).

Return of the Jedi   1983   (CBS)   *Color*
Director: Richard Marquand
Starring: Mark Hamill, Harrison Ford, Carrie Fisher, Billy Dee Williams, Anthony Daniels, David Prowse, Kenny Baker, Peter Mayhew, Frank Oz, Denis Lawson, Ian McDiarmid, Alec Guinness

Film three (and Episode VI) in the *Star Wars* saga, *Return of the Jedi* is the climax of the Luke Skywalker story. Here Luke reunites with Han and Leia and has his final confrontation with Darth Vader. Other highlights include Jabba the Hutt, the teddy bear–like Ewoks, and an airborne ride through a redwood frest. By now, Mark Hamill,

Harrison Ford, and Carrie Fisher are secure within their roles—and their performances are matched by Billy Dee Williams (Lando) and, under heavy disguise, Anthony Daniels (C-3PO), Kenny Baker (R2-D2), and Peter Mayhew (Chewbacca). The director of this installment, Richard Marquand, is also responsible for *The Legacy, Eye of the Needle,* and *Jagged Edge.* Returning as screenwriter is Lawrence Kasdan, this time abetted by George Lucas.

The Road Warrior   Australia 1981; U.S. 1982   (Warner)   *Color*
Director: George Miller
Starring: Mel Gibson, Bruce Spence, Vernon Wells, Mike Preston, Virginia Hay, Emil Minty, Kjell Nilsson

Known throughout most of the world as *Mad Max II*, this action-packed and emphatically violent futuristic adventure continues the exploits of Max (Mel Gibson), now a dispirited lone wolf wandering about post-Apocalypse Australia. Fuel is in short supply, and savage bikers roam the land in a pillaging, murderous spree. Reluctantly, Max joins forces with a small band of homesteaders and helps them annihilate the supervillains. The script—by Terry Hayes, Brian Hannant, and director George Miller—and the relentless pacing turn *The Road Warrior* into a mythic extravaganza. *The Road Warrior* built a mainstream following that rescued the original film, *Mad Max*, from obscurity in America, then led to a follow-up: *Mad Max: Beyond Thunderdome* (1985).

Rodan   1957   (Vestron)   *Color*
Director: Inoshiro Honda
Starring: Kenji Sawara, Yumi Shirakawa, Akihiko Hirato, Ako Kobori

Another production of Japan's Toho Studios, this science-fiction blockbuster is a thinly veiled remake of *Godzilla, King of the Monsters*—except this time the creature can fly. Rodan is a giant pterodactyl with a wingspread exceeding 200 feet. Watch out, Tokyo! *Rodan*, directed by horror movie veteran Inoshiro Honda *(Godzilla, Mothra)*, ascends from a screenplay by Tameshi Kimura and Takeo Murata and a story by Takashi Kuronuma. Isamu Ashida is the director of photography, and Eiji Tsuburaya is credited with the special effects. Dubbed in English.

Rosemary's Baby   1968   (Paramount)   ◆   *Color*
Director: Roman Polanski
Starring: Mia Farrow, John Cassavetes, Ruth Gordon, Sidney Blackmer, Ralph Bellamy, Maurice Evans, Elisha Cook, Jr., Patsy Kelly, Angela Dorian, Charles Grodin

Based on Ira Levin's horror novel, Roman Polanski's screen adaptation casts Mia Farrow and John Cassavetes as a young New York married couple. Rosemary and Guy have just moved into a cavernous Central Park West apartment complex. Rosemary, who is pregnant, has misgivings about some of the other tenants. Before long she learns that the building houses a coven of witches—and that she, her actor-husband, and their unborn child are in peril. Polanski's exercise in Gothic melodrama lifts most of Levin's original dialogue, then adds an element of spookiness that is the director's own. Ruth Gordon, in her best supporting Oscar role, plays a witch. *Rosemary's Baby* represents an early and auspicious credit for cinematographer William A. Fraker, who had just shot *The Fox* and went on to *Monte Walsh* (which he also directed), *Heaven Can Wait*, and *American Hot Wax*. Sequel: "Look What's Happened to Rosemary's Baby," a 1976 TV movie subsequently retitled "Rosemary's Baby II."

Star Trek: The Motion Picture   1979   (Paramount)   *Color*
Director: Robert Wise
Starring: William Shatner, Leonard Nimoy, DeForest Kelley, Stephen Collins, Persis Khambatta, James Doohan, Nichelle Nichols, Walter Koenig, George Takei, Majel Barrett, Grace Lee Whitney, Mark Lenard

The starship *Enterprise*, of three-season (1966–69) television fame, cruised onto the motion picture screen in this $40 million space spectacular. Reuniting most of the TV cast, the galactic adventure—penned by Harold Livingstone and Alan Dean Foster— tells of an alien force entering Federation territory and heading for Earth. Only one ship can stop the enemy. So Captain James T. Kirk (William Shatner) resumes command of the *Enterprise* and reassembles the crew: Mr. Spock (Leonard Nimoy), Dr. Leonard McCoy (DeForest Kelley), Sulu (George Takei), Uhura (Nichelle Nichols), Ensign Pavel Chekov (Walter Koenig), Engineer Montgomery Scott (James Doohan), et al.

Star Trek: The Wrath of Khan   1982   (Paramount)   *Color*
Director: Nicholas Meyer
Starring: William Shatner, Leonard Nimoy, DeForest Kelley, James Doohan, Walter Koenig, George Takei, Nichelle Nichols, Bibi Besch, Merritt Butrick, Paul Winfield, Kirstie Allen, Ike Eisenmann, John Vargas, Ricardo Montalban

Deep in the twenty-third century, Jim Kirk and the men and women of the starship *Enterprise* continue their explorations "where no man has gone before." This saga is a sequel to the TV series episode "Space Seed." In that installment, the evil genius Khan (Ricardo Montalban) was banished to a distant planet. But now he's back to destroy the *Enterprise* crew. Most viewers agree that this sequel is livelier than the 1979 feature—thanks to the screenplay of Jack B. Sowards and the direction by Nicholas Meyer (author of *The Seven-Per-Cent Solution* and director-screenwriter of *Time After Time*). The special visual effects were produced by Lucasfilm's Industrial Light & Magic.

Star Trek III: The Search for Spock   1984   (Paramount)   *Color*
Director: Leonard Nimoy
Starring: William Shatner, Leonard Nimoy, DeForest Kelley, James Doohan, Walter Koenig, George Takei, Nichelle Nichols, Christopher Lloyd, Robin Curtis, Merritt Butrick, James B. Sikking, Phil Morris, Scott McGinnis, John Larroquette, Robert Hooks, Joe W. Davis, Dame Judith Anderson

Round three in the big screen *Star Trek* cycle. At the end of Episode II, Mr. Spock (Leonard Nimoy) was killed. As this feature, directed by Nimoy, begins, Kirk and the *Enterprise* crew fly to the Genesis planet and from there to Vulcan, Spock's home, where they endeavor to protect their departed friend's soul. In villainous pursuit are the Klingons, a race of aliens. *The Search for Spock* was written by producer Harve Bennett. And the exploits continue: *Star Trek IV*, subtitled *The Voyage Home*, also directed by Nimoy, is set for release in 1987.

Star Wars   1977   (CBS)   ◆   *Color*
Director: George Lucas
Starring: Mark Hamill, Harrison Ford, Carrie Fisher, Peter Cushing, Alec Guinness, Anthony Daniels, Kenny Baker, David Prowse, Peter Mayhew

Star Wars is, after *E.T.*, the biggest box-office attraction in cinema history. It's not merely a movie legend, but a cultural phenomenon which captured the imagination of the entire world. The three films and their related products (T-shirts, board games, hot cocoa mugs) have grossed over a billion dollars. The saga began here with the story of interplanetary hero Luke Skywalker (Mark Hamill); rogue pilot Han Solo (Harrison Ford); volatile Princess Leia Organa (Carrie Fisher); Obi-Wan Kenobi (Alec Guinness), last of the Jedi knights and instructor in the ancient ways of the Force; and Darth Vader (David Prowse, with the voice of James Earl Jones), malignant Dark Lord of the Sith. Here, too, are the androids C-3PO and R2-D2 and that furry giant, Chewbacca the Wookie. Seven Academy Awards: music score (John Williams), costume design (John Mollo), sound, editing, visual effects, and a special Oscar to Benjamin Burtt, Jr., for his creation of the alien creatures and robot voices. The emblems of good and evil meet again in *The Empire Strikes Back* (1980) and *Return of the Jedi* (1983).

Starman 1984 (RCA) *Color*
Director: John Carpenter
Starring: Jeff Bridges, Karen Allen, Charles Martin Smith, Richard Jaeckel, Robert Phalen, Tony Edwards, John Walter Davis, Ted White, Dirk Blocker, M. C. Gainey, Sean Faro

After landing in Wisconsin one starry night, an extraterrestrial traveler (Jeff Bridges) assumes the shape of Jenny Hayden's dead husband. With a rudimentary knowledge of English, the starman forces Jenny (Karen Allen) to accompany him to meet a return satellite. Along the way, the alien develops a passion for Jenny, Dutch apple pie, and automotive transportation. *Starman* is appealing thanks to its lowkey humor and performances. This unemphatic "message" film achieved notoriety before its production because Columbia Pictures purchased Bruce A. Evans and Raynold Gideon's script in preference to *E.T., The Extraterrestrial*. A television series adaptation debuted in 1986, starring Robert Hays as the starman.

Superman 1978 (Warner) *Color*
Director: Richard Donner
Starring: Marlon Brando, Gene Hackman, Christopher Reeve, Ned Beatty, Jackie Cooper, Jeff East, Glenn Ford, Trevor Howard, Margot Kidder, Marc McClure, Phyllis Thaxter, Susannah York

The caped legend of comic books, radio, and TV soars onto the screen. Not for the first time, however. There were movie serials in 1948 and 1950 and a low-budget feature, *Superman and the Mole Men*, in 1951. In this lavish 1978 production, Christopher Reeve stars as the Man of Steel. The script by Mario Puzo, David Newman, Leslie Newman, and Robert Benton traces the hero's origins on the planet Krypton, where he was the son of Jor-El (Marlon Brando) and Lara (Susannah York). Invested with supernatural powers, the little boy arrives on Earth and is adopted by a Smallville, Kansas, farm couple—the Kents (Glenn Ford and Phyllis Thaxter), who dub their stepchild Clark. And the saga continues to Metropolis for adventures with the *Daily Planet* staff—editor Perry White (Jackie Cooper), newshound Lois Lane (Margot Kidder), and cub reporter Jimmy Olson (Marc McClure)—and mastervillain Lex Luthor (Gene Hackman) and his henchman Otis (Ned Beatty). *Superman* is an impeccable technical achievement from director Richard Donner, production designer John Barry, and cinematographer Geoffrey Unsworth (his last completed film). This initial installment in the reactivated series amassed $83 million in box-office rentals.

Superman II   Great Britain 1980; U.S. 1981   (Warner)   *Color*
Director: Richard Lester
Starring: Gene Hackman, Christopher Reeve, Ned Beatty, Jackie Cooper, Sarah Douglas,
Clifton James, Margot Kidder, E. G. Marshall, Marc McClure, Jack O'Halloran, Valerie
Perrine, Terence Stamp, Susannah York

It all began with a comic book and a syndicated strip created in the late thirties by two teenagers—writer Jerry Siegel and artist Joe Shuster. From there to radio, movie cartoons and live-action serials, the long-running television series starring George Reeves, and Saturday morning cartoon programs. Then in 1978 came *Superman—the Movie* and the rest, including, to date, three sequels, is history. Part II reassembles most of the cast of Part I. Herein Superman/Clark Kent falls in love with Lois Lane, faces a rematch with Lex Luthor, and meets a new team of arch-criminals: three renegades from the planet Krypton (Terence Stamp, Sarah Douglas, Jack O'Halloran) who overcome the hero with strength-ebbing Kryptonite, then proceed to destroy downtown Metropolis. This time the screenplay is credited to Mario Puzo, David Newman, and Leslie Newman—and Richard Lester is in the director's chair.

Them!   1954   (Warner)   *Black-and-White*
Director: Gordon Douglas
Starring: James Whitmore, Edmund Gwenn, Joan Weldon, James Arness, Onslow Stevens,
Sean McClory, Chris Drake, Sandy Descher, Fess Parker, Olin Howlin

In this science fiction movie, twelve-foot-high killer ants, mutated by atomic radiation, have bred in the New Mexico desert near Alamogordo. Their size is formidable and their touch, by way of injections of formic acid, is lethal. After reducing the human population of the desert, they head to Southern California. In hot pursuit are a team of soldiers (led by James Whitmore) and scientists (presided over by entomologist Edmund Gwenn). The chase leads to Los Angeles, where the giant ants have taken residence in the sewers. *Them!* is scripted by Ted Sherdeman from a story by George Worthing Yates; director Gordon Douglas makes the terror credible—abetted by Bronislau Kaper's score and the cinematography of Sid Hickox.

The Thing from Another World   1951   (RKO;   *Black-and-White*
      Nostalgia; VidAm; King of Video)
Director: Christian Nyby
Starring: Margaret Sheridan, Kenneth Tobey, Robert Cornthwaite, Douglas Spencer, James
Young, Dewey Martin, Robert Nichols, William Self, Eduard Franz, Sally Creighton,
James Arness

In the fifties, *The Thing . . .* was a major achievement in the cinema of the fantastic. At a U.S. research outpost in the Arctic, an expedition team frees a space traveler from his permafrost grave and takes him back to their headquarters. When the alien is accidentally thawed, he becomes a ferocious, unstoppable killing machine. Screenwriter Charles Lederer's inspiration for this amalgam of horror and science fiction is the John W. Campbell, Jr., short story, "Who Goes There?" Christian Nyby is credited with the direction, though it's widely speculated that Howard Hawks, who produced, or Orson Welles was the actual guiding force. (The film is accentuated by Hawksian overlapping dialogue and rapid-fire delivery; Russell Harlan's shadowy, atmospheric cinematography certainly suggests Welles.) James Arness is cast as the giant humanoid alien; but he doesn't get many close-ups and has no lines to speak. Remade in 1982 by John Carpenter.

The Time Machine   1960   (MGM)   ◆   *Color*
Director: George Pal
Starring: Rod Taylor, Yvette Mimieux, Alan Young, Sebastian Cabot, Tom Helmore, Whit Bissell, Doris Lloyd

In this time-travel fantasy, a young Victorian scientist (Rod Taylor) constructs a machine and is hurtled through time and space to the year 802701. The future, at least that far in the future, is not a pleasant place. The inventor becomes involved with two tribal factions: the Eloi, slaves who live under a decaying dome, and the Morlocks, shaggy cannibals who are now the rulers of civilization. A comic-book style adaptation of the H. G. Wells novel, *The Time Machine*—directed by George Pal from David Duncan's screenplay—is especially appropriate for children. Gene Warren and Tim Barr's special effects were honored by the Academy.

2001: A Space Odyssey   1968   (MGM)   ◆   *Color*
Director: Stanley Kubrick
Starring: Keir Dullea, Gary Lockwood, William Sylvester, Daniel Richter, Leonard Rossiter, Robert Beatty, Margaret Tyzack

Man's origins, his destiny, and the cyclical nature of life itself are the themes of this classic science fiction essay from Stanley Kubrick. Written by Kubrick and Arthur C. Clarke, whose story "The Sentinel" provided inspiration, *2001: A Space Odyssey* centers around the voyage of the space ship *Discovery*. Traveling on a half-billion-mile journey to Jupiter are astronauts David Bowman (Keir Dullea) and Frank Poole (Gary Lockwood). A HAL 9000 computer (voice by Douglas Rain) is in overall control of the vessel—and, after malfunctioning, it becomes irrational, marooning Poole in space and battling to the death with Bowman. Geoffrey Unsworth is the principal photographer, although some work was contributed by John Alcott. Oscars went to the special effects supervisors. Sequel: *2010*, released in 1984.

2010   1984   (MGM)   *Color*
Director: Peter Hyams
Starring: Roy Scheider, John Lithgow, Helen Mirren, Bob Balaban, Keir Dullea, Douglas Rain, Madolyn Smith, Dana Elcar, Tallesin Jaffe, James McEachin, Mary Jo Deschanel

2010 is the long-awaited sequel to Stanley Kubrick's *2001: A Space Odyssey*. Scientist Heywood Floyd (Roy Scheider) and cosmonaut Tanya Kirbuk (Helen Mirren) lead a joint U.S.-Soviet mission to locate the spacecraft *Discovery* and its crew. This latest probe seeks to clarify the mystery of the monolith and the malfunctioning of HAL (again given voice by Douglas Rain). David Bowman (Keir Dullea) returns with the message that "Something wonderful" will happen. In the film's climactic moments it does. Written and directed by Peter Hyams, from the Arthur C. Clarke novel, *2010*.

West World   1973   (MGM)   *Color*
Director: Michael Crichton
Starring: Yul Brynner, Richard Benjamin, James Brolin, Norman Bartold, Alan Oppenheimer, Victoria Shaw, Steve Franken, Mike Mikkler

A vast amusement center called Delos is the setting for this science fiction adventure. Visitors to Delos may choose among three holiday resorts—RomanWorld, MedievalWorld, or WestWorld—where, for a thousand dollars a day, they can live out their dreams of heroism, sexual abandon, or any other human desire. All three sites are totally computerized and served by humanoid robots. Delos is a fantasy world, but when the West World gunslinger robot (played by Yul Brynner) malfunctions and turns into a killing machine, Peter Martin (Richard Benjamin) and John Blane (James Brolin) are among those vacationers caught in the mêlée. Written and directed with consummate attention to detail by Michael Crichton, this feature represented the filmmaker's big-screen debut; he subsequently scripted and directed *Coma, The Great Train Robbery, Looker,* and *Runaway. FutureWorld,* realized by Richard T. Heffron in 1976, portrayed Delos a few years after the massacre recounted in *WestWorld.*

When a Stranger Calls   1979   (RCA)   *Color*
Director: Fred Walton
Starring: Charles Durning, Carol Kane, Colleen Dewhurst, Tony Beckley, Rachel Roberts, Ron O'Neal

Coscenarists Steve Feke and Fred Walton created a twenty-minute short called *The Sitter.* They shopped it with various studios in hopes of obtaining financing for an expanded, feature-length version. *When a Stranger Calls,* directed by Walton, is the result. A maniac-on-the-loose movie, it starts with a nightmarish premise: a babysitter (Carol Kane) receives eerie phone calls from a killer (Tony Beckley), realizing almost too late that he is in the house with her. She is rescued by a fast-thinking policeman (Charles Durning), but the terror starts again seven years later when the madman escapes from an asylum. To forewarn the squeamish: there is gore in this picture, but most scenes present the after-the-fact traces of violence. The writers have gone for tension rather than shock effects.

When Worlds Collide   1951   (Paramount)   ◆   *Color*
Director: Rudolph Maté
Starring: Richard Derr, Barbara Rush, Peter Hanson, Larry Keating, Judith Ames, John Hoyt, Mary Murphy, Laura Elliot, Stephen Chase, Sandro Giglio, Frank Cady, Hayden Rorke

The Earth's final hours are depicted in this apocalyptic thriller. Bellus, a runaway planet, is on a collision course with Earth. Scientists rush to complete a spaceship which will take forty passengers to Zyra, another planet, before the impact occurs. An Academy Award went to Gordon Jennings for his special effects. (Producer George Pal won in the same category a year earlier for *Destination Moon.*) Among the special visuals is the destruction of New York by a tidal wave. *When Worlds Collide* was adapted by Sidney Boehm from the novel by Edwin Balmer and Philip Wylie. John F. Seitz and W. Howard Greene shared the cinematography, and Rudolph Maté—a former cinematographer himself—was the director.

Musicals

All That Jazz   1979   (CBS)   *Color*
Director: Bob Fosse
Starring: Roy Scheider, Jessica Lange, Ann Reinking, Leland Palmer, Ben Vereen, Cliff Gorman, Erzsebet Foldi, Sandahl Bergman, John Lithgow, Deborah Geffner

The critical acclaim for *Cabaret* and the commendable results of *Lenny* seemed to raise viewers' expectations of Bob Fosse to unrealistic heights. Thus many viewers are still radically divided on *All That Jazz*. The musical drama is a semiautobiographical analysis of Fosse's alter ego, Joe Gideon (Roy Scheider). Joe, a moviemaker and Broadway director-choreographer, is at work on a stage musical; shooting a film about Lenny Bruce; marching in an endless parade of colleagues, lovers, and ex-wives. Chain-smoking, pill-popping Joe ultimately has a near-fatal heart attack, then bypass surgery. Not the traditional movie musical. But a colorful production, stunning dances, and Roy Scheider's performance hold it together. This very Felliniesque film was shot by Fellini's cinematographer Giuseppe Rotunno.

An American in Paris   1951   (MGM)   *Color*
Director: Vincente Minnelli
Starring: Gene Kelly, Leslie Caron, Oscar Levant, Georges Guétary, Nina Foch

This ambitious MGM musical was lauded in its heyday as revolutionary. (Vincente Minnelli and producer Arthur Freed inserted a twenty-minute ballet at the climax of *An American in Paris*—a gamble for a mass-market Hollywood production; but the gamble paid off handsomely.) Alan Jay Lerner's love triangle plot is the loose framework: ex-GI Kelly remains in Paris after World War II and falls in love with Caron, who is already engaged to Guétary; Kelly himself is pursued by wealthy patroness Foch. But, of course, the heart and soul of the picture are the dances, choreographed by Kelly, and the George and Ira Gershwin score. Among the songs: "I Got Rhythm," "Embraceable You," " 's Wonderful," "Nice Work If You Can Get It," "Our Love Is Here to Stay," and "I'll Build a Stairway to Paradise" (lyrics by Ray Goetz and Buddy DeSylva). The picture won six Oscars, including one for best film of the year and one for Lerner's story and screenplay. Also singled out were the cinematography, art direction/set decoration, costume design, and musical scoring. Additionally, the Academy voted a special career award to Kelly "in appreciation of his versatility as an actor, singer, director and dancer, and specifically for his brilliant achievements in the art of choreography on film."

Auntie Mame   1958   (Warner)   *Color*
Director: Morton DaCosta
Starring: Rosalind Russell, Forrest Tucker, Coral Browne, Fred Clark, Roger Smith, Patric Knowles, Peggy Cass, Jan Handzlik, Joanna Barnes, Pippa Scott, Lee Patrick, Willard Waterman, Connie Gilchrist

"Life is a banquet, and most poor suckers are starving to death." Mame Dennis's motto is a rallying cry for the perpetually young at heart. One who benefits the most from Mame's tutelage is her little nephew Patrick, who becomes her ward, and for the next twenty-odd years, her escort, confidant, and partner. The screenplay by Betty Comden and Adolph Green was adapted from Jerome Lawrence and Robert E. Lee's Broadway hit which, in turn, was derived from the Patrick Dennis novel. These incarnations eventually evolved into *Mame*, Jerry Herman's musical—and the film version thereof. Rosalind Russell, who had enacted the nonmusical Auntie on stage, reprises the performance and reconfirms her screen status as the quintessential breezy, devil-may-care sophisticate. Peggy Cass, Agnes Gooch on Broadway too, also shines. Another special performance: Coral Browne as venomous Vera Charles. Watch for character actress Margaret Dumont, the Marx Brothers's favorite foil, in a quick bit as a noblewoman.

The B and Wagon   1953   (MGM)   *Color*
Director: Vincente Minnelli
Starring: Fred Astaire, Cyd Charisse, Oscar Levant, Nanette Fabray, Jack Buchanan, James Mitchell, Robert Gist

One of the crowning achievements from the golden years of the MGM musical. Fred Astaire stars as a legendary song-and-dance man who returns to the stage in a production that goes more awry with every rehearsal—a musical morality play drawn from the Faust legend. Oscar Levant, Nanette Fabray, and Cyd Charisse are his colleagues and fellow sufferers; Jack Buchanan plays the arty director whose incessant bright ideas quite literally stop the show. The genius of Astaire and Minnelli is front and center, but there are plenty of opportunities for all the performers to make the most of Betty Comden and Adolph Green's screenplay. The Howard Dietz-Arthur Schwartz tunes include "By Myself," "Shine on Your Shoes," "Dancing in the Dark," "Louisiana Hayride," and the landmark "That's Entertainment."

Bells Are Ringing   1969   (MGM)   *Color*
Director: Vincente Minnelli
Starring: Judy Holliday, Dean Martin, Fred Clark, Eddie Foy, Jr., Jean Stapleton, Ruth Storey, Frank Gorshin, Gerry Mulligan

Bells Are Ringing represents Judy Holliday's last screen performance. The quintessential dumb blonde appears as an answering-service operator who gets involved in her clients' lives. One client to whom she provides wake-up calls is songwrite Dean Martin. When they meet face-to-face, love blooms. So do the Jule Styne-Betty Comden-Adolph Green songs: "Just in Time," "The Party's Over," "Drop That Name," "Long Before I Knew You," and—most melodious—"I'm Going Back to the Bonjour Tristesse Brassiere Company." Repeating her Broadway performance, Holliday is fresh and funny. Martin costars as the songsmith stumped for inspiration. Jean Stapleton, a decade before Edith Bunker made her a household name, plays the owner of the answering service. In the decade following *Bells Are Ringing*, director Vincente Minnelli concentrated on dramas—returning to the movie musical only one more time before the close of his career: *On a Clear Day You Can See Forever* (1970).

Brigadoon   1954   (MGM)   *Color*
Director: Vincente Minnelli
Starring: Gene Kelly, Van Johnson, Cyd Charisse, Elaine Stewart, Barry Jones, Hugh Laing, Albert Sharpe, Virginia Bosler, Jimmy Thompson, Tudor Owen, Eddie Quillan, Madge Blake, Dody Heath

Brigadoon is a village in the Scottish Highlands that springs to life for twenty-four hours every 100 years. The popular Alan Jay Lerner-Frederick Loewe musical, brought to the screen by Vincente Minnelli, features one of their most melodic scores. Some of the musical numbers: "The Heather on the Hill," "From This Day On," "I'll Go Home with Bonnie Jean," "It's Almost Like Being in Love," "Waiting for My Dearie," and the title song. Gene Kelly is both star and choreographer. Van Johnson plays his Highlands touring companion. George Chakiris, several years before his *West Side Story* stardom, is featured as one of the young men of the magical village.

Bye, Bye, Birdie   1963   (RCA)   *Color*
Director: George Sidney
Starring: Janet Leigh, Dick Van Dyke, Ann-Margret, Maureen Stapleton, Bobby Rydell, Jesse Pearson, Paul Lynde, Mary LaRoche, Michael Evans, Robert Paige, Gregory Morton, Bryan Russell, Milton Frome, Ed Sullivan

Rock 'n' roll idol Conrad Birdie is now an army draftee. For his farewell performance before heading off to boot camp, he is supposed to bestow one last kiss on an admiring fan on Ed Sullivan's TV show. Ann-Margret, in a pre-sex-symbol role, is the lucky girl who wins the kiss. This adaptation of Michael Stewart's stage musical, with songs by Charles Strouse and Lee Adams, contains a wealth of comedy. One highlight is Paul Lynde's condemnation of "Kids." ("Why can't they be like we were—perfect in every way?") Other songs: "Honestly Sincere," "Put on a Happy Face," "A Lot of Living to Do," "Rosie," "One Last Kiss," "One Boy," "How Lovely to Be a Woman," and the title tune. The choreographers are Onna White and Tom Panko. George Sidney, who started as a second-unit director, is an old pro with movie musicals; his credits extend to *Show Boat, Annie Get Your Gun,* and *Kiss Me, Kate*—to name a few.

Cabaret   1972   (CBS)   ◆   *Color*
Director: Bob Fosse
Starring: Liza Minnelli, Michael York, Joel Grey, Helmut Griem, Fritz Wepper, Marisa Berenson, Ralf Wolter, Elisabeth Neumann-Viertel

The plot originated in *Goodbye to Berlin*, Christopher Isherwood's collection of reminiscences about Germany at the twilight of the Weimar Republic. The stories were adapted, in sequence, as the stage play *I Am a Camera*, as a movie of the same name, then as *Cabaret*, the Tony-winning musical by Fred Ebb and John Kander, with a libretto by Joe Masteroff. Each reincarnation retained Isherwood's centers of focus: pre-Hitler Berlin and demimondaine Sally Bowles. In *Cabaret*, Liza Minnelli assumes the role of

Sally, the Kit Kat Klub's featured artiste; Joel Grey plays the cabaret's garish master of cermonies; and Michael York, as a naive young writer, is the stand-in for Isherwood. The Kit Kat's raucous (and sometimes sinister) production numbers, choreographed by Fosse and lensed by Geoffrey Unsworth, act as a commentary of the developments outside—the historical, political, economic, and social events that pave the way for Nazism. Jay Presson Allen, known primarily for her stage and screen version of *The Prime of Miss Jean Brodie,* wrote the screenplay. Fosse retains the best of Broadway songs and adds three new ones (also by Kander and Ebb): "Mein Herr," "Maybe This Time," and "Money, Money, Money." Beaten in the best film category, *Cabaret* was nonetheless tapped for eight Academy Awards. The winners: Fosse, Minnelli, cinematographer Unsworth, editor David Bretherton, score adapter Ralph Burns, the sound crew, the art direction/set decoration ensemble, and supporting actor Grey—who had captured a Tony in the same role.

Camelot   1967   (Warner)   *Color*
Director: Joshua Logan
Starring: Richard Harris, Vanessa Redgrave, Franco Nero, David Hemmings, Lionel Jeffries, Laurence Naismith, Pierre Olaf, Estelle Winwood, Anthony Rogers, Peter Bromilow

The Arthurian myth is one of the most beloved in literature. The legend of courtly love and the foundation of the Round Table reached its acme in T. H. White's novel, *The Once and Future King*—which inspired the Alan Jay Lerner-Frederick Loewe-Moss Hart musical, *Camelot.* The score includes the robust title song, "I Wonder What the King Is Doing Tonight," "The Simple Joys of Maidenhood," "C'est Moi," "The Lusty Month of May," "How to Handle a Woman," "Take Me to the Fair," "If Ever I Would Leave You," "I Loved You Once in Silence," and "What Do the Simple Folk Do?" All engage the viewer in the three-way love affair of Arthur (Richard Harris), Guinevere (Vanessa Redgrave), and Lancelot (Franco Nero). John Truscott designed the costumes and sets. The video version of *Camelot* restores some footage trimmed by Warner after the film's initial roadshow engagements. Careful viewers will spot an editing slip-up: Lionel Jeffries, as King Pellinore, is shown in the Arthur-Guinevere wedding montage—almost half an hour before Pellinore's first introduction to the king and queen.

Carousel   1956   (CBS)   *Color*
Director: Henry King
Starring: Gordon MacRae, Shirley Jones, Cameron Mitchell, Barbara Ruick, Claramae Turner, Robert Rounseville, Gene Lockhart, Audrey Christie, Susan Luckey, William Le Massena, John Dehner, Richard Deacon

Billy Bigelow, a roguish merry-go-round operator, courts, then marries, a shy cotton-mill worker named Julie. Their happiness is short-lived, though. Billy, after helping a friend in a holdup, is killed in a freak accident. But thanks to the compassion of a celestial Starkeeper, Billy returns briefly to Earth to discover what has happened to Julie—and Louise, the daughter he never lived to see. This film rendition of the Rodgers and Hammerstein musical play retains the songs ("Soliloquy," "If I Loved You," "A Real Nice Clambake," "You'll Never Walk Alone")—while contributing the visuals of the Maine locales. (There was some sound stage shooting, and that footage exists in stark contrast to the location photography.) Husband-and-wife team Henry and Phoebe Ephron, old pros with movie comedies and musicals, wrote the screenplay. First teamed in the 1955 film version of *OKLAHOMA!,* Gordon MacRae and Shirley Jones star as Billy and Julie. Gene Lockhart plays the kindly Starkeeper. Rod Alexander staged the lively dances. Ballet star Jacques D'Amboise is the dancing partner of Louise (Susan Luckey) for the dream ballet choreographed by Agnes De Mille.

A Chorus Line   1985   (Embassy)   *Color*
Director: Richard Attenborough
Starring: Michael Douglas, Terrence Mann, Alyson Reed, Cameron English, Vicki Frederick, Audrey Landers, Michael Blevins, Yamil Borges, Sharon Brown, Gregg Burge, Tony Fields, Nicole Fosse, Jan Gan Boyd, Michelle Johnston, Janet Jones

After more than eleven years on Broadway (and still running as of this writing), that "singular sensation" is now a movie. Joseph Papp's original stage production was "conceived, choreographed, and directed" by Michael Bennett, from a book by James Kirkwood and Nicholas Dante, and with music by Marvin Hamlisch and lyrics by Edward Kleban. *A Chorus Line* dramatizes the grueling chorus auditions for a Broadway musical. Zach, the director of the show within the show, announces to a stageful of hopeful dancers that he will hire only eight of them—four men, four women. The drama surfaces when the aspirants reveal themselves—often stripping carefully polished facades—in dialogue, song, and dance. Among the musical numbers: "I Hope I Get It," "I Can Do That," "At the Ballet," "Dance: Ten; Looks: Three," and the signature, "What I Did for Love." Only a few songs from the Broadway score have been dropped—and Hamlisch and Kleban have added one particulaly notable one: "Surprise, Surprise." Working from the format of the stage production, the chief adapters of the movie (screenwriter Arnold Schulman and director Richard Attenborough) honor the scope and special merits of the original.

Coal Miner's Daughter   *Listed under Biographies.*

The Cotton Club   *Listed under Dramas.*

Damn Yankees   1958   (Warner)   *Color*
Directors: George Abbott and Stanley Donen
Starring: Tab Hunter, Gwen Verdon, Ray Walston, Russ Brown, Shannon Bolin, Nathanael Frey, Jimmie Komack, Rae Allen, Robert Shafer, Jean Stapleton, Albert Linville

Joe Hardy, a middle-aged Washington Senators fan, is transformed by the devil into a young baseball star. That's the premise of this Hollywood adaptation of George Abbott's 1955 stage musical. *Damn Yankees,* with music and lyrics by Richard Adler and Jerry Ross, is conveyed to the screen by Abbott himself, directing with Stanley Donen. Tab Hunter stars as shoeless Joe Hardy, Russ Brown plays a nervous coach, and Jean Stapleton has the role of a flaky fan. Of note: Gwen Verdon and Ray Walston, re-creating their Broadway roles of Lola, the torrid vamp, and Applegate, her wily, hissing boss. The choreography comes courtesy of Bob Fosse, who can be glimpsed as a mambo dancer. Among the tunes: "Two Lost Souls," "Whatever Lola Wants," "You Gotta Have Heart," "Six Months Out of Every Year," and "Who's Got the Pain?"

Doctor Doolittle   1967   (CBS)   ◆   *Color*
Director: Richard Fleischer
Starring: Rex Harrison, Samantha Eggar, Anthony Newley, Richard Attenborough, Peter Bull, Muriel Landers, William Dix, Geoffrey Holder, Portia Nelson, Norma Varden

Hugh Lofting, an American born in Great Britain, wrote more than a dozen children's books featuring a nineteenth-century English doctor who resided in Puddleby-on-the-Marsh. Doctor Doolittle's cachet was that he could talk to animals. Rex Harrison does precisely that in the film version, an elaborate musical adaptation of Lofting by scenarist-lyricist-composer Leslie Bricusse. (Among the songs: "My Friend, the Doctor," "The Reluctant Vegetarian," "At the Crossroads," "I've Never Seen Anything Like It," "Beautiful," "When I Look in Your Eyes," "Like Animals," "After Today," "Fabulous Places," "I Think I Like You," and the Academy Award–winning "Talk to the Animals.") All the touchstones of the original books are on view: Jip the Dog, Chi-Chi the Chimp, Gub-Gub the Pig, and (seeing is believing) the Pushmi-Pullyu, a dancing two-headed llama. Cinematographer Robert Surtees's locations include Castle Combe in the English countryside and the Caribbean island of Santa Lucia. The dances were staged by Herbert Ross. Unfortunately, *Doctor Doolittle*'s $28 million budget, coupled with the decline of interest in musicals, doomed it to box-office failure.

Fiddler on the Roof   1971   (CBS)   *Color*
Director: Norman Jewison
Starring: Topol, Norma Crane, Leonard Frey, Molly Picon, Paul Mann, Rosalind Harris, Michele Marsh, Neva Small, Paul Michael Glaser, Raymond Lovelock, Elaine Edwards, Candy Bonstein, Zvee Scooler, Louis Zorich

One of the summits of the American musical theater, *Fiddler on the Roof* makes its screen transition with both heart and razzle-dazzle intact. The center of the work is Tevye, the poor Jewish dairyman in Czarist Russia who tries to preserve his heritage. The year is 1905, and Tevye lives with his wife and their daughters in a village in the Ukraine. The family disintegrates as the daughters are married and, later, as pogroms drive the villagers off their land—sending some on the trek to America. Norman Jewison's film retains the spirit and vision of the award-winning Broadway play, adapted from Sholem Aleichem's stories by Joseph Stein, who is also the author of the screenscript. The Sheldon Harnick-Jerry Bock score features "Tradition," "Matchmaker, Matchmaker," "Sunrise, Sunset," "Tevye's Dream," and "If I Were a Rich Man." Isaac Stern, offscreen, provides the violin music throughout. Under Jewison's direction, the tale is recounted with gusto by Topol (as Tevye) and the entire cast. Academy Awards: John Williams (music adaptation) and Oswald Morris (cinematography).

Finian's Rainbow   1968   (Warner)   *Color*
Director: Francis Ford Coppola
Starring: Fred Astaire, Petula Clark, Don Francks, Keenan Wynn, Tommy Steele, Barbara Hancock, Al Freeman, Jr., Ronald Colby, Dolph Sweet, Wright King

End of year 1968 witnessed the release of three adaptations of long-running stage musicals: *Oliver!*, *Funny Girl*, and *Finian's Rainbow*. Only the latter failed to duplicate its Broadway magic at the box office. But there is a small, fervid band who revere Coppola's film transcription. Fred Astaire, in his last big-screen role, is feisty Finian McLonergan, who leaves his native Ireland for America, where—in the verdant hills of Rainbow Valley, within shouting distance of Fort Knox—he plans to grow rich. Finian believes his pot of gold, stolen from Glocca Morra leprechauns, will proliferate when buried in the fertile ground adjacent to the fort. From this whimsical premise arises an energetic film bolstered by a dozen of the most highly acclaimed songs ever created for Broadway, including "That Old Devil Moon," "Necessity," and "When I'm

Not Near the Girl I Love." In Astaire's support are Tommy Steele (Og the Leprechaun), Barbara Hancock (Susan the Silent), and, as the lovers, Don Francks and Petula Clark.

Funny Girl   1968   (RCA)   ◆   *Color*
Director: William Wyler
Starring: Barbra Streisand, Omar Sharif, Walter Pidgeon, Anne Francis, Kay Medford, Lee Allen, Gerald Mohr, Frank Faylen

William Wyler's film version of *Funny Girl*, adapted by Isobel Lennart from her stage playscript, is the musical biography of Ziegfeld Follies headliner Fanny Brice. Barbra Streisand won an Oscar for her portrayal of Brice, the gifted comedienne whose private life was pure heartbreak. Most of the show tunes by Jule Styne and lyricist Bob Merrill are here, including "People," "Sadie, Sadie, Married Lady," "I'm the Greatest Star," and "Don't Rain on My Parade." For the finale, Streisand belts out an actual Fanny Brice standard, "My Man." Anne Francis enacts a Follies showgirl, Walter Pidgeon portrays Flo Ziegfeld, and Omar Sharif plays Brice's romantic interest—petty gangster Nicky Arnstein. William Wyler directed. Barbra also starred in the 1975 sequel, *Funny Lady*, which picked up Fanny Brice's story where *Funny Girl* left off. (*Funny Lady*'s John Kander-Fred Ebb score contains the hit song "How Lucky Can You Get?")

A Funny Thing Happened on the Way to the Forum   1966   (CBS)   *Color*
Director: Richard Lester
Starring: Zero Mostel, Phil Silvers, Buster Keaton, Jack Gilford, Michael Crawford, An-nette André, Patricia Jessel, Michael Hordern, Inga Nielsen, Leon Greene, Myrna White, Lucienne Bridou, Helen Funai, Jennifer Baker, Susan Baker, Pamela Brown, Alfie Bass, Roy Kinnear

The theatrical heritage inspiring this musical comedy runs the gamut from 1920s girly shows all the way back to Attic New Comedy (c. 200 B.C.). A raucous burlesque, *A Funny Thing Happened on the Way to the Forum*, set in ancient Rome, adopts its stock characters from the even-more-ancient Greek dramatist Plautus. On tap are the scheming slave (Zero Mostel as Pseudolus), his dopey foil (Jack Gilford as Hysterium), the lecherous masters (Phil Silvers and Michael Hordern as Lycus and Senex respectively), the braggart soldier (Leon Greene as Miles Gloriosus), and the love-starved youth (Michael Crawford as the aptly named Hero). Concocted for Broadway by Burt Sheve-love and Larry Gelbart, then screenscripted by Melvin Frank and Michael Pertwee, the puns and gags continue unabated; the lines are pelted by an ensemble of farceurs, who also get mileage out of Stephen Sondheim's lyrics in "Free," "Lovely," "Comedy Tonight," "Bring Me My Bride," and "Everybody Ought to Have a Maid." Directed by Richard Lester in the fragmented style he brought to the two Beatles films, *A Hard Day's Night* and *Help!* Lester's cinematographer is directing apprentice Nicolas Roeg.

Gentlemen Prefer Blondes   1953   (CBS)   *Color*
Director: Howard Hawks
Starring: Jane Russell, Marilyn Monroe, Charles Coburn, Elliott Reid, Tommy Noonan, George Winslow, Marcel Dalio, Taylor Holmes, Norma Varden, Howard Wendell, Steven Geray, Henri Letondal, Alex Frazer, George Chakiris, Robert Fuller, Harry Carey, Jr., Ray Montgomery

Dorothy (Jane Russell), a showgirl, and her dumb-blonde friend Lorelei (Marilyn Monroe) set sail for Paris. This version of the Joseph Fields-Anita Loos Broadway musical incorporates the tunes of two songwriting teams: Hoagy Carmichael-Harold Adamson and Jule Styne-Leo Robin. Among the numbers: "Bye, Bye, Baby," "When Love Goes Wrong," "Diamonds Are a Girl's Best Friend," and "Two Little Girls from Little Rock." The screenplay is by Charles Lederer. The production numbers were choreographed by Jack Cole. Of all the men smitten by the leads, surely the two funniest are seventyish Charles Coburn, of the bullfrog voice, and sevenish George Winslow, whose unique basso led him to be nicknamed (and often credited as) "Foghorn." A Paris-localed sequel, *Gentlemen Marry Brunettes,* was released in 1955, but the only returning participant was Jane Russell.

Gigi　　1958　　(MGM)　　　　　　　　　　　　　　◆　　*Color*
Director: Vincente Minnelli
Starring: Leslie Caron, Maurice Chevalier, Louis Jourdan, Hermione Gingold, Eva Gabor, Jacques Bergerac, Isabel Jeans, John Abbott, Edwin Jerome, Lydia Stevens, Maurice Marsac, Monique Van Vooren

This musical reverses a trend: originally conceived for the screen, it has subsequently been adapted for the stage. But the movie, directed by Vincente Minnelli, is the one that captured the hearts of critics and audiences. The Academy Award–winning best picture of 1958, *Gigi* is the story of a young turn-of-the-century Parisienne groomed by the women in her family to be a courtesan. But when Gigi (Leslie Caron) falls in love with her protector, Gaston (Louis Jourdan), she fools everyone by choosing respectability and persuades Gaston to marry her. Alan Jay Lerner's screenplay, derived from Colette, leaves spaces for these familiar tunes (lyrics by Lerner, music by Frederick Loewe): "It's a Bore," "The Parisians," "The Night They Invented Champagne," "Say a Prayer for Me Tonight," "Gossip," "Thank Heaven for Little Girls," "I Remember It Well," "I'm Glad I'm Not Young Any More," "Waltz at Maxim's (She's Not Thinking of Me)," and the Oscar-winning title song. Betty Wand provides Leslie Caron's singing voice. In sum, nine Academy Awards went to *Gigi*—plus a special Oscar to Maurice Chevalier "for his contributions to the world of entertainment for more than half a century."

Grease　　1978　　(Paramount)　　　　　　　　　　　　　*Color*
Director: Randal Kleiser
Starring: John Travolta, Olivia Newton-John, Stockard Channing, Jeff Conaway, Dinah Manoff, Didi Conn, Eve Arden, Frankie Avalon, Joan Blondell, Edd Byrnes, Sid Caesar, Alice Ghostley, Dody Goodman, Sha Na Na, Barry Pearl, Michael Tucci

Rydell High School is the principal setting for this salute to the fads, fashions, and sounds of the late fifties. The stage creation of Jim Jacobs and Warren Casey—by way of their book, music and lyrics—*Grease* had a seven-year New York run. This movie incarnation, founded on Bronte Woodard's screenplay, was retailored somewhat to fit John Travolta and Olivia Newton-John. Among the musical numbers: "Summer Nights," "Beauty School Dropout," and "We Go Together (Like Rama-Lama-Lama, Ka-Dinga Da Ding-Dong)." Several new tunes were added, including the Bee Gee's opening-credits title song and "Hopelessly Devoted to You," with music and lyrics by John Farrar. The cast is composed of energetic, hip-swiveling singers and dancers, among them Jeff Conaway, Stockard Channing, Dinah Manoff, and Didi Conn. *Grease* ultimately grossed over $97 million. (Randal Kleiser, directing his first big-screen feature, had worked once before with Travolta—in the latter's TV-movie debut, *The Boy in the Plastic Bubble*.) Sequel: *Grease 2* (1982).

Guys and Dolls   1955   (CBS)   *Color*
Director: Joseph L. Mankiewicz
Starring: Marlon Brando, Jean Simmons, Frank Sinatra, Vivian Blaine, Robert Keith, Stubby Kaye, B. S. Pully, Johnny Silver, Sheldon Leonard, Danny Dayton, George E. Stone, Regis Toomey, Kathryn Givney, Veda Ann Borg

Another representative from the golden age of movie musicals, *Guys and Dolls* is based on the 1950 stage play by Jo Swerling and Abe Burrows. Inspired by the stories of Damon Runyon, the show tells of sister Sarah Brown, of the Salvation Army, and her romance with gambler Sky Masterson. Meanwhile, Nathan Detroit, organizer of a "permanent floating crap game," tries to skirt the issue of marriage with the insistent Miss Adelaide. On the fringes are additional colorful characters: Nicely-Nicely Johnson, Benny Southstreet, Harry the Horse, Society Max, Angie the Ox, and other assorted Times Square types. Among Frank Loesser's songs (ten of them intact from the stage, and several new ones added): "Fugue for Tinhorns," "Follow the Fold," "The Oldest Established Permanent Floating Crap Game in New York," "I'll Know," "Adelaide's Lament," "If I Were a Bell," "Take Back Your Mink," "Luck Be a Lady," "Sit Down, You're Rockin' the Boat," "Sue Me," "Pet Me, Papa," "A Woman in Love," and the title number. (Michael Kidd is the choreographer.) Repeating their Broadway performances are Vivian Blaine (Adelaide), Stubby Kaye (Nicely-Nicely), B. S. Pully (Big Jule), and Johnny Silver (Benny Southstreet). Frank Sinatra plays Nathan Detroit, and the romantic leads are Marlon Brando and Jean Simmons—both of whom do their own singing.

Gypsy   1962   (Warner)   *Color*
Director: Mervyn LeRoy
Starring: Rosalind Russell, Natalie Wood, Karl Malden, Paul Wallace, Betty Bruce, Parley Baer, Harry Shannon, Suzanne Cupito, Ann Jillian, Diane Pace, Faith Dane, Roxanne Arlen, George Petrie, William Fawcett, Guy Raymond, Louis Quinn, Jean Willes

An abridged list of Rosalind Russell's credits includes *Craig's Wife*, *The Citadel*, *The Women*, *His Girl Friday*, *My Sister Eileen*, *Sister Kenny*, *Picnic*, and *Auntie Mame*. One of Russell's best roles—and her last great, starring role—was *Gypsy's* Mama Rose, originated on Broadway by Ethel Merman. In this musicalization of Gypsy Rose Lee's autobiography, Natalie Wood plays the title figure, the legendary queen of burlesque. But Russell dominates as the quintessential backstage mother. The film, with a screenplay of the Arthur Laurents original by Leonard Spigelgass, retains some Sondheim songs: "Let Me Entertain You," "Small World," "Baby June and Her Newsboys," "Some People," "Mr. Goldstone," "Little Lamb," "You'll Never Get Away from Me," "If Momma Was Married," "All I Need Is the Girl," "Wherever We Go," "You Gotta Get a Gimmick," and "Rose's Turn." Miss Russell's numbers, although she sang on stage before, were here partly dubbed with Lisa Kirk's voice.

Hair   1979   (CBS)   *Color*
Director: Miloš Forman
Starring: John Savage, Treat Williams, Beverly D'Angelo, Annie Golden, Dorsey Wright, Don Dacus, Cheryl Barnes, Nicholas Ray, Charlotte Rae, Miles Chapin

At the dawning of the age of Aquarius, hair length became a political statement. Miloš Forman's film version of the stage musical (book by Gerome Ragni and James Rado, music by Galt MacDermot) celebrates long hair, sunlight, and flower children. A young Oklahoma farm boy (John Savage) visits New York for a few days before being shipped to Vietnam. He becomes enamoured of a band of hippies, who work to change his thinking about war. Among the musical numbers: the title song, "Easy to Be Hard," "Frank Mills," "Aquarius," "Let the Sunshine In," and "Black Boys, White Boys." To some viewers there is already a dated quality to *Hair,* but the choreography of Twyla Tharp and Miroslav Ondricek's cinematography give the film a lift.

A Hard Day's Night   1964   (MPI)   *Color*
Director: Richard Lester
Starring: The Beatles (George Harrison, John Lennon, Paul McCartney, Ringo Starr), Wilfrid Brambell, Norman Rossington, John Junkin, Victor Spinetti, Anna Quayle, Michael Trubshawe, Richard Vernon, Deryck Guyler, Rosemarie Frankland, Patti Boyd, Kenneth Haigh

Nobody was surprised when the Beatles' first full-length movie became a runaway success. An off-the-wall experimental comedy that is framed as a semi-documentary to capture a day in the life of the Fab Four (a train ride from Liverpool to London, meeting with the fans, dashing for privacy, a TV studio concert), *A Hard Day's Night* reflects both the ebullience of the Beatles at the dawn of their careers and the creativity of director Richard Lester. Shot in a potpourri of styles, the picture manages to be as funny as it is innovative. The songs: "If I Fell," "This Boy" (Ringo's theme), "And I Love Her," "Tell Me Why," "She Loves You," "I Should Have Known Better," and "I'm Happy Just to Dance With You." Screenplay by Alun Owen.

The Harder They Come   1973   (Thorn)   *Color*
Director: Percy Henzell
Starring: Jimmy Cliff, Carl Bradshaw, Janet Bartley, Ras Daniel Hartman, Basil Keane, Bobby Charlton, Winston Stona

Ivan (reggae singer Jimmy Cliff), a young Jamaican, aspires to stardom as a recording artist. He arrives in Kingston, but finds career doors closed to him. Only after embarking on a well-publicized life of crime does he become famous as a singer. As depicted herein the focal points of Jamaica are poverty, drug-running, and law enforcement corruption. However, the rhythms of reggae—an amalgam of blues, calypso, and rock 'n' roll—alleviate this grim portrait of the island paradise. Among the songs, written and performed by Jimmy Cliff: "The Harder They Come," "Sitting in Limbo," "Many Rivers to Cross," and "You Can Get It If You Really Want." *The Harder They Come* has the distinction of being the first Jamaican feature filmed by locals. The director (and coauthor with Trevor D. Rhone) is Percy Henzell. Portions of the dialogue are spoken in a Rastafarian dialect.

Hello, Dolly!   1970   (CBS)   *Color*
Director: Gene Kelley
Starring: Barbra Streisand, Walter Matthau, Michael Crawford, Marianne McAndrew, E. J. Peaker, Tommy Tune, David Hurst, Louis Armstrong

This screen treatment of the Broadway musical showcases Barbra Streisand as Yonkers widow Dolly Levi, a matchmaker. Misanthropic millionaire Horace Vandergelder, played by Walter Matthau, is the match Dolly would like to make for herself. And, as a climax to a series of plot twists, she does. Writer-producer Ernest Lehman (*The Sound of Music* screenwriter) retains many of the features of the Michael Stewart libretto (adapted from Thornton Wilder's play *The Matchmaker*) and the Jerry Herman songs. Among the musical virtues: "So Long, Dearie," "Before the Parade Passes By," "Put on Your Sunday Clothes," and the title number, performed by acrobatic waiters at the Harmonia Gardens. Gene Kelly directed; Michael Kidd staged the dances.

Help!   1965   (MPI)   *Color*
Director: Richard Lester
Starring: The Beatles (George Harrison, John Lennon, Paul McCartney, Ringo Starr), Leo McKern, Eleanor Bron, Victor Spinetti, Roy Kinnear, Patrick Cargill, John Bluthall, Warren Mitchell, Peter Copley, Dandy Nichols

Richard Lester's second film starring the Beatles is more elaborate than *A Hard Day's Night,* but shares a common denominator: it is a freewheeling evocation of the musicians' personalities. In the script by Charles Wood and Marc Behm, a religious cult attempts to reclaim a sacred ring that is firmly affixed to one of Ringo's fingers, and a round-the-world chase ensues. The Lennon-McCartney score includes "Help!," "Ticket to Ride," "Another Girl," "The Night Before," "You've Got to Hide Your Love Away," and "You're Gonna Lose That Girl," with "I Need You," written by George Harrison. The cinematography is by David Watkin.

High Society   1956   (MGM)   *Color*
Director: Charles Walters
Starring: Bing Crosby, Grace Kelly, Frank Sinatra, Celeste Holm, John Lund, Louis Calhern, Sidney Blackmer, Louis Armstrong, Margalo Gillmore, Lydia Reed, Gordon Richards, Richard Garrick, Richard Keene

Cole Porter's music is coupled with Philip Barry's high society repartee in this musicalization of *The Philadelphia Story.* The adaptation by John Patrick uses some of the original's dialogue, thus providing ammunition for the sparring among Bing Crosby, Frank Sinatra, Grace Kelly, and Celeste Holm. Some critics believe the production isn't up to the standards of visual elegance of most other MGM musicals of the period—but most everyone remembers the songs: "True Love," "Well, Did You Evah?," "You're Sensational," "Little One," "Who Wants to Be a Millionaire," "Mind If I Make Love to You," "I Love You, Samantha," "Now You Has Jazz" (contributed by Louis Armstrong), and the title number. *High Society* was the last film of Louis Calhern, who died in May 1956, and of Grace Kelly, who, upon her marriage to Prince Rainier, retired from motion pictures.

Honeysuckle Rose   1980   (Warner)   *Color*
Director: Jerry Schatzberg
Starring: Willie Nelson, Dyan Cannon, Amy Irving, Slim Pickens, Joey Floyd, Charles Levin, Mickey Rooney, Jr., Pepe Serna, Lane Smith, Priscilla Pointer, Diana Scarwid, Rex Ludwick, Mickey Raphael

Country-western singer Buck Bonham has been on the road for over twenty years—busing to concert dates from St. Louis to Baton Rouge, Kansas City to Tulsa. According to one of his colleagues, Buck is "everybody's hero." Devoted to his wife, who remains at their ranch home, where she is the Bonham Band's tour manager, Buck also has a roving eye. This musical drama depicts his current extramarital dalliance with the young daughter of a fellow musician and its consequences for him, his family, and his band. Willie Nelson stars as Buck; Slim Pickens plays his longtime associate; Amy Irving plays Pickens's daughter and the band's new singer; Charles Levin and Pepe Serna portray two roadies; and Dyan Cannon is cast as Buck's gutsy, down-to-earth wife. Carol Sobieski, William Wittliff, and John Binder collaborated on the screenplay; Jerry Schatzberg (*Scarecrow*, *The Seduction of Joe Tynan*) directed. Richard Baskin, of *Nashville* fame, supervised the music, and the songs include "On the Road Again," "Whiskey River," and, from guest star Emmylou Harris, "So You Think You're a Cowboy."

The **J**azz Singer   1980   (Paramount)   *Color*
Director: Richard Fleischer
Starring: Neil Diamond, Laurence Olivier, Lucie Arnaz, Catlin Adams, Franklin Ajaye, Paul Nicholas, Mike Kellin, Sully Boyar

Al Jolson in 1927. Danny Thomas in 1953. And Neil Diamond in 1980. All have starred as *The Jazz Singer*. The plot essentials, as derived from the venerable Samson Raphaelson playscript, remain: an elderly Jewish cantor (here played by Laurence Olivier) wants his son to follow in his footsteps rather than using his singing voice for secular rewards. The scenarists, Herbert Baker and Stephen H. Foreman, have updated the original and made a few other changes; for instance, the mother played in the Jolson version by Eugenie Besserer is now a supportive girlfriend—thereby providing Lucie Arnaz a strong secondary role.

Jesus Christ Superstar   1973   (MCA)   *Color*
Director: Norman Jewison
Starring: Ted Neeley, Carl Anderson, Yvonne Elliman, Barry Dennen, Joshua Mostel, Bob Bingham, Kurt Yaghjian

Tim Rice and Andrew Lloyd Webber's rock opera evolved from a hit record album and staged concerts to fully mounted productions in London and New York to the Norman Jewison-Robert Stigwood film spectacle. Director Jewison and his coscenarist, Melvyn Bragg, add some embellishments: the musical drama is now framed by the arrival in and departure from the Holy Land of a busload of young tourists; these youths become passion players enacting episodes from the life of Christ. The leading actors are Ted Neeley (Jesus), Carl Anderson (Judas), Yvonne Elliman (Mary Magdalene), Barry Dennen (Pilate), Josh Mostel (Herod), Bob Bingham (Caiphas), and Kurt Yaghjian (Annas).

The **K**ing and I   1956   (CBS)   *Color*
Director: Walter Lang
Starring: Deborah Kerr, Yul Brynner, Rita Moreno, Martin Benson, Terry Saunders, Rex Thompson, Carlos Rivas, Patrick Adiarte, Alan Mowbray, Geoffrey Toone

Yul Brynner, in re-creating his Tony-winning Broadway performance as the King of Siam, also claimed a best actor Oscar. The Richard Rodgers (music) and Oscar Hammerstein (book and lyrics) stage success launched Brynner's theatrical career; this streamlining of the Broadway musical (by Ernest Lehman) did the same for his film career. The star, in the role he claimed to the end of his life, plays the dynamic Siamese ruler who wants to be an up-to-date (late nineteenth century) presence yet retain his privileges as absolute monarch. He, therefore, clashes ideologically with the democratic English schoolteacher (Deborah Kerr), brought to Siam to educate the royal offspring. Directed by Walter Lang, *The King and I*—derived from the 1946 *Anna and the King of Siam* (with Rex Harrison and Irene Dunne)—is an opulent production, accentuated by the score: "Getting to Know You," "Whistle a Happy Tune," "Hello, Young Lovers," "I Have Dreamed," "Something Wonderful," "We Kiss in a Shadow," and "Shall We Dance?" (Deborah Kerr's singing voice is dubbed by Marni Nixon—Natalie Wood's *West Side Story* dubber.) In 1972 Brynner joined with Samantha Eggar, as Anna, for the short-lived TV series entitled simply "Anna and the King."

King Creole   1958   (CBS)   *Black-and-White*
Director: Michael Curtiz
Starring: Elvis Presley, Carolyn Jones, Dolores Hart, Dean Jagger, Walter Matthau, Jan Shepard, Paul Stewart, Liliane Montevecchi, Vic Morrow

Harold Robbins's Chicago-set gangster novel *A Stone for Danny Fisher* is the unlikely source for this Elvis Presley vehicle, the singer's fourth feature. Ironically, *King Creole* (the locale is changed to New Orleans) is one of Elvis's best films and best performances—perhaps because the star was working with a major director: Michael Curtiz. The Herbert Baker-Michael V. Gazzo story involves a would-be delinquent who is first a busboy and then a singer in a crime-backed night club. Walter Matthau portrays the mob leader; Carolyn Jones plays his decent-hearted moll; and Dolores Hart is the pure girl who falls in love with the musician. Songs include "Hardheaded Woman," "Dixieland Rock," and the title ballad.

Kismet   1955   (MGM)   *Color*
Director: Vincente Minnelli
Starring: Howard Keel, Ann Blyth, Dolores Gray, Vic Damone, Monty Woolley, Sebastian Cabot, Jay C. Flippen, Mike Mazurki, Jack Elam

Luther Davis and Charles Lederer's Broadway musical transcription of the oft-filmed drama returns again to the screen—with much of the stage music retained: "Night of Nights," "Stranger in Paradise," "Baubles, Bangles, and Beads," et al. (Robert Wright's score is adapted from themes by Alexander Borodin.) This Arabian Nights spectacular presents Howard Keel in the role of the magician who overcomes a villainous vizier and wins the heart of a beggar's beautiful daughter (Ann Blyth). Old Bagdad, as constructed on the MGM sound stages, is shot by Joseph Ruttenberg's Eastmancolor camera. Jack Cole staged the show-stopping dances.

Kiss Me, Kate   1953   (MGM)   *Color*
Director: George Sidney
Starring: Kathryn Grayson, Howard Keel, Ann Miller, Keenan Wynn, Bobby Van, Tommy Rall, James Whitmore, Kurt Kasznar, Bob Fosse, Ron Randall, Willard Parker, Carol Haney

Kiss Me, Kate is widely heralded as the best screen showcasing of Cole Porter. Fourteen of the seventeen Broadway songs have been retained, among them the classics "Wunderbar," "So in Love," "Too Darn Hot," "Brush Up Your Shakespeare," and "Always True to You in My Fashion." The witty Samuel and Bella Spewack playscript, adapted by Dorothy Kingsley, juxtaposes a former married couple's backstage battling with their onstage performances in *The Taming of the Shrew*. Kathryn Grayson and Howard Keel portray the Katherine-Petruchio counterparts—tempestuous on both sides of the footlights. Other standouts are Ann Miller, Tommy Rall, and Bob Fosse (as Bianca and her suitors), and as the doltish gangsters, James Whitmore and Keenan Wynn. Choreography by Hermes Pan. Originally released in 3-D.

Les Girls   1956   (MGM)   *Color*

Director: George Cukor
Starring: Gene Kelly, Mitzi Gaynor, Kay Kendall, Taina Elg, Jacques Bergerac, Leslie Phillips, Henry Daniell, Patrick Macnee, Stephen Vercoe, Philip Tonge, Owen McGiveney, Maurice Marsac, Cyril Delevanti, Nestor Paiva

The songs of Cole Porter grace another sophisticated MGM musical. In addition to the title tune, the melodies include "Ladies in Waiting," "Flower Song," "C'est L'Amour," "You're Just Too, Too," and "Why Am I So Gone About That Gal?" The John Patrick plot, from a novel by Vera Caspary, features a *Rashomon*-like device of three different interpretations of the past. The flashbacks are spun by three ex-chorines (now ladies of society) who once supported hoofer Barry Nichols (Gene Kelly) in his stage act. (Two of Barry's former dancers are suing the third over her published memoirs about those song-and-dance days of yore.) Directed by George Cukor, who is aided by Jack Cole's choreography and Robert Surtees's cinematography. *Les Girls* was Kelly's last Hollywood musical. The film inspired the one-season (1963) TV sitcom "Harry's Girls," which starred Larry Blyden as vaudevillian Harry Burns.

Mary Poppins   *Listed under Family Viewing/Children's*

My Fair Lady   1964   (CBS)   *Color*

Director: George Cukor
Starring: Audrey Hepburn, Rex Harrison, Stanley Holloway, Wilfrid Hyde-White, Gladys Cooper, Jeremy Brett, Theodore Bikel, Isobel Elsom, Mona Washbourne, John Holland, John Alderson, John McLiam, Walter Burke, Owen McGiveney, Marjorie Bennett, Jack Greening, Moyna MacGill, Henry Daniell, Ben Wright, Alan Napier

Lerner and Loewe's Tony-winning musical, after running on Broadway from 1956 to 1962, came to the screen and captured eight Academy Awards. George Bernard Shaw's *Pygmalion* inspired this tale of Professor Henry Higgins (Rex Harrison), a linguist, elocution teacher, and confirmed bachelor. To win a wager, he takes Eliza Doolittle (Audrey Hepburn), a London street waif, and trains her to be a lady—first by fine-tuning her shrill Cockney into an aristocratic accent. Among the songs: "With a Little Bit of Luck," "The Rain in Spain," "I Could Have Danced All Night," "On the Street Where You Live," "Get Me to the Church on Time," "I've Grown Accustomed to Her Face," and "Wouldn't It Be Loverly?" *My Fair Lady* was named best picture, and other Oscars went to Harrison, director George Cukor, cinematographer Harry Stradling, score adapter André Previn, costumer Cecil Beaton, the Warner Bros. sound department, and the art direction/set decoration corps.

Nashville 1975 (Paramount) ✳ ✪ ◆ Color

Director: Robert Altman
Starring: David Arkin, Barbara Baxley, Ned Beatty, Karen Black, Ronee Blakley, Timo-thy Brown, Keith Carradine, Geraldine Chaplin, Robert DoQui, Shelley Duvall, Allen Garfield, Henry Gibson, Scott Glenn, Jeff Goldblum, Barbara Harris, David Hayward, Michael Murphy, Allan Nichols, Dave Peel, Cristina Raines, Bert Remsen, Lily Tomlin, Gwen Welles, Keenan Wynn

Robert Altman's panorama of American life, using Nashville as the microcosm, focuses on twenty-four people who are involved—as entertainers, backup men, or spectators—in a forthcoming political rally for Hal Phillip Walker, the Replacement Party's candidate for president. The screenplay is by Joan Tewkesbury, an Altman associate who also wrote *Thieves Like Us*. Among the characters parading by: rival country music queens (Ronee Blakley and Karen Black), a gospel singer (Lily Tomlin), no-talent hopefuls (Gwen Welles and Barbara Harris), a mainstream rock group (Keith Carradine, Cristina Raines, and Allan Nichols), a nitwit BBC interviewer (Geraldine Chaplin), a campaign advance man (Michael Murphy), a Grand Ole Opry superstar (Henry Gibson), and on and on. *Nashville* was chosen best picture of the year by the New York Film Critics and the National Society of Film Critics. The songs include "Bluebird," "Memphis," "200 Years," "Dues," "Rolling Stone," "Tapedeck in His Tractor," "One, I Love You," and two by Keith Carradine—"It Don't Worry Me" and "I'm Easy," the latter an Academy Award winner. Many of the actor-singers wrote their own songs; other numbers were created by musical director Richard Baskin (who appears on-screen as a pianist named Frog).

Night and Day *Listed under Biographies.*

Oklahoma! 1955 (CBS) ◆ Color

Director: Fred Zinnemann
Starring: Gordon MacRae, Gloria Grahame, Gene Nelson, Charlotte Greenwood, Shirley Jones, Eddie Albert, James Whitmore, Rod Steiger, Barbara Lawrence, Jay C. Flippen, Roy Barcroft, James Mitchell, Bambi Lynn

The landmark Richard Rodgers-Oscar Hammerstein stage success took more than a decade to reach the screen, but for most viewers, the result made the wait worthwhile. Plaudits to the creators—Rodgers for music, Hammerstein for book and lyrics—and to the adapters, Sonya Levien and William Ludwig. With Fred Zinnemann as director and Agnes De Mille retained as choreographer, the film edition is a festival of song and dance. Beyond the titular anthem to the Sooner State, the songs include "Oh, What a Beautiful Mornin'," "The Surrey with the Fringe on Top," "Everything's Up-to-Date in Kansas City," "Many a New Day," "Pore Jud," "All Er Nuthin," "I Can't Say No," "The Farmer and the Cowman," and "People Will Say We're in Love." Gene Nelson and Gloria Grahame are cast as the comic couple, Will and Ado Annie; Gordon MacRae and Shirley Jones play the romantic leads, Curly and Laurey; James Mitchell and Bambi Lynn portray the dream-sequence dancers for Curley and Laurey; Charlotte Greenwood plays Aunt Eller; Eddie Albert enacts the peddler Ali Hakim; and Rod Steiger plays Jud Fry. Two Academy Awards went to *Oklahoma!*—for Fred Hymes's sound recording and the score adaptation by Robert Russell Bennett, Jay Blackton, and Adolph Deutsch.

Oliver!   1968   (RCA)   ◆   *Color*
Director: Carol Reed
Starring: Ron Moody, Oliver Reed, Shani Wallis, Mark Lester, Jack Wild, Harry Secombe, Hugh Griffith, Sheila White, Joseph O'Conor, Leonard Rossiter, Peggy Mount, Megs Jenkins, Hylda Baker

Oliver!, in Carol Reed's film transcription, emphasizes the ebullience and deemphasizes the gloomy undertones of Lionel Bart's stage musical. Inspired by the Charles Dickens classic, the story introduces little Oliver Twist, the orphan who becomes involved with a den of child thieves, then is rescued from poverty by the kindly gentleman, Mr. Brownlow. Bart's libretto is adapted by Vernon Harris, and most of his original music remains. The songs include "Food, Glorious Food," "Consider Yourself," "It's a Fine Life," "As Long as He Needs Me," "You've Got to Pick a Pocket or Two," and the haunting "Who Will Buy?" Heading the versatile cast: Mark Lester as Oliver; Jack Wild as the Artful Dodger; Shani Wallis plays Nancy; Oliver Reed as Bill Sikes; and Ron Moody, who turns Fagin into a lovable rogue. *Oliver!* was cited by the Academy as best picture of the year; additionally, Carol Reed was named best director. Other Oscars: sound, art direction/set decoration, scoring adaptation, and a special award to Onna White for her choreography.

On a Clear Day You Can See Forever   1970   (Paramount)   *Color*
Director: Vincente Minnelli
Starring: Barbra Streisand, Yves Montand, Bob Newhart, Larry Blyden, Simon Oakland, Jack Nicholson, John Richardson, Pamela Brown, Irene Handl, Roy Kinnear, Mabel Albertson, John Le Mesurier, Leon Ames

Daisy Gamble (Barbra Streisand), a chain-smoking Brooklynite with amazing powers of extrasensory perception, tries to kick the tobacco habit through hypnosis. Under hypnosis, she regresses to a previous existence as a nineteenth-century English beauty from the court of the Prince Regent. Streisand's bell-like voice and her comic timing propel this adaptation of the Broadway stage success (music by Burton Lane, book and lyrics by Alan Jay Lerner). The principal songs are "Hurry! It's Lovely Up Here," "Melinda," "He Wasn't You," "Come Back to Me," "What Did I Have That I Don't Have?" and the title song. Director Vincente Minnelli, abetted by cameraman Harry Stradling, creates a disarming world for Daisy—in both her present and past lives. Yves Montand plays Daisy's psychiatrist. Jack Nicholson, as her brother, had his material, including a song, trimmed just before the film's release; his screen time is very limited.

On the Town   1949   (MGM)   ◆   *Color*
Directors: Gene Kelly and Stanley Donen
Starring: Gene Kelly, Frank Sinatra, Betty Garrett, Ann Miller, Jules Munshin, Vera-Ellen, Florence Bates, Alice Pearce, George Meader, Bern Hoffman, Lester Dorr, Bea Benadaret, Don Brodie, Hans Conried, Carol Haney

On the Town is a catalogue of events surrounding a twenty-four-hour leave undertaken by three sailors in New York City. Their goals are to see the sights and to meet girls. For all three—Gabey (Gene Kelly), Chip (Frank Sinatra), and Ozzie (Jules Munshin)—their dreams come true. This MGM musical is an adaptation of the Adolph Green-Betty Comden-Leonard Bernstein stage hit, with Green and Comden providing the screenscript. The Manhattan merry-go-round is enhanced by location photography in

Technicolor and these grand tunes: "New York, New York," "Miss Turnstiles," "Prehistoric Man," "Come Up to My Place," "Main Street," "Count on Me," "A Day in New York," and "On the Town." (An Academy Award went to Roger Edens and Lennie Hayton for their score, which also included some new songs.) The directorial collaboration of Gene Kelly and Stanley Donen continued with *Singin' in the Rain* (1952) and *It's Always Fair Weather* (1955).

Paint Your Wagon   1969   (Paramount)   *Color*
Director: *Joshua Logan*
Starring: *Lee Marvin, Clint Eastwood, Jean Seberg, Harve Presnell, Ray Walston, Tom Ligon, Alan Dexter, William O'Connell, Ben Baker, Alan Baxter, Paula Trueman, Robert Easton, John Mitchum*

Paint Your Wagon is the Alan Jay Lerner-Frederick Loewe songfest about immigrant sourdoughs, circa 1880, who inhabit the California mining settlement dubbed No Name City ("Population: Male"). As a stage presentation, *Paint Your Wagon* was lauded for its score—and criticized for its exceptionally banal book. Here the libretto—adapted by Lerner with Paddy Chayefsky—receives a major overhaul. The main story now revolves around two gold miners, Ben Rumson (Lee Marvin) and Pardner (Clint Eastwood), who form a menage à trois with a young Mormon woman (Jean Seberg). Director Joshua Logan alternates action sequences with musical segments—and he has assembled an enthusiastic, if unexpected, cast. Marvin interprets "Wand'rin' Star"and Eastwood has a go at "I Talk to the Trees." Harve Presnell, the only professional voice in the ranks, has the show's most famous song, "They Call the Wind Maria." Five Lerner-Loewe tunes from the original stage production have been eliminated, but five new numbers have been added by Lerner and André Previn.

The Rose   *Listed under Dramas.*

Royal Wedding   1951   (Discount Video Tapes)   *Color*
Director: *Stanley Donen*
Starring: *Fred Astaire, Jane Powell, Peter Lawford, Sarah Churchill, Keenan Wynn, Albert Sharpe, Viola Roache, Henri Letondal, James Finlayson, Alex Frazer, Jack Reilly, Mae Clarke*

Tom and Ellen Bowen (Fred Astaire and Jane Powell), starring as a brother and sister, are a song-and-dance team in London at the time of Princess Elizabeth's marriage to Prince Philip. Before this Alan Jay Lerner-Burton Lane musical comedy (with a screenplay by Lerner) concludes, they each hear wedding bells of their own. Tom falls for English show girl Anne Ashmond (Sarah Churchill), while Ellen hooks Lord John Brindale (Peter Lawford). The quartet of lovers pause occasionally for these songs: "Too Late Now," "I Left My Hat in Haiti," "How Could You Believe Me," "Every Night at Seven," "Open Your Eyes," "What a Lovely Day for a Wedding," "Sunday Jumps," and "You're All the World to Me"—the last showcasing Astaire, partnered with a coat rack, and tap dancing on the walls and ceiling of his hotel suite.

Saturday Night Fever   *Listed under Dramas.*

Seven Brides for Seven Brothers   1954   (MGM)   ◆   *Color*
Director: Stanley Donen
Starring: Howard Keel, Jane Powell, Jeff Richards, Russ Tamblyn, Tommy Rall, Virginia Gibson, Ian Wolfe, Marc Platt, Matt Mattox, Jacques D'Amboise, Howard Petrie

Dancing reigns in this Michael Kidd–choreographed musical. Based marginally on Stephen Vincent Benet's story "The Sobbin' Women," *Seven Brides for Seven Brothers* tells of seven fur-trapping backwoodsmen from Oregon and their search for mates. Adam (Howard Keel) and his six brothers—played by Jeff Richards, Russ Tamblyn, Tommy Rall, Marc Platt, Matt Mattox, and Jacques D'Amboise—are greenhorns at the courting game; but they sing and dance their way into the hearts of seven beauties. Jane Powell plays Milly, Adam's beloved, while the other brides are enacted by Virginia Gibson, Nancy Kilgas, Betty Carr, Norma Doggett, Julie Newmar (then billed as Newmeyer), and Ruta Lee (credited as Ruta Kilmonis). The songs are by Johnny Mercer and Gene De Paul: "Bless Your Beautiful Hide," "Wonderful, Wonderful Day," "When You're in Love," "Lament," "June Bride," "Sobbin' Women," and "Spring, Spring, Spring." Stanley Donen directed from a script by Frances Goodrich, Albert Hackett, and Dorothy Kingsley. Academy Award: Adolph Deutsch and Saul Chaplin for scoring.

1776   1972   (RCA)   *Color*
Director: Peter H. Hunt
Starring: William Daniels, Howard Da Silva, Ken Howard, Donald Madden, Ron Holgate, David Ford, Blythe Danner, John Myhers, Virginia Vestoff, John Cullum

1776 depicts the efforts of the Second Continental Congress to ratify the Declaration of Independence. An adaptation of the Broadway musical, *1776* is vitalized by the screenplay of Peter Stone—from his stage original—and the Sherman Edwards songs: "Molasses to Rum," "Commitment," "Momma, Look Sharp," "The Lees of Old Virginia," et al. The actor-singers (many of them reprising their Broadway performances) are William Daniels as John Adams; Virginia Vestoff as Abigail Adams; John Cullum as Edward Rutledge; Donald Madden as John Dickinson, the villain of the piece; Ron Holgate as Richard Henry Lee; Howard Da Silva as Benjamin Franklin; Ken Howard as Thomas Jefferson; and Blythe Danner as Martha Jefferson. Harry Stradling, Jr., is the director of photography.

Show Boat   1951   (MGM)   *Color*
Director: George Sidney
Starring: Kathryn Grayson, Ava Gardner, Howard Keel, Joe E. Brown, Marge Champion, Gower Champion, Robert Sterling, Agnes Moorehead, Adele Jergens, William Warfield, Leif Erickson, Owen McGiveney, Frances Williams, Regis Toomey, Chick Chandler, Fuzzy Knight

The third screen edition of the Jerome Kern-Oscar Hammerstein II musical stands as a vigorous and colorful remake. Again the score includes these Kern-Hammerstein standards: "Bill," "Make Believe," "Ol' Man River," "Can't Help Lovin' Dat Man," and "Why Do I Love You?"—with additional contributions from P. G. Wodehouse, notably "Life Upon the Wicked Stage." As before, the setting is a turn-of-the-century Mississippi show boat and the personnel include Captain Andy Hawks (Joe E. Brown), his daughter Magnolia (Kathryn Grayson), dashing Gaylord Ravenal (Howard Keel), strong man Joe (William Warfield), and sultry Julie Laverne (Ava Gardner, whose singing voice is Annette Warren). Marge and Gower Champion play the troupe's featured hoofers. The screenplay, from Edna Ferber's novel, is by John Lee Mahin; the director is George Sidney (*Anchors Aweigh; The Harvey Girls; Kiss Me, Kate*). Choreography by Robert Alton.

Silk Stockings 1957 (MGM) *Color*
Director: Rouben Mamoulian
Starring: Fred Astaire, Cyd Charisse, Janis Paige, Peter Lorre, Jules Munshin, George Tobias, Joseph Buloff, Barrie Chase

Silk Stockings is the screen revision of the Broadway musicalization of *Ninotchka*, the classic movie comedy starring Greta Garbo and Melvyn Douglas. The stage play of George S. Kaufman and Leueen McGrath is here adapted by Leonard Gershe and Leonard Spiegelgass—and most of the Cole Porter score is salvaged. Cyd Charisse, in the Garbo role, plays an icy Soviet agent sent to Paris to reclaim a defector—a composer who is writing a score for a Hollywood picture. Taking the (revamped) Melvyn Douglas part is Fred Astaire, who in this edition is a movie producer who must thaw the lady commissar. Janis Paige is featured as a showgirl; Peter Lorre and Jules Munshin play other Soviets seduced by capitalism. Song highlights: "All of You," "Stereophonic Sound," and "Fated to Be Mated." *Silk Stockings* was the last completed film of Rouben Mamoulian, whose directorial career spanned from *Applause,* the revolutionary 1929 talkie, through *City Streets*, the 1932 *Dr. Jekyll and Mr. Hyde, Queen Christina, Becky Sharp, The Gay Desperado, The Mark of Zorro, Blood and Sand,* and *Summer Holiday.*

Singin' in the Rain 1952 (MGM) *Color*
Directors: Gene Kelly and Stanley Donen
Starring: Gene Kelly, Donald O'Connor, Debbie Reynolds, Jean Hagen, Millard Mitchell, Cyd Charisse, Douglas Fowley, Rita Moreno, Madge Blake, King Donovan, Kathleen Freeman, Bobby Watson, Tommy Farrell, Jimmie Thompson, Mae Clarke, Dawn Addams, Elaine Stewart

A classic among screen musicals, this satire of Hollywood takes place in 1927 when silent movies gave way to talkies. The script by Adolph Green and Betty Comden incorporates a medley of Arthur Freed-Nacio Herb Brown songs: "Make 'Em Laugh," "You Were Meant for Me," "Good Morning," "All I Do Is Dream of You," "Fit As a Fiddle and Ready for Love," and many more—including the landmark title number; an added dividend is the Comden-Green-Roger Edens song, "Moses." Entangled in Monumental Pictures' transition to the sound era are cinematic heart-throb Don Lockwood (Gene Kelly); musician Cosmo Brown (Donald O'Connor), Don's former burlesque partner; song-and-dance ingénue Kathy Selden (Debbie Reynolds); and Lina Lamont (Jean Hagen), a movie queen who speaks in an ear-splitting shriek. Kelly, who directed with Stanley Donen, also staged the dance numbers.

The Sound of Music 1965 (CBS) *Color*
Director: Robert Wise
Starring: Julie Andrews, Christopher Plummer, Eleanor Parker, Richard Haydn, Peggy Wood, Charmian Carr, Heather Menzies, Nicolas Hammond, Duane Chase, Angela Cartwright, Debbie Turner, Kym Karath, Anna Lee, Portia Nelson, Ben Wright, Norma Varden, Marni Nixon

The Rodgers and Hammerstein Broadway hit in its panoramic screen incarnation. *The Sound of Music* was lauded with five Oscars: best picture, director (Robert Wise), sound, score adaptation (Irwin Kostal), and editing (William Reynolds). Julie Andrews, straight from her Academy Award–winning Mary Poppins interpretation, plays Maria von Trapp, the stepmother to a brood of children in pre–World War II Austria. Their idyllic life before the Nazi regime and their ultimate escape into Switzerland create the drama behind the music. (Ernest Lehman adapted the stage book by Howard Lindsay and Russel Crouse.) The songs include the title number, "Maria," "Morning Hymn," "I Have Confidence," "Do-Re-Mi," "Edelweiss," "My Favorite Things," "Sixteen Going on Seventeen," and "So Long, Farewell." Choreography: Marc Breaux and Dee Dee Wood. Marni Nixon, the off-screen dubber for dozens of nonsinging actresses, appears in the small role of Sister Sophia.

South Pacific   1958   (CBS)   ◆   *Color*
Director: Joshua Logan
Starring: Rossano Brazzi, Mitzi Gaynor, John Kerr, Ray Walston, Juanita Hall, France Nuyen, Russ Brown, Jack Mullaney, Ken Clark, Floyd Simmons, Candace Lee, Warren Haieb, Tom Laughlin, Beverly Aadland, Ron Ely, Doug McClure

1943 on a South Pacific island: the setting for Rodgers and Hammerstein's indestructible Pulitzer Prize musical. Transposed to film in 1958, the production profits from location shooting in the Fiji Islands and Hawaii. Beyond the real-life tropical locales, *South Pacific* remains virtually the same: U.S. Navy nurse Nellie Forbush (Mitzi Gaynor), a self-described cockeyed optimist—but with underpinnings of bigotry—falls in love with mysterious French planter Emile De Becque (Rossano Brazzi; singing voice by Giorgio Tozzi). Directed by Joshua Logan from Paul Osborn's screenplay—with its source in James Michener's *Tales of the South Pacific*—the picture retains the Broadway songs, among them "Some Enchanted Evening," "Younger Than Springtime," "Bali Hai," "Happy Talk," "You've Got to Be Taught," "My Girl Back Home," "There Is Nothing Like a Dame," "I'm Gonna Wash That Man Right Out of My Hair," "This Nearly Was Mine," and "I'm in Love With a Wonderful Guy." An Oscar went to the Todd-AO Sound Department. Unfortunately, time has treated the film stock badly— particularly the color-filtered Bali Hai sequences which, moreover, seemed oddly tinted even when the movie was first released.

A Star Is Born   1954   (Warner)   *Color*
Director: George Cukor
Starring: Judy Garland, James Mason, Charles Bickford, Jack Carson, Tommy Noonan, Lucy Marlow, Amanda Blake, Irving Bacon, James Brown, Joan Shawlee, Dub Taylor, Louis Jean Heydt, Bob Jellison, Chick Chandler

In effect, the third time around for the story—inspired by *What Price Hollywood* (1932) and the earlier *A Star Is Born* (1937)—this edition stars Judy Garland as Vicki Lester, née Esther Blodgett. The film, as directed by George Cukor from the Moss Hart script, showcases Garland in what many critics consider her most memorable adult performance. As Vicki's star is on the rise, her husband's—matinee idol Norman Maine (James Mason)—is on the decline. Therein lies the drama and the poignancy of this musical drama. The songs include "Born in a Trunk" by Leonard Gershe, and these Harold Arlen-Ira Gershwin standards: "The Man That Got Away," "Gotta Have Me Go With You," "It's a New World," and "Someone at Last." The resored version of *A Star Is Born,* as available on cassette, contains these formerly deleted numbers: "Lose That Long Face," "Shampoo Commercial," and "Here's What I'm Here For." The cinematographer is Sam Leavitt; choreographer is Richard Barstow. The plot made the circuit once again in 1976, under the same title, as a vehicle for Barbra Streisand and Kris Kristofferson.

That's Entertainment!   1974   (MGM)   *Color*
Director: Jack Haley, Jr.
Starring: Fred Astaire, Bing Crosby, Gene Kelly, Peter Lawford, Liza Minnelli, Donald O'Connor, Debbie Reynolds, Mickey Rooney, Frank Sinatra, James Stewart, Elizabeth Taylor

The above-named stars serve as hosts for this audio-visual scrapbook of MGM's musical past. The film clips range from 1929's *Broadway Melody* through the heyday of the forties and fifties. Many magnificent song-and-dance artists are highlighted—most of the on-screen hosts, for instance, along with Judy Garland, Ray Bolger, Eleanor Powell; but there are some actors not known as singers, too: Cary Grant, Clark Gable, and the very young James Stewart. Audiences in 1974 had either forgotten or were too young to remember the Esther Williams water ballets included here—and they were among the most-talked-about sequences. More moments were compiled for *That's Entertainment, Part 2* (1976) and *That's Dancing!* (1985).

That's Entertainment, Part 2   1976   (MGM)   *Color*
Director: Gene Kelly
Starring: Fred Astaire, Gene Kelly

A continuation of *That's Entertainment!*, MGM's salute to its golden years. Again, singing and dancing dominate; but this time there is comedy from Tracy and Hepburn, Laurel and Hardy, the Marx Brothers, and others. Fred Astaire and Gene Kelly are the cohosts—and, in their first reunion in thirty years, they perform a bit of terpsichorean magic. From MGM's archives: Kelly and Judy Garland perform "Be a Clown" from *The Pirate*; Astaire and Cyd Charisse romance one another in "All of You" from *Silk Stockings*; and the show continues with Louis Armstrong, Jack Buchanan, Nelson Eddy, Oscar Levant, Jeanette MacDonald, Ann Miller, Mickey Rooney. . . .

There's No Business Like Show Business   1954   (CBS)   *Color*
Director: Walter Lang
Starring: Ethel Merman, Donald O'Connor, Marilyn Monroe, Dan Dailey, Johnnie Ray, Mitzi Gaynor, Richard Eastham, Hugh O'Brian, Frank McHugh, Rhys Williams, Lee Patrick, Chick Chandler, Eve Miller, Robin Raymond, Lyle Talbot, Alvy Moore, Gavin Gordon, Jimmy Baird, Billy Chapin, Charlotte Austin

A songfest with music and lyrics by Cole Porter. Among the tunes are "A Pretty Girl," "Play a Simple Melody," "Alexander's Ragtime Band," "Remember," "Heat Wave," "If You Believe," "A Man Chases a Girl," "Lazy," "Let's Have Another Cup of Coffee," "When That Midnight Choo Choo Leaves for Alabam," "After You Get What You Want, You Don't Want It," and the ever-popular "There's No Business Like Show Business." Around the numbers is woven a story—scripted by Phoebe and Henry Ephron from a treatment by Lamar Trotti. The main action concerns the Donahues, a family of trouping vaudevillians. Dan Dailey and Ethel Merman play the song-and-dance mom and pop who thrust their children onstage as soon as they can walk. The secondary plot deals with what happens to the three Donahue offspring (Donald O'Connor, Mitzi Gaynor, and Johnnie Ray) when they reach adulthood. Marilyn Monroe plays a sizzling songbird who becomes a Donahue by marriage. Directed by Walter Lang *(The Bluebird, Tin Pan Alley, Coney Island, State Fair, Cheaper by the Dozen, On the Riviera, With a Song in My Heart, Call Me Madam, The King and I)*, and choreographed by Robert Alton.

Thoroughly Modern Millie   1967   (MCA)   ◆   *Color*
Director: George Roy Hill
Starring: Julie Andrews, Mary Tyler Moore, Carol Channing, James Fox, John Gavin, Beatrice Lillie, Jack Soo, Pat Morita, Philip Ahn, Cavada Humphrey, Anthony Dexter, Lou Nova, Michael St. Clair, Albert Carrier, Victor Rogers, Lizabeth Hush, Herbie Faye, Ann Dee, Benny Rubin, Mae Clarke

The Roaring Twenties set the scene for this musical comedy. Millie Dillmount (Julie Andrews) arrives in New York as an inhibited midwesterner, but she decides to be thoroughly modern. Bobbing her hair and lifting her hemline are only the beginning. She becomes a secretary, adopts flapper argot, falls for her boss (John Gavin), shares an apartment with a penny-pinching roommate (Mary Tyler Moore), and finds true love with a real nice boy named Jimmy Smith (James Fox). Millie and her newfound friends even unmask a white slave racket engineered by the malevolent Mrs. Meers (Beatrice Lillie). The Oscar-winning music was composed and directed by Elmer Bernstein. There are standards like "Baby Face," "Jazz Baby," and "Poor Butterfly"—along with "Jimmy" by Jay Thompson, "Tapioca" (a new dance craze), and the title song by James Van Heusen and Sammy Cahn. Richard Morris penned the screenplay and George Roy Hill directed.

Till the Clouds Roll By   1946   (MGM)   *Color*
Director: Richard Whorf
Starring: Robert Walker, Judy Garland, Lucille Bremer, Van Heflin, Joan Wells, Paul Langton, Dorothy Patrick, Mary Nash, Harry Hayden, Paul Maxey, Rex Evans, Dinah Shore, Van Johnson, June Allyson, Cyd Charisse, Gower Champion, Sally Forrest

This musical salute to composer Jerome Kern has among the guest stars such MGM contract players as Lena Horne ("Why Was I Born?"); Angela Lansbury ("How D'You Like to Spoon With Me?"); Frank Sinatra ("Ol' Man River"); and Kathryn Grayson, Tony Martin, Virginia O'Brien, and Caleb Peterson. Over twenty songs are rendered in this capsule version of *Show Boat*. In the story proper, Robert Walker stars as Kern; Judy Garland is Ziegfeld Follies girl Marilyn Miller; and Paul Langton plays Oscar Hammerstein. Richard Whorf directed from a screenplay written, in turn, by Guy Bolton, George Wells, Myles Connolly, and Jean Holloway.

The U̲nsinkable Molly Brown   1964   (MGM)   *Color*
Director: Charles Walters
Starring: Debbie Reynolds, Harve Presnell, Ed Begley, Jack Kruschen, Hermione Baddeley, Vassili Lambrinos, Fred Essler, Harvey Lembeck, Lauren Gilbert, Kathryn Card, Hayden Rorke, Martita Hunt, Audrey Christie, Vaughn Taylor, Grover Dale, Gus Trikonis, Anna Lee

The Richard Morris Broadway musical book, with music and lyrics by Meredith Willson *(The Music Man)*, gets a Hollywood reworking. The story is loosely patterned on the real-life Molly Brown, a poor young woman of turn-of-the-century Denver who strikes it rich with a silver mine, rises to the top of the city's society, and, in 1912, survives the tragedy of the *Titanic*. Molly, as played by Debbie Reynolds, is therefore unsinkable. This Charles Walters–directed feature is a bawdy, brassy presentation of her biography, as screenscripted by Helen Deutsch. The choreography is by Peter Gennaro. Costarring as the heroine's handsome, faithful husband is baritone Harve Presnell in his movie debut. Five numbers from the seventeen-song stage show are retained— "Colorado Is My Home," "I'll Never Say No," "Soliloquy," "Belly Up to the Bar, Boys," and "I Ain't Down Yet"; additionally, Willson wrote "He's My Friend" especially for the picture.

Victor/Victoria   1982   (MGM)   ◆ ▲   Color
Director: Blake Edwards
Starring: Julie Andrews, James Garner, Robert Preston, Lesley Ann Warren, Alex Karras, John Rhys-Davies, Graham Stark, Peter Arne, Sherloque Tanney, Michael Robbins

This musical farce about changing sex roles and mistaken identities won the French César as best foreign film. Inspired by the 1933 German film *Viktor und Viktoria* and the 1936 British remake *First a Girl*, *Victor/Victoria* showcases Julie Andrews as an impoverished singer in 1934 Paris. Coached by her gay mentor (Robert Preston), a cabaret artist himself, the young woman becomes the toast of café society by masquerading as a man who is a female impersonator. As far as the public is concerned, she is Victor—not Victoria. Show business success is hers, but the ruse complicates her love life. Directed by Blake Edwards from his own screenplay, *Victor/Victoria* profits from its slapstick origins, the color photography of Dick Bush, and the period score by Henry Mancini. (Mancini and Leslie Bricusse won an Academy Award for their original songs and adaptations.)

West Side Story   1961   (CBS)   ◆   Color
Directors: Robert Wise and Jerome Robbins
Starring: Natalie Wood, Richard Beymer, Rita Moreno, George Chakiris, Russ Tamblyn, Tucker Smith, Tony Mordente, Eliot Feld, David Winters, Burt Michaels, Robert Banas, Anthony Teague, Tommy Abbott, Gus Trikonis, Simon Oakland, Bill Bramley, Ned Glass, John Astin, Penny Santon

A contemporary *Romeo and Juliet*, this adaptation of the Broadway musical milestone adds spectacle to the Arthur Laurents-Jerome Robbins play (screenwritten by Ernest Lehman) and the music and lyrics of, respectively, Leonard Bernstein and Stephen Sondheim. *West Side Story* tells of the rivalry between two street gangs, the Jets and the Sharks—and the love that emerges between Tony (Richard Beymer, with the singing voice of Jimmy Bryant), an ex-Jet, and Maria (Natalie Wood, dubbed by Marni Nixon), whose brother is the leader of the Sharks. Song highlights: "Cool," "Maria," "Tonight," "Somewhere," "I Feel Pretty," "In America," "Something's Coming," "Gee, Officer Krupke," "A Boy Like That," and "There's a Place for Us." The dramatic dance sequences—restaged for the motion picture camera by Jerome Robbins, who choreographed the Broadway production—were shot almost entirely on location. For his achievement, Robbins was presented with an honorary Academy Award. *West Side Story* won ten Oscars in the competitive categories: best picture; director(s); supporting actor and actress (George Chakiris, Rita Moreno); cinematography (Daniel L. Fapp); art direction/set decoration (Boris Leven, Victor A. Gangelin); sound (Todd-AO and Samuel Goldwyn sound departments); editing (Thomas Stanford); costume design (Irene Sharaff); and scoring (Saul Chaplin, Johnny Green, Sid Ramin, and Irwin Kostal).

White Christmas   1954   (Paramount)   *Color*
Director: Michael Curtiz
Starring: Bing Crosby, Danny Kaye, Rosemary Clooney, Vera-Ellen, Dean Jagger, Mary Wickes, John Brascia, Anne Whitfield, Richard Shannon, Grady Sutton, Sig Rumann, Herb Vigran, Percy Helton, Barrie Chase, George Chakiris

Distinguished by Irving Berlin's title song, this quasi-remake of *Holiday Inn* (1942) follows the fortunes of two song-and-dance men—Bob Wallace (Bing Crosby) and Phil Davis (Danny Kaye)—as they entertain at a winter resort owned by their former army general (Dean Jagger). Two singing sisters, Betty (Rosemary Clooney) and Judy (Vera-Ellen), are part of the package. Other songs: "Snow," "Sisters," "The Old Man," "Blue Skies," "Count Your Blessings," "Love, You Didn't Do Right by Me," "Gee, I Wish I Was Back in the Army," and "The Best Things Happen While You're Dancing." A romantic comedy (with Kaye generating some laughs), *White Christmas* is directed by Michael Curtiz from a screenplay by Norman Krasna, Norman Panama, and Melvin Frank. Historical note: it's the first movie produced in VistaVision.

Yentl   1983   (CBS)   *Color*
Director: Barbra Streisand
Starring: Barbra Streisand, Mandy Patinkin, Amy Irving, Nehemiah Persoff, Steven Hill

Barbra Streisand coscripted, directed, and takes the title role in this musical adaptation of Isaac Bashevis Singer's tale "Yentl, the Yeshiva Boy." Set in turn-of-the-century Eastern Europe, the picture begins with the death of Yentl's rabbi father. A secret scholar, the girl decides to disguise herself as a boy in order to gain entrance to the all-male yeshiva and pursue Talmudic studies. (For the masquerade she dubs herself Anshel.) Yentl's dream of formal education is short-lived, though. To save the relationship of two good-hearted lovers—Avigdor (Mandy Patinkin) and Hadass (Amy Irving)—she must reveal her true identity. A balance of comedy and drama, *Yentl* also contains a series of soliloquy-songs by Michel Legrand (music) and Alan and Marilyn Bergman (lyrics).

Suspense and Mystery

Against All Odds   1984   (RCA)   *Color*
Director: Taylor Hackford
Starring: Rachel Ward, Jeff Bridges, James Woods, Alex Karras, Jane Greer, Dorian Harewood, Swoosie Kurtz, Saul Rubinek, Bill McKinney, Richard Widmark

When good-natured football player Jeff Bridges is dropped from his Los Angeles team, he accepts an offer of quick cash to find a runaway heiress. But before he and the heiress return to California, they're enmeshed in a web of blackmail, political machinations, and murder. An update (and sunnier interpretation) of the *film noir* classic *Out of the Past*, *Against All Odds* is directed by Taylor Hackford *(An Officer and a Gentleman, White Nights)*. Jane Greer, long absent from feature films, had the Rachel Ward role in the original; here she is Ward's mother. "Take a Look at Me Now," Phil Collins's haunting theme, is incorporated into the action, then sung by the composer-lyricist over the closing credits.

Airport   1970   (MCA)   ◆   *Color*
Director: George Seaton
Starring: Burt Lancaster, Dean Martin, Jean Seberg, George Kennedy, Jacqueline Bisset, Van Heflin, Maureen Stapleton, Helen Hayes, Barry Nelson, Dana Wynter, Lloyd Nolan, Barbara Hale

Melodrama reigns when, one night at a metropolitan airport, a winter storm and a psychopath combine to make flying even riskier than usual. This variation of *Grand Hotel* didn't impress critics in 1970 but it was popular at the box office (ultimately earning over $45 million in U.S./Canada theater rentals). Producer Ross Hunter and director-screenwriter George Seaton assembled one of the most star-filled casts of the era for their adaptation of the Arthur Hailey best-seller. Helen Hayes, an Oscar winner for best actress in 1932, picked up a second trophy for her supporting role as a stowaway in *Airport*. The film's success inspired three sequels: *Airport 1975*, *Airport '77*, and *The Concorde—Airport '79*.

Al Capone   *Listed under Biographies.*

Anatomy of a Murder   1959   (RCA)   *Black-and-White*
Director: Otto Preminger
Starring: James Stewart, Lee Remick, Ben Gazzara, Arthur O'Connell, Eve Arden, Kathryn Grant, George C. Scott, Orson Bean, Russ Brown, Murray Hamilton, Brooks West, John Qualen, Royal Beal, Duke Ellington, Joseph N. Welch

A courtroom melodrama. James Stewart is a small-town Michigan attorney who defends an Army lieutenant (Ben Gazzara) on a murder charge. Central issue: had the lieutenant's wife (Lee Remick) been raped by the murder victim? The controversial themes and (for 1959) explicit dialogue were no doubt the beacons that drew Preminger to the Robert Traver best-seller. (Traver was the pseudonym for Michigan Supreme Court Justice John D. Voelker.) Wendell Mayes was the script adapter. Standouts in the cast: the three nominal leads; Eve Arden as Stewart's Della Street; George C. Scott as the prosecuting attorney; and, as the presiding judge, Joseph N. Welch—who rose to celebrity as the Army-McCarthy hearings lawyer, then became a real-life judge before making his acting debut in *Anatomy of a Murder*. Music score by Duke Ellington, who has a cameo.

Back from Eternity   1956   (United)   *Black-and-White*
Director: John Farrow
Starring: Robert Ryan, Anita Ekberg, Rod Steiger, Phyllis Kirk, Keith Andes, Fred Clark, Beulah Bondi

John Farrow's *Back from Eternity* is a remake of *Five Came Back* (1939), a suspense film also directed by Farrow—and a rare instance of a director's reshooting the same script, often in frame-by-frame duplication. Both pictures recount what happens when an airplane is forced to land in the dense jungles of the Amazon. The stranded passengers are at the mercy of the elements and one another. When the plane is finally repaired, it can carry only five of the passengers to safety. Who will make it back: the pilot? the convict? the spunky stewardess? the copilot? the devoted elderly couple? the mysterious fashion plate? A genuine B-movie, first scripted by Nathanael West, Jerry Cady, and Dalton Trumbo, *Back from Eternity* is bolstered by the players' characterizations of both the good guys (Robert Ryan, Phyllis Kirk) and the bad (Rod Steiger). Farrow's first edition of this story established him as a promising director. His later assignments: *Wake Island, Two Years before the Mast, The Big Clock, Night Has a Thousand Eyes, Alias Nick Beal,* and *Hondo.*

The Bedford Incident   1965   (RCA)   *Black-and-White*
Director: James Harris
Starring: Richard Widmark, Sidney Poitier, James MacArthur, Martin Balsam, Wally Cox, Eric Portman, Donald Sutherland, Michael Kane

Richard Widmark is the commander of the USS *Bedford,* a destroyer on a routine submarine-scouting NATO patrol. Suddenly an unidentified sub is discovered deep in the waters off the coast of Greenland. To whom does it belong? Before the answer arrives—in a climactic confrontation—a lot of tension has accumulated. This Cold War thriller is as timely and controversial now as when it was released. Widmark, in the core role, is a neurotic skipper who has built his navy career on a doctrine of perfectionism. Contributing support as less colorful characters are journalist Sidney Poitier, doctor Martin Balsam, and cunning subofficer Michael Kane. Shot by writer-director James Harris in his feature debut, *The Bedford Incident* trades on the claustrophobia induced in a military ship, thereby existing as a precursor to the similar (though set during World War II) and equally scary *Das Boot.*

Berlin Express   1948   (Nostalgia)   *Black-and-White*
Director: Jacques Tourneur
Starring: Merle Oberon, Robert Ryan, Charles Korvin, Paul Lukas, Robert Coote

High-class entertainment for those who love mysteries set aboard trains. Set in post–
World War II Europe, *Berlin Express* is a fast-paced battle of wits between Allies and
underground Nazis. The latter, in an effort to keep Germany disunited, have sworn
to kidnap and kill an important German peace-keeping advocate. But the police of
several Western nations are guarding him on a train to Berlin. Harold Medford's
screenplay keeps one guessing. Cinematographer Lucien Ballard had one of his first
challenging assignments here, followed by numerous others in Sam Peckinpah movies.
Jacques Tourneur—master of the macabre in *Cat People, I Walked with a Zombie, The
Leopard Man,* and *Out of the Past*—was the perfect choice to direct *Berlin Express.*

The Big Fix   1978   (MCA)   *Color*
Director: Jeremy Paul Kagan
*Starring: Richard Dreyfuss, Susan Anspach, Bonnie Bedelia, John Lithgow, Ofelia Me-
dina, Fritz Weaver, F. Murray Abraham, John Cunningham*

Moses Wine was a Berkeley radical in the sixties; now he's a private eye—a wisecracking
gumshoe enmeshed in politics, weekend fatherhood, and, ultimately, a murder case
that hits close to home. Another mirror of this nation's post-Vietnam mood, *The Big
Fix* derives from Roger L. Simon's whodunit novel of the same name. (Simon also
provided the screenplay.) Half the movie is about refugees of sixties activism; the other
half concerns a dirty-tricks gubernatorial campaign that Moses is investigating. Before
long the dual plots become one. *The Big Fix* affords an alternately affectionate and
grim look at the recent past—in the guise of a thriller. F. Murray Abraham fans will
enjoy the actor as a sixties cult leader who has undergone a considerable transformation.

The Big Heat   1954   (RCA)   *Black-and-White*
Director: Fritz Lang
*Starring: Glenn Ford, Gloria Grahame, Jocelyn Brando, Alexander Scourby, Lee Marvin,
Jeanette Nolan, Peter Whitney, Willis Bouchey, Robert Burton, Adam Williams, Dorothy
Green, Carolyn Jones*

This police-corruption exposé is a *film noir* favorite from veteran director Fritz Lang.
Police lieutenant Glenn Ford's young wife (Jocelyn Brando) is killed in a bomb-rigged
car intended for him. When the crooked commissioner won't assist in solving the
murder, Ford resigns from the force and sets out for revenge on the mobster responsible. Before justice triumphs, a world of scandal, physical torture, and multiple murder
is unmasked. Among the characters that Ford encounters is Lee Marvin, who plays a
sullen sadist. Sidney Boehm's no-frills dialogue is distilled from a William P. McGivern
story. Lang brought Ford and Grahame together again right after *The Big Heat* for a
film version of Zola's *The Human Beast: Human Desire,* another brutal film.

The Birds   1963   (MCA)   *Color*
Director: Alfred Hitchcock
*Starring: Rod Taylor, Jessica Tandy, Suzanne Pleshette, Veronica Cartwright, Ethel Grif-
fies, Charles McGraw, Ruth McDevitt, Joe Mantell, Elizabeth Wilson, Lonny Chapman,
Tippi Hedren*

More terror in a sunshine setting (San Francisco and points north) from the master of
suspense. The Evan Hunter script was inspired by a Daphne du Maurier short story—
counting *Rebecca* and *Jamaica Inn,* it was the third time Hitchcock utilized a du Maurier

source. Bodega Bay, not far up the coast from San Francisco, is inundated by unprovoked attacks from birds. Recovering from a seagull's peck, socialite Tippi Hedren stays with Lawyer Rod Taylor in the home he shares with his mother (Jessica Tandy) and sister (Veronica Cartwright). Before the weekend is over, more and more birds have revolted against man, bringing horror and countless deaths to the small fishing village. The theme of *The Birds,* as the director explicitly stated on occasion, is complacency—the self-absorption of humankind. Even without that heavy burden, *The Birds* rates as a peculiarity in Hitchcock's career.

Black Sunday   1977   (Paramount)   *Color*
Director: John Frankenheimer
Starring: Robert Shaw, Bruce Dern, Marthe Keller, Fritz Weaver, Steven Keats, Bekim Fehmiu, Michael V. Gazzo, William Daniels

All Fall Down. Birdman of Alcatraz. The Manchurian Candidate. Seconds. These films attest to John Frankenheimer's impressive range of style in the sixties. But the director had endured a rough period in the decade after *Grand Prix* (1966), culminating in one completed feature—*Impossible Object*—which was never released. Taken from the Thomas Harris best-seller, *Black Sunday* is a strong commercial property. Focus is upon a squad of international terrorists who plan havoc on Super Bowl Sunday—with the president in the stands. As the race against time begins, Frankenheimer tightens the screws. Bruce Dern plays a crazed bomber who gains control of the Goodyear blimp—with its TV hook-up view of the game; Robert Shaw costars as Dern's pursuer. The picture is stamped with climactic aerial sequences designed to induce white knuckles.

Blood Simple   1984   (MCA)   *Color*
Director: Joel Coen
Starring: John Getz, Frances McDormand, Dan Hedaya, M. Emmet Walsh, Samm-Art Williams, Deborah Neuman, Raquel Gavia, Van Brooks

This sophisticated but bloody salute to *film noir* is, to many, a cut above independent films, the first by brothers Joel and Ethan Coen. Both wrote the screenplay, and Joel directed. Julian Marty (Dan Hedaya), the owner of the Neon Boot, a Texas honky tonk, is unbalanced. His possessiveness has driven his wife Abby (Frances McDormand) away and—ultimately—into the arms of bartender Ray (John Getz). Riddled with insane jealousy, Julian hires a private investigator (M. Emmet Walsh) to murder the lovers. With an acknowledgment to James M. Cain, the brothers Coen then devise an unbroken sequence of double (and triple) twists and fatal misapprehensions. Black humor elevates *Blood Simple* above the standard murder mystery. The art director is Jane Musky and the photography is by Barry Sonnenfeld. Grand performances all around; the first-time viewer will have no idea who to trust, which adds to the edginess. As the rotund private detective, M. Emmet Walsh's character is the personification of sleaze.

Blow Out   1981   (Warner)   *Color*
Director: Brian De Palma
Starring: John Travolta, Nancy Allen, John Lithgow, Dennis Franz, Peter Boyden

John Travolta plays a sound effects engineer for teen slasher movies. While recording background sounds one night, he witnesses a fatal car accident. Later, playing back his tapes, he is horrified to discover that the car wreck was not an accident but premeditated murder. Bit by bit, Travolta pieces together the clues to find there has been an attempt to cover up a politician's death. Writer-director Brian De Palma usually provides visual quotes from Hitchcock's work; but most prevailing references here are to Antonioni's *Blow-Up* and Coppola's *The Conversation*. De Palma's fans will be entertained by this conspiracy thriller, replete with the director's telltale marks: sex, paranoia, gruesome deaths, and imperturbable killers. Travolta appears as a rare De Palma character who generates wholehearted sympathy—in what the actor claimed was his first adult role.

Blue Thunder   1983   (RCA)   *Color*
Director: John Badham
Starring: Roy Scheider, Warren Oates, Candy Clark, Daniel Stern, Paul Roebling, Joe Santos, David S. Sheiner, Ed Bernard, Jason Bernard, Mario Machado, James Murtaugh, Malcolm McDowell

The Los Angeles Police Department's newly formed Blue Thunder team is a helicopter surveillance group. Roy Scheider stars as the Vietnam vet pilot, an officer who patrols L.A. streets from the air—in a silent, nearly impregnable chopper with ultrasensitive microphones; an infrared, see-through-walls camera; and imposing firepower (a machine-gun capable of expelling 4,000 rounds a minute). Scheider and Daniel Stern, his copilot, chance upon a government plot involving a colonel (Malcolm McDowell), a fiend of the first rank, who has ulterior plans for the super-duper aircraft. *Blue Thunder* is a spirited techno-thriller written by Dan O'Bannon and Don Jakoby and directed by John Badham as a warmup for his *War Games*. John A. Alonzo supervised the cinematography. Owing to its theatrical success, *Blue Thunder* became a television series—short-lived early in 1984—starring James Farentino in the Scheider role.

Body Heat   1981   (Warner)   *Color*
Director: Lawrence Kasdan
Starring: William Hurt, Kathleen Turner, Richard Crenna, Ted Danson, J. A. Preston, Mickey Rourke, Kim Zimmer, Jane Hallaren, Lanna Saunders

Ned Racine (William Hurt) is a small-town Florida lawyer sweltering in the summer heat and exercising his libido at every opportunity. One especially hot night he begins an affair with Matty Walker (Kathleen Turner), the wife of a millionaire (Richard Crenna) whose far-flung business ventures require frequent travel. Before long, the lovers have outlined the demise of the husband. Lawrence Kasdan's story contains echoes of *Double Indemnity* and *The Postman Always Rings Twice*. (Lust, greed, blackmail, and murder germinate.) But *Body Heat* is more than slick imitation; it's a crime-of-passion thriller that rejuvenates the genre. The cinematography by Richard H. Kline brings atmosphere to the tropic Florida locales, and the music of John Barry is an underscoring of the erotic (and homicidal) events. Kasdan's directorial debut revalidates his screenwriting skills.

The Border   1982   (MCA)   *Color*
Director: Tony Richardson
Starring: Jack Nicholson, Harvey Keitel, Valerie Perrine, Warren Oates, Elpidia Carrillo, Shannon Wilcox, Manuel Viesias, Jeff Morris, Dirk Blocker

An exploration of illegal immigration, this melodrama casts Jack Nicholson as a patrol guard on the Mexico border. He is shocked to discover that some of his associates are taking payoffs rather than arresting aliens. His wife, Valerie Perrine, urges him to follow suit. He does—for a while. Nicholson's inner turmoil of conscience and the conflict between him and corrupt border officials form the dramatic basis of *The Border*. Finally, justice prevails. This tale of the New West finds British director Tony Richardson working in Peckinpah territory. Mexican actress Elpidia Carrillo makes a strong impression as a young mother whom Nicholson helps.

The Boston Strangler   *Listed under Biographies.*

The Boys from Brazil   1978   (CBS)   *Color*
Director: Franklin J. Schaffner
Starring: Gregory Peck, Laurence Olivier, James Mason, Lilli Palmer, Uta Hagen, Bruno Ganz, Rosemary Harris, Steve Guttenberg, Denholm Elliott, John Dehner, John Rubinstein, Anne Meara, David Hurst, Michael Gough, Prunella Scales

Gregory Peck, radically cast against type, plays Nazi war criminal Dr. Josef Mengele, a geneticist hiding in the Brazilian jungles, where he continues the experimentation he began in the death camps. (Mengele's mad dream, in Ira Levin's novel and Heywood Gould's screen adaptation, is to clone Hitler.) Vowing to destroy Mengele is Ezra Leiberman (Laurence Olivier), an elderly Nazi hunter, based somewhat on the real-life Simon Wiesenthal. Cinematographer Henri Decaë, whose work has graced French films since 1949, shot this fascinating but gruesome horror story.

Bullitt   1968   (Warner)   ◆   *Color*
Director: Peter Yates
Starring: Steve McQueen, Robert Vaughn, Jacqueline Bisset, Don Gordon, Robert Duvall, Simon Oakland, Norman Fell, Georg Stanford Brown, Robert Lipton, Justin Tarr, Ed Peck, Al Checco, Victor Tayback

The picture opens with a gangland slaying and ends in retribution. In the interval, San Francisco police lieutenant Frank Bullitt must ferret out a double-dealing defector from the top levels of a Chicago mob. *Bullitt* is a formula film scrambled to keep viewers off-guard; the way scriptwriters Alan R. Trustman and Harry Keliner submerged plot and character was new in 1968—but the formula has been widely imitated since, as any "Miami Vice" viewer can testify. This was director Peter Yates's first American movie. Steve McQueen stars as the hero—flip, tanned, turtlenecked, and driving a flashy Mustang. A key scene of the production is the breathtaking auto chase through San Francisco's hilly streets shot by cinematographer William Fraker and edited by Oscar-winning Frank P. Keller. Inspired by Robert L. Pike's novel, *Mute Witness*.

Charade   1963   (MCA; Video Treasures; Goodtimes   *Color*
     Home Video Corp.)
Director: Stanley Donen
Starring: Cary Grant, Audrey Hepburn, Walter Matthau, James Coburn, George Kennedy, Ned Glass, Jacques Marin, Paul Bonifas

After her husband is murdered in their Paris apartment, Regina Lampert (Audrey Hepburn) is menaced by four sadistic badmen. They, in tandem with her late mate, stole a quarter of a million in gold during World War II—and they presume Regina knows the whereabouts of the fortune. To the lady's rescue comes an FBI agent and tax investigator with half a dozen aliases (Cary Grant). This thriller, with hints of Hitchcock in the black humor, was scripted by Peter Stone from his novel with French scenarist and *policier* writer Marc Behm. Director Stanley Donen shot *Charade* in Paris and the French Alps, then appended a haunting musical score by Henry Mancini; Johnny Mercer provided the lyrics for the title song. From this union arises a suspenseful romantic comedy. Also on view are Walter Matthau, James Coburn, and George Kennedy as the villains.

Charley Varrick 1973 (MCA) *Color*
Director: Don Siegel
Starring: Walter Matthau, Joe Don Baker, Felicia Farr, Andy Robinson, Sheree North, Norman Fell, Benson Fong, Woodrow Parfrey, William Schallert, Jacqueline Scott, Marjorie Bennett, Rudy Diaz, Charles Matthau, John Vernon

Another crime thriller from cult favorite Don Siegel *(Riot in Cell Block 11, Baby Face Nelson, Madigan, Coogan's Bluff, Dirty Harry)*. Walter Matthau plays Charley Varrick, a crop-duster pilot whose second career is more lucrative: bank robber. Charley, however, is conservative, low-risk, and low-profile. Known as "the last of the independents," he knocks off only small banks. Something goes awry in his latest stick-up: he unwittingly steals laundered Mafia money—and thus finds himself at odds with both the Mafia and the FBI. John Reese's novel, *The Looters,* was a straightforward, hard-nosed crime novel; but the screen adaptation by Howard Rodman and Dean Reisner invests the proceedings—and the principal character—with an undercurrent of humor. Matthau, again as a gruff good guy, has a field day outwitting his pursuers. Director Siegel, in Hitchcock style, does a walk-on—as a grizzled reprobate named Murph.

Chinatown 1974 (Paramount) ◆ *Color*
Director: Roman Polanski
Starring: Jack Nicholson, Faye Dunaway, John Hillerman, Perry Lopez, Burt Young, Bruce Glover, Joe Mantell, Roy Jensen, Diane Ladd, Dick Bakalyn, John Huston

The year: 1937. J. J. Gittes, formerly of the Los Angeles police force—and assigned to the Chinatown beat—is now a private eye. In the foreground of his investigation is a real estate corruption scam involving water rights. Soon awaiting Gittes's services is a case featuring incest and murder. Jack Nicholson plays the protagonist—brash, profane, cynical, but essentially scrupulous. The chief obstacle in his solution to the mystery is Faye Dunaway's character. John A. Alonzo's cinematography captures the tones of the time and place, and the period artifacts come to life in Richard Sylbert's art and set direction (and through his sister-in-law Althea's costumes). *Chinatown,* while acknowledging its thirties hardboiled origins, is both grimmer and grittier than its prototypes. A near-classic, it would have attained perfection had director Polanski filmed the ending—the final reckoning in Chinatown—that Robert Towne wrote, rather than the Gothic finale the finished movie bears. Towne—who contributed to *Bonnie and Clyde* rewrites (and wrote the Brando-Pacino garden scene in *The Godfather*) before receiving full credit for *The Last Detail*—perhaps had the last laugh. When the 1974 Oscars were parceled out, the only *Chinatown* recipient was best original screenplay: Robert Towne.

The Collector   1965   (RCA)   *Color*
Director: William Wyler
Starring: Terence Stamp, Samantha Eggar, Mona Washbourne, Maurice Dallimore, William Beckley, Gordon Barclay, David Haviland

Freddie Clegg is a lonely clerk in a London bank. Butterfly collecting is his avocation—and his only obsession until he decides to kidnap a young woman, Miranda Grey, and install her in the cellar of his house in the countryside. Terence Stamp stars as Freddie; Samantha Eggar plays his human butterfly. This psychological suspense tale, with crime from the criminal's point of view, has a screenplay by Stanley Mann and John Kohn—revamped from the dual-narration, twice-told construction of the John Fowles novel. *The Collector* is essentially a two-character movie—a contest of wills between captor and captive. Under William Wyler's deliberate pacing, it also becomes a solemn representation of psychosis. (Maurice Jarre provided the music.) At one point in the shooting, Wyler contemplated dismissing Miss Eggar and replacing her with Natalie Wood. Thanks to the unavailability of the latter, Eggar continued in the role—and critical raves and an Oscar nomination ensued.

Coma   1978   (MGM)   *Color*
Director: Michael Chrichton
Starring: Geneviève Bujold, Michael Douglas, Elizabeth Ashley, Rip Torn, Richard Widmark, Lois Chiles, Harry Rhodes, Lance LeGault

Geneviève Bujold uncovers a hospital conspiracy in this shocker from writer-director Michael Crichton. Bujold, a Boston surgeon, fears that young, healthy patients are deliberately being rendered comatose. Her misgivings lead her to a heavily guarded government institute where patients are placed on life-support systems—and their organs are auctioned off to the highest bidder. From this grisly premise, initially set forth by novelist Robin Cook, surfaces a fast-paced and not too graphic medical thriller. Bujold makes a fetching amateur sleuth—a lady in distress whose wild accusations are not believed (except by the audience). Michael Douglas plays the heroine's colleague and live-in boyfriend. Keep a sharp watch for a pre-"Magnum" Tom Selleck as one of the victims.

The Conversation   1974   (Paramount)   ✳   *Color*
Director: Francis Ford Coppola
Starring: Gene Hackman, John Cazale, Allen Garfield, Frederic Forrest, Cindy Williams, Michael Higgins, Elizabeth MacRae, Teri Garr, Harrison Ford, Mark Wheeler, Robert Shields, Phoebe Alexander

Gene Hackman stars as Harry Caul, a professional surveillance and security technician (wiretapper) working in San Francisco. Hired to eavesdrop on a young man and woman as they stroll in Ghirardelli Square, Harry utilizes his most sophisticated bugging equipment. Later, assembling a master tape in his editing studio, he comes across a key phrase (that the man whispered to the woman): "He'd kill us if he got the chance." Harry then concludes that the man who hired him—a high-level business executive (Robert Duvall in an unbilled cameo)—intends just that: murder. Harry decides to save the young couple from their fate. Soon, however, the tables are turned. Someone, Harry discovers, is spying on him. Hackman is excellent as the edgy, guilt-ridden snoop; he makes Harry Caul an unforgettably desperate figure. Supporting him are Harrison Ford as an enigmatic associate of Duvall's; Cindy Williams and Frederic Forrest as the couple who have the conversation; and—fleetingly—mime artist Robert Shields, engaging in a bit of street theater. Francis Ford Coppola, as scenarist and director, turns *The Conversation* into a chilling, complex quasi documentary—distinguished by Bill Butler's unadorned cinematography and Walter Murch's editing and sound engineering. *The Conversation* was completed in 1972, then shelved until 1974, when it won the Palme d'Or at Cannes.

Cutter's Way   1981   (MGM)   *Color*
Director: Ivan Passer
Starring: Jeff Bridges, John Heard, Lisa Eichhorn, Ann Dusenberry, Stephen Elliott, Arthur Rosenberg, Nina Van Pallandt, Patricia Donahue

Cutter's Way, first released as *Cutter and Bone*, failed to attract audiences under either title. Perhaps audiences primed for a murder mystery were unprepared for a sobering character study of three post-Vietnam misfits. Based on Newton Thornberg's novel *(Cutter and Bone)*, the film depicts the lives of Alex Cutter (John Heard), a crippled veteran; Richard Bone (Jeff Bridges), his beach bum friend; and Cutter's wife, Maureen (Lisa Eichhorn), who loves both men. The three friends become involved in a complex murder case when Bone chances upon the aftermath of a brutal slaying. Cutter, Bone, and Maureen suspect that a Santa Barbara oilman is the killer of a teenage girl, so they do some surreptitious sleuthing—with tragic results. Jeffrey Alan Fiskin wrote the screenplay. Czech emigré Ivan Passer's other films include *Born to Win, Law and Disorder,* and *Creator.*

Dark Passage   1947   (Key)   *Black-and-White*
Director: Delmer Daves
Starring: Humphrey Bogart, Lauren Bacall, Bruce Bennett, Agnes Moorehead, Tom D'Andrea, Houseley Stevenson

Convicted of murder by circumstantial evidence, a wrongly accused man escapes from San Quentin and undergoes plastic surgery. Humphrey Bogart stars with Lauren Bacall in this thriller, which breathes new life into the wrong man theme. Dramatized by Delmer Daves from the David Goodis novel, the story makes interesting use of subjective camera, particularly in the early passages before the hero is reborn with Bogart's face. Sid Hickox is the director of photography. *Dark Passage* was Bogie and Bacall's third screen teaming—preceded by *To Have and Have Not* (1944) and *The Big Sleep* (1946).

The Day of the Dolphin   1973   (Embassy)   *Color*
Director: Mike Nichols
Starring: George C. Scott, Trish Van Devere, Paul Sorvino, Fritz Weaver, Jon Korkes, Edward Herrmann, John Dehner, Elizabeth Wilson

This conspiracy story centers around a research foundation for the study of dolphins. A leading scientist, played by George C. Scott, heads a team of young marine biologists working off the coast of Florida. There they are defining the interrelationship between dolphin language and English. Scott's prize pupils are a pair of affectionate dolphins named Alpha and Beta—Fa and Be, for short. Some nefarious (and unspecified) government agency wants to use Fa and Be in a plot to blow up the president's yacht. *The Day of the Dolphin,* as adapted by Buck Henry, muffles the anti-American components of Robert Merle's novel and emphasizes the cuteness of Fa and Be. Had the producers deleted several violent episodes and the bitter ending, *The Day of the Dolphin* would make a fine fantasy-spy-adventure story for small children. The film was shot by William A. Fraker above water and Lamar Boren below.

Death on the Nile   1978   (Thorn)   ◆   *Color*
Director: John Guillermin
Starring: Peter Ustinov, Jane Birkin, Lois Chiles, Bette Davis, Mia Farrow, Jon Finch, Olivia Hussey, George Kennedy, Angela Lansbury, Simon MacCorkindale, David Niven, Maggie Smith, Jack Warden, Harry Andrews, I. S. Johar, Sam Wanamaker

Time: the mid-thirties. Place: the Nile steamer *Karnak*. On board for the luxury cruise up the Nile are several outlandish passengers, not the least being Hercule Poirot, the legendary Belgian detective. Joining him are an assortment of British and American tourists, representatives of the idle class—and all suspects when a young heiress on board is brutally murdered. Anthony Shaffer's screenplay is a translation of Agatha Christie's puzzler, and not above planting a few red herrings. As in *Murder on the Orient Express,* a well-known cast provides the fun of star-gazing. This time around Peter Ustinov assumes the Poirot role; he gives a droll, spirited interpretation. (Ustinov subsequently played Poirot in *Evil Under the Sun* and a series of made-for-TV movies.) Anthony Powell won an Oscar for his costume designs. *Death on the Nile,* first published in 1937, was Dame Agatha's favorite novel among all those she set in foreign locales.

Death Wish   1974   (Paramount)   *Color*
Director: Michael Winner
Starring: Charles Bronson, Hope Lange, Vincent Gardenia, Stuart Margolin, William Redfield, Steven Keats, Gregory Rozakis

Vigilante justice, New York City style, is the subject of this controversial and violent movie. Muggers rape architect Paul Kersey's daughter and murder his wife. When the police can't ascertain the killers' identities, Kersey takes the law into his own hands. Not only does he unearth his wife's murderers, but other criminals too, and when street crime plunges drastically, he becomes a hero (although of unknown identity). Charles Bronson plays Paul Kersey, Hope Lange his wife, and Vincent Gardenia the cop who tries to expose him. Wendell Mayes's screenplay, a rethinking of the Brian Garfield novel, comes down clearly in favor of vigilantism; Garfield's depiction wasn't so cut and dry. *Death Wish* is a thriller directed by Michael Winner—a frequent Bronson collaborator. (Their partnership is best represented by *The Mechanic.*) Winner, Bronson, and Gardenia met for an encore in 1982—*Death Wish II.* Only Winner and Bronson participated in the finale: *Death Wish 3* (1985).

Deathtrap   1982   (Warner)   *Color*
Director: Sidney Lumet
Starring: Michael Caine, Christopher Reeve, Dyan Cannon, Irene Worth, Henry Jones, Joe Silver, Tony Di Benedetto

After a series of box-office disasters, a once-celebrated Broadway dramatist (Michael Caine) is desperate for another winner. When one of his former students (Christopher Reeve) submits a well-crafted playscript, Caine is tempted to take full credit. His wife (Dyan Cannon) wonders: would he kill for a hit? With adultery, larceny, covert motives, and a red herring or two among its ingredients, *Deathtrap* emphasizes wit more than action. From Ira Levin's long-running Broadway edition, adapted by Jay Presson Allen, the premise is less whodunit than who will do it to whom. The dénouement, none too convincing in the stage version, is somewhat neatened up for the movie. In difficult roles, the three principals tread the delicate line between melodrama and a parody thereof. Sidney Lumet directed.

The Deep 1977 (RCA) *Color*
Director: Peter Yates
Starring: Robert Shaw, Jacqueline Bisset, Nick Nolte, Louis Gossett, Eli Wallach, Robert Tessier, Earl Maynard

Novice scuba divers David Sanders (Nick Nolte) and Gail Berke (Jacqueline Bisset) are hunting for sunken treasures. A Haitian named Cloche (Louis Gossett) and his gang of thugs are after a shipwrecked consignment of morphine. The two parties encounter one another in the waters off Bermuda—thereby setting the plot in motion. Nolte and Bisset soon realize that sharks and moray eels aren't the only dangers lurking in the deep. Peter Benchley's novel was a follow-up to *Jaws*, and in the screen adaptation, cowritten with Tracy Keenan Wynn, Robert Shaw plays the friendly old salt who comes to the young couple's rescue. As the rough-hewn adventurer, Shaw is one of the chief delights of the film. Another bonus: the underwater photography of Al Giddings and Stan Waterman. Director Peter Yates's climactic underwater scene could perhaps have been staged more carefully; all the characters are dressed in masks and wet suits and some viewers may be confused over which swimmers are the good guys, which the bad.

The Detective 1968 (CBS) *Color*
Director: Gordon Douglas
Starring: Frank Sinatra, Lee Remick, Jacqueline Bisset, Ralph Meeker, William Windom, Al Freeman, Jr., Tony Musante, Jack Klugman, Horace MacMahon, Lloyd Bochner, Robert Duvall

Frank Sinatra has the role of a time-toughened New York City cop with marital difficulties. *The Detective*, inspired by Roderick Thorp's popular novel, divides its concern between the hero's present caseload and his problems with his wife. Abby Mann's screenplay adopts Thorp's relatively gutsy approach to both plot threads. On view are the deglamourized, lower depths aspects of Manhattan—with Sinatra, after investigating a gruesome antigay murder, realizing that an innocent man has been sent to the electric chair. A tale punctuated by gore and clinical descriptions of corpse mutilations, *The Detective* was in its day a bona fide shocker.

Dial "M" for Murder 1954 (Warner) *Color*
Director: Alfred Hitchcock
Starring: Ray Milland, Grace Kelly, Robert Cummings, John Williams, Anthony Dawson, Leo Britt, Patrick Allen, George Leigh

Tony Wendice is a former tennis ace now comfortably supported by his loyal wife, Margot. Margot is, in turn, loved by Mark Halliday, a crime story writer. Jealous beyond all reason, Tony hatches a plot to murder his wealthy spouse—and use the writer as an alibi while blackmailing an old school chum into committing the murder. That's the starting point for this Alfred Hitchcock favorite. *Dial "M" for Murder* arises from Frederick Knott's London and New York theatrical success, adapted by the dramatist himself. The film only rarely opens up beyond the single set of the stage production. Ray Milland stars as the cunning husband; Grace Kelly, his intended victim; Robert Cummings, the detective fiction writer; and, as the real detective, John Williams, repeating his stage role as Inspector Hubbard. This picture was Hitchcock's only experiment in 3-D (a component forced on him by Jack Warner); however, because the 3-D fad was abating, the finished feature was originally released in a normal flat version. For quick eyes: Hitch's cameo arrives this time in the form of a photograph. A 1981 made-for-television version cast Christopher Plummer, Angie Dickinson, Michael Parks, and Anthony Quayle in the central roles.

Diamonds Are Forever   1971   (CBS)   *Color*
Director: Guy Hamilton
Starring: Sean Connery, Jill St. John, Charles Gray, Lana Wood, Jimmy Dean, Bruce Cabot, Bruce Glover, Bernard Lee, Lois Maxwell, Desmond Llewelyn, Leonard Barr, Laurence Naismith

For record-keepers: *Diamonds Are Forever* is the eighth James Bond caper, the sixth with Sean Connery as star, the second directed by Guy Hamilton, and the first set in American locales. Las Vegas, Reno, Palm Springs, and Los Angeles provide the backdrops as Agent 007 pursues a diamond smuggler. The plot, as always, is heavily revised from the Ian Fleming original—on this occasion by Richard Maibaum and Tom Mankiewicz. The scenarists have created a formula spy adventure, reliant on stunts and catastrophic explosions. As Ernst Blofeld, the main menace, Charles Gray is noteworthy.

Dirty Harry   1971   (Warner)   *Color*
Director: Don Siegel
Starring: Clint Eastwood, Harry Guardino, Reni Santoni, Andy Robinson, John Larch, John Mitchum, Mae Mercer, Lyn Edginton, Ruth Kobart, Woodrow Parfrey, Josef Sommer, William Paterson, James Nolan, John Vernon

This trend-setting urban cop thriller introduces Inspector Harry Callahan (Clint Eastwood) of the San Francisco police force. Harry is a soft-spoken troubleshooter who always draws tricky assignments. His latest case involves a slimy psychopath dubbed The Scorpio Killer, who is a sniper on the loose. An expert marksman, he has pledged to kill one person a day until he is caught. Harry, packing a .44 Magnum, does catch him; however, The Scorpio Killer is released through lack of evidence. Fed up with the justice system, Harry tosses away his badge, preferring to stalk his psychotic prey as a vigilante. *Dirty Harry* unfolds with a minimum of dialogue, and a lot of gore and brutality, supplied by husband-and-wife team Rita M. and Harry Julian Fink, with additional contributions by Dean Riesner. Men's action-adventure drama is director Don Siegel's *forte*. As the exalted cop hero, Clint Eastwood attracted an additional, non-Western audience. The continuing exploits of Harry Callahan have been dramatized in *Magnum Force, The Enforcer,* and *Sudden Impact* (the "Make my day" movie).

Dr. No   Great Britain 1962; U.S. 1963   (CBS)   *Color*
Director: Terence Young
Starring: Sean Connery, Jack Lord, Joseph Wiseman, Ursula Andress, Zena Marshall, Eunice Gayson, Lois Maxwell, Margaret LeWars, John Kitzmiller, Bernard Lee, Anthony Dawson, Lester Prendergast

Dr. No, the movie that launched an industry and created megastars and millionaires, was itself released with little fanfare. This initial cinema installment (*Casino Royale* was the first book) of the James Bond series cost a mere million—hardly the lavish, large budget spectacular that each of the subsequent entries became. To introduce Britain's foremost cloak-and-dagger hero to moviegoers, producers Harry Saltzman and Albert R. Broccoli chose *Dr. No,* wherein Agent 007 is dispatched to Kingston, Jamaica, to investigate the disappearance of another operative. To solve the mystery, Bond invades Crab Key, the secret island of arch-fiend Dr. No, a scientist working with SPECTRE (Special Executive for Counter-Terrorism, Revenge and Extortion). Joseph Wiseman plays Dr. No, Ursula Andress portrays Honey Ryan, the Venus who emerges scantily garbed from the sea, and Sean Connery stars as James Bond, as he would on six subsequent occasions. (The choice of too-handsome Connery didn't please novelist Ian Fleming. His ideal casting: a lean, tough type with a scar on his face—composer Hoagy Carmichael.) Also making the first of many appearances are Bernard Lee (M) and Lois Maxwell (Miss Moneypenny, M's private secretary). The screenplay credit reads Richard Maibaum, Johanna Harwood, and Berkley Mather; Terence Young directed. Young also guided these later 007 escapades: *From Russia with Love* and *Thunderball.*

Dragnet   1954   (MCA)   *Color*
Director: Jack Webb
Starring: Jack Webb, Ben Alexander, Richard Boone, Ann Robinson, Stacy Harris, Virginia Gregg, Victor Perrin, Georgia Ellis, James Griffith, Dick Cathcart, Malcolm Atterbury, Olan Soulé, Dub Taylor

Dragnet began as a radio show in 1949. The series was transferred to television for its (initial) eight-year run in 1952. Then, in 1954, the Emmy-winning police drama had a big screen outing. This theatrical film highlights all the trademarks of the series: the clipped dialogue (penned by Richard L. Breen), Walter Schumann's bold theme music, and adherence to the files of the Los Angeles Police Department. Jack Webb served as producer, director, and star. As LAPD plainclothesman Sergeant Joe Friday, he detects a pattern in a sequence of seemingly random murders. Ben Alexander, the perennial Officer Frank Smith, is Watson to Friday's Holmes. And one may see Dennis Weaver, honing his pre-"McCloud" police skills, as one of Friday's associates, a captain of homicide. Cliff Arquette makes an appearance as Charley Weaver. Edward Colman supervised the photography.

Dressed to Kill   1980   (Warner)   *Color*
Director: Brian De Palma
Starring: Michael Caine, Angie Dickinson, Nancy Allen, Keith Gordon, Dennis Franz, David Margulies

Dressed to Kill begins by dwelling upon a day in the life of a sexually frustrated housewife: her fantasies; unsatisfactory sex with her husband; a visit to her psychiatrist; a flirtation at the Metropolitan Museum of Art; then satisfactory sex at the apartment of the handsome stranger from the museum. Then, as she is leaving the stranger's building to return to her family, she is gruesomely murdered by a mad slasher. The woman's son, a science whiz, finds the killer with the help of a quick-witted prostitute whom the slasher is also stalking. Brian De Palma's film contains an explicitness (of sex *and* violence) that some may consider soft-core pornography—a limit the writer-director pushed even further in *Blow Out* and *Body Double.* Pino Donaggio's insistent musical score helps, as does the playing by the dominant actors. Note the performance by

Keith Gordon, later the proud owner of *Christine,* playing the teenage scientist who stumbles upon the identity of the psycho killer.

The Eagle Has Landed   1977   (CBS)   *Color*
Director: John Sturges
Starring: Michael Caine, Donald Sutherland, Robert Duvall, Jenny Agutter, Donald Pleasence, Anthony Quayle, Larry Hagman, Jean Marsh, Sven-Bertil Taube, John Standing, Judy Geeson, Maurice Roeves

This speculative historical thriller emanates from the same school as *The Day of the Jackal* and *Brass Target,* to name two recent graduates. Those movies (and their source books) involved assassination plots against, respectively, General De Gaulle and General Patton. *The Eagle Has Landed,* adapted by Tom Mankiewicz from the Jack Higgins adventure novel, uses Winston Churchill as a target. During World War II several Nazi paratroopers land near an English village where the Prime Minister will be visiting. Some of the Germans, impersonating genteel British folk, infiltrate the community in preparation for kidnapping and murdering Churchill. Although the outcome is foreknown, scenarist Maniewicz and director John Sturges create a series of suspenseful episodes. Part of the tension arises from the discovery that there are a few good guys among the German ranks and a few rotten ones among the village populace.

The Enforcer   1976   (Warner)   *Color*
Director: James Fargo
Starring: Clint Eastwood, Tyne Daly, Harry Guardino, Bradford Dillman, John Mitchum, DeVeren Bookwalter, John Crawford, Albert Popwell

Dirty Harry Callahan (Clint Eastwood) returns in installment three of the popular series. The mayor of San Francisco is kidnapped, so Harry finds himself battling an underground terrorist group, the Revolutionary Strike Force. Before the psychopathic hoodlums are put to rest, the film has lingered upon the requisite brutality and bloodshed (and several car chases). Stirling Silliphant and Dean Riesner's script follows the formula, while James Fargo, the assistant director on several previous Clint Eastwood films, is elevated to full status here. Eastwood's macho intensity pervades *The Enforcer,* but this time he is bolstered by Tyne Daly, playing his new female partner. Daly is the costar of TV's long-running "Cagney and Lacey."

Enter the Dragon   1973   (Warner)   *Color*
Director: Robert Clouse
Starring: Bruce Lee, John Saxon, Jim Kelly, Shih Kien, Bob Wall, Ahna Capri, Angela Mao Ying, Betty Chung, Geoffrey Weeks, Yang Sze, Peter Archer

In the last film Bruce Lee completed before his untimely death, he plays a Hong Kong martial arts expert who turns sleuth. He and costars John Saxon and Jim Kelly are hired by British intelligence to penetrate the island fortress of an Oriental drug-and-prostitution kingpin. As the three heroes gather evidence, they participate in a series of martial arts championships. At this juncture in Michael Allin's script, lunges, kicks, and leaping acrobatics—recorded by cinematographer Gilbert Hubbs—prevail. The climactic hand-to-hand competition finds Lee against the chief villain, who wears a hand mitt of knife blades. That finale is staged by director Robert Clouse in a hall of mirrors—à la Orson Welles's *The Lady from Shanghai.*

Evil Under the Sun   1982   (Thorn)   *Color*
Director: Guy Hamilton
Starring: Peter Ustinov, Jane Birkin, Colin Blakely, Nicholas Clay, James Mason, Sylvia Miles, Denis Quilley, Diana Rigg, Maggie Smith, Emily Hone, John Alderson, Paul Antrim, Cyril Conway, Barbara Hicks, Richard Vernon

In Guy Hamilton's film version of the 1941 Agatha Christie novel, from Anthony Shaffer's script, Peter Ustinov again plays Poirot. The redoubtable Belgian is on holiday at a resort hotel on an exotic island in the Adriatic (changed from Christie's original Devon seaside setting). Suddenly, a tragic death occurs—and there are intimations of an earlier unsolved murder. Poirot, however, is not deceived. *Evil Under the Sun* is another star-studded Christie whodunit. Shaffer's dialogue is copious with theatrical repartee and one-upmanship. (Shaffer, the twin brother of Peter Shaffer, also wrote the stage play and film *Sleuth.*) Contributing to the stylishness are the Cole Porter score, Anthony Powell's campy costumes, and the vibrant color cinematography of Christopher Challis. Filmed on location in Majorca.

Eye of the Needle   1981   (CBS)   *Color*
Director: Richard Marquand
Starring: Donald Sutherland, Kate Nelligan, Ian Bannen, Christopher Cazenove, Philip Martin Brown, Alex McCrindle

London, 1940. In this World War II spy thriller, a faithful adaptation of Ken Follett's international best-seller, Donald Sutherland plays a crafty German agent—Die Nagel—who has penetrated British intelligence. Having learned of plans for the D-Day invasion, he charters a boat for Europe. But a squall intervenes and he crashes on Scotland's Storm Island, inhabited by only four people. He is cared for by a loyal Englishwoman (Kate Nelligan), a devoted wife and mother. By the time she learns Die Nagel's true identity, she and her family are in jeopardy. Stanley Mann's screenplay generates tension of a Hitchcockian strain. The directorial reins are in the hands of Richard Marquand *(The Legacy, Return of the Jedi, Jagged Edge).* Alan Hume was the cinematographer.

Eyes of Laura Mars   1978   (RCA)   *Color*
Director: Irvin Kershner
Starring: Faye Dunaway, Tommy Lee Jones, Brad Dourif, René Auberjonois, Raul Julia, Frank Adonis, Lisa Taylor

Eyes of Laura Mars is a slasher film, photographed elegantly and in trendy settings with handsome stars. Successful fashion photographer Laura Mars (Faye Dunaway) specializes in layouts with SoHo-chic sadomasochist elements. While shooting a new spread, Laura begins to have premonitions about a psycho killer. In reality, a homicidal maniac embarks on a series of ice-pick murders—starting with Laura's sexy models. What is the link between her psychic visions and the unknown killer? A police lieutenant (Tommy Lee Jones) is assigned to protect Laura and solve the murders. This stylish whodunit, not for the squeamish, was written by John Carpenter (of *Halloween* fame), revised by David Zelag Goodman, and directed by Irvin Kershner. Cinematographer Victor J. Kemper and editor Michael Kahn are responsible for a good deal of the suspense. Raul Julia, as Laura's ex-husband, and René Auberjonois, her agent-manager, are among the supporting performers.

Eyewitness   1981   (CBS)   *Color*
Director: Peter Yates
Starring: William Hurt, Sigourney Weaver, Christopher Plummer, James Woods, Irene Worth, Kenneth McMillan, Pamela Reed, Steven Hill, Morgan Freeman

Two plots develop concurrently in this whodunit about a night janitor in a Manhattan office building who discovers a murder victim on his rounds, then romances the television newswoman assigned to report on the slaying. William Hurt is the janitor. Although not an eyewitness, he implies that he is in order to meet the beautiful TV journalist, played by Sigourney Weaver. As the suspects accumulate, the murder becomes more and more shrouded in mystery—and the lives of the two principals are placed in increasing jeopardy. *Eyewitness* constitutes a reunion, in a radically different genre, for Steve Tesich and Peter Yates, the writer and the director of *Breaking Away*.

The **Fallen Idol**   1948   (Prism; Budget Video;   ★   *Black-and-White*
      Cable Films; Western Film & Video Inc.; Movie Buff Video)
Director: Carol Reed
Starring: Sir Ralph Richardson, Michèle Morgan, Bobby Henrey, Sonia Dresdel, Jack Hawkins, Bernard Lee, Denis O'Dea, Dora Bryan

Graham Greene's imaginative suspense story "The Basement Room" is the source for this Carol Reed film. Greene, who also wrote the screen adaptation, tells of a small boy whose father is a London ambassador. Because his father is away so frequently, the youngster turns his affections to the good-natured household butler. This source of idolatry has a shrewish wife, the embassy cook. When the cook is killed in a fall, the ambassador's son mistakenly interprets the accidental death as murder—and suspects his friend. When a police investigating team arrive, the boy perjures himself in order to protect his idol. But the lies only add to the incriminating evidence. How will the butler prove his innocence? *The Fallen Idol* is a mystery-cum-character study, named best picture of the year by the British Film Academy. Nuanced acting is one of the hallmarks of Carol Reed's motion pictures, and here he is served by Sir Ralph Richardson in the title role, Michèle Morgan as the embassy clerk he loves, and Bobby Henrey playing the well-meaning child.

Family Plot   1976   (MCA)   *Color*
Director: Alfred Hitchcock
Starring: Karen Black, Bruce Dern, Barbara Harris, William Devane, Ed Lauter, Cathleen Nesbitt, Katherine Helmond, Warren J. Kemmerling, Edith Atwater, William Prince, Nicholas Colasanto, Marge Redmond

The Rainbird Pattern by British suspense veteran Victor Canning provides the springboard for this Alfred Hitchcock comedy-drama—the director's final film. Ernest Lehman's California-set screenplay, lighter in tone than Canning's novel, follows two couples: Blanche, a possibly fake spiritualist, and Lumley, her boyfriend, are trying to find a dying dowager's missing grandson; Fran and Adamson, two sinister figures, are hatching a kidnapping plot. It turns out that Adamson is the missing heir, but when he learns that Blanche and Lumley are snooping around, he mistakes their motives and decides to kill them. Hitchcock's tongue is planted firmly in cheek; *Family Plot* awakens memories of his other lighthearted thrillers, including *Young and Innocent* and *The Lady Vanishes*. Barbara Harris stars as Blanche, the madcap psychic. Bruce Dern, as Lumley, is her foil. William Devane and Karen Black play the sleek villains. TV sitcom fans will enjoy seeing Katherine Helmond, of "Soap" and "Who's the Boss?," and the late Nicholas Colasanto, Coach on "Cheers," in small but important roles. The obligatory Hitchcock cameo arrives this time as the famous silhouette is framed behind a frosted-window door marked Registrar of Births and Deaths. Two exquisite set pieces make *Family Plot* unmistakably Hitchcock: a runaway car sequence and a chase through a cemetery. (The cinematographer was Leonard J. South.) As lagniappe, the enterprise is capped by the music of John Williams.

Farewell, My Lovely   1975   (RCA)   *Color*
Director: Dick Richards
Starring: Robert Mitchum, Charlotte Rampling, John Ireland, Sylvia Miles, Anthony Zerbe, Harry Dean Stanton, Jack O'Halloran, Joe Spinell, Sylvester Stallone, Kate Murtagh, John O'Leary, Walter McGinn, Burton Gilliam

Raymond Chandler's hardboiled Los Angeles shamus has been embodied by a long line of screen idols. Among the diverse personalities to have portrayed Philip Marlowe are Humphrey Bogart *(The Big Sleep)*, Robert Montgomery *(Lady in the Lake)*, George Montgomery *(The Brasher Doubloon)*, James Garner *(Marlowe)*, Elliott Gould *(The Long Goodbye)*, and, considered by many the best of the bunch, Dick Powell in *Murder, My Sweet*—the earlier adaptation of *Farewell, My Lovely*. This time around Robert Mitchum assumes the role of Marlowe. The plot is essentially unchanged in this Dick Richards–directed version: the detective embarks on a search for an ex-con's missing girlfriend. The seedy forties milieux are re-created by cameraman John A. Alonzo and production designer Dean Tavoularis. Speaking Chandler's lines, as revised by scenarist David Zelag Goodman, are numerous fine actors. In her second Academy Award–nominated performance, Sylvia Miles appears briefly as Mrs. Florian. And there are good moments from John Ireland as Multy, Harry Dean Stanton as Billy Rolfe, John O'Leary as Marriott, and Sly Stallone as Jonnie. (Mitchum played Marlowe once again—in the 1978 remake and update of *The Big Sleep*, set in London.)

For Your Eyes Only   1981   (CBS)   *Color*
Director: John Glen
Starring: Roger Moore, Carole Bouquet, Topol, Lynn-Holly Johnson, Julian Glover, Jill Bennett, Jack Hedley, Lois Maxwell, Cassandra Harris, Desmond Llewelyn, Geoffrey Keen

James Bond is once again on Her Majesty's secret service. For his current mission he is dispatched to Greece. A mysterious sea crash has caused the sinking of a surveillance vessel. On board is a top-secret activating device for a nuclear submarine. Bond must recover the device before it falls into Soviet hands. In his fifth appearance as Ian Fleming's licensed-to-kill hero, Roger Moore thwarts yet another ruthless madman. This chase thriller, written by Richard Maibaum and Michael G. Wilson, bears no relation to the Fleming original. Even so, most 007 fans agree that of the Bond films starring Moore, *For Your Eyes Only* rates as the best. John Glen, a second-unit director on earlier Bonds, makes his full-fledged debut here. His other features include *Octopussy* (1983) and *A View to a Kill* (1985). Sheena Easton performs the title song, as written by Bill Conti (music) and Mick Leeson (lyrics).

Force 10 from Navarone   1978   (Warner)   *Color*
Director: Guy Hamilton
Starring: Robert Shaw, Harrison Ford, Barbara Bach, Edward Fox, Franco Nero, Carl Weathers, Richard Kiel, Alan Badel

This sequel to 1961's *The Guns of Navarone* involves some of the same World War II commandos in another high-risk mission. The special task group known as Force 10 is detailed to blow up a bridge linking the Nazis with partisans in Yugoslavia. In this adaptation by Robin Chapman of the Alistair MacLean adventure novel, there is a traitor on the team. The familiar derring-do is enlivened by Guy Hamilton's direction. Ron Goodwin wrote the music. Robert Shaw, in his next-to-last film role, portrays the Force 10 team leader. (Shaw died just before completing *Avalanche Express*; when that film was released in 1979, it was revealed that much of his dialogue had been dubbed by an impressionist.)

The French Connection   1971   (CBS)   *Color*
Director: William Friedkin
Starring: Gene Hackman, Fernando Rey, Roy Scheider, Tony LoBianco, Marcel Bozzuffi, Eddie Egan, Sonny Grosso

New York narcotics cop Popeye Doyle becomes mired in a cesspool of vice when he attempts to dethrone a drug king. The ring leader, a debonair Frenchman with a handy silver-handled umbrella, proves a wily and elusive prey. Ultimately, Popeye quells the French connection. Playing the pivotal character, Gene Hackman, after years of character-actor apprenticeship, validated his status as a leading man, winning an Oscar and worldwide recognition. Ernest Tidyman's screenplay derives from Robin Moore's fact-based book about the 1961 smashing of a New York heroin empire originating in Marseilles. (Supporting players Eddie Egan and Sonny Grosso, then NYPD employees, were real-life players in this operation.) *The French Connection*'s most unforgettable scene is the car chase sequence beneath a Brooklyn elevated subway, photographed by Owen Roizman. Academy Awards sweepstakes: Hackman, Friedkin, Tidyman's script adaptation, Jerry Greenberg's editing, and best picture of 1971. *The French Connection* inspired Hollywood to make a series of movies about cops, including one titled *French Connection 2*.

French Connection 2   1975   (CBS)   *Color*
Director: John Frankenheimer
Starring: Gene Hackman, Roy Scheider, Fernando Rey, Bernard Fresson, Jean-Pierre Castaldi, Charles Millot, Cathleen Nesbitt, Philippe Léotard

The return of Popeye Doyle. At the end of *The French Connection*, New York City cops smashed a major narcotics operation. The mastermind, however, escaped unscathed. In this sequel, Popeye (Gene Hackman) arrives in Marseilles to confront the Frenchman (Fernando Rey, re-creating his role from the original) on his home turf. The screenwriters—Alexander Jacobs, Robert Dillon, and Laurie Dillon—provide another strenuous adventure for the protagonist. The beauty (and drug-milieu squalor) of Southern France are captured by Claude Renoir's camera. *French Connection 2* is a more leisurely drama than its predecessor, concentrating on the contradictions in Popeye's character, his difficulties with the French language, his uneasy relationship with his Marseilles police force counterpart (Bernard Fresson), and the Frenchman's pernicious tricks.

Frenzy 1972 (MCA) *Color*
Director: Alfred Hitchcock
Starring: Jon Finch, Alec McCowen, Barry Foster, Billie Whitelaw, Anna Massey, Barbara Leigh-Hunt, Bernard Cribbins, Vivien Merchant, Michael Bates, Clive Swift, Elsie Randolph, Jean Marsh

London is rocked by a series of slayings by a sex criminal known as "the Necktie Murderer." As Scotland Yard investigates the rape-strangulation murders, the trail leads to an irascible, though charming, layabout named Richard Blany (Jon Finch). The dragnet, devised by one Inspector Oxford (Alec McCowen), tightens and ultimately traps Blany. Only then is it apparent that he is innocent. The wrong man theme is a favorite of Alfred Hitchcock and here it is united with various subplots, including a comic relief motif involving Inspector Oxford and his wife (Vivien Merchant), who fancies herself a gourmet cook. Anthony Shaffer's screenplay, based on Arthur La Bern's thriller, *Goodbye Piccadilly, Farewell Leicester Square*, features—in addition to the murder solution—a wealth of British slang. Predominating *Frenzy*, though, are Hitchcock's sardonicism and his distinctively visual world. To many, one overhead tracking shot, pulling away from the murderer's apartment as he enters with his latest victim, is vintage Hitchcock.

From Russia with Love 1964 (CBS) *Color*
Director: Terence Young
Starring: Sean Connery, Daniela Bianchi, Pedro Armendariz, Lotte Lenya, Robert Shaw, Bernard Lee, Eunice Gayson, Walter Gotell, Francis De Wolff, George Pastell, Nadja Regin, Lois Maxwell, Alizia Gur, Martine Beswick, Vladek Sheybal, Peter Bayliss, Peter Madden

For this second episode in the profitable 007 series, James Bond (Sean Connery) again challenges the nefarious SPECTRE (Special Executive for Counter-Terrorism, Revenge and Extortion). Suave, seemingly indestructible Bond must foil SPECTRE agents who try to purloin a Lektor decoding apparatus from the Soviet cryptographic headquarters in Istanbul. Placing Bond's life in jeopardy are enemy agent Rosa Klebb (Lotte Lenya) and muscleman Red Grant (a blond Robert Shaw). The screenplay, by Richard Maibaum and Johanna Harwood, follows the Ian Fleming original more closely than the later, increasingly techno-oriented productions. (Maibaum, either singly or in collaboration, has written more 007 screenscripts than anyone.) Other players: Bernard Lee as M, Eunice Gayson as Sylvia, and Lois Maxwell as Miss Moneypenney. The music is by John Barry, whose title song (with lyricist Lionel Bart) is performed by Matt Munro. (Monty Norman composed the James Bond theme—and starting with this film, the series' elaborate precredit mini-adventure was forged.)

The Getaway 1972 (Warner) *Color*
Director: Sam Peckinpah
Starring: Steve McQueen, Ali MacGraw, Ben Johnson, Sally Struthers, Al Lettieri, Slim Pickens, Jack Dodson

Doc McCoy (Steve McQueen) is a convicted thief. In return for his early release from a Texas penitentiary, Doc agrees to pull a bank robbery for a crooked member of the parole board. Then the double-crosses begin. *The Getaway* is probably the most commercial film in Sam Peckinpah's repertoire. It features two top stars, McQueen and then wife Ali MacGraw, both at the peak of their popularity; it also contains unrelieved action—without the brooding elements found in the director's darker films. Slow-motion death and destruction are given prominence: McQueen methodically blows apart a police car with a 20-gauge shotgun; blood-splattered bodies tumble to dusty earth with the speed of molasses. The script comes from a novel by *noir* writer Jim Thompson, as adapted by future director Walter Hill *(Hard Times, The Warriors, The Long Riders, Southern Comfort, 48 Hrs.).* Lucien Ballard is the cinematographer.

Goldfinger   1964   (CBS)   ◆   *Color*
Director: Guy Hamilton
Starring: Sean Connery, Gert Frobe, Honor Blackman, Shirley Eaton, Tania Mallett, Harold Sakata, Bernard Lee, Martin Benson, Cec Linder, Austin Willis, Lois Maxwell, Bill Nagy, Alf Joint, Varley Thomas, Nadja Regin, Raymond Young, Richard Vernon

With this feature, Auric Goldfinger joins the colorful gallery of James Bond super-villains. In 007's third screen adventure, Goldfinger is an international criminal who plans to capture Fort Knox, the gold depository, and there implant a nuclear device. The tongue-in-cheek script of Richard Maibaum and Paul Dehn enlivens the Ian Fleming original and Guy Hamilton, as director, brings the action to a fevered pitch. The characters include aviatrix Pussy Galore (Honor Blackman); the gold-hungry title character (Gert Frobe); Goldfinger's Oriental henchman, Oddjob (Harold Sakata), whose homburg is a deadly weapon; a sex kitten (Shirley Eaton) who is literally gilded to death; and the suave superspy himself (again enacted by Sean Connery). John Barry's title song is performed by Shirley Bassey. Academy Award: best sound effects.

Gorky Park   1983   (Vestron)   *Color*
Director: Michael Apted
Starring: William Hurt, Lee Marvin, Brian Dennehy, Ian Bannen, Joanna Pacula, Michael Elphick, Richard Griffiths, Rikki Fulton, Alexander Knox, Alexei Sayle

An urban police procedural mystery in a new locale: contemporary Moscow (though shot in Helsinki). This thriller opens with the discovery of a triple murder in Gorky Park. The three victims have, additionally, been mutilated, their faces and fingerprints removed. (The forensic evidence is fairly graphic and not for the squeamish.) Arkady Renko, a young police inspector, works to ascertain first the identities of the deceased, second to track down the murderer or murderers. When his investigation reveals Kremlin complicity, Renko is thrust into a battle of wills with his superiors—and a clandestine political-criminal ring. *Gorky Park,* with a screenplay by Dennis Potter from the best-selling novel by Martin Cruz Smith, draws power from its cast, headed by William Hurt as Renko and Lee Marvin as one of his adversaries. Britain's Michael Apted also directed *Stardust, Agatha, Coal Miner's Daughter,* and *Continental Divide.*

The Great Escape   1963   (CBS)   *Color*
Director: John Sturges
Starring: Steve McQueen, James Garner, Richard Attenborough, James Donald, Charles Bronson, Donald Pleasence, James Coburn, David McCallum, Gordon Jackson, John Leyton, Angus Lennie, Nigel Stock, Jud Taylor, William Russell, Robert Desmond, Tom Adams, Lawrence Montaigne, Hannes Messemer

The mesmerizing story of Allied officers in a German prison camp in 1942, screenscripted by James Clavell and hardboiled fiction writer W. R. Burnett, is fact-based—and inspired a book, also called *The Great Escape,* by Paul Brickhill. Under John Sturges's direction, the POWs' elaborate plans and subsequent escape make for hair-raising excitement. Heading the all-male international cast are Steve McQueen (as Cooler King), James Garner (The Scrounger), Richard Attenborough (Big X), James Coburn (The Manufacturer), and Charles Bronson (as Danny Velinski). Little known fact: *The Great Escape* is an unofficial remake of a 1958 British film, *Danger Within* (American release title: *Breakout*), with Richard Todd, Bernard Lee, Michael Wilding, Dennis Price, and, again, Richard Attenborough.

Green for Danger   Great Britain 1946; U.S. 1947   *Black-and-White*
   (Learning)
Director: Sidney Gilliat
Starring: Alastair Sim, Sally Gray, Rosamund John, Trevor Howard, Leo Genn, Judy Campbell, Megs Jenkins, Ronald Ward, Moore Marriott

An emergency hospital in the Kentish countryside is the setting for murder most British. Why (and how) was the patient killed as he lay on the operating table? Equally important: Who is responsible? Inspector Cockrill (Alastair Sim), of the local constabulary, is called in to snare the evildoer. But before he can, murder strikes again. Christianna Brand's classic suspense novel, set during World War II, is faithfully reconstructed by the producing team of Frank Launder and Sidney Gilliat, who wrote *The Lady Vanishes* for Hitchcock. (This time Gilliat directed and was assisted on the screenplay by Claud Gurney.) Beyond its plot, *Green for Danger* evokes a sense of atmosphere; the workaday routine in and around the hospital plays an important role and, as the death count escalates, the cinematography of Wilkie Cooper generates bona fide terror. The mad killer—masked and gowned, and stalking his prey in a dark, deserted dispensary—is the stuff of nightmares. The term "surprise ending" really applies here.

The Guns of Navarone   1961   (RCA)   ◆   *Color*
Director: J. Lee Thompson
Starring: Gregory Peck, David Niven, Anthony Quinn, Stanley Baker, Anthony Quayle, Irene Papas, Gia Scala, James Darren, James Robertson Justice, Richard Harris, Bryan Forbes, Allan Cuthbertson, Michael Trubshawe, Percy Herbert, Walter Gotell, Albert Lieven, Norman Wooland

Alistair MacLean's best-selling adventure novel is given deluxe screen treatment in this Carl Foreman-J. Lee Thompson feature. MacLean's plot, scripted by Foreman, sprouts from a courageous attempt of a small Allied raiding party to blow up two enormous German guns on a Greek island in World War II. Excitement dominates, but the tension is counterbalanced by philosophical observations and character revelations. The international cast is headed by Gregory Peck, David Niven, Anthony Quinn, and Stanley Baker. Shot on location on the rugged island of Rhodes. An Academy Award went to the special effects team. Sequel: *Force 10 from Navarone* (1978).

Harper   1966   (Warner)   *Color*
Director: Jack Smight
Starring: Paul Newman, Lauren Bacall, Julie Harris, Arthur Hill, Janet Leigh, Pamela Tiffin, Robert Wagner, Robert Webber, Shelley Winters, Harold Gould, Strother Martin, Roy Jensen, Martin West, Jacqueline De Wit

This replica of the private eye movies of the forties derives from *The Moving Target,* an installment in Ross MacDonald's Lew Archer series. For the film the hero's surname was changed to Harper, to conform with Paul Newman's run of luck in *H* films: *The Hustler, Hemingway's Adventures of a Young Man,* and *Hud,* to be followed by *Hombre.* Newman, as the flinty Los Angeles detective, is hired by Lauren Bacall to discover the whereabouts of her missing (and possibly murdered) husband. By dint of his adroit sleuthing, Harper cracks the case. Screenwriter William Goldman and director Jack Smight honor the conventions of the genre. Sequel, also starring Newman as Lew Harper: *The Drowning Pool* (1976).

Hombre   1967   (CBS)   *Color*
Director: Martin Ritt
Starring: Paul Newman, Fredric March, Richard Boone, Diane Cilento, Cameron Mitchell, Barbara Rush, Martin Balsam, Peter Lazer, Margaret Blye, Skip Ward, Frank Silvera, David Canary, Val Avery

Arizona in the 1880s. Russell (Paul Newman) is a white man raised among the Apache, then forced back into the white man's world. Unfortunately, Russell, derogatorily called "hombre," can identify with neither society—though his sympathies lie with the oppressed Indians. His allegiances are sorely tested when he is one of several stagecoach passengers at the mercy of a band of robbers. Elmore Leonard's novel has been turned into a suspenseful movie adventure. The adaptation is by director Martin Ritt's regular scenarists, Irving Ravetch and Harriet Frank, Jr., and the performances—with Newman, Fredric March, and, particularly, Barbara Rush cast against type—offer surprises.

Hopscotch   *Listed under Comedies.*

The Hot Rock   *Listed under Comedies.*

Hush . . . Hush, Sweet Charlotte   1965   (CBS)   *Black-and-White*
Director: Robert Aldrich
Starring: Bette Davis, Olivia de Havilland, Joseph Cotten, Agnes Moorehead, Cecil Kellaway, Victor Buono, Mary Astor, William Campbell, Wesley Addy, Bruce Dern, George Kennedy, Dave Willock, John Megna, Ellen Corby, Helen Kleeb, Marianne Stewart, Frank Ferguson

Grand Guignol gets a thorough workout in this Southern Gothic shocker. Among the ingredients of the Henry Farrell-Lukas Heller story are a nightmarish mansion, a severed hand, a bloodied cleaver, a gore-covered wedding dress, and a corpse who won't stay horizontal. In spinning this tale of the madness of sweet Charlotte Hollis, a reclusive Louisiana plantation belle, the screenwriters give glancing acknowledgment to earlier horror classics, predominantly *Diabolique.* Bette Davis stars as Charlotte; Olivia de Havilland plays her cousin Miriam; Joseph Cotten is cast as the family doctor; Mary Astor, in her screen farewell, portrays mystery woman Jewel Mayhew; and Academy Award—nominated Agnes Moorehead plays Velma, the housekeeper who is as loony as Charlotte. Intended, in part, as a follow-up to *What Ever Happened to Baby Jane?,* with the same director (Robert Aldrich), writers, and stars, this chiller evolved without the participation of the star, Joan Crawford, whom de Havilland replaced just before shooting started. Frank De Vol wrote the music and Mack David the lyrics for the title song.

I Confess   1953   (Warner)   *Black-and-White*
Director: *Alfred Hitchcock*
Starring: *Montgomery Clift, Anne Baxter, Karl Malden, Brian Aherne, O. E. Hasse,*
Roger Dann, Dolly Haas, Charles André, Judson Pratt, Ovila Legare, Gilles Pelletier

To many critics Hitchcock's excursion into blackmail, murder, and shared guilt qualifies as his starkest, most somber work. Father Michael Logan (Montgomery Clift) hears the confession of murderer Otto Keller (O. E. Hasse); refusing to violate the sanctity of the confessional, the priest harbors the killer's secret. In a twist of fate, Father Logan is presumed to be the murderer, and he is hounded by Inspector Larrue (Karl Malden). The performances and fresh setting (Quebec) counterbalance the pervading sense of doom; but there are no laughs—or even smiles. *I Confess,* developed from Paul Anthelme's 1902 play, *Nos Deux Consciences,* was adapted by many hands but ultimately credited to George Tabori and William Archibald. Music: Dimitri Tiomkin. The director's token cameo arrives early; he crosses the screen at the top of a staircase.

In Cold Blood   1967   (RCA)   *Black-and-White*
Director: *Richard Brooks*
Starring: *Robert Blake, Scott Wilson, John Forsythe, Paul Stewart, Gerald S. O'Loughlin,*
Jeff Corey, John Gallaudet, James Flavin, Charles McGraw, James Lantz, Will Geer,
John McLiam, Ruth Storey, Brenda C. Currin, Paul Hough, Vaughn Taylor, Teddy Eccles, Raymond Hatton

Richard Brooks's adaptation of the Truman Capote best-seller examines the real-life murder of a Kansas farm family by a pair of psychopathic drifters. The story of killers Perry Smith and Richard Hickock integrates documentary realism with the plot intricacies of a psychological thriller. Robert Blake and Scott Wilson are the epitome of evil as the ex-cons who slaughter the four members of the Clutter family; John Forsythe plays the chief detective on the case; and Paul Stewart, as a reporter, portrays the Capote stand-in. The incisive photography of Conrad Hall takes full advantage of the actual locales—Kansas, Missouri, Nevada, Colorado, Texas, and Mexico (the route Smith and Hickock followed after the murders).

In the Heat of the Night   1967   (CBS)   ◆   *Color*
Director: *Norman Jewison*
Starring: *Sidney Poitier, Rod Steiger, Warren Oates, Lee Grant, James Patterson, Quentin*
Dean, Larry Gates, William Schallert, Beah Richards, Scott Wilson, Jack Teter, Matt
Clark, Anthony James, Kermit Murdock, Khalil Bezaleel, Peter Whitney, William Watson,
Timothy Scott, Eldon Quick, Fred Stewart, Arthur Malet, Peter Masterson

In this Academy Award picture, set in sleepy Sparta, Mississippi (though shot in southern Illinois), a murder case is solved by two lawmen—one black, one white. Initially, the alliance is troublesome between slick Philadelphia police detective Virgil Tibbs (Sidney Poitier) and Bill Gillespie (Rod Steiger), Sparta's contemptuous, bombastic police chief; but they grow to like and respect one another—and they solve a murder puzzle. Norman Jewison's film benefits from strong performances, as well as Haskell Wexler's photography, and the editing style of Hal Ashby. Additional Academy honors were accorded Steiger for best actor; Stirling Silliphant's screenplay adaptation of John Ball's novel; and the sound department at the Samuel Goldwyn Studio. Ray Charles sings the title song, composed by Quincy Jones (with Alan and Marilyn Bergman lyrics). Poitier revived Virgil Tibbs for two follow-up features: *They Call Me Mister Tibbs!* (1970) and *The Organization* (1971).

Klute　1971　(Warner)　◆　*Color*
Director: Alan J. Pakula
Starring: Jane Fonda, Donald Sutherland, Charles Cioffi, Roy Scheider, Dorothy Tristan, Rita Gam, Vivian Nathan, Nathan George, Anthony Holland, Richard B. Shull, Jean Stapleton, Robert Milli

A missing-persons case in Pennsylvania leads to New York call girl Bree Daniels (Jane Fonda), who once saw the missing man. John Klute (Donald Sutherland) is a young policeman who leaves the force to find his missing friend. When he and Bree join ranks, they solve a very tangled mystery—arising from a series of call-girl killings. Fans of Claude Chabrol's shadowy, perverse psychological thrillers will recognize the French master's influence here. The screenplay by Andy and Dave Lewis emphasizes mood and character; the chief villain, a one-time client of Bree's, is not difficult to spot. Under Alan Pakula's direction, suspense is nonetheless maintained. Jane Fonda's performance as the emotionally detached Bree resulted in her first Oscar.

The Last of Sheila　1973　(Warner)　*Color*
Director: Herbert Ross
Starring: Richard Benjamin, Dyan Cannon, James Coburn, Joan Hackett, James Mason, Ian McShane, Raquel Welch

A show business whodunit, *The Last of Sheila* represents the joint screenwriting debut of actor Anthony Perkins and composer-lyricist Stephen Sondheim. Both games and puzzle aficionados, they have devised an ingenious conundrum. The plot begins when a Hollywood leading lady named Sheila is killed by a hit-and-run driver. A year later, the deceased actress's husband—an imperious producer (James Coburn)—invites six friends to his yacht, the *Sheila,* in the waters off Cannes. There he proposes a series of games which, he assures the participants, will solve the mystery surrounding his beloved's death. But soon other murders begin. *The Last of Sheila,* directed by Herbert Ross, will appeal to both detective fiction fans and those drawn to tales of the super-rich and the super-troubled. The music is by Billy Goldenberg, and Bette Midler's rendition of his "Friends" is used under the closing credits.

The Late Show　1977　(Warner)　*Color*
Director: Robert Benton
Starring: Art Carney, Lily Tomlin, Bill Macy, Eugene Roche, Joanna Cassidy, John Considine, Ruth Nelson, John Davey, Howard Duff

This ode to forties detective fiction, written and directed by Robert Benton, presents Art Carney as Ira Wells, an aging, overweight private eye with a perforated ulcer. When his friend Harry Regan (Howard Duff), another detective, is murdered, Ira vows to catch the culprit. Determined to help is a euphoric would-be actress named Margo (Lily Tomlin), who had hired Harry Regan to find her missing cat. Margo suggests to Ira that they could team up like Nick and Nora Charles. When they do—and become entangled with lowlife, freeloaders, and sinister killers—*The Late Show* takes flight. Robert Altman produced the film, which shows evidence of his inspiration; Carney, Tomlin, and other actors often give the impression of improvising and embroidering. Filmed on location in Los Angeles.

The List of Adrian Messenger   1963   (MCA)   *Black-and-White*
Director: John Huston
Starring: Tony Curtis, Kirk Douglas, Burt Lancaster, Robert Mitchum, Frank Sinatra,
George C. Scott, Dana Wynter, Clive Brook, Gladys Cooper, Herbert Marshall, Jacques
Roux, John Merivale, Marcel Dalio, Tony Huston, Noel Purcell

Anthony Veiller's adaptation of Philip MacDonald's famous suspense novel lays the
groundwork for this John Huston–directed whodunit. The film is a lark, and making
it Huston must have felt he was taking a holiday—particularly after the dark doings
of *The Roots of Heaven, The Unforgiven, The Misfits,* and *Freud.* The story concerns the
search by a retired British intelligence officer (George C. Scott) for a mass murderer
with a talent for disguise; this homicidal blackguard is rapidly disposing of eleven victims
on his list—each person mysteriously connected with a line of Irish peers. The scenes
alternate between Limehouse and Ireland, with its riding-to-hounds landed gentry.
Indeed, it's on a fox hunt that the investigating officer finally catches the murderer.
An added novelty of *The List of Adrian Messenger* is that five big names (Tony Curtis,
Kirk Douglas, Burt Lancaster, Robert Mitchum, and Frank Sinatra) costar in heavy
makeup (by Bud Westmore)—and some fun is generated in trying to spot them while
the central mystery is solved.

Live and Let Die   1973   (CBS)   *Color*
Director: Guy Hamilton
Starring: Roger Moore, Yaphet Kotto, Jane Seymour, Clifton James, David Hedison, Geof-
frey Holder, Bernard Lee, Lois Maxwell

Roger Moore's first outing as James Bond came in this spy adventure, number eight
in the series—not counting the spoofy, multiple-Bond *Casino Royale* released under
non-Broccoli-Saltzman auspices in 1967. In *Live and Let Die* the superagent's nemesis
is a black drug king (Yaphet Kotto) operating in the Caribbean. Tom Mankiewicz's
alternately violent and tongue-in-cheek script keeps the plot moving forward at a rapid
clip. Voodoo, heroin, exotic locales, thrilling chases, and hairbreadth escapes all figure
into the action. The title song is written and performed by Paul and Linda McCartney.

The **M**an on the Eiffel Tower   1949   (Movie Buff Video;   *Color*
    Classic Video Cinema Collector's Club; Cable Films; Discount Video Tapes)
Director: Burgess Meredith
Starring: Charles Laughton, Franchot Tone, Burgess Meredith, Robert Hutton, Jean Wal-
lace, Patricia Roc, Wilfrid Hyde-White, Belita

Charles Laughton incarnates Parisian police inspector Jules Maigret, hero of scores of
Georges Simenon mystery novels. The screenplay by Harry Brown is taken from
Simenon's *A Battle of Nerves,* and the film serves as the screen directing debut of actor
Burgess Meredith, who assumes a supporting role. Shot on location in France, *The
Man on the Eiffel Tower* dramatizes Maigret's methodical entrapment of a crazed mur-
derer. A taut piece of detective fiction with a suspense-packed climax.

The Man Who Knew Too Much   1956   (MCA)   ◆   *Color*
Director: Alfred Hitchcock
Starring: James Stewart, Doris Day, Brenda de Banzie, Bernard Miles, Daniel Gélin,
Ralph Truman, Mogens Wieth, Alan Mowbray, Hillary Brooke, Christopher Olsen, Reggie
Nalder, Yves Brainville, Richard Wattis, Alix Talton, Noel Willman, Carolyn Jones, Leo
Gordon, Richard Wordsworth

In Hitchcock's elaborate remake of his 1934 British thriller, a little boy is kidnapped by a gang of assassins to ensure his father's silence. Dr. Ben McKenna (James Stewart) and his family—wife Jo (Doris Day) and son Hank (Christopher Olsen)—are vacationing in French Morocco when the danger erupts. A mysterious stranger with evidence of an assassination plot in London is murdered, and Ben, unfortunately, becomes privy to the dying man's final words. When little Hank is spirited away to London, his parents set out to rescue him—and to prevent a political murder. The climax of the chase occurs at a symphony concert in Albert Hall (with composer Bernard Herrmann doing on-screen service as the conductor). The Oscar-winning Jay Livingston-Ray Evans song, "Qué Será Será," introduced here by Doris Day, is integral to the suspense. John Michael Hayes and Angus MacPhail wrote the screenplay.

The Manchurian Candidate   1962   (MGM)   *Black-and-White*
Director: John Frankenheimer
Starring: Frank Sinatra, Laurence Harvey, Janet Leigh, Angela Lansbury, Henry Silva, James Gregory, Leslie Parrish, John McGiver, Khigh Dhiegh, James Edwards, Douglas Henderson, Albert Paulsen, Barry Kelley, Lloyd Corrigan, Madame Spivy

Screenwritten by George Axelrod from Richard Condon's novel, *The Manchurian Candidate* conjures a nightmare vision of communist brainwashing. Raymond Shaw (Laurence Harvey) is a Korean War hero who has been brainwashed so thoroughly that, upon his return to the States, he goes into a hypnotic trance on a given signal—and will cold-bloodedly commit any murder suggested by his monitor. The monitor (whose identity comes as a shock in the last reel) commands him to assassinate a liberal presidential candidate. Among those who become aware of Raymond's deadly directive are his mother (Angela Lansbury); Bennett Marco, his best buddy (Frank Sinatra); a mystery woman name Rosie (Janet Leigh); and several high-ranking senators (John McGiver and James Gregory).

Marathon Man   1976   (Paramount)   *Color*
Director: John Schlesinger
Starring: Dustin Hoffman, Laurence Olivier, Roy Scheider, William Devane, Marthe Keller, Fritz Weaver, Marc Lawrence, Richard Bright

Szell (Laurence Olivier), a depraved ex-Nazi, emerges from Uruguay, where he has been hiding for decades. His destination: New York City, where a fortune in diamonds (derived from robbing death camp victims) awaits. This complex and sometimes bloody espionage thriller, scripted by William Goldman from his novel, presents two brothers as threats to Szell's mission. Doc (Roy Scheider) and Babe Levy (Dustin Hoffman) are the sons of a Jewish professor driven to suicide during the McCarthy era—and they work to outwit the evil war criminal. Directed by John Schlesinger, it has flesh-and-blood red herrings that include an enigmatic Swiss beauty (Marthe Keller) and a government agent (William Devane). Conrad Hall's camera traverses Manhattan, uptown and down, covering the glamourous thoroughfares and the seedy side streets.

Marooned   1969   (RCA)   ◆   *Color*
Director: John Sturges
Starring: Gregory Peck, Richard Crenna, David Janssen, James Franciscus, Gene Hackman, Lee Grant, Nancy Kovack, Mariette Hartley, Scott Brady

Movies used to be ballyhooed as "right out of today's headlines." Here's one that, in

1969, actually rose to the hyperbole—a space melodrama released almost concurrently with a problem-beset Apollo 13 mission. Timely then, *Marooned* can be enjoyed several decades later as a suspenseful story about a three-man Apollo crew stranded in space. The astronauts are played by Richard Crenna, James Franciscus, and Gene Hackman; Gregory Peck is the stalwart chief of the manned flight program. The screenplay, from Martin Caidin's novel, is credited to Mayo Simon. A visual and technical achievement, *Marooned* should captivate even today's more sophisticated viewer from blast-off through rescue operations all the way to reentry. The film received an Academy Award for Robbie Robertson's special effects.

Midnight Express   1978   (RCA)   ◆   *Color*
Director: Alan Parker
Starring: Brad Davis, Randy Quaid, John Hurt, Mike Kellin, Irene Miracle, Bo Hopkins, Paolo Bonacelli, Paul Smith, Norbert Weisser, Michael Ensign, Peter Jeffrey

This brutal and graphic account of the tribulations of a drug dealer was honored with two Academy Awards—one for the Giorgio Moroder score, the other for Oliver Stone's script, based on the memoirs of young student Billy Hayes. As portrayed in the film by Brad Davis, Billy is an American hashish smuggler who is caught red-handed and imprisoned, in brutal circumstances, in a Turkish jail. He is originally sentenced to four years for his felony; but when the sentence is inexplicably extended to thirty years, Billy decides to take the "midnight express" (to escape). The prison environment and atrocities are unforgettably realized by director Alan Parker; not for the squeamish.

The Mirror Crack'd   1980   (Thorn)   *Color*
Director: Guy Hamilton
Starring: Angela Lansbury, Geraldine Chaplin, Tony Curtis, Edward Fox, Rock Hudson, Kim Novak, Elizabeth Taylor, Marella Oppenheim, Wendy Morgan, Margaret Courtenay, Charles Gray, Maureen Bennett, Carolyn Pickles, Eric Dodson, Charles Lloyd-Pack, Pierce Brosnan

"The mirror crack'd from side to side;/'The curse is come upon me,' cried/The Lady of Shallot." Therein lies the clue that Jane Marple uses to solve this Agatha Christie murder mystery. Scripted from Dame Agatha's 1962 novel by Jonathan Hales and Barry Sandler, *The Mirror Crack'd* features not only Alfred Lord Tennyson's poem but a series of murders—all emanating from the production of a big-studio movie in an English village. Miss Marple (Angela Lansbury), sidelined with a game leg, must rely on others to do the footwork; but it is she who solves the puzzle. Governed by Guy Hamilton's direction and the production design of Michael Stringer, the film recaptures the genteel English manor mystery world depicted in films of the thirties and forties.

Missing   1982   (MCA)   ◆ ✳ *Color*
Director: Costa-Gavras
Starring: Jack Lemmon, Sissy Spacek, John Shea, Melanie Mayron, Janice Rule, Charles Cioffi, David Clennon, Joe Regalbuto, Richard Venture, Jerry Hardin, Richard Bradford

Another political thriller from filmmaker Costa-Gavras, *Missing*—derived from Thomas Hauser's book *The Execution of Charles Horman*—is the director's American debut. Working with coscenarist Donald Stewart, he draws a haunting portrait of a real-life tragedy. In the aftermath of the 1973 coup that drove Salvador Allende from power in Chile, a young American journalist (John Shea) disappears. His strong-willed young wife (Sissy Spacek) and ultra-conservative father (Jack Lemmon) must join forces in Santiago to investigate. Their discovery that the young man has been executed is only the first of many horrors they uncover. Recipient of the Palme d'Or at Cannes, the film also won an Oscar for screenplay adaptation.

Mr. Majestyk   1974   (MGM)   *Color*
Director: Richard Fleischer
Starring: Charles Bronson, Al Lettieri, Linda Cristal, Lee Purcell, Paul Koslo, Alejandro Rey, Taylor Lacher, Frank Maxwell, Jordan Rhodes

Unflappable is the word for Mr. Majestyk. A Vietnam veteran, he lives in Colorado, where he's an independent watermelon farmer. When he refuses to defer to racketeers, he becomes the target of a syndicate hitman. Mr. Majestyk, however, does not run for cover. Instead, he takes arms, literally, against his sea of troubles and confronts the Mafia man and his associates. Elmore Leonard's script is the basis for this action drama, which provides another iconographic role for Charles Bronson. Richard Fleischer, Bronson's director, later guided two performances by Arnold Schwarzenegger: *Conan the Destroyer* and *Red Sonja.*

Moonraker   1979   (CBS)   *Color*
Director: Lewis Gilbert
Starring: Roger Moore, Lois Chiles, Michael Lonsdale, Richard Kiel, Corinne Clery, Bernard Lee, Geoffrey Keen, Desmond Llewellyn, Lois Maxwell

Episode eleven in the James Bond saga places the hero (Roger Moore) in Venice, Rio de Janeiro, the upper Amazon, and in orbit around the Earth. Christopher Wood's screenplay, with barely a trace of Ian Fleming in it, starts with the disappearance of a moon shuttle during a test flight—and ends in outer space. In between, Agent 007 investigates the chicanery of a megalomaniacal fiend named Drax (Michael Lonsdale) who plans to wipe out humankind and breed an extraterrestrial totalitarian colony. *Moonraker,* directed by Bond veteran Lewis Gilbert, marks the return of Jaws (Richard Kiel), the villain of *The Spy Who Loved Me,* and the final appearance of the late Bernard Lee, who played M throughout the series.

Murder on the Orient Express   1974   (Paramount)   ◆   *Color*
Director: Sidney Lumet
Starring: Albert Finney, Lauren Bacall, Martin Balsam, Ingrid Bergman, Jacqueline Bisset, Jean-Pierre Cassel, Sean Connery, John Gielgud, Wendy Hiller, Anthony Perkins, Vanessa Redgrave, Richard Widmark, Michael York

Agatha Christie's intrepid Belgian sleuth Hercule Poirot (Albert Finney) is aboard the Calais coach when a wealthy American businessman is murdered. The luxury train— ultimately snowbound—is loaded with potential suspects, all with murky pasts. This Sidney Lumet film, adapted by Paul Dehn, provides the Tiffany treatment: exotic locales, sumptuous costumes, and the majestic train itself! For star-gazers, railway buffs, and fans of Christie's whodunits. The production received six Oscar nominations, including best actor for Finney, but only Ingrid Bergman, in the supporting actress category, carried away a statuette. (Christie's 1934 novel had its genesis in the Lindbergh kidnapping case.)

The Narrow Margin   1952   (RKO)   *Black-and-White*
Director: Richard Fleischer
Starring: Charles McGraw, Marie Windsor, Jacqueline White, Gordon Gebert, Queenie Leonard, David Clarke, Peter Virgo, Don Beddoe, Paul Maxey, Harry Harvey

This thriller mixes two popular mystery subgenres: hardboiled detective fiction and the train-set whodunit. The screenplay by Earl Felton, following an original story by Martin Goldsmith and Jack Leonard, tells of a toughened policeman (Charles McGraw) who is protecting a gangster's widow (Marie Windsor) aboard a Chicago–to–Los Angeles express. The widow is a vital prosecution witness in a grand jury exposé, and she's the target of hitmen—some of whom are on the train. *The Narrow Margin* is a fast-paced adventure with notable cinematography (in close quarters) by George E. Diskant.

The New Centurions   1972   (RCA)   *Color*
Director: Richard Fleischer
Starring: George C. Scott, Stacy Keach, Jane Alexander, Rosalind Cash, Scott Wilson, Clifton James, William Atherton, Erik Estrada, Isabel Sanford, James B. Sikking, Ed Lauter, Roger E. Mosley

Stirling Silliphant's adaptation of the Joseph Wambaugh novel preserves the original's grit and gore. The centurions of the title are to be found in Precinct 45 of the present-day Los Angeles police force. A veteran cop (George C. Scott) trains a rookie (Stacy Keach) in how to survive the dangers of the street. The episodic nature of their assignments provides the kind of action that later inspired the TV series "Police Story," for which Wambaugh was a consultant. There is authenticity in *The New Centurions*; violence is depicted side by side with the mundane aspects of police detection. Director Richard Fleischer shows the policemen living under heightened stress, emerging as a society unto themselves with a unique camaraderie.

Night of the Generals   1967   (RCA)   *Color*
Director: Anatole Litvak
Starring: Peter O'Toole, Omar Sharif, Tom Courtenay, Donald Pleasence, Joanna Pettet, Christopher Plummer, Philippe Noiret, Charles Gray, Coral Browne, John Gregson, Harry Andrews, Nigel Stock, Juliette Greco

This complex murder mystery asks: Which of a corps of elite Nazi generals is a psychopathic murderer whose victims are all prostitutes? A thriller in an original setting, *Night of the Generals* presents Philippe Noiret as a persistent French sleuth who, after the war, tracks down a killer who has long been at bay—a killer now eliminating anyone who suspects his sexual psychopathy. Director Anatole Litvak has shaped both a whodunit and a character study from Hans Helmut Hirst's best-selling novel. Paul Dehn and Joseph Kessel wrote the screenplay. Photographed by Henri Decaë in Warsaw and Paris.

Nighthawks   1981   (MCA)   *Color*
Director: Bruce Malmuth
Starring: Sylvester Stallone, Billy Dee Williams, Lindsay Wagner, Persis Khambatta, Nigel Davenport, Jamie Gillis, Einar Perry Scott, Rutger Hauer

New York City is the battleground as two undercover cops (Sylvester Stallone and Billy Dee Williams) in a special unit pursue one of Europe's most merciless terrorists

(Rutger Hauer). In David Shaber's screenplay, realized by debuting director Bruce Malmuth, the killer proves himself a brilliant adversary. As part of his campaign to capture publicity, he holds hostage passengers in a sky tram over the East River. Unexpected twists abound in this shocker, an urban thriller in the *French Connection* vein—with location photography by James A. Contner.

North by Northwest   1959   (MGM)   *Color*
Director: Alfred Hitchcock
Starring: Cary Grant, Eva Marie Saint, James Mason, Jessie Royce Landis, Leo G. Carroll, Philip Ober, Josephine Hutchinson, Martin Landau, Adam Williams, Edward Platt, Robert Ellenstein, Les Tremayne, Philip Coolidge, Edward Binns, Pat McVey, Ken Lynch, John Beradino

The United Nations building; the Plaza Hotel; Grand Central Station; Chicago's Ambassador East; the Indiana plains; the Black Hills of South Dakota—*North by Northwest* is an Alfred Hitchcock thriller taking supreme advantage of its location photography. Turning upon the Maestro's oft-utilized wrong-man premise, the story starts when New York advertising executive Roger Thornhill (Cary Grant) is mistaken for a spy. He is then chased by both foreign agents and interstate police who believe he is an assassin. Ernest Lehman, author of the screenplay, has constructed a whirlwind adventure, capped by two of the best-remembered moments in the Hitchcock repertoire: the sequence of the menacing crop-duster biplane and the climactic chase across the presidential profiles of Mount Rushmore. Grant and Eva Marie Saint are a sizzling romantic team, while James Mason is the epitome of sinister suavity. The director's cameo? He's the man who misses the bus. Music: Bernard Herrmann.

Notorious   1946   (CBS)   *Black-and-White*
Director: Alfred Hitchcock
Starring: Cary Grant, Ingrid Bergman, Claude Rains, Louis Calhern, Leopoldine Konstantin, Reinhold Schünzel, Moroni Olsen, Ivan Triesault, Alex Minotis, Wally Brown, Gavin Gordon, Bea Benadaret, Virginia Gregg

Vintage Hitchcock, this psychological suspense tale by Ben Hecht (who adapted *Spellbound* the year before) is for all enthusiasts of the genre. A chilling delineation of realistic—as opposed to movie-melodramatic—evil, *Notorious* thrusts Cary Grant and Ingrid Bergman into post–World War II espionage. T. R. Devlin (Grant), a spy for the State Department, convinces Alicia Huberman (Bergman) to marry, then collect evidence against, a neo-Nazi leader (Claude Rains) headquartered in Rio. By falling in love with Devlin, Alicia betrays her new husband in more ways than one. When her duplicity is discovered, her life is placed in jeopardy. Rains makes an oddly sympathetic villain; Grant and Bergman add texture as the not altogether likable good guys. Hitchcock's MacGuffin this time: uranium ore hidden in bottles in the wine cellar.

Obsession   1976   (RCA)   *Color*
Director: Brian De Palma
Starring: Cliff Robertson, Geneviève Bujold, John Lithgow, Sylvia Williams, Wanda Blackman, Patrick McNamara

Brian De Palma's tribute to Hitchcock themes and camera pyrotechnics refers most explicitly to *Vertigo*, but long-term fans of Sir Alfred may be able to draw further parallels. *Obsession*, De Palma's ninth feature, is the story of Michael Courtland (Cliff Robertson), a wealthy New Orleans land developer whose wife and young daughter are killed when kidnappers attempt to abduct them. Michael, suffused with guilt, never recovers from their deaths. Then, years after the event on a business trip to Florence, he meets Sandra Portinari (Geneviève Bujold), a dead ringer for his wife. Who is this mysterious woman? Paul Schrader's screenplay answers that and other relevant queries—en route to a climax that has Michael reliving the night of the fateful kidnapping-murder. For this thriller De Palma eschews his standard anthology of blood-splattering effects.

Odd Man Out   1947   (Learning)   *Black-and-White*
Director: Carol Reed
Starring: James Mason, Kathleen Ryan, Robert Newton, F. J. McCormick, Robert Beatty, Cyril Cusack, Fay Compton, Dan O'Herlihy, Denis O'Dea, Maureen Delany, Joseph Tomelty, William Hartnell, W. G. Fay, Elwyn Brook-Jones

Set in mid-winter Belfast, this suspense concentrates on Johnny MacQueen (James Mason), a gunman belonging to the Irish Republican Army. As the film opens, Johnny is wounded in a daring holdup in which he kills a man; he becomes a fugitive, trailed by the police and rival factions. Among those he encounters in his desperate flight are his future girl (Kathleen Ryan), an elderly priest (W. G. Fay), a half-crazed, drunken artist (Robert Newton), a pub keeper (William Hartnell), and the head constable (Denis O'Dea). Mason creates a pathetic central character, and there are notable contributions from some of the members of Dublin's Abbey Theatre players. R. C. Sherriff and F. L. Green wrote the screenplay from the latter's novel. *Odd Man Out* was remade in an American setting as *The Lost Man* (1969), with Sidney Poitier as the hunted criminal.

The Odessa File   1974   (RCA)   *Color*
Director: Ronald Neame
Starring: Jon Voight, Maximilian Schell, Mary Tamm, Maria Schell, Derek Jacobi, Peter Jeffrey, Noel Willman, Klaus Löwitsch

Nineteen sixty-three. A young German journalist (Jon Voight), while researching Nazi war crimes, comes upon the whereabouts of a former SS officer (Maximilian Schell). The reporter's investigations ultimately lead him to ODESSA, a top-secret *Schutzstaffel* organization. Jon Voight, playing against type (though with a convincing German accent), is effective as the Nazi-stalking hero. An ensemble of international stars support him. The Kenneth Ross-George Markstein screenplay reduces the plot but keeps the thrills of the Frederick Forsyth novel on which it is based. Andrew Lloyd Webber wrote the score.

The Onion Field   1979   (Embassy)   *Color*
Director: Harold Becker
Starring: John Savage, James Woods, Franklyn Seales, Ronny Cox, Ted Danson, David Huffman, Dianne Hull

The Onion Field is a grim delineation of the underside of police work and the vagaries of the criminal justice system. Based on a Los Angeles Police Department case history and the book (and screenplay) by Joseph Wambaugh, it's the story of two police officers, Hettinger and Campbell (John Savage and Ted Danson), and their night of terrorization by two psychotic criminals (James Woods and Franklyn Seales). The first act of this multipart drama ends when Campbell is savagely murdered in an onion field near Bakersfield—and Hettinger manages to escape. Thereafter, he must live with allegations of improper conduct even when the two culprits are brought to justice. A complex semidocumentary portrait.

The **P**arallax View   1974   (Paramount)   *Color*
Director: Alan J. Pakula
Starring: Warren Beatty, Hume Cronyn, William Daniels, Kenneth Mars, Walter McGinn, Kelly Thordsen, Jim Davis, Bill McKinney, Earl Hindman, Bill Joyce, William Jordan, Stacy Keach, Sr., Ford Rainey, Paula Prentiss

This murder mystery begins and ends with political assassination. Investigating the conspiracy behind the slaying of a senator is Oregon newspaper reporter Joe Frady (Warren Beatty). Witnesses to the assassination are systematically being murdered—and when Joe's probes continue, his own life is placed in jeopardy. This thriller, scripted by David Giler and Lorenzo Semple, Jr., from the Loren Singer novel, finds parallels in the aftermath of the JFK assassination. The hero's paranoia mounts as he finds evidence of a cover-up of major proportions. *The Parallax View* is directed by Alan J. Pakula and recalls such similarly themed works as *The Manchurian Candidate, Z,* and *Missing.* Gordon Willis is responsible for the cinematography.

Port of New York   1949   (Video Yesteryear;   *Black-and-White*
          Movie Buff Video; Discount Video Tapes)
Director: Laslo Benedek
Starring: Scott Brady, Richard Rober, K. T. Stevens, Yul Brynner, Lynn Carter

Directed by Laslo Benedek before he achieved recognition for *Death of a Salesman* and *The Wild One,* this low-budget gangster melodrama features Yul Brynner in his movie debut. Brynner plays Vicola, a master villain supervising the shipment of drugs into New York, and it's one of his rare screen appearances with a head of hair. *Port of New York,* from an original screenplay by Eugene Ling, utilizes a semidocumentary approach in its enactment of narcotics crack-downs by customs agents. Scott Brady, playing a G-man, infiltrates the mob and, with the assistance of good-bad girl K. T. Stevens, puts a temporary halt to the smuggling.

The Poseidon Adventure   1972   (CBS)   ◆   *Color*
Director: Ronald Neame
Starring: Gene Hackman, Ernest Borgnine, Red Buttons, Carol Lynley, Roddy McDowall, Stella Stevens, Shelley Winters, Jack Albertson, Pamela Sue Martin, Arthur O'Connell, Eric Shea, Leslie Nielsen

New Year's Eve on the passenger liner *Poseidon.* A tidal wave curtails the festivities, capsizing the cruise ship and sending it to the ocean's floor upside down. Survivors must crawl, climb, and swim their way to freedom. In the Stirling Silliphant-Wendell Mayes screenplay, only a half dozen members of the all-star passenger list make it to the closing credits. The sets and special effects prevail. Producer Irwin Allen is a master of the disaster extravaganza, as demonstrated here and in *The Towering Inferno.* The 1972 Oscar for best song went to Al Kasha and Joel Hirschhorn's "The Morning After."

Prince of the City   1981   (Warner)   *Color*
Director: Sidney Lumet
Starring: Treat Williams, Jerry Orbach, Richard Foronjy, Don Billett, Kenny Marino,
Carmine Caridi, Tony Page, Norman Parker, Paul Roebling, Bob Balaban, James Tolkan,
Steve Inwood, Lindsay Crouse, Matthew Laurance, Tony Turco, Ron Maccone, Ron Kara-
batsos, Tony Di Benedetto, Robert Christian, Lee Richardson, Lane Smith

Robert Daley's best-seller, *Prince of the City*, offered an inside account of New York
City police corruption. The Sidney Lumet film, from the director's screenplay with Jay
Presson Allen, is a fictionalized assessment of the real events. The main character,
Danny Ciello (Treat Williams)—based on actual undercover agent Robert Leuci—is a
narcotics detective who tries to expose department graft. But as an informant in the
Knapp Commission investigation, Ciello becomes more a victim than a hero. Lumet
goes for a semidocumentary presentation herein, and *Prince of the City*, with its theme
and *film noir* lighting (by cinematographer Andrzej Bartkowiak), may remind viewers
of Lumet's earlier *Serpico*.

The Prowler   1951   (VCII Inc.)   *Black-and-White*
Director: Joseph Losey
Starring: Van Heflin, Evelyn Keyes, John Maxwell, Katharine Warren, Emerson Treacy

Joseph Losey, before his exile as a result of the Hollywood blacklist, made this violent
homage to *Double Indemnity* and *The Postman Always Rings Twice*. A rookie patrolman
(Van Heflin) is summoned on a routine prowler case. The complainant is a rich but
bored housewife (Evelyn Keyes); when she and the cop meet, it's lust at first sight. In
time they dream of murdering her disc jockey husband. All for love—and money.
Quintessential *film noir* ingredients season the screenplay by Hugo Butler, based on a
story by Robert Thoeren and Hans Wilhelm.

Psycho   1960   (MCA)   *Black-and-White*
Director: Alfred Hitchcock
Starring: Anthony Perkins, Vera Miles, John Gavin, Martin Balsam, John McIntire,
Simon Oakland, Vaughn Taylor, Frank Albertson, Lurene Tuttle, Pat Hitchcock, John
Anderson, Mort Mills, Janet Leigh

Norman Bates (Anthony Perkins) is the focus of Alfred Hitchcock's *Psycho*. The Bates
Motel and the adjacent family mansion, off an isolated stretch of southern California
highway, are the sites of several gruesome murders. Various people investigate, to
Norman's chagrin, for his primary interest is in protecting his eccentric old mother.
Among those who discover mother's deadly secret are Marion Crane (Janet Leigh),
her beau Sam (John Gavin), her sister Lila (Vera Miles), a private eye named Arbogast
(Martin Balsam), and the local sheriff (John McIntire). Hitchcock's cameo comes at
the beginning: he's the cowboy-hatted man outside Marion Crane's Phoenix office.
Joseph Stefano wrote the screenplay from Robert Bloch's novel, John L. Russell is the
cinematographer, and longtime Hitchcock associate Bernard Herrmann composed the
score. *Psycho* inspired an onslaught of celluloid copies (*Homicidal, Straitjacket, Psy-*
chomania, Anatomy of a Psycho). However, there are two direct sequels: *Psycho II*,
directed by Hitchcock protégé Richard Franklin, and *Psycho III*, directed by and starring
Anthony Perkins.

The **R**acket   1951   (Nostalgia)   *Black-and-White*
Director: John Cromwell
Starring: Robert Mitchum, Robert Ryan, Lizabeth Scott, Ray Collins, William Talman, Joyce Mackenzie, Robert Hutton, William Conrad, Don Porter

A *film noir* gangster melodrama, *The Racket* is based on a 1927 Broadway drama, subsequently filmed (in 1928) by producer Howard Hughes and director Lewis Milestone. The story gets some updating in the 1951 version—by way of a screenscript from William Wister Haines and W. R. Burnett. The direction is by John Cromwell and (uncredited) Nicholas Ray. A big city police captain (Robert Mitchum) clashes with a racketeer (Robert Ryan). The mobster has been exercising his political muscle, so there's corruption in the upper ranks of city government and it's filtered into the police force. Costars William Talman and Ray Collins were later reteamed on TV's "Perry Mason."

Raggedy Man   1981   (MCA)   *Color*
Director: Jack Fisk
Starring: Sissy Spacek, Eric Roberts, Sam Shepard, William Sanderson, Tracey Walter, R. G. Armstrong, Henry Thomas, Carey Hollis, Jr.

Nostalgia and suspense combine in this feature directing debut for Jack Fisk, a former art director and Sissy Spacek's husband. Set in a small Texas town in 1944, *Raggedy Man* offers Spacek as a lonely divorcée (and mother of two boys) whose livelihood is earned as a switchboard operator. Trapped in the stifling, gossip-ridden atmosphere, the young woman plans to move away. Then she finds love with a sailor on leave. The William D. Wittliff screenplay also plants a mystery element: several enigmatic and potentially violent strangers stalk through the community by night. Eric Roberts plays the sailor, and—as the children—Carey Hollis, Jr., and a pre-*E.T.* Henry Thomas. Fisk directed Spacek again in *Violets Are Blue* (1986).

Raiders of the Lost Ark   1981   (Paramount)   *Color*
Director: Steven Spielberg
Starring: Harrison Ford, Karen Allen, Denholm Elliott, Ronald Lacey, John Rhys-Davies, Wolf Kahler, Paul Freeman

The first Indiana Jones adventure. Dr. Jones (Harrison Ford), globe-trotting professor of archaeology, is enlisted to thwart the Nazis in their desires to locate the fabled Ark of the Covenant. Legend states that an army that carries the Ark before it will be invincible. So the race is on! The creators of this legend (director Spielberg, executive producer George Lucas, and screenwriter Lawrence Kasdan) are avid students of American popular culture. *Raiders* is a 1980s offspring of *Don Winslow of the Navy* and other cliff-hanging serials of yesteryear. Saturday matinees are the unquestioned inspiration for Indy's wardrobe (battered fedora and bullwhip), the hairbreadth escapes, and the whirlwind disaster-a-minute plot. Spielberg et al. must have tapped directly into the audience's escapist fantasies: *Raiders* is now sixth among all-time money-making movies. *Indiana Jones and the Temple of Doom*, a prequel released in 1984, almost emulated the runaway success of *Raiders*: it ranks seventh on the box-office chart.

Rear Window   1954   (MCA)   *Color*
Director: Alfred Hitchcock
Starring: James Stewart, Grace Kelly, Wendell Corey, Thelma Ritter, Raymond Burr, Ju-

dith Evelyn, Ross Bagdasarian, Georgine Darcy, Sara Berner, Frank Cady, Jesslyn Fax, Rand Harper, Irene Winston, Harris Davenport, Marla English, Kathryn Grant

Magazine photographer L. B. Jeffries (James Stewart) is sidelined by a broken leg. Temporarily confined to his Greenwich Village apartment in a wheelchair and a hip-to-toe plaster cast, Jeff amuses himself by studying his courtyard neighbors through binoculars and telephoto lenses. It's all a game—until he becomes convinced that one neighbor, Lars Thorwald (Raymond Burr), is a wife-murderer. In this Alfred Hitchcock chiller, derived by John Michael Hayes from a Cornell Woolrich short story, the suspense evolves from the director's experimentation with subjective viewpoint: nearly all the action is seen from the wheelchair perspective of the photographer-hero. Grace Kelly plays a socialite, and Thelma Ritter a sharp-tongued nurse. Hitchcock's walk-on? He's a butler winding a clock. Screenwriter Hayes won an Edgar Award from the Mystery Writers of America for *Rear Window*.

The Red House   1947   (Budget Video; Discount   *Black-and-White*
    Video Tapes; Classic Video Cinema Collector's Club; Kartes Productions)
Director: Delmer Daves
Starring: Edward G. Robinson, Lon McCallister, Allene Roberts, Judith Anderson, Rory Calhoun, Julie London, Ona Munson

In this psychological thriller Edward G. Robinson stars as a farmer tormented by a decrepit old house in the nearby woods. A violent crime was once committed in the red house, and the farmer was the only witness; but others—including his young ward (Allene Roberts) and a callow hired hand (Lon McCallister)—want to unravel the dwelling's secret. The plot arises from the novel by George Agnew Chamberlain; Delmer Daves *(Dark Passage, 3:10 to Yuma, Cowboy, Parrish, Spencer's Mountain)* is both screenwriter and director. *The Red House* is a Hitchcock-like tale of suspense, enhanced by a moody score by Miklos Rozsa.

Repulsion   1965   (Vid Dim; Sheik Video; Video   *Black-and-White*
    Connection)
Director: Roman Polanski
Starring: Catherine Deneuve, Ian Hendry, John Fraser, Yvonne Furneaux, Patrick Wymark, Renée Houston, Valerie Taylor, James Villiers, Helen Fraser, Hugh Futcher, Mike Pratt, Monica Merlin, Imogen Graham

In *Repulsion*, Roman Polanski's first English-language film, the director reorchestrates his familiar theme of innocence amidst corruption. Carol (Catherine Deneuve) is a beautiful Belgian girl working as a manicurist in London. Shy of men, she is the opposite side of the coin from her sister (and apartment mate) Helen (Yvonne Furneaux). When Helen and her lover vacate the flat for several weeks, Carol grows despondent, then terrified. The city seems to pose a constant threat of sexual assault, so the young woman locks herself up in the apartment. Even there, she can't escape her hallucinations— which ultimately inspire her to commit murder. A psychological mystery with horror touches, *Repulsion* (in Polanski's screenplay with Gérard Brach) charts Carol's descent into madness.

Rider on the Rain   1970   (Embassy)   *Color*
Director: René Clément
Starring: Charles Bronson, Marlène Jobert, Gabriele Tinti, Jill Ireland, Jean Gaven, Jean

Piat, Corinne Marchand, Annie Cordy, Ellen Bahl, Steve Eckhardt, Jean-Daniel Ehrman, Marika Green, Yves Massart, Marc Mazza

This cat-and-mouse murder mystery's main character is Mellie (short for Mélancolie), a young woman from a coastal town near Marseilles who becomes involved with a violent stranger, a stolen cash box of $15,000, and the discovery of a long-buried murder victim. Suddenly, Harry Dobbs (Charles Bronson), an Army investigator with a Cheshire cat smile, appears searching for an escaped lunatic. The complex script by Sébastien Japrisot *(The Sleeping Car Murders)* is directed by René Clément *(Forbidden Games, Gervaise, Purple Noon)*. Francis Lai's alternately romantic and hackle-raising score contributes further sophistication. Marc Mazza enacts the title role—a silent menace named, in honor of Hitchcock, MacGuffin.

Riot in Cell Block 11   1954   (Republic)   *Black-and-White*
Director: Don Siegel
Starring: Neville Brand, Emile Meyer, Frank Faylen, Leo Gordon, Robert Osterloh, Paul Frees, Don Keefer

The title tells it all. In this grim prison drama, founded on an original screenplay by Richard Collins, three inmates at California's Folsom State Prison wrest control of their cell block. With guards as their captives, they demand redress for penal injustices. When the revolt becomes a media event, the convicts take advantage of the publicity. A touch action melodrama, *Riot in Cell Block 11*, under Don Siegel's direction, also has the feel of a true crime documentary.

Rope   1948   (MCA)   *Color*
Director: Alfred Hitchcock
Starring: James Stewart, John Dall, Farley Granger, Sir Cedric Hardwicke, Constance Collier, Douglas Dick, Edith Evanson, Dick Hogan, Joan Chandler

In Patrick Hamilton's playscript, as adapted for the screen by Hume Cronyn and Arthur Laurents, two young men, Brandon and Philip (John Dall and Farley Granger), murder a college friend for a thrill. Brandon is the mastermind for whom "the power to kill can be just as satisfying as the power to create"; to celebrate, he throws a cocktail party, hiding the body in a trunk used as the buffet table. One of the party guests is Brandon Cadell (James Stewart), an ultralogical former professor who becomes suspicious of the two hosts. The heralded gimmick behind this thriller is that it's an experiment in unbroken continuity: Hitchcock shot *Rope* on one set in ten-minute takes (stopping only to place new film in the camera magazine). The eighty-minute running length is both real and reel time.

The S̲et-Up   1949   (Blackhawk Films; Nostalgia)   *Black-and-White*
Director: Robert Wise
Starring: Robert Ryan, Audrey Totter, George Tobias, Alan Baxter, James Edwards, Wallace Ford

A punch-drunk prizefighter refuses to play down-and-dirty tricks. The story is old, but the retelling, in this Robert Wise–directed feature, incorporates fresh side plots. Art Cohn's screenplay takes its inspiration from an unlikely source: a poem by Joseph Moncure March. Robert Ryan plays Stoker Thompson, the righteous boxer who wants to keep his record honest. He keeps plugging away, often at much younger opponents. The fight depicted in this film is a set-up, but Stoker doesn't know it; his manager (George Tobias) has taken a bribe, pledging that the ex-champ will take a fall. *The Set-Up,* photographed by Milton Krasner, has a violent climax in the ring—followed by a gruesome dénouement.

Seven Days in May   1964   (Paramount)   *Black-and-White*
Director: John Frankenheimer
Starring: Burt Lancaster, Kirk Douglas, Fredric March, Ava Gardner, Edmond O'Brien, Martin Balsam, George Macready, Whit Bissell, Hugh Marlowe, Bart Burns, Richard Anderson, Jack Mullaney, Andrew Duggan, John Larkin, John Houseman

This nuclear-age tale of suspense hypothesizes a military scheme to take over the U.S. government. Certain radical elements in high echelons of the Air Force and the Joint Chiefs of Staff believe that President Jordan Lyman (Fredric March) is too pacifistic. The president has just signed a nuclear disarmament treaty with the Soviet Union, an act that General James Scott (Burt Lancaster) and his right-wing henchmen deplore as treasonous. So the takeover plot is set in motion. *Seven Days in May,* adapted by Rod Serling from the Fletcher Knebel-Charles W. Bailey II best-seller, ranks among the best political thrillers of the sixties. Melodramatic situations emerge, but the performances—by March, Lancaster, Kirk Douglas, Ava Gardner, Edmond O'Brien, and others—are realistically modulated.

The Silent Partner   Canada 1978; U.S. 1979   (Vestron; Time)   *Color*
Director: Daryl Duke
Starring: Elliott Gould, Christopher Plummer, Susannah York, Celine Lomez, Michael Kirby, Ken Pogue, John Candy

In this offbeat suspense comedy—adapted by Curtis Hanson from Anders Bodelson's novel, *Think of a Number*—Elliott Gould plays a mild-mannered Toronto bank teller. Beneath his sheepish smile and his stuffed shirt resides a larcenous heart. When the clerk learns in advance of a robbery, he pulls a switch on the heist's psychotic mastermind (Christopher Plummer). Reprisal arrives in a fairly savage way. (Viewers should be warned that there are some graphically depicted deaths as a counterbalance to the overall levity.) Directed by Daryl Duke, whose earlier film *Payday* is a cult favorite and whose later "The Thorn Birds" was a TV ratings giant. Cinematographer: Stephen Katz; music by jazz great Oscar Peterson.

Sleuth   1972   (Media)   *Color*
Director: Joseph L. Mankiewicz
Starring: Laurence Olivier, Michael Caine, Alec Cawthorne, Margo Channing, John Matthews, Teddy Martin

Andrew Wyke is an aging writer of mystery novels; Milo Tindle is a gigolo—and Andrew's wife's lover. When the two men meet at the novelist's remote country manor house in Wiltshire, England, the stage is set for deceit, disguise, madness, and murder. *Sleuth* is a cat-and-mouse melodrama featuring homicidal psychosis lodged behind civility. The plot began as Anthony Shaffer's West End thriller, which later transferred to Broadway. Shaffer, whose twin brother Peter is the author of *Equus* and *Amadeus,* also wrote the screenplay. Laurence Olivier, as Andrew, and Michael Caine, as Milo, make lively antagonists; Marguerite, Andrew's wife, makes a token appearance—as a living-room portrait of Joanne Woodward.

Split Second   1953   (RKO)   *Black-and-White*
Director: Dick Powell
Starring: Stephen McNally, Alexis Smith, Jan Sterling, Paul Kelly, Keith Andes, Arthur Hunnicutt, Richard Egan, Robert Paige

A hardboiled crime thriller, *Split Second* represents Dick Powell's directorial debut. (Before his death in 1963, he directed four more features, notably *The Enemy Below*.) The William Bowers and Irving Wallace screenplay evolves from a suspenseful premise: several escaped convicts hold hostages in a Nevada ghost town, which has been designated as an atomic bomb testing site. All are unaware that in an hour's time the town and surrounding area will be obliterated; the minutes tick down to seconds. An archetypal countdown mystery, *Split Second* profits from its taut script and direction—and the solid performances by its cast.

The Spy Who Loved Me   1977   (CBS)   *Color*
Director: Lewis Gilbert
Starring: Roger Moore, Barbara Bach, Curt Jurgens, Richard Kiel, Caroline Munro, Bernard Lee, Lois Maxwell, Walter Gotell, George Baker, Desmond Llewelyn, Edward De Souza

Another chapter in the biography of secret agent 007. Bond (Roger Moore) teams up with a glamourous Soviet spy (Barbara Bach) to outwit Stromberg (Curt Jurgens), an unbalanced shipping magnate. Stromberg has built an underwater city in anticipation of his nuclear annihilation of the earth's surface. Before eliminating the criminal mastermind, Bond must contend with an indefatigable steel-toothed giant named Jaws (Richard Kiel). Directed by Lewis Gilbert from the Christopher Wood-Richard Maibaum screenplay, *The Spy Who Loved Me* is number ten in the series. Marvin Hamlisch's theme, "Nobody Does It Better," is sung by Carly Simon.

Stage Fright   1950   (Warner)   *Black-and-White*
Director: Alfred Hitchcock
Starring: Jane Wyman, Marlene Dietrich, Michael Wilding, Richard Todd, Sybil Thorndike, Kay Walsh, Miles Malleson, Hector MacGregor, Joyce Grenfell, André Morell, Patricia Hitchcock, Ballard Berkeley, Alastair Sim

The backstage London theater world gives grit to this Alfred Hitchcock whodunit. Taken from *Man Running*, a novel by Selwyn Jepson, as adapted by Whitfield Cook, Ranald MacDougall, and Alma Reville, *Stage Fright* presents drama students Eve Gill (Jane Wyman) and Jonathan Cooper (Richard Todd)—desperate to prove that the latter is not implicated in the murder of celebrated actress Charlotte Inwood's husband. The two students believe that Charlotte (Marlene Dietrich) is the guilty party and they begin spying on her. Eve, in a hazardous move, takes a job as the star's maid in hopes of collecting damaging evidence. Supporting the leads are Michael Wilding as Wilfrid ("Ordinary") Smith, a detective; Alastair Sim as Eve's father; Patricia Hitchcock as Chubby Bannister; and Joyce Grenfell as a daffy shooting gallery attendant.

Stalag 17   1953   (Paramount)   ◆   *Black-and-White*
Director: Billy Wilder
Starring: William Holden, Don Taylor, Otto Preminger, Robert Strauss, Harvey Lembeck, Richard Erdman, Peter Graves, Neville Brand, Sig Rumann, Michael Moore, Peter Baldwin, Robinson Stone, Robert Shawley, William Pierson, Gil Stratton, Jr., Ross Bagdasarian, Robin Morse, Tommy Cook

William Holden, in his Oscar-winning performance, is Sergeant Sefton. One of a group of American servicemen in a German prisoner-of-war camp, Sefton is not trusted by the other internees—who ultimately accuse him of being a spy. In this adaptation of the Donald Bevan-Edmund Trzinski stage drama, the cynical sergeant must prove his innocence by ferreting out the real culprit. With director Billy Wilder and his co-scenarist Edwin Blum behind the scenes, there is comedy mixed with mystery. Brightly played by Holden and his colleagues: Don Taylor as Lieutenant Dunbar; Robert Strauss and Harvey Lembeck providing comic relief as Stosh and Harry; Richard Erdman as Hoffy; Peter Graves as Price; Neville Brand as Duke; and, playing the camp commandant, Otto Preminger.

Strangers on a Train   1951   (Warner)   *Black-and-White*
Director: Alfred Hitchcock
Starring: Robert Walker, Farley Granger, Ruth Roman, Leo G. Carroll, Patricia Hitchcock, Marion Lorne, Laura Elliott, Jonathan Hale, Howard St. John, John Brown, Norma Varden, Robert Gist, John Doucette

Guy Haines (Farley Granger), an unhappily married tennis pro, is forced by psychopathic Bruno Anthony (Robert Walker) into a bizarre scheme to trade murders. Bruno strangles Guy's unfaithful, shrewish wife (Laura Elliott); he then expects Guy to reciprocate—by dispatching Bruno's father (Jonathan Hale). This tension-filled Alfred Hitchcock classic originates from Patricia Highsmith's novel; the adaptation was effected by Whitfield Cook, then carried through several screenplay drafts by Raymond Chandler before Czenzi Ormonde, Alma (Reville) Hitchcock, and others wrote the shooting script. The climactic merry-go-round sequence is among the most richly visual moments in all of Hitchcock. The director himself can be viewed, early on, as the man boarding the train with an enormous bass fiddle. Cinematography is by Robert Burks. *Strangers on a Train* was remade in 1969 as *Once You Kiss a Stranger*, with the backgrounds transferred from tennis to the golf world.

Straw Dogs   1971   (CBS)   *Color*
Director: Sam Peckinpah
Starring: Dustin Hoffman, Susan George, Peter Vaughan, T. P. McKenna, Del Henney, Ken Hutchinson, Colin Welland, Jim Norton, Sally Thomsett, Donald Webster, Len Jones, Michael Mundell, Peter Arne, Robert Keegan, June Brown, Chloë Franks, David Warner

This contemporary shocker from Sam Peckinpah contains exploitation film ingredients (simulations of savage sex and graphic violence—for which it became a *succès de scandale*); but it has been critically hailed in certain corners. David (Dustin Hoffman), an American mathematics professor, has rented a remote Cornish farm near the town where his wife Amy (Susan George) grew up. Amy is a sexual tease, taunting the men who knew her as a townie. David, the cool, rational academic, espouses pacifism but his philosophy changes when he, in turn, is taunted by the village roughnecks. After several of them rape and sodomize Amy, David engineers a bloody revenge. David Zelag Goodman's screenplay is based on *The Siege of Trencher's Farm,* a novel by Gordon M. Williams. Colin Welland, who plays Minister Hood, later wrote screenplays himself—*Chariots of Fire* and *Twice in a Lifetime,* among others.

The Taking of Pelham 1 2 3   1974   (CBS)   *Color*
Director: *Joseph Sargent*
Starring: *Walter Matthau, Robert Shaw, Martin Balsam, Hector Elizondo, Earl Hindman, James Broderick, Dick O'Neill, Jerry Stiller, Tony Roberts, Doris Roberts, Kenneth McMillan, Julius Harris, Sal Viscuso*

The Taking of Pelham 1 2 3 is a police procedural to restore one's faith in the genre. Peter Stone's screenplay, patterned closely upon the novel by John Godey, capitalizes on a terror intrinsic to many New Yorkers: something *else* has gone wrong with the subways! In this instance four armed hooligans hijack a train on the Pelham line and hold the passengers hostage. The gunmen demand a ransom of a million dollars in cash which is to be authorized by the mayor's office and delivered in one hour. A racing-with-the-clock thriller, *The Taking of Pelham 1 2 3* also contains patches of humor. Walter Matthau plays his transit detective role on several levels of irony, while Robert Shaw induces chills as the mastermind of the hijack. Cinematographer Owen Roizman, who also shot *The French Connection,* captures the squalor of the New York transit system.

They Live by Night   1949   (Budget Video)   *Black-and-White*
Director: *Nicholas Ray*
Starring: *Farley Granger, Cathy O'Donnell, Howard Da Silva, Jay C. Flippen, Helen Craig, Ian Wolfe, Marie Bryant*

Nicholas Ray, beforehand an assistant of Elia Kazan, made his directing debut with this crime drama. Set in the 1930s, the film takes its strength from Charles Schnee's screenplay and forceful, non-clichéd characterizations. There is a kind of tragic poetry in this tale of young lovers (Farley Granger and Cathy O'Donnell) who, in their association with two hardened criminals, are driven to crime themselves. The youngsters marry, but their grim life has already ensnared them and they must remain fugitives. *They Live by Night* is based on Edward Anderson's 1937 novel, *Thieves Like Us,* remade under that title in 1974 by Robert Altman—who adhered more closely to the book's tone and period evocation. Both films initially failed to attract an audience; time, however, has enhanced their reputations.

They Won't Believe Me   1947   (Nostalgia)   *Black-and-White*
Director: *Irving Pichel*
Starring: *Robert Young, Susan Hayward, Jane Greer, Rita Johnson, Tom Powers, Don Beddoe, Frank Ferguson*

Jonathan Latimer's script for *They Won't Believe Me* has elements of Hitchcock and James M. Cain. The tension and twists of the former combine with the hardboiled touches of the latter. Neither Hitchcock nor Cain is directly involved here, but their influence is felt. A philandering man-about-town (Robert Young) wants to ditch his wealthy wife (Rita Johnson) and run away with his latest girlfriend (Jane Greer). But, checkbook in hand, the wife convinces him to move from New York to Los Angeles. They'll start a new life there, she reasons. Then another attractive woman (Susan

Hayward) catches the playboy's eye. As the film begins, the greedy protagonist is standing trial for murder; the events leading to his arrest are shown in flashback. Many surprising turns await. *They Won't Believe Me* is directed by Irving Pichel and the cinematography is by Harry J. Wild.

Thief   1981   (CBS)   *Color*
Director: Michael Mann
Starring: James Caan, Tuesday Weld, Willie Nelson, Robert Prosky, James Belushi, Tom Signorelli, Dennis Farina, Nick Nickeas, W. R. Brown, Norm Tobin, Del Close

A high-tech crime melodrama, *Thief* is the feature film debut of writer-director Michael Mann. His earlier claim to fame was the TV movie *The Jericho Mile*; his post-*Thief* credits are *The Keep, Manhunter,* and *Miami Vice,* for which he is executive producer. The pulsating music here is by Tangerine Dream. Mann himself, as the guiding hand, provides the street realism and the blunt violence. Derived from Frank Hohimer's novel, *The Home Invaders,* the picture describes the private and professional life of an ex-con (James Caan) whose talents as a world-class thief place him in jeopardy with mobsters and crooked cops.

The Third Man   Great Britain 1949; U.S. 1950   ◆   *Black-and-White*
(Media; Prism; Budget Video; Video Yesteryear; Vid Dim.; Sheik Video; Video Connections; Discount Video Tapes; Cable Films; Western Film & Video Inc.; Cinema Concepts; Classic Video Cinema Collector's Club; Hal Roach Studios; Goodtimes Home Video Corp.)
Director: Sir Carol Reed
Starring: Joseph Cotten, Alida Valli, Orson Welles, Trevor Howard, Bernard Lee, Wilfrid Hyde-White, Ernst Deutsch, Erich Ponto, Siegfried Breuer, Paul Hoerbiger

This thriller was written by Graham Greene—from a story he later published. As directed by Carol Reed, *The Third Man* is a classic of cold war suspense. Set in post–World War II Vienna (and filmed there), the story begins as an American pulp novelist named Martins (Joseph Cotten) learns that his old friend Harry Lime (Orson Welles) has been killed in an accident. In fact, Harry Lime is alive; but as a corrupt black marketeer, he is a man on the run—sought by his mistress (Alida Valli), a crafty British intelligence officer (Trevor Howard), and by an increasingly puzzled Martins. As the manhunt ensues, so does a striking depiction of malevolence—by way of the dialogue and direction, Anton Karas's zither music, Robert Krasker's Oscar-winning cinematography, and the interpretations of the leading and featured players.

Three Days of the Condor   1975   (Paramount)   *Color*
Director: Sydney Pollack
Starring: Robert Redford, Faye Dunaway, Cliff Robertson, Max von Sydow, John Houseman, Walter McGinn, Addison Powell, Tina Chen, Michael Kane, Don McHenry, Michael Miller, Helen Stenborg, Carlin Glynn

Joseph Turner (Robert Redford) is a New York–based CIA operative whose job it is to read spy thrillers. One day in the midst of a downpour, he dashes from his office for lunch; when he returns, all his colleagues have been murdered. The hired assassin (Max von Sydow) realizes that Joseph has escaped the carnage—so he starts tracking him to earth. Joseph, in turn, soon realizes that the killer has been employed by another department of the CIA. Why? All is revealed in the climax of this man-on-the-run thriller by Lorenzo Semple, Jr., and David Rayfiel—based loosely on James Grady's *Six Days of the Condor*. Faye Dunaway plays a landscape photographer who shelters the hunted hero for a time. (The suspense, generated by director Sydney Pollack, builds over three—rather than the novel's six—days.)

Thunderball   1965   (CBS)   ◆   *Color*
Director: Terence Young
Starring: Sean Connery, Claudine Auger, Adolfo Celi, Luciana Paluzzi, Rik Van Nutter, Bernard Lee, Martine Beswick, Guy Doleman, Molly Peters, Desmond Llewelyn, Lois Maxwell, Roland Culver, Earl Cameron, Paul Stassino, Rose Alba, Philip Locke, Edward Underdown, Reginald Beckwith

A special effects Oscar went to this fourth chapter in the James Bond series, wherein the hero encounters an old foe: SPECTRE. Terror erupts when 007's adversary Emilio Largo (Adolfo Celi)—evil incarnate in his black eyepatch—hijacks a NATO aircraft equipped with a nuclear bomb. Largo threatens to detonate the bomb (upon Miami and Cape Canaveral) unless he is supplied with a one-million-pound ransom in diamonds. The Richard Maibaum-John Hopkins screenplay capitalizes on both tension and tongue-in-cheek dialogue—with the by-now obligatory double meanings. The underwater photography of Ted Moore and his crew rates as one of the highlights of *Thunderball*. Tom Jones sings the Don Black-John Barry title theme. (The basic plot here was reutilized in 1983's aptly titled *Never Say Never Again*—Sean Connery's return to Bond after an absence of twelve years.)

Tiger Bay   1959   (Learning)   *Black-and-White*
Director: J. Lee Thompson
Starring: John Mills, Horst Buchholz, Hayley Mills, Yvonne Mitchell, Megs Jenkins, Anthony Dawson, George Selway

Hayley Mills in her starring debut—and the first of four films she made with her father. The dockland of Cardiff in Wales is the setting for this unusual chiller. A twelve-year-old slum girl (Mills) is a witness when a Polish sailor (Horst Buchholz) murders his mistress. When the killer abducts the little girl, a police manhunt is instigated. The characterizations are the foundation of *Tiger Bay*; beyond Hayley's impressive performance, there are solid turns by Buchholz and, as the detective on the case, John Mills. Directed by J. Lee Thompson from a screenplay by John Hawkesworth and Shelley Smith. (The other pictures in which John and Hayley starred are *The Chalk Garden, The Truth about Spring*, and *The Family Way*.)

Time After Time   1979   (Warner)   *Color*
Director: Nicholas Meyer
Starring: Malcolm McDowell, David Warner, Mary Steenburgen, Charles Cioffi, Joseph Maher, Geraldine Baron, Michael Evans, James Garrett, Keith McConnell, Read Morgan, Kent Williams

From his home base of 1893 London, young H. G. Wells (Malcolm McDowell) travels in time to present-day San Francisco in pursuit of psychopath John Leslie Stevenson (David Warner), commonly known as Jack the Ripper. Before catching up with the Ripper, Wells encounters Hari Krishnas, fast-food McDonald's, a skyscraping Hyatt Regency, and liberated womanhood—in the person of Amy Catherine Robbins (Mary Steenburgen). When hero and villain finally reunite, the latter points to televised violence—Palestinian bombers, Saturday morning cartoons, political assassinations—and proclaims with pride: "I belong here completely and utterly. I'm home . . . the world has caught up with and surpassed me." *Time After Time* is an adult fantasy thriller, written and directed by Nicholas Meyer after a story by Karl Alexander and Steve Hayes. Photographed by Paul Lohmann and scored by Miklos Rozsa.

To Catch a Thief   1955   (Paramount)   *Color*
Director: Alfred Hitchcock
Starring: Cary Grant, Grace Kelly, Jessie Royce Landis, John Williams, Charles Vanel, Brigitte Auber, Jean Martinelli, Georgette Anys, Roland Lesaffre, Jean Hebey, René Blancard

Hitchcock's romantic thriller finds inspiration, by way of David Dodge's novel, in the adage "It takes a thief to catch a thief." John Robie (Cary Grant), a former cat burglar who has retired to the French Riviera, is suspected of committing a series of jewel thefts in and around Cannes. But he's innocent—the real culprit is craftily emulating Robie's modus operandi. In the interest of self-protection, the wrongly accused hero goes after the cagey newcomer. John Michael Hayes's dialogue, replete with innuendo between Grant and leading lady Grace Kelly, gives an added charge to this comedy-mystery. The on-location photography is courtesy of Hitchcock regular Robert Burks. The director's traditional walk-on is here a sit-on; for a few seconds he's sitting next to Grant on a bus.

Topkapi   1964   (CBS)   ◆   *Color*
Director: Jules Dassin
Starring: Melina Mercouri, Peter Ustinov, Maximilian Schell, Robert Morley, Akim Tamiroff, Gilles Segal, Jess Hahn, Joseph Dassin, Despo Diamantidou

English suspense novelist Eric Ambler, by way of his *The Light of Day*, gave inspiration to this heist adventure. Director Jules Dassin and his scenarist, Monja Danischewsky, offer both comedy and terror as six jewel thieves gather in Istanbul to steal a valuable dagger from the Topkapi Palace Museum. The intrepid sextet are played by Maximilian Schell, Melina Mercouri, Robert Morley, Gilles Segal, Jess Hahn, and, as the fumbling Arthur Simpson, Peter Ustinov—who won an Oscar for his interpretation. (This was Ustinov's second award in the supporting actor category; he also won in 1960 for *Spartacus.*) *Topkapi* maintains the grand tradition of Dassin's *Rififi* but with more of an accent on humor. The picture owes much of its vibrancy to Henri Alekan's cinematography and the score of Manos Hadjidakis.

The Towering Inferno   1974   (CBS)   ◆   *Color*
Directors: John Guillermin and Irwin Allen
Starring: Steve McQueen, Paul Newman, William Holden, Faye Dunaway, Fred Astaire, Susan Blakely, Richard Chamberlain, Jennifer Jones, O. J. Simpson, Robert Vaughn, Robert Wagner, Susan Flannery, Sheila Mathews, Normann Burton, Jack Collins, Don Gordon, Felton Perry, Gregory Sierra, Dabney Coleman, Scott Newman

An all-star cast populates this disaster epic codirected by John Guillermin and Irwin Allen. (The latter is credited with staging the action sequences.) William Holden stars as a San Francisco business tycoon who has used "alternate building materials" to cut corners in the construction of a newly opened skyscraper. Paul Newman plays his architect. And Steve McQueen enacts the fire chief called in when the building is engulfed in flames. The screenplay by Stirling Silliphant is derived from two similar novels: Richar Martin Stern's *The Tower* and *The Glass Inferno* by Thomas M. Scortia and Frank M. Robinson. Academy Awards: best song—"We May Never Love Like This Again" by Al Kasha (music) and Joel Hirschhorn (lyrics)—and best cinematography by Fred Koenekamp and Joseph Biroc.

Trapped   1949   (Movie Buff Video)   *Black-and-White*
Director: Richard Fleischer
Starring: Lloyd Bridges, Barbara Payton, John Hoyt, James Todd, Russ Conway, Tommy Noonan

The glossy look of the film and director Richard Fleischer's pacing belie the fourteen-day shooting schedule and the outlay of under $200,000. The hero of Earl Felton and George Zuckerman's story is an FBI agent named Downey (John Hoyt). In an effort to stamp out the counterfeit racket, Treasury agents allow a known forger to escape their custody. Stewart (Lloyd Bridges), a fence for the fake money, becomes trapped in the middle. Ultimately, the trail leads to the ringleader (James Todd). Felicitous plot twists add to the suspense.

The Treasure of the Sierra Madre   1948   (Key)   ◆   *Black-and-White*
Director: John Huston
Starring: Humphrey Bogart, Walter Huston, Tim Holt, Bruce Bennett, Barton MacLane, Alfonso Bedoya, A. Soto Rangel, Manuel Donde, José Torvey, Margarito Luna, Jacqueline Dalya, Bobby Blake, Spencer Chan, Julian Rivero, John Huston, Jack Holt

John Huston, as writer and director, is the major creative force behind this adaptation of the novel by B. Traven. At the center of the plot are three gold prospectors— toothless Howard (Walter Huston); Curtin (Tim Holt), an honest youngster; and Fred C. Dobbs (Humphrey Bogart), Curtin's hobo-companion. This trio is stranded in 1920s Mexico, where they unite to strike it rich in the bandit-ridden Sierra Madre. Good fortune is with them, but—as in Traven's original—gold can turn friends into strangers. *The Treasure of the Sierra Madre* is a sardonic fable performed by the three leads— and by Alfonso Bedoya, as the villainous Gold Hat. Academy Awards: best director, best screenplay, best supporing actor (Walter Huston). The elder Huston reportedly told son John years earlier, "If you ever become a writer or director, please find a good part for your old man." John himself may be seen early in the film as the American tourist in the white suit. Bobby Blake, who plays the Mexican boy, grew into the adult actor Robert Blake, TV's "Baretta."

The Trouble with Harry   1955   (MCA)   *Color*
Director: Alfred Hitchcock
Starring: Edmund Gwenn, John Forsythe, Shirley MacLaine, Mildred Natwick, Mildred Dunnock, Jerry Mathers, Royal Dano, Parker Fennelly, Philip Truex

This black comedy about the discovery of a body outside a tranquil Vermont village presents Hitchcock in a whimsical mode. Several people come upon Harry's corpse in the woods and, because they either feel responsible for his death or think a loved one may be responsible, they try to dispose of the body. Participating in the macabre game of get rid of the body are Captain Albert Wiles (Edmund Gwenn in his fourth Hitchcock role); artist Sam Marlowe (John Forsythe); Mrs. Wiggs (Mildred Dunnock), the general store owner; Miss Graveley (Mildred Natwick), a sweet-natured spinster with designs on the Captain; and little Arnie Rogers (Jerry "The Beaver" Mathers) and his mother, Jennifer (Shirley MacLaine in her film debut). Taken from the novel by Jack Trevor Story, as adapted by John Michael Hayes, *The Trouble with Harry* was photographed—as were most of Hitchcock's films of the fifties—by Robert Burks. This is the first collaboration between the director and composer Bernard Herrmann.

Vertigo 1958 (MCA) *Color*
Director: Alfred Hitchcock
Starring: James Stewart, Kim Novak, Barbara Bel Geddes, Tom Helmore, Henry Jones, Raymond Bailey, Ellen Corby, Konstantin Shayne, Lee Patrick

Alfred Hitchcock's psychological suspense drama collected mixed reviews in its initial release, but today it is regarded by many as his masterpiece. Drawn by scenarists Alec Coppel and Samuel Taylor from the Pierre Boileau-Thomas Narcejac novel *D'Entre Les Morts, Vertigo* is a tale of romantic obsession. James Stewart, in his fourth and final film for Hitchcock, stars as John "Scottie" Ferguson, an ex-detective forced to retire from the San Francisco police department because of his fear of heights. But danger occurs at ground level when Scottie is hired to shadow Madeleine Elster (Kim Novak), a woman who is convinced that a long-dead relative has returned to possess her. During a trancelike wandering, Madeleine tries to commit suicide by jumping into San Francisco Bay. Scottie rescues the troubled woman—and soon finds himself falling in love with her. Barbara Bel Geddes costars as the hero's erstwhile fiancée, and the traditional Hitchcock team has been assembled behind the camera: photographer Robert Burks, editor George Tomasini, art director Hal Pereira, and composer Bernard Herrmann.

Victory 1981 (CBS) *Color*
Director: John Huston
Starring: Sylvester Stallone, Michael Caine, Max von Sydow, Pelé, Daniel Massey, Carole Laure, Bobby Moore, George Mikell, Tim Pigott-Smith, Osvaldo Ardiles

In this John Huston action tale, guided by the Evan Jones and Yabo Yablonsky screenplay, Huston generates tension as German officials organize a soccer match between their pro players and a group of Allied war prisoners, some of whom were civilian footballers. The Germans intend the game as Master Race propaganda, but the POW's plan to turn the event to their own advantage. (To this point, *Victory* plays like a war-set variant on *The Longest Yard*.) Ultimately, an elaborate escape plot is hatched—to be executed on the day of the big match. The heroes of this thriller are Sylvester Stallone and Michael Caine, abetted by Brazilian soccer champ Pelé. Max von Sydow plays their nemesis, a Nazi officer. Director of photography: Gerry Fisher, whose work enhanced *Accident, The Go-Between*, and *Juggernaut*.

Wait Until Dark 1967 (Warner) *Color*

Director: Terence Young
Starring: Audrey Hepburn, Alan Arkin, Richard Crenna, Jack Weston, Efrem Zimbalist, Jr., Samantha Jones, Julie Herrod, Frank O'Brien, Gary Morgan

This chiller is based on the 1966 Broadway success by creator Frederick Knott. Susy Hendrix (Audrey Hepburn) is a blind housewife whose Greenwich Village apartment becomes the focal point for three desperate criminals. Susy is the unknowing possessor of an antique doll stuffed with heroin. Her photographer-husband Sam (Efrem Zimbalist, Jr.) is lured away on a wild goose chase, and the villainous trio—Carlino (Jack Weston), Mike Talman (Richard Crenna), and psychotic mastermind Harry Roat, Jr. (Alan Arkin)—begin their campaign of terror. Only then does Susy discover that the doll is on the premises. Directed by Terence Young from Robert and Jane Howard-Carrington's screenplay. The claustrophobic setting was designed by George Jenkins, and the eerie theme music is by Henry Mancini.

War Games   1983   (CBS)   *Color*
Director: John Badham
Starring: Matthew Broderick, Dabney Coleman, John Wood, Ally Sheedy, Barry Corbin, Juanin Clay

Teenage electronics wizard David Lightman (Matthew Broderick), believing he's previewing a new line of video games, taps into a NORAD—North America Air Defense—computer. Unwittingly, he challenges the computer to World War III. Pentagon officials arrest David, then, with his help, race to prevent a global thermonuclear catastrophe. This science fiction thriller, directed by John Badham, takes full advantage of both the humor and the horror in the Lawrence Lasker-Walter F. Parkes screenplay. Broderick's dual-edged performance is supported by John Wood as a reclusive scientist and Dabney Coleman as an arrogant war room official. William A. Fraker is the cinematographer.

What Ever Happened to Baby Jane?   1962   (Warner)   *Black-and-White*
Director: Robert Aldrich
Starring: Bette Davis, Joan Crawford, Victor Buono, Marjorie Bennett, Maidie Norman, Anna Lee, B. D. Merrill, Wesley Addy, Julie Allred, Gina Gillespie, Dave Willock, Ann Barton, Bert Freed, Russ Conway, Robert Cornthwaite, Bobs Watson

Jane Hudson (Bette Davis) is an egomaniacal harridan, a monster obsessed by the fact that she was once a saccharine child star named Baby Jane. Her sister Blanche (Joan Crawford) also had a show biz career—until she was crippled in a mysterious car wreck. Now Jane and Blanche are recluses, sharing a roomy, once-glamourous home in Los Angeles. A psychopathic relationship exists between the two sisters, sparked by lifelong jealousy. As written by Lukas Heller and directed by Robert Aldrich, *What Ever Happened to Baby Jane?* is a macabre horror tale. B. D. Merrill, Miss Davis's daughter, plays her next-door neighbor Liza.

White Heat   1949   (CBS)   *Black-and-White*
Director: Raoul Walsh
Starring: James Cagney, Virginia Mayo, Edmond O'Brien, Margaret Wycherly, Steve Cochran, John Archer, Wally Cassell, Mickey Knox, Ian MacDonald, Fred Clark

This classic gangster drama was a comeback film for James Cagney after several box-office mediocrities. Gunsel Cody Jarrett is one of the actor's most enduring characterizations—an epileptic psychopath. While imprisoned, he learns that his mother (Margaret Wycherly) has been killed, so he breaks out of jail—with an undercover Treasury agent (Edmond O'Brien) who's been masquerading as his cellmate. The T-man then infiltrates Cody's reactivated gang. And Cody stalks his mother's murderer. Directed by *auteur* favorite Raoul Walsh, *White Heat* has a screenplay by Ivan

Goff and Ben Roberts (from a story by Virginia Kellogg). Cinematographer: Sid Hickox.

White Nights   1985   (RCA)   ◆   *Color*
Director: Taylor Hackford
Starring: Mikhail Baryshnikov, Gregory Hines, Geraldine Page, Helen Mirren, Jerzy Sko-limowski, John Glover, Stefan Gryff, William Hootkins, Shane Rimmer, Isabella Rossellini

Ballet star Nikolai "Kolya" Rodchenko (Mikhail Baryshnikov), a Soviet citizen, has defected to the United States, where he has been working for several years. On his way to a dancing engagement in Tokyo, the plane in which he is traveling is forced to make a crash-landing near a Siberian military installation. He is taken prisoner and transferred to Moscow—where he is placed in the care of Raymond Greenwood (Gregory Hines), a black American tap dancer. Raymond, too, is a defector, but in the opposite direction. Now, however, he and his Russian wife would like to leave. He is told by Colonel Chaiko (Jerzy Skolimowski), a KGB man, that he must convince Kolya to renounce his defection and perform once again in Kirov. Suspense and dazzling dance work in counterpoint as the story evolves into an escape thriller. Chosen for the prestigious Royal Film Performance, *White Nights* was directed by Taylor Hackford from the James Goldman-Eric Hughes screenplay and photographed by David *(Out of Africa)* Watkin. The score includes two hit songs: "Separate Lives," by Stephen Bishop, sung by Phil Collins, and the Oscar-winning "Say You, Say Me," written and performed by Lionel Richie.

The White Tower   1950   (Budget Video)   *Color*
Director: Ted Tetzlaff
Starring: Glenn Ford, Claude Rains, Alida Valli, Oscar Homolka, Sir Cedric Hardwicke, Lloyd Bridges, June Clayworth

A tension-packed mountaineering adventure, *The White Tower* is set in Switzerland, where six people have six different reasons for tackling an Alpine peak. The screenplay, devised by Paul Jarrico after a novel by James Ramsay Ullman, concentrates on their life-risking ascent. A mixture of character drama and action, the film is directed by Ted Tetzlaff, revered principally for *The Window* (1949), another exercise in suspense. Also performing yeoman work behind the camera is director of photography Ray Rennahan. Roy Webb wrote the score.

The Window   1949   (Nostalgia)   ◆   *Black-and-White*
Director: Ted Tetzlaff
Starring: Barbara Hale, Bobby Driscoll, Arthur Kennedy, Paul Stewart, Ruth Roman

This near-forgotten suspense film was a sleeper hit in its day. Spun from the boy-who-cried-wolf motif (and specifically inspired by Cornell Woolrich's 1947 story "The Boy Who Cried Murder"), *The Window* presents an over-imaginative, tale-spinning Hell's Kitchen tenement kid (Bobby Driscoll) who witnesses a murder. His parents (Barbara Hale, Arthur Kennedy) don't believe him; but the killers (Paul Stewart, Ruth Roman) do. Driscoll was presented with a miniature Oscar as "the outstanding juvenile actor of 1949." Scripted by Mel Dinelli, directed by Ted Tetzlaff, and photograhed in *film noir* trappings by William Steiner. Woolrich's story also served as the source for *The Boy Who Cried Murder* (1966) and *Cloak and Dagger* (1984).

Witness   1985   (Paramount)   ◆   *Color*
Director: Peter Weir
Starring: Harrison Ford, Kelly McGillis, Josef Sommer, Danny Glover, Lukas Haas, Alexander Godunov, Patti LuPone, Jan Rubes

An Amish boy (Lukas Haas) who has never been far from his Lancaster County, Pennsylvania, farm witnesses a murder in a Philadelphia train station. He and his mother (Kelly McGillis), a young widow, are interrogated by police captain John Book (Harrison Ford). When the youngster identifies the killer as another cop, Book opens the door on a widespread departmental conspiracy. In order to protect both himself and his witness, he accompanies mother and child back to their farm and tries to assimilate himself into their community. But the corrupt cops are on their trail. *Witness,* Australian director Peter Weir's first American movie, gives Harrison Ford an opportunity to step beyond his superhero typecasting. (Director and actor reunited for *The Mosquito Coast.*) The screenplay by Earl W. Wallace, William Kelley, and Pamela Wallace won not only an Academy Award but the prestigious Edgar from the Mystery Writers of America. A second Oscar went to Thom Noble for his editing.

Witness for the Prosecution   1957   (CBS)   *Black-and-White*
Director: Billy Wilder
Starring: Tyrone Power, Marlene Dietrich, Charles Laughton, Elsa Lanchester, John Williams, Henry Daniell, Ian Wolfe, Una O'Connor, Torin Thatcher, Francis Compton, Norma Varden, Philip Tonge, Ruta Lee

Agatha Christie's long-running London and New York stage play is a wonderful screen thriller, as adapted by director Billy Wilder and his coscenarist Harry Kurnitz. Centrally a courtroom drama about a sensational London murder, *Witness for the Prosecution* begins as Leonard Vole (Tyrone Power), a charming ne'er-do-well, is accused of killing Emily French (Norma Varden), a wealthy unmarried woman. Convinced of Vole's innocence, aging, ailing barrister Sir Wilfrid Robarts (Charles Laughton) agrees to stand for the defense. A surprise witness for the prosecution, however, is Vole's wife, Christine (Marlene Dietrich). Under Wilder's aegis, this is a production which respects the formulas of the genre and contributes more besides. The camera work is by Russell Harlan. A 1982 TV remake starred Beau Bridges as Vole, Diana Rigg as Christine, and Ralph Richardson as Sir Wilfrid.

The Wrong Man   1957   (Warner)   *Black-and-White*
Director: Alfred Hitchcock
Starring: Henry Fonda, Vera Miles, Anthony Quayle, Harold J. Stone, Charles Cooper, John Heldabrand, Esther Minciotti, Doreen Lang, Laurinda Barrett, Norma Connolly, Nehemiah Persoff, Lola D'Annunzio, Robert Essen, Kippy Campbell, Richard Robbins

A partial documentary, this Alfred Hitchcock drama is a clinical depiction of justice gone wrong. As revealed in the screenplay by Maxwell Anderson and Angus MacPhail—based on Herbert Brean's *Life* magazine article, "A Case of Identity"—Christopher Emmanuel Balestrero (Henry Fonda) is a jazz musician at New York's Stork Club; on January 14, 1953, he is arrested and charged with armed robbery. Unreliable witnesses and circumstantial evidence combine to place Balestrero behind bars. Only when the real thief strikes again, is trapped, and confesses does the truth emerge. Costarring in *The Wrong Man* are Vera Miles as Rose, the victim's wife; Esther Minciotti as his mother; and Quayle as lawyer Frank O'Connor. The real-life O'Connor served as a technical consultant to Hitchcock.

You Only Live Twice   1967   (CBS)   *Color*

Director: Lewis Gilbert
Starring: Sean Connery, Akiko Wakabayashi, Tetsuro Tamba, Mie Hama, Teru Shi-mada, Karin Dor, Lois Maxwell, Desmond Llewelyn, Bernard Lee, Charles Gray, Tsai Chin, Donald Pleasence, Alexander Knox, Robert Hutton, Burt Kwouk

For record-keepers: *You Only Live Twice* is the fifth feature in the Bond of the British Secret Service series. The script by Roald Dahl uses little more than the title of Ian Fleming's novel. This film introduces SPECTRE mastermind Ernst Stavros Blofeld (here played by Donald Pleasence), determined to hijack U.S. and Soviet space capsules to incite the major powers to declare war on each other. Sean Connery again portrays 007, and he contends with piranhas, sumo wrestlers, and being dropped by helicopter into the crater of an inactive volcano—where the badmen have housed a rocket-launching pad. The music, as before, is by John Barry; Nancy Sinatra performs the title song.

Young Sherlock Holmes   1985   (Paramount)   *Color*

Director: Barry Levinson
Starring: Nicholas Rowe, Alan Cox, Sophie Ward, Anthony Higgins, Susan Fleetwood, Freddie Jones, Nigel Stock, Roger Ashton Griffiths, Donald Eccles, Patrick Newell, Earl Rhodes

This speculative fantasy explores the schoolboy experiences of Sherlock Holmes. Eighteen-year-old Sherlock (Nicholas Rowe) attends an upper-class London public school. Among his friends is young John Watson (Alan Cox), who hopes to be a doctor one day. The two mates decide to play detective when a series of unexplained deaths occur. (The victims have been dispatched by a fiend with an Egyptian blowgun and poisoned darts.) The screenplay by Chris Columbus honors (for a while at least) the Holmesian conceits fabricated by Sir Arthur Conan Doyle. Scares galore dot Sherlock and John's investigation. Directed by Barry Levinson *(Diner, The Natural)*, with cinematography by Stephen Goldblatt and music by Bruce Broughton.

War

■

Apocalypse Now   1979   (Paramount)   ◆   *Color*
Director: Francis Ford Coppola
Starring: Marlon Brando, Robert Duvall, Martin Sheen, Frederic Forrest, Albert Hall,
Sam Bottom, Larry Fishburne, Dennis Hopper, G. D. Spradlin, Harrison Ford

Coppola's movie found its source in Joseph Conrad's *Heart of Darkness*. In the film update, set during the war in Vietnam, Army captain Martin Sheen travels upriver to locate and murder a Green Beret colonel (Marlon Brando) gone mad. Three years in production and with a budget of over $30 million, *Apocalypse Now* was only a middling success when it finally premiered in the spring of 1979—its box-office potential blunted by mixed reviews and the national release several months earlier of another war-related drama: the 1978 Oscar champ, *The Deer Hunter*. (In time, though, *Apocalypse Now* actually eclipsed the other picture in box-office receipts.) There were several Academy Award nominations for Coppola and company, notably best picture, director, and screenplay (Coppola teamed with John Milius); but *Apocalypse Now* secured only two Oscars—one for the sound team, one for Vittorio Storaro's cinematography.

Battle Cry   1955   (Warner)   *Color*
Director: Raoul Walsh
Starring: Van Heflin, Aldo Ray, Mona Freeman, Nancy Olson, James Whitmore, Ray-
mond Massey, Tab Hunter, Dorothy Malone, Anne Francis, William Campbell, John
Lupton, Justus McQueen, Perry Lopez

This star-studded salute to the U.S. Marine Corps is based on Leon Uris's novel, his first in a string of popular successes. Uris also wrote the screenplay. World War II is the setting as a group of recruits undergoes rigorous boot camp training before engaging in action in the Pacific. Although sweeping and actional, there is time off for romance: Nancy Olson loves Aldo Ray; Dorothy Malone seduces Tab Hunter; Anne Francis is attracted to several people. In the intervals between nonstop action at home and in battle, the film provides an early look at Fess Parker and at the familiar (albeit young) face belonging then to Justus McQueen—whom we now know as L. Q. Jones, the name of his character in *Battle Cry*. Veteran men's adventure director Raoul Walsh came to this project toward the end of his fifty-year career; the final product is one of his enduring achievements. Musical score by Max Steiner, of *King Kong* and *Gone with the Wind* fame.

Battle of the Bulge   1965   (Warner)   *Color*
Director: Ken Annakin
Starring: Henry Fonda, Robert Shaw, Robert Ryan, Dana Andrews, George Montgomery,
Ty Hardin, Pier Angeli, Barbara Werle, Charles Bronson, Werner Peters, Hans Christian
Blech, James MacArthur, Telly Savalas

This cinematic retelling of a major crisis situation in World War II was shot in Spain
and originally released in Cinerama. Home viewers won't be compromised though;
expert cinematographer Jack Hildyard's framing and depth of focus can be appreciated
even without a rectangular screen. Explosive action is at the forefront of *Battle of the
Bulge*; emphasis lies not with the characters, but on strategy, troop deployments, and
battle skirmishes. Ken Annakin, the director, started in the British film industry by
making small-scale documentary films. He's at the opposite end of the spectrum here,
guiding a mammoth historical reenactment. When the film premiered, the Philip Yor-
dan-Milton Sperling-John Nelson screenplay was criticized by veterans' groups for its
inaccuracies and distortions.

Battleground   1949   (MGM)   ◆   *Black-and-White*
Director: William Wellman
Starring: Van Johnson, John Hodiak, Ricardo Montalban, George Murphy, Marshall
Thompson, Jerome Courtland, Don Taylor, Bruce Cowling, James Whitmore, Douglas
Fowley, Leon Ames, Guy Anderson, Thomas E. Breen, Denice Darcel, Richard Jaeckel

A detail of airborne troops, led by top sergeant James Whitmore, is trucked into
Bastogne after the German invasion. Many viewers consider this one of the best fiction
films concerning the Battle of the Bulge. A military drama that honors authenticity,
Battleground is also one of the most moving in the canon because it concentrates on
the humans involved; the battles occur, for the most part, only in montages. War
pictures were one of William Wellman's specialties; this film fits alongside other Wellman classics from *Wings* to *The Story of G.I. Joe*. *Battleground* captured two Oscars—
for Paul C. Vogel's black-and-white photography and for the original screenplay by
Robert Pirosh, who was at Bastogne himself. Star alert: young James Arness as a skinny
G.I. called Garby.

The Big Red One   1980   (CBS)   *Color*
Director: Samuel Fuller
Starring: Lee Marvin, Mark Hamill, Robert Carradine, Bobby Di Cicco, Kelly Ward,
Perry Lang, Siegfried Rauch, Stephane Audran, Serge Marquand

Samuel Fuller's semiautobiographical account of a World War II rifle squadron is the
capstone of an illustrious, though not always critically heralded, career. The story
concentrates on four young soliders and their tough-but-caring first sergeant (Lee
Marvin) upon their landing in North Africa as part of "the Big Red One"—the U.S.
Army's legendary First Infantry Division. The war, as visualized by Fuller, is presented
in relatively small scale—no major bombardments. War as madhouse is given literal
interpretation at the climax when the heores invade an asylum that is being used as a
German stronghold. Fuller fills the screen of *The Big Red One* with enough suspense
and good moviemaking to captivate even those who don't like war films.

The Boys in Company C   1978   (RCA)   *Color*
Director: Sidney J. Furie
Starring: Stan Shaw, Andrew Stevens, James Canning, Michael Lembeck, Craig Wasson,
Scott Hylands, James Whitmore, Jr., Santos Morales, Lee Ermey

This drama follows a company of marine recruits as they go through basic training, then ship out to Vietnam in 1967. The boys are a cross-pollination of ethno-cultural types, and they are played by an ensemble of then unknowns—many of whom gained fame on TV or in more highly touted pictures. *The Boys in Company C*, politically incorrect in 1978, was a comparative failure—its box office profits far lower than *The Green Berets*, with which it has superficial similarities. James Whitmore, Jr., is notable in a role that, twenty-odd years earlier, his father played. (See *Battleground.*) And a bona fide ex-marine sergeant (Lee Ermey) contributes a touch of realism as he takes the recruits through their basic training. The action scenes devised by Sidney J. Furie and his coscenarist Rick Natkin are reasonably graphic, and their dialogue is appropriately raw. In 1984 Furie and Natkin collaborated again on a Vietnam story—*Purple Hearts*—this time focusing on nonbattlefront aspects: the romance between a nurse and a navy medic.

The Bridge on the River Kwai   1957   (RCA)   ◆   *Black-and-White*
Director: David Lean
Starring: William Holden, Alec Guinness, Jack Hawkins, Sessue Hayakawa, James Don-
ald, Geoffrey Horne, André Morell, Peter Williams, John Boxer, Percy Herbert, Harold
Goodwin, Ann Sears

World War II Burma. British soldiers, commanded by a stern colonel, are taken prisoner by the Japanese. The POW's are ordered to build a railroad bridge for their captors. The colonel (Alec Guinness) sees the operation as a way of restoring morale and discipline. Ultimately, he begins to take the enterprise personally. Meanwhile, two soldiers (William Holden, Jack Hawkins), assigned to rescue the prisoners, plan to demolish the bridge. David Lean's epic was honored with seven Academy Awards: best picture, director, actor (Guinness), cinematography (Jack Hildyard), editing (Peter Taylor), music scoring (Malcolm Arnold), and adapted screenplay. Pierre Boulle, upon whose novel the film was founded, couldn't read or write English; he was given screen credit for the script because the real scenarists, Michael Wilson and Carl Foreman, were still blacklisted in 1957. In 1985 belated Oscars were awarded to the widows of Wilson and Foreman.

A Bridge Too Far   1977   (CBS)   *Color*
Director: Richard Attenborough
Starring: Dirk Bogarde, James Caan, Michael Caine, Sean Connery, Edward Fox, Elliott
Gould, Gene Hackman, Anthony Hopkins, Hardy Krüger, Laurence Olivier, Ryan O'Neal,
Robert Redford, Maximilian Schell, Liv Ullmann

A Bridge Too Far, Cornelius Ryan's posthumous book, is the exhaustive account of a World War II setback for the Allies. The objective was to shorten the war by putting the Dutch Rhine bridges out of commission. But in 1944 an airdrop behind German lines went awry, culminating in the mistake-ridden attack on the bridge at Arnhem. Joseph Levine's screen version, directed by Richard Attenborough, assembled such talents as Sean Connery, Ryan O'Neal, and Robert Redford. The celebrity-laden production still wasn't a commercial success—partly because of the astronomical budget (reportedly $25 million), partly because American filmgoers were not interested in seeing a story of war disaster. William Goldman wrote the screenplay. Geoffrey Unsworth was the cinematographer.

Catch-22   1970   (Paramount)   *Color*
Director: Mike Nichols
Starring: Alan Arkin, Martin Balsam, Richard Benjamin, Art Garfunkel, Jack Gilford, Buck Henry, Bob Newhart, Anthony Perkins, Paula Prentiss, Jon Voight, Orson Welles, Martin Sheen, Susanne Benton

Satirist Joseph Heller's story takes place during World War II at a U.S. Air Force base in the Mediterranean. Pilots are losing their lives daily. Captain Yuri Yossarian wants to be certified insane so he won't have to fly any more missions. Working his way through military red tape, Yossarian encounters Catch-22: if he's sane enough not to want to fly, then how can he be insane? Back to the cockpit. Buck Henry's adaptation of the Heller novel retains the deadpan black humor and the lunatic characters—from Major Major Major (Bob Newhart) to Milo Minderbinder (Jon Voight) to the very sane protagonist (Alan Arkin). The laughing-in-death's-face scenario and Mike Nichols's chilly direction weren't acceptable to the mass audience in 1970—but now *Catch-22* the film has almost as strong a cult following as *Catch-22* the book. Cinematographer David Watkin's experimental use of color and lighting extended the work he began in *Help!* and the *The Charge of the Light Brigade* (1968 version), then continued in the Richard Lester *Musketeers* movies, *Robin and Marian,* and *Chariots of Fire.*

The Colditz Story   Great Britain 1955; U.S. 1957   (Thorn)   *Black-and-White*
Director: Guy Hamilton
Starring: John Mills, Eric Portman, Christopher Rhodes, Lionel Jeffries, Bryan Forbes, Ian Carmichael, Richard Wattis, Frederick Valk, Anton Diffring, Eugene Deckers, Theodore Bikel

A near-forgotten prisoner-of-war thriller. In World War II a group of British POW's are impounded in a maximum security prison within Colditz Castle in Germany. Colditz is reputedly escape-proof, but a band of stalwart prisoners attempts a breakout anyway. Guy Hamilton, a specialist in action pictures, started as an assistant director for Carol Reed; he also assisted John Huston on *The African Queen.* His later reputation arises from his 007 association (from *Goldfinger* through *The Man with the Golden Gun*) and his direction of two Christie-derived movies *(The Mirror Crack'd* and *Evil under the Sun).* Of his early work, *The Colditz Story* best demonstrates his expertise with suspense. Hamilton's screenplay with Ivan Foxwell was the basis for a 1972 English teleseries starring David McCallum—later syndicated in America.

The Cruel Sea   1953   (Thorn)   *Black-and-White*
Director: Charles Frend
Starring: Jack Hawkins, Donald Sinden, Stanley Baker, John Stratton, Denholm Elliott, John Warner, Virginia McKenna, Bruce Seton, Moira Lister, June Thorburn

Eric Ambler's concise script, from the autobiographical novel by Nicholas Monsarrat, encapsulates the Battle of the Atlantic in the story of one corvette—the *Compass Rose*—and its crew's encounters with German U-boats. *(Das Boot* provides a seen-through-the-other-periscope perspective.) Heading the cast, under Charles Frend's direction, are Donald Sinden as a thinly disguised version of Monsarrat, a lieutenant who rises to the rank of lieutenant-commander, and Jack Hawkins as the captain of the *Compass Rose*.

The **D**am Busters   1955   (Thorn)   *Black-and-White*
Director: Michael Anderson
Starring: Richard Todd, Michael Redgrave, Ursula Jeans, Basil Sydney, Patrick Barr, Ernest Clark, Derek Farr, Charles Carson, Stanley Van Beers, Colin Tapley, Raymond Huntley

The best moments in this historical drama depict the meticulous preparation for—and subsequent commission of—a perilous World War II operation. Special bombs are produced for the destruction of the Moehne and Eder dams in Germany, and a flight crew must be assembled. *The Dam Busters* is a realistic vision of war, compactly written and directed by R. C. Sherriff and Michael Anderson, respectively. Amazingly, suspense is maintained in portraying even the most mundane events. In the large cast, Michael Redgrave stands out as the scientist, Dr. Barnes Wallis, who creates the devastating bombs.

Das Boot   *Listed under Foreign Language.*

The Desert Fox   1951   (CBS)   *Black-and-White*
Director: Henry Hathaway
Starring: James Mason, Jessica Tandy, Sir Cedric Hardwicke, Luther Adler, Everett Sloane, Leo G. Carroll, George Macready, Richard Boone, Eduard Franz, Desmond Young

Field Marshal Erwin Rommel led Germany's North African operations in World War II. Considered by many historians to be a brilliant and formidable opponent, as commander of the Afrika Korps he earned the nickname "desert fox." This movie biography recounts Rommel's string of victories, his defeat at El Alamein, and his return, in disillusionment, to Germany. The field marshal, who ultimately opposed Hitler, is presented in a heroic light—with James Mason the protagonist. Jessica Tandy costars as his wife, and Luther Adler plays a vivid Hitler. Of other interest, the screenplay is by Nunnally Johnson, from Desmond Young's biography, *Rommel*. Director Henry Hathaway's pacing gives the film a documentary feel, a quality he also brought to *The House on 92nd Street* and *Kiss of Death*. Hathaway startled 1951 audiences by beginning *The Desert Fox* with a lengthy precredit action sequence—a standard practice today. Mason played Rommel again in the 1953 *The Desert Rats*.

The Dirty Dozen   1967   (MGM)   ◆   *Color*
Director: Robert Aldrich
Starring: Lee Marvin, Ernest Borgnine, Charles Bronson, Jim Brown, John Cassavetes, Richard Jaeckel, George Kennedy, Trini Lopez, Ralph Meeker, Robert Ryan, Telly Savalas, Clint Walker, Robert Webber, Donald Sutherland

The twelve title figures of action director Robert Aldrich's World War II adventure are a commando group composed of convict-soldiers serving time in a stockade. They are reprieved to train for a perilous mission: the elimination of top-ranking Nazi officers in occupied France. Coaching the dirty dozen and leading them on the final assault is a hard-bitten major played by Lee Marvin. The frequently bloody tale emerges from a novel by E. M. Nathanson, transferred to the screen by Nunnally Johnson and Lukas Heller. The Academy cited John Poyner for his sound effects. *The Dirty Dozen* was oft-imitated *(The Devil's Brigade, Dayton's Devils, The Devil's Eight,* and uncountable telemovies with and without devil in the title); but the original is still the best. As popular as the film was, eighteen years passed before a sequel was fashioned; in a 1985 TV movie, *The Dirty Dozen: The Next Mission,* three returnees—Marvin, Ernest Borgnine, and Richard Jaeckel—re-created their original roles.

The Dogs of War   Great Britain 1980; U.S. 1981   (CBS)   *Color*
Director: John Irvin
Starring: Christopher Walken, Tom Berenger, Colin Blakely, Hugh Millais, Paul Freeman, JoBeth Williams, Robert Urquhart

Christopher Walken is cast as a soldier of fortune whose assignments take him to political hot spots all over the globe. A solitary man with a secret profession, he is an enigma to his few friends and loved ones. Walken's current mission involves him with a specially selected band of international mercenaries; under his command they will help to overthrow a corrupt West African dictator. Based on the Frederick Forsyth best-seller, the Gary De Vore-George Malko script is an action- and irony-packed adventure. *The Dogs of War* is not all blood and guts; it works as a fascinating character study and a sobering reflection on the precariousness of power. John Irvin, whose first theatrical feature this was, has also directed *Ghost Story, Champions, Turtle Diary,* and the television version of John Le Carré's *Tinker, Tailor, Soldier, Spy.*

El Cid   1961   (Lightning Video; United Home Video)   *Color*
Director: Anthony Mann
Starring: Charlton Heston, Sophia Loren, Raf Vallone, Geneviève Page, John Fraser, Gary Raymond, Hurd Hatfield, Massimo Serato, Herbert Lom, Andrew Cruickshank, Christopher Rhodes, Michael Hordern, Tullio Carminati, Ralph Truman, Gérard Tichy, Frank Thring

Rodrigo Diaz, known as El Cid and romanticized in the poetry and drama of many languages, is the eleventh-century Christian soldier who freed Spain from Moorish invaders. This action adventure, written by Frederic M. Frank and Philip Yordan, chronicles the Spanish national hero's battles against the Moors and his love for Chimene. Handsome castles, stunning vistas, and numerous battles (including the siege of Valencia) are all captured by Robert Krasker's lens. The finale, with the mortally wounded El Cid lashed to his horse and riding against the foe, is not to be missed. Director Anthony Mann built his reputation with Western dramas such as *Winchester '73, Bend of the River, The Naked Spur, The Man from Laramie,* but his hand is sure here too. Charlton Heston is the hero, and Sophia Loren plays his lady love.

Exodus   1960   (CBS)   ◆   *Color*
Director: Otto Preminger
Starring: Paul Newman, Eva Marie Saint, Ralph Richardson, Peter Lawford, Lee J. Cobb, Sal Mineo, John Derek, Hugh Griffith, Gregory Ratoff, Felix Aylmer, David Opatoshu, Jill Haworth, Marius Goring, Alexandra Stewart, Michael Wager, Martin Benson, Paul Stevens, Victor Maddern, George Maharis

Exodus, from the Leon Uris epic, concerns the birth of the state of Israel in 1947. At the forefront of the Israeli fight for independence is resistance leader Ari Ben Canaan (Paul Newman). He and other Jewish immigrants defy the British Governor of Cyprus (Ralph Richardson) and run the blockade to the homeland. On the sidelines is a sympathetic army nurse (Eva Marie Saint) enamored of Ari. The sprawling novel is given an episodic translation by Dalton Trumbo (the first screenwriting credit under his own name since his 1947 blacklisting). *Exodus* rates as one of Otto Preminger's best-directed features, particularly in its first half. Notable in the large cast are Sal Mineo as young Dov Landau and Peter Lawford as Major Caldwell. An Academy Award went to Ernest Gold for his score.

The **F**inal Countdown   1979   (Vestron)   *Color*
Director: Don Taylor
Starring: Kirk Douglas, Martin Sheen, Katherine Ross, James Farentino, Charles Durning, Ron O'Neal

In this action-packed fantasy melodrama, the U.S.S. *Nimitz,* the world's largest nuclear-powered aircraft carrier, is on maneuvers near Hawaii. Suddenly, in the midst of a storm, the ship passes through a time warp. Captain Matthew Yelland (Kirk Douglas) and his crew find themselves hurtled back to December 1941—just hours before the Japanese attack on Pearl Harbor. With a squadron of F-14's on board, the *Nimitz* could easilty tilt the scales and alter the course of history. Will Captain Yelland make that fateful decision? Don Taylor *(Escape from the Planet of the Apes, Damien—Omen II, The Island of Dr. Moreau)* directed the original screenplay by David Ambrose, Gerry Davis, Thomas Hunter, and Peter Powell.

From Here to Eternity   *Listed under Dramas.*

Gallipoli   1981   (Paramount)   *Color*
Director: Peter Weir
Starring: Mark Lee, Mel Gibson, Bill Kerr, Robert Grubb, David Argue, Tim McKenzie, Bill Hunter

Australia during World War I. Two young men, after trekking eastward across the desert from Perth, enlist in the armed forces. Bound by their mutual athletic interests, the two become friends. They train together and jointly serve in the Gallipoli campaign—the British Empire's futile attempt to secure the Dardanelles, capture Constantinople, and thereby connect with Russia. David Williamson's script examines that fateful battle on the beach of Gallipoli, while reflecting on the special nature of wartime friendship. Mel Gibson and Mark Lee play the young soldiers. Among director Peter Weir's other accomplishments are *Picnic at Hanging Rock, The Last Wave, The Year of Living Dangerously, Witness,* and *The Mosquito Coast.* Camera work by Russell Boyd.

Go Tell the Spartans   1978   (Vestron)   *Color*
Director: Ted Post
Starring: Burt Lancaster, Craig Wasson, Marc Singer, Jonathan Goldsmith, Dennis Howard, Joe Unger, Evan Kim, John Megna, Hilly Hicks, David Clennon, Dolph Sweet, Clyde Kusatsu

Go Tell the Spartans dramatizes the early days of U.S. involvement in Vietnam. The time is 1964 and American military advisers are making their presence felt. When further inroads are considered, one tight-lipped major, played by Burt Lancaster, begins to have doubts. Of the young actors playing the recruits, Marc Singer, Craig Wasson, and Hilly Hicks are most prominent. Action specialist Ted *(Magnum Force)* Post is the director; while his story erupts in violence, Post (with his cinematographer Harry Stradling, Jr.) finds ways of minimizing the blood and violence. The realistic dialogue and plot, adapted by Mendell Mayes, are from Daniel Ford's novel, *Incident at Muc Wa*.

The Guns of Navarone   *Listed under Suspense and Mystery.*

The Horse Soldiers   1959   (CBS)   *Color*
Director: John Ford
Starring: John Wayne, William Holden, Constance Towers, Althea Gibson, Hoot Gibson, Anna Lee, Russell Simpson, Stan Jones, Carleton Young, Basil Ruysdael, Judson Pratt, Willis Bouchey, William Leslie, Ken Curtis, Bing Russell, Walter Reed, Bill Henry, O. Z. Whitehead, Strother Martin, Denver Pyle

A late-career Civil War epic from John Ford. The year is 1863, and Colonel John Marlowe (John Wayne) leads the Union cavalry behind Confederate lines to sabotage a crucial railroad junction. In the raiding party is Major Henry Kendall (William Holden), a doctor with pacifist leanings. Inevitably, the two officers clash philosophically. But in the John Lee Mahin-Martin Rackin screenplay, from a Harold Sinclair novel, they join ranks for the final confrontation against the enemy. Wayne and Holden are joined by two uncommon leading ladies: tennis great Althea Gibson and musical-comedy-star-turned-dramatic-actress Constance Towers. The song, "I Left My Love," was written by Stan Jones, who plays General Ulysses S. Grant.

King Rat   1965   (RCA)   *Color*
Director: Bryan Forbes
Starring: George Segal, Tom Courtenay, James Fox, Patrick O'Neal, Denholm Elliott, James Donald, Todd Armstrong, Alan Webb, Leonard Rossiter, Geoffrey Bayldon, John Mills

Singapore, as occupied by the Japanese during World War II, is the setting for this prisoner-of-war drama. The plot, taken by writer-director Bryan Forbes from James Clavell's novel, concerns the Allied inmates' struggles for survival in a Japanese POW camp. In the title role, George Segal is an American corporal who curries favor with his captors. The other prisoners feel he is treading a thin line between self-protection and collaboration. The film is a bleak character study, highlighted by the playing of Segal and of Tom Courtenay and James Fox as British airmen who first oppose, then come to an understanding with, the King Rat. Imaginatively shot by Burnett Guffey.

The **L**ongest Day   1962   (CBS)   ◆   *Black-and-White*
Directors: Ken Annakin, Andrew Marton, Bernhard Wicki
Starring: Eddie Albert, Paul Anka, Arletty, Jean-Louis Barrault, Richard Beymer, Bour-
vil, Richard Burton, Red Buttons, Sean Connery, Mark Damon, Ray Danton, Irina
Demick, Fabian, Mel Ferrer, Henry Fonda, Steve Forrest, Donald Houston, Jeffrey
Hunter, Peter Lawford, Dewey Martin, Roddy McDowall, Sal Mineo, Robert Mitchum,
Kenneth More, Edmond O'Brien, Ron Randell, Madeleine Renaud, Robert Ryan, Tommy
Sands, Rod Steiger, Richard Todd, Tom Tryon, Robert Wagner, John Wayne, Stuart
Whitman

June 6, 1944, D-Day: the Allied invasion of Normandy. This beginning of the end to
World War II was chronicled in Cornelius Ryan's book, a kaleidoscopic account of the
people and events of that fateful day. Ryan also scripted most of the episodes in the
mammoth ($10 million) Darryl F. Zanuck film version. (Other screenplay contributors:
Romain Gary and James Jones.) To bring this epic tale to the screen, Fox and Zanuck
employed an international cast and three directors: Andrew Marton (for the American
involvement), Ken Annakin (British sequences), and Bernhard Wicki (German sequences). Two Academy Awards: Jean Bourgoin and Walter Wottitz's cinematography
and the special effects by Robert MacDonald and Jacques Maumont.

Men in War   1957   (King of Video; World Video   *Black-and-White*
     Pictures)
Director: Anthony Mann
Starring: Robert Ryan, Aldo Ray, Robert Keith, Philip Pine, Vic Morrow, James Edwards,
Scott Marlowe, Victor Sen Yung, Nehemiah Persoff

When an American infantry platoon in Korea is cut off from battalion headquarters,
a dangerous situation becomes even more so. The infantrymen must scale a treacherous
hill to wipe out an enemy bunker. This small-scale war drama—directed by Anthony
Mann from Philip Yordan's adaptation of the Van Van Praag novel, *Combat*—is distinguished by realistic heroics and a diminution of genre clichés. Robert Ryan stars
and the cast includes Vic Morrow, who in 1962 would begin a five-year stint in TV's
"Combat." Music: Elmer Bernstein.

Midway   1976   (MCA)   *Color*
Director: Jack Smight
Starring: Charlton Heston, Henry Fonda, Robert Mitchum, Glenn Ford, Edward Albert,
James Coburn, Glenn Corbett, Christopher George, Hal Holbrook, Monte Markham, To-
shiro Mifune, Pat Morita, Ed Nelson, Cliff Robertson, James Shigeta, Robert Wagner,
Robert Webber, Kevin Dobson, Robert Ito

The 1942 battle of Midway Island in the Pacific provides the backdrop for this air-
and-sea war drama. (Newsreel footage alternates with newly staged combat sequences.)
Charlton Heston is the lead, defending Midway against the Japanese navy, and Edward
Albert plays his ensign son—who happens to be in love with a Japanese girl. The epic
battle itself is depicted through both Allied and Japanese viewpoints. The screenplay
by Donald S. Sanford gives employment to an array of Hollywood superstars in small
parts, à la *The Longest Day* and *A Bridge Too Far*. Jack Smight *(Harper, No Way to Treat
a Lady, Airport 1975)* is the director. Alert viewers will recognize stock photography
from *Thirty Seconds over Tokyo* and catch Tom Selleck in a walk-on.

Paths of Glory   1957   (CBS)   *Black-and-White*
Director: Stanley Kubrick
Starring: Kirk Douglas, Adolphe Menjou, Ralph Meeker, George Macready, Wayne Morris, Richard Anderson, Timothy Carey, Joseph Turkel

One of the strongest pacifist films ever created, *Paths of Glory* documents a shameful incident from World War I. Adapted from Humphrey Cobb's novel by Calder Willingham, Jim Thompson, and director Stanley Kubrick, the picture dramatizes the court martial and execution of three innocent French soldiers on charges of cowardice—only to assuage the ruthlessness of two vain, discipline-mad generals (George Macready and Adolphe Menjou). Kubrick's detached presentation, with a deemphasis on histrionics, makes the horrifying situation all the more compelling. *Paths of Glory* was banned in France for many years.

The Pride and the Passion   1957   (CBS)   *Color*
Director: Stanley Kramer
Starring: Cary Grant, Frank Sinatra, Sophia Loren, Theodore Bikel, John Wengraf, Jay Novello, José Nieto, Philip Van Zandt, Paco el Laberinto, Carlos Larranaga

Producer-director Stanley Kramer's adaptation of C. S. Forester's *The Gun* was filmed on location in Spain. The plot, as scenarized by Edna and Edward Anhalt, turns upon the search for a powerful cannon to be used by Spanish guerrillas holding out against Napoleon. The year is 1810, and Anthony Trumbull (Cary Grant), a British naval officer, is engaged by Miguel (Frank Sinatra), Juana (Sophia Loren), and a few other resistance fighters to assist them in finding the cannon and deploying it for battle. Their united efforts result in stirring, indeed thunderous, action. Franz Planer is the cinematographer. Georges Antheil wrote the music; Peggy Lee performs the theme song.

Run Silent, Run Deep   1958   (CBS)   *Black-and-White*
Director: Robert Wise
Starring: Clark Gable, Burt Lancaster, Jack Warden, Brad Dexter, Joe Maross, H. M. Wynant, Nick Cravat, Don Rickles

This World War II submarine melodrama is highlighted by the contest of wills between a veteran commander (Clark Gable) and his executive officer (Burt Lancaster). The strife, both inside and out, mushrooms as their sub passes from Pearl Harbor to Tokyo Bay. Awaiting the crew is a climactic confrontation with an enemy destroyer. *Run Silent, Run Deep* is an undersea adventure, adapted by John Gay from Edward L. Beach's novel. Directing an all-male cast, Robert Wise derives suspense from the claustrophobia, the unnerving wait, and the explosive finale. The Franz Waxman score packs a wallop too.

The Sand Pebbles   1966   (CBS)   *Color*
Director: Robert Wise
Starring: Steve McQueen, Richard Attenborough, Richard Crenna, Candice Bergen, Maryat Andriane, Mako, Larry Gates, Charles Robinson, Simon Oakland, Ford Rainey, Joe Turkel, Gavin MacLeod, Richard Loo, Gus Trikonis, Beulah Quo, James Hong, Barney Phillips

This $12 million action extravaganza depicts the involvement of the *San Pablo,* an American gunboat, in the affairs of revolution-ridden 1926 China. Stationed on the Yangtze River, the ship is the setting for both external and internal discord. Jake Holman (Steve McQueen) is the engineer, a seaman who believes in isolationism. His philosophy changes as the political situation explodes. Helping Jake nourish his humanitarianism is Shirley Eckert (Candice Bergen), a schoolteacher at an American mission. A highly pictorial drama—shot by Joseph MacDonald—*The Sand Pebbles* is derived by Robert Anderson from Richard McKenna's novel; some of McKenna's plot parallels America's intervention in Vietnam. Filmed in Taiwan and Hong Kong.

Sands of Iwo Jima   1949   (Republic)   *Black-and-White*
Director: Allan Dwan
Starring: John Wayne, John Agar, Adele Mara, Forrest Tucker, Arthur Franz, Julie Bishop, Richard Jaeckel, Wally Cassell, James Brown, Richard Webb, James Holden, Peter Coe, Martin Milner

John Wayne stars as a tough Marine Corps sergeant in this tribute to the heroes of the World War II Pacific campaign. (Over 6,000 soldiers died in capturing the eight-square-mile island of Iwo Jima from the Japanese.) Molding the raw recruits into fighting men is Sergeant John M. Stryker (Wayne); his biggest obstacle is a cocky young private named Peter Conway (John Agar). Conway, an officer's son, has no love for the Corps, but Stryker turns him around. The screenplay for *Sands of Iwo Jima* is by Harry Brown and James Edward Grant, action specialists—as is director Allan Dwan, a cult icon for his low-budget genre favorites *(Up in Mabel's Room, Brewster's Millions, Getting Gertie's Garter, The Wild Blue Yonder, The Woman They Almost Lynched, Tennessee's Partner, Hold Back the Night, Slightly Scarlet,* and scores of others). Three of the six Marines who survived the historic flag-raising on Mount Suribachi portray themselves: Ira H. Hayes, Rene A. Gagnon, and John H. Bradley.

Tora! Tora! Tora!   1970   (CBS)   ◆   *Color*
Directors: Richard Fleischer, Toshio Masuda, Kinji Fukasaku
Starring: Martin Balsam, Joseph Cotten, E. G. Marshall, Jason Robards, James Whitmore, Wesley Addy, Edward Andrews, Leon Ames, Neville Brand, Leora Dana, George Macready, Takahiro Tamura, Soh Yamamura

Almost documentary in tone, *Tora! Tora! Tora!* is a reconstruction of the attack on Pearl Harbor. The events of December 7, 1941, are told from both American and Japanese points of view. This $25 million battle extravaganza, under the direction of Richard Fleischer and two Japanese filmmakers, is based on historical accounts which are woven into a scenario by Larry Forrester, Hideo Oguni, and Ryuzo Kikushima. The harrowing special visual effects by L. B. Abbott and A. D. Flowers were honored with an Academy Award. Music: Jerry Goldsmith.

Twelve O'Clock High   1949   (CBS)   ◆   *Black-and-White*
Director: Henry King
Starring: Gregory Peck, Hugh Marlowe, Gary Merrill, Millard Mitchell, Dean Jagger, Robert Arthur, Paul Stewart, John Kellogg, Robert Patten, Lee MacGregor, Sam Edwards, Richard Anderson, Lawrence Dobkin, Kenneth Tobey

It's England, 1942. Frank Savage (Gregory Peck), a young U.S. Air Force general, takes command of a bomber group stationed near London. The 918th Bombardment Group is a second-rank outfit when Savage arrives, but he soon turns it into a proud and aggressive unit. Unfortunately, the general, faced with mission upon mission, begins to crack under the pressure. *Twelve O'Clock High* is directed by longtime Twentieth Century-Fox house director Henry King *(Ramona, Seventh Heaven, In Old Chicago, Alexander's Ragtime Band, The Song of Bernadette, Wilson, Margie, The Gunfighter, Love Is a Many-Splendored Thing)*. The screenplay is by Sy Bartlett and Beirne Lay, Jr., based on their novel. Supporting actor Dean Jagger was singled out by the Academy for his interpretation of Major Harvey Stovall; another Oscar went to the Fox sound department. The novel and film inspired a two-and-a-half-season teleseries that starred Robert Lansing as General Savage and Frank Overton as Major Stovall.

Uncommon Valor   1983   (Paramount)   *Color*
Director: Ted Kotcheff
Starring: Gene Hackman, Robert Stack, Fred Ward, Reb Brown, Patrick Swayze, Randall "Tex" Cobb, Harold Sylvester, Tim Thomerson, Gail Strickland

The central action of this post-Vietnam adventure involves one man's search for American GI's missing in action. (The theme was duplicated in later pictures, *Rambo* and *Missing in Action* to name two.) In *Uncommon Valor* a retired army colonel (Gene Hackman) returns on a rescue mission to find his son, reported as a prisoner of war. Bankrolled by a Texas oil man (Robert Stack), the colonel leads five marines on a commando raid on a Laotian POW camp. The screenplay by Joe Gayton creates heroic characters and places them in one suspenseful situation after another. One of the top-grossing movies of 1983, *Uncommon Valor* is directed by Ted Kotcheff.

Von Ryan's Express   1965   (CBS)   *Color*
Director: Mark Robson
Starring: Frank Sinatra, Trevor Howard, Raffaella Carra, Brad Dexter, Sergio Fantoni, John Leyton, Edward Mulhare, Wolfgang Preiss, James Brolin, John van Dreelen, Adolfo Celi, Vito Scotti, Richard Bakalyn, Michael Goodliffe, Michael St. Clair.

A World War II prisoner-escape melodrama, *Von Ryan's Express* centers on an unpopular American colonel, Joseph Ryan (Frank Sinatra). Ryan is in charge of the Allied soldiers in an Italian POW camp. His brashness is not to the other men's liking until he masterminds their escape by commandeering a German freight train. The Wendell Mayes-Joseph Landon screenplay, based on the novel by David Westheimer, creates suspense as Axis pilots fly in pursuit of the escapees. Directed by Mark Robson, with cinematography by William A. Daniels.

Westerns

The **A**lamo   1960   (CBS)   ◆   *Color*
Director: John Wayne
Starring: John Wayne, Richard Widmark, Laurence Harvey, Carlos Arruza, Frankie Avalon, Patrick Wayne, Chill Wills, Linda Cristal, Joan O'Brien, Joseph Calleia, Richard Boone

An account of the events leading up to the fight for the famous Texas mission-fort— against overwhelming Mexican odds. John Wayne, as director-star, set out to confirm the mythic status of Davy Crockett, Jim Bowie, William Travis, Sam Houston, and other figures of the American frontier. (John Ford helped briefly, though his footage was never used.) In depicting the heroes, James Edward Grant's screenplay often resorts to long speeches. ("Republic," says Wayne's Crockett, "I like the sound of the word. . . . One of those words that makes me tight in the throat.") The climactic battle, however, is electrifying, well worth the film's historical inaccuracies. *The Alamo* was nominated for several Oscars, including best film and best supporting actor (Chill Wills), but received only one—for sound.

Apache   1954   (CBS)   *Color*
Director: Robert Aldrich
Starring: Burt Lancaster, Jean Peters, John McIntire, Charles Buchinsky, John Dehner, Paul Guilfoyle, Ian MacDonald, Walter Sande, Morris Ankrum, Monte Blue

After the surrender of Geronimo in 1886, a young Indian pacifist sentenced to a Florida prison escapes en route. He marries a white woman and tries to become a farmer and raise a family. Neither the prejudice of white locals nor the continued presence of the U.S. Cavalry alleviates his misfortune. Burt Lancaster as the renegade Indian and Jean Peters as his young wife make a photogenic duo. The James R. Webb scenario, from Paul Wellman's novel *Bronco Apache*, is enriched by Ernest Laszlo's color cinematography and Alan Crosland's editing. This adult Western is one of the seminal early works that Lancaster produced jointly with Harold Hecht; their association continued with *Vera Cruz, Trapeze,* and *Separate Tables*. Charles Buchinsky, Lancaster's antagonist, made career strides when, shortly after *Apache,* he changed his surname to Bronson.

The **B**allad of Cable Hogue   1970   (Warner)   *Color*
Director: Sam Peckinpah
Starring: Jason Robards, Stella Stevens, David Warner, Strother Martin, Slim Pickens, L. Q. Jones, Peter Whitney, R. G. Armstrong, Gene Evans, Kathleen Freeman

Sam Peckinpah's valentine to the Old West is a far cry from his customary blood-and-guts approach. The story of a grizzled prospector who, abandoned in the desert, finds "water where there isn't any" and who proceeds to build thereon a way station for the stage line, the film is at root a romantic version of the decline of the frontier—an event heralded and spurred by "the coming of the Machine." Old Cable Hogue has a singularly unlucky skirmish with the Machine—as embodied in a newfangled motor car. Serio-comic, much in the manner of *Butch Cassidy and the Sundance Kid.* The camera work is by Lucien Ballard. The main ingredients in the picture are the performances of Jason Robards as Hogue; Stella Stevens as Hildy, the floozy with dreams of San Francisco society; and David Warner as the unscrupulous preacher and founder of a doctrine of his own "revelation."

Bite the Bullet   1975   (RCA)   *Color*
Director: Richard Brooks
Starring: Gene Hackman, Candice Bergen, James Coburn, Ben Johnson, Jan-Michael Vincent, Ian Bannen, Robert Donner, Paul Stewart, Dabney Coleman

A Western action-adventure in the tradition established by Richard Brooks in *The Last Hunt* and *The Professionals.* Not primarily a Western director, Brooks seems comfortable with saddles and sagebrush. *Bite the Bullet* documents an endurance horse race over more than 600 miles of rough terrain—from Denver to Kansas City. The entrants are a colorful bunch: an over-the-hill cowpoke, a proud Englishman, a lawman, a hard-bitten youth with an itchy trigger finger. The panorama is rendered by director of photography Harry Stradling, Jr. and the finale at the finish line, recorded in slow motion, is rousing.

Blazing Saddles   *Listed under Comedies.*

Butch Cassidy and the Sundance Kid   1969   (CBS)   *Color*
Director: George Roy Hill
Starring: Paul Newman, Robert Redford, Katharine Ross, Strother Martin, Henry Jones, Cloris Leachman, Jeff Corey, George Furth, Ted Cassidy, Kenneth Mars

Set in the American Southwest and along the Texas-Mexican border at the turn of the century, *Butch Cassidy and the Sundance Kid* employs the identical trappings of *The Wild Bunch,* including the same theme: two bank and train robbers pursued by a relentless posse. Ultimately, to make their grand getaway, Butch (Redford) and Sundance (Newman) flee to Latin America—but not before they establish themselves as unconventional folk heroes along the way. William Goldman wrote the lighthearted script. Katharine Ross, fresh from another costarring stint with Redford *(Tell Them Willie Boy Is Here),* redefines smoldering sexuality as Etta Place, the schoolteacher who accompanies the boys to Bolivia. Oscars went to William Goldman (best original screenplay), Conrad Hall (best cinematography), Burt Bacharach (best original score), and Bacharach and Hal David (for the song "Raindrops Keep Fallin' on My Head").

Cat Ballou   *Listed under Comedies.*

Chisum   1970   (Warner)   *Color*
Director: Andrew V. McLaglen
Starring: John Wayne, Forrest Tucker, Christopher George, Ben Johnson, Glenn Corbett, Bruce Cabot, Andrew Prine, Patric Knowles, Richard Jaeckel, Lynda Day George, Geoffrey Deuel, John Agar, Lloyd Batista, Robert Donner, Ray Teal, Glenn Langan, Christopher Mitchum, Pedro Armendariz, Jr.

As enacted by John Wayne, John Simpson Chisum is a hero in the classic Western mold. Frontier justice is under consideration. A cattle baron troubled by corrupt influences in small town government joins forces with Billy the Kid and Pat Garrett to smash the evil forces. The scriptwriter, Andrew J. Fenady, is more renowned for his detective fiction (*The Man with Bogart's Face*). Director Andrew V. McLaglen, son of Victor, worked as an assistant for John Ford and William Wellman before graduating to his own features; among the many other John Wayne films he directed are *McClintock* (the first, in 1963), *Hellfighters,* and *The Undefeated.*

The Comancheros   1961   (CBS)   *Color*
Director: Michael Curtiz
Starring: John Wayne, Stuart Whitman, Lee Marvin, Ina Balin, Bruce Cabot, Nehemiah Persoff, Michael Ansara, Patrick Wayne, Edgar Buchanan

The Comancheros, contrary to expectations, aren't Indians. Rather they are white renegades who are running guns to the Comanches. Bent on suppressing both Comanches and Comancheros is Texas Ranger Jack Cutter (John Wayne). Along for the dusty ride is Paul Regret (Stuart Whitman), a wily gambler who is first Captain Cutter's prisoner, then his partner. *The Comancheros* emerges as an all-for-fun adventure, evolved from Paul I. Wellman's novel by long-standing Western writers James Edward Grant and Clair Huffaker. Elmer Bernstein wrote the musical score. *The Comancheros* was the last film of Michael Curtiz, whose directing career spanned fifty years and embraced films such as *The Adventures of Robin Hood, Casablanca, Mildred Pierce,* and *Life with Father.*

Comes a Horseman   1978   (CBS)   *Color*
Director: Alan J. Pakula
Starring: James Caan, Jane Fonda, Jason Robards, George Grizzard, Richard Farnsworth, Jim Davis, Mark Harmon, Basil Hoffman, James Keach

Another contemporary Western, *Comes a Horseman* is set in post–World War II Colorado, where ranchwoman Jane Fonda is hounded by malignant cattle king Jason Robards. Robards is a land grabber—and his erstwhile romance with Fonda will not prevent him from seizing her ranch. Siding with the lady to oppose her antagonist are James Caan and Richard Farnsworth. In the New West, justice triumphs, though not without sacrifice. Dennis Lynton Clark's script furnishes moments of brio for the actors, though occasionally it only skims the surface of the cattle baron-versus-ranchers formula. Former stuntman Richard Farnsworth, who later played *The Grey Fox,* was nominated for an Oscar for his performance as Fonda's trusty ranch hand.

The Cowboys   1972   (Warner)   *Color*
Director: Mark Rydell
Starring: John Wayne, Roscoe Lee Browne, Bruce Dern, Colleen Dewhurst, Slim Pickens, Lonny Chapman, Charles Tyner, A Martinez, Alfred Barker, Jr., Robert Carradine, Sean Kelly, Clay O'Brien, Sarah Cunningham, Allyn Ann McLerie, Matt Clark

Because a gold strike has lured his men away, rancher Will Andersen (John Wayne) hires eleven schoolboys for a cattle drive of 400 miles. Before the boys reach their destination, they confront weather hazards, internecine squabbling, a friendly madam (Colleen Dewhurst), and a cattle-rustling scoundrel named Long Hair (Bruce Dern). Ultimately, the novice cowmen learn harsh lessons about the code of the West. Wayne is supported by an impressive cast: Dern, Dewhurst, Roscoe Lee Browne as the trail cook, and the eleven young men of the title—notably Robert Carradine and A Martinez. The screenplay by husband-and-wife team Irving Ravetch and Harriet Frank, Jr., may raise a few eyebrows for its climactic bloodshed—replicated from William Dale Jennings's novel. A 1974 television series—also called *The Cowboys*—was derived from the novel; four of the boys from the movie (Carradine, Martinez, Sean Kelly, and Clay O'Brien) saddled up for the TV version.

E l Dorado 1967 (Paramount) *Color*
Director: Howard Hawks
Starring: John Wayne, Robert Mitchum, James Caan, Charlene Holt, Michele Carey, Edward Asner, Arthur Hunnicutt, R. G. Armstrong, Paul Fix, Christopher George, Johnny Crawford, Robert Donner

A gunfighter (John Wayne) and a good-natured young gambler (James Caan) help an alcoholic sheriff (Robert Mitchum) out of a serious jam. The three join forces to defeat an evil cattle baron and suppress a range war. If all this sounds familiar, it's because *El Dorado* is Howard Hawks's unofficial remake of his own *Rio Bravo* (1959). The 1967 film has Robert Mitchum standing in for Dean Martin, while James Caan has the role formerly played by Ricky Nelson. (In *Rio Bravo*, Nelson was Colorado; here Caan is named Mississippi.) The screenwriter is Leigh Brackett.

G unfight at the O.K. Corral 1957 (Paramount) *Color*
Director: John Sturges
Starring: Burt Lancaster, Kirk Douglas, Rhonda Fleming, Jo Van Fleet, John Ireland, Lyle Bettger, Frank Faylen, Earl Holliman, Ted De Corsia, Dennis Hopper, Whit Bissell, George Matthews, John Hudson, DeForest Kelley, Martin Milner, Kenneth Tobey

The events surrounding the O.K. Corral shootout have provided inspiration for hundreds of Western novels and, by conservative estimate, half a dozen feature films. *My Darling Clementine* (1946), *Hour of the Gun* (1967) and *Doc* (1971) are variations on the familiar tale—but to many this 1957 release is the most memorable. The Leon Uris screenplay recounts in rugged fashion (and almost minute-by-minute) the day of the fateful encounter between Wyatt Earp and Doc Holliday, on the side of justice, and the reprehensible Clanton gang. Burt Lancaster plays Wyatt Earp; Kirk Douglas portrays Doc Holliday. Playing Wyatt's brothers are John Hudson, DeForest Kelley, and Martin Milner. Lyle Bettger is cast as dastardly Ike Clanton and perennial Western badmen Lee Van Cleef and Jack Elam have small roles. Dimitri Tiomkin's score and Frankie Laine's interpretation of the title song (by Tiomkin and lyricist Ned Washington) punctuate the gunplay.

Heartland   1979   (Thorn)   *Color*
Director: Richard Pearce
Starring: Rip Torn, Conchata Ferrell, Barry Primus, Lilia Skala, Megan Folson, Amy Wright

A mail-order companion is the heroine of this frontier drama. In 1910 a courageous widow living in Denver is hired through a newspaper ad by a rancher from Wyoming. She and her young daughter trek across the prairies of the Wyoming wilderness to their new home. Employed as a housekeeper by the stoic ranchman, the widow struggles to improve her lot in life. Beth Ferris's fact-based screenplay is inspired by the diary of a pioneer woman named Elinore Randall Stewart. Directed by Richard Pearce (before *Threshold* and *Country*). Conchata Ferrell and Rip Torn are rugged and real as the widow and employer whose bumpy relationship forms the theme of *Heartland*.

High Noon   1952   (Republic)   ◆   *Black-and-White*
Director: Fred Zinnemann
Starring: Gary Cooper, Thomas Mitchell, Lloyd Bridges, Katy Jurado, Grace Kelly, Otto Kruger, Lon Chaney, Harry Morgan, Ian MacDonald, Eve McVeagh, Harry Shannon, Lee Van Cleef, Bob Wilke, Sheb Wooley

Carl Foreman's landmark Western centers on the archetypal confrontation: sheriff versus badmen on the streets of a frontier town. In the Foreman script, however, Sheriff Will Kane (Gary Cooper) stands alone—forsaken by the townspeople he is trying to protect. One of the main villains is played by Lee Van Cleef, who doesn't utter a word; he only sneers and plays the harmonica. Oscars went to the star (his first Academy recognition was for *Sergeant York)* and to the Dimitri Tiomkin score. Tiomkin and Johnny Mercer's theme, "Do Not Forsake Me, Oh My Darlin'," is sung by Tex Ritter.

Hombre   *Listed under Suspense and Mystery.*

How the West Was Won   1963   (MGM)   ◆   *Color*
Directors: John Ford, Henry Hathaway, George Marshall
Starring: Carroll Baker, Lee J. Cobb, Henry Fonda, Carolyn Jones, Karl Malden, Gregory Peck, George Peppard, Robert Preston, Debbie Reynolds, James Stewart, Eli Wallach, John Wayne, Richard Widmark, Brigid Bazlen, Walter Brennan, David Brian, Andy Devine, Raymond Massey, Agnes Moorehead, Harry Morgan, Thelma Ritter, Russ Tamblyn

This epic paean to the founding of the West also casts a few sidebar salutes to the frontier spectacles of Cecil B. De Mille. James R. Webb's script is sprawling—from the earliest days on the Erie Canal to the Oregon and California trail drives to the laying of the transcontinental railroad. The concept employs three veteran directors: Henry Hathaway, shouldering the major burden, handles "The Rivers, The Plains, The Outlaws"; John Ford's episode is called "The Civil War"; and George Marshall contributes an essay on "The Railroad." The three sequences are given continuity in Spencer Tracy's narration and the folk melodies of Dave Guard and the Whiskeyhill Singers. An all-star history lesson, originally released in old-style Cinerama (with the three-screen technique and the three-camera process of cinematography). Oscars went to the James Webb screenplay, to Harold F. Kress for his editing, and to the MGM sound department.

Jeremiah Johnson   1972   (Warner)   *Color*
Director: Sydney Pollack
Starring: Robert Redford, Will Geer, Stefan Gierasch, Allyn Ann McLerie, Charles Tyner,
Delle Bolton, Josh Albee, Joaquín Martinez, Paul Benedict, Matt Clark, Jack Colvin

An ex-soldier, the protagonist of this Western drama is addressed as "Pilgrim." (The screenplay by John Milius and Edward Anhalt, with contributions by David Rayfiel, is set in the post–Mexican-American War era.) Pilgrim (also known as Jeremiah Johnson) survives as a trapper in the Utah mountains. When the army enlists his services to rescue a stranded wagon train, the mountain man makes the mistake of profaning a Crow Indian burial ground—thus instigating a series of massacres. Robert Redford stars as the legendary title character; Will Geer plays the ancient trapper who teaches Pilgrim the ways of the wilderness; and Allyn Ann McLerie has one harrowing scene as the maddened survivor of an Indian attack. This was Sydney Pollack's second time directing Redford; preceding *Jeremiah Johnson* was *This Property Is Condemned*—with *The Way We Were, Three Days of the Condor, The Electric Horseman,* and *Out of Africa* as collaborations yet to come. The brutal wilderness landscapes are captured by Andrew Callaghan's cinematography. Songs by John Rubinstein and the late Tim McIntire.

Little Big Man   1970   (Key)   *Color*
Director: Arthur Penn
Starring: Dustin Hoffman, Faye Dunaway, Martin Balsam, Richard Mulligan, Chief
Dan George, Jeff Corey, Alan Oppenheimer, Amy Eccles, Cal Bellini, Robert Little Star

This Western saga presents Dustin Hoffman in one of his most celebrated roles: Jack Crabb. The Calder Willingham adaptation of Thomas Berger's novel introduces Crabb as a 121-year-old man being interviewed about the adventures of his youth. Central to the account (and fully dramatized in flashback) is his recollection of General George A. Custer's campaign against the Cheyenne; Crabb, in fact, is the only white survivor of Custer's stand at Little Bighorn. Under Arthur Penn's direction, Hoffman's depiction of the hero (from young adult to decrepit old age) is an amazement. Supporting him are Richard Mulligan as General Custer, Jeff Corey as Wild Bill Hickok, Chief Dan George as Old Lodge Skins, Martin Balsam as a swindler tortured by the Indians, and Faye Dunaway as a parson's wife who turns to prostitution.

Lonely Are the Brave   1962   (MCA)   *Black-and-White*
Director: David Miller
Starring: Kirk Douglas, Gena Rowlands, Walter Matthau, Michael Kane, Carroll O'Con-
nor, William Schallert, George Kennedy, Karl Swenson, Bill Raisch

Edward Abbey's novel *Brave Cowboy* provides the inspiration for this contemporary Western. Kirk Douglas portrays a rebellious ranch hand, the last of his breed—displaced by time and fate. He finds himself a fugitive from justice, pursued cross country by a tough but decent sheriff (Walter Matthau). A cruel lesson awaits: the horseback cow-poke is no match for a mid-twentieth-century posse, bolstered with jeeps, trucks, and helicopters. Dalton Trumbo's adaptation of the Abbey novel has been directed by David Miller, whose credits reach back to 1941's *Billy the Kid* and forward to *Sudden Fear, The Oppoite Sex* (MGM's musicalization of *The Women*), *Happy Anniversary, Midnight Lace, Back Street,* and *Captain Newman, M.D.*; since the late seventies, television movies have claimed his attention. Director of photography: Philip Lathrop.

The Magnificent Seven   1961   (CBS)   *Color*
Director: John Sturges
Starring: Yul Brynner, Eli Wallach, Steve McQueen, Horst Buchholz, Robert Vaughn,
James Coburn, Charles Bronson, Brad Dexter, Vladimir Sokoloff, Rosenda Monteros

The gunslingers of the title are embodied by a pleiad of well-known stars: Steve McQueen, James Coburn, Robert Vaughn, Charles Bronson, Horst Buchholz, Brad Dexter, and—as their mastermind—Yul Brynner. In this John Sturges Western, scripted by William Roberts, the seven are hired as protection men by Mexican villagers besieged by bandits. Leading the bandidos is Eli Wallach. This popular and influential adventure movie is essentially the Hollywood version of *The Seven Samurai*; it replicates both the violence and the comedy of the Kurosawa model. The Elmer Bernstein score was Oscar-nominated at the time and later cannibalized for television commercials. Three sequels: *Return of the Seven* (1966), *Guns of the Magnificent Seven* (1969), and *The Magnificent Seven Ride!* (1972).

A Man Alone   1955   (Republic)   *Color*
Director: Ray Milland
Starring: Ray Milland, Mary Murphy, Ward Bond, Raymond Burr, Arthur Space, Alan
Hale, Jr., Lee Van Cleef

In an acting career that spanned fifty-five years and encompassd well over a hundred movies, Ray Milland also took time to direct five films, all of which he appeared in. His directorial debut came with this Western melodrama. *A Man Alone*, written by John Tucker Battle, places Milland in gunslinger guise; he is a fugitive who has been framed—by the real perpetrators—for the massacre of a stagecoach party. With both lawmen and badmen in pursuit, his only hope for salvation is a small-town sheriff's daughter (Mary Murphy). For the record, Milland's other directing efforts include *Lisbon* (1956), *The Safecracker* (1958), *Panic in the Year Zero* (1962), and *Hostile Witness* (1968).

A Man Called Horse   1970   (CBS)   *Color*
Director: Elliot Silverstein
Starring: Richard Harris, Dame Judith Anderson, Jean Gascon, Manu Tupou, Corinna
Tsopei, Dub Taylor

Elliot Silverstein, the director of *Cat Ballou*, returned to a Western milieu for this 1970 action film; only this time the themes were dead serious. Richard Harris plays an English aristocrat traveling in the Dakotas in 1825. Captured by the Yellow Hand Sioux, the Englishman is forced to live with the tribe. In time he is converted to the Indian way of life and, to prove his worth as a Sioux leader, undergoes the torturous sun vow ceremony. *A Man Called Horse*, derived from a story by Dorothy M. Johnson, presents an unromantic view of man and nature; it's much more brutal than the traditional Old West saga. Two sequels featured Harris again in the title role: *The Return of a Man Called Horse* (1976) and *Triumphs of a Man Called Horse* (1983).

One-Eyed Jacks   1961   (Paramount)   *Color*
Director: Marlon Brando
Starring: Marlon Brando, Karl Malden, Katy Jurado, Pina Pellicer, Slim Pickens, Ben
Johnson, Sam Gilman, Larry Duran, Timothy Carey, Miriam Colon, Elisha Cook, Jr.

Marlon Brando's directing debut came in this delineation of vengeance and violence in a Western town. (Brando dismissed Stanley Kubrick shortly before shooting began.) The filmmaker also stars as Rio, an outlaw just released from a five-year prison stretch and in search of a friend who double-crossed him. Karl Malden, playing Dad Longworth, is that scoundrel, now a sheriff in Old California. Their paths intersect again, and a bitter rivalry ensues. The scenario by Gus Trosper and Calder Willingham emerges from Charles Neider's novel, *The Authentic Death of Hendry Jones*. *One-Eyed Jacks* is what was once called an adult Western—to distinguish films of its stripe from Saturday matinee kiddie fare; even today it seems relentlessly brutal. Larry Duran, Brando's stand-in since *Viva Zapata!,* made his acting debut herein playing a border *hombre* named Modesto.

The Outlaw Josey Wales   1976   (Warner)   *Color*
Director: Clint Eastwood
Starring: Clint Eastwood, Chief Dan George, Sondra Locke, Bill McKinney, Paula True-man, Sam Bottoms, John Vernon

Josey Wales (Clint Eastwood) is a peaceable farmer in the post–Civil War South. But, when renegade Union soldiers murder his wife and son, he seeks revenge—his motto becomes "Blood for blood." In part a rerun of plot situations that Eastwood met in *A Fistful of Dollars* and his other Westerns, Eastwood directs from a screenplay by Phil Kaufman and Sonia Chernus. (The novel *Gone to Texas,* by Forrest Carter, was the source.) John Vernon has the role of Fletcher. Bruce Surtees's cinematography captures both a barrage of ferocity and the raptures of the landscape. Sequel: *The Return of Josey Wales* (1986), starring Michael Parks in the Eastwood role.

The Professionals   1966   (RCA)   *Color*
Director: Richard Brooks
Starring: Burt Lancaster, Lee Marvin, Robert Ryan, Jack Palance, Claudia Cardinale, Ralph Bellamy, Woody Strode, Joe De Santis, Rafael Bertrand

Written, produced, and directed by Richard Brooks, this Western adventure take its premise from *A Mule for the Marquesa,* a novel by Frank O'Rourke. A rich railroad owner (Ralph Bellamy) hires four soldiers of fortune (Burt Lancaster, Lee Marvin, Robert Ryan, and Woody Strode) to rescue his kidnapped wife (Claudia Cardinale). It appears that she's been carried across the border into Mexico by a bandit named Jesus Raza (Jack Palance). The rescue squad sets out—and the excitement begins. Photographed by Conrad Hall.

Red River   1948   (Key)   *Black-and-White*
Director: Howard Hawks
Starring: John Wayne, Montgomery Clift, Joanne Dru, Walter Brennan, Coleen Gray, John Ireland, Noah Beery, Jr., Harry Carey, Sr., Harry Carey, Jr., Paul Fix, Mickey Kuhn, Chief Yowlachie, Hank Worden, Tom Tyler, Glenn Strange

Howard Hawks's classic saga of the West, *Red River* dramatizes the first cattle drive up the Chisholm Trail (from Texas to Kansas). Leading the drive is empire-building Tom Dunson (John Wayne), the original rugged individualist. With Tom are his step-son, Matthew Garth (Montgomery Clift), a tenderfoot, and a crew of experienced drovers. The conflict arises in stampedes, gunfights, Indian battles, and the antagonism between Tom and Matthew. Borden Chase and Charles Schnee wrote the screenplay; Russell Harlan was the cinematographer; and Dimitri Tiomkin composed the score. *Red River* represented the screen debut of Montgomery Clift, although his second feature, *The Search,* was released first. Clift's *A Place in the Sun* costar, Shelley Winters, here takes the role of a dancehall girl.

Rio Bravo   1959   (Warner)   *Color*
Director: Howard Hawks
Starring: John Wayne, Dean Martin, Ricky Nelson, Angie Dickinson, Walter Brennan, Ward Bond, John Russell, Pedro Gonzalez-Gonzalez, Estelita Rodriguez, Claude Akins, Malcolm Atterbury, Harry Carey, Jr., Bob Steele, Myron Healey

Old pros behind and in front of the camera make *Rio Bravo* a model Western comedy-adventure. It all began with a short story by B. H. McCampbell; amplified in the Jules Furthman-Leigh Brackett screenplay, the tale is further enhanced by the direction of Howard Hawks, here reunited with his favorite leading man: John Wayne. The Duke plays John T. Chance, a Texas border town sheriff forced to rely on a group of misfits to maintain law and order. Siding with Chance against an evil gun gang are Dude (Dean Martin), an alcoholic ex-deputy; Colorado (Ricky Nelson), a singing cowpoke; and Stumpy (Walter Brennan), a cackling cripple. Songs by Dimitri Tiomkin and Paul Francis Webster. (See *El Dorado* in this section.)

The Searchers   1956   (Warner)   *Color*
Director: John Ford
Starring: John Wayne, Jeffrey Hunter, Vera Miles, Ward Bond, Natalie Wood, John Qualen, Olive Carey, Henry Brandon, Ken Curtis, Harry Carey, Jr., Antonio Moreno, Pat Wayne, Hank Worden, Lana Wood, Dorothy Jordan, Pippa Scott

Little Debbie Edwards (Lana Wood) is kidnapped by Comanche marauders after they slaughter her mother and father. In pursuit of the Indians is Ethan Edwards (John Wayne), Debbie's uncle, a Civil War veteran. Martin Pawley (Jeffrey Hunter), a young bronco-buster, accompanies Ethan. After five years, they find the girl (now grown into Natalie Wood). A Western adventure, many critics consider *The Searchers* one of John Ford's masterworks. Directed from a script by Frank S. Nugent and the source novel by Alan Le May, the picture also provides Wayne with one of his most complex roles. Max Steiner composed the music. Shot in the Mounument Valley of Utah and Arizona and in Gunnison, Colorado, and Alberta, Canada.

Shane   1953   (Paramount)   ◆   *Color*
Director: George Stevens
Starring: Alan Ladd, Jean Arthur, Van Heflin, Brandon de Wilde, Jack Palance, Ben Johnson, Edgar Buchanan, Emile Meyer, Elisha Cook, Jr., Douglas Spencer, John Dierkes, Ellen Corby, Edith Evanson, Nancy Kulp, Beverly Washburn

A mysterious range rider comes to the rescue of some Wyoming homesteaders in this classic Western. Shane (Alan Ladd) is a former gunslinger who wants to put his past behind him. When he protects the Starrett family (Van Heflin and Jean Arthur) against cut-throat businessmen and hired killers, the newcomer is hero-worshiped by the Starretts's son, Joey (Brandon de Wilde). Suggested by Jack Schaefer's novel, *Shane* is coscripted by A. B. Guthrie, Jr., and Jack Sher. It ranks—with *Gunga Din, Woman of the Year, Talk of the Town, A Place in the Sun, Giant,* and *The Diary of Anne Frank*— as one of director George Stevens's most admirable achievements. Lloyd Griggs won an Academy Award for his cinematography. A 1966 television series starred David Carradine in the title role.

She Wore a Yellow Ribbon   1949   (Media; Nostalgia;   ◆   *Color*
      VidAm; King of Video)
Director: John Ford
Starring: John Wayne, Joanne Dru, John Agar, Ben Johnson, Harry Carey, Jr., Victor McLaglen, Mildred Natwick, George O'Brien, Arthur Shields, Noble Johnson, Cliff Lyons, Tom Tyler

The second installment of John Ford's cavalry trilogy (bookended by *Fort Apache* and *Rio Grande*), this feature centers on Captain Nathan Cutting Brittles (John Wayne playing a character twenty years his elder). Brittles is about to retire, but he refuses to abandon his undermanned cavalry outpost while there's the threat of an Apache uprising. The Frank Nugent-Laurence Stallings screenplay evolved from a *Saturday Evening Post* story by James Warner Bellah. Winton Hoch's cinematography won him an Oscar. The central performance by Wayne is bolstered by Ford's regular stock company: Victor McLaglen, Harry Carey, Jr., Ben Johnson, Mildred Natwick, George O'Brien, et al.

Shenandoah   1965   (MCA)   *Color*
Director: Andrew V. McLaglen
Starring: James Stewart, Doug McClure, Glenn Corbett, Patrick Wayne, Rosemary Forsyth, Phillip Alford, Katharine Ross, Charles Robinson, Paul Fix, Denver Pyle, George Kennedy, Tim McIntire, James McMullan, James Best, Warren Oates, Strother Martin, Dabbs Greer, Harry Carey, Jr., Gregg Palmer, Bob Steele

An all-star cast illuminates this sentimental drama. Written by James Lee Barrett and directed by Andrew V. McLaglen, *Shenandoah* dramatizes the plight of a Virginia agricultural dynasty during the Civil War. Charlie Anderson (James Stewart) is an isolationist farmer whose family of seven is pulled into the brother-against-brother strife. (The plot line served as the basis for the Tony Award–winning Broadway musical of the same name.) The film's homespun quality is its long suit. Memorable performances and an emotion-rousing finale contribute. Joseph Gershenson is the musical supervisor.

The Shootist   1976   (Paramount)   *Color*
Director: Don Siegel
Starring: John Wayne, Lauren Bacall, Ron Howard, James Stewart, Richard Boone, John Carradine, Scatman Crothers, Rick Lenz, Harry Morgan, Bill McKinney, Sheree North, Hugh O'Brian

Bat Masterson is only one of scores of legendary figures known intimately by J. B. Books (John Wayne), given to outrageous pronouncements—and now himself the celebrated last of a dying breed: the tall-in-the-saddle gunfighter. Wracked by cancer, the erstwhile hero comes to Carson City, Nevada, in 1901, rents a room in the boardinghouse of widow Bond Rogers (Lauren Bacall), then prepares to die. Bond's teenage son Gillom (Ron Howard) holds Books in great esteem; others in town, however, want to put the gunman's renowned fast draw to one last test. *The Shootist* was John Wayne's final movie. It was directed by Don Siegel from a screenplay by Miles Hood Swarthout and Scott Hale. (The source is Glendon Swarthout's novel of the same name.)

Silverado   1985   (RCA)   *Color*
Director: Lawrence Kasdan
Starring: Kevin Kline, Scott Glenn, Rosanna Arquette, John Cleese, Kevin Costner, Brian Dennehy, Danny Glover, Jeff Goldblum, Linda Hunt

Four gunfighters are drawn together as reluctant heroes in this intricately plotted Western. Written by brothers Lawrence and Mark Kasdan (and directed by the former), *Silverado* introduces Paden (Kevin Kline), an eccentric loner; Mal (Danny Glover), a muscular, tenderhearted wrangler; Jake (Kevin Costner), a nimble daredevil; and Emmett (Scott Glenn), Jake's elder brother—a taciturn cowpuncher. The heroes mount up to counteract a cunning sheriff (Brian Dennehy) and various desperadoes. The screenplay and performances lift this ode to the West far above genre limitations. Linda Hunt, the Oscar-winning actress of *The Year of Living Dangerously*, plays a frontier town barmaid. Among other contributors are cinematographer John Bailey, editor Carol Littleton, and composer Bruce Broughton.

Skin Game   1971   (Warner)   *Color*
Director: Paul Bogart
Starring: James Garner, Louis Gossett, Susan Clark, Brenda Sykes, Edward Asner, Andrew Duggan, Henry Jones, Neva Patterson

In this pre–Civil War Southern comedy, James Garner stars as a diligent con man. To increase his repertoire of tricks, he teams up with a black city-slicker (Lou Gossett) from the North. Together, they pose as master and slave—with the latter being sold again and again to the highest bidder, then escaping to replay the scam in other towns throughout the Old South. Ultimately, a female bunco artist (Susan Clark) becomes their sidekick. In time, the stunt gets all three partners in hot water. A comic tale, *Skin Game* is written by Peter Stone (under the pseudonym Pierre Martin) and Richard Alan Simmons. The director is Paul Bogart, whose film work extends from *Marlowe* (1969) to *Oh God! You Devil* (1984), but whose principal renown comes through his long association with TV's "All in the Family." A 1974 television movie/series pilot, entitled "Sidekicks" and directed by Burt Kennedy, starred Gossett again, with Larry Hagman in the Garner role.

Soldier Blue   1970   (Embassy)   *Color*
Director: Ralph Nelson
Starring: Candice Bergen, Peter Strauss, Donald Pleasence, John Anderson, Jorge Rivero, Dana Elcar, James Hampton

The foundation for this antiwar Western is the real-life Sand Creek Massacre—the U.S. Cavalry's slaughter of Cheyenne warriors and their families. Instead of detailing gore and ghoulishness for their own sake, though, the picture uses the white man's inhumane treatment of the Indians as punctuation in an intelligent adventure tale. Derived from Theodore V. Olsen's novel, *Arrow in the Sun*, the John Gay screenplay presents Candice Bergen and Peter Strauss as two white survivors of an Indian attack in Cheyenne territory; their subsequent trek across the desert leads them to Sand Creek—where they are eyewitnesses to the massacre. Directed by Ralph Nelson *(Re-*

quiem for a Heavyweight, Lilies of the Field, Soldier in the Rain, Father Goose, Charly).

Support Your Local Sheriff *Listed under Comedies.*

3:10 to Yuma 1957 (RCA) *Black-and-White*
Director: Delmer Daves
Starring: Glenn Ford, Van Heflin, Felicia Farr, Leora Dana, Richard Jaeckel, Henry Jones, Robert Emhardt

A suspense film that happens to be set in the Old West, *3:10 to Yuma* arises from a story by Elmore Leonard. As screenwritten by Halsted Welles, the plot centers on notorious killer Ben Wade (Glenn Ford). The badman is now in the custody of peace-loving farmer Dan Evans (Van Heflin). Captor and captive are waiting in a dusty Southwest cow town for the arrival of the 3:10 train—and the U.S. marshal thereon who will convey Ben to a Yuma prison. But before the train pulls in, Ben's outlaw gang, bent on reprisal, invades the town. The action is staged by director Delmer Daves *(Destination Tokyo, The Red House, Dark Passage, Broken Arrow, Cowboy, The Hanging Tree)* and his cinematographer, Charles Lawton, Jr.

True Grit 1969 (Paramount) ◆ *Color*
Director: Henry Hathaway
Starring: John Wayne, Glen Campbell, Kim Darby, Jeremy Slate, Robert Duvall, Strother Martin, Dennis Hopper, Jeff Corey, Alfred Ryder, John Fiedler, Donald Woods, Edith At-water

Mattie Ross (Kim Darby), a young frontier girl from Dardanelle, Yell County, Arkansas, seeks vengeance on the bad men who murdered her father. When she espies hard-drinking, one-eyed U.S. Marshal Rooster Cogburn (John Wayne), Mattie can't be sure if he has true grit or not. But he soon proves his worth. *True Grit*, adapted from the Charles Portis novel by Marguerite Roberts, is the film that finally netted the Duke his Oscar. He reprised his role of the gruff marshal in *Rooster Cogburn* (1975), costarring Katharine Hepburn. A 1978 television movie entitled "True Grit" offered Warren Oates as Cogburn.

Winchester '73 1950 (MCA) *Black-and-White*
Director: Anthony Mann
Starring: James Stewart, Shelley Winters, <u>Dan Duryea</u>, Stephen McNally, Charles Drake, Millard Mitchell, John McIntire, Will Geer, Jay C. Flippen, Rock Hudson, John Alex-ander, Steve Brodie, James Millican, Abner Biberman

The rifle of the title is reputedly "the gun that won the West." Unfortunately, cowboy Lin McAdam's prize Winchester is stolen, and as he and several other interested parties trace its whereabouts, violence and murder erupt. This all-star Western drama took enormous strides in reestablishing the genre in post–World War II America. Indeed, director Anthony Mann and the lead, James Stewart (here playing McAdam), did their utmost to keep fifties audiences supplied with quality Westerns. Although they made several movies separately, they worked together on *Bend of the River* (1952), *The Naked*

Spur (1953), *The Far Country* (1955), and *The Man from Laramie* (1955). There's an opportunity in *Winchester '73* to observe two actors early in their careers: Rock Hudson plays a renegade Indian named Young Bull, while Tony (billed as Anthony) Curtis is a soldier called Doan. The screenplay, heavy on action, is by Robert L. Richards and Borden Chase—and William Daniels is the cinematographer. A television movie remake was first broadcast in 1967.

Editors' Choice Appendix

These English language films released prior to 1946 are available on videocassette. So many of them are in the public domain that the distributors are not listed—most of the films should be available from several distributors.

Abe Lincoln in Illinois   (1939)
All Quiet on the Western Front
  (1930)
Animal Crackers   (1929)
The Awful Truth   (1937)

The Bells of St. Mary's   (1945)
The Blue Angel   (1930)
  Both dubbed and subtitled.
Bringing up Baby   (1938)

Carefree   (1938)
Casablanca   (1943)
Citizen Kane   (1941)
City Lights   (1931)

Day at the Races   (1937)
Dinner at Eight   (1933)
Dodsworth   (1936)
Dracula   (1931)
Duck Soup   (1933)
Dumbo   (1941)

Foreign Correspondent   (1940)
Forty-Second Street   (1933)
Frankenstein   (1932)

Gaslight   (1944)
Gold-Diggers   (1933)
Gold Rush   (1925)
Gone with the Wind   (1939)
Goodbye, Mr. Chips   (1939)
Grand Hotel   (1932)

Grand Illusion   (1937)
The Grapes of Wrath   (1940)
The Great Ziegfeld   (1936)
Gunga Din   (1939)

Holiday   (1938)
How Green Was My Valley   (1941)
The Human Comedy   (1943)
The Hunchback of Notre Dame
  (1939)

The Informer   (1935)
It Happened One Night   (1934)

King Kong   (1933)

The Lady Vanishes   (1938)
Laura   (1944)
Little Caesar   (1930)
The Little Foxes   (1941)
Lost Horizon   (1937)

The Magnificent Ambersons   (1942)
The Maltese Falcon   (1941)
Modern Times   (1936)
Mr. Smith Goes to Washington
  (1939)
Mrs. Miniver   (1942)
Mutiny on the Bounty   (1935)
My Man Godfrey   (1936)

Night at the Opera   (1935)
Now, Voyager   (1942)

Our Town   (1940)

The Philadelphia Story   (1940)
Pinocchio   (1940)
The Private Life of Henry the VIII
   (1933)
The Public Enemy   (1931)

Rebecca   (1940)
Rules of the Game   (1939)

Scarface   (1932)
Stage Door   (1937)
Stagecoach   (1939)
A Star Is Born   (1937)
Steamboat Bill, Jr.   (1928)

Suspicion   (1941)
Swing Time   (1936)

A Tale of Two Cities   (1935)
The Thin Man   (1934)
The Thirty-Nine Steps   (1935)
Top Hat   (1935)
Topper   (1937)

Watch on the Rhine   (1943)
The Wizard of Oz   (1939)
The Women   (1939)
Wuthering Heights   (1939)

Yankee Doodle Dandy   (1942)
You Can't Take It with You   (1938)

Index of Movie Listings